17th Nordic Conference of Computational Linguistics (NODALIDA 2009)

NEALT Proceedings Series Volume 4

Odense, Denmark
14 – 16 May 2009

Editors:

Kristiina Jokinen
Eckhard Bick

ISBN: 978-1-5108-3465-1

NEALT PROCEEDINGS SERIES
VOL. 4

Proceedings of the
17th Nordic Conference of Computational Linguistics
NODALIDA 2009

May 14-16, 2009
Odense, Denmark

Editors

Kristiina Jokinen and Eckhard Bick

NORTHERN EUROPEAN ASSOCIATION FOR LANGUAGE TECHNOLOGY

Contents

Preface

We are pleased to present the Proceedings of NODALIDA 2009, the 17th Nordic Conference of Computational Linguistics, held 14-16 May 2009 in Odense, Denmark.

The NODALIDA conference has always been an important meeting for the Nordic computational linguistics and language technology community. In recent years, especially through the establishment of the Northern European Association of Language Technology (NEALT), it has emerged as a major conference covering the geographical area of the Nordic countries as well as the Baltic countries and Northwest Russia. The previous NODALIDA conference was a success along the new dimension of being both a regional and an international character, and the current NODALIDA conference follows these lines. Although smaller in numbers, it shows similar recognition on the international level, as witnessed by a fair amount of submissions from outside the core geographical areas in Europe, and also from the US, India, and Japan.

We received altogether 82 submissions from 24 countries in the five categories of regular full papers, regular short papers, student papers, demos and workshops. The review process was rigorous and aimed at high scientific standards: each submission received three reviews and borderline cases were further subjected to discussion among the reviewers and the Programme Committee members. This resulted in the acceptance of 43 high-quality papers which appear in these proceedings, as well as five workshops which will produce their own proceedings. Of the accepted papers in the main conference, nine are short papers, three are student papers, and five are demos. The low number of student papers was disappointing, and we hope this will improve in future conferences.

The conference also features two distinguished invited speakers. Their talks concern language research and technological applications that allow us to address challenges encountered in the multilingual and multimodal contexts. Jean Carletta (University of Edinburgh) talks about interdisciplinary work on corpus collection, analysis of group dynamics, and interaction management in her keynote talk "Developing Meeting Support Technologies: From Data to Demonstration (and Beyond)". Ralf Steinberger (EC - Joint Research Centre) presents the cross-lingual functionality of a news analysis system and highlights various language technology topics in a rich multilingual environment (between 19 and 43 languages) in his keynote talk "Linking News Content Across Languages".

Besides presenting novel research, another important goal of the NODALIDA conference is to establish a series of tutorials concerning state-of-the-art language technology and computational linguistics research. In this conference, Graham Wilcock (University of Helsinki) presents an overview of linguistic annotation using open source tools in his tutorial "Text Annotation with OpenNLP and UIMA".

The conference programme also includes five workshops as specialised meetings on various relevant topics. We are proud to offer the following workshops, held immediately before the main conference:

W1: Nordic Perspectives on the CLARIN Infrastructure of Common Language Resources

W2: Multimodal Communication: from Human Behaviour to Computational Models

W3: Lexical Semantic Resources for NLP Purposes - the Interplay between Lexical Semantics, Lexicography, Terminology and Formal Ontologies

W4: Extraction and Use of Constructions in NLP

W5: Constraint Grammar and Robust Parsing

The conference has also attracted two satellite events, held before the workshops: the student and board meetings of the NGSLT (The Nordic Graduate School of Language Technology), and the project-related workshop "Linguistic Theory and Raw Sound" organised by Peter Juel Henrichsen (Copenhagen Business School). Moreover, during the conference there will be the second NEALT business meeting.

The organisation of a conference of this size is not possible without the efforts of several people working together in a friendly yet efficient manner. We would first like to thank our international Review Committee for their wonderful work on reviewing. Their prompt and constructive judgments greatly assisted us in putting together the current, exciting programme. We also wish to thank the Program Committee for their insightful comments, inviting the reviewers, and in general sharing their views on many complicated issues dealing with the structure and format of the conference. A big thank you goes to the Local Organisation Committee at the University of Southern Denmark for all their hard work concerning conference logistics and practical issues for the conference, and to the Institute of Language and Communication for financial and logistic support. Special thanks go to Mare Koit, Editor-in-Chief of the NEALT Publication Series at University of Tartu, for her kind help in the production of the electronic proceedings.

Finally, on behalf of the organisers, we would like to thank all the conference speakers and participants. Your interactions and enthusiasm will make the actual conference into what it aims to be: a forum for fruitful conversations and discussions which contribute to connections and work for years to come.

We wish you inspiring, useful, and enjoyable conference days at NODALIDA 2009.

Kristiina Jokinen

Programme Chair

NODALIDA 2009

Eckhard Bick

Local Chair

NODALIDA 2009

Committees

PROGRAM COMMITTEE

Kristiina Jokinen (CHAIR), University of Helsinki and University of Tartu
Robin Cooper, University of Göteborg
Anna Korhonen, University of Cambridge
Kaili Müürisep, University of Tartu
Joakim Nivre, Uppsala University
Patrizia Paggio, University of Copenhagen
Koenraad de Smedt, University of Bergen
Roman Yangarber, University of Helsinki

LOCAL ORGANIZATION COMMITTEE

Eckhard Bick (CHAIR), University of Southern Denmark
Poul Søren Kjærsgaard, University of Southern Denmark
Klaus Robering, University of Southern Denmark
Anette Wulff, University of Southern Denmark

REVIEWERS

Helena Ahonen-Myka, University of Helsinki, Finland
Lars Ahrenberg, University of Linköping, Sweden
Tanel Alumäe, Technical University of Tallinn, Estonia
Antti Arppe, University of Helsinki, Finland
Gemma Boleda, Universitat Politècnica de Catalunya, Spain
Francis Bond, NICT, Japan
Lars Borin, University of Gothenburg, Sweden
Rolf Carlson, KTH, Sweden
Mathias Creutz, Helsinki University of Technology, Finland
Antoine Doucet, University of Caen, France
Elisabet Engdahl, University of Gothenburg, Sweden
Stefan Evert, University of Osnabrück, Germany
Björn Gambäck, SICS, Sweden
Barbara Gawronska, University of Skövde, Sweden
Jeroen Geertzen, University of Cambridge, UK
Janne Bondi Johannessen, University of Oslo, Norway
Christer Johansson, University of Bergen, Norway
Heiki-Jaan Kaalep, University of Tartu, Estonia
Kaarel Kaljurand, University of Tartu, Estonia
Viggo Kann, KTH, Sweden
Jussi Karlgren, SICS, Sweden
Mare Koit, University of Tartu, Estonia
Dimitrios Kokkinakis, University of Gothenburg, Sweden
Kimmo Koskenniemi, University of Helsinki, Finland
Udo Kruschwitz, University of Sussex, UK
Yuval Krymolowski, Bar-Ilan University, Israel
Marco Kuhlmann, Uppsala University, Sweden
Krista Lagus, Helsinki University of Technology, Finland
Miro Lehtonen, University of Helsinki, Finland

Ian Lewin, EBI, UK
Krister Lindén, University of Helsinki, Finland
Ramón López-Cózar Delgado, University of Granada, Spain
Jan Tore Lønning, University of Oslo, Norway
Bente Maegaard, University of Copenhagen, Denmark
Beáta Megyesi, Uppsala University, Sweden
Kadri Muischnek, University of Tartu, Estonia
Costanza Navarretta, University of Copenhagen, Denmark
Pierre Nugues, University of Lund, Sweden
Jussi Piitulainen, University of Helsinki, Finland
Ari Pirkola, University of Tampere, Finland
Gábor Prószéky, Pázmány University, Hungary
Eiríkur Rögnvaldsson, University of Reykyavik, Iceland
Bolette Sandford Pedersen, University of Copenhagen, Denmark
Inguna Skadiņa, Tilde, Latvia
Torbjørn Svendsen, Norwegian University of Science and Technology, Norway
Anders Søgaard, University of Copenhagen, Denmark
Jürgen Wedekind, University of Copenhagen, Denmark
Aline Villavicencio, University of Rio Grande do Sul, Brazil
Martin Volk, University of Stockholm, Sweden
Atro Voutilainen, Connexor, Finland
Michael Zock, LIF, CNRS, Marseille, France

Conference program
NODALIDA-2009

Corpus, annotation, and their use (Chair: Rickard Domeij)	
11.00-11.30	Janne Bondi Johannessen, Joel Priestley, Kristin Hagen, Tor Anders Åfarli and Øystein Alexander Vangsnes. *The Nordic Dialect Corpus - an advanced research tool*
11.30-12.00	Nathan Green, Paul Breimyer, Vinay Kumar and Nagiza F. Samatova. *WebBANC: Building Semantically-Rich Annotated Corpora from Web User Annotations of Minority Languages*
12.00-12.30	Olga Lashevskaja and Olga Mitrofanova. *Disambiguation of Taxonomy Markers in Context: Russian Nouns*
12.30-13.00	Krister Lindén and Jussi Tuovila. *Corpus-based Paradigm Selection for Morphological Entries*

<table>
<tr><td colspan="2">Morphology and Syntax (Chair: Koenraad de Smedt)</td></tr>
<tr><td>11.00-11.30</td><td>Krister Lindén and Tommi Pirinen. Weighted Finite-State Morphological Analysis of Finnish Compounding with HFST-LEXC</td></tr>
<tr><td>11.30-12.00</td><td>Miikka Silfverberg and Krister Lindén. Conflict Resolution Using Weighted Rules in HFST-TWOLC</td></tr>
<tr><td>12.00-12.30</td><td>Hrafn Loftsson, Ida Kramarczyk, Sigrún Helgadóttir and Eiríkur Rögnvaldsson. Improving the PoS tagging accuracy of Icelandic text</td></tr>
<tr><td>12.30-13.00</td><td>Katri Haverinen, Filip Ginter, Veronika Laippala and Tapio Salakoski. Parsing Clinical Finnish: Experiments with Rule-Based and Statistical Dependency Parsers</td></tr>
</table>

<table>
<tr><td colspan="2">Semantic Classification (Chair: Robin Cooper)</td></tr>
<tr><td>11.00-11.30</td><td>Michael Wiegand and Dietrich Klakow. Predictive Features in Semi-Supervised Learning for Polarity Classification and the Role of Adjectives</td></tr>
<tr><td>11.30-12.00</td><td>Jari Björne, Filip Ginter, Juho Heimonen, Sampo Pyysalo and Tapio Salakoski. Learning to Extract Biological Event and Relation Graphs</td></tr>
<tr><td>12.00-12.30</td><td>Jacob Persson, Richard Johansson and Pierre Nugues. Text Categorization Using Predicate-Argument Structures</td></tr>
<tr><td>12.30-13.00</td><td>Peter Kolb. Experiments on the difference between distributional similarity and relatedness</td></tr>
</table>

13.00-14.00 **Lunch**

14.00-14.45 **Demos** (Chair: Eiríkur Rögnvaldsson)

Eckhard Bick. *DeepDict - A Graphical Corpus-based Dictionary of Word Relations*

Sandra Derbring, Peter Ljunglöf and Maria Olsson. *SubTTS: Light-weight automatic reading of subtitles*

Peter Ljunglöf, Staffan Larsson, Katarina Mühlenbock and Gunilla Thunberg. *TRIK: A talking and drawing robot for children with communication disabilities*

Arne Martinus Lindstad, Anders Nøklestad, Janne Bondi Johannessen and Øystein A. Vangsnes. *The Nordic Dialect Database: Mapping Microsyntactic Variation in the Scandinavian Languages*

Bodil Nistrup Madsen and Hanne Erdman Thomsen. *CAOS - A Tool for the Construction of Terminological Ontologies*

14.45-15.30 **Student posters** (Chair: Kaili Müürisep)

Maria Eskevich. *Prominence detected by listeners for future speech synthesis application*

Okko Räsänen and Joris Driesen. *A comparison and combination of segmental and fixed-frame signal representations in NMF-based word recognition*

Bálint Sass. *Verb Argument Browser for Danish*

Regular poster

Anders Søgaard. *A linear time extension of deterministic pushdown automata*

15.30-16.00 **Coffee**

16.00-17.00   **Tutorial** (Chair: Joakim Nivre)
Graham Wilcock (University of Helsinki). *Text Annotation with OpenNLP and UIMA*

19.00   **Conference dinner**

16 May
9.00-10.00   **Invited Talk** (Chair: Kristiina Jokinen)
Ralf Steinberger (EC - Joint Research Centre). *Linking News Content Across Languages*

10.00-10.30   **Coffee**

10.30-11.30   **Regular papers** (3 parallel sessions)

Semantics (Chair: Costanza Navarretta)
10.30-11.00   Bolette Sandford Pedersen and Anna Braasch. *What do we need to know about humans? A view into the DanNet database*
11.00-11.30   Kristina Nilsson and Hans Hjelm. *Using Semantic Features Derived from Word-Space Models for Swedish Coreference Resolution*

Parallel Corpora and Translation (Chair: Inguna Skadiņa)
10.30-11.00   Hercules Dalianis, Martin Rimka and Viggo Kann. *Using Uplug and SiteSeeker to construct a cross language search engine for Scandinavian languages*
11.00-11.30   Christian Hardmeier and Martin Volk. *Using Linguistic Annotations in Statistical Machine Translation of Film Subtitles*

Algorithms (Chair: Kimmo Koskenniemi)
10.30-11.00   Anders Søgaard. *Verifying context-sensitive treebanks and heuristic parses in polynomial time*
11.00-11.30   Anssi Yli-Jyrä. *An Efficient Double Complementation Algorithm for Superposition-Based Finite-State Morphology*

11.30-12.30   **Posters** (Chair: Eckhard Bick)

Lene Antonsen, Trond Trosterud and Saara Huhmarniemi. *Interactive pedagogical programs based on constraint grammar*

Eva Forsbom. *Extending the View: Explorations in Bootstrapping a Swedish PoS Tagger*
Tatiana Gornostay and Inguna Skadina. *Pattern-based English-Latvian Toponym Translation*

Yves Lepage and Chooi Ling Goh. *Towards automatic acquisition of linguistic features*

Miguel A. Molinero, Benoit Sagot and Lionel Nicolas. *Building a morphological and syntactic lexicon by merging various linguistic resources*

Magnus Rosell. *Part of Speech Tagging for Text Clustering in Swedish*

Natalie Schluter and Josef van Genabith. *Dependency Parsing Resources for French: Converting Acquired Lexical Functional Grammar F-Structure Annotations and Parsing F-Structures Directly*

12.30-13.30   **Lunch**

13.30-14.30   **Short regular papers** (3 parallel sessions)

Parsing and Tagging (Chair: Janne Bondi Johannessen)

13.30-13.50	Mark Fishel and Joakim Nivre. *Voting and Stacking in Data-Driven Dependency Parsing*
13.50-14.10	Rashmi Gangadharaiah, Ralf Brown and Jaime Carbonell. *Active Learning in Example-Based Machine Translation*
14.10-14.30	Beata B. Megyesi. *The Open Source Tagger HunPoS for Swedish*

Semantic Analysis (Chair: Poul Søren Kjærsgaard)

13.30-13.50	Eckhard Bick and M. Pilar Valverde Ibáñez. *Automatic Semantic Role Annotation for Spanish*
13.50-14.10	Manfred Klenner, Angela Fahrni and Stefanos Petrakis. *PolArt: A Robust Tool for Sentiment Analysis*
14.10-14.30	Lilja Øvrelid. *Cross-lingual porting of distributional semantic classification*

Applications (Chair: Klaus Robering)

13.30-13.50	Inguna Skadiņa and Edgars Bralitis. *English-Latvian SMT: knowledge or data?*
13.50-14.10	Karin Friberg Heppin. *MedEval - Six Test Collections in One*
14.10-14.30	Anton Karl Ingason, Skúli Bernhard Jóhannsson, Eiríkur Rögnvaldsson, Hrafn Loftsson and Sigrún Helgadóttir. *Context-Sensitive Spelling Correction and Rich Morphology*

14.30-15.30   **NEALT Business meeting**

15.30-16.00   **Closing**

16.00-16.30   **Coffee**

I Invited Papers

Developing Meeting Support Technologies:

From Data to Demonstration (and Beyond)

Jean Carletta
University of Edinburgh
Edinburgh, Scotland
`jeanc@inf.ed.ac.uk`

Abstract

In 2004, the AMI Consortium set out to collect a multimodal meeting corpus that would give us all the raw material we needed to demonstrate a whole range of meeting support technologies, most of which we knew we hadn't thought of yet. In this keynote, I will talk about how we designed the corpus to grow an interdisciplinary community that would collectively understand not just the technologies but how groups work, and then I will describe some of the novel applications we have built using the data and are currently showing to industrial end users.

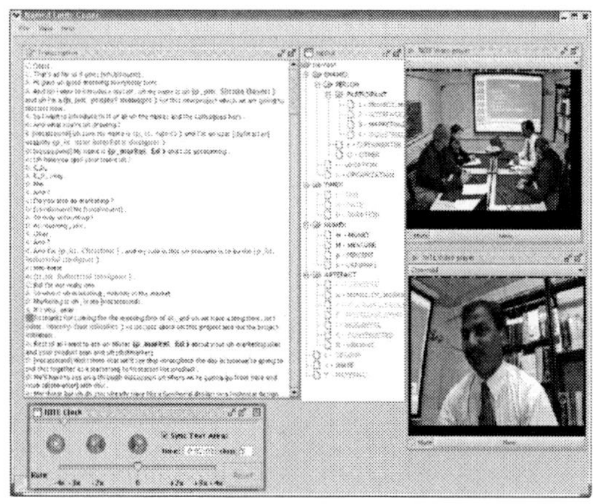

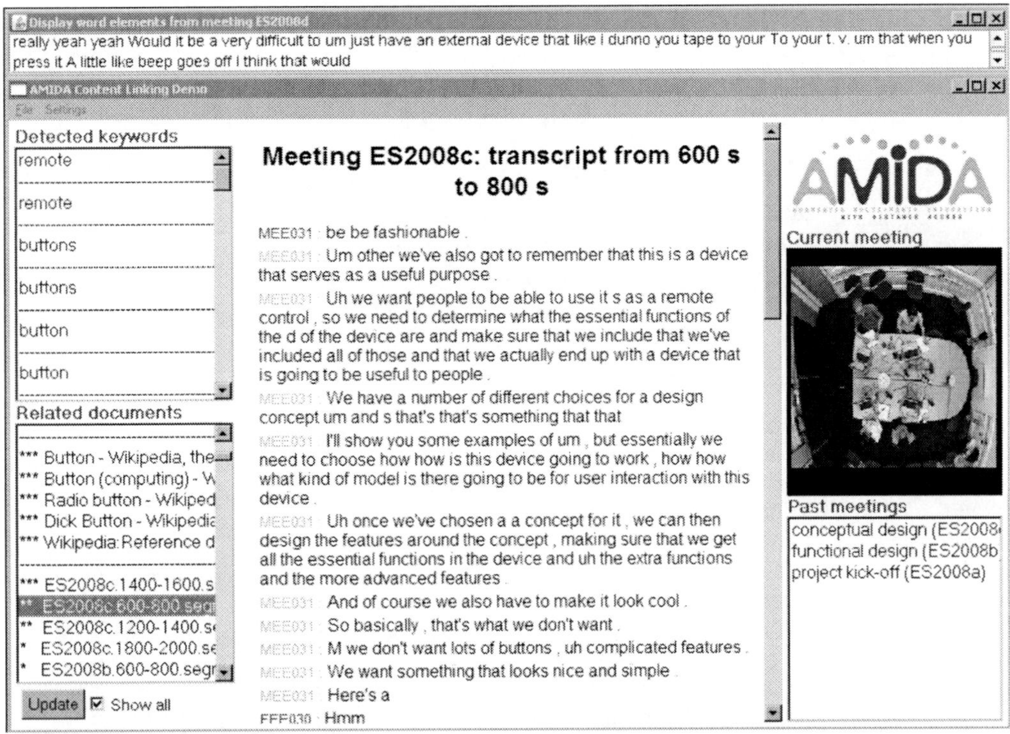

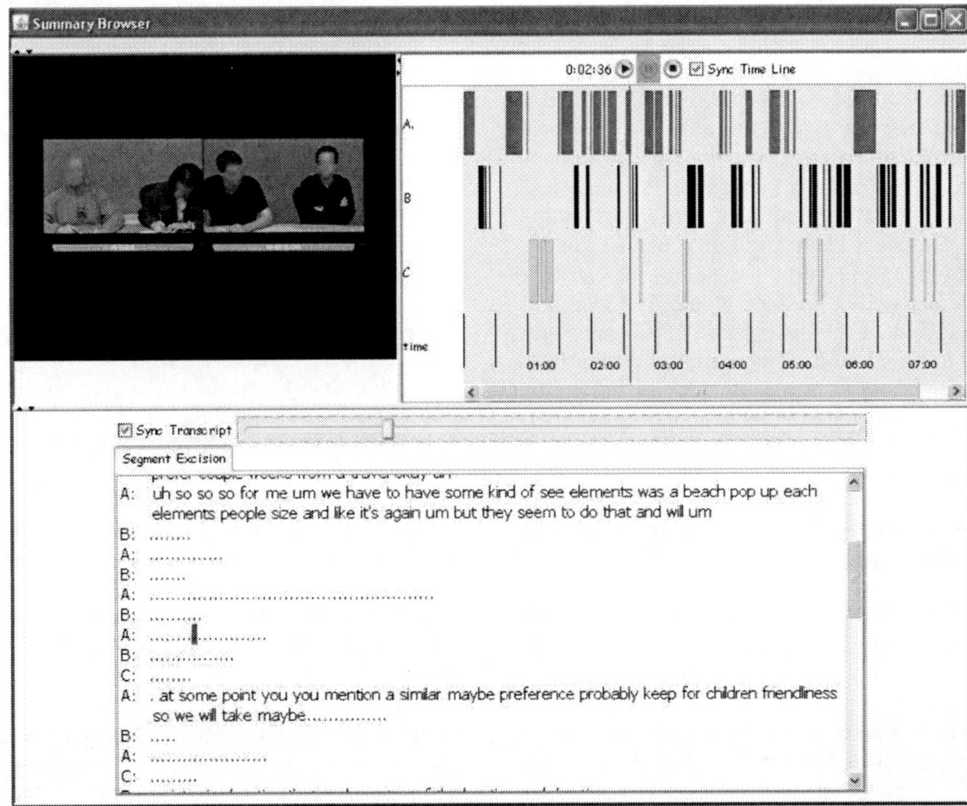

ISSN 1736-6305 Vol. 4
http://hdl.handle.net/10062/9206

Linking News Content Across Languages

Ralf Steinberger
European Commission – Joint Research Centre
21027 Ispra (VA), Italy
http://langtech.jrc.it/ – http://press.jrc.it/overview.html
Ralf.Steinberger@jrc.it

1   Introduction

Organisations and individuals that need to monitor what the media say about certain issues face an extreme information overload, especially if they are interested in the news written in more than one language. News aggregators sometimes pre-filter potentially user-relevant articles or automatically group related articles into clusters. However, the enormous amount of available online information calls for further automatic information processing to enable users to sieve through even larger amounts of textual data in less time and to navigate and explore the document collections efficiently.

2   NewsExplorer

NewsExplorer is a freely available news analysis system that offers such functionality in 19 languages. NewsExplorer integrates various text analysis applications including clustering, multi-label document classification, named entity recognition, name variant matching across languages and writing systems, topic detection and tracking, and more. The purpose of this presentation is to present this news exploration and analysis system and to especially address the multilinguality issue and the cross-lingual functionality of the application. References to prior art will be made, where appropriate.

3   News Data and the EMM family of applications

NewsExplorer is part of the Europe Media Monitor (EMM) family of applications (http://press.jrc.it/overview.html). EMM gathers a daily average of 80,000 news articles from about 2,200 web news sources in 43 languages. *NewsBrief* and the Medical Information System *MedISys* classify the news, cluster related articles and alert users of breaking news when unexpected spikes are detected. *EMM-Labs* gives access to data visualisation tools and to the results of a collection of advanced text processing tools such as relation extraction, event scenario template filling, and various types of social networks. The freely available EMM online applications attract between one and two Million hits per day.

References

Steinberger Ralf, Bruno Pouliquen & Camelia Ignat (2008). *Using language-independent rules to achieve high multilinguality in text mining.* In: Françoise Fogelman-Soulié, Domenico Perrotta, Jakub Piskorski & Ralf Steinberger (eds): Mining Massive Data Sets for Security. IOS-Press, Amsterdam, Holland.

Pouliquen Bruno & Ralf Steinberger (2009). *Automatic Construction of Multilingual Name Dictionaries.* In: Cyril Goutte, Nicola Cancedda, Marc Dymetman & George Foster (eds.): Learning Machine Translation. MIT Press, NIPS series.

Pouliquen Bruno, Ralf Steinberger & Camelia Ignat (2003). *Automatic Annotation of Multilingual Text Collections with a Conceptual Thesaurus.* In: Proceedings of the EUROLAN Workshop Ontologies and Information Extraction at the Summer School The Semantic Web and Language Technology - Its Potential and Practicalities. Bucharest, Romania.

Pouliquen Bruno, Marco Kimler, Ralf Steinberger, Camelia Ignat, Tamara Oellinger, Ken Blackler, Flavio Fuart, Wajdi Zaghouani, Anna Widiger, Ann-Charlotte Forslund, Clive Best (2006). *Geocoding multilingual texts: Recognition, Disambiguation and Visualisation.* Proceedings of the 5th International Conference on Language Resources and Evaluation LREC, pp. 53-58. Genoa, Italy.

Pouliquen Bruno, Ralf Steinberger & Clive Best (2007). *Automatic Detection of Quotations in Multilingual News.* In: Proceedings of the International Conference Recent Advances in Natural Language Processing RANLP. Borovets, Bulgaria.

Pouliquen Bruno, Olivier Deguernel & Ralf Steinberger (2008). *Story tracking: linking similar news over time and across languages*. In: Proceedings of the CoLing'2008 workshop: Multi-source, multilingual information extraction and summarization, Manchester, August 2008.

Acknowledgements

NewsExplorer and the other EMM media monitoring applications are complex applications, which were built in a group effort. I would thus like to thank the whole EMM team for their good work and especially Bruno Pouliquen, who was the main driving force behind the development of NewsExplorer.

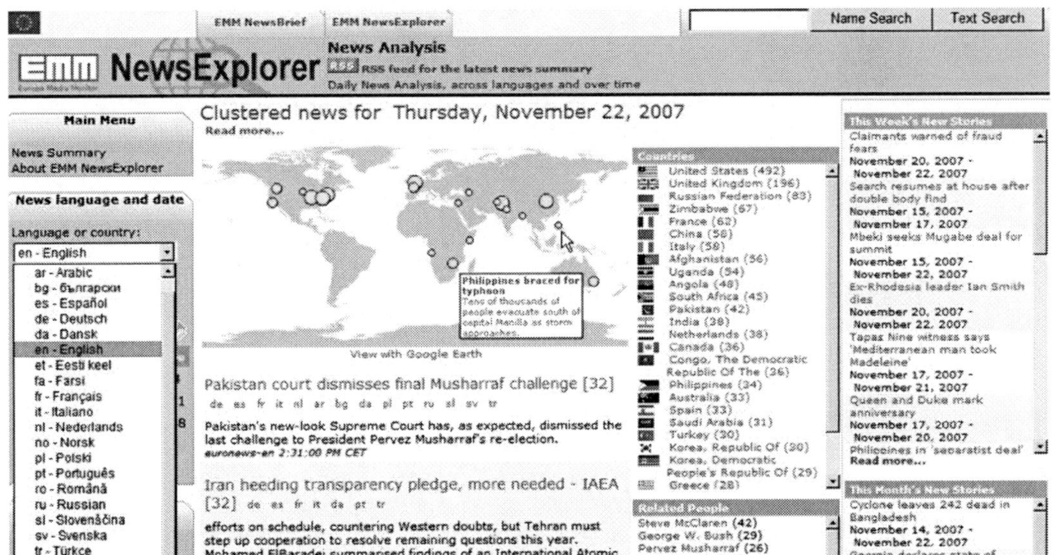

Figure 1. Screenshot of NewsExplorer, showing a map with the location of today's news, the largest English language news clusters, links to related news in the other 18 languages, lists of countries, people and organizations mentioned in the news that day, and lists of the biggest 'stories' (daily news clusters linked over time) this week, month and year.

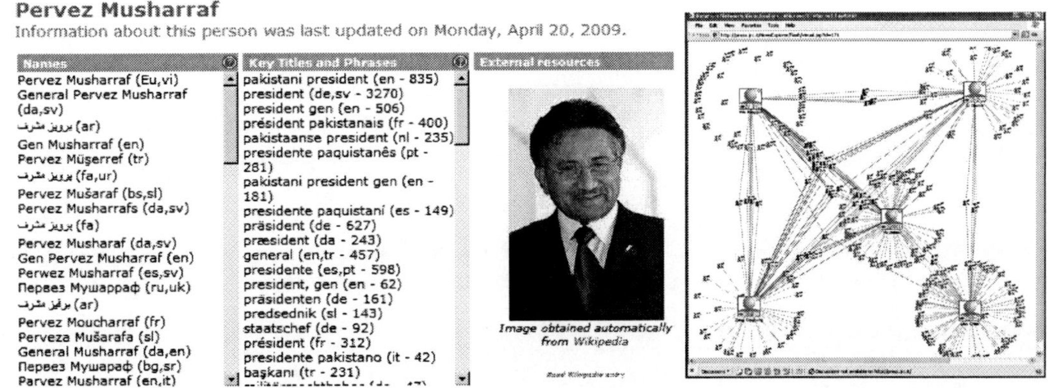

Figure 2. Screenshot of (part of) NewsExplorer's page on Pakistani President Pervez Musharraf. That page shows automatically collected name variants (including variants in different scripts such as Arabic, Farsi, and Russian), titles, lists of related persons, lists of related news clusters, quotations by and about Musharraf, multi-day 'stories' in which he is mentioned, and more. Relations between two or more persons can be visualised graphically.

ISSN 1736-6305 Vol. 4
http://hdl.handle.net/10062/9206

II Tutorial

Text Annotation with OpenNLP and UIMA

Graham Wilcock
University of Helsinki
`graham.wilcock@helsinki.fi`

Abstract

The tutorial presents a practical overview of automatic linguistic annotation of texts using freely available open source tools.

1 OpenNLP

Text annotation typically involves tasks at several linguistic levels, such as sentence boundary detection, tokenization, part-of-speech tagging, phrase chunking, syntactic parsing, named entity recognition, coreference resolution, and semantic role labelling. Most of these tasks can be done with appropriate combinations of OpenNLP tools (`http://opennlp.sourceforge.net`).

Practical examples will show annotations of a short English text. OpenNLP outputs annotations in a simple plain text format.

The OpenNLP tools do a good job of creating annotations automatically, but a number of issues arise. Although the OpenNLP tools themselves are open source Java and platform-independent, the annotation pipelines (where the output of one component is input to the next component) are created by Linux shell scripts and Windows .bat files that are platform-dependent and error-prone. Apache Ant can be used to gain platform-independence, but Ant requires technical skills.

2 WordFreak

OpenNLP tools can also be used in WordFreak (`http://wordfreak.sourceforge.net`) as plugins. WordFreak provides an attractive, easy-to-use GUI for linguistic annotations. It is open source Java and platform-independent, and is convenient for manually correcting annotations made by the OpenNLP tools. However, Word-Freak creates annotations in its own specific XML stand-off annotation format.

This raises the issue of interoperability. How can annotations be interchanged between tools that use different annotation formats? This can be done by XSLT transformations, for example WordFreak XML format can be transformed by XSLT to OpenNLP plain text annotation format. However, writing such XSLT stylesheets requires specific technical skills.

3 UIMA

UIMA (Unstructured Information Management Architecture) provides solutions to many of the above issues. UIMA is open-source Java (`http://incubator.apache.org/uima`). It aims to support interoperability and scalability.

In UIMA, annotators run in analysis engines. New annotators are written in Java, and existing annotation tools such as the OpenNLP tools are converted to UIMA annotators by Java wrappers. Pipelines of annotators run in aggregate analysis engines. Pipelines can be configured by writing XML descriptors (similar in some ways to Ant tasks), or by means of an easy-to-use graphical configuration tool in the Eclipse GUI (Figure 1).

UIMA supports interoperability at the level of annotation formats by adopting XML Metadata Interchange (XMI), which has been proposed as an interchange standard. Instead of having its own specific XML annotation format, the UIMA annotation format is XMI.

UIMA also supports interoperability at the level of annotation tools by means of a type system that defines annotation types and their features. Types are used to check that output from one component is the right type for input to the next component.

Practical examples will show how to configure and use pipelines of OpenNLP tools in UIMA, and how to view the annotations in UIMA (Figure 2).

References

Graham Wilcock. 2009. *Introduction to Linguistic Annotation and Text Analytics*. Morgan and Claypool.

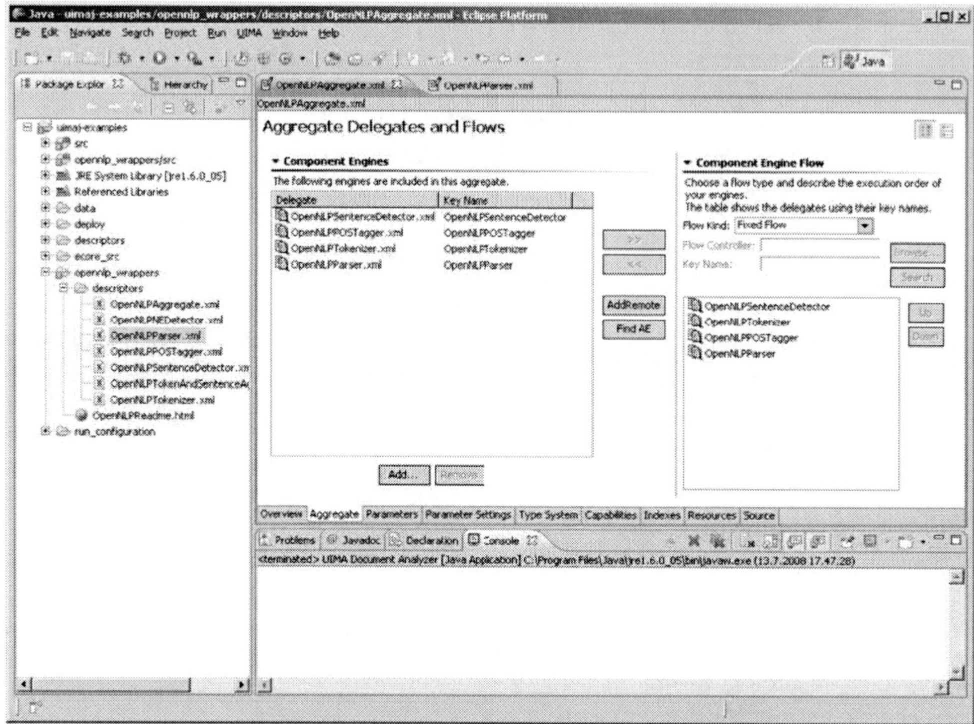

Figure 1: Configuring an OpenNLP annotation pipeline in UIMA

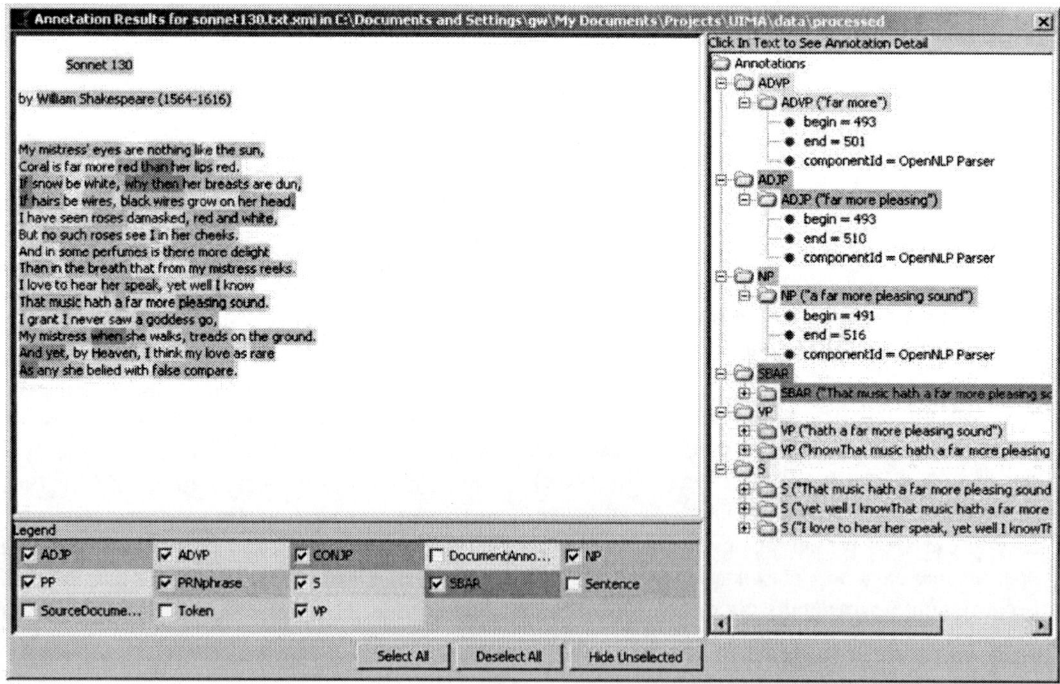

Figure 2: Viewing annotations by OpenNLP Parser in UIMA

ISSN 1736-6305 Vol. 4
http://hdl.handle.net/10062/9206

III Regular Papers

Interactive pedagogical programs based on constraint grammar

Lene Antonsen
University of Tromsø
Norway
lene.antonsen
@uit.no

Saara Huhmarniemi
University of Tromsø
Norway
saara.huhmarniemi
@helsinki.fi

Trond Trosterud
University of Tromsø
Norway
trond.trosterud
@uit.no

Abstract

This article presents a set of interactive parser-based CALL programs for North Sámi. The programs are based on a finite state morphological analyser and a constraint grammar parser which is used for syntactic analysis and navigating in the dialogues. The analysers provide effective and reliable handling of a wide variety of user input. In addition, relaxation of the grammatical analysis of the user input enables locating grammatical errors and reacting to the errors with appropriate feedback messages.

1 Introduction

This paper describes the implementation a set of CALL (Computer Assisted Language Learning) programs for learners of North Sámi (a Uralic language), based on a finite state transducer (fst) and constraint grammar (CG) technology.

The pedagogical programs are available on a web-based learning platform OAHPA!, accessible at http:\\oahpa.uit.no. There are six programs altogether: A word quiz (Leksa), a numeral quiz (Numra), basic morphological exercises (Morfa-S), morphological exercises in a sentential frame (Morfa-C), a question-answer (QA) drill (Vasta), and a dialogue program (Sahka).

The OAHPA! platform is implemented in Django, a Python-based web development framework, combined with a Mysql database.

In section 2 we describe the initial linguistic resources and the pedagogical motivation behind the programs. Section 3 presents the pedagogical lexicon and the morphological analyser. The fourth section presents the parser-based CALL programs and shows how the CG-parser was utilised for error detection and navigation in the programs accepting free sentence input. Section 5 contains an evaluation of the programs.

2 Background

2.1 Basic grammatical analysis

The pedagogical programs in OAHPA! are based upon three pre-existing language technology resources developed at the University of Tromsø: a morphological analyser/generator, a CG parser for North Sámi and a number word generator compiled with the Xerox compiler xfst.

The morphological analyser/generator is implemented with fst and compiled with the Xerox compilers twolc and lexc (Beesley and Karttunen, 2003). Sámi languages have large morphological paradigms for each lexeme – verbs and adjectives have more than 100 inflected forms. In addition, some of the paradigm members have a very low text frequency. Due to the limited amount of electronically available text resources, an fst analyser was used, rather than e.g. an HMM tagger (Trosterud, 2007). The lexicon contains 97.500 lemmata – almost half of them proper nouns. We made two different variants of the analyser/generator: one tolerant, with morphological patterns based upon actual usage, and the other one normative, adhering to the written standard.

The morphological disambiguator is implemented in the CG-framework (Karlsson et. al, 1995). The CG-framework is based upon manually written rule sets and a syntactic analyser which selects the correct analysis in case of homonymy and adds grammatical function and dependency relations to the analysis. We used vislcg3 for the compilation of CG rules. Vislcg3 is a new, improved version of the open source compiler vislcg (visl, 2008). The CG-framework is presented in section 4.1.

2.2 Previous accounts on parser-based CALL

Even if many interactive parser-based CALL programs are described in the literature, see (Gamper and Knapp, 2002; Heift and Schulze, 2007), very few of them are available for actual use online and most systems have remained at a prototype level. One of very few exceptions is e-tutor, a program for teaching German to foreigners (Heift, 2001; Heift and Nicholson, 2001), at `http://e-tutor.org`. e-tutor gives very good feedback to student's errors, but the possible input is restricted to small, fixed vocabularies, and there is no dialogue. The grammar formalism used is Head-driven Phrase Structure Grammar (HPSG).

Vislcg3 is used in the VISL-suite of games for teaching grammatical analysis on the Internet `http://visl.sdu.dk`. Most of the games in VISL are based on pre-analysed sentences, but one of the programs accepts free user input in some of the 7 supported languages. The input is analysed or changed into grammar exercises (Bick, 2005).

2.3 The pedagogical motivation

The main goal of the development of OAHPA! was to develop a language tutoring system going beyond simple multiple-choice questions or string matching algorithms, with free-form dialogues and sophisticated error analysis. Immediate error feedback and advice about morphology and grammar were seen as important requirements for the program.

In addition, the programs were designed to be flexible so that the student could choose exactly which aspect of the language and on which level of difficulty she would like to train. To better integrate the tools to the instruction, the vocabulary was designed so that it may be restricted to particular textbooks. Finally, the programs were made freely accessible via Internet.

Due to its complex morphology, Sámi languages demand a lot of practising before the student reaches a level of fluency required for everyday conversation. Since Sámi is a minority language, learners often do not have enough opportunities to practise the language in a natural setting. Our programs give a practical supplement to the instruction given at school or university. In addition, the dialogue program consists of everyday topics, with underlying pedagogical goals such as practicing verb inflection, choice of correct case form or vocabulary learning.

The student may choose between two main North Sámi dialects. Especially when training morphology, it is important that the forms that are presented for the user, are the same that the ones used in the language society or taught during instruction. Still, the program accepts any correct orthographic word form provided by the student.

North Sámi is used in three countries, and therefore the programs have several metalanguages (Norwegian, Finnish, North Sámi, English). We are also considering extending the programs to other Sámi languages.

3 Pedagogical lexicon

3.1 The structure of the lexicon

All the OAHPA! programs share a set of common resources: a pedagogical lexicon and a morphological generator that is used for generating the different word forms that appear in the programs. The dialectal variation is taken into account in the lexicon as well as in the morphology. In addition, the morphological properties of words are used when making a detailed feedback on morphological errors.

The pedagogical lexicon forms a collection of words that are considered relevant for the learners of North Sámi in schools and universities. The words occur in different forms in the tasks. The pedagogical lexicon contains additional information about the lemmata, such as Norwegian and Finnish translation, semantic class, dialect and information about the inflection. The words in the pedagogical lexicon were collected from the key textbooks for North Sámi and the source information is included in the lexicon entry. In addition, homonymy in both base form and inflection is dealt with using ids for lexicon entries instead of lemmata. The lexicon consists of 1538 nouns, 500 verbs and 194 adjectives, in addition to a small lexicon for closed parts of speech. Figure 1 shows an example of an entry in the noun lexicon.

The word forms that are used in the program are pre-generated with a transducer that contains of the full North Sámi vocabulary, the inflectional and derivational morphology, and the non-segmental morphological processes (consonant gradation, diphthong simplification, etc.). Similar transducer is used in live analysis of user input in the programs Vasta and Sahka, which are described in section 4.

The contents of the pedagogical lexicon as well as full paradigms for each lexicon entry are stored in the Mysql database. The database allows effective processing of queries and multiple simultaneous users. In addition, generating the word forms

```
<entry id="monni">
  <lemma>monni</lemma>
  <pos class="N"/>
  <translations>
    <tr xml:lang="nob">egg</tr>
    <tr xml:lang="fin">muna</tr>
  </translations>
  <semantics>
    <sem class="FOOD-GROCERY"/>
  </semantics>
  <stem class="bisyllabic" diphthong="no"
    gradation="yes" soggi="i" rime="0"/>
  <dialect class="NOT-KJ"/>
  <sources>
    <book name="d1"/>
    <book name="sara"/>
    <book name="algu"/>
  </sources>
</entry>
```

Figure 1: An entry in the pedagogical lexicon.

and storing them to the database provides better control over the inflected word forms and e.g. different dialectal forms. The handling of dialectal variation is described in the next section.

3.2 Handling the dialectical variation

When generating sentences or providing the correct answers for the user, we wanted to control the selection of word forms to allow only normative forms in the correct dialect. On the other hand, the live analyser used for the analysis of the user input should be tolerant and accept all correct variants of the same grammatical word. Therefore we compiled different analysers/generators for different purposes: one normative but variation-tolerant transducer for analysing the input, and two strict ones for different dialects for sentence generation.

The variation between the main dialects Kárášjohka and Guovdageaidnu was in the source code (lexc) marked in one of the following ways:

(a) NOT-KJ (not generated for KJ-dialect)

(b) NOT-GG (not generated for GG-dialect)

We also marked entries in the pedagogical lexicon-files as in Figure 1. This system can easily be expanded with more dialects. Figure 2 contains an example of how the dialectal information is handled in the morphological analyser.

3.3 Feedback on morphological errors

The inflectional information of words contained in pedagogical lexicon is used for generating feed-

```
+A+Comp:i%>X4b BUStem ; !  NOT-KJ
+A+Comp:á%>X4b BUStem ; !  NOT-GG
```

Figure 2: Handling of dialectal variation in the morphological analyser.

back to the student. If the user does not inflect the lemma correctly, she can ask for hints about the inflection, and try once more, instead of getting the correct answer straight away.

The feedback messages are determined by the combination of morphological features in the lexicon and the inflection task at hand. Consider a part of the feedback specification in the Figure 3. It specifies the morphological rule that there is a vowel change in illative singular for bisyllabic nouns that end with the vowel *i*. The corresponding feedback message instructs the user to remember the vowel change.

```
<stem class="bisyllabic" soggi="i">
  <msg case="Ill" number="Sg">i_á</msg>
  <note>láibi > láibái </note>
</stem>

<message id="i_á">Vowel change i > á.
</message>
```

Figure 3: The features in the lexicon are used to determine the correct feedback message, in this case the message is "Vowel change i > á".

The feedback may consist of several parts so that the user also receives information about e.g. stem class. All the feedback messages that match the feature definition in the given task, are collected and given to the user in a specified order.

4 CG-parser in live analysis programs Vasta and Sahka

4.1 Syntactic analyses of the student's answer

We have chosen not to use multiple-choice, but rather let the student formulate her own answer. To a certain question one may give many kinds of acceptable answers. In Sámi one may change word order, and also add many kinds of particles.

We use vislcg3 for analysing the student's answer. The reason for choosing CG as parser platform was that only CG is robust enough for handling unconstrained input, and at the same time accurate enough to identify errors. The program contains manually written, context dependent rules, mainly used for selecting the correct analysis in case of homonymy. Each rule adds, removes, selects or replaces a tag or a set of grammatical tags in a given sentential context. Context conditions may be linked to any tag or tag set of any word anywhere in the sentence, either locally (in a fixed subdomain of the context) or globally (in the whole context). Context conditions in the same rule may be linked, i.e. conditioned upon each other, negated or blocked by interfering words or tags. Vislcg3 is documented at (visl, 2008). Grammars for Danish and Norwegian based on CG achieve very good F-scores (Bick, 2003).

The question and the answer are merged, and given to the analyser as one text string. We use a ruleset file which disambiguates the student's input only to a certain extent, because there will probably be grammatical and orthographic errors. The last part of the file consists of rules for giving feedback to the student's grammatical errors, and rules for navigating to the correct next question of in the dialogue, due to the student's answer. How to generate feedback or navigation instructions is explained in section 4.2 and 4.6.

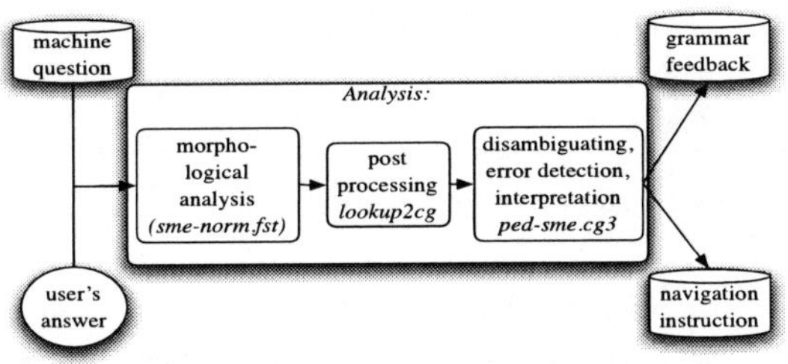

Figure 4: An overview of the analysis process.

The question mark is exchanged for a special symbol ("qst" QDL), cf. figure 5. Instead of a sentence delimiter, we want to be able to refer to the question and the answer separately in the rules.

4.2 Tutorial feedback

Tutorial feedback is feedback about grammar errors (CG prefix *&grm*), and in Figure 6 we see a rule for assigning a tag if the student has not used accusative, when the question requires it. If the interrogative pronoun is in accusative, we expect an accusative in the answer. The rule assigns a *&grm-missing-Acc* tag to the interrogative pronoun if there is no accusative or negation verb in the answer.

```
"<Maid>"
    "maid" Adv
    "maid" Interj
    "mii" Pron Interr Pl Acc
    "mii" Pron Interr Sg Acc
    "mii" Pron Rel Pl Gen
    "mii" Pron Interr Pl Gen
    "mii" Pron Rel Sg Acc
    "mii" Pron Rel Pl Acc
"<don>"
    "dot" Pron Dem Sg Gen
    "don" Pron Pers Sg2 Nom
    "dot" Pron Dem Sg Acc
"<lohket>"
    "lohkat" V TV Ind Prs Pl3
    "lohkat" V TV Imprt Prs Pl2
    "lohkat" V TV Ind Prt Sg2
"<ikte>"
    "iktit" V TV Ind Prt Pl3
    "iktit" V TV Ind Prs Du1
    "ikte" Adv
"<^qst>"
    "^qst" QDL
"<Ikte>"
    "iktit" V TV Ind Prt Pl3
    "iktit" V TV Ind Prs Du1
    "ikte" Adv
"<mun>"
    "mun" Pron Pers Sg1 Nom
"<lohken>"
    "lohkat" V TV Ind Prt Sg1
"<boares>"
    "boaris" A Attr
"<girji>"
    "girji" N Sg Nom
"<.>"
    "." CLB
```

Figure 5: Between analysis and disambiguation.

```
LIST TARGETQUESTION-ACC = ("mii" Acc) ("gii" Acc)
("galle" Acc) ("gallis" N Acc) ;

MAP (&grm-missing-Acc) TARGET TARGETQUESTION-ACC IF
(*1 QDL BARRIER WORK-V LINK NOT *1 Acc OR Neg
BARRIER S-BOUNDARY);
```

Figure 6: Rule assigning missing Acc -tag.

Figure 7 shows how the vislcg3 file has disambiguated and added the error tag to the input which is the analysis from Figure 5. The tag generates feedback to the student. The object is in Nom instead of Acc, and the grammar adds the error tag.

The most difficult problem for the grammatical analysis are the student's misspellings. A misspelling may be left unrecognized in the analysis or it can produce another word form for the same lemma, or from some other lemma.

When the word form is not recognized during the analysis, the feedback message to the student points to the unrecognized word form asking the student to check the spelling. To the extent that misspellings are the most common type of errors, the current feedback does not provide enough in-

```
"<Maid>"
   "mii" Pron Interr Pl Acc &grm-missing-Acc
   "mii" Pron Interr Sg Acc &grm-missing-Acc
"<don>"
   "don" Pron Pers Sg2 Nom
"<lohket>"
   "lohkat" V TV Ind Prt Sg2
"<ikte>"
   "ikte" Adv
"<^qst>"
   "^qst" QDL
"<Ikte>"
   "ikte" Adv
"<mun>"
   "mun" Pron Pers Sg1 Nom
"<lohken>"
   "lohkat" V TV Ind Prt Sg1
"<boares>"
   "boaris" A Attr
"<girji>"
   "girji" N Sg Nom
"<.>"
   "." CLB

<message id="grm-missing-Acc">The answer should
   contain an accusative.</message>
```

Figure 7: QA with missing Acc -tag added because the object *girji* is in Nom (What did you read yesterday? Yesterday I read an old book-SgNom).

structions for the student to improve the spelling. However, in order to give better feedback to certain misspellings, we have added e.g. place names with small initial letter to the fst, together with an error tag, so that the student gets a precise feedback. We will implement more that kind of rules and consider usage of a spell checker to help the student to find the correct word form.

For misspellings that produce another word form of the same lemma, we have written rules that are based on the grammatical context. The real problem emerges when the spelling error gives rise to an unintended lemma. Then the challenge is to give a feedback according to what the student thinks she has written. In this case, feedback has to be tailored using the knowledge about the student's interlanguage. We have created sets for typical unintended lemmata. Combined with contextual rules we can then give the user a good feedback due to the misspelling instead of the unintended lemma.

E.g. if the student uses the Sg2 form of the main verb after the negative verb, instead of the correct ConNeg form, then the erroneous form can be a ConNeg form of a derivated verb, and the normal feedback will be: "You should answer with the same verb as in the question." The student will not understand this, because she thinks that the word

form in the answer is an instance of the same verb. The solution was to generate all these forms of the verbs in the questions, make a set of them, and make a rule for in the right context, give the feedback: "The negative form is not correct."

4.3 The open QA drill – Vasta

In between the "natural" dialogues, mimicking real life dialogues, and the pure grammar training session, inquiring paradigm forms, we have made a question-answer drill. The drill has two question types: Yes/no questions and wh-questions.

There are two motives for making this program type. First, our tailored dialogues run the risk of getting quickly consumed. With a QA drill we may generate an indefinite number of questions. Second, the students need to automate the question-answer routine – answer with the correct verb, inflect the finite verb correctly and choose the correct case form.

The questions are generated, and then the question and answer are analysed together, and the student gets feedback, as described in 4.1. The question matrices are marked with level, so there is a level option. Only one question is presented at a time. The student can answer what she wants, but she has to use a full sentence (containing a finite verb), and use the same verb as in the question. There are 111 matrix questions.

4.4 Sentence generator

One of the main goals of the programs in OAHPA! is to practice language in natural settings with variation in the tasks. In order to provide variation in programs that involve sentential context we implemented a sentence generator. The sentence generator is used in the morphology in sentential context program (Morfa-C), and for generating questions to the QA drill (Vasta). Figure 8 contains an example of sentence matrix that is used in the sentence generator.

The question matrix contains two types of elements: constants and grammatical units. The constants such as *go* and *ikte* in the Figure 8 are present in each generated sentence as such, whereas grammatical units allow more variation. Both the inflection and the content of the grammatical units may vary from question to question, and from program to program. E.g. in the question in Figure 8 the MAINV is fixed to past tense, but the person and number inflection may vary freely. In addition, certain elements such as the sentence

```
<q level="2" id="go_ikte">
  <qtype>PRT</qtype>
  <question>
    <text>MAINV go SUBJ ikte</text>
    <element id="MAINV">
  <grammar tag="V+Ind+Prt+Person-Number"/>
  <sem class="ACTIVITY"/></element>
    <element id="SUBJ">
  <sem class="HUMAN"/>
  <grammar pos="N"/></element></question>
</q>
```

Figure 8: Example showing question generation (MAINV question-particle SUBJ yesterday).

subject (SUBJ) have default inflection in nominative, but the default inflection may be overridden. The selection of words for the sentence is constrained by semantic sets. Semantic sets are also used as an option in the word quiz (Leksa).

The sentence generator handles agreement e.g. between subject and the main verb. The agreement may be explicitly marked between any two elements, which indicates that the two elements share the same number and person inflection.

In addition to generating questions, the sentence generator is used for generating answer templates. In this case, the sentence generator takes into account the agreement inside a sentence, but also the content and agreement between the question and the answer. For example, the person and number inflection in the answer is restricted by the question. We chose not to accept an inclusive interpretation of the pronouns in Pl1 and Du1, because we wanted the student to exercise also 2. person verb inflection. Table 1 shows how the question Person-Number (QPN) Sg1 requires answer Person-Number (APN) Sg2, and so on. Pl1 as an answer to Pl1 is thus not accepted by the system.

Table 1: Provided question-answer agreement.

QPN	APN	QPN	APN	QPN	APN
Sg1	Sg2	Du1	Du2	Pl1	Pl2
Sg2	Sg1	Du2	Du1	Pl2	Pl1
Sg3	Sg3	Du3	Du3	Pl3	Pl3

4.5 The dialogue program – Sahka

The idea behind the dialogue program is that the student may exercise North Sámi in a natural set-ting, and at the same time receive feedback about errors. Each dialogue is based on a scenario, such as meeting a person for the first time or going to a grocery store. In addition, each scenario has a set of underlying pedagogical goals. E.g. in the Grocery-dialogue the student is telling what kind of food she wants to buy and the underlying pedagogical goal is to exercise inflecting objects in accusative.

Each dialogue consists of branches to different topics. The program asks questions, comments on the student's answers and starts a new topic according to the answer. The dialogue forms a continuum and contains only accepted answers. The feedback concerning grammatical errors is given on a separate window and the user is allowed to correct the answer until it is accepted.

A topic starts with an opening utterance which is either a question or a comment followed by a question. Thus, the user expected to provide answers to the questions throughout the dialogue. The dialogue proceeds to an appropriate utterance inside the current topic. In the end of the topic, there is always a closing comment after which the dialogue proceeds to next topic. Both the next utterance and the next topic may be selected based on the information in the user's answer. For example, if the question is about having a car, a positive answer will navigate to a branch with a follow-up questions. In the next section, we describe the navigation inside the dialogue in more detail.

The dialogue system itself is quite simple. Only the program can make initiatives, and all the utterances from the program are ready-made, addressing topics that the program is able to handle. In other words, the sentence generation mechanism used in Vasta is not utilised in the dialogue program. Developing the program to the direction of free dialogue, where also the student is able to take initiatives, requires among other things an analyser which maps semantic roles to the student's input and a semantically enriched lexicon.

4.6 Navigating in the Sahka dialogue

Navigating inside the dialogue is implemented in CG-rules. The user input is tagged during analysis with information on whether the answer is interpreted as affirmative or negative. In addition, a special tag indicates whether the sentence contains some information that should be stored for the following questions or utterances. The program is thus able to store simple information such as the student's name, place where she lives and for example the type of her car and use this information in tailored utterances.

Every utterance contains one or more links to other utterances. The link is selected according to the tag assigned to the question-answer pair, e.g. *&dia-neg* for a negative answer, *&dia-pos* for a positive answer, or *&dia-target* for a certain word, e.g. target="hivsset", like in Figure 9. In Figure 10 we see how the *&dia-target* tag is mapped to the noun in illative. The question is "In which room do we put the TV?" One of the alternatives for the navigation is due to the target tag being assigned to the lemma *hivsset* ("WC"). The answer will be "That is not a good idea. Make a new try."

```
<utt type="question" name="gosa_bidjat_TV">
 <text>Gude latnjii moai bidje mu TV?</text>
 <alt target="hivsset" link="gosa_bidjat_TV">
 <text>Dat gal ii heive! Geahčcal oddasit.</text>
      </alt>
 <alt target="default" link="gosa_bidjat_beavddi">
<text>Moai gudde dan ovttas dohko.</text></alt></utt>
```

Figure 9: Rule for navigating according to answer.

Figure 10 shows a general rule, not connected to any particular question, for adding a target-tag to the NP-head in illative after a question with the interrogate *guhte* + a noun in illative (= "to which").

```
MAP (&dia-target) TARGET NP-HEAD + Ill IF
(*-1 QDL BARRIER S-BOUNDARY LINK **-1 (N Ill)
LINK -1 ("guhte"))(NOT 0 NOTHING) ;
```

Figure 10: Case tag adding triggered by question.

Every question has its own unique id, which is used in navigating between questions. In addition, the CG-rules may be tailored for specific questions. An answer from the student about her age will induce a tag (Figure 11), which functions as a link when moving to the next dialogue branch. Figure 12 gives an example of how to navigate to the next question or branch, with help of the tag. The question introducing the choice is "How old are you?"

5   Evaluation

At the time of writing, the programs have been in public use for approximately two months. All user input the word quiz Leksa, the numeral quiz Numra, the bare morphological task Morfa-S and

```
# Adding age-tags
MAP (&dia-adult) TARGET Num (*-1 QDL LINK 0
(Man_boaris_don_leat))(0 ("[2-9][0-9])"r))  ;
MAP (&dia-young) TARGET Num (*-1 QDL LINK 0
(Man_boaris_don_leat))(0 ("[1][0-9])"r))  ;
MAP (&dia-child) TARGET Num (*-1 QDL LINK 0
(Man_boaris_don_leat))(0 ("[1-9])"r))  ;
```

Figure 11: Rules for giving age-tag to the input.

```
<utt type="question" name="Man_boaris_don_leat">
 <text>Man boaris don leat?</text>
 <alt target="young" link="at_school_young"/>
 <alt target="child" link="begin_school_child"/>
 <alt target="adult" link="job_adult"/>
 <alt target="default" link="job_adult"/>
</utt>
```

Figure 12: Navigating to the next question or branch, with help of a tag.

the contextual morphology task Morfa-C has been logged from the very beginning. Unfortunately the programs Vasta and Sahka, have been logged for a couple of days only. The log contains 32475 queries (679 queries/day for the 4 programs logged the whole period), of these, approximately 600, or under 2%, were nonsense answers.

Table 2:   Answers to the programs (Vasta and Sahka were logged at the end of the period only).

Program	Correct	Wrong	Total	%
Morfa-S	6920	6323	13243	52.3
Leksa	5659	4248	9907	57.1
Numra	3086	2512	5598	55.1
Morfa-C	1349	1613	2962	45.5
Sahka	322	322	644	50.0
Vasta	19	102	121	15.7
Total	17355	15120	32475	53,44

As can be seen from Table 2, slightly more than half of the queries resulted in correct answers. When confronted with an error feedback, the user is offered grammatical help, and thereafter she has the possibility to give a new answer to the same query. An investigation of 1500 queries to Morfa-C showed that 444, or 30%, were such repeated answers. Even though we have no log info of the use of the morphological feedback (section 3.3), our impression from classroom experience is that the users are actively using the feedback system. This indicates that what we are witnessing is a truly interactive process, where users err in half of the queries, and then follow up with a new try, possibly after having read the morphological advice from the program.

The error log for Sahka shows that one fourth of the errors are due to orthographical errors (Table 3). Most of the "no finite verb" errors are elliptical answers, and these are not accepted, for pedagogical reasons. The remaining cases are errors where the misspelled verb is an existing word. Also for the other grammatical errors verb errors are dominating. The main goal of the program was to train verb forms in a dialogue, and the error log shows that the program is able to capture such errors.

The logs may not only be used for evaluating the programs, but also for monitoring the learning process as such. To take just one example, the Morfa logs give the error rate for each and every morphosyntactic property and stem type, thereby giving valuable information as to which parts of the verbal paradigm are the most problematic ones.

Table 3: Error types for Sahka, ordered after type.

Error type	#	Error type	#
no finite verb	85	wr. case for V-arg	22
orth. error	83	wr. case after Num	10
wrong S-V agr	46	wrong tense	9
no infinite V	30	no postposition	6
wrong V choice	24	wrong word	7

6 Conclusion

By using a sloppy version of the syntactical analyser for North Sámi, combined with a set of error-detection rules, we have been able to build a flexible CALL resource. The programs are modular, and the modules may be improved by adding more materials – words, tasks, dialogues, levels, words from textbooks. The CG parser framework was originally chosen as parser framework for Sámi due to its extraordinary results for free-text parsing. The present project has shown that CG is well fit for making pedagogical dialogue systems as well.

The program suite is something quite new among pedagogical programs for Sámi, and indeed its dialogue and open QA-programs are quite rare within the field of parser-based CALL. The QA and the dialogue program are tolerant towards variation in student answer (not only string matching), and the random generation of tasks more or less in all of the programs allows the student to use them over and over again.

Acknowledgments

Thanks to the faculty of Humanities at the University of Tromsø, and the Sámi Parliament in Norway, for funding the project.

References

Kenneth R. Beesley and Lauri Karttunen. 2003. *Finite State Morphology*. CSLI publications in Computational Linguistics. USA.

Eckhard Bick. 2003. PaNoLa: Integrating Constraint Grammar and CALL applications for Nordic languages. Holmboe, Henrik (ed.): *Nordic Language Technology, Årbog for Nordisk Sprogteknologisk Forskningsprogram 2000-2004*. 183–190, København: Museum Tusculanums Forlag.

Eckhard Bick. 2005. Live use of Corpus data and Corpus annotation tools in CALL: Some new developments in VISL. Holmboe, Henrik (ed.): *Nordic Language Technology, Årbog for Nordisk Sprogteknologisk Forskningsprogram 2000-2004*, 171–185. København: Museum Tusculanums Forlag.

Johann Gampfer and Judith Knapp. 2001. A review of intelligent CALL systems. *Computer Assisted Language Learning* 15(4):329–342.

Trude Heift. 2001. Intelligent Language Tutoring Systems for Grammar Practice. *Zeitschrift fur Interkulturellen Fremdsprachenunterricht [Online]* 6(2).

Trude Heift and Devlan Nicholson. 2001. Web Delivery of Adaptive and Interactive Language Tutoring. *International Journal of Artificial Intelligence in Education* 12(4):310–325.

Trude Heift and Mathias Schulze. 2007. *Errors and intelligence in computer-assisted language learning: parsers and pedagogues*. Routledge studies in computer-assisted language learning 2. New York : Routledge.

Fred Karlsson and Atro Voutilainen and Juha Heikkilä and Arto Anttila. 1995. *Constraint grammar: a language-independent system for parsing unrestricted text*. Mouton de Gruyter.

Trond Trosterud. 2007. *Language technology for endangered languages: Sámi as a case study*. http://giellatekno.uit.no/background/rvik.pdf University of Tromsø, Norway.

VISL-group. 2008. *Constraint Grammar*. http://beta.visl.sdu.dk/constraint_grammar.html University of Southern Denmark.

ISSN 1736-6305 Vol. 4
http://hdl.handle.net/10062/9206

Learning to Extract Biological Event and Relation Graphs

Jari Björne[1], Filip Ginter[1], Juho Heimonen[2], Sampo Pyysalo[3] and Tapio Salakoski[1,2]
[1]Department of IT, University of Turku
[2]Turku Centre for Computer Science (TUCS)
Joukahaisenkatu 3-5, 20520 Turku, Finland
`firstname.lastname@utu.fi`
[3]Department of Computer Science, University of Tokyo
7-3-1 Hongo, Bunkyo-ku, 113-0033 Tokyo, Japan
`smp@is.s.u-tokyo.ac.jp`

Abstract

While the overwhelming majority of information extraction efforts in the biomedical domain have focused on the extraction of simple binary interactions between named entity pairs, some recently published corpora provide complex, nested and typed event annotations that aim to accurately capture the diversity of biological relationships. We present the first machine learning approach for extracting such relationships, utilizing both a graph kernel and a novel, task-specific feature set. We show that relationships can be predicted with 77% F-score, or 83% if their type and direction is disregarded. Using both gold standard and generated parses, we determine the impact of parsing on extraction performance. Finally, we convert our predicted complex relationships to binary interactions, recovering binary annotation with 62% F-score, relating the new method to the large body of work available on binary interactions.

1 Introduction

The previous decade has brought about an ever-increasing interest in the application of natural language processing methods to address information overload challenges in the biomedical domain (see, e.g., the recent review by Zweigenbaum et al. (2007)). Most domain information extraction (IE) efforts have focused on relationships between biologically interesting molecules. Among these, the most prominent IE target are protein-protein interactions (PPIs). The overwhelming majority of proposed approaches cast the task as determining which pairs of co-occurring entities are related (binary interactions). Many methods further specify the nature of these relationships by

assigning them types or specifying the roles (e.g. agent/patient) that the entities play. While this extraction model has supported considerable advances in biomedical IE and has served as the basis for real-world applications for e.g. assisted database curation (Alex et al., 2008), its limitations, such as the restriction to events between entity pairs commonly referred to as binary interactions in the domain literature, are increasingly recognized by the biomedical NLP community. In this paper, we argue for an alternate model and present the first machine-learning approach to the extraction of structured, complex events and relationships among bioentities.

To overcome the limitations of the pairwise approach to biomedical IE, two recent corpora, BioInfer (Pyysalo et al., 2007a) and the GENIA Event corpus (Kim et al., 2008a) annotate events and static relationships using a more expressive formalism that differs from the prevailing approach in several key aspects: First, type, direction and the trigger statement in the text stating the relationship (often a verb) are annotated. Second, events can have more than two participants whose roles are specified, allowing the accurate representation of statements such as *proteins A, B and C form a complex*. Finally, events can also act as arguments of other events, enabling the annotation of nested events such as *A causes B to bind C* (Figure 1A). These representations largely resemble *event extraction* as formulated in (later) Message Understanding Conferences (MUC) (see, e.g., Sundheim (1995)) and in the Automatic Content Extraction (ACE) program (see, e.g., Doddington (2004)). BioInfer also annotates static relations (e.g. *substructure*) and both BioInfer and GENIA annotate non-biological relationships (e.g. coreferences) with specialized mechanisms. In this paper, we use the term *complex relationship* to encompass both event and generic relationship annotation.

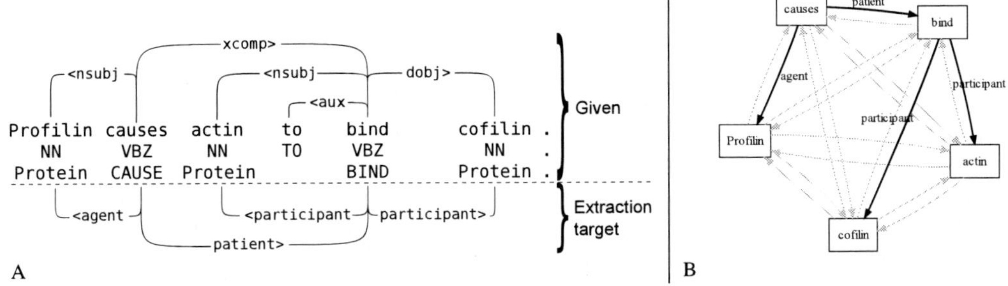

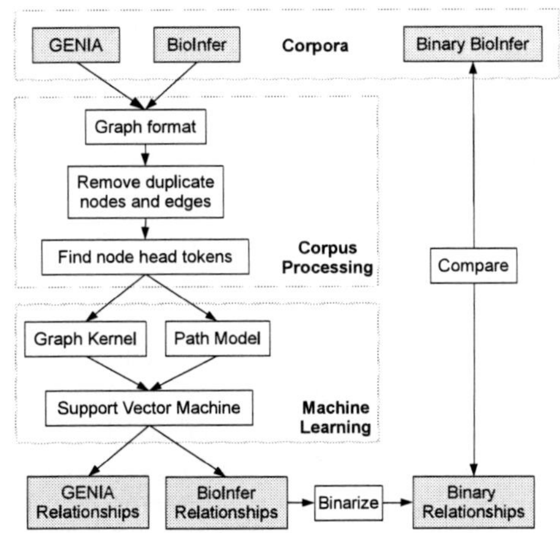

Figure 1: **A.** An example sentence that shows the dependency parse and the relationship graph, whose edges we aim to predict. **B.** Relationship edges can exist between any of the annotated entities and events. For each pair, there can be one undirected or two directed relationships.

In this paper we first introduce the corpora used and their conversion to examples usable for machine learning, then the criteria used for evaluating the system followed by our results. The distinct task of binarization is discussed in its own section. Finally we provide an overview of the related work in this field followed by conclusions.

2 Methods

2.1 Corpora and the Extraction Task

BioInfer consists of 1100 sentences with both semantic and syntactic annotation. For GENIA, we use the 1968 sentence intersection of the GENIA Treebank (syntactic annotation) and GENIA Event corpus (semantic annotation). For developing our system, we used half of each corpus. The other half alone was used for the final experiments to avoid overfitting our system to the data.

In order to use the two corpora for IE, their annotations have to be cast in a single, consistent representation (Figure 1A). Here we follow Björne et al. (2008) and Heimonen et al. (2008) in representing the semantic annotations as graphs whose nodes correspond to entities and events, and labeled directed edges to their relationships. The relationship edges describe *themes* and *causes* of events, structural relations between physical entities such as *substructure* and also non-biological relations such as coreferences. These graphs capture the several distinct forms of annotation in the corpora in a unified, yet expressive format.

The corpora are further processed for our IE task (Figure 2). All entities and events must be represented by a trigger in the text, a constraint imposed to assure that they can be recognized using regular text tagging methods. Some event nodes, like the semantic equality in *actin A (ActA)* that

Figure 2: Outline of the experiments. Corpora are converted to a shared graph representation from which the edges are learned. Binarization of predicted BioInfer relationships allows comparison with a binary version of the corpus.

defines a relationship between *actin A* and *ActA* do not have an explicit trigger word. This type of node and its participant edges are collapsed into an equivalent relationship edge.

Dependency representations of syntax are commonly applied in IE. We use both hand-annotated gold-standard data provided with the corpora as well as parses generated using the Charniak-Lease parser (Lease and Charniak, 2005), which is one of the best-performing parsers in the biomedical domain, achieving an F-score of 81.3% on GENIA and 79.4% on BioInfer (Pyysalo et al., 2007b). All parses are transformed to the Stanford dependency scheme using the tools of de Marneffe et al. (2006). As illustrated in Figure 1A, the dependencies of the parse form a graph that often closely resembles the relationship graph. Roughly 60% of BioInfer and GENIA relationship edges correspond to a single dependency (Björne et al., 2008).

While the nodes of the dependency graph are tokens, the nodes of the relationship graph are entities and events whose triggers can span multiple tokens. To align the graphs, the trigger of each entity or event is associated with one token, its semantic head. This mapping produces a text-bound semantic graph representation (*relationship graph*) that is largely equivalent in information content to the original corpus annotations.

We note that multiple entities or events can occasionally have the same trigger. Since IE systems start from a trigger, producing multiple events or entities of the same type is a non-trivial task which is outside the scope of this study. We represent these cases with one node in the relationship graph. Especially in the case of events, this can lead to some loss of information. In situations like *A and B bind C and D, respectively*, there are two distinct events with the same trigger *bind*.

To summarize, we cast our IE task as one of generating the edges of the relationship graph (Figure 1B) given its nodes, i.e. events and entities. Here we follow the standard division of IE research into identification of entities and subsequent extraction of their relationships, focusing on the subtask of relationship extraction. This definition was chosen as it most resembles the related task of extracting binary protein-protein interactions, which can be viewed as a special case of relationship edges. This allows the straightforward application of already existing methods.

Note that both GENIA and BioInfer only annotate events with explicitly stated participants. Therefore an event with no participants in the relevant span of text (a sentence in BioInfer and a document in GENIA) are not annotated and thus will not be considered for potential relationships.

We perform two main information extraction experiments. First, we extract *untyped undirected* relationships, i.e. detect whether a pair of nodes has a relationship of any type or direction. Second, we extract *typed directed* relationships, where we determine if two nodes have a relationship, in which direction it is defined, and what its type is.

2.2 Defining examples

If a single pair has several relationships of the same direction but different types , these would re-

sult in identical examples. To be able to use standard classifiers that give one classification per example, we merge the types of such examples into one compound type. As seen in Tables 2 and 3 this is extremely rare. We define one example per pair per direction for the typed directed task and one example per pair for the untyped undirected task (Figure 1B). Pairs with an annotated relationship are the positive examples and, as per the closed world assumption, those with no relationship are the negative examples.

For machine learning, each example is represented as a set of features. We compare two feature generation methods (Figure 2). The graph kernel was chosen as we represent the complex relationships in a graph format. For an overview of this recent state-of-the-art method and its use in the extraction of binary interactions we refer to Airola et al. (2008) and Miwa et al. (2008). Since the graph kernel has high memory and processing time requirements, we also developed a new, smaller feature set specifically targeting complex relationships.

2.3 Path Model

The Path Model feature set was developed to be highly specific for the extraction of complex relationships. For each pair of nodes, a number of features are generated. Most of these are based on the shortest path in the syntactic dependency graph (Figure 1A). While the graph kernel uses weights to emphasize tokens and dependencies on the shortest path, our path model aims to capture their relations explicitly.

The shortest path is defined as the shortest undirected path in the dependency graph that connects the head tokens of the two nodes (entities/events) of the example pair. Since multiple paths can exist between tokens in the Stanford dependency scheme, there can be several shortest paths. In such cases, all of them are used to generate features. If no path exists, only the head tokens of the node pair are used for generating features.

Most features are built from the attributes of the tokens and dependencies of the parse. For tokens, these attributes include the text of the token, the part of speech tag (using the Penn Treebank tagset) and the entity/event type (such as *protein* for an entity or *bind* for an event). If the token belongs to a named entity (e.g. a known protein name like *actin*) its text is replaced with a generic placeholder to prevent the system from making predictions based on the frequency of relationships between specific names. The attributes of a dependency are its type (e.g. *subject*) and direction relative to its surrounding dependencies. Unless otherwise stated, all features are binary, that is, they have a value of 1 or 0 (present/absent).

N-grams For each shortest path, a number of *n*-grams are generated by merging the attributes of 2-4 consecutive tokens. Similarly, *n*-grams are built from the types and directions of consecutive dependencies. For each token (resp. dependency), an additional 3-gram merging its attributes with the attributes of its two flanking dependencies (resp. tokens) is defined. Finally, a 2-gram is defined for each pair of consecutive tokens, arranged in the order of their governor-dependent relationship. All of these *n*-grams aim to explicitly state the structural relations that the graph kernel defines only indirectly.

Hanging Dependency Features Tokens immediately outside the path connected by dependencies to the terminal tokens of the path contain information about the context of the two nodes of the example pair. These dependencies "hanging" at the ends of the path are used to define features, as are the tokens they link to.

Individual Component Features For all of the tokens and dependencies on the shortest paths, features are also defined based only on their attributes in isolation of their context. Tokens within the triggers of the two nodes of the example pair are tagged to explicitly state this role. Additional features are defined for each token stating its position at either the terminus or the interior of the path.

Frequency Features The number of tokens in the shortest path is defined as the value of the *length*-feature, as well as explicitly as a *length_n* feature. The number of occurrences of each entity/event type (such as *protein* or *bind*) in the sentence are defined as values of specific features.

Relationship Graph Node Features For the two nodes of each example, features are defined from the combination of their categories (*entity* or *event*) as well as their types (such as *protein* or *bind*). If the triggers of both nodes have the same head token, a feature is defined explicitly representing this potential self-loop.

2.4 Machine Learning

For classification, we use the support vector machine as implemented in SVM^{light} (for the untyped undirected task) and $\text{SVM}^{multiclass}$ (for the typed directed task) by Joachims (1999). All experiments are performed using ten-fold cross-validation. Examples are divided into ten sets on the basis of articles, avoiding the information leak between training and testing described by Sætre et al. (2007). For each of the ten folds, the classifier is trained on the union of eight of the sets. One set is used for a grid search for the optimal SVM regularization parameter C and the remaining set is the test set, separating parameter selection from testing.

2.5 Evaluation Criteria

We use two measures to evaluate our results: the standard F-score metric (the harmonic mean of precision and recall) and AUC.

F-score is a common metric for evaluating relationship extraction, but is sensitive to the class distribution of the data. For binary classification (untyped undirected relationships), the true/false positives/negatives from which F-score is calculated are easily defined. For multiclass classification (typed directed relationships), we have a negative class (i.e. no relationship) and a number of positive classes (the relationship types). F-scores are micro-averaged to take into account the number of instances in each class. For the micro-average, correctly classified non-negative examples are true positives, examples incorrectly classified as instances of a non-negative class are false positives and non-negative examples incorrectly classified as negatives are false negatives.

AUC, or area under the receiver operating characteristic curve, is a class distribution invariant binary performance measure (Hanley and McNeil, 1982). This and other advantages have led to AUC becoming widely adopted in machine learning.

3 Results and Discussion

The performance of the feature generation methods for both the untyped undirected and the typed directed tasks is shown in Table 1. Performance on both tasks is well above the trivial all-positive baseline. For the untyped undirected task, detecting the presence of an edge has the highest F-score of 83% on BioInfer with gold standard parses. As expected, F-score is lower with parses generated

corpus	parse	features	untyped undirected				typed directed		
			P	R	F	AUC	P	R	F
BioInfer	GS	PM	84.4	82.1	83.1±2.3	89.4±1.8	78.7	76.7	77.7±2.6
		GK	74.9	70.6	72.6±2.6	82.6±2.2	72.6	56.8	63.6±2.5
	CL	PM	76.6	67.3	71.5±4.6	81.4±2.6	73.5	61.9	67.0±3.7
		GK	66.8	61.4	63.8±2.4	77.3±1.5	64.2	47.1	54.1±4.1
GENIA	GS	PM	75.5	63.1	68.7±1.5	80.5±1.2	70.2	60.9	65.2±2.4
	CL	PM	72.3	57.4	63.8±2.8	77.6±2.1	65.6	55.5	60.1±3.0

Table 1: Performance of relationship extraction using gold standard (GS) and Charniak-Lease (CL) parses. Examples are classified based on either the path model (PM) or features produced by the graph-kernel (GK). (P)recision, (R)ecall, (F)-score and AUC are shown with standard deviations for F and AUC. For the *typed directed* task, all scores are micro-averaged. The all-positive baseline F-score for the *untyped undirected* task is 31% for BioInfer and 17.1% for GENIA.

by the Charniak-Lease parser (71% on BioInfer), showing the extent to which the parser limits extraction performance.

The path model outperforms the graph kernel for both untyped undirected and typed directed extraction. Despite weighting the shortest path, the graph kernel produces features from the entire sentence for each example, thus resulting in a large number of potentially misleading features. The graph kernel also lacks all explicit n-grams of the path model. Due to its excessive computational requirements, we only apply the graph kernel to the smaller BioInfer dataset.

Predicting types and directions turns the problem into a multi-class classification task. The micro-averages in Table 1 show that this does not notably decrease performance. Compared to the untyped undirected task, F-scores are 3-6 percentage points lower with the path model and 9-10 percentage points lower with the graph kernel. This relatively small difference is promising for future work, as type and direction are important for defining meaningful complex relationships.

Information extraction performance for individual BioInfer relationship edge types is shown in Table 2. Promisingly the most important group for defining biologically interesting relationships, the event-group, shows high precision and recall for all of its types. Many static relationships, e.g. edges of type *identity*, *possessor* and *sub* (we refer to Heimonen (2008) for definitions) can be extracted with even higher reliability, perhaps due in part to a close correspondence to specific syntactic structures, such as prepositional phrases. On the other hand, edges representing complex syntactic structures, such as coreferences (*corefer*) are recovered with lower accuracy, as can be expected since coreference resolution is best addressed us-

group	type	count	P	R	F
event	participant	836	80.0	77.2	78.6
	patient	655	79.7	77.4	78.5
	agent	428	75.5	66.8	70.9
static	identity	289	86.5	88.9	87.7
	sub	134	85.5	79.1	82.2
	possessor	119	83.2	83.2	83.2
	member	105	64.8	43.8	52.3
	super	59	78.2	72.9	75.4
	nesting	20	66.7	50.0	57.1
non-biol.	equal	120	60.5	60.0	60.3
	corefer	66	55.6	22.7	32.3
	rel-ent	22	0.0	0.0	0.0
merged	contain+sub	20	0.0	0.0	0.0
	member+agent	3	0.0	0.0	0.0
	agent+patient	3	0.0	0.0	0.0
	f-contain+sub	2	0.0	0.0	0.0

Table 2: Per-type results of extraction of *typed directed* relationships from BioInfer using gold standard parses and the path model. Count shows the number of examples of a given type from a total of 31674 including negatives.

ing a specialized method. Merged edges are a result of having one edge per pair of nodes per direction (see Section 2.2). These very rare cases are not recovered by the learning-based approach.

Performance per GENIA edge type is shown in Table 3. Non-biological relationships, such as coreferences, are syntactically diverse structures and have unsurprisingly a low performance. *Cause* and *theme* types define the participants of events and roughly correspond to the *agent* and *patient* types of BioInfer, respectively. The *participant* type of BioInfer describes relationships that can be thought of as either *agent* or *patient*. GENIA uses the *theme* type for such cases.

The high performance for both BioInfer and GENIA typed directed relationship extraction is especially noticeable in light of the very high class imbalance. Even for the most common types the

group	type	count	P	R	F
event	theme	3164	73.6	65.1	69.1
	cause	1202	65.3	54.7	59.5
non-biol.	coref	252	51.2	25.4	34.0
	scatter	169	40.0	17.8	24.6
merged	cause+theme	1	0.0	0.0	0.0

Table 3: Per-type results of extraction of *typed directed* relationships from GENIA using gold standard parses and the path model. Count shows the number of examples of a given type from a total of 104198 including negatives.

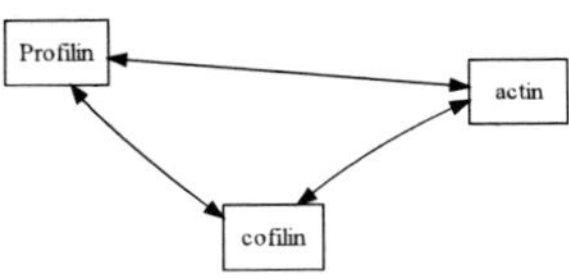

Figure 3: Untyped undirected binary relationships. Compare with Figure 1B. In this example, all possible binary relationships exist.

positive/negative ratio is about 0.03. The most common BioInfer type, *participant*, has 836 positives vs. 30838 negatives (Table 2). For GENIA, the most common type, *theme*, has 3164 positives vs. 101034 negatives (Table 3).

We tested the impact of the feature groups defined in Section 2.3 by disabling one group at a time. F-score decreased at most less than 2 percentage points, indicating a substantial overlap of information between the groups. We also tried defining the features without entity/event types, which reduced F-score by 4.4 percentage points, indicating that this information is important but not critical for the system.

4 Binarization

The prevailing approach in the domain is to extract binary interactions, that is, relationships restricted to occurring between pairs of physical entities (most often proteins). To compare the performance of the proposed approach to these existing extraction systems, the semantically rich relationship graphs must be reduced into a less-expressive, binarized form. Examples of binary relationships are shown in Figure 3.

The transformation from a complex to a binary relationship graph has been shown to be possible for BioInfer (Heimonen et al., 2008). This binarization process aims to express as binary relationships the biologically relevant information present

corpus	parse	P	R	F
BioInfer	GS	74.2	53.7	62.3
	CL	70.7	42.9	53.4

Table 4: Performance of binary relationship extraction measured against the binarized gold standard BioInfer relationship annotation for which the F-score of the all-positive baseline is 40.8%.

in complex relationships, while minimizing the inevitable loss of information. Consider, for example, the sentence *Phosphorylation of cofilin regulates actin polymerization*, which expresses the events *regulation, phosphorylation* and *polymerization* among the proteins *cofilin* and *actin*. It can be summarized with a binary relationship *regulation* while the information regarding *phosphorylation* and *polymerization* is lost.

The predicted typed directed complex relationship graphs for BioInfer were binarized using the software of Heimonen et al. (2008). The output was evaluated against the binarized gold standard BioInfer relationship annotation. To compare with previously published results on this dataset, we treat the relationships as untyped undirected. The results of the evaluation are presented in Table 4. The F-score of 53.4% for the Charniak-Lease parsed data should be related to the F-score of 61.3% reported by Airola et al. (2008). This difference can be partly explained by the fact that the binarizer was developed for hand-annotated data rather than noisy, automatically generated data. Also, the precision of 70.7% suggests that complex relationships recovered by the system to the point that they could be binarized were often correct. We have thus shown that the output of an IE system targeting complex relationship graphs can be binarized, although this process currently results in lower performance than extraction methods directly targeting binary interactions.

5 Related Work

Extraction of protein relationships is a key task in biomedical NLP, and has been widely studied in the simple setting of recognizing pairs of related co-occurring entities. The problem has been considered in recent shared tasks (Nedéllec, 2005; Krallinger et al., 2008) as well as in dozens of studies employing a variety of different corpora for training and evaluation (Pyysalo et al., 2008).

Several recently proposed extraction methods

make use of dependency representations of syntax (Kim et al., 2008b; Miwa et al., 2008), including the Stanford dependency representation (Airola et al., 2008; Van Landeghem et al., 2008; Katrenko and Adriaans, 2008). Many of the features we apply are standard in relation extraction studies; for a recent study of "ACE-style" feature sets see the study by Buyko et al. (2008).

By contrast to the wealth of IE studies focusing on pairs of related entities, has received much less attention. While hand-written systems capable of extracting structured events (Friedman et al., 2001) have been proposed, the present study is to the best of our knowledge the first to consider the task of learning to extract events as represented in the BioInfer and GENIA corpora. Further, while task settings similar to ours have been widely considered in the MUC and ACE evaluations and part of the task setting shares many characteristics with semantic role labeling as considered e.g. in the recent CoNLL evaluation (Surdeanu et al., 2008), meaningful comparison across domains and resources would be difficult to establish. In relating our results to those of previously proposed methods, we will thus only consider biomedical relationship extraction results as they relate to our results for binarized relation extraction.

Due to the difficulty of meaningful comparison of reported results across different corpora (Airola et al., 2008; Van Landeghem et al., 2008), we will consider our results in comparison with recently proposed methods evaluated on the AIMed corpus (Bunescu et al., 2005), which is frequently used in domain studies (Bunescu et al., 2005; Giuliano et al., 2006; Airola et al., 2008; Van Landeghem et al., 2008; Miyao et al., 2008; Miwa et al., 2008) and can be seen as an emerging *de facto* standard for biomedical relationship extraction method evaluation. Among these comparable studies, the best results are reported by Miwa et al. (2008) using the graph kernel of Airola et al. (2008), considered also in the present study. We note that Airola et al. (2008) report an F-score of 61% on the BioInfer corpus for the binary relationship extraction task. Given that our method is not primarily intended for this type of binary PPI extraction and that our binarization method was not originally developed to deal with noisy input, we find our result of 53% F-score on BioInfer (62% with gold standard parses) encouraging.

The system described in this paper formed the basis for the best-performing system in the primary task of the BioNLP'09 Shared Task on Event Extraction,[1] further validating the presented approach and results (Björne et al., 2009).

6 Conclusions

We provide the first system designed for extracting complex relationships as defined in the BioInfer and GENIA Event corpora, using the complex semantic annotation they provide that allows interaction extraction between a broader set of biological concepts than only named molecules. The unified graph format abstracts from the various information extraction tasks and defines a shared representation for the layers of annotation in both BioInfer and the GENIA Event corpus. This abstraction provides a representation approachable for the general NLP community lacking extensive knowledge of the biological details.

Classification performance of the system, even on typed and directed data, was good, and having a system that predicts typed events (e.g. binding or phosphorylation) provides valuable data when extracting specific information about a defined biological issue. By binarizing our predicted relationship graphs, we have shown that complex relationship extraction need not be a completely separate problem from binary interaction extraction.

As a contribution to the emerging field of complex relationship extraction, we will publish the software used to convert GENIA and BioInfer to the shared graph format, the extraction system and the software used for binarizing the extracted complex relationships.

Acknowledgments

This work was funded by the Academy of Finland. We thank CSC - IT Center for Science Ltd. for providing computational resources.

References

A. Airola, S. Pyysalo, J. Björne, T. Pahikkala, F. Ginter, and T. Salakoski. 2008. All-paths graph kernel for protein-protein interaction extraction with evaluation of cross-corpus learning. *BMC Bioinformatics*, 9(Suppl 11):S2.

B. Alex, C. Grover, B. Haddow, M. Kabadjov, E. Klein, M. Matthews, S. Roebuck, R. Tobin, and X. Wang. 2008. Assisted curation: Does text mining really help? In *Proc. of PSB'08*.

---

[1] http://www-tsujii.is.s.u-tokyo.ac.jp/GENIA/SharedTask

J. Björne, S. Pyysalo, F. Ginter, and T. Salakoski. 2008. How complex are complex protein-protein interactions? In *Proc. of SMBM'08*, pages 125–128.

J. Björne, J. Heimonen, F. Ginter, A. Airola, T. Pahikkala, and T. Salakoski. 2009. Extracting complex biological events with rich graph-based features sets. In *Proc. of the BioNLP'09 Workshop at NAACL-HLT 2009*. To appear.

R. Bunescu, R. Ge, R. Kate, E. Marcotte, R. Mooney, A. Ramani, and Y. Wong. 2005. Comparative experiments on learning information extractors for proteins and their interactions. *Artificial Intelligence in Medicine*, 33(2):139–155.

E. Buyko, E. Beisswanger, and U. Hahn. 2008. Testing different ACE-style feature sets for the extraction of gene regulation relations from MEDLINE abstracts. In *Proc. of SMBM'08*, pages 21–28.

G. Doddington, A. Mitchell, M. Przybocki, L. Ramshaw, S. Strassel, and R. Weischedel. 2004. The Automatic Content Extraction (ACE) program: Tasks, data, and evaluation. In *Proc. of LREC'04*, pages 837–840.

C. Friedman, P. Kra, H. Yu, M. Krauthammer, and A. Rzhetsky. 2001. GENIES: A natural-language processing system for the extraction of molecular pathways from journal articles. *Bioinformatics*, 17(Suppl. 1):S74–S82.

C. Giuliano, A. Lavelli, and L. Romano. 2006. Exploiting shallow linguistic information for relation extraction from biomedical literature. In *Proc. of EACL'06*, pages 401–408.

J. A. Hanley and B. J. McNeil. 1982. The meaning and use of the area under a receiver operating characteristic (ROC) curve. *Radiology*, 143(1):29–36.

J. Heimonen, S. Pyysalo, F. Ginter, and T. Salakoski. 2008. Complex-to-pairwise mapping of biological relationships using a semantic network representation. In *Proc. of SMBM'08*.

T. Joachims, 1999. *Advances in Kernel Methods - Support Vector Learning*, chapter Making large-Scale SVM Learning Practical. MIT-Press.

S. Katrenko and P. Adriaans. 2008. A local alignment kernel in the context of nlp. In *Proc. of Coling'08*.

J-D. Kim, T. Ohta, and Tsujii J. 2008a. Corpus annotation for mining biomedical events from literature. *BMC Bioinformatics*, 9(1):10.

S. Kim, J. Yoon, and J. Yang. 2008b. Kernel approaches for genic interaction extraction. *Bioinformatics*, 24(1):118–126.

M. Krallinger, F. Leitner, C. Rodriguez-Penagos, and A. Valencia. 2008. Overview of the protein-protein interaction annotation extraction task of BioCreative II. *Genome Biology*, 9(Suppl 2):S4.

M. Lease and E. Charniak. 2005. Parsing biomedical literature. In *Proc. of the Second International Joint Conference on Natural Language Processing*, Lecture notes in computer science, pages 58–69.

M.-C. de Marneffe, B. MacCartney, and C. D. Manning. 2006. Generating typed dependency parses from phrase structure parses. In *Proc. of LREC'06*, pages 449–454.

M. Miwa, R. Sætre, Y. Miyao, T. Ohta, and J. Tsujii. 2008. Combining multiple layers of syntactic information for protein-protein interaction extraction. In *Proc. of SMBM'08*.

Y. Miyao, R. Sætre, K. Sagae, T. Matsuzaki, and J. Tsujii. 2008. Task-oriented evaluation of syntactic parsers and their representations. In *Proc. of ACL'08*, pages 46–54.

C. Nedéllec. 2005. Learning Language in Logic – genic interaction extraction challenge. In *Proc. of the 4th ICML Workshop on Learning Language in Logic*, pages 31–37, Aug.

S. Pyysalo, F. Ginter, J. Heimonen, J. Björne, J. Boberg, J. Järvinen, and T. Salakoski. 2007a. BioInfer: A corpus for information extraction in the biomedical domain. *BMC Bioinformatics*, 8(1):50.

S. Pyysalo, F. Ginter, V. Laippala, K. Haverinen, J. Heimonen, and T. Salakoski. 2007b. On the unification of syntactic annotations under the stanford dependency scheme: A case study on BioInfer and GENIA. In *Proc. of BioNLP'07*, pages 25–32.

S. Pyysalo, A. Airola, J. Heimonen, J. Björne, F. Ginter, and T. Salakoski. 2008. Comparative analysis of five protein-protein interaction corpora. *BMC Bioinformatics*, 9(Suppl 3):S6.

R. Sætre, K. Sagae, and J. Tsujii. 2007. Syntactic features for protein-protein interaction extraction. In *Second International Symposium on Languages in Biology and Medicine short papers*.

B. M. Sundheim. 1995. Overview of results of the MUC-6 evaluation. In *Proc. of MUC-6*, pages 13–31.

M. Surdeanu, R. Johansson, A. Meyers, L. Màrquez, and J. Nivre. 2008. The CoNLL-2008 shared task on joint parsing of syntactic and semantic dependencies. In *Proc. of CoNLL'08*, pages 159–177.

S. Van Landeghem, Y. Saeys, B. De Baets, and Y. Van de Peer. 2008. Extracting protein-protein interactions from text using rich feature vectors and feature selection. In *Proc. of SMBM'08*.

P. Zweigenbaum, D. Demner-Fushman, H. Yu, and K. B. Cohen. 2007. Frontiers of biomedical text mining: current progress. *Briefings in Bioinformatics*, 8(5):358–375.

ISSN 1736-6305 Vol. 4
http://hdl.handle.net/10062/9206

Using Uplug and SiteSeeker to construct a cross language search engine for Scandinavian languages

Hercules Dalianis   **Martin Rimka**   **Viggo Kann** *

Dept of Computer and System Sciences, School of Computer Science and Communication*
KTH and Stockholm University
Forum 100, 164 40 Kista, Sweden
Email: `hercules@dsv.su.se`, `rimka@dsv.su.se`, `viggo@csc.kth.se`

Abstract

This paper presents how we adapted a website search engine for cross language information retrieval, using the Uplug word alignment tool for parallel corpora. We first studied the monolingual search queries posed by the visitors of the website of the Nordic council containing six different languages. In order to compare how well different types of bilingual dictionaries covered the most common queries and terms on the website we tried a collection of ordinary bilingual dictionaries, a small manually constructed trilingual dictionary and an automatically constructed trilingual dictionary, constructed from the news corpus in the website using Uplug. The precision and recall of the automatically constructed Swedish-English dictionary using Uplug were 71 and 93 percent, respectively. We found that precision and recall increase significantly in samples with high word frequency, but we could not confirm that POS-tags improve precision. The collection of ordinary dictionaries, consisting of about 200 000 words, only cover half of the top 100 search queries at the website. The automatically built trilingual dictionary combined with the small manually built trilingual dictionary consists of about 2000 words and covers 27 of the top 100 search queries.

Key words: Cross language information retrieval, parallel corpora, word alignment, Swedish, Danish, Norwegian.

1   Introduction

Scandinavian languages as Swedish, Norwegian, and Danish are comprehensible for Scandinavians. A typical Swede will for example understand written and to a certain degree spoken Danish, but is not able to speak Danish, that is he has a passive understanding of Danish (and vice versa for the other speakers).

The development of Internet has caused a new problem: the Scandinavians have difficulty finding information in the other neighboring languages since they do not have active knowledge in the other languages and therefore cannot write correct search queries.

The Nordic council experiences exactly such a problem on its website http://www.norden.org, since it has information in the main Nordic languages: Swedish, Danish, Norwegian, Icelandic, Finnish as well as English. The three languages Swedish, Danish and Norwegian are by the Nordic council considered to be one language – Scandinavian – and intercomprehensible, and are therefore not translated into their counterparts. Both employed and visitors at the website have difficulty finding information since the information in the Scandinavian languages are not overlapping and the users are not active users of two or more of the Scandinavian languages. The Nordic council therefore sponsored a research project to construct a Nordic on-line dictionary (Kann & Hollman 2007) and a cross language search engine to make it possible to search in for example Swedish and also find information in Danish and Norwegian. The research presented in this paper was done in this project.

2   Previous research

Most approaches to cross language information retrieval use general bilingual dictionaries, for example Indonesian-English, the MUST system, (Lin 1999) Amharic-English, CLEF, (Argaw et al 2004), Chinese-Japanese-English-Spanish-German, web search engine, (Zhou et al 2005), French-English, Questioning answer system (Plamondon & Foster 2003). One interesting approach in cross language information retrieval is the approach in Järvelin et al (2006) using fuzzy matching as the only translation technique for the two closely related languages Swedish and Norwegian.

There is a lack of bilingual dictionaries between small languages. A solution would be to use existing bilingual dictionaries between a small and a large language to create a bilingual dictionary for two small languages. This method is called pivot alignment and is argued for in Borin (2000). Borin writes that "Pivot alignment in-creases word alignment recall, without sacrificing precision", but in Zhou et al (2004) pivot language translation is said to make a 52% drop in performance compared to direct translation.

Charitakis (2007) used Uplug for aligning words in a Greek-English parallel corpus. The corpus was comparably sparse and unannotated, containing 200 000 words from each language downloaded from two different real bilingual websites. A sample of 498 word-pairs from Uplug were evaluated by expert evaluators and the result was 51 percent correct translated terms (frequency >3). When studying high frequent word pairs (>11), there were 67 percent correct translated terms. Velupillai & Dalianis (2008) showed 94 percent correct translation (in average) on the closely related languages Swedish, Danish and Norwegian using Uplug.

The ITools suite for word alignment was used in Nyström et al (2006) on a medical parallel corpus containing 174 000 Swedish words and 153 000 English words, thereby creating 31 000 terms with 76 percent precision and 77 percent recall.

It is well known that stemming in information retrieval increases precision and recall (e.g. Carlberger et al 2001), therefore one could assume that stemming eventually would improve word alignment. However, Strömbäck (2005) has experimented to use lemmatization before executing Uplug on an English-Swedish corpus, and his results do not give any clear indication whether stemming is useful in word alignment.

Schrader (2004) shows that lemmatization and tagging of English and German parallel text decrease precision but improve recall in word alignment.

Toutanova et al (2002) showed up to 16 percent error reduction in word alignment for English and French (Hansard parallel corpora) using POS tagging.

Compound splitting, which can be done automatically with high accuracy (Sjöbergh and Kann 2006), is another approach that could give good results before performing word alignment, see Popoviç et al (2006), though they do not write how large the improvement is.

Thus, the previous research raised a number of important research questions and problems: Does POS-tagging improve word alignment quality? What is the optimal size of the parallel corpus to obtain good quality bilingual dictionaries? Is lemmatization or stemming before word alignment a good approach to increase precision/recall? How useful is a pivot language in the process of creating bilingual dictionaries, and what is the best pivot language to use in this project? What is the lowest word frequency for a good quality word alignment?

3 Content of website and search behavior

The website experimented on was the website of the Nordic council containing around 40 000 web pages written in six different languages. To find out the search behavior of the users and also find out what type of information (and in which languages) is available at the website of the Nordic council, we connected the commercial search engine SiteSeeker and its search box to the Nordic council's web site and let the search engine run for six months. By this experiment we found the most common search queries, the search queries with no answers, in which languages the queries were written, etc.

Around 10 000 search queries are made per month on the website. The queries are in many different languages, most often in Swedish, English and Finnish.

Very early we took the 100 most common search queries posed to the website of the Nordic council and translated them manually to the other Scandinavian languages, i.e. manually created and customized a Scandinavian dictionary. When we later got better statistics of the search queries we found that this trilingual dictionary in fact only covers 24 of the 100 most common search queries.

From the website we also extracted from each of four languages the 200 words with the highest tf-idf, that is the most significant words in each language on the website. These 800 words hence gave us a picture of the website.

We compared these words with a collection of bi- and trilingual dictionaries that we had access to, to find the coverage of the dictionaries. The dictionaries were the Lexin dictionaries Swedish-English, English-Swedish, Danish-Swedish, and Norwegian-Swedish-English, and the Nordic council Skandinavisk ordbok which is Swedish-Danish-Norwegian. The dictionaries contain altogether about 200 000 unique words. We found that of the 200 most common terms in each language on the website, on average 73 percent were covered by these dictionaries. The manual dictionary of 231 words covered 9 percent of the 800 most common search words on the website and 24 percent of the 100 most common search queries.

The collection of dictionaries covered only half (54) of the 100 most common search queries. It was reassuring to see that the entire website covered 98 of the 100 most common search queries (in practice 100 percent, since the only uncovered search queries "indtaste søgeord" and "skrifið leitarorð", meaning "Enter search words", were predefined queries at the website).

In order to be really useful for cross language searching the bi- and trilingual dictionaries have to be extended to all four languages (Danish, Norwegian, Swedish, and English). Even if this was done the amount of covered most common queries would probably still be about half.

Dalianis (2002) showed that one cannot use ordinary dictionaries for good quality automatic spell checking of queries to search engines. Ordinary dictionaries do not really match the very domain specific content on a website. Our covering results confirm this.

4 Corpora

The covering analysis motivated us to automatically build a trilingual dictionary using parallel news texts from the Nordic council website.

The news texts are mostly written in one language and then translated to three other languages, so that each article will exist in English, Finnish, Icelandic, and Scandinavian. Swedish, Danish, and Norwegian are thus considered to be one language, and therefore news written in one of these languages is not translated to the other Scandinavian languages. For example, a news text written in Swedish is translated into English, Finnish, and Icelandic, but not to Danish or Norwegian.

The consequence of this is that English, Icelandic, and Finnish can be considered to be pivot languages for Swedish, Danish, and Norwegian.

We extracted 4 873 news articles in RSS format, written in Swedish, Danish, Norwegian, and English. These articles were comparably short, in average containing 160 words per article, in total 260 000 words per language, except for English where there were 865 000 words, see table 1. Each English version of a news article had always a parallel version written in either Swedish, Danish, or Norwegian.

Parallel texts	No of news texts	English words	Swe/Dan/Nor words
Eng-Swe	1 569	259 364	229 215
Eng-Dan	1 638	299 992	272 516
Eng-Nor	1 666	305 866	278 626
Total	4 873	865 222	780 357

Table 1. Number of news texts and words in different corpora

Apart from the news texts, the Nordic Council website contains other parallel or semi-parallel texts, for example organization, regulations, procedures, fact sheets etc. However, these documents are very few compared to the news texts.

5 Word alignment

As a word alignment tool we decided to use Uplug, since many researchers recommended it and Uplug has been used with successful results for other languages, e.g. Swedish and Turkish (Megyesi & Dahlqvist 2007).

Uplug is a word alignment tool for parallel corpora and was developed at Uppsala University by Jörg Tiedemann (Tiedemann 2003, Uplug 2008). Uplug works excellent (we have used version 0.1.9d) even though it can be memory consuming, mostly when doing sentence alignment in large corpora. The memory problem, however, can be easily solved with 'hard delimiter' tags (Gale and Church 1991).

We executed Uplug on the parallel texts written in English and Swedish, English and Danish, and English and Norwegian.

The news articles were extracted from the RSS file, language classified with LingPipe (2006), and merged into one corpus file per language. To allow sentence alignment only within article boundaries, we added hard delimiters.

The corpus files were tokenized with built-in Uplug scripts and aligned with a sentence aligner based on the statistical model of sentence length (Gale and Church 1991). The output was then word aligned with Uplug, which uses a combination of statistical and linguistic information to align single and multi-word units (Tiedemann 2003). The Uplug output was presented both in XML format (with word link certainty and other clues) and in text format, as a frequency table with word frequency, source and target terms (table 2).

40	sustainable	hållbar
40	responsibility	ansvar
40	proposal	förslag
40	increase	öka

Table 2. English-Swedish frequency table

According to rough manual estimation, word links with frequency 3 and higher had much better precision than links with low frequency (1-2).

We also executed Uplug on corpora that were lemmatized with CST Lemmatiser (Jongejan and Haltrup 2005); however, we could not see any

significant improvement in the Uplug output. We attributed this fact to insufficient accuracy in the lemmatization rules, and thus continued to use corpora with inflected forms remaining. The English-Swedish, English-Danish, and English-Norwegian frequency tables were used to create a Swedish-Danish-Norwegian dictionary using English as pivot language (Borin 2000, Sjöbergh 2005). The Swedish, Danish, and Norwegian tokens which were linked to the identical English tokens were considered to be equivalents. For example, Swedish *hållbar*, Danish *bæredygtig*, and Norwegian *bærekraftig* were linked in the Uplug output to the English word *sustainable* (table 3); therefore the three Scandinavian words could be aligned to each other.

This method is rather approximate and may align words which do not have the same meaning. Nevertheless, we found it useful in creating multi-lingual dictionaries for expanding search queries. To achieve better precision, we extracted only links with frequency 3 or above.

Frequency table	Word link	
Eng-Swe	*sustainable*	*hållbar*
Eng-Dan	*sustainable*	*bæredygtig*
Eng-Nor	*sustainable*	*bærekraftig*

Table 3. Example with Swedish, Danish, and Norwegian tokens aligned to an English token

One spin-off effect of such pivot alignment method was that we obtained synonym lists in each of the aligned languages. For example, if English *production* was linked to Swedish *produktion* and *tillverkning*, then both Swedish words could be considered synonyms and obtained using the same software as for extracting Scandinavian triplets. The same method was used by Kann and Rosell (2005) constructing possible synonym pairs that were later evaluated by Internet users.

Coverage	200 000 words in dictionaries	231 words in manual dictionary	1984 words in half-automatic dictionary	Complete website
800 most common words on website	76 %	9%	24%	100%
100 most common search queries	54 %	24%	27%	98%
250 most common search queries	36 %	14%	17%	98%

Table 4. Coverage of the website and queries by dictionaries

For production purposes, we obtained 805 triplets in Swedish-Danish-Norwegian (1834 unique words), from Uplug results and after pivot alignment that later were manually corrected (half-automatic dictionary) and merged with the manually constructed trilingual dictionary. This merged dictionary containing 1984 unique words was integrated in the SiteSeeker search engine to support the cross-lingual information retrieval on the Nordic council website. We investigated how this half-automatic dictionary covers the common words and queries of the website of the Nordic council. The coverage is about half of that for the 100 times larger collection of dictionaries, and it is more useful for cross-language searching, since it is not just bilingual. Table 4 summarizes the coverage results for evaluation purpose. We aligned the Swedish and English corpus with and without part-of-speech (POS) tags. The corpus was tagged using the TNT tagger (Brants 2000). The English model was trained on the Penn Treebank corpus. The Swedish model was trained on the Stockholm-Umeå Corpus (SUC) annotated with the Parole tagset (Megyesi 2001).

6   Evaluation

To evaluate the Uplug output, we used a prior evaluation method with gold standards (Ahrenberg et al 2000). This evaluation requires additional tailor-made software. However, one can re-use the gold standards for different types of parallel corpora (e.g. with and without POS-tags). In addition, prior evaluation allows for more accurate measurement of the system output because it is based on the corpora used by the system.

The gold standards were built by manually annotating links in the sentence-aligned Swedish-English parallel corpora, in accordance to the manual annotation guidelines (Merkel 1999). We omitted, however, the definite articles in the gold standards in order to make them more consistent with the bilingual lexicons required for the query expansion. The articles and other stop words are not included in such lexicons because these words have low significance in normal search.

To build the gold standard, we used a sample of the 5 000 most frequent search queries from the Nordic council website. We chose this type of sample in order to examine how the extracted bilingual lexicon can support the query expansion in parallel corpora.

We established that 647 terms (13% of the sample) could be found in the Swedish corpus used by Uplug in word alignment. These terms were divided into three frequency categories (table 5). The terms from each frequency category were then used to build a separate gold standard. The fourth gold standard was built by merging the first three gold standards, i.e. it contained terms from all frequency categories (337 terms).

We intended to make the gold standards as extensive as possible, but we also applied certain limitations on the sample to make it more close to the bilingual dictionary needed to support query expansion. Thus, the gold standards included only Swedish nouns and adjectives with different spelling than their English equivalents. The words with identical spelling as their translations (most of the proper names and abbreviations) were omitted because they did not require query expansion, and hence, were not important for evaluation. The sample terms with missing or indirect translations were also left out, i.e. only 'regular' links were allowed in the gold standards.

Frequency category	Sample terms found in Swedish corpus	Sample terms included in gold standards
1-2	229	91
3-10	206	111
>10	212	138

Table 5. Distribution of sample terms across frequency categories

The evaluation was done with the built-in Uplug script *evalalign.pl* which uses the MWU measures (Tiedemann 2003). These measures are tailored to produce more reliable values for precision and recall in the system links which contain multi-word units (MWU).

Table 6 presents precision values for the Swedish-English corpora measured against the four gold standards. We evaluated word alignment in the two types of Swedish-English corpora – without linguistic information (default pre-processing) and with it (POS-tags).

The main purpose of this evaluation was to measure the quality of Uplug used on the Nordic council corpus. We also wanted to examine whether POS-tags can improve word alignment.

Frequency category	Corpora with default pre-processing	Corpora with POS-tags
1-2	54%	54%
3-10	70%	67%
>10	83%	76%
all freq	**71%**	67%

Table 6. Precision in the Swedish-English corpora

Several conclusions can be made from this table. First, not surprisingly, words with higher frequency are aligned with better precision. For example, rare words which occur only once or twice in Swedish corpus show 54% precision, whereas words with frequency above 10 have 83% precision. These results are also very close to the results of Strömbäck (2005).

Next, the gold standard based on the middle frequency category (3-10) returns similar precision value as the gold standard consisting of terms in all frequency categories. In other words, the middle category is representative of all frequency categories together.

These two observations are consistent across both the default and POS-tagged corpora.

Finally, precision of the POS-tagged corpora in all frequencies (67%) is lower than precision of the corpora without POS-tags (71%). We can also observe that the difference between the default and POS-tagged corpus increases in middle and high frequency categories. Thus, the lowest frequency category shows almost identical precision for both types of corpora, whereas the difference between the precision values in the highest frequency category reaches 7%.

Frequency category	Corpora with default pre-processing	Corpora with POS-tags
1-2	82%	83%
3-10	95%	92%
>10	98%	96%
all freq	**93%**	91%

Table 7. Recall in the Swedish-English corpora

Table 7 presents recall values for the Swedish-English corpora. In this table, we can observe similar tendency across the recall values – the words with high frequency produce better recall values compared to the words with low frequency. Furthermore, the corpus with POS-tags has lower recall value than the corpus without POS-tags, except for the lowest frequency category.

On the other hand, the difference among the recall values in the default and POS-tagged corpus is not as distinct as among the precision values.

7   SiteSeeker uses bilingual dictionaries

The cross language dictionary with the 805 triplets in Swedish, Danish and Norwegian was connected to the SiteSeeker search engine. The search works as a query expansion expanding the original term to terms in the others languages provided the original term has a translation to another term. The interface can filter the hit lists based on language, see figure 1. 30 percent of the top 100 queries used cross-lingual information retrieval. The top 100 queries compose 8 percent of the total queries, and the top 5 000 queries compose 50 percent of the total queries. Of the top 100 queries 24 percent were proper nouns that of course were not translated.

Figure 1 shows an example of the cross language search on the Nordic council website. The Swedish word *arbetsmarknad* in the original search query *nordisk arbetsmarknad* is expanded to the Danish word *arbejdsmarked* which allows retrieving the relevant documents in Danish.

During 2006, the search statistics of Site-Seeker showed 36 percent queries with no hits. During 2008, with the cross language dictionary connected to SiteSeeker, we obtained only 19 percent queries with no hits, about half of the 2006 value, even though the site had about the same amount of indexed pages as in 2006.

8   Conclusions

Our conclusions from the experiments with the website of the Nordic council are that it is very difficult to obtain a large enough parallel corpus to automatically create a large enough bilingual or trilingual dictionary covering all types of queries from the users.

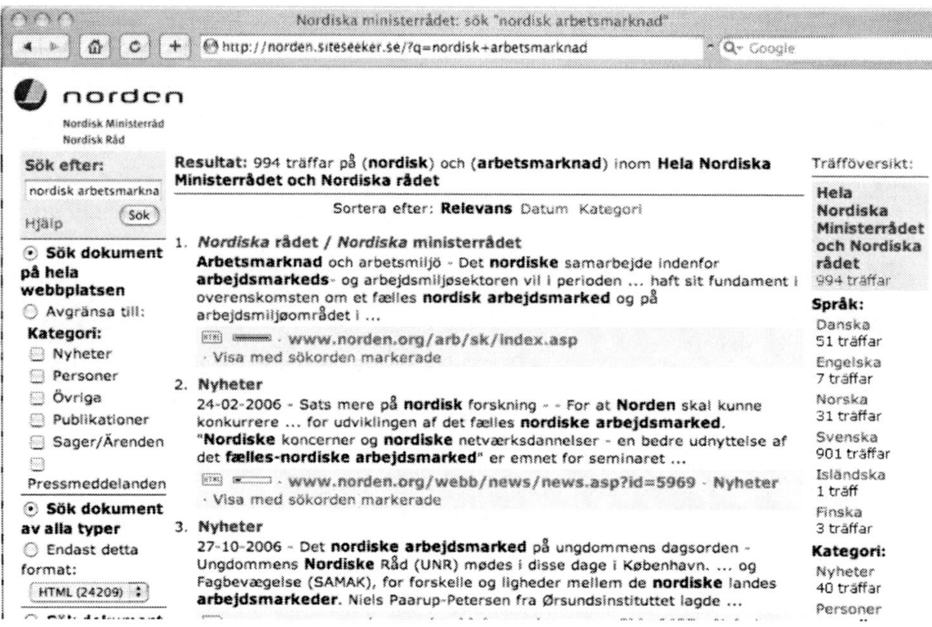

Figure 1. Cross language search on the Nordic council website

In order to improve the coverage a supplementary trilingual dictionary could be manually built using statistics of the top queries.

Word alignment quality using Uplug was high considering the small corpus. Also, we discovered that POS-tagging did not improve word alignment.

Pivot alignment is a useful trick that made our work possible. The similarity between the Scandinavian languages made the drop in performance due to the pivot alignment too small to be visible.

We post-processed the dictionary removing duplicate translations and translations that contained words that were shorter than four characters. This increased the quality and usefulness of the trilingual dictionary considerably.

The extracted words of the 4 873 news texts did not really cover the words in the 40 000 web pages, but when combined with a small hand-made trilingual dictionary they covered the most common search queries reasonably well.

Future work will encompass the impact of lemmatization in word alignment and as well as the use of other word alignment tools.

References

Ahrenberg, L., M. Merkel, A. Sågvall Hein and J. Tiedemann. 2000. Evaluation of word alignment systems. In Proc. LREC 2000, Athens.

Argaw, A., L. Asker, R. Cöster and J. Karlgren 2004. Dictionary-based Amharic - English Information Retrieval. In Proc. Cross Language Evaluation Forum (CLEF 2004), Bath, UK.

Borin L. 2000. You'll take the high road and I'll take the low road: Using a third language to improve bilingual word alignment. In Proc. 18th International Conference on Computational Linguistics. COLING 2000, Vol. 1. Saarbrücken: Universität des Saarlandes. 97-103.

Brants, T. 2000. TnT - A Statistical Part-of-Speech Tagger. In Proc. Sixth Applied Natural Language Processing Conference ANLP-2000, Seattle, WA.

Carlberger, J., H. Dalianis, M. Hassel, and O. Knutsson 2001. Improving Precision in Information Retrieval for Swedish using Stemming. In Proc. Nodalida 2001, Uppsala, Sweden

Charitakis K. 2007. Using parallel corpora to create a Greek-English dictionary with Uplug. In Proc. Nodalida 2007, Tartu, Estonia.

Dalianis, H. 2002. Evaluating a Spelling Support in a Search Engine. In Proc. Natural Language Processing and Information Systems, 6th International Conference on Applications of Natural Language to Information Systems, NLDB 2002 (Eds.) B. Andersson, M. Bergholtz, P. Johannesson, Stockholm, Sweden, June 27-28, 2002. Lecture Notes in Computer Science. Vol. 2553. pp. 183-190. Springer Verlag.

Gale, W. A. and K. W. Church 1991. A program for aligning sentences in bilingual corpora. In Proc. 29th annual meeting on Association for Computational Linguistics, p.177-184, 1991, Berkeley, California.

Jongejan, B. and D. Haltrup 2005. The CST Lemmatiser. Center for Sprogteknologi, University of Copenhagen, version 2.9 (October 6, 2005), http://cst.dk/download/cstlemma/current/doc/

Järvelin, A., S. Kumpulainen, A. Pirkola and E. Sormunen 2006. Dictionary-independent translation in CLIR between closely related languages. In Proc. Dutch-Belgian Information Retrieval Workshop, TNO ICT, Delft, The Netherlands, 2006.

Kann, V. and J. Hollman 2007. Tvärslå – Defining an XML exchange format and then building an on-line Nordic dictionary. In Proc. Automatic Treatment of Multilinguality in Retrieval, Search and Lexicography, Workshop in Copenhagen 2007.

Kann, V. and M. Rosell 2005. Free construction of a Swedish dictionary of synonyms. In Proc. Nodalida 2005, Joensuu.

Lin, C-Y. 1999. Machine Translation for Information Access across Language Barrier: the MuST System. In Machine Translation Summit VII, Singapore.

LingPipe 2006. LingPipe is a suite of Java libraries for the linguistic analysis of human language, http://www.alias-i.com/lingpipe/

Megyesi, B. 2001. Data-Driven Methods for PoS tagging and Chunking of Swedish. In Proc. Nodalida 2001, Uppsala.

Megyesi, B. and B. Dahlqvist 2007. The Swedish-Turkish Parallel Corpus and Tools for its Creation. In Proc. Nodalida 2007, Tartu, Estonia.

Merkel, M. 1999. Annotation Style Guide for the PLUG Link Annotator. Technical report, Linköping University.

Nyström, M., M. Merkel, L. Ahrenberg, P. Zweigenbaum, H. Petersson and H. Åhlfeldt. 2006. Creating a medical English-Swedish dictionary using interactive word alignment in BMC medical informatics and decision making.

Plamondon, L. and G. Foster. 2003. Quantum, a French/English Cross-language Question Answering System. In Proc. Cross-Language Evaluation Forum (CLEF 2003), Trondheim.

Popović, M., D. Stein and H. Ney 2006. Statistical Machine Translation of German Compound Words. In Proc. FinTAL, 5th International Conference on Natural Language Processing, Springer Verlag, LNCS, pages 616-624, Turku.

Sarr, M. 2003. Improving precision and recall using a spell checker in a search engine. In Proc. Nodalida 2003, Reykjavik.

Schrader, B. 2004. Improving Word Alignment Quality Using Linguistic Knowledge. In Proc. International Conference on Language Re-sources and Evaluation, LREC 2004, Lissabon.

Sjöbergh, J. 2005. Creating a free digital Japanese-Swedish lexicon. In Proc. PACLING 2005, pages 296-300, Tokyo.

Sjöbergh, J. and V. Kann 2006. Vad kan statistik avslöja om svenska sammansättningar (What can statistics reveal about Swedish compounds), Språk och Stil 2006, vol. 16, pages 199-214.

Strömbäck, P. 2005. The Impact of Lemmatization in Word Alignment, Master thesis, Department of Linguistics and Philology, Uppsala University.

Tiedemann, J. 2003. Recycling Translations - Extraction of Lexical Data from Parallel Corpora and their Application in Natural Language Processing, Doctoral Thesis, Studia Linguistica Upsaliensia 1, ISSN 1652-1366, ISBN 91-554-5815-7.

Toutanova, K., H. T. Ilhan and C. D. Manning 2002. Extensions to HMM-based Statistical Word Alignment Models. In Proc. ACL Language Processing (EMNLP), Philadelphia, 2002, pp. 87-94.

Uplug 2008. Uplug is a collection of tools for linguistic corpus processing, word alignment and term extraction from parallel corpus, http://uplug.sourceforge.net/

Velupillai, S. and Dalianis, H. (2008). Automatic Construction of Domain-specific Dictionaries on Sparse Parallel Corpora in the Nordic Languages. In Proc. 2nd MMIES Workshop: Multi-source, Multilingual Information Extraction and Summarization, held in conjunction with COLING-2008, Manchester.

Zhou, Y., J. Qin, H. Che and J. F. Nunamaker 2005. Multilingual Web Retrieval: An Experiment on a Multilingual Business Intelligence. In Proc. 38th Hawaii International Conference on System Sciences 2005.

ISSN 1736-6305 Vol. 4
http://hdl.handle.net/10062/9206

Extending the View
Explorations in Bootstrapping a Swedish PoS Tagger

Eva Forsbom
Department of Linguistics and Philology, Uppsala University
Graduate School of Language Technology
evafo@stp.lingfil.uu.se

Abstract

State-of-the-art statistical part-of-speech taggers mainly use information on tag bi- or trigrams, depending on the size of the training corpus. Some also use lexical emission probabilities above unigrams with beneficial results. In both cases, a wider context usually gives better accuracy for a large training corpus, which in turn gives better accuracy than a smaller one. Large corpora with validated tags, however, are scarce, so a bootstrap technique can be used. As the corpus grows, it is probable that a widened context would improve results even further.

In this paper, we looked at the contribution to accuracy of such an extended view for both tag transitions and lexical emissions, applied to both a validated Swedish source corpus and a raw bootstrap corpus. We found that the extended view was more important for tag transitions, in particular if applied to the bootstrap corpus. For lexical emission, it was also more important if applied to the bootstrap corpus than to the source corpus, although it was beneficial for both. The overall best tagger had an accuracy of 98.05%.

1 Introduction

Given the limitations of computational and human resources, state-of-the-art statistical taggers mostly use context information on tag bigrams, for smaller training corpora, or trigrams, for larger training corpora. Some also use lexical emission probabilities above unigrams, although with a rather limited context view, with beneficial results (e.g. Thede and Harper, 1999; Toutanova et al., 2003). But as computational power grows, and (semi)automatic annotation becomes more correct over time, resulting in large almost-correct training corpora, it would be interesting to see if it's worth extending the view.

For Swedish, several statistical part-of-speech taggers have been trained on the Swedish Stockholm-Umeå Corpus (SUC, Ejerhed et al., 2006), which has become a *de facto* standard for training and evaluating part-of-speech taggers. Most of them are based on hidden Markov models (e.g. Carlberger and Kann, 1999; Hall, 2003; Megyesi, 2002; Nivre, 2000; Sjöbergh, 2003b), with bi- or trigram tag transition probabilities.

As SUC is a balanced corpus (not just news texts) with a fairly large tagset, it is too small to be used alone as training data for any higher-accuracy tagger, so it has also been used to bootstrap a much larger, unannotated, corpus, that can be added as training data. In previous studies, bootstrapping has proved to be a viable approach (cf. Forsbom, 2008b; Merialdo, 1994; Nivre and Grönqvist, 2001; Sjöbergh, 2003a).

A recent open-source tagger, HunPos (Halácsy et al., 2007), include the range of parameters we would like to explore for extended context views for tag transition and lexical emissions.

In the following, we first describe the method, tagger and data sets used (Section 2), before describing the parameters used (Section 3). Results from experimental runs are then discussed and explored using a regression tree (Section 4).

2 Bootstrapping

In order to explore the effect of extending the view, large corpora are needed. Unfortunately, large validated training corpora are scarce, so in the abscence of such a desired resource, we have to build our own. And we do this by using a smaller-sized validated (source) corpus to bootstrap an order of magnitude larger (bootstrap) corpus, which will contain some noise, but in general, will be correct.

2.1 Method

The following bootstrap procedure was used:

1. Train a training model on the entire source corpus.

2. Tag the bootstrap corpus using the training model.

3. Train an evaluation model on the tagged bootstrap corpus (not including the source corpus). For other taggers than TnT (Brants, 2000), train a TnT lexical model on the same data, to use for evaluation statistics on known/unknown words.

4. Evaluate the evaluation model on 10 folds of the source corpus (if possible, drilled-down by genre).

5. (Train a final tag model on a concatenation of the source corpus and the tagged bootstrap corpus.)

The procedure is part of an ongoing project where various taggers and bootstrap corpora are compared (cf. Forsbom, 2006, 2008a,b). Therefore, evaluation is done with the same evaluation program, `tnt-diff`, to get comparable results on known/unknown words regardless of tagger. The known/unknown statistics should therefore be seen from a "TnT perspective", while the overall results are tagger-neutral.

Although we do not use proper 10-fold cross-validation (as we use the entire source corpus for bootstrapping), we still evaluate separately on 10 folds to be able to measure standard deviation.

In the optional fifth step, a final tag model which includes the source corpus and most likely gives even better results, could be trained and used in applications. Models from the experiment reported here are, for example, used in two other projects for summarisation and measuring readability.

2.2 Tagger

In this experiment, we use HunPos (Halácsy et al., 2007), which is a recent open-source implementation of many of the features included in TnT (Brants, 2000). As hidden Markov model taggers,

both use a state transition probability for the current tag given a history of previous tags, and a lexical emission probability for the current word given a history of previous tags (see further in Section 3).

Unknown words are handled by suffix probability estimates from low-frequency words. HunPos also uses the same linear interpolation smoothing technique as in TnT. For HunPos, it is currently the only smoothing choice, while TnT also includes alternative techniques. If HunPos is trained using trigram state transitions and unigram lexical emission, it behaves as TnT with default settings.

The main reason for using HunPos here is the possibility to vary the history both for state transitions and lexical emissions, while in TnT, the history for lexical emission is fixed and for state transition limited to uni-, bi-, and trigrams.

2.3 Source corpus

We have chosen to use SUC (Ejerhed et al., 2006) as a source corpus for two reasons apart from it being a *de facto* standard: it contains validated tags, and it is a balanced corpus, and therefore possibly a better representative of general language than a single-genre corpus.

SUC contains modern Swedish prose covering approximately 1.2 million word tokens. The 1,040 text samples are from the years 1990 to 1994, and are meant to mirror what a Swedish person might read in the early nineties.

The distribution of tokens between genres (or main categories) is shown in Table 1.

ID	Genre	Tokens (%)
a	Press: Reportage	9.1
b	Press: Editorial	3.5
c	Press: Reviews	5.6
e	Skills and Hobbies	11.5
f	Popular Lore	9.4
g	Biographies, essays	5.2
h	Miscellaneous	13.9
j	Learned and scientific writing	16.4
k	Imaginative prose	25.4

Table 1: Distribution of tokens/genre in SUC.

2.3.1 Choice of tagset

The SUC corpus has two interchangeable tagsets: SUC (Ejerhed et al., 1992) and PAROLE (see Section 2.4). An alternative to the SUC tagset is the Granska tagset, which in general gives better accuracy (2% improvement). The Granska tagset is a slight modification of the SUC tagset. Modifications include merging of infrequent tags, adding information on auxiliary verbs, reclassification of present participles to adjectives, and adding information on set- and date-describing words (Carlberger and Kann, 1999).

In a study of the contribution of the modifications, Forsbom (2008a) found that a distinction between main and auxiliary verbs was beneficial for copulas and temporal auxiliaries, but maybe not for modal verbs. The addition of the number feature singular to singular numbers, and the semantic feature date to names of days and months, was also beneficial, but to a lesser degree. These modifications are revertible without loss of information.

Some other modifications were also beneficial, but not revertible, e.g. conflation of past participle tags with the corresponding tags for adjectives.

To benefit from the improved accuracy that some of the Granska tags give, we have here used the SUC tagset with revertible Granska modifications for copulas, auxiliaries, singular numbers, and dates.

A comparison of accuracy for the three tagsets is shown in Table 2[1].

Tagset	Overall	Known	Unknown
SUC	95.52±0.15	96.31±0.13	86.26±0.99
Granska	95.68±0.14	96.42±0.13	87.09±0.91
Modified	95.61±0.14	96.40±0.12	86.37±0.96

Table 2: Estimated accuracy and standard deviation for the SUC, Granska and modified tagsets (10-fold cross-validation on SUC). Proportion of unknown words is 7.87 ± 0.20.

2.4 Bootstrap corpus

There are not many available large corpora of Swedish texts, and even fewer balanced corpora representing general language. Of the ones that do exist, the balanced Swedish PAROLE corpus has been used with success for bootstrapping (Forsbom, 2008b). The PAROLE corpus (University of Gothenburg) was collected for the EU project PAROLE (Preparatory Action for Linguistic Resources Organisation for Language Engineering) finished in 1997. The corpus contains around 19.4 million words of written texts from various categories, mainly sampled from The Swedish Language Bank (see Table 3). The texts have been part-of-speech tagged with PAROLE tags using a statistical tagger by Daniel Ridings (University of Gothenburg).

Text category	Period	Tokens (%)
Novels	1976–1981	22.7
Newspapers	1976–1997	70.1
Magazines	1995–1996	2.1
Web texts	1997	5.2

Table 3: Distribution of tokens/genre in PAROLE.

In order to harmonise the PAROLE corpus with SUC, we made some changes to the original corpus:

- A set of known multi-word abbreviations have been treated as one token, with any whitespace replaced by an underscore.

- Sentence boundaries have been introduced with a simplistic sentence splitter (i.e. new sentence after .,!,? if the following line starts with capital, digit, or -).

- The original tags were replaced during bootstrap by the modified tagset used here.

3 Exploring possible views

We were interested in seeing the effect of widening the view, from the commonly used bi- or trigrams to as high an n-gram as we could compute. In the hidden Markov model, the state transition probability of a tag is based on the previous k tags (the tag order). For the default trigram tag order, $k = 2$, the probability of t_3 is $P(t_3|t_1, t_2)$.

We also wanted to explore the effect of the lexical emission order. For the default bigram emission order in HunPos, $k = 2$, the probability of w_2 is $P(w_2|t_1, t_2)$. Emission probability in TnT is fixed to $k = 1$.

In HunPos, there are also other possible parameters to tune, e.g. suffix length and rare word frequency for the handling of unknown words. For Swedish, however, changing these parameters have minor, if any, effect (Megyesi, 2008), so we used the default settings. And, unlike TnT, there are no smoothing parameters to tweak from the command line.

In the experiment, we therefore concentrated on the parameters for tag and emission order in the hidden Markov model. We used nodes (accessing maximally 4GB RAM during training[2]) in the UPPMAX computer grid[3], which could maximally

---

[1]The comparison was done with TnT.

[2]Most nodes have a total of 8GB RAM, but not consecutive, so HunPos cannot use all of it.

[3]Uppsala Multidisciplinary Center for Advanced Computational Science. URL: http://www.uppmax.uu.se/.

train models for 5-grams for tag transition (tag order 4) and 4-grams for lexical emission (emission order 4). We varied both settings for both the source and the bootstrap corpus from 1 to 4, giving 256 combinations in all.

4 Results

Not surprisingly, as lexical models are larger than tag models and more so for large corpora, both memory usage and CPU time were mostly affected by emission order for the bootstrap corpus. The tagger with the widest view (4.4.4.4) maximally occupied 3.2GB, and took 1.5 hours to train and evaluate, while the tagger with the narrowest view (1.1.1.1) used a maximum of 0.5 GB and took 10 minutes. The 4.4.4.4 tagger also had the best overall accuracy of all taggers, 98.05%. The training phase requires more RAM than tagging. And although it takes a second or two to load the model before tagging starts, it is practically possible to use it in a computer with 2GB RAM. Furthermore, if the tagger is wrapped in a server, the model need only be loaded once.

Accuracy for the 2.2.2.2 (default) and 4.4.4.4 (best) tagger, respectively, is shown in Table 4, drilled-down by genre in SUC, and by known and unknown words. The 4.4.4.4 tagger overall improved .85 points over the 2.2.2.2 tagger. Most of the improvement lies in a better model for known words. For unknown words, on the other hand, the result is actually worse than for the 2.2.2.2 tagger. Forsbom (2008b) showed that genre composition of the bootstrap corpus had an effect on accuracy, both overall and drilled-down by genre. Here, we can see that the context size also matters. Fiction, for example, has above average overall accuracy with the 4.4.4.4 tagger, and below with the 2.2.2.2 one. Whether it has to do with a more formulaic language or not remains to be seen.

As the context size affects known and unknown words differently, we looked at the top 10 models for each of them. The ranking for the top 10 models for known words (see Table 6) follows the overall top 10 models (see Table 5) except for rank 9. The top 10 for unknown words (see Table 7) have only one model in common with the overall and known words top 10, namely rank 6, the 3.3.3.3 model. In a context where many unknown words are expected, the 3.3.3.3 model is a good compromise candidate.

To see the effect on accuracy of each setting, we used an Anova regression tree (Breiman et al., 1984; Therneau and Atkinson, 2004), where the accuracy for each combination is the response variable and each setting is a predictor variable. The regression tree was built using binary recursive partitioning of the data from the runs, where each split has a certain cost complexity. The cost complexity in combination with a cross-validation error, i.e. the "one standard-deviation rule" (Maindonald and Braun, 2003, p. 273f), was used to

	Settings				Accuracy		
Rank	SE	ST	BE	BT	Overall	Known	Unknown
1	4	4	4	4	98.05+0.10	98.50+0.08	85.28+1.03
2	3	4	3	4	97.97+0.10	98.41+0.07	85.51+1.03
3	4	4	3	4	97.96+0.09	98.39+0.07	85.38+0.99
4	3	4	4	4	97.93+0.11	98.37+0.08	85.15+1.07
5	4	3	4	3	97.89+0.12	98.32+0.08	85.54+1.02
6	4	4	4	3	97.88+0.11	98.32+0.10	85.26+1.01
7	4	3	4	4	97.86+0.13	98.30+0.10	84.95+0.98
8	3	3	3	3	97.83+0.11	98.24+0.09	85.78+0.98
9	3	3	4	3	97.81+0.11	98.23+0.09	85.57+0.96
10	4	3	3	3	97.80+0.11	98.23+0.10	85.62+0.99

Table 5: Top 10 models if sorted by overall accuracy. S=source model, B=bootstrapped model, E=emission order, T=tag order.

	Settings				Accuracy		
Rank	SE	ST	BE	BT	Overall	Known	Unknown
1	4	4	4	4	98.05+0.10	98.50+0.08	85.28+1.03
2	3	4	3	4	97.97+0.10	98.41+0.07	85.51+1.03
3	4	4	3	4	97.96+0.09	98.39+0.07	85.38+0.99
4	3	4	4	4	97.93+0.11	98.37+0.08	85.15+1.07
5	4	3	4	3	97.89+0.12	98.32+0.08	85.54+1.02
6	4	4	4	3	97.88+0.11	98.32+0.10	85.26+1.01
7	4	3	4	4	97.86+0.13	98.30+0.10	84.95+0.98
8	3	3	3	3	97.83+0.11	98.24+0.09	85.78+0.98
9	4	3	3	4	97.78+0.11	98.23+0.09	85.15+0.97
10	4	3	3	3	97.80+0.11	98.23+0.10	85.62+0.99

Table 6: Top 10 models if sorted by accuracy for known words. S=source model, B=bootstrapped model, E=emission order, T=tag order.

	Settings				Accuracy		
Rank	SE	ST	BE	BT	Overall	Known	Unknown
1	1	3	1	3	97.12+0.12	97.51+0.11	86.10+0.92
2	1	3	2	3	97.19+0.12	97.58+0.10	86.01+0.98
3	2	3	2	3	97.54+0.12	97.95+0.10	85.94+1.03
4	1	4	1	4	97.43+0.09	97.83+0.08	85.89+1.07
5	2	3	1	3	97.16+0.12	97.55+0.11	85.82+0.97
6	3	3	3	3	97.83+0.11	98.24+0.09	85.78+0.98
7	1	4	1	3	97.14+0.12	97.53+0.10	85.78+0.90
8	1	4	2	4	97.48+0.10	97.89+0.08	85.75+1.01
9	3	3	2	3	97.54+0.11	97.95+0.09	85.73+1.01
10	4	3	2	3	97.54+0.11	97.95+0.09	85.70+1.00

Table 7: Top 10 models if sorted by accuracy for unknown words. S=source model, B=bootstrapped model, E=emission order, T=tag order.

Genre	2.2.2.2			4.4.4.4			
	Overall	Known	Unknown	Overall	Known	Unknown	Prop. unknown
All	97.20±0.12	97.61+0.11	85.55±0.94	98.05±0.10	98.50±0.08	85.28±1.03	3.35±0.24
a	97.59±0.20	97.89±0.13	87.02±2.72	98.43±0.20	98.75±0.15	87.52±2.62	2.79±0.28
b	97.74±0.38	97.90±0.35	90.00±3.76	98.48±0.20	98.69±0.15	88.46±4.85	2.00±0.37
c	97.41±0.40	97.73±0.37	88.38±2.35	98.16±0.41	98.52±0.34	87.99±3.19	3.33±0.48
e	97.21±0.27	97.60±0.23	85.99±4.08	98.16±0.19	98.60±0.12	85.47±3.94	3.38±0.67
f	97.51±0.40	97.76±0.39	89.20±2.04	98.37±0.33	98.66±0.28	89.02±2.49	2.91±1.05
g	97.38±0.26	97.62±0.20	90.24±4.59	98.17±0.24	98.43±0.21	89.53±3.95	2.80±0.96
h	97.52±0.23	98.00±0.22	86.89±2.00	98.19±0.29	98.69±0.22	86.80±2.10	4.21±0.88
j	96.77±0.46	97.72±0.22	81.92±3.16	97.34±0.33	98.37±0.11	81.29±3.11	5.93±0.84
k	96.96±0.22	97.13±0.21	87.42±2.30	98.08±0.15	98.27±0.13	87.40±2.10	1.75±0.16

Table 4: Estimated accuracy and standard deviation for the 2.2.2.2 (default) and 4.4.4.4 (best) HunPos bootstrapped, drilled-down by SUC genre (10-fold cross-validation on SUC).

prune the resulting regression tree, to limit the risk of overfitting to the data. The rule says to prune a tree at the cost complexity of the first subtree with a cross-validation error larger than the minimal cross-validation error + 1 cross-validation standard deviation. For our overall tree, only one node was pruned.

The pruned regression tree, with a cross-validation error rate of 2%, is shown in Figure 1. As can be seen, the tag order plays the major role, both for the source and bootstrap corpora, and the main splits are between bigrams and trigrams. The setting used for the bootstrap corpus also seems more important than for the source corpus.

For unknown words, only the settings for tag order were used in building the regression tree. The tree, with one node pruned and a cross-validation error rate of as much as 8%, is shown in Figure 2. One thing that is more clear in the regression than when looking at the top 10 models is that for unknown words 4-grams seem optimal, while a wider context decreases the accuracy. In cases where many unknown words are expected, for example when moving to a new domain, it may therefore be wise to choose a lower tag order to get better results, whereas a good compromise could be the 3.3.3.3 model (cf. Tables 5–7).

As was the case for the top 10 models, the regression tree for known words (not included here) show a similar pattern to the overall tree. The only difference in tree structure is a missing subtree for known words, which corresponds to two nodes that were pruned from the known words tree.

5   Concluding remarks

In the paper, we looked at the effect of widening the context view, for tag transitions and lexical emissions, when bootstraping a raw corpus with a tagger trained on a validated source corpus.. Given current hardware limitations, we stopped at 5-grams (fourth order). A 5-gram hidden Markov model tagger, for example, gave better overall accuracy than a trigram tagger. Although memory requirements for training extend the average user's available RAM, tagging can be done in a reasonably equipped personal computer, even if loading the model takes time.

By means of a regression tree, we found in our experiment that a widened view was more important for tag transitions, and in particular for the bootstrap corpus. For lexical emission, it was also more important for the bootstrap corpus, although it was beneficial for both corpora. The main splits were between bigrams and trigrams. The best overall tagger was the one with the widest view for both tag transition and lexical emission, used for both corpora. It had an accuracy of 98.05%, compared to a bootstrapped tagger with only default settings, 97.20%. The improvement mainly occurred for known words, while the results for unknown words were actually worse. The optimal setting for unknown words was with 4-gram tag transition for both source and bootstrap corpora. The best compromise, if handling of unknown words is crucial, was the 3.3.3.3 model, 97.83%.

The widened view affected various genres in different degrees. Fiction, for example, benefited very much from it.

A selection of the models and accompanying information are available at `http://stp.lingfil.uu.se/~evafo/ resources/taggermodels/`.

Acknowledgements

We would like to thank Anna Sågvall Hein and the anonymous reviewers for valuable comments,

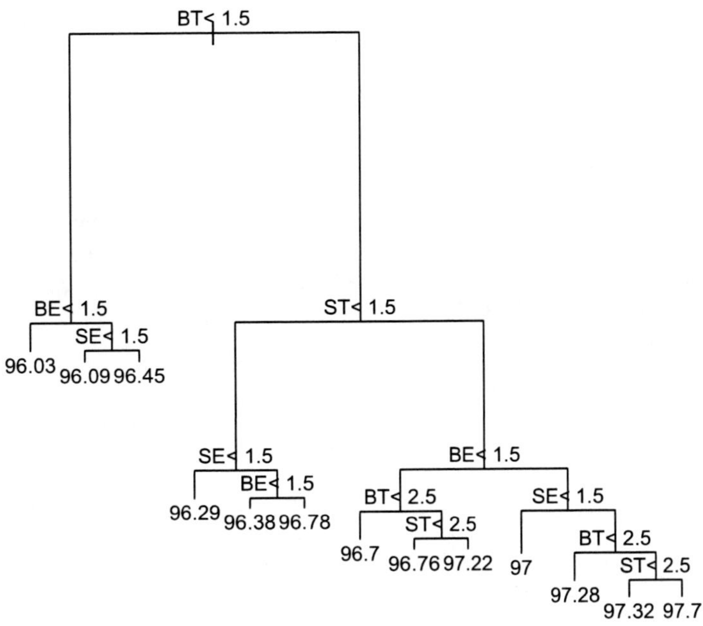

Figure 1: Regression tree for overall accuracy of bootstrapped models for various combinations of HunPos settings (10-fold cross-validation error rate=2%). S=source model, B=bootstrapped model, E=emission order, T=tag order.

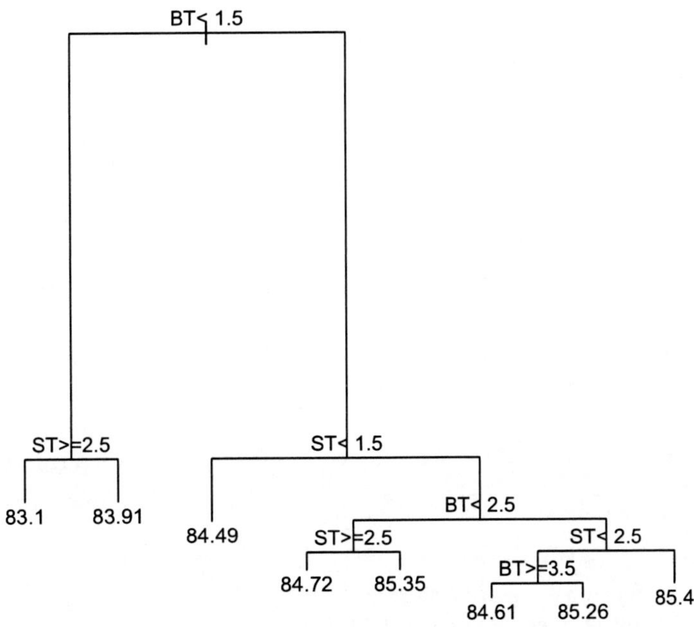

Figure 2: Regression tree for accuracy of unknown words in bootstrapped models for various combinations of HunPos settings (10-fold cross-validation error rate=8%). S=source model, B=bootstrapped model, E=emission order, T=tag order.

UPPMAX for letting us use their computer grid, Jonas Sjöbergh for a lexer which we based our PAROLE to Granska conversion script on, Johan Hall, Jens Nilsson and Joakim Nivre for a SUC version with Granska tags, which we used to tune the conversion script, and finally GSLT and NGSLT for funding.

References

Thorsten Brants. TnT - a statistical part-of-speech tagger. In *Proceedings of ANLP-2000*, Seattle, Washington, 2000.

Leo Breiman, Jerome H. Friedman, Richard A. Olshen, and Charles J. Stone. *Classification and Regression Trees*. Wadsworth International Group, Belmont, California, 1984.

Johan Carlberger and Viggo Kann. Implementing an efficient part-of-speech tagger. *Software Practice and Experience*, 29(9), 1999.

Eva Ejerhed, Gunnel Källgren, Ola Wennstedt, and Magnus Åström. The linguistic annotation system of the Stockholm–Umeå corpus project. Report DGL-UUM-R-33, Dep. of General Linguistics, University of Umeå, 1992.

Eva Ejerhed, Gunnel Källgren, and Benny Brodda. Stockholm-Umeå corpus version 2.0. Stockholm University, Dep. of Linguistics and Umeå University, Dep. of Linguistics, 2006.

Eva Forsbom. Big is beautiful: Bootstrapping a PoS tagger for Swedish, 2006. Poster presentation at GSLT retreat, Gullmarsstrand.

Eva Forsbom. Good tag hunting: Tagability of Granska tags. In *Resourceful Language Technology: Festschrift in Honor of Anna Sågvall Hein*. Uppsala University, 2008a.

Eva Forsbom. Size is not everything. genre balance in bootstrapping a Swedish PoS tagger. In *Proceedings of SLTC'08*, Stockholm, 2008b.

Péter Halácsy, András Kornai, and Csaba Oravecz. HunPos – an open source trigram tagger. In *Proceedings of ACL'07*, Prague, Czech Republic, 2007.

Johan Hall. A probabilistic part-of speech tagger with suffix probabilities. MSI report 03015, School of Mathematics and Systems Engineering, Växjö University, 2003.

John Maindonald and John Braun. *Data Analysis and Graphics Using R: An Example-based Approach*. Cambridge University Press, Cambridge, UK, 2003.

Beáta Megyesi. *Data-Driven Syntactic Analysis. Methods and Applications for Swedish*. Institution for Speech, Music and Hearing, Royal Institute of Technology, Stockholm, 2002.

Beáta Megyesi. The open source tagger HunPoS for Swedish. Report, Dep. of Linguistics and Philology, Uppsala University, 2008.

Bernard Merialdo. Tagging English text with a probabilistic model. *Computational Linguistics*, 20(2), 1994.

Joakim Nivre. Sparse data and smoothing in statistical part-of-speech tagging. *Journal of Quantitative Linguistics*, 7(1), 2000.

Joakim Nivre and Leif Grönqvist. Tagging a corpus of spoken Swedish. *International Journal of Corpus Linguistics*, 6(1), 2001.

Jonas Sjöbergh. Bootstrapping a free part-of-speech lexicon using a proprietary corpus. In *Proceedings of ICON-2003*, Mysore, India, 2003a.

Jonas Sjöbergh. Combining POS-taggers for improved accuracy on Swedish text. In *Proceedings of NoDaLiDa 2003*, Reykjavik, Iceland, 2003b.

Scott M. Thede and Mary P. Harper. A second-order hidden Markov model for part-of-speech tagging. In *Proceedings of ACL99*, College Park, Maryland, 1999.

Terry M. Therneau and Beth Atkinson. *rpart: Recursive Partitioning*, 2004. R package version 3.1-20. R port by Brian Ripley.

Kristina Toutanova, Dan Klein, Christopher D. Manning, and Yoram Singer. Feature-rich part-of-speech tagging with a cyclic dependency network. In *Proceedings of HLT-NAACL'03*, Edmonton, Canada, 2003.

University of Gothenburg. The PAROLE corpus at The Swedish Language Bank. URL http://spraakbanken.gu.se/parole/.

ISSN 1736-6305 Vol. 4
http://hdl.handle.net/10062/9206

Pattern-based English-Latvian Toponym Translation

The paper on similar issues will be presented at European Association for Machine Translation conference.

Tatiana Gornostay
Tilde, Latvia
tatjana.gornostaja@tilde.lv

Inguna Skadiņa
Tilde, Latvia
inguna.skadina@tilde.lv

Abstract

Due to their linguistic and extra-linguistic nature toponyms deserve a special treatment when they are translated. The paper deals with issues related to automated translation of toponyms from English into Latvian. Translation process allows us to translate not only toponyms from a dictionary, but out-of-vocabulary toponyms as well. Translation of out-of-vocabulary toponyms is divided into three steps: source string normalization, translation, and target string normalization. Translation step implies application of translation strategies and linguistic toponym translation patterns. 10,000 UK-related toponyms from Geonames were used as a development set. The developed methods have been evaluated on a test set: the accuracy of translation is 67% for the whole test set, 58% for one-word toponymic units, and 81% for multi-word toponyms.

1 Introduction

Toponyms in general are studied by toponymy, they represent names of places comprising the following types:

- hydronyms (names of bodies of water: bays, streams, lakes, lagoons, oceans, ponds, seas, etc.);

- oronyms (names of mountains, cliffs, craters, rocks, points, etc.);

- geonyms (general names for streets, squares, lines, avenues, paths, alleys, roads, embankments, etc.);

- oeconyms (names of populated places: an administrative division, country, city, town, house or other building);

- cosmonyms or astronyms (names of stars, constellations or other heavenly bodies).

The paper aims to research a complicated task of machine translation (MT) and cross-language information retrieval (CLIR) – automated translation of toponyms. Most of toponym translation approaches are data-driven (see, e.g. Meng et al., 2001; Al-Onaizan and Knight, 2002; Sproat et al., 2006; Alegria et al., 2006; Wentland et al., 2008) since they deal with widely used languages which have enough linguistic resources for development.

Taking into account an under-resourced status of the Latvian language with few available corpus resources, especially parallel bilingual corpora, a rule-based approach is proposed for the English-Latvian toponym translation.

There are several commonly used translation strategies for toponyms (Babych and Hartley, 2004): transference strategy (i.e., do-not-translate), transliteration strategy (i.e., phonetic or spelling rendering), translation strategy (i.e., translation itself) and combined strategy.

Transference strategy with a do-not-translate list is often used for translation of toponyms which do not need any rendering at all and are often left not translated, e.g. organization names (Babych and Hartley, 2003) or names of hotels in our system.

The most common transliteration techniques are phoneme-based and grapheme-based (Zhang et al., 2004). The phoneme-based approach (Knight and

Graehl, 1998; Meng et al., 2001; Oh and Choi, 2002; Lee and Chang, 2003) implies conversion of a source language word into a target language word via its phonemic representation, i.e., grapheme-phoneme-grapheme conversion. The grapheme-based technique converts a source language word into a target language word without any phonemic representation (grapheme-grapheme conversion) (Stalls and Knight, 1998; Li et al., 2004).

The first part of the paper presents an overview of the concept and nature of toponyms. In the second part we focus on the English-Latvian toponym translation, including the description of translation strategies (TS) and linguistic toponym translation patterns (LTTP).

2   Concept and Nature of Toponyms

Although Geoffrey Leech (1981) accepts a special status of toponyms as proper names without a conceptual meaning since any componential analysis cannot be performed for them, we should bear in mind and admit the fact that many toponyms are at least meaningful etymologically, e.g *Cambridge* – bridge over the river *Cam* (Leidner, 2007).

Toponyms are also ambiguous. Leidner (2007) describes three types of toponymical ambiguity:

- morpho-syntactic ambiguity: a word itself may be a toponym or may be a non-toponym, e.g. *Liepa* as a populated place in Latvia versus *liepa* (lime-tree) as a common noun;

- referential ambiguity: a toponym may refer to more than one place of the same type, e.g. *Riga* as a populated place and the capital of Latvia and *Riga* as a populated place in the USA, state Michigan;

- feature type ambiguity: a toponym may refer to more than one place of a different type, e.g. *Ogre* as a populated place and a river in Latvia.

Another type of toponymical ambiguity is eponymical ambiguity when places are named after people or deities, e.g., *Vancouver* after George Vancouver. Sometimes the same place is known by different names – endonyms (names of places used by inhabitants, self-assigned names) and exonyms (names of places used by other groups, not locals),

e.g. *Firenze* for its inhabitants and *Florence* for English.

Furthermore, metonymy also contributes to the issue. This linguistic phenomenon was studied from the toponymical point of view by Markert and Nissim (2002). The authors stated that metonymic use of toponyms is regular and productive. It can reach up to 17% of all of toponyms as it was proved by the example of the English language. The most frequent and conventional case of toponymical metonymy is as in the *"government of ..."* pattern, e.g. *"Latvia announced ..."* means *"the government of Latvia announced ..."*.

Finally, toponyms are changed frequently since they themselves and the places they refer to are not constant. Therefore, when dealing with toponyms it is also very important to take into consideration historical and cultural facts.

Thus, the abovementioned linguistic and extra-linguistic features make toponym processing difficult, i.e., their resolution, retrieval, and especially translation.

3   English-Latvian Toponym Translation

In the overall MT, English-Latvian toponym translation problems have not been researched in before. The existing literature describes general principles of rendering of the English proper names, mostly anthroponyms, into Latvian. Therefore we studied three main issues related to MT of the English-Latvian toponyms:

- orthographic, phonetic and grammatical distinctions between these languages;

- potential toponym translation strategies;

- potential linguistic toponym translation patterns.

Although English and Latvian are Indo-European languages and share some grammatical features, they have a lot of differences. At first, English belongs to the Germanic language group while Latvian belongs to the group of the Baltic languages. In morphological typology the English language is an analytical language in contrast to a synthetic Latvian with a rich set of inflections.

The linguistic features of Latvian toponymic units were studied to ensure that translations correspond to common rules of the Latvian grammar and orthography. For instance, Latvian multi-word units can be translated in several ways, however, a compound is preferable if the source toponymic unit could be reconstructed (Ahero, 2006).

The lack of orthographic and phonetic convergence in English (26 letters to 44 phonemes), historical changes and traditions in spelling, origin language of a toponym, and ambiguity were the main difficulties we faced.

3.1 Source String Normalization

The process of translation of a toponymic unit is divided into three steps: source string normalization, translation, i.e., application of translation strategy (TS) and linguistic toponym translation patterns (LTTP), and target string normalization according to the Latvian grammar and orthography rules.

Source string normalization implies the following changes:

- all tabs and double space characters, including the string beginning, are normalized to single space characters;

- the so-called "zero-fertility words" (Al-Onaizan and Knight, 2002) of English are normalized to zero-translations into Latvian, e.g. the indefinite article *a* is omitted;

- hyphenated words are replaced with non-hyphenated ones;

- some abbreviations are expanded to full words, e.g. *St.* to *Saint*;

- signs, if possible, are replaced with words, e.g. *&* to *and*;

- punctuation marks are normalized to zero-translations.

3.2 Translation: English-Latvian Toponym Translation Strategies

The English-Latvian transliteration strategy is based on the grapheme-to-grapheme approach, which implies direct mapping of English letter sequences into Latvian ones, formalized in a set of transliteration rules. Transliteration strategy is language dependent (Karimi et al., 2007). It is not a trivial task, due to issues described above, as well as due to many exceptions (see Castañeda-Hernández, 2004 about general toponym translation problem).

The set of English-Latvian transliteration rules consists of about 110 transliteration patterns describing English-Latvian grapheme-to-grapheme correspondences. All foreign names (those of non-English origin) are rendered according to English pronunciation standards. The main principle is the possibility to reconstruct the source toponymic unit (Ahero, 2006).

The result of transliteration may vary, as there are several ways of rendering English letter combinations into Latvian, e.g., *-c-* stands for *-k-* before consonants (except *-h-*), and *-a-, -o-, -u-,* for *-s-* before *-i-, -e-, -y-,* and for *-č-* in the combination with *-h-*.

Transference strategy is applied to both unprocessed toponymic units, which are not described by any of linguistic toponym translation patterns, and organization and hotel names.

There are cases when multi-word toponyms are not transferred or transliterated but translated into Latvian, e.g., *East Anglian Heights, North West Highlands* are translated into Latvian as *Austrumanglijas augstiene, Ziemeļskotijas kalnāji* correspondingly. Single word units are transliterated, as a rule.

Transliteration strategy can be also applied to multi-word units in parallel with translation which is infrequent and conventional.

Toponym translation strategies are closely related with LTTPs and are language dependent. Therefore combined strategy is also used when treating different types of toponyms.

3.3 Translation: Linguistic Toponym Translation Patterns

Most of popular toponyms, such as names of countries and capitals, seas and oceans, are translated using an English-Latvian dictionary, e.g., *Lisbon − Lisabona, Brussels − Brisele, Cologne − Ķelne, Antwerp − Antverpene, Great Britain − Lielbritānija, Atlantic Ocean − Atlantijas okeāns*. If a toponym is an out-of-vocabulary (OOV) word then one of the LTTPs is applied.

To determine common LTTPs for toponyms which are not in dictionaties we used a list of 10,000 UK-related toponyms from Geonames and analyzed 59 most common toponym types.

LTTPs determine ways how source toponymic units are rendered into target toponymic units. We distinguish two types of LTTPs: in-word patterns and multi-word patterns.

The in-word LTTP describes word transformation model based on English-Latvian transliteration rules, including the most frequent prefixes, suffixes, and letter combinations. There are about 300 in-word LTTPs described, e.g.: *new-* to *ņū-*, *deep-* to *dīp-*, *mc-* to *mak-*, *-worth* to *–vērt*, *-islet* to *–ailet*, etc.

Multi-word LTTPs involve three translation strategies. The first translation strategy S_1 is based on transliteration rules. Translation strategy S_2 combines the translation strategy S_1 with the insertion of a nomenclature word, e.g., *Bebington* (as a railroad station) – *Bebingtonas stacija*. If a nomenclature word is included in a source toponymic unit, as it is in the pattern S_3, it is either translated (*Newton Point - Ņūtona zemesrags, Gog Magog Hills - Gogmagogu kalni*) or transliterated (*Green Isle – Grīnaila, North East Coast – Nortīstkosta*) in the target language.

We have described 40 nomenclature words which are translated under certain conditions. Auxiliary words, such as prepositions, are also either translated or transliterated, e.g., *Horse of Copinsay – Horsofkopinsejs* (transliteration), *Milford upon Sea - Milforda pie jūras* (translation).

Examples of LTTPs are presented in Table 1. X_n is a toponymic unit in a source language, S_n is a translation strategy, Y_n is a toponymic unit in a target language, and $P_n\{X_n, S_n, Y_n\}$ is a corresponding LTTP.

3.4 Target String Normalization

Target string normalization modifies a toponymic unit according to the Latvian grammar and orthography rules, e.g. all populated places are feminine gender (see P2): *Newcastle* → *Ņūkāsla* which is indicated by the ending *–a* (feminine, singular nominative).

English Toponym X_n	**Translation Pattern P_n**	**Translation Strategy S_n**	**Latvian Toponym Y_n**
$P_1\{X_1, S_1, Y_1\}$			
X1: N *Knocklayd*	P1: N → N	S1: transliteration	Y1: N masculine singular *Nokleids*
$P_2=\{X_1, S_1, Y_2\}$			
X1: N *Newcastle*	P2: N → N	S1: transliteration	Y2: N feminine singular *Ņūkāsla*
$P_3=\{X_1, S_2, Y_3\}$			
X1: N *Bebington*	P3: N → N + N	S2: transliteration + nomenclature word	Y3: N feminine singular genitive + N *Bebingtonas stacija*
$P_4=\{X_2, S_1, Y_2\}$			
X2: N's + N *Bishop's Stortford*	P4: N's + N → N	S1: transliteration	Y2: N feminine singular *Bišopsstortforda*
$P_5=\{X_3, S_1, Y_2\}$			
X3: N + N's + N *St. Bishop's Town*	P5: N + N's + N → N	S1: transliteration	Y2: N feminine singular *Sentbišopsatauna*
$P_6=\{X_4, S_1, Y_2\}$			
X4: N + N *Bishop Auckland* *North Ronaldsay*	P6: N + N → N	S1: transliteration	Y2: N feminine singular *Bošopoklenda* *Nortronaldseja*
$P_7=\{X_5, S_1, Y_2\}$			
X5: A + N *South Ribble, Green Isle*	P7: A + N → N	S1: transliteration	Y2: N feminine singular *Sautribla* *Grīnaila*
$P_8=\{X_6, S_3, Y_4\}$			
X6: N + P + N *Milford upon Sea*	P8: N + P + N → N + P + N	S3: transliteration + translation	Y4: N feminine singular genitive + P + N

Stratford upon Avon			*Milforda pie jūras, Stradforda pie Avona*
$P_9=\{X_6, S_1, Y_5\}$			
X6: N + P + *Longville in the Dale*	P9: N + P + N → N + N	S1: transliteration	Y5: N feminine singular genitive + N feminine singular locative *Longvila Deilā*
$P_{10}=\{X_7, S_1, Y_2\}$			
X7: A + A + N *North East Coast*	P10: A + A + N → N	S1: transliteration	Y2: N feminine singular *Nortīstkosta*
$P_{11}=\{X_8, S_2, Y_3\}$			
X8: N + C + N *Sandal & Agbrigg*	P11: N + C + N → N + N	S2: transliteration + nomenclature word	Y3: N feminine singular genitive + N *Sendalendagbrigas stacija*
$P_{12}=\{X_4, S_3, Y_6\}$			
X4: N + N *Newton Point*	P12: N + N → N + N	S3: transliteration + translation	Y6: N masculine singular genitive + N *Ņūtona zemesrags*
$P_{13}=\{X_6, S_1, Y_1\}$			
X6: N + P + N *Horse of Copinsay*	P:13 N + P + N → N	S1: transliteration	Y1: N masculine singular *Horsofkopinsejs*
$P_{14}=\{X_7, S_3, Y_7\}$			
X7: N + N + N *Gog Magog Hills*	P14: N + N + N → N + N	S3: transliteration + translation	Y7: N masculine plural genitive +N *Gogmagogu kalni*

Table 1. Examples of English-Latvian Linguistic Toponym Translation Patterns

4 Evaluation and Limitations

The current MT evaluation theory and practice lacks in evaluation methods for toponym translation task. One of the reasons could be that it is not clear what the correct toponym translation is, since results may vary and more than one target toponymic unit is acceptable. As a result, scores calculated with a single target variant will underestimate translation accuracy. Moreover, human translations are often inaccurate as well.

Existing English-Latvian MT systems[1] do not implement any OOV algorithms to translate toponymic units. Thus, we had no possibility to compare our algorithm with other MT performance.

For evaluation purposes we compared translation results of our translation module with reference (human) translations from two bilingual dictionaries. 330 English toponymic units of different types with Latvian translation equivalents were manually extracted from dictionaries and processed with our OOV toponym translation module. We set the following evaluation scores:

- if the translation result coincides with the corresponding linguistic toponym translation pattern then the translation is *accurate* and the score is 1;

- if the translation result deviates from the corresponding linguistic toponym translation pattern then the translation is *inaccurate*, and the score is 0,5 for one distinction and 0 for more distinctions.

We accept variants as they were also described by linguistic toponym translation patterns (in transliteration rules). As a result, the accuracy of translation is 67% on the whole test set, 58% on the set containing one-word toponymic units, and 81% on multi-word test set.

---

[1] English-Latvian Pragma Expert: www.acl.lv, English-Latvian Google: http://translate.google.com, English-Latvian Tilde http://www.tilde.lv/English/portal/go/tilde/3777/en-US/DesktopDefault.aspx (November, 2008)

5   Conclusions and Future Work

We have described the pattern-based toponym translation approach developed for the English-Latvian language pair. The focus of the paper is on the detailed description of OOV toponym processing and describes possible translation strategies and linguistic toponym translation patterns with examples and evaluation results.

We can conclude that for the implemented rule-based approach there is much room for possible improvements, and evaluation results prove this statement. The main reason, why toponym processing is such a challenge for an MT task, is the necessity of knowledge of toponym rendering rules, variety of languages as well as a considerable amount of history and culture (Castañeda-Hernández, 2004). It is impossible to formalize this process completely and it is obvious that there can be mistakes in automated translation of toponymic units.

Corpus-based approach has not been applied in this research due to the lack of monolingual and bilingual linguistic resources. However, the issue of compiling a multilingual corpus of toponym-referenced texts for the Latvian language is being studied.

We consider the present research as the starting point for such tasks as multilingual cross-language MT of toponyms and application to other languages, especially Cyrillic or other non-Latin scripts.

Acknowledgement

We would like to thank Raivis Skadiņš for his comments and remarks on the article, Lars Ahrenberg for discussions on toponym machine translation, and Lars Borin for general discussions on toponymy.

This research was carried out in the framework of the project no. 045335 – TRIPOD project (TRIPartite multimedia Object Description) co-funded by the European Commission within the Sixth Framework Programme.

References

Antonija Ahero. 2006. *English Proper Name Rendering into the Latvian Language* (Angļu Īpašvārdu Atveide Latviešu Valodā). Zinātne, Rīga.

Iñaki Alegria, Nerea Ezeiza, Izaskun Fernandez. 2006. Named entities translation based on comparable cor-pora. *Proceedings of the 11ᵗʰ Conference of the European Chapter of the Association for Computational Linguistics, Workshop on Multi-word expressions in a Multilingual Context*, Italy. Pp.1-8.

Yaser Al-Onaizan and Kevin Knight. 2002. Translating named entities using monolingual and bilingual resources. *Proceedings of the 40ᵗʰ Meeting of the Association for Computational Linguistics*, USA. Pp.400-408.

Bogdan Babych and Anthony Hartley. 2003. Improving Machine Translation Quality with Automatic Named Entity Recognition. *Proceedings of the 7ᵗʰ European Association for Machine Translation Workshop Improving machine translation through other language Technology Tools*, Hungary. Pp.1-8.

Bogdan Babych and Anthony Hartley. 2004. Selecting Translation Strategies in MT using Automatic Named Entity Recognition. *Proceedings of the 9ᵗʰ European Association for Machine Translation Workshop Broadening horizons of machine translation and its applications*, Malta. Pp.18-25.

Gilberto Castañeda-Hernández. 2004. Navigating through Treacherous Waters: The Translation of Geographical Names. *Translation Journal*, 8(2): [electronic resource]: http://accurapid.com/journal/28names.htm#1

Sarvnaz Karimi, Falk Scholer, and Andrew Turpin. 2007. Collapsed consonant and vowel models: new approaches for English-Persian transliteration and back-transliteration. *Proceedings of the 45ᵗʰ Annual Meeting of the Association for Computational Linguistics*, Czech Republic. Pp.648-655.

Kevin Knight and Jonathan Graehl. 1998. Machine Transliteration. *Computational Linguistics*, 24(4):599-612.

Chun-Jen Lee and Jason S. Chang. 2003. Acquisition of English-Chinese Transliteration Word Pairs from Parallel-Aligned Texts using a Statistical Machine Translation Model. *Proceedings of Human Language Technologies – The North American Chapter of the Association for Computational Linguistics Workshop: Building and Using parallel Texts Data Driven Machine Translation and Beyond*, Canada. Pp.96-103.

Geoffrey Leech. 1981. *Semantics. The Study of Meaning*. 2ⁿᵈ edition. Penguin, London, England, UK.

Jochen L. Leidner. 2007. *Toponym Resolution in Text: Annotation, Evaluation and Applications of Spatial Grounding of Place Names*. PhD thesis. Institute for Communicating and Collaborative Systems School of Informatics, University of Edinburgh.

Haizhou Li, Min Zhang, and Jian Su. 2004. A joint source-channel model for machine transliteration. *Proceedings of the 42nd Annual Meeting on association for Computational Linguistics*. Spain. Pp.159–166.

Katja Markert and Malvina Nissim. 2002. Towards a corpus annotated for metonymies: the case of location names. *Proceedings of the 3rd International Conference on Language Resources and Evaluation*, France. Pp.1385-1392.

Helen M. Meng, Wai-Kit Lo, Berlin Chen, and Karen Tang. 2001. Generate Phonetic Cognates to Handle Named Entities in English-Chinese cross-language spoken document retrieval. *Proceedings of Institute of Electrical and Electronics Engineers Automatic Speech Recognition and Understanding Workshop*, Italy.

Jong-Hoon Oh and Key-Sun Choi. 2002. An English-Korean Transliteration Model Using Pronunciation and Contextual Rules. *Proceedings of the 19th International Conference on Computational Linguistics*, Taiwan, 1:1-7.

Richard Sproat, Tao Tao, and Cheng-Xiang Zhai. 2006. Named entity transliteration with comparable corpora. *Proceedings of the 44th Annual meeting of the Association for Computational Linguistics*, Australia. Pp.73-80.

Bonnie Glover Stalls and Kevin Knight. 1998. Translating Names and Technical Terms in Arabic Text. *Proceedings of the Coling / Association for Computational Linguistics Workshop on Computational Approaches to Semitic Languages*, Canada. Pp.365-266.

Wolodja Wentland, Johannes Knopp, Carina Silberer, and Matthias Hartung. 2008. Building a Multilingual Lexical Resource for Named Entity Disambiguation, Translation and Transliteration. *Proceedings of the 6th Language Resources and Evaluation Conference*, Morocco.

Min Zhang, Haizhou Li, and Jian Su. 2004. Direct Orthographical Mapping for Machine Transliteration. *Proceedings of the 20th International Conference on Computational Linguistics*, Switzerland.

ISSN 1736-6305 Vol. 4

http://hdl.handle.net/10062/9206

WebBANC: Building Semantically-Rich Annotated Corpora from Web User Annotations of Minority Languages

Nathan Green[1,2,*]   Paul Breimyer[1,2,*]   Vinay Kumar[1]   Nagiza F. Samatova[1,2,∓]

[1]**North Carolina State University**
890 Oval Drive
Raleigh, NC 27695

[2]**Oak Ridge National Laboratory**
1 Bethel Valley Rd
Oak Ridge, TN 37831

Abstract

Annotated corpora are sets of structured text used to enable Natural Language Processing (NLP) tasks. Annotations may include tagged parts-of-speech, semantic concepts assigned to phrases, or semantic relationships between these concepts in text. Building annotated corpora is labor-intensive and presents a major obstacle to advancing machine translators, named entity recognizers (NER), part-of-speech taggers, etc. Annotated corpora are specialized for a particular language or NLP task. Hence, a majority of the world's 6000+ languages lack NLP resources, and therefore remain *minority*, or *under-resourced*, languages in modern language technologies.

In this paper we present WebBANC, a framework for Building Annotated NLP Corpora from user annotations on the Web. With WebBANC, a casual user can annotate parts of HTML or PDF text on any website and associate the text with semantic concepts specific to an NLP task. User annotations are combined by WebBANC to produce annotated corpora potentially comparable in diversity to corpora in English, minority languages, and human generated categories, such as those on Yahoo.com, with an average precision and recall of 0.80, which is comparable to automated NER tools on the CoNLL benchmark.

---
* Both authors contributed equally
∓ Corresponding author: samatovan@ornl.gov

1   Introduction

The Web is the holy grail of linguistic data (Rayson et al., 2006). It has recently gained popularity as a resource for *minority* (Ghani and Mladenic, 2001), or *under-resourced*, languages that lack automatic Natural Language Processing (NLP) resources, even from the Basic Language Resource Kit (BLARK) (Krauwer, 2003). "Web as Corpus" has been especially valuable for constructing text corpora from the Web for these languages (Scannell, 2007; Baroni and Bernardini, 2004). Language specific corpora are useful for many language technology applications, including named entity recognition, machine translation, spelling correction, and machine-readable dictionaries. The An Crúbadán Project, for example, has succeeded in creating corpora for more than 400 of the world's 6000+ languages by web crawling. With a few exceptions, most of the 400+ corpora, however, lack any linguistic annotations due to the limitations of the annotation tools (Rayson et al., 2006).

In spite of the many documented advantages of linguistically annotated data over raw data (Mair, 2005), annotated corpora are quite sparse. The majority of previous work on corpus annotation has utilized manual coding by linguistic experts, automated software tagging systems, and semi-automatic combinations of the two approaches. Uren et al. provide a comprehensive survey of existing semantic annotation tools, including some community-driven projects (2006). While yielding high quality and enormous value, manual corpus annotation is both tedious and time-consuming. For example, the GENIA corpus contains 9,372 sentences, curated by five part-time annotators, one senior coordinator, and one junior coordinator over 1.5 years (Kim et al., 2008). In contrast, software tagging systems, such as those for annotating web corpora are automatic and fast, but primarily exist for *majority* languages.

For *minority* languages, however, few automated corpora annotation systems exist and different approaches are needed. In this paper, we hypothesize that the Web, coupled with web user community efforts, represent a paradigm shift in annotated corpora construction. We extend the concept of community-based web content creation, such as Wikipedia (Zesch et al., 2007), by assuming that websites, especially frequently visited ones, present an ideal platform for large-scale community-level annotations for NLP tasks. We also argue that if given an opportunity to link annotations with semantic concepts, such as those represented in the form of ontologies, the web community can potentially create semantically-rich annotated corpora at an unprecedented scale.

The actual impact of web user annotated corpora creation remains to be seen, but the potential benefits of such a framework are manifold. It may reduce the time required to create annotated corpora for NLP tasks potentially from months to days. For NER tasks, for example, commercial applications currently support a handful of entities. For instance, NetOwl Extractor is a commercial application that supports seven entity types and seventy subtypes, including people, organizations, places, etc. The lack of entity breadth is explained by the intense human-labor required for entity type development.

A framework could potentially enable building semantically richer and larger corpora by supporting any ontology, which would allow researchers to introduce new levels of semantic richness into corpora. For example, the Gene Ontology (GO) (Ashburner et al., 2000) contains over 100,000 biological concepts that can enrich annotations and the correspondingly generated corpora.

A web user annotation framework may also enable automatic processing of minority languages by supporting minority corpora generation. The Open American National Corpus (OANC) (Ide and Macleod, 2001) is a major initiative meant to parallel the British National Corpus (Burnard, 1995), which contains over 100 million words. Minority languages do not enjoy the same support as American and British English, and it is unlikely that similar scale corpora will be generated for minority languages. The WebBANC framework can potentially enable annotated corpora generation of many less common domains, such as minority lan-

guages, by distributing the annotation effort over many users.

2   WebBANC Framework

We introduce a framework that leverages user annotations on the *Web* to *Build Annotated NLP Corpora* (WebBANC). We show that given such a framework, user annotations of commonly visited websites may contain enough linguistically diverse text to create sufficiently diverse corpora for various NLP tasks. To evaluate the results, we compare corpora created from the most visited websites to the human organized categories on Yahoo.com, and to commonly used corpora such as the OANC (Ide and Macleod, 2001), a freely available massive collection of American English texts with over fourteen million words.

We also compare the corpora against a minority language corpus generated from the Icelandic Frequency Dictionary (IFD) (Pind et al., 1991), a balanced corpus including Icelandic Fiction, Translated Fiction, and other categories compiled from text fragments written between 1980-1989 (Helgadttir, 2004). We show, through large-scale simulation, that aggregate user annotations covering approximately 50% of the words in the top 100 most visited websites can generate corpora that represent 35%-70% of the diversity of these corpora at 70%-90% precision. Small-scale user studies show that the average precision and recall for English named entity recognition (NER) tasks are comparable with those achieved by more than a dozen automatic NER tools when tested against the widely accepted CoNLL benchmark (Sang and Meulder, 2003).

2.1   Requirements

To be successful, a distributed free-text annotation framework must support annotations of most web-pages that the *layman* user regularly encounters on the Web. For this reason, the framework should allow users to annotate both PDF and HTML documents, including pages built by underlying technologies that display HTML, such as PHP. Building corpora using distributed annotations should adhere to standards in the machine learning community, such as those proposed by the W3C, to enable standardized interfaces between clients and the framework. These standards may include the *Resource Description Framework* (RDF) (Klyne and Carroll, 2004) to communicate between the web browser (the client) and the annotation manager (the server) and *XPointers* (DeRose et al., 1998) to locate text in HTML documents, allowing users to annotate any text on a webpage.

The framework should also provide easy-to-use annotation plug-ins for diverse web browsers with intuitive Graphical User Interfaces, potentially customized for individual NLP tasks. A simple drag-and-drop or right-mouse-click-and-select interface to choose a semantic concept, such as person or location for a highlighted word or phrase on the webpage, can serve as an example interface for NER tasks. Designing a simple and functional interface for different NLP tasks, such as entity relationships, may not be trivial.

A major issue for future minority language NLP developments is the need to generate and use *consistent* annotations (Leitner and Valencia, 2008). The framework should use standard semantic tags and allow user communities to supply their own standards; various scenarios are described below.

The framework should allow users to supply their own semantic tags for annotations. However, maintaining consistency may be quite difficult and may ultimately restrict the resulting annotated corpora uses for NLP tools.

The framework should permit users to choose semantic concepts and/or relationships from collections of controlled vocabularies, synonymous sets, and standard ontologies. Ontologies are formal representations of a set of domain concepts and the relationships between those concepts, and can provide a natural and standard hierarchy to tag a document. The W3C Web Ontology Language (OWL) (Bechhofer et al., 2004) is a standard for well-structured representations. Different domains have developed domain-specific ontologies, such as the Gene Ontology (GO) terms in Biology (Ashburner et al., 2000), but they may be too complex and require some adaptation to facilitate use by layman users, as well as domain experts. While the framework should allow users to select from a set of default ontologies, individual users and user communities should be free to create and integrate their own ontologies into the framework.

The framework should support semi-automated NLP tools or models to pre-annotate possibly relevant terms using existing NLP tools. The tools should use standard collections of semantic tags and offer the tagged annotations to users for validation via easy-to-use graphical interfaces. Semi-

automated predictive models exist for some NLP tasks, such as part-of-speech and NER (Sang and Meulder, 2003). These models can be leveraged by the framework to validate manual annotations and may help identify poor annotations. Incorporating both ontologies and automated NLP annotation tools into the framework should be realized through the use of webservices (Alonso, 2004) using standard communication protocols.

Two critical and non-trivial issues for such a framework are annotation quality and the quality-control mechanisms. Unlike manually annotated corpora by domain experts, annotations by web users will likely be noisy. Although such annotated web corpora can still be utilized for manual curation, it would be desirable for the framework to provide analytical intelligence to make decisions about collating and resolving possibly conflicting and uncertain annotations from potentially numerous users and/or various NLP tools. This is an open area of research and deserves an active investigation.

2.2 Framework Architecture

The current implementation of the WebBANC framework consists of the following main components: an Annotation Server, the Annotation database, an OWL Ontology Interface, a Query and Retrieval Interface, and an Annotation Frontend.

The Annotation Frontend is a Firefox plug-in that uses XUL and JavaScript and supports two interfaces: one handles standard text and the other annotates PDF documents. The browser implementation allows distributed users to annotate websites. Users highlight words or phrases to annotate and link them to semantic tags by dragging or double-clicking the tag. The plain text interface builds upon the W3C Annotea project (Kahan et al., 2002). The PDF client leverages jPDFNotes (2008) and is compiled with Java 5.

The WebBANC framework lets developers expose any ontology by extending a Java class or implementing specific webservices. The OWL Ontology Interface sends available ontologies from the server to the Annotation Frontend through an OWL API. WebBANC uses OWL for ontology communication because it is a W3C standard and will allow others to develop new semantic tags and relationships as well as ease the development of new Annotation Frontends.

The Annotation Server handles communication between the Annotation Frontend and the backend database, which uses MySQL 5. Communication between clients and servers uses XML, and specifically either RDF or OWL, depending on the request context. The MySQL database is stored on an annotation server to support permanent storage and querying of manually annotated text. This allows NLP models to refine their prediction algorithms and also allows WebBANC to generate corpora in multiple formats. We intend to extend the framework with the ability to plug-in NLP models to support semi-automation, thereby allowing users to curate model-specific tags.

3 Results

We evaluated WebBANC at two levels: small-scale actual user annotation performance and large-scale simulation-based results. The purpose of the former is to determine the efficacy and accuracy of annotated corpora generated by untrained casual users. The latter was designed to draw conclusions regarding the diversity of user annotations generated on the Web and to compare the generated corpora with existing corpora in English, minority languages, and human generated categories, such as those found on Yahoo.com.

3.1 Small-Scale Study of Casual Annotators

To examine the effectiveness of untrained annotators using a web based annotation platform, Web-BANC was released to several users. The purpose of this study was to test whether volunteer casual annotators are effective in terms of accuracy and throughput.

3.1.1 Evaluation Methodology

To examine the effectiveness of untrained annotators we conducted a study of users annotating web pages of their choosing for a named entity task. While annotating, users were restricted to the tags Person, Organization, and Location and were instructed to only use the system for fifteen minutes a day over four consecutive days. Users were also instructed for one of those days to annotate approximately 60 sentences extracted from the 2003 Conference on Natural Language Learning (CoNLL) training corpus with the same entity types; the sentences were un-tagged prior to the experiment. We refer to the training corpus as the CoNLL corpus, and selected it for our evalu-

ation due to its widespread adoption as a benchmark corpus.

3.1.2 Small-Scale Study Results

The seven users created a corpus of 1,634 annotations: 1028 for general web pages and 606 for CoNLL data. Volunteer casual annotators with no previous annotation experience demonstrated high throughput, in comparison to the GENIA corpus (Kim et al., 2008).

Table 1: Recall and Precision for CoNLL annotations.

	Per	Loc	Org	Avg	CoNLL Avg
Recall (All Data)	1.00	0.94	0.82	0.92	0.81
Precision (All Data)	0.70	0.82	0.42	0.58	0.82

Table 2: Precision for CoNLL annotations with filtering.

	Per	Loc	Org	Avg
Precision (Majority Voting)	0.76	0.86	0.48	0.64
Precision (Coverage Req.)	0.73	0.90	0.55	0.69
Precision (Majority Voting + Coverage Req.)	0.79	0.95	0.69	0.79

While throughput is important, the accuracy of the annotations directly impacts the usefulness of the corpus. To test users' annotation accuracy we directly compared their annotations to the expertly created standard CoNLL corpus. Table 1 shows that the users collectively annotated every Person entity tagged by CoNLL, giving a recall of 1. User-level annotation of the Location entity also achieved a high recall of 0.94, but the Organization entity yielded a lower recall of 0.82. The average recall over the three entities is 0.92, which is an improvement over the average recall of 0.81 provided by the sixteen automated predictive tools in CoNLL.

User-level annotations demonstrated the following precision: 0.79, 0.95, and 0.69 for Person, Location, and Organization entities, respectively, with an average of 0.79. These results, shown in

Table 2, were calculated using majority voting after removing annotations with singular coverage. Based on users' feedback, annotating the Organization entity was the most unclear of the three. The average precision for the Person and Location entities was 0.87. Again, the casual user-level precision was comparable with the automated tools that attained an average precision of 0.82 over the three entities. For user-level annotations of arbitrary web pages of their choosing, 42.1%(31.2%) of the web pages were found the top 70(50) web pages viewed in the United States according to Alexa.com, an internet traffic rating site. Due to these results, the subsequent evaluation considered up to the top 100 websites in the United States in an effort to better represent possibly annotated websites. The webpage categories annotated included News, Politics, Technology, Blogs, Science, and others, showing a range of diverse entity types that casual users may annotate using Web-BANC.

3.2 Large-Scale System Generated Simulations

Section 3.1 shows WebBANC's potential for high throughput and accuracy, but effectiveness is dependent on regularly visited web pages containing words that are useful to NLP annotated corpora. Therefore, our experiment compares the content of frequently visited web sites to established corpora.

3.2.1 Evaluation Methodology

For large-scale simulation-based evaluation, we conducted three experiments comparing different sets of corpora to web generated corpora. The first experiment identified human-curated categories using Yahoo.com, which has about twenty primary categories, such as Health, Politics, and Weather. The corpora generated from these categories allowed us to evaluate category-specific corpora, for example, a Sports corpus. The second experiment used the most commonly visited web sites for a minority language, specifically Icelandic, and compared the results to a half-million word Icelandic corpus published by the Institute of Lexicography in 1991 (Pind et al., 1991) and produced from the IFD, supplied by the Árni Magnússon Institute for Icelandic Studies. The final experiment is compared against the OANC to assess the potential for building general English corpora.

A simple examination of word counts and word diversity derived from web corpus annotations from popular websites can help determine the likelihood of creating a diverse corpus, and therefore assess whether the generated corpus is likely to be useful. However, the rate at which users collectively annotate words encountered during regular web browsing, which we call the *annotation percentage*, directly affects the expected word counts and will vary. We considered *annotation percentages* from 100%, 90%, ..., 50% to simulate different user scenarios.

The experiments contained simulations that permute the recursive depth searched, the annotation percentage, and the number X of frequently visited sites explored. To simulate the web pages a casual user might browse on a daily basis we used data from Alexa.com to identify the most popular X websites in the United States, where $X \in \{10, 25, 50, 100\}$, referred to as the *top X* sites. The depth is varied to simulate different user behavior; some users will only visit the main web page, while others will drill-down into sublevels. Corpora generated from depth 0 contain the text on the front page of each URL; depth 1 corpora contain all text from depth 0, and all text gathered by following URL links at depth 0; similarly, depth 2 corpora contain all text obtained from the depth 1 traversal, including text collected by following all links discovered at depth 1. The number of links, or URLs, harvested for the top 100 corpus at depth 2 (see Table 3) became too large to process and were left out of the results. We used the *wget* Unix program to recursively follow these links. These 3 depths, 4 groupings of popularities and 6 annotation percentages generated 72 datasets (3*4*6=72) per corpus.

Table 3: The number of documents harvested for the top X corpora at each depth.

	Depth 0	Depth 1	Depth 2
Top 10	10	207	2,266
Top 25	25	940	16,576
Top 50	50	2,272	33,239
Top 100	100	5,047	111,188

We used *recall* and *precision* to compare performance in our top X generated corpora. Given an established corpus or category system, called a *base word list*, and a generated word list from the top X websites, we calculate precision and recall after the following pre-processing: for each site in a URL list or base corpus, apply a Perl module from BootCaT (Baroni and Bernardini, 2004) to retrieve the text from that URL and remove all HTML tags; remove all punctuation and words that appear in the stop word filter; apply Porter stemming; and generate a unique term list.

3.2.2 Large-Scale Study Results

Human-Curated Corpora: To evaluate Web-BANC's ability to generate category or entity specific corpora, we ran several simulations varying the traversal depth and quantity of top X sites. This experiment was designed to compare category recognition between the top X corpora and humanly-curated corpora. The results indicate that both the value of X and the traversal depth affect the quality of generated corpora.

Table 4 shows unique word counts for a select set of Yahoo.com categories including Nutrition, Sports, and Technology. Due to the limited text at depth 0 and the great expansion of text at depth 2, the decision was made to examine the human-curated categories at depth 1. There are fewer web pages to annotate at depth 1 than depth 2, and therefore depth 1 may better simulate likely user behavior.

Table 4: Unique word counts for human-curated corpora from Yahoo.com.

	Depth 0	Depth 1	Depth 2
Nutrition	417	7,071	16,452
Sports	796	17,760	74,840
Technology	432	16,440	100,163

As Table 4 shows, depth had less impact on the Nutrition corpus size. The pages retrieved at consecutive depths for Nutrition returned similar words, which negatively affected the uniqueness and diversity of the corpus. Sports benefited greatly from increased depth due to its hierarchical information content. Similar to Sports, information content for the Technology category was organized in a product-driven hierarchy, resulting in a higher dependence on the depth level.

We examined the top 100 most visited sites, compared them to three Yahoo.com human-curated corpora, both at depth 1, and examined the results with annotation percentages ranging from 100% to 50%. Figure 1 shows maximum recall of 67%, 70%, and 57% for the Nutrition, Sports, and Technology corpora, respectively. In the less

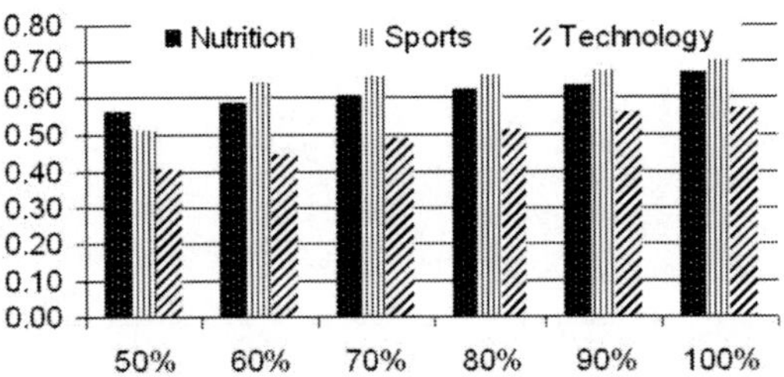

Figure 1: Recall of the top 100 corpus (depth 1) vs. human-curated Yahoo.com corpora (depth 1).

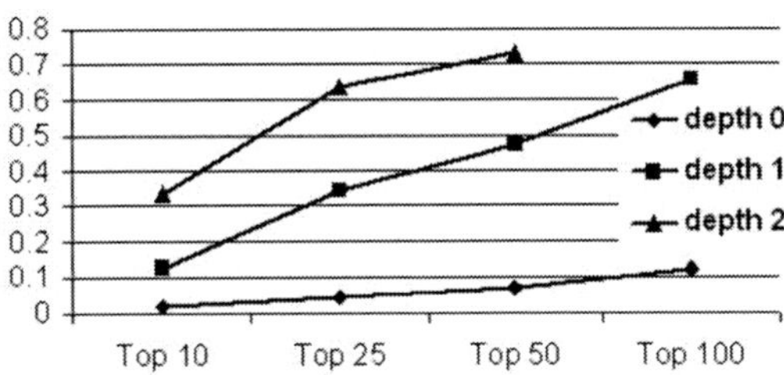

Figure 2: Recall of top X corpora at depths 0, 1, and 2 vs. Sports Yahoo.com corpus (depth 1) with annotation percentage of 70%.

ideal scenario, in which users collectively only annotate half of what they see, Figure 1 shows recall above 50% for two of the three Yahoo.com categories, indicating that users collectively annotating half of all encountered words can cover about half the possible words in a specialized corpus.

Finally, we examined recall of the top X corpora at different depths against the Sports corpus at depth 1 using an annotation percentage of 70% to demonstrate X's effect on word diversity. As Figure 2 shows, recall improved from depths 0 to 1 for the top 10 and top 100 sites by a factor of eight (1.6% to 12.9%) and a smaller factor of 5.3 (12.4% to 66.5%), respectively. The top 100 sites did not perform as well because increasing X decreases word uniqueness, which attenuates the benefits. As X increases for the top X sites, Figure 2 suggests that recall increases. The figure also shows that similar recall performance can be achieved at smaller X values by increasing the depth. fGiven that our results showed higher recall with larger X values and increased depth, it would be interesting to harvest larger numbers of websites in future work to determine if a saturation point for the number of documents examined exists.

Minority Language Corpora: The lack of an-

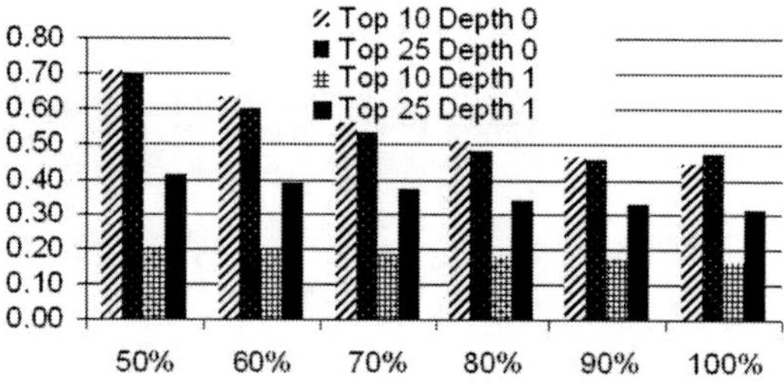

Figure 3: Precision of Icelandic top X corpora vs. IFD corpus.

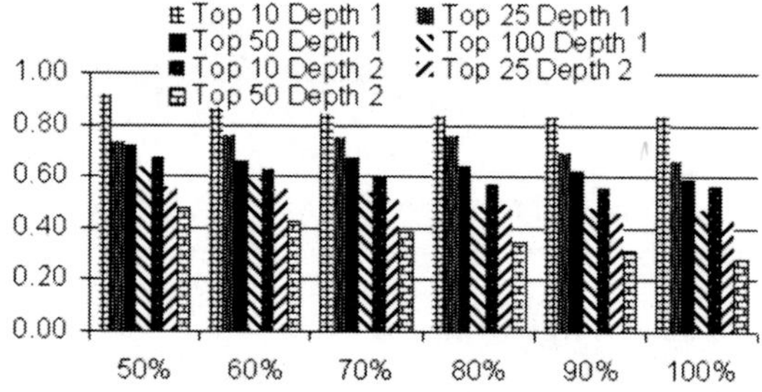

Figure 4: Precision comparison at different annotation percentages between OANC and the top X corpora.

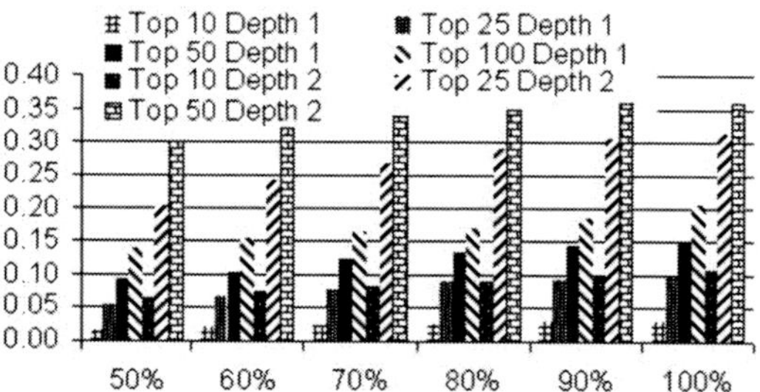

Figure 5: Recall comparison at different annotation percentages between OANC and the top X corpora.

notated corpora for minority languages is a primary cause for the dearth of machine learning tasks in these languages. The following experiment is designed to show that minority language speakers can annotate words during their daily browsing to aid in the construction of annotated corpora using the Icelandic language.

Figure 3 compares the precision of Icelandic top X corpora to the IFD corpus. The results suggest that words in the top X sites are useful for corpora generation, but diversity may be less than desirable, although 70% precision is attained for the top 10 and top 25 Icelandic websites at 50% annotation percentage. The results indicate that words encountered by Icelandic speakers in everyday web browsing may yield relatively precise Icelandic corpora.

Recall for Icelandic top X corpora is relatively low, around 30%, in comparison to the other experiments, for several reasons. Unlike the English corpora results, we did not apply a complete stemming or morphological tool, such as the Porter stemmer, and therefore many Icelandic words did not match their root words in the base corpora. In this simulation only a basic stemmer was applied (e.g. umlauts were not taken into account) causing some words to differ from their root words with the same semantic meaning. Future experiments on this topic should make use of newer lemmatization software for Icelandic, such as Lemmald (Ingason et al., 2008). IFD's use of literature is also a likely cause for the low recall since the most popular websites are news related.

The IFD corpus contained 35,883 unique words after applying a suffix stemmer and removing punctuation. Similar to the English corpora results for the top X sites, the Icelandic equivalents had low unique word counts for the top 10 (2,819) and top 25 (3,178) depth 0 searches, but increased at

depth 1. For example, the top 25 contained 22,661 unique words, which more closely approximates the size of the IFD corpus. The majority of depth 0 corpora exclusively contain Icelandic words, however, examining corpora at depth 1 shows that other languages, mostly English, pollute the corpora due to depth 0 sites linking to web sites in other languages, although some English phrases are filtered by the stop word list.

General Corpora: To encourage corpus creation from the Web, it is important to determine if the Web represents the breadth of a particular language, which this experiment addresses by comparing the top X corpora to the OANC corpora.

Figure 4 suggests that the top X corpora may be useful, with precision values almost 70%, if users annotate text at the top X sites at depths 0 and 1. The precision values decline at depth 2; this may be caused by pages at increased depth containing more category specific language that does not represent American English as precisly.

The recall results in Figure 5 compare OANC, the base corpus, to the top X sites at depths 1 and 2 and show low performance, peaking at 36.2%.

This is partly caused by OANC being a balanced collection of texts, which includes categories seldom found in the top X sites, such as Fiction and Technical, although the results for $X \in \{25, 50\}$ at depth 2 represent dramatic improvements over depths 0 and 1.

The precision results support the hypothesis that the Web may be useful for annotating the American Nation Corpus (ANC) for specific genres or categories that are covered in-depth on the Web, such as Technology, Business, or Sports documents. However, the recall results validate work by Ide, Reppen and Suderman (Ide et al., 2002) claiming that general corpora constructed from web documents would not cover the same breadth of topics as the ANC, which is a testament to the scope of the ANC project.

4   Conclusion and Future Work

Annotated corpora generation presents a major obstacle to advancing modern Natural Language Processing technologies, especially for minority languages. In this paper we introduced the Web-BANC framework, which aims to leverage a distributed web user community to build sufficiently diverse, semantically-rich, and large-scale corpora from user annotations. Accuracy and throughput were examined through a small-scale user study with promising results. We evaluated the diversity of the web-based corpora by comparing statistics against (a) corpora built from human-curated Yahoo.com categories, (b) a minority language corpus generated from the IFD, and (c) established domain corpora, such as OANC and CoNLL. Using up to 100 of the most commonly visited websites, according to Alexa.com, captured 35%-70% of the diversity of these base corpora at 70%-90% percent precision even using just half of the words encountered in these webpages. The actual user studies demonstrated a relatively high accuracy for the NER task that was comparable in performance to the majority of automatic NER tools.

The success of collaborate annotation projects, such as WebBANC rely heavily on user involvement. To increase the possibility of success for multi-lingual projects in the future we are developing other interfaces, such as collaborative games, that are beyond the scope of this paper. Collaborative annotation is likely to benefit from filtering and weighting techniques, as shown in Table 2, and our future work will incorporate inter-annotator agreement such as Kappa statistics.

Acknowledgments

We would like to thank the Fulbright Program for the year of support for Nathan Green in Iceland as well as the Árni Magnússon Institute for Icelandic Studies for supplying the Icelandic corpus. This work was funded by the Scientific Data Management Center under the Department of Energy's Scientific Discovery through Advanced Computing program. Oak Ridge National Laboratory is managed by UT-Battelle for the LLC U.S. D.O.E. under contract no. DEAC05-00OR22725.

References

G. Alonso. Web Services: Concepts, Architectures and Applications. Springer, 2004.

M. Ashburner, C. A. Ball, J. A. Blake, D. Botstein, H. Butler, J. M. Cherry, A. P. Davis, K. Dolinski, S. S. Dwight, and J. T. Eppig. Gene Ontology: tool for the unification of biology. *Nature Genetics*, 25:25, 2000.

M. Baroni and S. Bernardini. BootCaT: Bootstrapping corpora and terms from the web. *The 4th International Conference on Language Resources and Evaluation (LREC2004)*, Lisbon, Portugal, 2004.

S. Bechhofer, F. van Harmelen, J. Hendler, I. Horrocks, D. L. McGuinness, P. F. Patel-Schneider, and L. A. Stein. OWL Web Ontology Language Reference. W3C Recommendation, 10:2006–01, 2004.

L. Burnard. The Users Reference Guide for the British National Corpus. British National Corpus Consortium. *Oxford University Computing Service*, 1995.

S. DeRose, R. D. Jr., and E. Maler. XML Pointer Language (XPointer). *World Wide Web Consortium Working Draft*. March, 1998.

S. Helgadóttir. Testing data-driven learning algorithms for POS tagging of Icelandic. *Nordisk Sprogteknologi*, pages 2000–2004, 2004.

N. Ide and C. Macleod. The American National Corpus: A Standardized Resource of American English. *Corpus Linguistics*, pages 274–280, 2001.

N. Ide, R. Reppen, and K. Suderman. The American National Corpus: More than the web can provide. *The Third Language Resources and Evaluation Conference*, pages 839–844, 2002.

jPDFNotes Development Team. jPDFNotes. http://www.qoppa.com/pdfnotes/jpnindex.html.

J. Kahan, M. R. Koivunen, E. Prud'Hommeaux, and R. R. Swick. Annotea: an open RDF infrastructure for shared Web annotations. *Computer Networks*, 39:589–608, 2002.

J.D. Kim, T. Ohta, and J. Tsujii. Corpus annotation for mining biomedical events from literature. *BMC Bioinformatics*, 9:10, 2008.

G. Klyne and J. J. Carroll. Resource Description Framework (RDF): Concepts and Abstract Syntax. W3C Recommendation, 10, 2004.

D. Krafzig, K. Banke, and D. Slama. Enterprise SOA: Service-Oriented Architecture Best Practices. *Prentice Hall Ptr*, 2004.

S. Krauwer. The Basic Language Resource Kit (BLARK) as the First Milestone for the Language Resources Roadmap. *The International Workshop Speech and Computer (SPECOM 200)*, Moscow, Russia, 2003.

Y. Labrou and T. Finin. Yahoo! as an ontology: using Yahoo! categories to describe documents. *The eighth international conference on Information and knowledge management*, pages 180–187, 1999.

F. Leitner and A. Valencia. A text-mining perspective on the requirements for electronically annotated abstracts. *FEBS Letters*, 582:1178–1181, 2008.

C. Mair. The corpus-based study of language change in progress: The extra value of tagged corpora. *The AAACL/ICAME Conference*, Ann Arbor, 2005.

J. Pind, F. Magnússon, and S. Briem. The Icelandic Frequency Dictionary. The Institute of Lexicography, University of Iceland, Reykjavik, Iceland, 1991.

R. Ghani and D. Mladenic. Mining the Web to Create Minority Language Corpora. The 10th international conference on Information and knowledge management, pages 279–286, Athens, Georgia, 2001.

P. Rayson, J. Walkerdine, W. H. Fletcher, and A. Kilgarriff. Annotated web as corpus. A. Kilgarriff and M.Baroni, editors, *The 2nd International Workshop on Web as Corpus* (EACL06), pages 27–34, Trento, Italy, 2006.

E. Sang and F. D. Meulder. Introduction to the CoNLL-2003 shared task: language-independent named entity recognition. *The seventh conference on Natural language learning at HLT-NAACL* 2003-Volume 4, pages 142–147, 2003.

K. Scannell. The Crúbadán Project: Corpus building for under-resourced languages. C. Fairon, H. Naets, A. Kilgarriff, and G.-M. de Schryver, editors, *Building and Exploring Web Corpora*, pages 5–15, Louvain-la-Neuve, Belgium, 2007.

V. Uren, P. Cimiano, J. Iria, S. Handschuh, M. Vargas-Vera, E. Motta, and F. Ciravegna. Semantic annotation for knowledge management: Requirements and a survey of the state of the art. *Web Semantics: Science, Services and Agents on the World Wide Web*, 4:14–28, 2006.

A. Ingason, S. Helgadóttir, H. Loftsson, and Eiríkur Rögnvaldsson A Mixed Method Lemmatization Algorithm Using a Hierarchy of Linguistic Identities (HOLI). *Advances in Natural Language Processing*, 205–216, 2008.

T. Zesch, I. Gurevych, and M. Mühlhäuser. Analyzing and Accessing Wikipedia as a Lexical Semantic Resource. *Biannual Conference of the Society for Computational Linguistics and Language Technology*, pages 213–221, 2007.

ISSN 1736-6305 Vol. 4
http://hdl.handle.net/10062/9206

Using Linguistic Annotations in
Statistical Machine Translation of Film Subtitles

Christian Hardmeier
Fondazione Bruno Kessler
Human Language Technologies
Via Sommarive, 18
I-38050 Povo (Trento)
`hardmeier@fbk.eu`

Martin Volk
Universität Zürich
Inst. für Computerlinguistik
Binzmühlestrasse 14
CH-8050 Zürich
`volk@cl.uzh.ch`

Abstract

Statistical Machine Translation (SMT) has been successfully employed to support translation of film subtitles. We explore the integration of Constraint Grammar corpus annotations into a Swedish–Danish subtitle SMT system in the framework of factored SMT. While the usefulness of the annotations is limited with large amounts of parallel data, we show that linguistic annotations can increase the gains in translation quality when monolingual data in the target language is added to an SMT system based on a small parallel corpus.

1 Introduction

In countries where foreign-language films and series on television are routinely subtitled rather than dubbed, there is a considerable demand for efficiently produced subtitle translations. Although superficially it may seem that subtitles are not appropriate for automatic processing as a result of their literary character, it turns out that their typical text structure, characterised by brevity and syntactic simplicity, and the immense text volumes processed daily by specialised subtitling companies make it possible to produce raw translations of film subtitles with statistical methods quite effectively. If these raw translations are subsequently post-edited by skilled staff, production quality translations can be obtained with considerably less effort than if the subtitles were translated by human translators with no computer assistance.

A successful subtitle Machine Translation system for the language pair Swedish–Danish, which has now entered into productive use, has been presented by Volk and Harder (2007). The goal of the present study is to explore whether and how the quality of a Statistical Machine Translation (SMT) system of film subtitles can be improved by using linguistic annotations. To this end, a subset of 1 million subtitles of the training corpus used by Volk and Harder was morphologically annotated with the DanGram parser (Bick, 2001). We integrated the annotations into the translation process using the methods of factored Statistical Machine Translation (Koehn and Hoang, 2007) implemented in the widely used Moses software. After describing the corpus data and giving a short overview over the methods used, we present a number of experiments comparing different factored SMT setups. The experiments are then replicated with reduced training corpora which contain only part of the available training data. These series of experiments provide insights about the impact of corpus size on the effectivity of using linguistic abstractions for SMT.

2 Machine translation of subtitles

As a text genre, subtitles play a curious role in a complex environment of different media and modalities. They depend on the medium film, which combines a visual channel with an auditive component composed of spoken language and non-linguistic elements such as noise or music. Within this framework, they render the spoken dialogue into written text, are blended in with the visual channel and displayed simultaneously as the original sound track is played back, which redundantly contains the same information in a form that may or may not be accessible to the viewer. In their linguistic form, subtitles should be faithful, both in contents and in style, to the film dialogue which they represent. This means in particular that they usually try to convey an impression of orality. On the other hand, they are constrained by the mode of their presentation: short, written captions superimposed on the picture frame.

According to Becquemont (1996), the characteristics of subtitles are governed by the interplay of two conflicting principles: *unobtrusiveness* (discrétion) and *readability* (lisibilité). In order to provide a satisfactory experience to the viewers, it is paramount that the subtitles help them quickly understand the meaning of the dialogue without distracting them from enjoying the film. The amount of text that can be displayed at one time is limited by the area of the screen that may be covered by subtitles (usually no more than two lines) and by the minimum time the subtitle must remain on screen to ensure that it can actually be read. As a result, the subtitle text must be shortened with respect to the full dialogue text in the actors' script. The extent of the reduction depends on the script and on the exact limitations imposed for a specific subtitling task, but may amount to as much as 30 % and reach 50 % in extreme cases (Tomaszkiewicz, 1993, 6).

As a result of this processing and the considerations underlying it, subtitles have a number of properties that make them especially well suited for Statistical Machine Translation. Owing to their presentational constraints, they mainly consist of comparatively short and simple phrases. Current SMT systems, when trained on a sufficient amount of data, have reliable ways of handling word translation and local structure. By contrast, they are still fairly weak at modelling long-range dependencies and reordering. Compared to other text genres, this weakness is less of an issue in the Statistical Machine Translation of subtitles thanks to their brevity and simple structure. Indeed, half of the subtitles in the Swedish part of our parallel training corpus are no more than 11 tokens long, including two tokens to mark the beginning and the end of the segment and counting every punctuation mark as a separate token. A considerable number of subtitles only contains one or two words, besides punctuation, often consisting entirely of a few words of affirmation, negation or abuse. These subtitles can easily be translated by an SMT system that has seen similar examples before.

The orientation of the genre towards spoken language also has some disadvantages for Machine Translation systems. It is possible that the language of the subtitles, influenced by characteristics of speech, contains unexpected features such as stutterings, word repetitions or renderings of non-standard pronunciations that confuse the system. Such features are occasionally employed by subtitlers to lend additional colour to the text, but as they are in stark conflict with the ideals of unob-

trusiveness and readability, they are not very frequent.

It is worth noting that, unlike rule-based Machine Translation systems, a statistical system does not in general have any difficulties translating ungrammatical or fragmentary input: phrase-based SMT, operating entirely on the level of words and word sequences, does not require the input to be amenable to any particular kind of linguistic analysis such as parsing. Whilst this approach makes it difficult to handle some linguistic challenges such as long-distance dependencies, it has the advantage of making the system more robust to unexpected input, which is more important for subtitles.

We have only been able to sketch the characteristics of the subtitle text genre in this paper. Díaz-Cintas and Remael (2007) provide a detailed introduction, including the linguistics of subtitling and translation issues, and Pedersen (2007) discusses the peculiarities of subtitling in Scandinavia.

3   Constraint Grammar annotations

To explore the potential of linguistically annotated data, our complete subtitle corpus, both in Danish and in Swedish, was linguistically analysed with the DanGram Constraint Grammar (CG) parser (Bick, 2001), a system originally developed for the analysis of Danish for which there is also a Swedish grammar. Constraint Grammar (Karlsson, 1990) is a formalism for natural language parsing. Conceptually, a CG parser first produces possible analyses for each word by considering its morphological features and then applies constraining rules to filter out analyses that do not fit into the context. Thus, the word forms are gradually disambiguated, until only one analysis remains; multiple analyses may be retained if the sentence is ambiguous.

The annotations produced by the DanGram parser were output as tags attached to individual words as in the following example:

```
$-
Vad   [vad] <interr> INDP NEU S NOM @ACC>
vet   [veta] <mv> V PR AKT @FS-QUE
du    [du] PERS 2S UTR S NOM @<SUBJ
om    [om] PRP @<PIV
det   [den] <dem> PERS NEU 3S ACC @P<
$?
```

In addition to the word forms and the accompanying lemmas (in square brackets), the annotations contained part-of-speech (POS) tags such as INDP for "independent pronoun" or V for "verb", a morphological analysis for each word (such as NEU S NOM for "neuter singular nominative") and a tag specifying the syntactic function of the word in the sentence (such as @ACC>, indicating that the sentence-initial pronoun is an accusative object of the following verb). For some words, more fine-grained part-of-speech information was specified in angle brackets, such as <interr> for "interrogative pronoun" or <mv> for "verb of movement". In our experiments, we used word forms, lemmas, POS tags and morphological analyses. The fine-grained POS tags and the syntax tags were not used.

4 Factored Statistical Machine Translation

Statistical Machine Translation formalises the translation process by modelling the probabilities of target language (TL) output strings T given a source language (SL) input string S, $p(T\,|\,S)$, and conducting a search for the output string $\hat{T}$ with the highest probability. In the Moses decoder (Koehn et al., 2007), which we used in our experiments, this probability is decomposed into a log-linear combination of a number of feature functions $h_i(S,T)$, which map a pair of a source and a target language element to a score based on different submodels such as translation models or language models. Each feature function is associated with a weight λ_i that specifies its contribution to the overall score:

$$\hat{T} = \arg\max_T \, \log p(T\,|\,S)$$

$$= \arg\max_T \sum_i \lambda_i\, h_i(S,T)$$

The *translation models* employed in factored SMT are phrase-based. The phrases included in a translation model are extracted from a word-aligned parallel corpus with the techniques described by Koehn et al. (2003). The associated probabilities are estimated by the relative frequencies of the extracted phrase pairs in the same corpus. For *language modelling*, we used the SRILM toolkit (Stolcke, 2002); unless otherwise specified, 6-gram language models with modified Kneser-Ney smoothing were used.

The SMT decoder tries to translate the words and phrases of the source language sentence in the order in which they occur in the input. If the target language requires a different word order, reordering is possible at the cost of a score penalty. The translation model has no notion of sequence, so it cannot control reordering. The language model can, but it has no access to the source language text, so it considers word order only from the point of view of TL grammaticality and cannot model systematic differences in word order between two languages. *Lexical reordering models* (Koehn et al., 2005) address this issue in a more explicit way by modelling the probability of certain changes in word order, such as swapping words, conditioned on the source and target language phrase pair that is being processed.

In its basic form, Statistical Machine Translation treats word tokens as atomic and does not permit further decomposition or access to single features of the words. Factored SMT (Koehn and Hoang, 2007) extends this model by representing words as vectors composed of a number of features and makes it possible to integrate word-level annotations such as those produced by a Constraint Grammar parser into the translation process. The individual components of the feature vectors are called *factors*. In order to map between different factors on the target language side, the Moses decoder works with *generation models*, which are implemented as dictionaries and extracted from the target-language side of the training corpus. They can be used, e. g., to generate word forms from lemmas and morphology tags, or to transform word forms into part-of-speech tags, which could then be checked using a language model.

5 Experiments with the full corpus

We ran three series of experiments to study the effects of different SMT system setups on translation quality with three different configurations of training corpus sizes. For each condition, several Statistical Machine Translation systems were trained and evaluated.

In the *full data* condition, the complete system was trained on a parallel corpus of some 900,000 subtitles with source language Swedish and target language Danish, corresponding to around 10 million tokens in each language. The feature weights were optimised using minimum error rate training (Och, 2003) on a development set of 1,000 subtitles that had not been used for training, then the system was evaluated on a 10,000 subtitle test set that had been held out during the whole development phase. The translations were evaluated with the widely used BLEU and NIST scores (Papineni et al., 2002; Doddington, 2002). The outcomes of different experiments were compared with a randomisation-based hypothesis test (Cohen, 1995, 165–177). The test was two-sided, and the confidence level was fixed at 95 %.

The results of the experiments can be found in table 1. The baseline system used only a translation model operating on word forms and a 6-gram language model on word forms. This is a standard setup for an unfactored SMT system. Two systems additionally included a 6-gram language model operating on part-of-speech tags and a 5-gram language model operating on morphology tags, respectively. The annotation factors required by these language models were produced from the word forms by suitable generation models.

In the *full data* condition, both the part-of-speech and the morphology language model brought a slight, but statistically significant gain in terms of BLEU scores, which indicates that abstract information about grammar can in some cases help the SMT system choose the right words. The improvement is small; indeed, it is not reflected in the NIST scores, but some beneficial effects of the additional language models can be observed in the individual output sentences.

One thing that can be achieved by taking word class information into account is the disambiguation of ambiguous word forms. Consider the following example:

Input: Ingen vill bo mitt emot en ismaskin.
Reference: Ingen vil bo lige over for en ismaskine.
Baseline: Ingen vil bo mit imod en ismaskin.
POS/Morphology: Ingen vil bo over for en ismaskin.

Since the word *ismaskin* 'ice machine' does not occur in the Swedish part of the training corpus, none of the SMT systems was able to translate it. All of them copied the Swedish input word literally to the output, which is a mistake that cannot be fixed by a language model. However, there is a clear difference in the translation of the phrase *mitt emot* 'opposite'. For some reason, the baseline system chose to translate the two words separately and mistakenly interpreted the adverb *mitt*, which is part of the Swedish expression, as the homonymous first person neuter possessive pronoun 'my', translating the Swedish phrase as ungrammatical Danish *mit imod* 'my against'. Both of the ad-

ditional language models helped to rule out this error and correctly translate *mitt emot* as *over for*, yielding a much better translation. Neither of them output the adverb *lige* 'just' found in the reference translation, for which there is no explicit equivalent in the input sentence.

In the next example, the POS and the morphology language model produced different output:

Input: Dåliga kontrakt, dålig ledning, dåliga agenter.
Reference: Dårlige kontrakter, dårlig styring, dårlige agenter.
Baseline: Dårlige kontrakt, dårlig forbindelse, dårlige agenter.
POS: Dårlige kontrakt, dårlig ledelse, dårlige agenter.
Morphology: Dårlige kontrakter, dårlig forbindelse, dårlige agenter.

In Swedish, the indefinite singular and plural forms of the word *kontrakt* 'contract(s)' are homonymous. The two SMT systems without support for morphological analysis incorrectly produced the singular form of the noun in Danish. The morphology language model recognised that the plural adjective *dårlige* 'bad' is more likely to be followed by a plural noun and preferred the correct Danish plural form *kontrakter* 'contracts'. The different translations of the word *ledning* as 'management' or 'connection' can be pinned down to a subtle influence of the generation model probability estimates. They illustrate how sensitive the system output is in the face of true ambiguity. None of the systems presented here has the capability of reliably choosing the right word based on the context in this case.

In three experiments, the baseline configuration was extended by adding lexical reordering models conditioned on word forms, lemmas and part-of-speech tags, respectively. As in the language model experiments, the required annotation factors on the TL side were produced by generation models.

The lexical reordering models turn out to be useful in the *full data* experiments only when conditioned on word forms. When conditioned on lemmas, the score is not significantly different from the baseline score, and when conditioned on part-of-speech tags, it is significantly lower. In this case, the most valuable information for lexical reordering lies in the word form itself. Lemma and part of speech are obviously not the right abstractions to model the reordering processes when sufficient data is available.

Table 1 Experimental results

	full data		symmetric		asymmetric	
	BLEU	NIST	BLEU	NIST	BLEU	NIST
Baseline	53.67 %	8.18	42.12 %	6.83	44.85 %	7.10
Language models						
parts of speech	⋆ 53.90 %	8.17	⋆ 42.59 %	6.87	∘ 44.71 %	7.08
morphology	⋆ 54.07 %	8.18	⋆ 42.86 %	6.92	⋆ 44.95 %	7.09
Lexical reordering						
word forms	⋆ 53.99 %	8.21	42.13 %	6.83	∘ 44.72 %	7.05
lemmas	53.59 %	8.15	⋆ 42.30 %	6.86	∘ 44.71 %	7.06
parts of speech	∘ 53.36 %	8.13	⋆ 42.33 %	6.86	∘ 44.63 %	7.05
Analytical translation	53.73 %	8.18	⋆ 42.28 %	6.90	⋆ 46.73 %	7.34

⋆   BLEU score significantly above baseline ($p < .05$)

∘   BLEU score significantly below baseline ($p < .05$)

Another system, which we call the *analytical translation* system, was modelled on suggestions by Koehn and Hoang (2007) and Bojar (2007). It used the lemmas and the output of the morphological analysis to decompose the translation process and use separate components to handle the transfer of lexical and grammatical information. In order to achieve this, the baseline system was extended with additional translation tables mapping SL lemmas to TL lemmas and SL morphology tags to TL morphology tags, respectively. In the target language, a generation model was used to transform lemmas and morphology tags into word forms. The results reported by Koehn and Hoang (2007) strongly indicate that this translation approach is not sufficient on its own; instead, the decomposed translation approach should be combined with a standard word form translation model so that one can be used in those cases where the other fails. This configuration was therefore adopted for our experiments.

The analytical translation approach fails to achieve any significant score improvement with the full parallel corpus. Closer examination of the MT output reveals that the strategy of using lemmas and morphological information to translate unknown word forms works in principle, as shown by the following example:

Input: Molly har visat mig bröllopsfotona.
Reference: Molly har vist mig fotoene fra brylluppet.
Baseline: Molly har vist mig bröllopsfotona.
Analytical: Molly har vist mig bryllupsbillederne.

In this sentence, there can be no doubt that the output produced by the analytical system is superior to that of the baseline system. Where the baseline system copied the Swedish word *bröllopsfotona* 'wedding photos' literally into the Danish text, the translation found by the analytical model, *bryllupsbillederne* 'wedding pictures', is both semantically and syntactically flawless. Unfortunately, the reference translation uses different words, so the evaluation scores will not reflect this improvement.

The lack of success of analytical translation in terms of evaluation scores can be ascribed to at least three factors: Firstly, there are relatively few vocabulary gaps in our data, which is due to the size of training corpus. Only 1.19 % (1,311 of 109,823) of the input tokens are tagged as unknown by the decoder in the baseline system. As a result, there is not much room for improvement with an approach specifically designed to handle vocabulary coverage, especially if this approach itself fails in some of the cases missed by the baseline system: Analytical translation brings this figure down to 0.88 % (970 tokens), but no further. Secondly, employing generation tables trained on the same corpus as the translation tables used by the system limits the attainable gains from the outset, since a required word form that is not found in the translation table is likely to be missing from the generation table, too. Thirdly, in case of vocabulary gaps in the translation tables, chances are that the system will not be able to produce the optimal translation for the input sentence. Instead, an approach like analytical translation aims to find the best translation that can be derived from the available models, which is certainly a reasonable thing to do. However, when only one reference translation is used, current evaluation methods will not allow alternative solutions, uniformly penalising all deviating translations instead. While using more reference translations could potentially alleviate this problem, multiple references are expensive to produce and just not available in many situations. Consequently, there is a systematic bias against the kind of solutions analytical translation can provide: Often, the evaluation method will assign the same scores to untranslated gibberish as to valid attempts at translating an unknown word with the best means available.

6 Experiments with reduced corpora

We tested SMT systems trained on reduced corpora in two experimental conditions. In the *symmetric* condition, the systems described in the previous section were trained on a parallel corpus of 9,000 subtitles, or around 100,000 tokens per language, only. This made it possible to study the behaviour of the systems with little data. In the *asymmetric* condition, the small 9,000 subtitle parallel corpus was used to train the translation models and lexical reordering models. The generation and language models, which only rely on monolingual data in the target language, were trained on the full 900,000 subtitle dataset in this condition. This setup simulates a situation in which it is difficult to find parallel data for a certain language pair, but monolingual data in the target language can be more easily obtained. This is not unlikely when translating from a language with few electronic resources into a language like English, for which large amounts of corpus data are readily available.

The results of the experiments with reduced corpora follow a more interesting pattern. First of all, it should be noted that the experiments in the *asymmetric* condition consistently outperformed those in the *symmetric* condition. Evidently, Statistical Machine Translation benefits from additional data, even if it is only available in the target language.

The training corpus of 9,000 segments or 100,000 tokens per language used in the *symmetric* experiments is extremely small for SMT; in comparison to the training sets used in most other studies, this set is tiny. Consequently, one would expect the translation quality to be severely impaired by data sparseness issues, making it difficult for the Machine Translation system to handle unseen data. This prediction is supported by the experiments: The scores are improved by all extensions that allow the model to deal with more abstract representations of the data and thus to generalise more easily. The highest gains in terms of BLEU and NIST scores result from the morphology language model, which helps to ensure that the TL sentences produced by the system are well-formed.

Interestingly enough, the relative performance of the lexical reordering models runs contrary to the findings obtained with the full corpus. Lexical reordering models turn out to be helpful when conditioned on lemmas or POS tags, whereas lexical reordering conditioned on word forms neither helps nor hurts. This is probably due to the fact that it is more difficult to gather satisfactory information about reordering from the small corpus. The reordering probabilities can be estimated more reliably after abstracting to lemmas or POS tags.

In the *asymmetric* condition, the same phrase tables and lexical reorderings as in the *symmetric* condition were used, but the generation tables and language models were trained on a TL corpus 100 times as large. The benefit of this larger corpus is obvious already in the baseline experiment, which is completely identical to the baseline experiment of the *symmetric* condition except for the language model. Clearly, using additional monolingual TL data for language modelling is an easy and effective way to improve an SMT system.

Furthermore, the availability of a larger data set on the TL side brings about profound changes in the relative performance of the individual systems with respect to each other. The POS language model, which proved useful in the *symmetric* condition, is detrimental now. The morphology language model does improve the BLEU score, but only by a very small amount, and the effect on the NIST score is slightly negative. This indicates that the language model operating on word forms is superior to the abstract models when it is trained on sufficient data. Likewise, all three lexical reordering models hurt performance in the presence of a strong word form language model. Apparently, when the language model is good, nothing can be gained by having a doubtful reordering model trained on insufficient data compete against it.

The most striking result in the *asymmetric* condition, however, is the score of the analytical translation model, which achieved an improvement of impressive 1.9 percentage points in the BLEU score along with an equally noticeable increase of the NIST score. In the *asymmetric* setup, where the generation model has much better vocabulary coverage than the phrase tables, analytical translation realises its full potential and enables the SMT system to produce word forms it could not otherwise have found.

In sum, enlarging the size of the target language corpus resulted in a gain of 2.7 percentage points BLEU on the baseline score of the *symmetric* condition, which is entirely due to the better language model on word forms and can be realised without linguistic analysis of the input. By integrating morphological analysis and lemmas for both the SL and the TL part of the corpus, the leverage of the additional data can be increased even further by analytical translation, realising another improvement of 1.9 percentage points, totalling 4.6 percentage points over the initial baseline.

7 Conclusion

Subject to a set of peculiar practical constraints, the text genre of film subtitles is characterised by short sentences with a comparatively simple structure and frequent reuse of similar expressions. Moreover, film subtitles are a text genre designed for translation; they are translated between many different languages in huge numbers. Their structural properties and the availability of large amounts of data make them ideal for Statistical Machine Translation. The present report investigates the potential of incorporating information from linguistic analysis into the Swedish–Danish phrase-based SMT system for film subtitles presented by Volk and Harder (2007). It is based on a subset of the data used by Volk and Harder, which has been extended with linguistic annotations in the Constraint Grammar framework produced by the DanGram parser (Bick, 2001). We integrated the annotations into the SMT system using the factored approach to SMT (Koehn and Hoang, 2007) as offered by the Moses decoder (Koehn et al., 2007) and explored the opportunities offered by factored SMT with a number of experiments, each adding a single additional component into the system.

When a large training corpus of around 900,000 subtitles or 10 million tokens per language was used, the gains from adding linguistic information were generally small. Minor improvements were observed when using additional language models operating on part-of-speech tags and tags from morphological analysis. A technique called analytical translation, which enables the SMT system to back off to separate translation of lemmas and morphological tags when the main phrase table does not provide a satisfactory translation, afforded slightly improved vocabulary coverage. Lexical reordering conditioned on word forms also brought about a minor improvement, whereas conditioning lexical reordering on more abstract categories such as lemmas or POS tags had a detrimental effect.

On the whole, none of the gains was large enough to justify the cost and effort of producing the annotations. Moreover, there was a clear tendency for complex models to have a negative effect when the information employed was not selected carefully enough. When the corpus is large and its quality good, there is a danger of obstructing the statistical model from taking full advantage of the data by imposing clumsily chosen linguistic categories. Given sufficient data, enforcing manually selected categories which may not be fully appropriate for the task in question is not a promising approach. Better results could possibly be obtained if abstract categories specifically optimised for the task of modelling distributional characteristics of words were statistically induced from the corpus.

The situation is different when the corpus is small. In a series of experiments with a corpus size of only 9,000 subtitles or 100,000 tokens per language, different manners of integrating linguistic information were consistently found to be beneficial, even though the improvements obtained were small. When the corpus is not large enough to afford reliable parameter estimates for the statistical models, adding abstract data with richer statistics stands to improve the behaviour of the system. Compared to the system trained on the full corpus, the effects involve a trade-off between the reliability and usefulness of the statistical estimates and of the linguistically motivated annotation, respectively; the difference in the results stems from the fact that the quality of the statistical models strongly depends on the amount of data available, whilst the quality of the linguistic annotation is about the same regardless of corpus size. The close relationship of Swedish and Danish may also have impact: For language pairs with greater grammatical differences, the critical corpus size at which the linguistic annotations we worked with stop being useful may be larger.

Our most encouraging findings come from experiments in an asymmetric setting, where a very small SL corpus (9,000 subtitles) was combined with a much larger TL corpus (900,000 subtitles). A considerable improvement to the score was realised just by adding a language model trained on the larger corpus, which does not yet involve any linguistic annotations. With the help of analytical translation, however, the annotations could be successfully exploited to yield a further gain of almost 2 percentage points in the BLEU score. Unlike the somewhat dubious improvements in the other two conditions, this is clearly worth the effort, and it demonstrates that factored Statistical Machine Translation can be successfully used to improve translation quality by integrating additional monolingual data with linguistic annotations into an SMT system.

References

Daniel Becquemont. 1996. Le sous-titrage cinématographique : contraintes, sens, servitudes. In Yves Gambier, editor, *Les transferts linguistiques dans les médias audiovisuels*, pages 145–155. Presses universitaires du Septentrion, Villeneuve d'Ascq.

Eckhard Bick. 2001. En Constraint Grammar parser for dansk. In *8. Møde om udforskningen af dansk sprog*, pages 40–50, Århus.

Ondřej Bojar. 2007. English-to-Czech factored Machine Translation. In *Proceedings of the Second Workshop on Statistical Machine Translation*, pages 232–239, Prague.

Paul R. Cohen. 1995. *Empirical methods for Artificial Intelligence*. MIT Press, Cambridge (Mass.).

Jorge Díaz-Cintas and Aline Remael. 2007. *Audiovisual Translation: Subtitling*, volume 11 of *Translation Practices Explained*. St. Jerome Publishing, Manchester.

George Doddington. 2002. Automatic evaluation of machine translation quality using *n*-gram co-occurrence statistics. In *Proceedings of the second International conference on Human Language Technology Research*, pages 138–145, San Diego.

Fred Karlsson. 1990. Constraint Grammar as a framework for parsing running text. In *COLING-90.*

Papers presented to the 13th International conference on Computational Linguistics, pages 168–173, Helsinki.

Philipp Koehn and Hieu Hoang. 2007. Factored translation models. In *Conference on empirical methods in Natural Language Processing*, pages 868–876, Prague.

Philipp Koehn, Franz Josef Och, and Daniel Marcu. 2003. Statistical phrase-based translation. In *Proceedings of the 2003 conference of the North American chapter of the Association for Computational Linguistics on Human Language Technology*, pages 48–54, Edmonton.

Philipp Koehn, Amittai Axelrod, et al. 2005. Edinburgh system description for the 2005 IWSLT speech translation evaluation. In *International workshop on spoken language translation*, Pittsburgh.

Philipp Koehn, Hieu Hoang, et al. 2007. Moses: open source toolkit for statistical machine translation. In *Annual meeting of the Association for Computational Linguistics: Demonstration session*, pages 177–180, Prague.

Franz Josef Och. 2003. Minimum error rate training in Statistical Machine Translation. In *Proceedings of the 41st annual meeting of the Association for Computational Linguistics*, pages 160–167, Sapporo (Japan).

Kishore Papineni, Salim Roukos, Todd Ward, and Wei-Jing Zhu. 2002. BLEU: a method for automatic evaluation of machine translation. In *Proceedings of the 40th annual meeting of the Association for Computational Linguistics*, pages 311–318, Philadelphia. ACL.

Jan Pedersen. 2007. *Scandinavian subtitles. A comparative study of subtitling norms in Sweden and Denmark with a focus on extralinguistic cultural references*. Ph.D. thesis, Stockholm University, Department of English.

Andreas Stolcke. 2002. SRILM: an extensible language modeling toolkit. In *Proceedings of the International Conference on Spoken Language Processing*, Denver (Colorado).

Teresa Tomaszkiewicz. 1993. *Les opérations linguistiques qui sous-tendent le processus de sous-titrage des films*. Wydawnictwo Naukowe UAM, Poznań.

Martin Volk and Søren Harder. 2007. Evaluating MT with translations or translators. What is the difference? In *Proceedings of MT Summit XI*, pages 499–506, Copenhagen.

ISSN 1736-6305 Vol. 4
http://hdl.handle.net/10062/9206

Parsing Clinical Finnish: Experiments with Rule-Based and Statistical Dependency Parsers

Katri Haverinen,[1] **Filip Ginter,**[1] **Veronika Laippala,**[1,2] **and Tapio Salakoski**[1]
[1]Department of Information Technology
[2]Department of French Studies
University of Turku
Joukahaisenkatu 3-5
20520 Turku, Finland
`first.last@utu.fi`

Abstract

In this paper, we present a new syntactically annotated corpus consisting of daily notes from an intensive care unit in a Finnish hospital. Using the corpus, we perform experiments with both rule-based and statistical parsers. We apply an existing rule-based parser specifically developed for this clinical language and create a set of conversion rules for transforming the constituency scheme of this parser into the dependency scheme of the corpus. The statistical parser is induced from the corpus using the MaltParser system.

We find that even with a modestly-sized corpus, the statistical parser achieves results comparable to those previously reported on a number of languages using considerably larger corpora. The accurate constituency-to-dependency conversion improves the applicability of the rule-based parser by inferring grammatical roles, thus deepening its analyses.

1   Introduction

The potential advantages of applying natural language processing methods in the clinical domain are numerous, with many useful applications in decision support, patient management and profiling, and mining trends (see, e.g., the recent review by Friedman and Johnson (2006)). While certain applications, such as document retrieval and trend mining, can solely rely on word frequency-based statistical methods, a number of applications build on a detailed analysis of the text, typically involving syntactic parsing.

In this paper, we describe experiments on full parsing of Finnish intensive care unit (ICU) nursing documents written in a specific language referred to as ICU Finnish throughout the paper. The main contributions of this work are a corpus of ICU Finnish, syntactically annotated in an adapted version of the Stanford dependency (SD) scheme, and both rule-based and statistical parsing experiments on this corpus. We apply the rule-based parser of Laippala et al. (2009) developed for ICU Finnish, and develop a conversion from its native constituency scheme to the SD scheme. We also conduct experiments with a statistical parser induced from the ICU Finnish corpus using the MaltParser (Nivre et al., 2007) system. This allows us to evaluate and contrast the relative advantages of the two parsing approaches in this domain.

2   Related work

There are numerous applications of full syntactic parsers in the clinical domain. For instance, the Stanford parser has been applied to the extraction of noun phrases with full phrase structures and to negation detection in clinical radiology reports (Huang and Lowe, 2007; Huang et al., 2005). There have also been many studies on the adaptation of existing parsers to the specific domain of biomedical language. For example, Szolovits (2003) describes a method for expanding the Link Grammar (LG) lexicon with UMLS Specialist lexicon terms to improve its applicability to medical texts and Pyysalo et al. (2006) incorporate into LG a domain-adapted part-of-speech tagger.

The different ways to represent natural language syntax can be broadly distinguished into two categories. A constituency analysis divides the sentence into nested phrases, whereas a dependency analysis consists of a set of labelled dependencies between pairs of words. In this work, we focus on dependency parsing because of its benefits in applications and parser evaluation (see for example Lin (1998), Clegg and Shepherd (2007), and Nivre (2008b)), as well as its applicability to languages with a relatively free word order, such

Yövuoro	Nightshift
Potilas levoton, valittaa kipua.	Patient restless, complains of pain.
Annettu 100mg [lääke] hieman rauhottui.	Given 100mg [drugname] a little calmed down.
HENGITS: Hapettuu hyvin repiraattorissa.	BREATING: Oxidates well in repirator.
Putkesta hiukan nest. illalla.	A little liq. from the drain in the evening.
Diureesi: riittävää.	Diuresis: sufficient.
Hemodyn: annettu 50 mg/h [lääke],	Hemodyn: given 50 mg/h [drugname],
heikohko vaste vaihdettu [lääke].	rather weak response changed to [drugname].
OMAISET: vaimo soittanut jutellut lääkärin kanssa.	RELATIVES: wife called talked to doctor.

Figure 1: Example of ICU Finnish (left column) and its exact translation (right column), including spelling errors, capitalization, and the like.

as Finnish. We apply the Stanford dependency scheme (de Marneffe et al., 2006; de Marneffe and Manning, 2008), which has recently been employed in several studies especially in the biomedical domain, but also in other contexts. For an extensive list of applications, we refer to the review by de Marneffe and Manning (2008).

While numerous corpora and parsers exist for English and many other languages, resources for Finnish are scarce. For instance, there is no publicly available syntactically annotated corpus suitable for statistical parser induction. The only publicly available full parser is Connexor Machinese Syntax,[1] a closed-source commercial dependency parser for the general language. Other tools include FinTWOL and FinCG,[2] a morphological analyzer and a Constraint Grammar parser that resolves morphological ambiguity (Koskenniemi, 1983; Karlsson, 1990). The rule-based parser of Laippala et al. (2009) used in this work was developed for the clinical domain, and builds full constituency analyses on top of the morpholexical analyses provided by FinTWOL and FinCG.

3 ICU Finnish in the Stanford dependency scheme

ICU Finnish differs from standard Finnish in many ways (for details, see the discussion by Laippala et al. (2009)). Some of the most distinguishing features present in ICU Finnish, as well as many clinical sublanguages, are frequent misspellings, abbreviations and technical terms, telegraphic sentences, syntactic structures that would not be allowed in standard language, and frequent omissions of main verbs, subjects and copulas. Figure 1 is an illustration of ICU Finnish.[3] The effects of

ICU Finnish features on analyzing the syntax will be more thoroughly discussed in Section 3.2.

3.1 The SD scheme

In the SD scheme, the syntactic structure of a sentence is represented as a directed graph where the nodes correspond to words and the edges correspond to dependencies. Unlike in most dependency schemes, SD graphs are not necessarily trees and may even contain directed cycles. Each dependency is labelled with a dependency type that represents the syntactic function of the dependent word. In the latest version of the SD scheme (de Marneffe and Manning, 2008), there are in total 55 dependency types.

We have chosen the SD scheme due to its numerous successful applications in different contexts. Further, de Marneffe and Manning find the scheme applicable in parser comparison. This particular aspect of the scheme is of importance with respect to this work, as one part of this study is a comparison of two parsers. Alternative schemes, such as Grammatical Relations (Carroll et al., 1998) and the Connexor Machinese Syntax scheme, were also considered. The former has been suggested by its authors to be suitable for multiple languages, and the latter is a scheme designed for standard Finnish.

3.2 Applying the SD scheme to ICU Finnish

The SD scheme was designed for standard English. In this section, we describe the modifications made in order to adapt it to ICU Finnish. These modifications include both those that are required by Finnish in general, and those implied by the nature of the ICU sublanguage. For an illustration of the modified SD scheme, see Figure 2. As a detailed description of the SD scheme is beyond the scope of this paper, we only discuss our modifications to it and refer to the description by de Marneffe and Manning (2008).

---

[1]http://www.connexor.eu

[2]http://www.lingsoft.fi

[3]Due to the confidential nature of the patient data, these, as well as all examples used in this paper, are not actual sentences from the data, but rather illustrative examples.

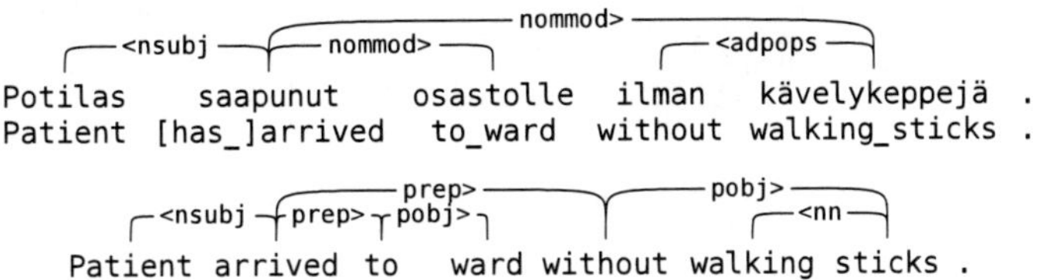

Figure 2: The modified SD scheme. Note the following features: nominal modifiers (*nommod* dependencies), dependencies between sentences (*sdep*), null verbs that represent omitted main verbs, explicit marking of copula subjects (*nsubj-cop*), and the use of direct object (*dobj*) in passive sentences. The sentence can be roughly translated as *Liquid from the drain, condition otherwise OK, evening drug given.*

Figure 3: Top: usage of the new dependency types *nommod* and *adpos*. Bottom: the corresponding English sentence and annotation in the SD scheme. Note that the type *nommod* is used both for nominal inflection and prepositional phrases.

3.2.1 Prepositional phrases

In the Finnish language, prepositions are relatively rare. Most English clauses with prepositional phrases have Finnish equivalents that use nominal inflection. For an example of a typical case, see Figure 2.

Seeing that inflectional and prepositional structures are semantically similar, it would be desirable to represent them in a similar manner also in the dependency structure. Therefore, we introduce a new dependency type, *nommod* (*nominal modifier*), to represent inflectional structures. This same type can also be used in sentences with actual pre- and postpositions. Only one additional type is needed for prepositional structures, a type named *adpos* (*adposition*). For an illustration of the usage of these two types, see Figure 3. The structure given to prepositional phrases is similar to that used in the scheme of the Pro3Gres parser (Schneider et al., 2004).

3.2.2 Passive subjects

Certain Finnish clause types, contrary to their English counterparts, do not require a subject. One that has a particular effect on our work is the passive voice. The surface subject in English passive clauses corresponds to both surface and deep object in Finnish. Therefore, we have not used the dependency type *nsubjpass* at all, and have used *dobj* instead.

3.2.3 Dependencies between sentences

A third modification to the SD scheme is required by the nature of the ICU language: sentence boundaries are often not clearly marked, or they lack punctuation altogether (see Figure 4). We split the text into separate sentences only when there is explicit punctuation that marks the sentence boundary. Recovering sentence boundaries that have no explicit surface marking is left to the parser, as recognizing them would be difficult for standard sentence splitters that lack syntax information. We have thus introduced a new dependency type, *sdep*, to connect these isolated sentences that are not explicitly coordinated or subordinated. To produce an analysis that is æsthetic from a scheme design point of view, if several *sdep* dependencies are needed in the same surface sentence, they are chained. This is to avoid unnecessarily long dependencies that are difficult for parsers to recover.

3.2.4 Omissions

In ICU Finnish, a frequent syntactic feature that has a notable effect on parsing the language is the omission of different sentence elements. One example of this is the omission of copulas and auxiliaries, which have little effect on sentence semantics. Consider, for example, *The patient is awake* vs. *The patient awake*.

In some cases, it is even possible to omit the main verb of a sentence. For instance, the structure

```
               ---------- sdep> ----------  ---------- sdep> ----------
  ┌ <nsubj-cop ┤        ┌ <nsubj-cop ┤           ┌ <nsubj ┤ ------- sdep> ------ ┌ nommod> ─── ┌ adpos> ┐
Potilas   hereillä  pulssi    70-80 ,   veli     soittanut   ,   jutellut   lääkärin  kanssa .
Patient   awake     pulse     70-80 , brother [has_]called , [has_]talked   doctor    with   .
```

Figure 4: The purpose of the *sdep* dependencies is to combine the independent sentences under one surface sentence into a single analysis. Without the dashed *sdep* dependencies, the analysis would contain separate islands. This sentence can be roughly translated as *Patient awake pulse 70-80, brother called, talked with the doctor.*

```
        ┌── <nommod ──┬─ nsubj> ─┐
    Putkesta      *null*  nestettä .
From_the_drain    *null*  liquid   .
```

Figure 5: Missing main verbs are represented by a null verb, in order to construct a dependency analysis for sentences such as this. The sentence can be roughly translated as *Liquid from the drain.*

```
      ┌── <nsubj-cop ──┐
      │  ┌--- <cop --┤
  Pulssi  [on]  normaali .
  Pulse   [is]  normal   .
```

Figure 6: The new dependency type *nsubj-cop*, used instead of *nsubj* in copula clauses. Note that the analysis stays essentially the same, regardless of the presence or absence of the copula.

Putkesta nestettä (*Liquid from the drain*) is common in ICU Finnish, though it would be judged fragmentary in standard Finnish. Here, the case of the noun *putkesta* (*from the drain*) expresses the direction of the liquid, and the actual verb (*to come*) can therefore be omitted, as its meaning is clear in the context. This poses a problem for most dependency schemes, as the main verb of a clause is also its head word. To be able to analyze the sentences with a missing main verb (21% of the sentences in the corpus), we have manually introduced a *null verb* in those sentences to represent the missing verb. See Figure 5 for an illustration of this solution.

Because the purpose of the null verb is to represent a word that is absolutely necessary for the construction of an SD analysis, null verbs are introduced only when the main verb is omitted. Copulas and auxiliaries never act as governors in the SD scheme and thus do not require a null verb to be inserted.

Finally, the frequent omissions of copulas require another minor modification to the SD scheme, the introduction of the dependency type *nsubj-cop*. The *nsubj* type used in the original SD scheme for both standard and copula subjects is in our version of the scheme replaced by *nsubj-cop* in copula clauses. This is to differentiate the special case of copula subjects, where, in the SD scheme, the governor of the dependency is not a verb but, for example, an adjective. For an illustration of the use of *nsubj-cop*, see Figure 6.

4 Performance measures

When evaluating the quality of our corpus, as well as the performance of the parsers in the experiments described below, we use the following measures.

Precision (P) is defined as the proportion of dependencies in the parser output that are also present in the gold standard. *Recall (R)*, in turn, is the proportion of dependencies in the gold standard that are also present in the parser output. These two are combined into an *F-score*, defined as $F = \frac{2PR}{P+R}$.

Labelled attachment score (A_L) is the proportion of tokens that are assigned the correct head and dependency label according to the gold standard, and *unlabelled attachment score (A_U)* is the proportion of tokens that are assigned the correct head, regardless of the dependency label (Nivre, 2008a). Note that A_L and A_U are defined for tree structures where each token has exactly one head. As noted previously, analyses in the SD scheme are not necessarily trees, and thus the two measures are not directly applicable to it.

5 Corpus annotation and statistics

As one of the primary contributions of this work, we have annotated a corpus of 1019 ICU Finnish sentences with 7614 tokens of which 6082 are non-punctuation. The text of the corpus consists of notes written by nurses about the condition of a patient, often with respect to standard topics such as breathing, hemodynamics, diuresis and relatives.

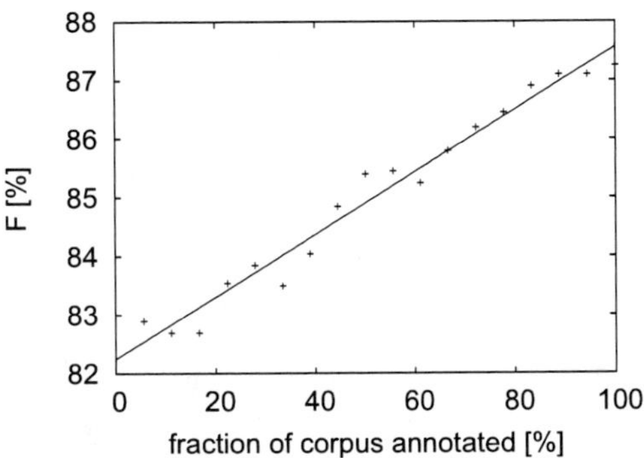

Figure 7: Inter-annotator agreement in F-score at various stages of the corpus annotation with a trend line. Note that the A_L and A_U measures are not reported, as the SD analyses are not necessarily trees.

The corpus currently consists of sentences from four different patient reports, as we decided to annotate full reports rather than randomly selected individual sentences, to enable further research, for example in report summarization.

The dependency annotation has in total 5194 dependencies. Only 2.9% of all sentences and 0.5% of all tokens are non-projective. The effect of non-projectivity on parsing ICU Finnish is thus negligible.

We used full double annotation, that is, each sentence was independently annotated by two annotators, and disagreements were jointly resolved. To evaluate the quality of the corpus, we measured inter-annotator agreement, defined as the average of the agreements of the two annotators against the final annotation. The average inter-annotator agreement on the whole corpus was 87.25% F-score. Figure 7 illustrates the growth of the inter-annotator agreement as the annotators become familiar with the task and the scheme.

We estimate that the current corpus has taken 70 man-hours of annotation work to develop, including both the independent annotation work by individual annotators and the joint resolving of disagreements. The disagreement resolving took in total approximately 30 man-hours. We used a custom software for annotation and disagreement resolution.

6   Experiments on the corpus

In this section, we discuss the experiments that the newly built corpus has enabled us to perform. We first describe our experiments on the rule-based approach, including the conversion rules required for the evaluation of the parser. We then present results of another experiment, which uses a statistical approach.

In order to be able to use the A_L and A_U performance measures described in Section 4, as well as to maintain comparability of results with Malt-Parser which produces tree analyses, the treeness of all analyses in all experiments was assured by breaking the possible cycles present in the gold standard. Punctuation tokens were excluded from all performance measurements and the null verbs representing omitted verbs were preserved in the parser input.

6.1   Parsing experiments with a rule-based parser

As the first part of our experiments, we apply the rule-based parser of Laippala et al. (2009) whose reported coverage is up to 75% of ICU Finnish sentences with an oracle best parse performance of above 90% in terms of the PARSEVAL metric (Black et al., 1991).

6.1.1   The dependency conversion

The parser natively produces constituency output. Thus, in order to evaluate the parser on the ICU Finnish corpus as well as to improve its applicability in the domain, we produce a conversion from this constituency scheme to the SD scheme. Note that, as illustrated in Figure 8, using a constituency scheme for ICU Finnish often results in complex representations which do not contain information about syntactic roles of the constituents. Inferring these roles is one of the aims of our conversion.

The conversion is implemented using hand-written rules. The parser assigns a head word for each phrase, and these heads are then used to produce the structure of the dependency graph by placing dependencies from the head word of each constituent to the head words of its sub-constituents. The conversion rules are generally only needed to assign types to these dependencies. There are few exceptions, such as the *sdep* dependencies (see Section 3.2.3) and certain auxiliary structures, where the structure in the SD scheme does not correspond to that induced from the head words. The rules can restrict on the structure of a subtree, that is, a rule can require a phrase as well as its sub-phrases, at any depth, to be of specific types. Our conversion approach closely fol-

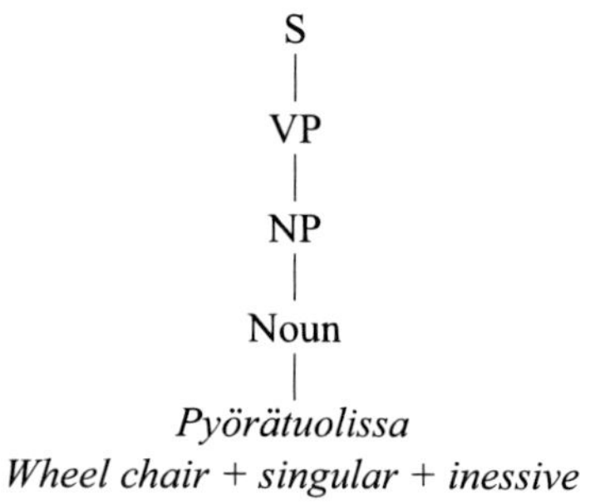

Figure 8: The constituency output of the parser of Laippala et al. (2009). The example sentence can be roughly translated as *In wheel chair*. The direct derivation of the VP from the NP is explained by the missing main verb that would in a corresponding SD analysis be represented by a null verb. Note the size of the tree, despite the fact that the sentence only consists of one word.

lows that of the Stanford tools (de Marneffe et al., 2006), as both utilize heads of phrases and subtree search to produce the structure and labels of the dependency parse.

The conversion rules were developed using the 80-sentence development set previously used by Laippala et al. (2009). We have annotated these sentences in the SD scheme to complement their existing constituency annotation.

6.1.2 Performance of the parser and conversion rules

When interpreting the results it is crucial to note that the rule-based parser does not have a ranking component that would select a single preferred analysis among the generated parses. The parser generates, on average, 33 parses per sentence and the figures reported are measured using the best parse with respect to the labelled attachment score (*oracle performance*). Further, the coverage of the parser in terms of the proportion of sentences that receive at least one analysis is 75% on our corpus and the performance values reported are calculated on these sentences, disregarding sentences that receive no analysis. The results are thus rather an upper limit of the performance to be expected in a real-world setting.

We find that the rule-based parser augmented with our conversion achieves an A_L of 75.2%, A_U of 84.5%, and F-score of 70.2%. Given the A_U of 84.5%, the parser itself assigns incorrect heads for 15.5% of tokens. This is the starting point for the

conversion rules, which result in the overall A_L of 75.2%. The difference of 9.3 percentage points between A_U and A_L is divided between errors of the conversion rules and errors of the parser who may assign correct heads but incorrect nonterminal labels, thus preventing correct interpretation of the parse. To establish this division of errors, we have performed a limited manual analysis of 16 randomly selected sentences (75 dependencies) and found that the conversion rules are responsible for 5.3 percentage points and the parser and FinTWOL for the remaining 4 percentage points.

6.2 Statistical parsing experiments with MaltParser

To complement the rule-based dependency parsing experiments, we also apply a statistical parser induced from the ICU Finnish corpus using the MaltParser system[4] (Nivre et al., 2007). We use the arc-eager parsing algorithm characterized as a deterministic, linear-time algorithm that generates a single projective dependency tree in a left-to-right pass through the sentence. The choice of a projective parsing algorithm is justified by the negligible amount of non-projective tokens in the corpus. The algorithm is based on the well-known shift-reduce bottom-up parsing strategy that processes the sentence from a token queue and maintains a stack of partially-processed tokens. At each point in the parsing process, the next transition applied by the parser is decided by a support vector machine (SVM) classifier based on features extracted from the sentence tokens as well as the partially-built dependency tree.

In training the parser, we use the MaltParser default feature model for the arc-eager parsing algorithm. Broadly stated, this model considers morpholexical properties of the first four tokens in the queue and the first two tokens on the stack as well as partially-built dependency structure features of the top items on the stack and the queue. The corpus text is first morphologically disambiguated using FinCG, thus obtaining a single morpholexical reading for each token. A separate feature is then generated for each morpholexical property produced by FinCG[5] for a given token (e.g. the POS, number, and case). Whenever the token wordform does not carry a particular property (e.g. nouns do not have a tense and verbs do not have a case), the

---

[4]Version 1.2, http://www.maltparser.org

[5]See http://www2.lingsoft.fi/doc/fintwol/intro/tags.html for the full set of tags given by FinTWOL/FinCG

feature is set to *null*. Rather than wordforms, we use word lemmas in the feature model to reduce training data sparseness.

All results reported in this section are obtained using ten-fold cross-validation, where in each fold 80% of the data is used for training, 10% for parameter estimation, and 10% for testing. In preliminary experiments on a small portion of the data, we selected the second degree polynomial kernel for the parser SVM classifier. The values of the SVM regularization parameter C and the kernel parameter γ were selected for each fold separately, using a joint grid search on the parameter estimation set. The best-performing parameter combination in terms of A_L on the parameter estimation set was then used in parsing the test set, thus avoiding parameter over-fitting. All other parameters were left at their default values.

The results are shown in Table 1 for varying sizes of the training sets, in order to estimate the learning curve of the parser. The overall parser performance, 69.9% A_L, can be contrasted with the results of Nivre (2008a) who reports an average A_L of 79.77% across 13 languages. The results for individual languages, however, range from 64.7% for Turkish to 90.1% for Japanese. In that respect, the results for ICU Finnish are among the lower ones, but arguably well within the typical range to be expected. This is particularly encouraging given that the ICU Finnish corpus is currently relatively small, consisting of 1019 sentences and 6082 non-punctuation tokens. As a point of comparison, Nivre has used corpora of 5000 sentences with 58000 tokens, and 17000 sentences with 151000 tokens for Turkish and Japanese, respectively.

The statistical parser yields a lower absolute performance than the rule-based parser. However, the two results are not directly comparable. First, the oracle best-parse strategy had to be used for the rule-based parser. Second, the results of the rule-based parser include only those sentences for which the parser has given at least one analysis (75% of all sentences). Taking these measurement limitations into account, it would seem likely that with a larger corpus available for training and other further improvements, a statistical parsing approach based on MaltParser will be preferable over the rule-based parser of Laippala et al. It is worth noting that the parsing speed of the statistical parser is on the order of 10 sentences per

sample [%]	A_L[%]	A_U [%]	F [%]
100	69.9±2.0	77.1±2.5	66.6±2.2
75	68.4±2.8	75.8±2.2	65.0±3.2
50	65.8±2.0	73.6±1.5	62.0±2.3
25	57.2±2.7	67.5±1.7	52.6±3.2

Table 1: MaltParser results with varying training set size. The *sample* column gives the size to which the training sets in the ten-fold cross-validation were downsampled. Performance figures are given together with their standard deviation on the ten folds.

second, whereas the rule-based parser parses one sentence in approximately 2 to 3 seconds.

7 Conclusions and discussion

In this paper, we have presented a new syntactically annotated corpus of ICU Finnish, the language used in daily nursing notes in an intensive care unit. The corpus is annotated in the Stanford dependency scheme which we find suitable for ICU Finnish with only minor modifications. We have performed parsing experiments on this corpus using two approaches: by converting the constituency output of an existing rule-based parser (Laippala et al., 2009) to a dependency scheme, and by inducing a statistical parser from the new corpus using MaltParser (Nivre et al., 2007).

The rule-based parser, together with the constituency-to-dependency conversion developed for the purposes of this work, achieved the oracle labelled attachment score of 75.2%. In a separate evaluation of the conversion rules, we find that the rules contribute roughly 5 percentage points to the overall error rate.

The statistical parser trained on the rather modestly sized corpus achieved a labelled attachment score of 69.9%, approaching the results presented by Nivre (2008a) for parsers trained on significantly larger corpora. The comparability of results of the rule-based and the statistical parsers is difficult to establish given that the rule-based parser does not provide a single preferred analysis.

Our results on the statistical parsing of ICU Finnish, particularly encouraging when taking into consideration the modest size of the corpus, might suggest that full parsing of the intensive care language is, perhaps somewhat counterintuitively, not a very difficult task, relative to the general language. For a more definitive conclusion, a considerably broader study, beyond the scope of this paper, would need to be performed. In particular, possible features allowing the parser to better capture the idiosyncrasies of the ICU sublanguage need to be explored more thoroughly.

The first obvious future work direction is to further increase the size of the corpus and find a legal way to release the corpus annotation while protecting patient privacy. One option could, for example, be to release an unlexicalized version of the corpus with morphological and syntactic annotation only. The second direction is to complement the preliminary experiments with MaltParser presented in this paper by carefully exploring the possible feature models, parsing algorithms and parser training parameters in order to maximize the performance of the induced parser. The final direction is to develop a method for inserting the null verbs necessary in the dependency analysis, either as a separate pre-processing step, or directly as part of parsing.

Acknowledgments

We would like to thank Lingsoft Ltd. for making FinTWOL and FinCG available to us. This work has been supported by the Academy of Finland and Tekes, the Finnish Funding Agency for Technology and Innovation.

References

E. Black et al. 1991. A procedure for quantitatively comparing the syntactic coverage of English grammars. In *Proceedings of the Fourth DARPA Speech and Natural Language Workshop*, pages 306–312.

J. E. Carroll, E. Briscoe, and A. Sanfilippo. 1998. Parser evaluation: a survey and a new proposal. In *Proceedings of LREC'98*, pages 447–454.

A. B. Clegg and A. Shepherd. 2007. Benchmarking natural-language parsers for biological applications using dependency graphs. *BMC Bioinformatics*, 8(1):24.

C. Friedman and S. Johnson. 2006. Natural language and text processing in biomedicine. In *Biomedical Informatics*, pages 312–343. Springer.

Y. Huang and H. J. Lowe. 2007. A novel hybrid approach to automated negation detection in clinical radiology reports. *Journal of the American Medical Informatics Association*, 14(3):304–311.

Y. Huang, H. J. Lowe, D. Klein, and R. J. Cucina. 2005. Improved identification of noun phrases in clinical radiology reports using a high-performance statistical natural language parser augmented with the UMLS Specialist Lexicon. *Journal of the American Medical Informatics Association*, 12(3):275–285.

F. Karlsson. 1990. Constraint Grammar as a framework for parsing unrestricted text. In *Proceedings of COLING'90*, pages 168–173.

K. Koskenniemi. 1983. Two-level model for morphological analysis. In *Proceedings of the 8th International Joint Conference on Artificial Intelligence*, pages 683–685.

V. Laippala, F. Ginter, S. Pyysalo, and T. Salakoski. 2009. Towards automatic processing of clinical finnish: A sublanguage analysis and a rule-based parser. *International Journal of Medical Informatics, Special Issue on Mining of Clinical and Biomedical Text and Data*. In press.

D. Lin. 1998. A dependency-based method for evaluating broad-coverage parsers. *Natural Language Engineering*, 4(2):97–114.

M-C. de Marneffe and C. Manning. 2008. Stanford typed hierarchies representation. In *Proceedings of COLING'08, Workshop on Cross-Framework and Cross-Domain Parser Evaluation*, pages 1–8.

M-C. de Marneffe, B. MacCartney, and C. Manning. 2006. Generating typed dependency parses from phrase structure parses. In *Proceedings of LREC'06*, pages 449–454.

J. Nivre, J. Hall, J. Nilsson, A. Chanev, G. Eryiğit, S. Kübler, S. Marinov, and E. Marsi. 2007. MaltParser: A language-independent system for data-driven dependency parsing. *Natural Language Engineering*, 13(2):95–135.

J. Nivre. 2008a. Deterministic incremental dependency parsing. *Computational Linguistics*, 34(4):513–553.

J. Nivre. 2008b. Sorting out dependency parsing. In *Proceedings of GoTAL'08*, pages 16–27.

S. Pyysalo, S. Aubin, A. Nazarenko, and T. Salakoski. 2006. Lexical adaptation of Link Grammar to the biomedical sublanguage: a comparative evaluation of three approaches. In *Proceedings of SMBM'06*, pages 60–67.

G. Schneider, F. Rinaldi, and J. Dowdall. 2004. Fast, deep-linguistic statistical dependency parsing. In *Proceedings of COLING'04 Workshop on Recent Advances in Dependency Grammar*, pages 33–40.

P. Szolovits. 2003. Adding a medical lexicon to an English parser. In *Proceedings of AMIA'03*, pages 639–643.

ISSN 1736-6305 Vol. 4
http://hdl.handle.net/10062/9206

The Nordic Dialect Corpus – an advanced research tool

Janne Bondi Johannessen
University of Oslo
Oslo, Norway
jannebj@iln.uio.no

Joel Priestley
University of Oslo
Oslo, Norway
joeljp@gmail.com

Kristin Hagen
University of Oslo
Oslo, Norway
kristiha@iln.uio.no

Tor Anders Åfarli
Norwegian Univ. of Science & Tech.
Trondheim, Norway
tor.aafarli@hf.ntnu.no

Øystein Alexander Vangsnes
University of Tromsø
Tromsø, Norway
oystein.vangsnes@hum.uit.no

Abstract

The paper describes the first part of the Nordic Dialect Corpus. This is a tool that combines a number of useful features that together makes it a unique and very advanced resource for researchers of many fields of language search. The corpus is web-based and features full audio-visual representation linked to transcripts.

1 Credits

The Nordic Dialect Corpus is the result of close collaboration between the partners in the research networks Scandinavian Dialect Syntax and Nordic Centre of Excellence in Microcomparative Syntax. The researchers in the network have contributed in everything from decisions to actual work ranging from methodology to recordings, transcription, and annotation. Some of the corpus (in particular, recordings of informants) has been financed by the national research councils in the individual countries, while the technical development has been financed by the University of Oslo and the Norwegian Research Council, plus the Nordic research funds NOS-HS and NordForsk.

2 Introduction

In this paper, we describe the first, completed part of the Nordic Dialect Corpus. The corpus has a variety of features that combined makes it a very advanced tool for language researchers. These features include: Linguistic contents (dialects from five closely related languages), annotation (tagging and two types of transcription), search interface (advanced possibilities for combining a large array of search criteria and results presentation in an intuitive and simple interface), many search variables (linguistics-based, informant-based, time-based), multimedia display (linking of sound and video to transcriptions), display of informant details (number of words and other information on informants), advanced results handling (concordances, collocations, counts and statistics shown in a variety of graphical modes, plus further processing). Finally, and importantly, the corpus is freely available for research on the web.

We give examples of both various kinds of searches, of displays of results and of results handling.

3 Why the Nordic Dialect Corpus was developed

The Nordic Dialect Corpus was developed after a need for research material was voiced by members of NORMS (Nordic Centre of Excellence in Micro-comparative Syntax) and the ScanDiaSyn networks.

The overarching goal for these researchers is to study the dialects of the North-Germanic languages, i.e., the Nordic languages spoken in the Nordic countries, as dialects of the same language. The languages are closely related to each other, and three of them are mutually intelligible (Norwegian, Swedish and Danish), as are two others (Faroese and Icelandic). All of them have some mutual intelligibility with each other if we consider written forms.

Studying the dialects only within the confines of each national language was therefore considered to be misguided from a theoretical and principled point of view. Second, doing research across dialects over such a big area, covering six countries (Denmark, Faroe Islands, Finland, Iceland, Norway, and Sweden), would be almost impossible if each researcher should get hold of relevant data on their own.

Third, the research in NORMS and ScanDiaSyn focusses on syntax – in which case data of many different kinds were necessary. Questionnaires for specific phenomena were needed (but will not be discussed in this paper), and recordings of spontaneous speech as it is used in ordinary conversations were very important. The latter need is satisfied by the Nordic Dialect Corpus.

4   Description of the Corpus

4.1   Linguistic contents and numbers

The corpus contains dialect data from the national languages Danish, Faroese, Icelandic, Norwegian, and Swedish. It is steadily growing, since there are still new recordings that are being done, or planned, while other recordings are in various stages of finishing. At the moment, it contains speech data from approximately 170 informants with 466 000 words, unevenly spread between the five countries. Eventually, this will rise to around 600 informants and the number of words will likely be more than doubled. The numbers for the corpus as of today are given below.

Country	No of informants	No of words
Denmark	7	19 088
Faroe Islands	3	16 794
Finland	0	0
Iceland	4	10 287
Norway	45	132 417
Sweden	125	287 639
Sum	**184**	**466 225**

Table 1: Corpus contents by 9. January 2009.

Due to differences in the financing of the data collection in the different countries, the data are less uniform than one might have wanted ideally. (Some recordings and transcriptions were done for this corpus, while others were already done, such as most of the Swedish ones, which were generously given us by the earlier project Swedia 2000.)

Some recordings, such as those from Norway, the Swedish dialect of Oevdalian and the Danish dialect of Western Jutlandic, have two kinds of recordings per informant: one semi-formal interview (informant and project assistant), and one informal conversation between two informants. Some dialects have recordings of both young and old informants, while others are only represented by old ones. Some dialects are represented by both old and new recordings, where old ones are generally around fifty years old. Some dialects have been recorded by audio only, while others have been recorded by both audio and video. All the dialects have recordings of informants belonging to both genders. Most importantly, however, all the recordings represent spontaneous speech.

4.2   Annotation: transcription and tagging

All the dialect data have been transcribed by at least one transcription standard, and this work has been done for the most par in the individual countries: Each dialect has been transcribed by the standard official orthography of that country. (For Norwegian, which has two standard orthographies, Bokmål was chosen since there exist important computational tools for this variant.) In addition, all the Norwegian dialects and some Swedish ones have also been transcribed phonetically.[1] For the Norwegian dialects and the

---

[1] The Norwegian phonetic transcription follows that of Papazian and Helleland (2005). The transcription of the Oevdalian dialect follows the Oevdalian orthography (stan-

Oevdalian Swedish ones that have two transcriptions, the first transcription to be done was in each case the phonetic one, and then the phonetic transcription was translated to an orthographic transcription via a semi-automatic dialect transliterator developed for the project. The fact that there are two transcriptions for dialects that are very different from the standard national orthography makes it possible to search with both transcriptions in the corpus, and present search results in both, as illustrated below for the Swedish dialect of Oevdalian:

```
eð  bellum   wi:ð fel djærå um kumum å:

det  kan   vi ju göra om kommer på ı

it can.1PL we well do if
come.1PL on

'We can possibly do it if we
remember it.'
```

Figure 1. Two transcriptions for Oevdalian.

The Text Laboratory at the University of Oslo has the responsibility for the further technical devopment, including tagging. The whole corpus will be grammatically tagged with POS and selected morpho-syntactic features language by language. So far, the Norwegian data have been tagged, while the Swedish data will be tagged soon. Tagging speech data is different from tagging written data. Speech contains disfluencies, interruptions and repetitions, and there are rarely clear clause boundaries (Allwood, Nivre and Ahlsén 1989, Johannessen and Jørgensen 2006). This is usually reflected in the transcription of speech, which generally does not contain clause boundary or sentential markers such as full stops and exclamation marks (Jørgensen 2008, Rosén 2008). Any tagger developed for written language will therefore be difficult to use directly for spoken language. (Though Nivre and Grönqvist 2001 did this, on a material different from ours). The Norwegian speech tagger was developed for the NoTa Corpus (Norwegian speech corpus – Oslo part). Søfteland and Nøklestad (2008) describe how the corpus was first tagged with the Oslo-Bergen tagger for written Norwegian (Hagen et al. 2000), and then trained with a TreeTagger (Schmid 1994) on the resulting,

manually repeatedly corrected file. The TreeTagger gained an accuracy of 96.9 %. This tagger has then been used unchanged for the dialect corpus, under the assumption that the speech as represented in the dialects and in Oslo are sufficiently similar once they are all transcribed by the same transcription standard. The Swedish tagger is being trained in the same way. A written language TnT tagger developed by Sofie Johansson Kokkinakis (2003) has been applied to the Swedish dialect transcriptions (their standard orthographic version). The new data will be used as training data for a new Swedish speech Tree-Tagger.

4.3 Search Interface

The corpus uses an advanced search interface and results handling system Glossa (Nygaard 2007, Johannessen et al. 2008). The system allows for a large variety of search combinations making it possible to do very advanced and complex searches, even though the interface is very simple, with pull-down menus, and boxes that expand only when prompted by the user. The corpus search system Corpus Work Bench (Christ 1994, Evert 2005) is used, so that the simple corpus queries are translated to regular expressions before querying – something that is invisible to the user.

Several of the features in the search interface and the results display follow suggestions by participants in ScanDiaSyn and NORMS.

Searching for lemmas and part of words: For those parts of the corpus that are tagged and lemmatised, it is possible to search for the lemma only. This way we get all inflected forms of one lexeme. This feature is very useful when there is suppletion in the stem of the word. For example, search for the Norwegian lemma *gås* ('goose') will give the results *gås, gåsa, gjess, gjessene* (various combinations of number and definiteness).

The same box where the user can write a full search word or a lemma can also be used to write part of a search word. This way the user can, for example, search for a particular suffix. Below, the user has searched for the suffix *–ig*, which can be found in Norwegian, Swedish, and Danish.

---

dardised in 2005 by the *Råðdjärum* (The Oevdalian Language Council).

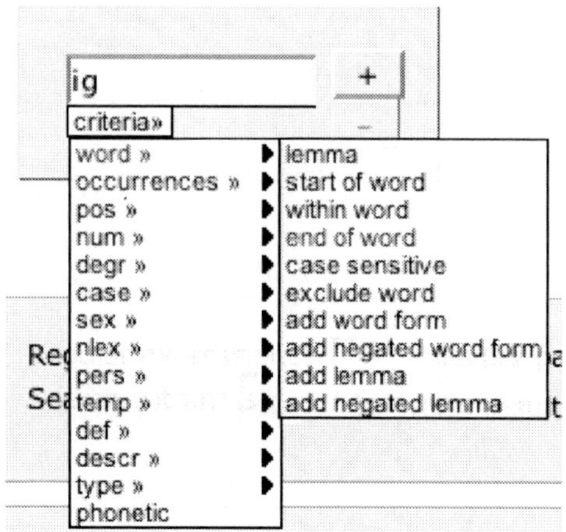

Figure 2: Search for suffix -*ig*

Notice that since nothing else was specified, this search would querying the whole corpus, i.e. amongst all the languages. Below we can see some of the many hits for the frequent adjectival suffixes –*ig* and -*lig* in the mainland Nordic languages, and a couple of occurrences of words containing the same sequence of letters in the insular Nordic languages (not representing these suffixes, however).

Freq.	Word found	Transla-tion	Lan-guage
7	særlig	espe-cially	No, Da
7	farlig	danger-ous	No, Sw, Da
7	þannig	thus	Ice
7	kjedelig	boring	No
6	väldig	very	Sw
5	rigtig	right	Da
5	otrolig	unbeliev-able	Sw
4	konstig	strange	Sw
1	sjómanna slig	sailor-like	Fa

Table 2: Some results from the –*ig* search

Searching for more than one word: In order to specify a search for more than one word, the user clicks on the plus sign in the first box, which gives one more box, with the possibility of specifying a number words in between:

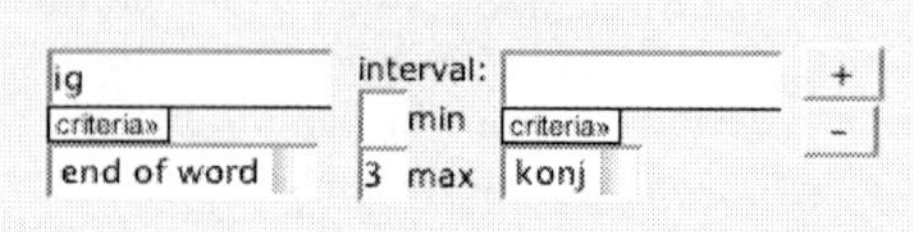

Figure 3. Searching for two words.

The illustration shows a search for a word ening in –*ig* separated by at most three words from a conjunction to the right.

Searching for part of speech: The tagged part of the corpus can also be queried directly by part-of-speech tags. This is exemplified in the figure above, where the second word is specified to be a conjunction. The user can choose whether a search word is specified by a word form (or part of one) and a part of speech or both. The pull-down menus in figure 2 exemplifies many of the search options that are available for a word.

Phonetic querying: The user can choose to query the corpus by specifying a phonetically specified string. This works only for the dialects that have two transcriptions (cf. section 4.2). An example of a situation in which this is useful will be where we want to query person-number inflection on verbs. Here, tagging will not help, since each tagger is trained on the standard orthographic version of the texts, and person-number inflection is only a dialect feature. Searching for this feature in Oevdalian, we can simply write for example the 1pl suffix as it is:

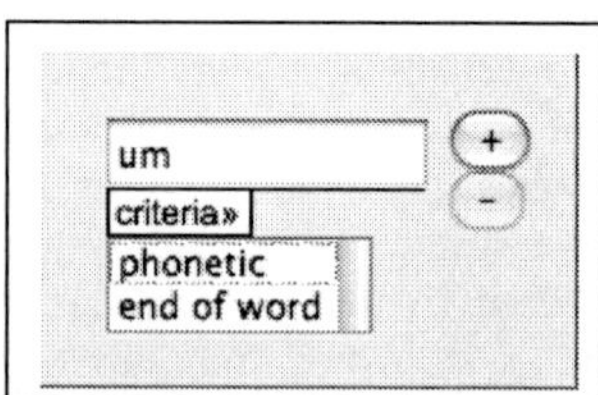

Figure 4. Searching in phonetic mode.

This will give results that would have been impossible to get from the orthographic text only. We refer to Figure 1 for an illustration, where the dialectal *bellum* ('can' 1PL) is represented by the standard *kan* ('can').

Informant-based querying: There are a number of ways to query the corpus in addition to the linguistics-based ones that we have seen above. All the details that are known about each informant are also searchable in the search interface. Thus, it is possible to specify as search criteria: age, sex, recording year, place of residence, country, region and area. Below, we show how we can choose individual places from the complete list, to be able to query only the informants from these places, which happen to be the area of Älvdalen in Sweden.

Figure 5. Delimiting the corpus by choosing some places from the full list.

4.4 Displaying of search results

Each search in the corpus gives a standardised view of the results in the form of a classical KWIC concordance. The results can be viewed in a number of additional ways which we will present below.

Multimedia display: The corpus includes trancribed speech from five countries and spans four decades. Some of the speech was naturally recorded using a tape recorder and later mp3 recorder, and some was recorded by videocamera. The result is accompanied by a clickable symbol to show the audio and video of that particular speech sequence. This is illustrated below.

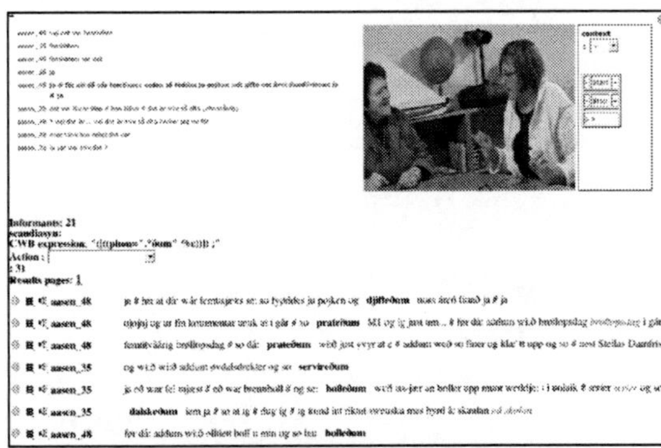

Figure 6. The multimedia results window.

Display of transcriptions and tagging: For those linguistic variants that have two transcriptions, either transcription can be chosen for displaying the result. The grammatical tags and the phonetic transcription of each standard orthographic word are visible in a window when navigating the mouse over the text:

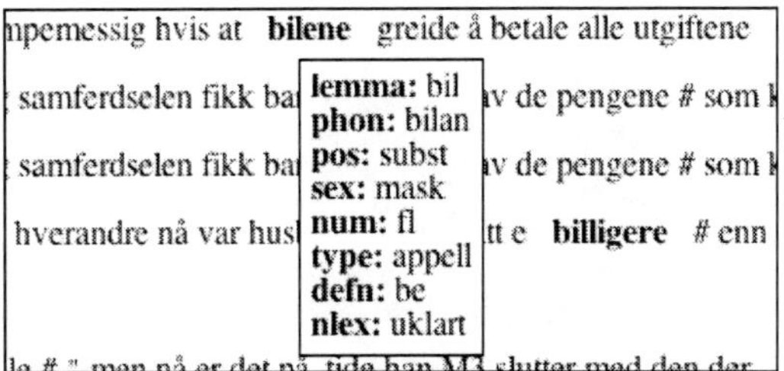

Figure 7. A window shows all information for each word that is moused over.

Action menu: On the results page there is an Action menu with a selection of choices for further displaying of results and results handling (the latter of which will be presented in section 4.6). The functionalities that follow in this subsection are choices in this menu.

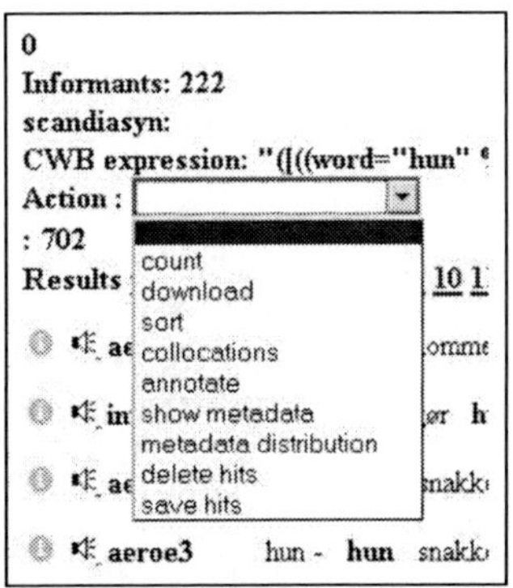

Figure 8. Action menu in results window.

Count: Choosing the Count option gives the search results as a list of all the hits sorted by frequency. Below, a bit of a list is shown as a result of the search for nouns starting with *bil-* in Norwegian.

occurences	match
40	bil
20	bilen
14	biler
11	bilde
7	bilene
4	bildet
1	bilkjøringa
1	bilbasert
1	bilder
1	bilveg
1	bildeler

Figure 9. Some nouns beginning with *bil-* ('car').

The count results can be shown in a number of ways, such as histograms and pie charts. The same result as above is shown below as a pie chart:

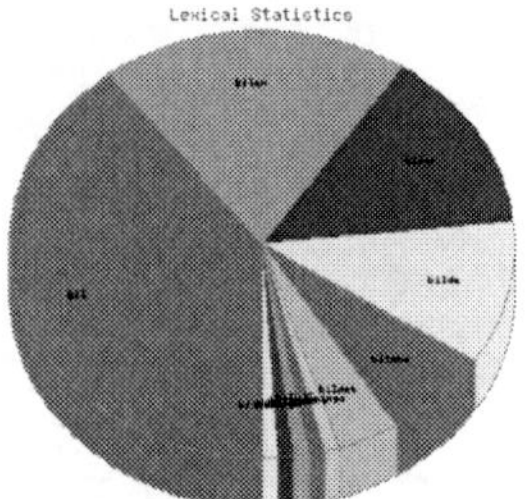

Figure 10. The same information as in figure 9.

Sort: The results are by default sorted according to the geographical residence of the informants. However, they can be displayed in many other ways as well. The most useful ones are perhaps those that sort the matches by the next word to the right or left.

Collocations: The results can be shown as collocations according to many different statistical measurements such as dice coeffiency, log-likelihood ration etc., with a choice between neighbouring bigrams and trigrams. The example below illustrates the collocations for the word *bil* 'car', used in the three mainland Nordic countries. The value of this choice is clearly illustrated in the example; the frequencies of the collocations are the same independently of language.

Left context				Right context			
ngram	rank	AM	occ	ngram	rank	AM	occ
en **	1	0.3304	19	** og	2	0.1628	7
ha **	5	0.0800	4	** och	3	0.1412	6
har **	5	0.0800	4	** #	3	0.1412	6
åker **	5	0.0800	4	** då	4	0.0964	4
åka **	5	0.0800	4	** ?	6	0.0732	3
med **	7	0.0606	3	** eller	6	0.0732	3
köra **	7	0.0606	3	** som	6	0.0732	3
æ **	7	0.0606	3	** på	6	0.0732	3
kjøre **	7	0.0606	3	** för	8	0.0494	2
ikke **	7	0.0606	3	** ##	8	0.0494	2
egen **	7	0.0606	3	** här	8	0.0494	2
ingen **	9	0.0408	2	** (uforståelig)	8	0.0494	2
vi **	9	0.0408	2	** nå	10	0.0250	1
kjørte **	9	0.0408	2	** stående	10	0.0250	1
ja **	9	0.0408	2	** dit	10	0.0250	1
någon **	9	0.0408	2	** ner	10	0.0250	1
kjører **	9	0.0408	2	** hver	10	0.0250	1
kör **	9	0.0408	2	** kommer	10	0.0250	1
* **	11	0.0206	1	** hemma.	10	0.0250	1

Figure 11. Some collocations for *bil* 'car'.

4.5 Displaying information on informants

There are two ways of finding information on the informants.

Via results page: Each concordance line has an "i" symbol on its very left. Clicking on this symbol reveals the following information on the informant in question: informant code, sex, age

group, country, place, number of words, recording year.

Via search page: There is a button called "Show Texts", which shows information on which informants are included in a particular query. For example, if the user wants to query the corpus on Swedish data only, (s)he can press this button and immediately see how many informants are represented in the selection, how many words each informant has uttered etc., like above, and this information can also be sorted by category to present for example number of words in a descending order. This way, we can see how different the informants are in this respect. One old man from Skreia, Norway, utters 1.300 words during his session, while another old man, from nearby Stange, utters more than 6.400 words.

4.6 Further processing of results

Deleting or choosing some results: In a corpus search it is often the case that the user get more results than intended. Sometimes the search expression just was not good enough, which can best be corrected by a new and more precise search. However, sometimes it is impossible to formulate better search criteria, whether it is because there is too much homonymy in the corpus, or because it just is not annotated for all imaginable research features. Let us use a simple example: We want to find all and only the occurrences of the 3sgF pronoun ('she') used as a determiner with something between and then a noun. This search will give a lot of unwanted hits that we want to remove. We choose the Delete option from the Action menu and get the figure below:

Figure 12. Results window with Delete option.

Notice in the figure that by having chosen the Delete option, the results come with a little box on the left hand side. In this box we tick the examples that we want to remove. If we suspected that there would only be a few examples that were appropriate for our research, we could instead have chosen the Choose option, which functions in the same way.

Annotating results: The individual researcher often needs to further annotate the results, for example according to pronunciation of certain sounds or words, or specific syntactic patterns. Below, we have chosen to annotate the examples by two categories: Demonstrative or Other:

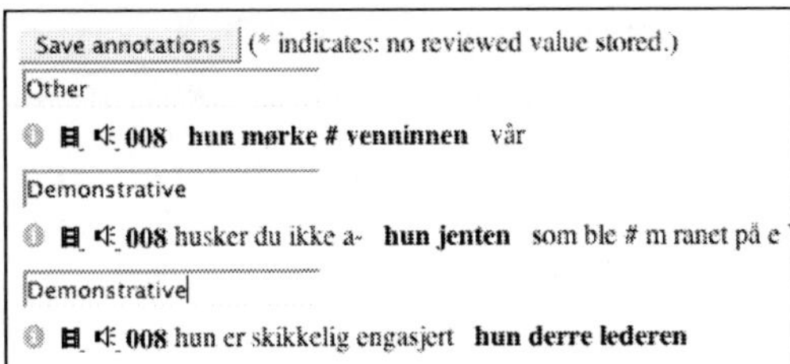

Figure 13. Results window with Annotate option.

The annotations can be edited and saved as annotation sets, for later reuse with other results.

Saving and downloading results: All results can be saved and/or downloaded, whether we choose the raw results or those that we have further processed by deletion, choice or annotation. By saving we get the opportunity to look at the results later, and with exactly the same possibilities for further processing and displaying of results in the corpus interface. Downloaded results, on the other hand, are not thus available in the corpus system, but can be imported as for instance tab-separated text.

5 Comparison with Other Dialect Corpora

There are some other dialect resources on the web, but there are to our knowledge few or no available web-based dialect corpora for other languages. One interesting resource is *Sounds familiar? Accents and Dialects of the UK*. It contains information on British dialects, and recordings of the dialects with transcripts, all presented via a web map. However, it is pedagogical, and not aimed at researchers. For example, there is no search option in the transcripts and no grammatical annotation.

The Scottish Corpus of Text and Speech contains 4 million words, 20% of which is spoken texts, provided with orthographic transcription, synchronised with the audio or video. It is not grammatically annotated and is not representative. However, it has a nice search interface.

The British National Corpus contains 10 million words of spoken English, which have been categorised into 28 different dialects. However, it says in their own search interface distribution that this categorisation is unreliable. Further, as a dialect corpus, the BNC has limited value, since it is not represented with audio, and the speech is transcribed orthographically.

The DynaSand web-based dialect database consists of information on various syntactic features and their distribution geographically in the Netherlands and Belgium. It contains recorded material from the project's questionnaire sessions, but the conversations contain to a large extent read sentences and meta-linguistic discussions, and less spontaneous speech.

The Spoken Dutch Corpus is transcribed orthographically, some of it also phonetically, and it is morphologically tagged. It contains spoken standard Dutch, not dialect data, and is not available by a web-interface.

There might be web-based dialect corpora for other languages, but information about these is hard to find, and they do not seem to be available on the web. One such corpus under development is Corpus of Estonian Dialects. Another is Spoken Japanese Dialect Corpus (GSR-JD), available on DVD. Finally we should mention a small dialect corpus of Norwegian (Talesøk). It contains audio and transcriptions, and is available on the web.

There are some general web-based speech corpora that do not focus on dialect classification. For an overview of some Northern European ones, and their state of art w.r.t. topics like technical solutions and audio-visual availability, we refer to Johannessen et al. (2007).

Finally, we would like to mention that Paul Thompson at the University of Reading had a posting at Corpora List on November 30 2008 asking for information on corpus projects in which the developers have linked digital audio and/or video files to the transcripts, to allow access to the precise segment(s) of the audiovisual files that relates to a part of the transcript. In his summary of 15 responses there was only one dialect corpus – our own Nordic Dialect Corpus.

6 Conclusion

We have presented the first version of the Nordic Dialect Corpus. It contains nearly half a million words of Nordic dialects. Most of them have been collected recently, but we have also included some old speech data. The Nordic Dialect Corpus has an advanced interface for searching and results handling. It is already a great resource for dialect researchers and linguists interested in the Nordic languages. The next version of the corpus will contain more dialect data. Part-of-speech taggers adapted for speech will be developed for alle the languages, and all present and future texts will be tagged.

Acknowledgements

In addition to participants in the ScanDiaSyn and NORMS networks, we would like to thank three anonymous NODALIDA-09 reviewers for valuable comments.

References

Allwood, Jens, Joakim Nivre, Elisabeth Ahlsén. 1989. Speech Management - On the Non-Written Life of Speech. *Gothenburg Papers in Theoretical Linguistics*. University of Gothenburg.

Christ, Oli. 1994. A modular and flexible architecture for an integrated corpus query system. COMPLEX'94, Budapest.

Evert, Stefan. 2005. The CQP Query Language Tutorial. Institute for Natural Language Processing, University of Stuttgart. URL www.ims.unistutgart.de/projekte/CorpusWorkbench/CQPTutorial.

Hagen, Kristin, Janne Bondi Johannessen and Anders Nøklestad. 2000. A Constraint-based Tagger for Norwegian. I Lindberg, Carl-Erik og Steffen Nordahl Lund (red.): *17th Scandinavian Conference of Linguistics*. Odense Working Papers in Language and Communication 19, 31-48, University of Southern Denmark, Odense.

Johannessen, Janne Bondi, Kristin Hagen, Joel Priestley and Lars Nygaard. 2007. An Advanced Speech Corpus for Norwegian. In: *NODALIDA Proceedings*. Tartu: University of Tartu, p. 29-36

Johannessen, Janne Bondi and Kristin Hagen. 2008. *Språk i Oslo. Ny forskning omkring talespråk.* Novus forlag, Oslo.

Johannessen, Janne Bondi, Lars Nygaard, Joel Priestley and Anders Nøklestad. 2008. Glossa: a Multilingual, Multimodal, Configurable User Interface. In: *Proceedings of the Sixth International Language Resources and Evaluation (LREC'08).* Paris: European Language Resources Association (ELRA).

Johannessen, Janne Bondi and Fredrik Jørgensen. 2006. Annotating and Parsing Spoken Language. In Peter Juel Henrichsen, Peter Rossen Skadhauge (eds.): *Treebanking for Discourse and Speech.* København: Samfundslitteratur. s. 83-103

Johansson, Sofie Kokkinakis. 2003. *En studie över påverkande faktorer i ordklasstaggning. Baserad på taggning av svensk text med EPOS.* (PhD dissertation). Gothenburg University.

Jørgensen, Fredrik. 2008. Automatisk gjenkjenning av ytringsgrenser i talespråk. In Johannessen and Hagen (eds.).

Nivre, Joakim and Leif Grönqvist. 2001. Tagging a Corpus of Spoken Swedish. *International Journal of Corpus Linguistics 6(1)*, 47-78.

Nygaard, Lars. 2007. The Glossa Manual. The Text Laboratory. www.hf.uio.no/tekstlab/glossa.html

Papazian, Eric and Botolv Helleland. 2005. *Norsk talemål.* Høyskoleforlaget, Kristiansand.

Rosén, Victoria. 2008. Mot en trebank for talespråk. In Johannessen and Hagen (eds).

Schmid, Helmut. 1994. Probabilistic Part-of-Speech Tagging Using Decision Trees. *Proceedings of International Conference on New Methods in Language Processing*.

Søfteland, Åshild and Anders Nøklestad. 2008. Manuell morfologisk tagging av NoTa-materialet med støtte fra en statistisk tagger. Johannessen and Hagen, 226-234.

Thompson, Paul. 2008. Summary on Info of audio-visual corpora. *Corpora List*, 15 December 2008.

Corpora and web resources

Barbiers, S. et al (2006). Dynamic Syntactic Atlas of the Dutch dialects (DynaSAND). Amsterdam, Meertens Institute. URL: http://www.meertens.knaw.nl/sand/

British National Corpus: http://www.natcorp.ox.ac.uk/

Corpus Gesprochen Nederlands. http://lands.let.kun.nl/cgn/ehome.htm

Nordic Dialect Corpus: http://omilia.uio.no/glossa/html/index_dev.php?corpus=scandiasyn

NoTa Corpus (Norwegian speech corpus – Oslo part) http://www.tekstlab.uio.no/nota/oslo/

Sounds familiar? http://www.bl.uk/learning/langlit/sounds/index.html

Scottish Corpus of Text and Speech. http://www.scottishcorpus.ac.uk/

Spoken Japanese Dialect Corpus (GSR-JD) http://research.nii.ac.jp/src/eng/list/detail.html#GSR-JD

Swedia 2000. http://swedia.ling.gu.se/

Talesøk. http://helmer.aksis.uib.no/talekorpus/Hovedside.htm

Text Laboratory, UiO: http://www.hf.uio.no/tekstlab/English/index.html

ISSN 1736-6305 Vol. 4
http://hdl.handle.net/10062/9206

Experiments on the difference between semantic similarity and relatedness

Peter Kolb
Universität Potsdam
Potsdam, Germany
`kolb@ling.uni-potsdam.de`

Abstract

Recent work has pointed out the difference between the concepts of semantic similarity and semantic relatedness. Importantly, some NLP applications depend on measures of semantic similarity, while others work better with measures of semantic relatedness. It has also been observed that methods of computing similarity measures from text corpora produce word spaces that are biased towards either semantic similarity or relatedness. Despite these findings, there has been little work that evaluates the effect of various techniques and parameter settings in the word space construction from corpora. The present paper experimentally investigates how the choice of context, corpus preprocessing and size, and dimension reduction techniques like singular value decomposition and frequency cutoffs influence the semantic properties of the resulting word spaces.

1 Introduction

A growing number of applications in natural language processing rely on knowledge about the semantic similarity between words. These similarities are used for example in ontology learning (Cimiano et al., 2005), information retrieval (Müller et al., 2007), and word sense disambiguation (Patwardhan et al., 2007).

One has to differentiate between semantic "similarity" and semantic "relatedness" (Budanitsky and Hirst, 2006). The first is a narrower concept that holds between lexical items having a similar meaning, like *palm* and *tree*. It is usually defined via the lexical relations of synonymy and hyponymy. (Geffet and Dagan, 2005) require that semantically similar words can be substituted for each other in context, which must not be true for semantically related words.

The broader concept semantic relatedness holds between lexical items that are connected by any kind of lexical or functional association. Dissimilar words can be semantically related, e.g. via relations like meronymy (*palm – leaf*), or when they belong to the same semantic field (*palm – coconut*). (Turney, 2008) seems to equate "related" with "associated" and defines: "Two words are associated when they tend to co-occur (*doctor* and *hospital*)".

Unfortunately, measures of semantic similarity and relatedness rely on hand-crafted lexical resources like WordNet, which are not available for many languages and have limited coverage, particularly in specialized domains. Therefore, (Kilgarriff, 2003) and others have argued for using "distributional similarity" as a proxy for semantic similarity. Distributional semantics is based on the assumption that words with similar meaning occur in similar contexts (Harris, 1968). Several successful methods to compute the distributional similarity of words from text corpora have been proposed, including (Landauer and Dumais, 1997), (Grefenstette, 1994), and (Sahlgren, 2001).

(Budanitsky and Hirst, 2006) emphasize the difference between semantic and distributional similarity. Methods that measure the similarity of the distributional behaviour of words do not take into account the different senses a word has, and therefore mix up the similar words for all the word senses. While semantic similarity is a relation between concepts, distributional similarity is a relation between words.

Finally, (Mohammad and Hirst, 2005) differentiate between distributional relatedness and distributional similarity. Two words are distributionally similar if they have many common co-occurring words in the same syntactic relations. By contrast, distributional measures that use a bag-of-words context capture distributional relatedness. (Kilgarriff and Yallop, 2000) call these two variants "tight" and "loose" word similarities. (Sahlgren, 2006) comes to the conclusion that word spaces based on direct co-occurrences capture relatedness, while spaces that are based on indirect or second-order co-occurrences capture similarity.

The difference between semantic similarity and relatedness is not only of theoretical interest. In fact some NLP applications require measures of semantic similarity, while others perform better with semantic relatedness. (Sahlgren and Karlgren, 2008) give an example from the area of text mining. For the analysis of opinions in blogs and discussion forums it is useful to automatically detect synonyms and spelling variants for an interesting term like *recommend*, thereby discovering terms that are used similarly in the given sublanguage, for example *love, lurve, looove* and *recomend*. To solve this task, measures of semantic similarity are much better suited. On the other hand, to find out what people associate with a target word like *Xbox*, measures of semantic relatedness should be preferred.

Other applications where a strict notion of similarity is more appropriate are automatic thesaurus generation and paraphrasing. In contrast, for word sense disambiguation the semantically related context word *coconut* is as useful as the similar word *tree* to disambiguate between the meanings of *palm*.

As these example applications show it is important to employ a word space with the right type of relations for use with a given application. But while (Rapp, 2002) and especially (Sahlgren, 2006) have investigated the effects of context choice and co-occurrence type on the semantic properties of the resulting word spaces, we are only aware of (Peirsman et al., 2007) to have tested the influence of dimension reduction techniques (namely Random Indexing and frequency cutoffs) on the outcome. The aim of the present paper is to experimentally confirm that the application of other dimension reduction techniques like singular value decomposition (SVD) and corpus preprocessing techniques like lemmatization also have considerable effect on the nature of the resulting word space.

In the next section we present our method for computing distributional similarity, in section 3 we describe three other systems we have chosen for comparison. Section 4 evaluates the performance

of the systems against human relatedness judgements and similarities based on WordNet. We report on a series of experiments concerning the size of the input corpus, the choice of context (syntactic vs. window-based), corpus preprocessing and filtering by word frequency. In section 5 we discuss the findings, and in the last section we summarize our contributions.

2 Our Method: DISCO

Our method for computing the distributional similarity between words is called DISCO (*extracting DIStributionally similar words using CO-occurrences*) and works as follows. In a preprocessing step, the corpus at hand is tokenized and highly frequent function words are eliminated. Since we want to keep the method independent from language-specific resources, neither part of speech tagging nor lemmatization are performed, and we use a simple context window of size ± 3 words for counting co-occurrences. Our evaluations showed that it is beneficial to take the exact position within the window into account, as has been done by (Rapp, 1999). This can be seen as a crude approximation of syntactic dependency relations. Instead of syntactic dependency triples like *<donut*, OBJ-OF, *eat>* we get triples of the form *<donut*, -2, *eat>*. Consequently, the features that describe a word's distribution are not just words as in a pure bag-of-words approach, but ordered pairs of word and window position.

Consider the example in table 1. It shows two occurrences of the word *palm* in a context of ± 3 words. When taking the exact window position into account, then *palm* is described by the five different features that result from the two occurrences (we ignore function words), listed on the lower left of the table. The features *<*, -3, oil>* and *<*, +1, oil>* are distinct and have nothing more in common than *<*, +3, hand>* and *<*, -1, provides>*. If the exact position is not observed, we get only four features (lower right of table 1), since the two occurrences of *oil* can not be distinguished any more. A context that observes the exact window position leads to tighter similarities than a window without exact position. In section 4.4 we evaluate the effect the window-position context bears on the resulting similarities.

Moving the window over our corpus gives us a co-occurrence matrix. Every row of the matrix describes a word, and is also called a "word vector".

-3	-2	-1		$+1$	$+2$	$+3$
oil	into	the	palm	of	his	hand
the	nuts	provides	palm	oil	while	the
<palm, -3, oil>	1			<palm, oil>		2
<palm, +3, hand>	1			<palm, hand>		1
<palm, -2, nuts>	1			<palm, nuts>		1
<palm, -1, provides>	1			<palm, provides>		1
<palm, +1, oil>	1					

Table 1: Example of using window position triples (WPT) as context for counting co-occurrences. WPT features are shown in the 1st column of the lowest row, the bag-of-words features in the 4th column.

The matrix size is not $v \times f$ as usual (with v being the number of words for which word vectors are built, f being the number of words used as features), but $v \times f \cdot r$ (r is the window size). The next step is to transform the absolute counts in the matrix fields into more meaningful weights. For this feature weighting we found the measure proposed by (Lin, 1998c), which is based on mutual information, to be optimal:

$$g(w, w', r) = \log \frac{(f(w, r, w') - 0,95)f(*, r, *)}{f(w, r, *)f(*, r, w')} \tag{1}$$

where w and w' stand for words and r for a window position (or a dependency relation, respectively), and f is the frequency of occurrence.

To arrive at a word's distributionally similar words the next step is to compare every word vector with all other word vectors. For vector comparison we use Lin's information theoretic measure ((Lin, 1998a)) as given in equation (2). Because a word vector represents the distribution of a word in the corpus, this vector comparison gives us the words which are used in similar contexts. Put differently, it finds the words that share a maximum number of common co-occurrences. For example, if *bread* co-occurs with *bake*, *eat*, and *crispy*, and *cake* also co-occurs with these three words, then *bread* and *cake* will be distributionally similar. Note that *bread* and *cake* do not need to co-occur themselves a single time to be regarded as similar.

As an example of the outcome, the twelve distributionally most similar words for *palm* are listed here:

palms (0.1345) coconut (0.1059) olive (0.0870) pine (0.0823) citrus (0.0745) oak (0.0677) mango (0.0652) cocoa (0.0645) banana (0.0627) bananas (0.0623) trees (0.0570) fingers (0.0560)

Such a list of distributionally similar words can in turn be seen as the "second order" word vector of the given word, containing not only the words which occur together with it, but those that occur in similar contexts. We can now compare two words based on their second order word vectors, too. This use of higher-order co-occurrences is to some extent comparable to what is achieved in LSA by singular value decomposition (Kontostathis and Pottenger, 2006).

In conclusion, DISCO provides two different similarity measures: DISCO1, that compares words based on their sets of co-occurring words, and DISCO2, that compares words based on their sets of distributionally similar words (i.e. DISCO2 compares the second order word vectors).

3 Description of the other Systems

LSA. Latent semantic analysis (Landauer and Dumais, 1997) is arguably the most popular variant of word space. Its core step is a dimension reduction technique called singular value decomposition (SVD). SVD computes the least mean square error projection of a matrix onto a lower dimensional matrix. It achieves a kind of generalization by combining columns that represent words with similar meanings. In our experiments we used the LSA implementation accessible at `http://lsa.colorado.edu`.

PMI-IR (pointwise mutual information - information retrieval). (Turney, 2001) presents a method for computing the similarity between arbitrary words that utilizes the WWW search engine AltaVista[1] according to the following for-

---

[1] `http://www.altavista.com`

$$lin(w, w') = \frac{\sum_{p=1}^{r} \sum_{w_i=1}^{v} \begin{cases} g(w, w_i, p) + g(w', w_i, p) & : \quad g(w, w_i, p) > 0 \quad \text{and} \quad g(w', w_i, p) > 0 \\ 0 & : \quad \text{else} \end{cases}}{\sum_{p=1}^{r} \sum_{w_i=1}^{v} (g(w, w_i, p) + g(w', w_i, p))} \tag{2}$$

mula, adapted from pointwise mutual information:

$$PMI\text{-}IR(w_1, w_2) = log \frac{H(w_1 NEAR \, w_2)}{H(w_1)H(w_2)} \tag{3}$$

where $H(w)$ is the number of hits the search engine returns for the query w. The more often two words co-occur near each other on a web page, the higher is their PMI-IR score. We computed the PMI-IR similarity values for our evaluation data by querying AltaVista on 4/10/2008.

WordNet::Similarity. WordNet::Similarity (Pedersen et al., 2004) is a Perl module based on WordNet that has been widely used in a variety of natural language processing tasks. It implements three measures of semantic relatedness (namely Hirst-St.Onge (hso), Lesk (lesk) and vector pairs (vp)) and six measures of semantic similarity (Jiang and Conrath (jcn), Leacock and Chodorow (lch), Lin (lin), path length (path), Resnik (res), and Wu and Palmer (wup)). The latter utilize the *is-a* relations in WordNet. Since there are only *is-a* relations between nouns and between verbs in WordNet, the similarity measures cannot be applied to adjectives or across part of speech.

4 Evaluation

4.1 Data

We built several DISCO word spaces according to the method outlined above. The first word space is based on 300,000 articles from the English Wikipedia[2], amounting to some 267 million tokens. We considered all words with a corpus frequency of at least 100, resulting in a vocabulary size of v =226,000, and used the f =101,000 most frequent words as feature words. This word space is employed in experiments 1 and 2 (sections 4.2 and 4.3).

In experiment 3 (section 4.4) we tested different parameter settings, which meant we had to build a number of word spaces. To limit the computational effort we decided to use a smaller corpus: the British National Corpus which consists

[2] http://en.wikipedia.org

of roughly 110 million tokens.

(Finkelstein et al., 2001) prepared a list of 353 noun-noun pairs and employed 16 subjects to estimate their semantic relatedness on a scale from 0 to 10. We use this list as our evaluation data. As seven word pairs contained at least one word that was unknown to WordNet, we deleted them from the list, leaving 346 word pairs for testing.

4.2 Correlation with Human Judgements of Semantic Relatedness

Our first experiment measures the correlation (according to the Pearson correlation coefficient) of the candidate systems with the averaged semantic relatedness scores assigned to the 346 word pairs by the human subjects. Table 2 shows the results. The first two correlation values in the first row of the table are taken from (Finkelstein et al., 2001). Among the systems listed in the first row, DISCO1 shows the lowest correlation with the human judgements, comparable to that of Finkelstein et al.'s vector approach. DISCO2 performs much better, but is still worse than LSA. The best score is achieved by PMI-IR, which is in accordance with other results reported in the literature (Turney, 2001).

The WordNet-based measures (shown in the second row of the table) perform worse, which comes as no surprise for the six measures of similarity, since they are not intended to measure relatedness. But the three measures of relatedness (hso, lesk, and vp) do not perform much better. The best scoring vector pairs measure (vp) only achieves the same score as DISCO1.

4.3 Correlation with WordNet::Similarity

We now take the semantic similarity values produced by the six WordNet similarity measures as gold standard and compare the correlation of the other test systems with these similarities. We assume that the six measures provide a sensible similarity gold standard since they are based exclusively on WordNets IS-A noun hierarchy and do not take into account other lexical relations or associations.

	Vector-based	LSA	PMI-IR	DISCO1	DISCO2		
	0.41	0.56	**0.63**	0.39	0.51		
hso	lesk	vp	jcn	lch	lin	path	res	wup
0.35	0.21	0.39	0.23	0.35	0.30	0.38	0.36	0.30

Table 2: Correlation of several systems with the semantic relatedness values assigned by humans.

	jcn	lch	lin	path	res	wup	avg.
PMI-IR	0.14	0.12	0.06	0.15	0.22	0.11	0.13
LSA	0.16	0.26	0.21	0.29	0.28	0.22	0.24
DISCO1	**0.38**	0.39	0.33	**0.45**	0.43	0.33	**0.38**
DISCO2	0.15	**0.40**	**0.39**	0.35	**0.44**	**0.40**	0.36

Table 3: Correlation between WordNet-based semantic similarity and four systems based on word distributions.

In this task, PMI-IR performs worst (cf. table 3), whereas DISCO1 shows the highest correlation on average. The behaviour of the two DISCO measures is difficult to compare, because DISCO1 scores higher than DISCO2 three times, but DISCO2 also scores higher than DISCO1 four times. If we take the averaged score, DISCO1 turns out slightly better. In any case, both DISCOs perform much better than PMI-IR and LSA.

4.4 Effect of different parameter settings and techniques

Our third experiment tests various parameter settings for the DISCO1 measure. As DISCO2, which was meant as a substitute for LSA, performed worse than LSA in the first experiment, we do not further evaluate this measure. Instead, we combine DISCO1 with SVD in the last part of experiment 3.

In the previous experiments a 267 million token corpus from the English Wikipedia was used, in the following we use a smaller corpus, namely the British National Corpus, which consists of only about 110 million tokens, i.e. has only 40% of the size of the Wikipedia corpus.

The reduced size of the input data has a noticeable effect on the computation of semantic relatedness (first row in table 4). While in the previous experiments DISCO1 achieved a correlation of 0.39 with the Finkelstein gold standard for semantic relatedness (abbreviated as *finkel353* in table 4), the same method now only scores 0.34 on the same task, which constitutes a decrease by 12.8%.

To quantify the effect of corpus size on semantic similarity we compute the correlation with Word-

	finkel353	res
DISCO1 WPT	0.34	**0.43**
DISCO1 without WPT	0.32	0.12
DISCO1 WPT lemmatized	**0.36**	0.41
DISCO1 dependency	**0.36**	0.39

Table 4: Experiment 3: Correlation between DISCO1 and two gold standards for different parameter settings.

Net::Similarity's Resnik measure from experiment 2 (*res* in table 4). As one can see from tables 3 and 4, the reduced size of the corpus has no negative effect on semantic similarity: the correlation stands at 0.43.

To quantify the benefit of our poor man's dependency triples – the window position triples (WPT) as explained in section 2 – we built a word space with a simple bag-of-words window as context. The size of the window remains the same (three words on either side of the target word), but the position inside the window is not observed any more. The result is shown in the second row of table 4. The correlation with the semantic relatedness gold standard drops from 0.34 to 0.32 (-5.9%). The correlation with the similarity reference crashes down by 72.1% from 0.43 to 0.12.

Next we lemmatized the corpus before applying DISCO using the well known Tree Tagger (Schmid, 1994). While lemmatization has a positive effect on semantic relatedness (cf. the third row in table 4) it has an almost equally strong negative effect on semantic similarity.

In the next part of experiment 3 we ran the Minipar (Lin, 1998b) robust dependency parser over

f	finkel353	res
101,000	0.34	0.43
50,000	0.37	0.43
20,000	0.40	0.45
10,000	**0.41**	**0.46**
5,000	0.40	0.43
1,000	0.38	0.43
500	0.36	0.33

Table 5: Frequency cutoff: Correlation of DISCO1 with the two gold standards for different quantities of feature words.

our corpus to extract syntactic dependency triples. This increases the correlation with the semantic relatedness gold standard from 0.34 to 0.36 (last row in table 4). That is, robust parsing has the same effect as lemmatization. Since Minipar automatically does lemmatization, we can conclude that syntactic dependency triples are no better than our window position triples.

Surprisingly, the correlation with the semantic similarity gold standard drops from 0.43 to 0.39 (-9.3%). We hypothesize that this might be the effect of noise produced by the parser.

Recall from section 2 that the size of the co-occurrence matrix is given by $v \times f \cdot r$ with v being the number of vocabulary items for which word vectors are collected, f being the number of feature words (the words that are used to populate the word vectors), and r being the window size. As stated in section 4.1, for all experiments so far we chose $f = 101,000$, i.e. we used the 101,000 most frequent words in the corpus as feature words. We will now systematically decrease this parameter. The effect of this adjustment can be seen in table 5. As the number of feature words decreases, the correlation with both gold standards increases, peaking at $f = 10,000$. For f lower than $1,000$, the performance of semantic similarity drops sharply, whereas semantic relatedness seems to suffer relatively less from such a dramatic decrease of the number of features. Note that for the optimal setting of this parameter the performance for semantic relatedness is now even better than with the much bigger corpus from the previous experiments (0.41 as compared to 0.39 in table 2). The same holds for the correlation with the semantic similarity gold standard (0.46 vs. 0.43, cf. table 3).

The frequency cutoff at $f = 10,000$ lead to

a considerable reduction of the size of our co-occurrence matrix which enabled us to apply the singular value decomposition to it. We used SVDLIBC[3] to reduce the matrix to its 300 principal components (i.e. we reduced the matrix size from $v \times 10,000 \cdot r$ to $v \times 300$). The result is shown in table 6. The use of SVD significantly increases the correlation with the relatedness gold standard, whereas it decreases the correlation with all six similarity measures.

5 Discussion

In the first experiment (see section 4.2) we found that PMI-IR scored best at the task of computing semantic relatedness, outperforming LSA and even more DISCO. The most interesting result of experiment 1 was that DISCO2 scored much better than DISCO1. Since the only difference between the two measures is the use of second order co-occurrences by DISCO2, we can conclude that for computing semantic relatedness higher-order co-occurrences can substitute for SVD – not fully, but at least to a certain degree.

We also observed that the three WordNet-based measures of semantic relatedness performed quite badly. The reason for this is unclear.

Experiment 2 (section 4.3) evaluated the correlation of different methods with semantic similarities produced by WordNet::Similarity. It was shown that DISCO1 scored much better in this task than PMI-IR and LSA. Moreover, the higher-order co-occurrences of DISCO2 did not seem to have a consistent positive effect. From this result we can conclude that singular value decomposition and higher-order co-occurrences increase the performance when computing semantic relatedness, but they do not help in computing semantic similarity. This conclusion is confirmed by the last part of experiment 3 (section 4.4), where we combined DISCO1 with SVD, leading to a significant performance increase for the relatedness gold standard, but to a decrease for all six similarity measures.

The poor performance of PMI-IR in the second experiment can be explained by the type of co-occurrence it is based on. While DISCO1 compares words based on their collocation sets, thereby finding words that are used similarly, PMI-IR's similarities *are* collocations. Therefore it rather produces very loose word similarities, i.e.

---

[3]http://tedlab.mit.edu/~dr/SVDLIBC/

	finkel353	jcn	lch	lin	path	res	wup
DISCO1-10K	0.41	**0.62**	**0.52**	**0.50**	**0.52**	**0.46**	**0.47**
DISCO1-10K-SVD	**0.55**	0.46	0.37	0.41	0.39	0.38	0.35

Table 6: Performance of DISCO1 after frequency cutoff at f = 10,000 with and without singular value decomposition (SVD)

words that are topically similar.

Experiment 3 (section 4.4) suggests that measures of relatedness highly profit from more input data. This is confirmed by the finding of experiment 1 that PMI-IR outperforms LSA, despite the fact that both methods use co-occurrence in a short piece of text as context. While LSA additionally employs SVD, there is nothing in PMI-IR that would explain its strong performance except the huge size of the corpus it is based on (the web).

Experiment 3 also confirms that the recording of the position within the context window has an enormous positive effect on computing semantic similarity, while the effect on semantic relatedness is less significant. This could be expected from the discussion of the relevant literature in section 1, where distributional similarity is explicitly defined by the use of a strict context that pays attention to syntactic features like word order. Our experiments indicate that any method which "blurs" the context (bag-of-words window, lemmatization, SVD) decreases the quality of semantic similarity. Instead, a "naked" approach based on indirect co-occurences should be chosen. This finding is in line with (Peirsman et al., 2007) who state that "severely reducing the dimensionality of the word vectors leads to a retrieval of more loosely related words." One should presume that consequently a syntactic context would score best, since this is the strictest imaginable context. Therefore, it is a bit surprising that the use of Minipar did not lead to an improvement. (Rapp, 2004) seems sceptical about the advantages of syntactic dependency triples over simple window approaches and assumes that the employment of a part-of-speech tagger will result in the same performance as the use of a parser. This hypothesis is confirmed by our results. (Grefenstette, 1996) and recently (Padó and Lapata, 2007) and (Peirsman et al., 2007) compared syntactic and window based approaches, and found that syntactic contexts performed superior. However, they used bag-of-words windows without taking into account the position inside the window. We propose that our window position triples should be rather seen as a syntactic context and not as a bag-of-words context. Yet we believe that for languages with a less strict word order than English (like for example Czech) syntactic dependency triples will outperform our window position triples.

Another interesting finding of experiment 3 resulted from the application of a frequency filter. We found that limiting the size of the co-occurrence matrix to the 10,000 most frequent feature words yielded the highest performance for both semantic similarity and relatedness.

6 Conclusion

In the present paper we have reported on several experiments regarding the influence of dimension reduction techniques, corpus size, and choice of context on the semantic properties of the resulting word spaces.

For future work we propose to carry out application-centered evaluations in order to confirm the practical relevance of the similarity–relatedness distinction put forth in this paper. DISCO is freely available for research purposes at `http://www.linguatools.de/disco_en.html`.

References

A. Budanitsky and G. Hirst. 2006. Evaluating WordNet-based Measures of Lexical Semantic Relatedness. *Computational Linguistics*, 32(1).

P. Cimiano, A. Hotho, and S. Staab. 2005. Learning Concept Hierarchies from Text Corpora using Formal Concept Analysis. *Journal of Artificial Intelligence Research*, 24:305–339.

L. Finkelstein, E. Gabrilovich, Y. Matias, E. Rivlin, Z. Solan, G. Wolfman, and E. Ruppin. 2001. Placing search in context: the concept revisited. In *WWW '01: Proceedings of the 10th international conference on World Wide Web*, pages 406–414, New York, NY, USA. ACM.

M. Geffet and I. Dagan. 2005. The distributional inclusion hypotheses and lexical entailment. In *Proc.*

of the 43rd Annual Meeting of the ACL, pages 107–114.

G. Grefenstette. 1994. *Explorations in Automatic Thesaurus Discovery*. Kluwer, Dordrecht.

G. Grefenstette. 1996. Evaluation techniques for automatic semantic extraction: comparing syntactic and window based approaches. In B. Boguraev and J. Pustejovsky, editors, *Corpus Processing for Lexical Acquisition*, pages 205 – 216. MIT Press, Cambridge, MA.

Z.S. Harris. 1968. *Mathematical Structures of Language*. Interscience Publishers, New York.

A. Kilgarriff and C. Yallop. 2000. What's in a thesaurus? In *Proceedings of the Second Conference on Language Resources and Evaluation*, pages 1371–1379, Athens.

A. Kilgarriff. 2003. Thesauruses for Natural Language Processing. In *Proceedings of Natural Language Processing and Knowledge Engineering (NLPKE)*, Beijing.

A. Kontostathis and W.M. Pottenger. 2006. A framework for understanding latent semantic indexing (LSI) performance. *Information Processing and Management*, 42(1):56–73, January.

T.K. Landauer and S.T. Dumais. 1997. A Solution to Plato's Problem: The Latent Semantic Analysis Theory of Acquisition, Induction and Representation of Knowledge. *Psychological Review*, 104(2):211–240.

D. Lin. 1998a. Automatic Retrieval and Clustering of Similar Words. In *Proceedings of COLING-ACL 1998*, Montreal.

D. Lin. 1998b. Dependency-based Evaluation of MINIPAR. In *Workshop on the Evaluation of Parsing Systems*, Granada, Spain.

D. Lin. 1998c. Extracting Collocations from Text Corpora. In *Workshop on Computational Terminology*, pages 57–63, Montreal, Kanada.

S. Mohammad and G. Hirst. 2005. Distributional Measures as Proxies for Semantic Relatedness. Unpublished.

C. Müller, I. Gurevych, and M. Mühlhäuser. 2007. Integrating Semantic Knowledge into Text Similarity and Information Retrieval. In *Proceedings of the First IEEE International Conference on Semantic Computing*, pages 57–63, Montreal, Kanada.

S. Padó and M. Lapata. 2007. Dependency-based Construction of Semantic Space Models. *Computational Linguistics*, 33(2):161–199.

S. Patwardhan, S. Banerjee, and T. Pedersen. 2007. UMND1: Unsupervised Word Sense Disambiguation Using Contextual Semantic Relatedness. In *SemEval-2007: Proceedings of the 4th International Workshop on Semantic Evaluations*, pages 390–393, Prague, Czech Republic, June.

T. Pedersen, S. Patwardhan, and J. Michelizzi. 2004. WordNet::Similarity - Measuring the Relatedness of Concepts. In *Proceedings of Fifth Annual Meeting of the North American Chapter of the Association for Computational Linguistics (NAACL-04)*, pages 38–41, Boston, MA., May.

Y. Peirsman, K. Heylen, and D. Speelman. 2007. Finding semantically related words in Dutch. Co-occurrences versus syntactic contexts. In *Workshop on Contextual Information in Semantic Space Models (CoSMo 2007)*, Roskilde.

R. Rapp. 1999. Automatic Identification of Word Translations from Unrelated English and German Corpora. In *Proceedings of ACL*, pages 519–526.

R. Rapp. 2002. The Computation of Word Associations: Comparing Syntagmatic and Paradigmatic Approaches. In *Proceedings of COLING-02*, Taipeh.

R. Rapp. 2004. A Freely Available Automatically Generated Thesaurus of Related Words. In *Proceedings of LREC 2004*, pages 395–398.

M. Sahlgren and J. Karlgren. 2008. Buzz Monitoring in Word Space. In *European Conference on Intelligence and Security Informatics (EuroISI 2008)*. Esbjerg, Denmark.

M. Sahlgren. 2001. Vector-based Semantic Analysis: Representing Word Meanings Based on Random Labels. In Alessandro Lenci, Simonetta Montemagni, and Vito Pirrelli, editors, *The Acquisition and Representation of Word Meaning*. Kluwer Academic Publishers.

M. Sahlgren. 2006. *The Word-Space Model: Using distributional analysis to represent syntagmatic and paradigmatic relations between words in high-dimensional vector spaces*. Ph.D. thesis, Stockholm.

H. Schmid. 1994. Probabilistic Part-of-speech Tagging Using Decision Trees. *International Conference on New Methods in Language Processing*.

P.D. Turney. 2001. Mining the Web for Synonyms: PMI-IR versus LSA on TOEFL. In *Proc. of the Twelth European Conference on Machine Learning*, pages 491–502.

P.D. Turney. 2008. A uniform approach to analogies, synonyms, antonyms, and associations. In *Proceedings of the 22nd International Conference on Computational Linguistics (Coling 2008)*, pages 905–912, Manchester, UK.

ISSN 1736-6305 Vol. 4
http://hdl.handle.net/10062/9206

Weighted Finite-State Morphological Analysis of Finnish Compounding with HFST-LEXC

Krister Lindén
University of Helsinki
Helsinki, Finland
`Krister.Linden@helsinki.fi`

Tommi Pirinen
University of Helsinki
Helsinki, Finland
`Tommi.Pirinen@helsinki.fi`

Abstract

Finnish has a very productive compounding and a rich inflectional system, which causes ambiguity in the morphological segmentation of compounds made with finite state transducer methods. In order to disambiguate the compound segmentations, we compare three different strategies, which are all cast in the same probabilistic framework and compared for the first time. We present a method for implementing the probabilistic framework as part of the building process of LexC-style morpheme sub-lexicons creating weighted lexical transducers. To implement the structurally disambiguating morphological analyzer, we use the HFST-LEXC tool which is part of the open source *Helsinki Finite-State Technology*. Using our Finnish test corpus with 53 270 compounds, we demonstrate that it is possible to use non-compound token probabilities to disambiguate the compounding structure. Non-compound token probabilities are easy to obtain from raw data compared with obtaining the probabilities of prefixes of segmented and disambiguated compounds.

1 Introduction

In languages with productive multi-part compounding, such as Finnish, German and Swedish, approximately 9-10 % of the word tokens in a corpus are compounds (Hedlund, 2002) and approximately 2/3 of the dictionary entries are compounds, cf. a publicly available Finnish dictionary (Research Institute for the Languages of Finland, 2007).

There have been various attempts at curbing the potential combinatorial explosion of segmentations that a prolific compounding mechanism produces. Karlsson (1992) showed that for Swedish the most significant factor in disambiguating compounds was the counting of the number of parts in the analysis, where the analysis with the fewest parts almost always was the best candidate. This has later been corroborated by others, e.g. (Sjöbergh and Kann, 2004). In particular, it was the main disambiguation criterion formulated by (Schiller, 2005) on German compounding. In addition, Schiller used frequency information for disambiguating between compounds with an equal number of parts. Schiller estimated her figures from compound part frequencies calculated from lists of segmented compounds, which requires a considerable amount of manual labor in order to create the training corpora consisting of attested compound words and their correct segmentations.

We suggest two modifications to the strategies of Karlsson and Schiller. First we suggest that the word segment probabilities can be estimated from non-compound word frequencies in the corpus. The motivation for our approach is that compounds are formed in order to distinguish between instances of frequently occurring phenomena and therefore compounds are more often formed for more frequently discussed phenomena. We assume that the frequency by which phenomena are discussed is reflected in the non-compound word form frequencies, i.e. high-frequency words should in general have more compounds. To further simplify the estimation process, we assume that the frequencies of the word tokens directly affect the probability of the forms used in the compound formation, which can be motivated by an analogy of use.

In addition, we suggest that the special word border penalty suggested by Karlsson and maintained by Schiller is unnecessary when framing the problem in a probabilistic framework. This has also been suggested by others, see e.g. Marek (2006). However, this is the first time the disambiguation principles of Karlsson and of Schiller are compared with a probabilistic approach on the same corpus.

Previously, there has been no publicly available general framework for conveniently integrating both a full-fledged morphological description and for representing probabilities for general morphological compound and inflectional analysis. Karlsson (1992) applied a post-processing phase to count the parts, and Schiller (2005) used the proprietary weighted finite-state compiler of Xerox (Kempe et al., 2003), which compiles regular expressions. We therefore introduce the open source software tool HFST-LexC[1], which is similar to the Xerox LexC tool (Beesley and Karttunen, 2003). In addition to the fact that HFST-LexC compiles LexC-style lexicons, it also has a mechanism for adding weights to compound parts and morphological analyses.

The remainder of the article is structured as follows. In Sections 2 and 3, we introduce a version of Finnish morphology for compounding. In Section 4, we introduce the probabilistic formulation of the methods for weighting the lexical entries. In Section 5, we briefly introduce the test and training corpora. In Section 6, we present the results. Finally, in Sections 7, 8 and 9, we give some notes on the implementation, discuss the results and draw the conclusions.

2   Inflection and Compounding in Finnish

In Finnish morphology, the inflection of typical nouns produces several thousands of forms for the productive inflection. Finnish compounding theoretically allows nominal compounds of arbitrary length to be created from initial parts of certain noun forms. The final part may be inflected in all possible forms.

For example the compounds describing ancestors are compounded from zero or more of *isän* 'father SINGULAR GENITIVE' and *äidin* 'mother SINGULAR GENITIVE' and then one of any inflected forms of *isä* or *äiti*, creating forms such as *äidinisälle* 'grandfather (maternal) SINGULAR ALLATIVE' or *isänisänisänisä* 'great great grandfather SINGULAR NOMINATIVE'. As for the potential ambiguity, Finnish also has the noun *nisä* 'udder', which creates ambiguity for any paternal grandfather, e.g. *isän#isän#isän#isä*, *isän#isä#nisän#isä*, *isä#nisä#nisä#nisä*, ...

However, much of the ambiguity in Finnish compounds is aggravated by the ambiguity of the inflected forms of the head words. For example *isän*, has several possible analyses, e.g. ISÄ+SG+GEN, ISÄ+SG+ACC and ISÄ+SG+INS.

Finnish compounding also includes forms of compounding where all parts of the word are inflected in the same form, but this is limited to a small fraction of adjective initial compounds and to the numbers if they are spelled out with letters. In addition, some inflected verb forms may appear as parts of compounds. These are much more rare than nominal compounds (Hakulinen et al., 2008) so they do not interfere with the regular compounding. We therefore did not consider them in this paper.

3   Morphological analysis of Finnish

Pirinen (2008) presented an open source implementation of a finite state morphological analyzer for Finnish. We use that implementation as a baseline for the compounding analysis as Pirinen's analyzer has a fully productive compounding mechanism. Fully productive compounding means that it allows compounds of arbitrary length with any combination of nominative singulars, genitive singulars, or genitive plurals in the initial part and any inflected form of a noun as the final part.

The morphotactic combination of morphemes is achieved by combining sublexicons as defined in (Beesley and Karttunen, 2003). We use the open source software called HFST-LexC with a similar interface as the Xerox LexC tool. The HFST-LexC tool includes preliminary support for weights on the lexical entries.

For the purpose of this experiment, each lexical entry constitutes one full word form, i.e., we create a full form lexicon using the previously mentioned

---

[1] http://kitwiki.csc.fi/twiki/bin/view/ KitWiki/HfstLexC

analyzer (Pirinen, 2008). This creates a huge text file for the purely inflectional morphology of approximately 40 000 non-compound lexical entries for Finnish, which were stored in a single CompoundFinalNoun lexicon as shown in Figure 1. The figure demonstrates an unweighted lexicon and also shows how we model the compounding by dividing the word forms into two categories: compound non-final (i.e., nominative singular, genitive singular, and genitive plural) and compound final forms allowing us to give weights to each form or compound part as needed.

```
LEXICON Root
## CompoundNonFinalNoun ;
## CompoundFinalNoun ;

LEXICON Compound
#:0 CompoundNonFinalNoun "weight: 0" ;
#:0 CompoundFinalNoun "weight: 0" ;

LEXICON CompoundNonFinalNoun
isä     Compound   "weight: 0" ;
isän    Compound   "weight: 0" ;
äiti    Compound   "weight: 0" ;
äidin   Compound   "weight: 0" ;

LEXICON CompoundFinalNoun
isä:isä+sg+nom      ## "weight: 0" ;
isän:isä+sg+gen     ## "weight: 0" ;
isälle:isä+sg+all   ## "weight: 0" ;

LEXICON ##
## # ;
```

Figure 1: Unweighted lexicon.

Compounding implemented with the unweighted sublexicons in Figure 1 is equivalent to the original baseline analyzer. The root sublexicon specifies that we can start directly with compound final noun forms, forming single part words, or start with compound initial forms, forming multi-word compounds. The compound initial lexicon is a listing of all nominative singulars, genitive singulars and genitive plurals, which is followed by a compound boundary marker in a separate sublexicon. After the compound boundary marker another word follows either from the compound initial sublexicon or from the compound final sublexicon. The compound final sublexicon, for the purposes of this experiment, contains a list of all possible forms of all words and their analyses.

4 Methodology

We define the weight of a token through its probability to occur in the corpus, i.e. we use the count, c, which is proportional to the frequency with which a token appears in a corpus divided by the corpus size, cs. The probability, $p(a)$, for a token, a, is defined by Equation 1.

$$p(a) = c(a)/cs \qquad (1)$$

Tokens known to the lexicon but unseen in the corpus need to be assigned a small probability mass different from 0, so they get $c(x) = 1$, i.e. we define the count of a token as its corpus frequency plus 1 as in Equation 2.

$$c(a) = 1 + \text{frequency}(a) \qquad (2)$$

If a token, e.g. *isän*, has several possible analyses, e.g. ISÄ+SG+GEN and ISÄ+SG+ACC, the total count for *isän* will be distributed among the analyses in a disambiguated training corpus. If the disambiguation result removes all readings ISÄ+SG+ACC from the disambiguated result, the count for this reading is still at least 1 according to Equation 2. We need the total probability mass of all the non-compound tokens in the lexicon to sum up to 1, so we define the corpus size as the number of all lexical token counts according to Equation 3.

$$cs = \sum_x c(x) \qquad (3)$$

To use the probabilities as weights in the lexicon we implement them in the tropical semi-ring, which means that we use the negative log-probabilities as defined by Equation 4.

$$w(a) = -\log(p(a)) \qquad (4)$$

For an illustration of how the weighting scheme is implemented in the lexicon, see Figure 2.

According to Karlsson (1992) and Schiller (2005), we may need to ensure that the weight of the compound segmentation *ab* of a word always is greater than the weight of a non-compound analysis *c* of the same word, so for compounds we use Equation 5, where a is the first part of the compound and x is the remaining part, which may be split into additional parts applying the equation recursively.

$$w(ax) = w(a) + M + w(x) \qquad (5)$$

```
LEXICON Root
## CompoundNonFinalNoun ;
## CompoundFinalNoun ;

LEXICON Compound
0:# CompoudNonFinalNoun "weight: 0" ;
0:# CompoudFinalNoun "weight: 0" ;

LEXICON CompoundNonFinalNoun
isä    Compound  "weight: -log(c(isä)/cs)" ;
isän   Compound  "weight: -log(c(isän)/cs)" ;
äiti   Compound  "weight: -log(c(äiti)/cs)" ;
äidin Compound  "weight: -log(c(äidin)/cs)" ;

LEXICON CompoundFinalNoun
isä:isä+sg+nom      ## "weight:-log(c(isä+sg+nom)/cs)" ;
isän:isä+sg+gen     ## "weight:-log(c(isä+sg+gen)/cs)" ;
isälle:isä+sg+all   ## "weight:-log(c(isä+sg+all)/cs)" ;
isin:isä+pl+ins     ## "weight:-log(c(isä+sg+all)/cs)" ;

LEXICON ##
## # ;
```

Figure 2: Structure weighting scheme using token penalties.

In particular, it is true that $w(ab) > w(c)$ if M is defined as in Equation 6.

$$M = -\log(1/(cs+1)) \qquad (6)$$

For an illustration of how a structure weighting scheme with compound penalties is implemented in the lexicon, see Figure 3.

```
LEXICON Root
## CompoundNonFinalNoun ;
## CompoundFinalNoun ;

LEXICON Compound
0:# CompoundNonFinalNoun "weight: -log(1/(cs+1))" ;
0:# CompoundFinalNoun "weight: -log(1/(cs+1))" ;

LEXICON CompoundNonFinalNoun
isä    Compound  "weight: -log(c(isä)/cs)" ;
isän   Compound  "weight: -log(c(isän)/cs)" ;
äiti   Compound  "weight: -log(c(äiti)/cs)" ;
äidin Compound  "weight: -log(c(äidin)/cs)" ;

LEXICON CompoundFinalNoun
isä:isä+sg+nom      ## "weight:-log(c(isä+sg+nom)/cs)" ;
isän:isä+sg+gen     ## "weight:-log(c(isä+sg+gen)/cs)" ;
isälle:isä+sg+all   ## "weight:-log(c(isä+sg+all)/cs)" ;
isin:isä+pl+ins     ## "weight:-log(c(isä+sg+all)/cs)" ;

LEXICON ##
## # ;
```

Figure 3: Structure weighting scheme using token and compound border penalties.

In order to compare with the original principle suggested by Karlsson (1992), we create a third lexicon for which structural weights are placed on the compound borders only, so for compounds we use Equation 7.

$$w(ax) = M + w(x) \qquad (7)$$

For an illustration of how a weighting scheme with the compound penalty suggested by Karlsson is implemented in the lexicon, see Figure 4.

```
LEXICON Root
## CompoundNonFinalNoun ;
## CompoundFinalNoun ;

LEXICON Compound
0:# CompoundNonFinalNoun "weight: -log(1/(cs+1))" ;
0:# CompoundFinalNoun "weight: -log(1/(cs+1))" ;

LEXICON CompoundNonFinalNoun
isä    Compound  "weight: 0" ;
isän   Compound  "weight: 0" ;
äiti   Compound  "weight: 0" ;
äidin Compound  "weight: 0" ;

LEXICON CompoundFinalNoun
isä:isä+sg+nom      ## "weight:-log(c(isä+sg+nom)/cs)" ;
isän:isä+sg+gen     ## "weight:-log(c(isä+sg+gen)/cs)" ;
isälle:isä+sg+all   ## "weight:-log(c(isä+sg+all)/cs)" ;
isin:isä+pl+ins     ## "weight:-log(c(isä+sg+all)/cs)" ;

LEXICON ##
## # ;
```

Figure 4: Structure weighting scheme using compound border penalties.

5 Training and Test Data

For training and testing purposes, we use a compilation of three years, 1995-1997, of daily issues of Helsingin Sanomat, which is the most wide-spread Finnish newspaper. The data actually spanned 2.5 years with 1995 and 1996 of equal size and 1997 only half of this. This collection contained approximately 2.4 million different words, i.e. types. We disambiguated the corpus using Machinese for Finnish[2] which provided

____
[2]Machinese is available from Connexor Ltd., www.connexor.com

one reading in context for each word based on syntactic parsing.

To create the test material from the corpus, we selected all word forms with more than 20 characters for which our baseline analyzer (Pirinen, 2008) gave a compound analysis, i.e. 53 270 types. The compounds were evenly distributed among the three years of data. Of these, we selected the types which had a structural ambiguity and found 4 721 such words, i.e. approximately 8.9 % of all the compound words analyzed by our baseline analyzer. Of the remaining more than 20-character compounds 63.7 % contained no ambiguities or only inflectional ambiguities. At most, the combination of structural and inflectional ambiguities amounted to 30 readings in three different words which after all is a fairly moderate number. On the average, the structural and inflectional ambiguity amounts to 2.79 readings per word. Examples of structurally ambiguous words are *aktivointimahdollisuuksien* with the ambiguity *aktivointi#mahdollisuus* 'of the opportunities to activate' vs. *akti#vointi#mahdollisuus* 'of the opportunities to act health' and *hiihtoharjoittelupaikassa* with the ambiguity *hiihto#harjoittelu#paikka* 'in the ski training location' vs. *hiihto#harjoittelu#pai#kassa* 'ski training pie cashier'.

The characteristics of all the compounds in the corpus is presented in Table 1.

# of Characters			# of Segments		
Min.	Max.	Avg.	Min.	Max.	Avg.
2	44	15.34	2	6	2.19

Table 1: Evaluation of compounds, segments and readings.

Examples of six-part compounds are:

- *elo#kuva#teatteri#tuki#työ#ryhmä*
  'movie theater support workgroup'

- *jatko#koulutus#yhteis#työ#toimi#kunta*
  'higher education cooperation committee'

- *lähi#alue#yhteis#työ#määrä#raha*
  'regional cooperation reserve'

The longest compound found in the corpus is *liikenne#turvallisuus#asiain#neuvottelu#kunnassa* 'in the road safety issue negotiating committee'

6   Tests and Results

We estimated the probabilities for the non-compound words in the 1995 part of the corpus. We then repeated the experiment and estimated the probabilities on the non-compound words of the 1996 part of the corpus. Since we do not use the compounds for training we can test on the compounds of all three years.

We evaluated the weighting schemes described in Section 4, i.e. the probabilistic method without compound boundary weighting, the probabilistic method combined with compound weighting and the traditional pure compound weighting. The precision and recall is presented in Table 2. Since we only took the first of the best results, the precision is equal to recall.

In both tests, we found the exact same result, i.e. there were two words out of 4721 structurally ambiguous words that failed when we used the compound weighting only. These were *puunostopolitiikkaansa* which had the structural ambiguities *puun#osto#politiikkaansa* 'timber purchasing policy' vs *puu#nosto#politiikkaansa* 'timber lifting policy' and *vuorotteluvapaalaisille* with the structural ambiguity *vuorottelu#vapaa#laisille* 'for persons on exchange sabbatical' vs. *vuorottelu#vapa#alaisille*[3] 'for exchange rod subjugates'.

We found no word that could be said to have a structural misinterpretation due to the estimated probabilities, but we found some words that were interpreted differently by the statistics from the two years, e.g. *laihdutuskuurilaisilla* with the ambiguity *laihdutus#kuurilaisilla* 'diet # program participants' vs. *laihdutuskuuri#laisilla* 'diet program # participants' and e.g. *avaruuslentotukikohta* with the ambiguity *avaruus#lentotukikohta* 'space # flight base' vs. *avaruuslento#tukikohta* 'space flight # base'.

Parameters	Prec. & Rec.
Only compound penalty	99.96 %
Compound penalty and prefix weights	100.00 %
No compound penalty but prefix weights	100.00 %

Table 2: Precision equals recall for the test results when we use only the first result.

---

[3]Strictly speaking this particular error is possible only because we did not enforce the Finnish orthography rule that the same vowel on both sides of the compound border requires a hyphen in-between.

We started with 53 270 compounds. With the probabilistic approach, we were hard pressed to find even some structural misinterpretations. With the word boundary penalty, we found two structural errors in the compound disambiguation.

7 Implementation Note

In HFST-LEXC, we use OpenFST (Allauzen et al., 2007) as the underlying finite-state software library for handling weighted finite-state transducers. The estimated probabilities are encoded as weights in the tropical semi-ring, see (Mohri, 1997). To extract the n-best results, we use a single-source n-best paths algorithm, see (Mohri and Riley, 2002).

8 Discussion and Further Research

Previous results for structural compound disambiguation for German using word probabilities and compound penalties (Schiller, 2005) or using only word probabilities (Marek, 2006) also achieved results with precision and recall in the region of 97-99 %. In German the ambiguities of long compounds may produce even 120 readings, but on the average the ambiguity in compounds is between 2-3 readings (Schiller, 2005), which is on par with the ambiguity of 2.8 readings found for long Finnish compounds. As pointed out initially (Hedlund, 2002), the amount of compounds occurring in Finnish, Swedish and German texts is also on a comparable level.

For some words the compound form has a linking element or a glue element. In Swedish, as pointed out by Karlsson (1992), the linking element is sometimes a structure indicator, e.g. the "-s-" in "[peppar#kak]s#burk" (ginger-bread jar) indicates a bracketing which is different if the "-s-" is missing as in "peppar#[kak#burk]" (pepper # cookie jar). However, in German the linking elements most often coincide with inflected forms (Fuhrhop, 1996), in which case they are called paradigmatic linking elements. The only exceptional or non-paradigmatic linking element in German is "-s-" for words ending in "-ung, -heit, -keit" and "-ion", in which case it is also mandatory, so the fact that it does not appear as an inflected form of non-compounds in a corpus is a non-issue from a probabilistic point of view. In this case, it is sufficient to estimate the frequency of the form without an "-s-". Finnish only has one systematic non-paradigmatic linking element,

i.e. the linking element for nouns and adjectives ending in "-nen" which is "-s-" in compounds, e.g. "yhteinen" (common) becomes "yhteis-" in compounds. In addition, a handful of words have exceptional forms, e.g. "suuri" (big) may also be "suur-" when used as a compound prefix. All other linking elements are paradigmatic, i.e. the compound prefixes coincide with inflected forms.

As the astute reader may have noticed, Equation 5 gives us a non-tight distribution for the complete set of words generated by the lexicon, although the distribution we estimate is tight for non-compounds. The consequence of this is that we cannot claim that the weights we derive for compounds correspond to the true probabilities of the productively formed compounds. What they do reflect, however, is whether the parts are more likely than surprise to form a productive compound from the parts observed in a corpus or whether the word is more likely to be an attested non-compound. E.g. the Swedish word "bollfot" (ball foot) is more likely to be formed by productive compounding from the parts "boll" (ball) and "fot" (foot) than to be observed as a single token, whereas the Swedish word "fotboll" (football) is more likely to be one token in the corpus than a productive compound. In English, this phenomenon is reflected in the orthography with some delay by tending to write very frequent or lexicalized compounds without intervening spaces.

If a disambiguated corpus is not available for calculating the word analysis probabilities, it is possible to use only the string token probabilities to disambiguate the compound structure without saying anything about the most likely morphological reading.

In Finnish, using only the structural penalties may also be an acceptable replacement. However, we need to note that a similar strategy in German, i.e. using only compound penalties on all compound prefixes, did not seem to perform as well (Schiller, 2005). This may be due to the fact that German contains a high number of very short one-syllable words which interfere with the compounding, whereas Finnish is more restricted in the number of short words.

Scandinavian languages are similar to German in that they have a number of short one-syllable nouns. Several different approaches for Swedish compound disambiguation are demonstrated in

(Sjöbergh and Kann, 2004). They show results of 86 % accuracy of compound segmenting when using compound component frequencies estimated from compounds and 90 % when using the number of compound components. However, they do not try a fully probabilistic approach and they do not try to estimate probabilities or any other weights for prefixes from non-compound words. So it is a question for further research whether a purely probabilistic approach could fare as well for Swedish and other Scandinavian languages as it seems to work for Finnish and German.

9 Conclusions

For Finnish, weighting compound complexity gives excellent results around 99.9 % almost regardless of the approach. However, from a theoretical point of view, we can still verify the two hypotheses we postulated initially. Most importantly, there seems to be no need to extract the counts from lists of disambiguated compounds, i.e., it is quite feasible to use general word occurrence probabilities for structurally disambiguating compounds. In addition, we can also corroborate the observation that when using word probabilities, it is possible to forego a specific structural penalty and rely only on the word probabilities. From a practical point of view, we introduced the open source tool, HFST-LEXC, and demonstrated how it can be successfully used to encode various compound weighting schemes.

Acknowledgments

This research was funded by the Finnish Academy and the Finnish Ministry of Education. We are also grateful to the HFST–Helsinki Finite State Technology research team and to the anonymous reviewers for various improvements of the manuscript.

References

Cyril Allauzen, Michael Riley, Johan Schalkwyk, Wojciech Skut, and Mehryar Mohri. 2007. OpenFst: A general and efficient weighted finite-state transducer library. In *Proceedings of the Ninth International Conference on Implementation and Application of Automata, (CIAA 2007)*, volume 4783 of *Lecture Notes in Computer Science*, pages 11–23. Springer. http://www.openfst.org.

Kenneth R. Beesley and Lauri Karttunen. 2003. *Finite State Morphology*. CSLI Publications. http://www.fsmbook.com.

Nanna Fuhrhop, 1996. *Deutsch - typologisch*, chapter Fugenelemente. de Gruyter, Berlin/New York.

Auli Hakulinen, Maria Vilkuna, Riitta Korhonen, Vesa Koivisto, Tarja Riitta Heinonen, and Irja Alho. 2008. *Iso suomen kielioppi*. Suomalaisen Kirjallisuuden Seura. refered on 31.12.2008, available from http://scripta.kotus.fi/visk.

Turid Hedlund. 2002. Compounds in dictionary-based cross-language information retrieval. *Information Research*, 7(2). http://InformationR.net/ir/7-2/paper128.html.

Fred Karlsson. 1992. Swetwol: A comprehensive morphological analyzer for swedish. *Nordic Journal of Linguistics*, 15(2):1–45.

André Kempe, Christof Baeijs, Tamás Gaál, Franck Guingne, and Florent Nicart. 2003. Wfsc - a new weighted finite state compiler. In *Proceedings of CIAA'03*, volume 2759 of *Lecture Notes in Computer Science*, pages 108–120. Springer.

Torsten Marek. 2006. Analysis of german compounds using weighted finite state transducers. Technical report, Eberhard-Karls-Universität Tübingen.

Mehryar Mohri and Michael Riley. 2002. An efficient algorithm for the n-best-strings problem. In *Proceedings of the International Conference on Spoken Language Processing 2002 (ICSLP '02)*.

Mehryar Mohri. 1997. Finite-state transducers in language and speech processing. *Computational Linguistics*, 23(2).

Tommi Pirinen. 2008. Suomen kielen äärellistilainen automaattinen morfologinen analyysi avoimen lähdekoodin keinoin. Master's thesis, Helsingin yliopisto.

Research Institute for the Languages of Finland. 2007. Kotimaisten kielten tutkimuskeskuksen nykysuomen sanalista. http://kaino.kotus.fi/sanat/nykysuomi/.

Anne Schiller. 2005. German compound analysis with *wfsc*. In *FSMNLP*, pages 239–246.

Jonas Sjöbergh and Viggo Kann. 2004. Finding the correct interpretation of Swedish compounds a statistical approach. In *Proceedings of LREC-2004*, pages 899–902, Lisbon, Portugal. http://dr-hato.se/research/sjobergh_kann_04.ps.

ISSN 1736-6305 Vol. 4
http://hdl.handle.net/10062/9206

Corpus-based Paradigm Selection
for Morphological Entries

Krister Lindén
University of Helsinki
Helsinki, Finland
Krister.Linden@helsinki.fi

Jussi Tuovila
University of Helsinki
Helsinki, Finland
Jussi.Tuovila@helsinki.fi

Abstract

Language software applications encounter new words, e.g., acronyms, technical terminology, loan words, names or compounds of such words. To add new words to a lexicon, we need to indicate their inflectional paradigm. In this article, we evaluate a lexicon-based method augmented with data from a corpus or the internet for selecting the inflectional paradigm of new words in Finnish. As an entry generator often produces numerous suggestions, it is important that the best suggestions be among the first few, otherwise it may become more efficient to create the entries by hand. By generating paradigm suggestions with an entry guesser and then further generating key word forms for the suggested paradigms, we were able to find support for the paradigms in a corpus. Our method has 79-83 % precision and 86-88 % recall, i.e. an F-score of 83-86 %, i.e. the first correctly generated entry is on the average found as the first or the second candidate.

1 Introduction

New words are constantly finding their way into daily language use. This is particularly prominent in rapidly developing domains such as biomedicine and technology. The new words are typically acronyms, technical terminology, loan words, names or compounds of such words. They are likely to be unknown by most hand-made morphological analyzers. In many applications, hand-made guessers are used for covering the low-frequency vocabulary or the strings are simply added as such.

Mikheev (1996, 1997) pointed out that words unknown to the lexicon present a substantial problem for part-of-speech tagging, and he presented a very effective supervised method for inducing English guessers from a lexicon and an independent training corpus. Oflazer & al. (2001) presented an interactive method for learning morphologies and pointed out that an important issue in the wholesale acquisition of open-class items is that of determining which paradigm a given citation form belongs to.

Recently, unsupervised acquisition of morphologies from scratch has been studied as a general problem of morphology induction in order to automate the morphology building procedure. For overviews, see Wicentowski (2002) and Goldsmith (2007). If we do not need a full analysis, but only wish to segment the words into morph-like units, we can use segmentation methods like Morfessor (Creutz & al., 2007). For a comparison of some recent successful segmentation methods, see the Morpho Challenge (Kurimo & al., 2007).

Although unsupervised methods have some advantages for less-studied languages, for the well-established languages, we have access to fair amounts of lexical training material in the form of analyses in the context of more frequent words. Especially for Germanic and Fenno-Ugric languages, there are already large-vocabulary descriptions available and new words tend to be compounds of acronyms and loan words with existing words. In English, compound words are written separately or the junction is indicated with a hyphen, but in other Germanic languages and in the Fenno-Ugric languages, there is usually no word boundary indicator within the compounds. It has previously been demonstrated by Lindén (2008) that already training sets as small as 5000 inflected word forms and their manually determined base forms will give a reasonable result for guessing base forms of new words by analogy, which was tested on a set of languages from different language families, i.e. English, Finnish, Swedish and Swahili.

In addition, there are a host of large but shallow hand-made morphological descriptions available, e.g., the Ispell collection of dictionaries (Kuenning, 2007) for spell-checking purposes, and many well-documented morphological analyzers are commercially available, e.g. Lingsoft[1]. It has also been demonstrated by Lindén (2009) that there is a simple but efficient way to derive an entry generator from a full-scale morphological analyzer implemented as a finite-state transducer. Such an entry generator can be used as a baseline for more advanced entry guessing methods.

In this work, we propose and evaluate a new method for *selecting the inflectional paradigm for an inflected word form* of a new word by generating paradigm suggestions with an entry generator and then further generating key words forms for the suggested paradigms in order to *find support for the paradigms in a corpus*. In Section 2, we outline the directly related previous work. In Section 3, we describe the new method. In Section 4, we present the training and test data. In Section 5, we evaluate the model. In Section 6, we discuss the method and the test results in light of the existing literature and some similar methods.

2 Lexicon-based Entry Generator

To create entries for a morphological analyzer from previously unseen words, we need an entry generator. Ideally, we can use information that is already available in some existing morphological description to encode new entries in a similar fashion. Below, we briefly outline a general method for creating lexicon-based entry generators that was introduced by Lindén (2009). In his article, Lindén demonstrates that the method works well for English, Finnish and Swedish.

Assume that we have a finite-state transducer lexicon T which relates base forms, $b(w)$, to inflected words, w. Let w belong to the input language L_I and $b(w)$ to the output language L_O of the transducer lexicon T. Our goal is to create an entry generator for inflected words that are unknown to the lexicon, i.e. we wish to provide the most likely base forms $b(u)$ for an unknown input word $u \notin L_I$. In order to create an entry generator, we first define the left quotient and the weighted universal language with regard to a lexical transducer. For a general introduction

to automata theory and weighted transducers, see e.g. Sakarovitch (2003).

If L_1 and L_2 are formal languages, the left quotient of L_1 with regard to L_2 is the language consisting of strings w such that xw is in L_1 for some string x in L_2. Formally, we write the left quotient as in Equation 1.

$$L_1 \setminus L_2 = \{ a \mid \exists x ((x \in L_2) \wedge (xa \in L_1)) \} \qquad (1)$$

We can regard the left quotient as the set of postfixes that complete words from L_2, such that the resulting word is in L_1.

If L is a formal language with alphabet Σ, a universal language, U, is a language consisting of strings in Σ^*. The weighted universal language, W, is a language consisting of strings in Σ^* with weights $p(w)$ assigned to each string. For our purposes, we define the weight $p(w)$ to be proportional to the length of w. We define a weighted universal language as in Equation 2.

$$W = \{ w \mid \exists w (w \in \Sigma) \} \qquad (2)$$

with weights $p(w) = C \mid w \mid$, where C is a constant.

A finite-state transducer lexicon, T, is a formal language relating the input language L_I to the output language L_O. The pair alphabet of T is the set of input and output symbol pairs related by T. An identity pair relates a symbol to itself.

We create an entry generator, G, for the lexicon T by constructing the weighted universal language W for identity pairs based on the alphabet of L_1 concatenating it with the left quotient of T with regard to the universal language U of the pair alphabet of T as shown in Equation 3.

$$G(T) = W \, T \setminus U \qquad (3)$$

Lindén (2009) proves that it is always possible to create an entry generator, $G(T) = W \, T \setminus U$, from a weighted lexical transducer T.

The model is general and requires no information in addition to the lexicon from which the entry generator is derived. Therefore Lindén suggests that it be used as a baseline for other entry generator methods.

3 Corpus-based Paradigm Selection

To score the top paradigms suggested by an entry generator, we generate some of the key word forms of a paradigm and compare them against a corpus. A paradigm whose key word forms are well-attested, i.e. used many times, is more likely to be correct than a paradigm whose word forms only have a few documented cases. Rare forms may even be spelling errors. By scoring all the paradigms provided by the paradigm guesser according to the frequency of the word forms and then comparing the scores, we find the paradigm that is most likely to be correct.

We define a method for scoring possible paradigms of an unknown word. Let us define a set of paradigms of an unknown word $U_p = \{P_1, P_2, P_3, ... P_n\}$. Each paradigm P_n has a set that consists of the paradigm's key words, $W_n = \{w_1, w_2, w_3, ... w_m\}$. A distinct word form w_K may simultaneously belong to the key word sets of several paradigms.

Each distinct word form w_K has a number of occurrences $o_c(w_K)$ in the corpus. If a key word belongs to the key word sets of more than one paradigm, the key word does not differentiate well between those paradigms. Therefore each key word w_m only receives a score o_{w_m} equal to the number of occurrences $o_c(w_K)$ in the corpus divided by the number $o_p(w_m)$ of key words w_m matching w_K in the set of paradigms U_P. The score of a key word is defined in Equation 4.

$$o_{w_m} = \frac{o_c(w_K)}{o_p(w_m)}, \quad w_K = w_m \quad (4)$$

We add the scores, o_w, of the key words in a paradigm and divide the sum by the number, $|W_p|$ of key words in the paradigm. The score of a paradigm is defined in Equation 5:

$$Score_{P_n} = \frac{\sum O_w}{|W_p|}, w \in W_n \quad (5)$$

A key word form can have several variants, e.g. the genitive plural of Finnish nouns may have up to three different variants for each word in a paradigm. The variants all represent a single word form, i.e. genitive plural. We select the largest variant score to represent the score of the word form.

The method orders the suggestions from the entry generator. If the method does not differentiate between two suggestions, the order proposed by the generator prevails.

The method can be used with any data that reflects the occurrence of the paradigm key words. Although we refer to the source of word frequency data as a corpus, the method can be used with other data sources as well. As is described in section 5, we have successfully tested the method using both corpus material and page frequencies returned by a web search engine. In theory, the method should work with any data source that reflects the occurrence of words in language use.

4　　Training and Test Data

To test our method for corpus-based paradigm selection of paradigms generated by a lexical entry generator, we used the entry generator for Finnish created by Lindén (2009) implemented with the *Helsinki Finite-State Technology* (HFST, 2008). In 4.1, we briefly describe the lexical resources used for the finite-state transducer lexicon which was subsequently converted into an entry generator.

Words unknown to the lexicon were drawn from a language-specific text collection. The correct entries for a sample of the unknown words were manually determined. In 4.2, we describe the text collections and the sample used as test data. In 4.3, we describe the evaluation method and characterize the baseline.

4.1　　Lexical Data for a Finnish Finite-State Transducer Lexicon and Entry Generator

Lexical descriptions relate look-up words to other words and indicate the relation between them. A morphological finite-state transducer lexicon relates a word in dictionary form to all its inflected forms. For an introduction, see e.g. Koskenniemi (1983).

Our current Finnish morphological analyzer was created by Pirinen (2008) based on the Finnish word list *Kotimaisten kielten tutkimuskeskuksen nykysuomen sanalista* (2007), which contains 94 110 words in base form. Of these, approximately 43 000 are non-compound base forms classified with paradigm information. The word list consists of words in citation form annotated with paradigm and gradation pattern. There are 78 paradigms and 13 gradation patterns. For example, the entry for käsi (= 'hand') is 'käsi 27' referring to paradigm 27 without gradation, whereas the word pato (= 'dam') is given as 'pato 1F' indicating paradigm 1 with gradation pattern F. From this description a lexical transducer is compiled with a cascade of finite-state operations. For nominal paradigms, i.e. nouns and adjectives, inflection includes case inflection, possessive suffixes and clitics creating more than 2 000 word forms for each nominal. For the verbal inflection, all tenses, moods and personal forms are counted as inflections, as well as all infinitives and participles and their corresponding nominal forms creating more than 10 000 forms for each verb. In addition, the Finnish lexical transducer also covers nominal compounding.

This finite-state transducer lexicon was converted into an entry generator using the procedure outlined in Section 2

4.2 Test Data

As test data, we use the *Finnish Text Collection,* which is an electronic document collection of the Finnish language. It consists of 180 million running text tokens. The corpus contains news texts from several current Finnish newspapers. It also contains extracts from a number of books containing prose text, including fiction, education and sciences. Gatherers are the Department of General Linguistics, University of Helsinki; The University of Joensuu; and CSC–Scientific Computing Ltd. The corpus is available through CSC [www.csc.fi].

We use the same test data as Lindén (2009), which is a set of previously unseen words in inflected form for which we wish to determine the inflectional paradigm. In order to extract word forms that represent relatively infrequent and previously unseen words, 5000 word and base form pairs had been drawn at random from the frequency rank 100 001-300 000. To get new words, only inflected forms that were not recognized by the lexical transducer were kept. However, from the test data, strings containing numbers, punctuation characters, or only upper case characters were also removed, as such strings require other forms of preprocessing as well in addition to some limited morphological analysis.

1. **ulkoasu**   *1 noun*   (appearance)
   ulkoasu ulkoasun ulkoasua ulkoasuun
   ulkoasut ulkoasujen ulkoasuja ulkoasuihin
2. **ulkoasu**   *2 noun*   (appearance)
   ulkoasu ulkoasun ulkoasua ulkoasuun ulkoasut
   ulkoasujen~ulkoasuitten~ulkoasuiden
   ulkoasuja~ulkoasuita ulkoasuihin
3. **ulkoasullata**   *73 I verb*   (to stuff sth from the outside)
   ulkoasullata ulkoasultaan ulkoasultasi
   ulkoasultaisi ulkoasullannee ulkoasullatkoon
   ulkoasullannut ulkoasullattiin
4. **ulkoasu**   *21 noun*   (appearance)
   ulkoasu ulkoasun ulkoasuta ulkoasuhun
   ulkoasut ulkoasuiden ulkoasuita ulkoasuihin

Picture 1. Word form *ulkoasultaan* (= by its appearance) and the combinations of **base form**, *paradigm information*, (English gloss added for readability of this picture only) and *key word forms* to be selected from.

Of the randomly selected strings, 1715 represented words not previously seen by the lexical

transducer. For these strings, correct entries were created manually. Of these, only 48 strings had a verb form reading. The rest were noun or adjective readings. Only 43 had more than one possible reading.

A sample of test strings are: *ulkoasultaan* (by its appearance), *euromaan* (of the euroland), *työvoimapolitiikka* (labour market policy), *pariskunnasta* (from the couple), *vastalausemyrskyn* (of the protest storm), *ruuanlaiton* (of the cookery), *valtaannousun* (of the rise to power), *suurtapahtumaan* (for the major event), …

In Picture 1, we see an example of the word form *ulkoasultaan* and the suggested paradigms as they have been generated by the entry generator and expanded with key word forms in order for an evaluator to determine the correct paradigm for the morphological entry.

4.3 Evaluation Measures, Baselines and Significance Test

We report our test results using recall and average precision at maximum recall. *Recall* means all the inflected word forms in the test data for which an accurate base form suggestion is produced. *Average precision at maximum recall* is an indicator of the amount of noise that precedes the intended paradigm suggestions, where n incorrect suggestions before the m correct ones give a precision of $1/(n+m)$, i.e., no noise before a single intended base form per word form gives 100 % precision on average, and no correct suggestion at maximum recall gives 0 % precision. The *F-score* is the harmonic mean of the recall and the average precision.

The random baseline for Finnish is that the correct entry is one out of 78 paradigms with one out of 13 gradations, i.e. a random correct guess would on the average end up as guess number 507.

As suggested by Lindén (2009), we use the automatically derived entry generator from Section 4.1 as a baseline. Using his test data, the test results will be directly comparable to the baseline provided in Table 1 with recall 82 %, average precision 76 % and the F-score 79 %.

The significance of the difference between the baselines and the tested methods is tested with matched pairs. The Wilcoxon Matched-Pairs Signed-Ranks Test indicates whether the changes in the ranking differences are statistically significant. For large numbers the test is almost as sensitive as the Matched-Pairs Student t-test even if it does not assume a normal distribution of the ranking differences.

Rank	Freq	Percentage
#1	1140	66,5 %
#2	186	10,8 %
#3	64	3,7 %
#4	17	1,0 %
#5	4	0,2 %
#6	2	0,1 %
#7-∞	302	17,6 %
Total	1715	100,0 %

Table 1. Baseline for Finnish entry generator.

5 Evaluation

We test how well the entry selection procedure outlined in Section 3 is able to select the correct paradigm for an inflected word form using the test data described in Section 4.2. Word forms representing previously unseen words were used as test data in the experiment. The generated entries are intended for human post-processing, so the first correct entry suggestion should be among the top 6 candidates, otherwise the ranking is considered a failure. In 5.1, we test the paradigm selection procedure against a Finnish text corpus. In 5.2, we also test the paradigm selection procedure using page counts from the internet.

5.1 Corpus-based Paradigm Ranking

We evaluate the paradigm selection method on paradigms generated by the lexicon-based entry generator against the *Finnish Text Collection* described in Section 4.2.

Rank	Freq	Percentage
#1	1316	76,7 %
#2	110	6,4 %
#3	34	2,0 %
#4	25	1,5 %
#5	11	0,6 %
#6	9	0,5 %
#7-∞	210	12,2 %
Total	1715	100,0 %

Table 2. Ranks of all the first correct entries by the Finnish entry generator when ranking suggestions against the *Finnish Text Collection*.

The Finnish entry generator generated a correct entry among the top 6 candidates for 88 % of the test data as shown in Table 2, which corresponds to an average position of 1.9 for the first correct entry with 88 % recall and 83 % average precision, i.e. an 86 % F-score.

5.2 Page Count-based Paradigm Ranking

We also evaluate the paradigm selection method on paradigms generated by the lexicon-based entry generator against the Word-Wide Web using page counts for pages retrieved over a period of some weeks from Google for key words of the paradigms. We retrieved the data from pages which Google gave a Finnish language code. We used this as way to verify the method on an independent corpus.

Rank	Freq	Percentage
#1	1229	71,7 %
#2	115	6,7 %
#3	77	4,5 %
#4	28	1,6 %
#5	18	1,0 %
#6	11	0,6 %
#7-∞	231	13,5 %
Total	1715	100,0 %

Table 3. Ranks of all the first correct entries by the Finnish entry generator when ranking suggestions against the World-Wide Web.

The Finnish entry generator generated a correct entry among the top 6 candidates for 86 % of the test data as shown in Table 3, which corresponds to an average position of 2.1 for the first correct entry with 86 % recall and 79 % average precision, i.e. an 83 % F-score.

5.3 Significance

The selection of the paradigms from the morphological entry generator was statistically highly significantly better than the lexical baseline according to the Wilcoxon Matched-Pairs Signed-Ranks Test. The difference between the corpus and the internet might be statistically significant, but has no real practical implications. The improvement in the F-score of 4-8 percentage points from the baseline model in two separate test settings is significant in practice.

6 Discussion

In this section, we discuss the results and give a brief overview of some related work. In 6.1, we compare test results with previous efforts. In 6.2, we discuss future work.

6.1 Discussion of Results

The problem when dealing with relatively low-frequency words is that an approach to generate additional word forms for their paradigms may not contribute much. It might well be that the word we are looking at is the only instance in the corpus. In that sense, turning to the internet for help seems like a good idea. It is interesting but not surprising to note that a relatively clean corpus still provides a slightly better basis for ranking word paradigms than the Internet. The most plausible explanation for this would be a larger amount of misspelled word forms which reduces the distinctions between paradigm suggestions, an effect that was observed during the evaluation.

Sometimes the misspelling was more common than the correctly spelled word. E.g., the sixth highest scoring word in our material was "seuraavä", with approx. 21 000 000 page counts, while its correctly spelled form, "seuraava", had almost 500 000 page counts less. This was in most cases corrected by a higher average frequency of the remaining word forms in the correct paradigm. Sometimes the incorrect paradigms happened to contain a homonym of some frequently occurring words, which raised the score of the paradigm above that of the correct paradigm candidate.

It is significant to note that our experiment demonstrates that the ranking can be performed using page counts instead of word counts with a sufficiently large corpus, which is by no means self-evident. Essentially page counts mean that we use the semantic context of a word. Many of the inflected forms will refer to the same pages, which also opens up avenues for future research. One could perhaps check how many pages contain the base form in addition to some inflected form of a paradigm in order to reduce the noise.

The fact that as a source of data, the corpus data fared slightly better than the internet may in our case also be attributable to the fact that Finnish word forms in the frequency range 100 000-300 000 may not be so rare after all due to the rich morphology and productive compounding mechanism of Finnish.

From a practical point of view, we are able to significantly reduce the workload of encoding lexical entries as most of the task can be accomplished automatically. However, a significant change is that assigning paradigms to words, which previously required an expert lexicographer, can now be accomplished by a native speaker making a choice, in practice, between the first two or at most three suggestions from the computer.[2]

---

[2] http://www.ling.helsinki.fi/cgi-bin/omor/omorfi-cgi-demo.py

6.2 Comparison with similar or related efforts

A related idea of expanding key word forms of paradigms to identify new words and their paradigms has been suggested by Hammarström & al (2006). However, their approach was to automatically deduce rules for which they could find as much support as was logically possible in order to make a safe inference. This leads to safely extracting words that already have a number of word forms in the corpus, i.e. mid- or high-frequency words, which for all practical purposes have already been encoded and are readily available in public domain morphological descriptions like the Ispell dictionaries (Kuenning, 2007) or more advanced descriptions like the Finnish dictionary *Kotimaisten kielten tutkimuskeskuksen nykysuomen sanalista* (2007). It should be noted that Hammarström & al (2006) came to the conclusion that it is recommendable that a linguist writes the extraction rules.

The approach suggested by Mikheev (1996, 1997) aims at solving the issue of unknown words in the context of part-of-speech taggers. However, in this context the problem is slightly easier as the guesser only needs to identify a likely part of speech and not the full inflectional paradigm of a word. He suggests an automatic way of extracting prefix and postfix patterns for guessing the part of speech. A related approach aiming at inducing paradigms for words and inflectional morphologies for 30 different languages is suggested by Wicentowski (2002).

Since there is a growing body of translated text even for less studied languages, there are interesting approaches using multi-lingual evidence for inducing morphologies, see e.g. Yarowski and Wicentowski (2000). This approach is particularly fruitful if we can use relations between closely related languages.

If we cannot find enough support for any particular paradigm of a word, e.g. if the word is too infrequent so that there are no other inflections, we need a way to make inferences based on related or similar strings. We need to make inferences based on the analogy with already known words as suggested e.g. by Goldsmith (2007) or Lindén (2008, 2009).

6.3 Future Work

The current approach only extracts inflectional information in the form of paradigms, even if the context of a new word also contributes other types of lexical information such as part of speech, argument structure and other more advanced types of syntactic and semantic information.

The Internet as a source of data also provides context for a search word, some of it specific to this particular data source. Our current approach does not yet take into account the nature of this source of data, such as an increased occurrence of misspellings, colloquial word forms and mixed-language content. Also, as the Internet is an ever-changing medium, any linguistic data derived form it is subject to constant change. The effect of this change to the reliability of evaluation needs to be further investigated.

7 Conclusions

We have proposed and successfully tested a new method for selecting paradigms generated for inflected forms of new words using additional corpus information for key forms of the paradigms suggested by en entry generator. We tested the model on Finnish, which is a highly inflecting language with a considerable set of inflectional paradigms and stem change categories. Our model achieved 79-83 % precision and 86-88 % recall, i.e. an F-score of 83-86 %. The average position for the first correctly generated entry was 1.9-2.1. The method was highly statistically significantly better than a non-trivial baseline and the improvement is also significant in practice.

Acknowledgments

We are grateful to the Finnish Academy and to the Finnish Ministry of Education for the funding and to the members of the HFST team at the University of Helsinki for fruitful discussions.

References

Creutz, M., Hirsimäki, T., Kurimo, M., Puurula, A., Pylkkönen, J., Siivola, V., Varjokallio, M., Arisoy, E., Saraçlar, M., Stolcke, A. 2007 Morph-based speech recognition and modeling of out-of-vocabulary words across languages. In *ACM Transactions on Speech and Language Processing*, 5(1) article 3.

Forsberg, M., Hammarström, H., and Ranta, A. 2006. Morphological Lexicon Extraction from Raw Text Data. *FinTAL 2006*, LNCS 4139, pages 488-499, 2006.

Goldsmith, J. A. 2007. Morphological Analogy: Only a Beginning, http://hum.uchicago.edu/ ~jagoldsm/ Papers/analogy.pdf

HFST–Helsinki Finite-State Technology. 2008. http://www.ling.helsinki.fi/kieliteknologia/ tutkimus/hfst/index.shtml

Koskenniemi, K.. 1983. Two-Level Morphology: A General Computational Model for Word-Form Recognition and Production. PhD Thesis. Department of General Linguistics, University of Helsinki, Publication No. 11.

Kotimaisten kielten tutkimuskeskuksen nykysuomen sanalista, 2007. Reseach Institute for the Languages of Finland. http://kaino.kotus.fi/sanat/ nykysuomi/

Kuenning, G. 2007 Dictionaries for International Ispell, http://www.lasr.cs.ucla.edu/geoff/ispell-dictionaries.html

Kurimo, M., Creutz, M., Turunen, V. 2007. Overview of Morpho Challenge in CLEF 2007. In *Working Notes of the CLEF 2007 Workshop*, pages 19-21.

Lindén, K. 2008. A Probabilistic Model for Guessing Base Forms of New Words by Analogy. In *9th International Conference on Intelligent Text Processing and Computational Linguistics*, Haifa, Israel, LNCS 4919, pages 106-116.

Lindén, K. 2009. Guessers for Finite-State Transducer Lexicons. In *CICling-2009, 10th International Conference on Intelligent Text Processing and Computational Linguistics*, March 1-7, 2009, Mexico City, Mexico.

Mikheev, A. 1997. Automatic Rule Induction for Unknown-Word Guessing. In *Computational Linguistics,*. 23(3), pages 405-423.

Mikheev, A. 1996. Unsupervised Learning of Word-Category Guessing Rules. In: *Proc. of the 34th Annual Meeting of the Association for Computational Linguistics (ACL-96)*, pages 327-334.

Oflazer, K., Nirenburg, S., McShane, M. 2001. Bootstrapping Morphological Analyzers by Combining Human Elicitation and Machine Learning. In *Computational Linguistics*, 27(1), pages 59-85.

Pirinen, T. 2008. Open Source Morphology for Finnish using Finite-State Methods (in Finnish). Technical Report. Department of Linguistics, University of Helsinki.

Sakarovitch, J. 2003. *Éléments de théorie des automates.* Vuibert

Wicentowski, R. 2002. Modeling and Learning Multilingual Inflectional Morphology in a Minimally Supervised Framework. PhD Thesis, Baltimore, USA.

Yarowsky, D. and Wicentowski. R. 2000. Minimally Supervised Morphological Analysis by Multimodal Alignment. In *Proceedings of the 38th Annual Meeting of the Association for Computational Linguistics*.

ISSN 1736-6305 Vol. 4
http://hdl.handle.net/10062/9206

Improving the PoS tagging accuracy of Icelandic text

Hrafn Loftsson   Ida Kramarczyk
School of Computer Science
Reykjavik University
Reykjavik, Iceland
{hrafn,ida07}@ru.is

Sigrún Helgadóttir
Árni Magnússon Institute
for Icelandic Studies
Reykjavik, Iceland
sigruhel@hi.is

Eiríkur Rögnvaldsson
Department of Icelandic
University of Iceland
Reykjavik, Iceland
eirikur@hi.is

Abstract

Previous work on part-of-speech (PoS) tagging Icelandic has shown that the morphological complexity of the language poses considerable difficulties for PoS taggers. In this paper, we increase the tagging accuracy of Icelandic text by using two methods. First, we present a new tagger, by integrating an HMM tagger into a linguistic rule-based tagger. Our tagger obtains state-of-the-art tagging accuracy of 92.31% using the standard test set derived from the IFD corpus, and 92.51% using a corrected version of the corpus. Second, we design an external tagset, by removing information from the internal tagset which reflects distinctions that are not morphologically based. Using the external tagset for evaluation, the tagging accuracy further increases to 93.63%.

1   Introduction

Icelandic is a morphologically complex language for which the task of part-of-speech (PoS) tagging has turned out to be difficult, both for data-driven and linguistic rule-based taggers (Helgadóttir, 2005; Loftsson, 2006; Loftsson, 2008; Dredze and Wallenberg, 2008). Before the work presented in this paper, the current state-of-the-art tagging accuracy was 92.06%, obtained using a bidirectional sequence classification method (Dredze and Wallenberg, 2008) and testing using the Icelandic Frequency Dictionary (IFD) corpus (Pind et al., 1991).

There are at least three reasons for this low accuracy – all of them are manifestations of the fact that the Icelandic language is morphologically complex. First, the large tagset used (about 700 tags) and the relatively small training corpus (about 590k tokens) causes data sparseness prob-

lems. Second, inherent long range tag dependencies in Icelandic text are difficult for many PoS tagging methods to resolve. Third, the tagset reflects distinctions which may be difficult to resolve at the level of PoS tagging, because some of them are not morphologically based.

The main material in this paper is threefold. First (in Section 2), we review previous tagging approaches for Icelandic and present a new tagger by integrating a Hidden Markov Model (HMM) tagger into a linguistic rule-based tagger in a novel way. Our tagger obtains an accuracy of 92.31%, which amounts to about a 3.2% error reduction rate compared to the previous best result. Furthermore, the accuracy increases to 92.51% when testing using a corrected version of the IFD corpus.

Second (in Section 3), we propose an external tagset (the tagset used for evaluation) by removing information from the internal tagset (the tagset used by a tagger) which reflects distinctions that are not morphologically based. These reductions should not affect the effectiveness of the tagset in practical applications. The tagging accuracy further increases to 93.63% using the external tagset.

Third (in Section 4), we discuss the results and provide directions for future work on tagging Icelandic.

2   Tagging Icelandic

In this section, we first describe the corpus used for training, developing and testing PoS taggers for Icelandic and the underlying tagset. Second, we review, in some detail, previous work on tagging Icelandic. Third, we describe our new tagging method, which results in a new state-of-the-art tagging accuracy. Finally, we evaluate our method using a corrected version of the original corpus.

2.1   The IFD corpus

All published tagging results hitherto for Icelandic have been based on the IFD corpus (Pind et al.,

1991). The IFD corpus is a balanced corpus, consisting of about 590k tokens. All 100 text fragments in the corpus were published for the first time in 1980–1989. The corpus comprises five categories of texts, i.e. Icelandic fiction, translated fiction, biographies and memoirs, non-fiction and books for children and youngsters. No two texts are attributed to the same person and all texts start and finish with a complete sentence. The corpus was semi-automatically tagged using a tagger based on linguistic rules and probabilities (Briem, 1989).

The main Icelandic tagset, constructed in the compilation of the IFD corpus, consists of about 700 possible tags, which is large compared to related languages. In this tagset, each character in a tag has a particular function. The first character denotes the *word class*. For each word class there is a predefined number of additional characters (at most six), which describe morphological features, like *gender*, *number* and *case* for nouns; *degree* and *declension* for adjectives; *voice*, *mood* and *tense* for verbs, etc. To illustrate, consider the word "*strákarnir*" ('(the) boys'). The corresponding tag is "nkfng", denoting noun (*n*), masculine (*k*), plural (*f*), nominative (*n*), and suffixed definite article (*g*).

2.2 Previous tagging results

The first tagging results for Icelandic were based on an experiment using several data-driven taggers (Helgadóttir, 2005; Helgadóttir, 2007). The highest tagging accuracy, 90.4%, was obtained by the *TnT* tagger (Brants, 2000), a popular HMM tagger. By using a simplified version of the tagset the accuracy of TnT increased to 91.83%, and further to 98.14% when only considering the word class (the first letter of a tag). All results were obtained using 10-fold cross-validation and the corresponding data-splits now form the standard training (90%) and test corpora (10%) for evaluating taggers for Icelandic. The average unknown word ratio using this data-split is 6.8%.

Data sparseness, non-local tag dependencies and fine-grained distinctions in the tagset are mainly to blame for the relatively low tagging accuracy obtained by (at the time) state-of-the-art data-driven taggers. This motivated the development of a linguistic rule-based tagger for Icelandic (Loftsson, 2008). The tagger, *IceTagger*, is reductionistic in nature, i.e. it removes inappropriate

tags from words in a given context. IceTagger first applies local rules (175 in total) for initial disambiguation and then uses a set of heuristics (global rules) for further disambiguation. The heuristics, for example, enforce feature agreement between subjects and verbs, between subjects and predicative complements, and between prepositions and the following nominals. If a word is still ambiguous after the application of the heuristics, the default heuristic is simply to choose the most frequent tag for the word.

An important part of IceTagger is the unknown word guesser, *IceMorphy* (Loftsson, 2008). It guesses the *tag profile* (the set of tags; sometimes called the *ambiguity class*) for unknown words by applying morphological analysis and ending analysis. In addition, IceMorphy can fill in the *tag profile gaps*[1] in the dictionary for words belonging to certain morphological classes.

For the sake of being easily able to compare the tagging accuracy between different methods, IceTagger and IceMorphy only use data resources based on the IFD corpus, i.e. data which is also available to data-driven taggers. The tagging accuracy of IceTagger is about 91.6%, a large improvement on the accuracy obtained by the TnT tagger. The tenth data file in the standard data-split was used for the development of IceTagger. Therefore, the average tagging accuracy is based on testing using the first nine test corpora.

Furthermore, by using the idea of a serial combination of a rule-based and a statistical tagger (Hajič et al., 2001), specifically making an HMM tagger, *TriTagger*, disambiguate words which IceTagger cannot fully disambiguate, the tagging accuracy increases to about 91.8% (Loftsson, 2006). In Table 1, we refer to this tagger as *Ice+HMM*[2].

Loftsson (2008) has also experimented with improving the tagging accuracy of the TnT tagger. The improvement consists of using IceMorphy to generate a "filled" dictionary, i.e. a dictionary for which tag profile gaps for certain words have been filled. Using such a dictionary significantly increases the tagging accuracy of TnT, from about 90.5% to about 91.3%. We refer to this tagger as the *TnT** tagger (see Table 1).

Before our current work, the state-of-the art

---

[1] A tag profile gap for a word occurs when a tag is missing from the tag profile. This occurs, for example, if not all possible tags for a given word are encountered during training.

[2] In (Loftsson, 2006), this tagger is called *Ice**.

Tagger	Unknown	Known	All
TnT	71.82	91.82	90.45
TnT*	72.98	92.60	91.25
IceTagger	75.30	92.78	91.59
Ice+HMM	75.63	93.01	91.83
BI+WC+CT	69.74	93.70	92.06
HMM+Ice	76.10	93.36	92.19
HMM+Ice+HMM	76.04	93.49	92.31

Table 1: Average tagging accuracy (%) using the original IFD corpus

tagging accuracy on Icelandic text[3] was obtained by Dredze and Wallenberg (2008) by applying a bidirectional sequence classification method (Shen et al., 2007). In this method, the classifier assigns the potential PoS tags (hypothesis) to a subsequence of words (called a span) based on features selected by the developer of the classifier. In each round, the highest scoring hypothesis is selected and the guessed tags are assigned to the span. Unassigned words are then reevaluated using the new information. Words either to the left or to the right of the previous assigned span can be chosen next – hence the name bidirectional classification.

Drezde and Wallenberg used the fact that data-driven methods are good at assigning correct word classes (the first letter of a tag in the IFD tagset) to words. Therefore, they divided the learning phase into separate learning problems. First, they constructed a word class (WC) tagger which classifies a word according to one of eleven word classes. Then the tagger only evaluates tags that are consistent with that class. This dramatically reduces the number of tags considered at each step during the bidirectional tagging algorithm. Secondly, noting that most tagging errors are due to errors in case, they constructed a case tagger (CT) that retags case on nouns, adjectives and pronouns, given the predicted tags from the WC tagger. Their combination of a bidirectional tagger, a WC tagger and a CT tagger (BI+WC+CT) resulted in an accuracy of 92.06% (see Table 1). The tenth data file was used for the development of the features used and the average accuracy is thus based on testing using the first nine test corpora.

2.3 Our tagging method

The motivation behind our method is twofold. First, when only considering the word class we noted that the tagging accuracy of IceTagger (97.61%) is significantly lower than the corresponding tagging accuracy of an HMM tagger like TnT (98.14%). This may be due to the limited amount of local rules in IceTagger. Secondly, as discussed above, determining the word class first can simplify the remainder of the disambiguation task.

Thus, we borrow the word class tagger idea from Drezde and Wallenberg and apply it by developing a new tagger based on IceTagger and TriTagger. The main idea is to use TriTagger (the HMM tagger; see Section 2.2) for choosing the word class and then use IceTagger to perform tagging which is consistent with the chosen class, but based on the whole tag string. We are not aware of similar work, i.e. in which a data-driven tagger is integrated into a linguistic rule-based tagger in the form of a pre-processing step. More specifically, the following steps are carried out for each input sentence:

1. IceTagger starts by looking up the tag profile for known tokens in the dictionary and uses IceMorphy for filling in tag profile gaps and generating the tag profile for unknown tokens.

2. For each token and its tag profile, a copy is made. A version of TriTagger, trained on the complete tag strings, disambiguates the copied tokens by using the standard HMM method of finding the tag sequence that maximises the product of contextual probabilities and lexical probabilities (Brants, 2000). The result is one proposed tag for each token.

3. For each token, the proposed tag t from TriTagger is used to eliminate tags from the corresponding token in IceTagger that are not consistent with the word class of tag t.

4. Finally, the standard version of IceTagger is run using (possibly) a reduced tag profile for each token.

We refer to this new tagger as the HMM+Ice tagger. It is an integrated tagger and, consequently, runs like a single tagger. Note that our method should be feasible for other morphologically complex languages for which an HMM tagger and a linguistic rule-based tagger already exist.

The tagging accuracy of HMM+Ice is 92.19% (see Table 1), which amounts to about a 7.1% and 1.6% error reduction rate compared to IceTagger and the BI+WC+CT tagger, respectively. As expected, the number of tags needed to be considered by IceTagger drops significantly when using TriTagger for initial disambiguation. The ambiguity rate (total number of tags divided by total number of tokens) for known ambiguous tokens in the standard version of IceTagger is 2.77. In the HMM+Ice tagger the corresponding number is 2.40, which amounts to a 13.4% drop in ambiguity rate.

Note that the HMM+Ice tagger applies the HMM before IceTagger runs, but, conversely, the Ice+HMM tagger (described in Section 2.2), applies the HMM after IceTagger. By combining these two methods, we obtain a more accurate tagger which runs in the following manner. It starts by following steps 1-3 described above. Then, in step 4, it runs the Ice+HMM tagger, instead of only running IceTagger. We refer to this method as the HMM+Ice+HMM tagger. The tagging accuracy of the HMM+Ice+HMM tagger is 92.31%, which amounts to about a 8.6% and 3.2% error reduction rate compared to IceTagger and the BI+WC+CT tagger, respectively. The difference between the HMM+Ice tagger and the HMM+Ice+HMM tagger is that the former chooses the most frequent tag for words which are still ambiguous after the application of IceTagger, whereas the latter applies the HMM model again to disambiguate those words.

Table 1 summarises the accuracy of all the PoS taggers discussed above (using the average from the first nine test corpora). The table shows that our HMM+Ice+HMM tagger outperforms the BI+WC+CT tagger because of higher accuracy for unknown words, but the accuracy obtained by the BI+WC+CT tagger for known words is superior by 0.21 percentage points. We hypothesised that this could partly be explained by the following. IceTagger uses a dictionary generated from a training corpus, consisting of each word encountered along with the tag profile for each word. Thus, the tag profile for a word w only contains tags that were found in a training corpus for w, in addition to missing tags generated by the tag profile

gap filling mechanism of IceMorphy (discussed in Section 2.2). In contrast, a tagger based on the bidirectional classification method evaluates all possible tags in the tagset to select the top tag for a word. Consequently, during tagging it does not look up the tag profile in a dictionary for a given word. This means, for example, that the BI+WC+CT tagger is able to assign a noun tag to a word w even though w is never tagged as a noun in the training corpus.

To verify this hypothesis, we analysed the output generated by the BI+WC+CT tagger. For each test corpus, it assigns, on average, 559 tags that are not included in the corresponding dictionary (filled with tags from IceMorphy) derived during training. The average size of a test corpus is 59,081 tokens and therefore the "out-of-dictionary" tags are 1.02% of the total tag assignments. However, only 160 of the 559 tags are actually correct tag assignments. Nevertheless, 0.29% of the tagging accuracy for known words $(160/59,081)$ can be attributed to these 160 correct tags. This supports our hypothesis, because the tagging accuracy of the BI+WC+CT tagger for known words would be a little less than the corresponding accuracy of the HMM+Ice+HMM tagger if the former tagger could not use out-of-dictionary tag assignments.

It is important to note that tagging time is very important in practical applications. According to Dredze and Wallenberg (2008b), the WC tagger alone processes 179 tokens per second (processing time for the CT tagger is not given). In comparison, our HMM+Ice+HMM tagger processes about 2350 tokens per second[4] (running on a Dell Precision M4300 2 Duo CPU, 2.20 GHz).

2.4 Using the corrected corpus

Loftsson (2009) has produced a version of the IFD corpus in which a number of tagging errors (1,334 in total) have been corrected. His reevaluation of the taggers TnT, TnT*, IceTagger and Ice+HMM showed a significant improvement in tagging accuracy compared to using the original corpus. We repeat his tagging results in Table 2, along with the results for the BI+WC+CT tagger and our HMM+Ice and HMM+Ice+HMM taggers. For the taggers TnT, TnT*, Ice+HMM, HMM+Ice, and HMM+Ice+HMM the results are presented after

---

[4]The standard version of IceTagger (without HMM integration) processes more than 6600 tokens per second.

Tagger	Unknown	Known	All
TnT	71.97	92.06	90.68
TnT*	73.10	92.85	91.50
IceTagger	75.36	92.95	91.76
Ice+HMM	75.70	93.20	92.01
BI+WC+CT	69.80	93.85	92.21
HMM+Ice	76.17	93.59	92.40
HMM+Ice+HMM	76.13	93.70	92.51

Table 2: Average tagging accuracy (%) using the corrected IFD corpus

Char #	Category/ Feature	Symbol – signification
1	Word class	**n**–noun
2	Gender	**k**–masculine, **v**–feminine, **h**–neuter, **x**–unspecified
3	Number	**e**–singular, **f**–plural
4	Case	**n**–nominative, **o**–accusative, **þ**–dative, **e**–genitive
5	Article	**g**–with suffixed article
6	Proper noun	**m**–person, **ö**–place, **s**–other proper name

Table 3: The signification of the tags for nouns

retraining on the corrected corpus. IceTagger does not need retraining because it does not derive a language model from a training corpus. Note that since we only had access to the output generated by the BI+WC+CT (not the tagger itself), we were not able to retrain that tagger. Thus, presumably, the accuracy of the BI+WC+CT in Table 2 is somewhat underestimated (and the same applies for the accuracy numbers which we present in Section 3).

Our HMM+Ice+HMM tagger achieves an accuracy of 92.51% for all words when testing using the corrected corpus. We suggest that researchers use the corrected version of the IFD corpus as a gold standard in future work[5].

3 Tagset Reduction

There are two main methods used when reducing tagsets in the context of PoS tagging – we refer to them as *tagset change* and *tagset mapping*. In the former method, the tagset is simplified and the training corpus updated to reflect the change in the tagset. Taggers are then retrained on the updated corpus and during testing the taggers thus produce tags according to the simplified tagset.

In the latter method, tagset mapping, the only change needed is in the testing (evaluation) part. When comparing a particular tag t_1 in the output of a tagger to a tag t_2 in the gold standard, the tags t_1 and t_2 are mapped to new simplified tags m_1 and m_2, respectively. Then, the tags m_1 and m_2 are compared instead of t_1 and t_2. When using the tagset mapping method, the tagset used by the tagger is called the *internal tagset* and the tagset used for evaluation called the *external tagset* (Brants, 1997). The motivation for using

the tagset mapping method is that often the internal (larger) tagset encodes information that can help disambiguate words in context.

The size of the current IFD tagset is a direct consequence of the morphological complexity of Icelandic and most of the distinctions that the tagset makes reflect morphosyntactic features which must be marked for the tagging to be useful. However, we believe that it is possible to make certain reductions which do not affect the effectiveness of the tagset in practical applications. In this section, we thus propose an external tagset, which can be used as an alternative to the original (internal) one used hitherto[6]. Our work is inspired by the tag simplification experiments by Helgadóttir (2005). We present four simplifications to the original tagset, implemented as tagset mappings[7], and evaluate taggers based on these different versions. In all cases, the tagging accuracy gained is presented relative to the accuracy obtained using the original tagset.

As discussed in Section 2.1, the current IFD tagset is large and makes fine-grained distinctions. Moreover, the tagset reflects distinctions which may be impossible (or at least very difficult) to resolve at the level of PoS tagging.

The most obvious example is the type of proper nouns, denoted by the sixth letter in the tags for nouns (see Table 3). This information is not of syntactic nature and to our knowledge this is not part of tagsets for other languages. Therefore, a separate natural language processing module, a

---

[5]The original IFD corpus and its corrected version is available for research purposes at The Árni Magnússon Institute for Icelandic Studies.

[6]We use linguistic knowledge when reducing the tagset. Another way, for example, would be to look at the precision and recall rates for each tag to motivate the tagset reduction.

[7]For the TnT tagger we indeed experimented with the tagset change method, but the tagging accuracy was either equivalent or substantially lower than using tagset mapping.

Tagger	Original tagset	Ignoring type of proper nouns	c=ct	Ignoring type of pronouns	Prep.= adverbs	All four mappings
TnT*	91.50	91.56	91.61	91.61	92.51	92.80
IceTagger	91.76	91.83	91.85	91.88	92.61	92.90
BI+WC+CT	92.21	92.27	92.27	92.31	92.89	93.12
HMM+Ice+HMM	92.51	92.57	92.62	92.62	93.35	93.63

Table 4: Average tagging accuracy (%) for all words using external tagsets

Named Entity Recogniser, is usually responsible for determining the type of proper nouns. Consequently, for the first simplification of the tagset, we remove the type information for proper nouns. During testing we thus perform a mapping which ignores the distinction made in the last letter of proper noun tags. This reduces possible proper noun tags from 144, in the internal tagset, to 48, in the external tagset. As can be seen by comparing columns 2 and 3 in Table 4, this increases the accuracy of the taggers by 0.06-0.07 percentage points.

In the IFD tagset, the tag "c" denotes a conjunction and "ct" a relativizer (a conjunction used to indicate a relative clause). The typical relativizer, "sem" ('that') can also be a comparative conjunction and it is often difficult, even for experienced linguists, to determine which function it has in a given sentence. Furthermore, this distinction must be based on syntactic and contextual information which is not available to a PoS tagger. The second simplification thus consists of mapping the "ct" tag to "c", i.e. removing the "ct" tag from the external tagset. This increases the tagging accuracy of the taggers by 0.06-0.11 percentage points (see column four of Table 4).

Tags starting with the letter "f" denote pronouns in the IFD tagset. The second letter, one of "[abeopst]" specifies type information, i.e. demonstrative, reflexive, possessive, indefinite, personal, interrogative or relative. In most cases, ignoring this type information does not lead to any loss of information, since most of the pronouns can only belong to one class anyway. In the few cases where a pronominal word form is ambiguous between pronoun classes, the distinction is either syntactically based or based on contextual information which is arguably beyond the realm of a PoS tagger. In the third simplification, we therefore perform a mapping which ignores the type of the pronoun. This reduces possible pronoun tags from 184, in the internal tagset, to 40, in the external tagset, and increases the tagging accuracy of the taggers by 0.10-0.12 percentage points (see column five of Table 4).

The three simplifications described above do not, however, help in reducing the most common tagging mistakes. Table 5 shows that out of the top six errors made by our HMM+Ice+HMM tagger, five are related to prepositions (tags "ao","aþ") and adverbs (tag "aa"), i.e. tagging words as prepositions governing the wrong case or tagging words as prepositions instead of adverbs, or vice versa. Notice that these tags are outsiders anyway, since they do not reflect any morphological distinctions in the words they are attached to, but only indicate the effect (case government) that these words have on their complements. However, the case is of course marked on the complement itself, so the case tag on the preposition/adverb is completely redundant but leads to a number of tagging errors. To illustrate, consider the phrase "í bæinn" ('to town') tagged as "ao nkeog". The second letter of the preposition tag "ao" denotes the case governed by the preposition and the fourth letter of the complement (noun) tag "nkeog" denotes the corresponding accusative case inflection. Only on the noun, therefore, does "o" signify morphologically marked grammatical information.

In the last simplification of the tagset, we therefore map the following seven tags "ao", "aþ", "ae", "aþm", "aþe", "aam", "aae" (preposition tags and adverbs in comparative and superlative form) to the adverb tag "aa", effectively disregarding the difference between prepositions and adverbs and reducing the external tagset by 7 tags. This increases the tagging accuracy by 0.68-1.01 percentage points (see column six of Table 4).

Finally, the last column of Table 4 shows the accuracy of the taggers when applying all the four tagset mappings at once. The overall tagging accuracy gain for the taggers is 0.91-1.30 percentage points when compared to using the original tagset. The size of the external tagset using all four map-

No.	Proposed tag > correct tag	Error rate	Cumulative rate
1.	aþ>ao	3.09%	3.09%
2.	aa>ao	1.69%	4.78%
3.	ao>aþ	1.68%	6.47%
4.	nveþ>nveo	1.66%	8.13%
5.	ao>aa	1.56%	9.70%
6.	aa>aþ	1.43%	11.13%
7.	nhen>nheo	1.00%	12.13%
8.	sfg3fn>sng	0.99%	13.12%
9.	nveo>nveþ	0.97%	14.09%
10.	nkeþ>nkeo	0.88%	14.97%

Table 5: The top ten most frequent errors made by the HMM+Ice+HMM tagger

pings is about 450 tags and our HMM+Ice+HMM tagger achieves an accuracy of 93.63% using this tagset.

4 Discussion and Future Work

Comparison in tagging accuracy between languages is difficult because of different levels of morphological complexity, different tagsets, different corpora, etc. However, for the sake of making one comparison to a related language, let us consider Swedish. An accuracy of about 95% was obtained for Swedish by a standard version of the TnT tagger, using a tagset consisting of 139 tags, a training corpus of 500k tokens, and an unknown word ratio of 8.1% (Megyesi, 2001). This can be compared to the 93.63% accuracy of our HMM+Ice+HMM tagger, obtained using a tagset of about 450 tags. According to this, there is still quite a large gap in tagging accuracy between the languages. Partly, it may be explained by the difference in tagset sizes, but, on the other hand, one would also expect that the tagging accuracy of Swedish could be increased by using a more sophisticated tagger than the standard version of TnT (e.g. a tagger similar to our HMM+Ice+HMM tagger). Due to the fact that Icelandic has considerably more complex inflectional morphology than Swedish, one may conclude that it will be difficult to achieve tagging accuracy numbers for Icelandic comparable to Swedish. Nevertheless, in order to further increase the tagging accuracy of Icelandic text, we foresee at least four possibilities.

First, one might try to minimise the ratio of unknown words. As mentioned in Section 2.2,

the average unknown word ratio using the standard data-split is 6.8%. Since the tagging accuracy of all the taggers for unknown words is only about 70-76% (see Table 1), it is important to minimise this ratio (the experiment by Helgadóttir (2005) using "a backup lexicon" showed good results). One possibility is to use the comprehensive Morphological Database of Icelandic Inflections (MDII) (Bjarnadóttir, 2005) for this purpose. The MDII contains about 270,000 entries, over 5.8 million word forms. The database does not, however, contain any frequency information. The data from the MDII could be used to extend the dictionaries used by the taggers (for the HMM taggers a uniform distribution could be assumed in the tag profile for a word), which should result in a dramatic drop in the unknown word ratio and, presumably, an increased tagging accuracy for all words.

Second, one might consider implementing a tagger (and a parser) using the framework of Constraint Grammar (CG) (Karlsson et al., 1995), which has been applied to several languages. The main advantage of CG systems is high accuracy (Samuelsson and Voutilainen, 1997), but the main disadvantage is the labour-intensive development – for example, the Norwegian CG project took seven man labour years (Hagen et al., 2000). Regardless, we think that a CG system should be developed for Icelandic. Note that the existence of the MDII could reduce the development time, i.e. with regard to the morphological analyser which is a crucial part of a CG system.

Third, one could explore further combining data-driven and linguistic rule-based methods. For example, since the accuracy of the BI+WC+CT tagger for unknown words is the least of all the taggers (see Table 1), it can presumably be increased by integrating a morphological component like IceMorphy.

Finally, as pointed out by Dredze and Wallenberg (2008), a considerable proportion of the errors are mistakes in case assignments of verb subjects and objects (rows no. 4, 9, and 10 of Table 5 illustrate the latter). Finding ways to minimise these errors is therefore part of the challenge ahead.

5 Summary

In this paper, we first presented a new state-of-the-art tagger for Icelandic, HMM+Ice+HMM, by integrating an HMM tagger into a linguistic rule-based tagger in a novel way. Our method should be feasible for other morphologically complex languages for which an HMM tagger and a linguistic rule-based tagger already exist. Evaluation shows that our HMM+Ice+HMM tagger obtains an accuracy of 92.31% using the standard test set derived from the IFD corpus. Furthermore, the accuracy increases to 92.51% using a corrected version of the corpus.

Second, we proposed an external tagset by removing information from the internal tagset which reflects distinctions that are not morphologically based. The accuracy of HMM+Ice+HMM increases to 93.63% using the external tagset.

Finally, we discussed the results and provided directions for future work.

Acknowledgments

The work in this paper was supported by the Icelandic Research Fund, grant 070025023. We thank Mark Drezde and Joel Wallenberg for providing access to the output of their tagger.

References

Kristín Bjarnadóttir. 2005. Modern Icelandic Inflections. In H. Holmboe, editor, *Nordisk Sprogteknologi 2005*, pages 49–50. Museum Tusculanums Forlag, Copenhagen.

Thorsten Brants. 1997. Internal and External Tagsets in Part-of-Speech Tagging. In *Proceedings of Eurospeech 97*, Rhodes, Greece.

Thorsten Brants. 2000. TnT: A statistical part-of-speech tagger. In *Proceedings of the 6th Conference on Applied Natural Language Processing*, Seattle, WA, USA.

Stefán Briem. 1989. Automatisk morfologisk analyse af islandsk tekst. In *Papers from the Seventh Scandinavian Conference of Computational Linguistics*, Reykjavik, Iceland.

Mark Dredze and Joel Wallenberg. 2008. Icelandic Data Driven Part of Speech Tagging. In *Proceedings of the 46th Annual Meeting of the Association for Computational Linguistics: Human Language Technologies*, Columbus, OH, USA.

Mark Dredze and Joel Wallenberg. 2008b. Further Results and Analysis of Icelandic Part of Speech Tagging. Technical report, Department of Computer and Information Science, University of Pennsylvania.

Kristin Hagen, Janne B. Johannessen, and Anders Nøklestad. 2000. A Constraint-Based Tagger for Norwegian. In C.-E. Lindberg and S.-N. Lund, editors, 17th *Scandinavian Conference of Linguistics. Odense Working Papers in Language and Communication*, volume 19, pages 31–48. University of Southern Denmark, Odense.

Jan Hajič, Pavel Krbec, Karel Oliva, Pavel Květoň, and Vladimír Petkevič. 2001. Serial Combination of Rules and Statistics: A Case Study in Czech Tagging. In *Proceedings of the 39th Association of Computational Linguistics Conference*, Toulouse, France.

Sigrún Helgadóttir. 2005. Testing Data-Driven Learning Algorithms for PoS Tagging of Icelandic. In H. Holmboe, editor, *Nordisk Sprogteknologi 2004*, pages 257–265. Museum Tusculanums Forlag, Copenhagen.

Sigrún Helgadóttir. 2007. Mörkun íslensks texta. [Tagging Icelandic text.]. *Orð og tunga*, 9:75–107.

Fred Karlsson, Atro Voutilainen, Juha Heikkilä, and Arto Anttila. 1995. *Constraint Grammar: A Language-Independent System for Parsing Unrestricted Text*. Mouton de Gruyter, Berlin.

Hrafn Loftsson. 2006. Tagging Icelandic text: an experiment with integrations and combinations of taggers. *Language Resources and Evaluation*, 40(2):175–181.

Hrafn Loftsson. 2008. Tagging Icelandic text: A linguistic rule-based approach. *Nordic Journal of Linguistics*, 31(1):47–72.

Hrafn Loftsson. 2009. Correcting a PoS-tagged corpus using three complementary methods. In *Proceedings of the 12th Conference of the European Chapter of the ACL (EACL 2009)*, Athens, Greece.

Beáta Megyesi. 2001. Comparing Data-Driven Learning Algorithms for PoS Tagging of Swedish. In *Proceedings of the Conference on Empirical Methods in Natural Language Processing (EMNLP 2001)*, Pittsburgh, PA, USA.

Jörgen Pind, Friðrik Magnússon, and Stefán Briem. 1991. *Íslensk orðtíðnibók [The Icelandic Frequency Dictionary]*. The Institute of Lexicography, University of Iceland, Reykjavik.

Christer Samuelsson and Atro Voutilainen. 1997. Comparing a Linguistic and a Stochastic tagger. In *Proceedings of the 8th Conference of the European Chapter of the ACL (EACL 1997)*, Madrid, Spain.

Libin Shen, Giorgio Satta, and Aravind K. Joshi. 2007. Guided learning for bidirectional sequence classification. In *Proceedings of the 45th Annual Meeting of the Association for Computational Linguistics*, Prague, Czech Republic.

ISSN 1736-6305 Vol. 4
http://hdl.handle.net/10062/9206

Disambiguation of Taxonomy Markers in Context: Russian Nouns

Olga Lashevskaja
University of Tromsø
Tromsø, Norway

olesar@gmail.com

Olga Mitrofanova
St. Petersburg State University,
Universitetskaya emb. 11,
199034, St. Petersburg, Russia
alkonost-om@yandex.ru

Abstract

The paper presents experimental results on WSD, with focus on disambiguation of Russian nouns that refer to tangible objects and abstract notions. The body of contexts has been extracted from the Russian National Corpus (RNC). The tool used in our experiments is aimed at statistical processing and classification of noun contexts. The WSD procedure takes into account taxonomy markers of word meanings as well as lexical markers and morphological tagsets in the context. A set of experiments allows us to establish preferential conditions for WSD in Russian texts.

1 Introduction

Word sense disambiguation (WSD) plays a crucial role in corpora development and use. A rich variety of reliable WSD techniques such as knowledge- (or rule-) based, statistical corpus-based WSD or their hybrids have been worked out and tested [Agirre & Edmonds 2007; Mihalcea & Pedersen 2005; Navigli 2009]. Knowledge-based WSD is performed with the help of semantic information stored in electronic lexicographic modules (e.g., WordNet, FrameNet). Corpus-based WSD implies extraction and statistical processing of word collocations which makes it possible to distinguish separate meanings of lexical items in context (e.g., [Pedersen 2002; Schütze 1998], etc.). Hybrid WSD brings into action both lexical resources and corpus analysis (e.g., [Leacock et al. 1998; Mihalcea 2002], etc.).

Richly annotated corpora prove to be valuable sources of linguistic evidence necessary for exploring word meanings, their interrelations, extracting lexical-semantic classes, developing taxonomies, etc. Statistical algorithms implemented in contemporary corpora processing tools ensure extraction of information on the frequency distributions of semantic, lexical and morphological markers. These data are indispensable for classification of word contexts and, thus, for proper identification of word senses in contexts [Mitrofanova et al. 2008a, Mitrofanova et al. 2008b].

Major WSD techniques were enabled in experiments on semantic ambiguity resolution in Russian texts. The use of lexical databases for Russian (e.g., an electronic thesaurus RuTes [Lukashevich & Chujko 2007], the RNC semantic dictionary [Rakhilina et al. 2006], RussNet lexical database [Azarova et al. 2008]) provides rather high quality of WSD. If lexicographic information is not available, statistical WSD techniques are indispensable in processing Russian texts. As experimental data have shown, it is possible to identify word meanings in contexts taking into account POS tag distributions [Azarova & Marina 2006] and lexical markers [Kobricov et al. 2005]; hybrid WSD seems to be effective as well [Toldova et al. 2008].

The purpose of the present project is statistical WSD in Russian texts which entails fulfilment of certain research tasks, such as: (1) development of a WSD tool for Russian; (2) experiments on WSD in Russian texts with various parameters; (3) studying preferential conditions for WSD in Russian. It should be noted that the present study is aimed at Targeted WSD (and not All Words WSD).

The scope of the project encompasses statistical WSD procedure in three modes – with regard to three types of contextual information: (1) lexical markers of word meanings in contexts (lemmas of lexical items co-occurring with ambiguous words in contexts); (2) taxonomy markers (semantic tagsets referring to lexical-semantic classes) of context items; (3) grammatical markers (morphological tagsets referring to POS and other grammatical features) of context items – and to compare reliability of these WSD approaches. It should be noted that experiments on WSD based on semantic annotation have no precedent in Russian corpus linguistics.

2 Linguistic data

Contexts for Russian nouns referring to tangible objects and abstract notions serve as an empirical basis of the study (such polysemous and/or homonymic words as *dom* 'building, private space, family, etc.', *organ* 'institution, part of body, musical instrument, etc.', *luk* 'onion, bow', *glava* 'head, chief, cupola, chapter, etc.', *vid* 'view, form, document, image, verbal aspect, kind, species', *kl'uč* 'key, clue, clef, spring, etc.', *sovet* 'advice, council, etc.', *ploš'ad'* 'square, space, etc.', *kosa* 'braid, scythe, peninsula', etc.). Although the nouns considered in course of experiments belong to different lexical-semantic groups, they reveal regular types of relations between meanings of polysemous words or between homonymic items. That's why the set of words in question should be regarded as representative of noun class in general.

Sets of contexts were extracted from the Russian National Corpus (RNC, http://www.ruscorpora.ru/), the largest annotated corpus of Russian texts containing about 150 M tokens. The texts included in the RNC are supplied with morphological (morphosyntactic) and semantic annotation. The majority of nouns in the RNC are assigned markers according to coarse-grained taxonomy (e.g. 'concrete', 'human', 'animal', 'space', 'construction', 'tool', 'container', 'substance', 'movement', 'diminutive', 'causative', 'verbal noun', and other lexical-semantic classes, cf. http://www.ruscorpora.ru/en/corpora-sem.html). Taxonomy markers assigned to a particular lexical item in a context account for the set of its registered meanings, so that a WSD procedure is often required.

WSD has to be performed for nouns with various frequencies of particular meanings (cf. Table 1).

Uses of the given nouns represented in the RNC by 10 or more occurrences for each word sense were analysed. Word senses with fewer contexts in the corpus (such as *dom* 'common space' or *dom* 'dynasty') were excluded from the study. In course of experiments on Targeted WSD manual disambiguation was performed for a training set of contexts for a particular word, the remaining ambiguous contexts were subjected to statistical WSD.

3 WSD procedure

A Python-based WSD software was developed to perform statistical WSD procedure in three modes, taking into account (1) lexical markers occurring in contexts; (2) taxonomy markers of context elements; and (3) grammatical markers – morphological tagsets assigned to context elements. An automatic word clustering (AWC) tool was adapted [Mitrofanova et al. 2007]. The AWC tool facilitates formation of clusters of similar contexts extracted from the RNC. Adjustment of AWC software for WSD purposes required implementation of machine learning and pattern recognition modules.

WSD procedure is carried out in stages. The first stage implies pre-processing of contexts in experimental set E. Semantically and morphologically unambiguous contexts are selected to form a training set S required for machine learning, while ambiguous contexts are treated as a trial set T. Machine learning is performed at the second stage. For each meaning of a word its statistical pattern is formed taking into account frequencies of taxonomy markers, lexical markers and morphological tagsets of context elements. Further, patterns of meanings, as well as trial contexts, are represented as vectors in a word space model. The third stage implies pattern recognition, i.e. selection of patterns nearest to vectors that correspond to ambiguous contexts. Three similarity measures based on the distance between patterns and vectors of trial contexts are calculated in different ways, so that the user can choose between Hamming measure, Euclidean measure, and Cosine measure. As a result, meanings exposed by particular patterns are automatically assigned to processed contexts.

Table 1. Russian nouns *dom, organ, luk, vid, glava*: taxonomy markers and frequencies of meanings (number of contexts in the RNC)

Word meanings and taxonomy markers	Number of contexts in the RNC
dom	3000 (total)
dom 'building' <r:concr t:constr top:contain>	1694
dom 'private space' <r:concr t:space>	95
dom 'family' <r:concr t:group pt:set sc:hum>	72
dom 'common space' <r:concr t:space der:shift der:metaph>	4
dom 'institution' <r:concr t:org>	292
dom 'dynasty' <r:concr pt:set sc:hum>	1
dom (merged meanings)	842
organ	834 (total)
organ 'institution' <r:concr t:org hi:class>	660
organ 'part of body' <r:concr pt:partb pc:hum pc:animal hi:class>	130
organ 'musical instrument' <r:concr t:tool:mus>	27
organ 'means' <r:concr der:shift dt:partb>	9
organ 'publication' <r:concr t:media hi:class>	8
luk	2200 (total)
luk 'onion' <r:concr t:plant t:fruit t:food pt:aggr>	1600
luk 'bow' <r:concr t:tool:weapon top:arc>	600
vid	2866 (total)
vid 'view' <r:abstr t:perc der:v>	1144
vid 'form' <r:abstr der:shift>	1075
vid 'document' <r:concr t:doc >	7
vid 'image' <r:concr t:workart>	10
vid 'expectation' <r:abstr t:ment>	10
vid 'kind, species' <r:abstr r:concr pt:set sc:X>	617
vid 'verbal aspect' <r:abstr >	3
Word meanings and taxonomy markers	Number of contexts in the RNC
glava	1073 (total)
glava 'head, part of body' <r:concr pt:partb pc:hum>	8
glava 'leading position' <r:concr der:shift dt:partb>	140
glava 'cupola' <r:concr pt:part pc:constr >	12
glava 'chief' <r:concr t:hum >	301
glava 'chapter' <r:concr t:text pt:part pc:text>[1]	612

---

[1] In this table, the following semantic tags are used: 1) top categories *r:concr* (concrete noun), *r:abstr* (abstract noun); 2) taxonomic classes *t:hum* (human beings), *t:org*

Series of tests were performed (1) to evaluate several parameters that can influence test results: context window size, proportional expansion of training sets of contexts for each meaning, etc.; (2) to estimate correlation between taxonomic, lexical and morphological criteria, to compare reliability of these WSD approaches and to ascertain preferential conditions of their application.

Evaluation of WSD quality was performed: results of automatic WSD were compared with results of manual WSD, precision P and recall R were defined in all series of tests.

4 General results of experiments

Thorough analysis of contexts shows that the appropriate choice of similarity measure (Cosine measure) alongside with expansion of a training set ($S = 100\ldots500$ contexts) ensures over 85% correct decisions on average ($P \approx 0.85$). Under such conditions, in series of experiments the number of correct decisions turned out to be no less than $50\ldots60\%$ ($P \approx 0.50\ldots0.60$), in some cases up to $95\ldots100\%$ ($P \approx 0.95\ldots1$).

The Cosine measure proves to be the most reliable similarity measure as it is the least sensitive to meaning frequencies. Hamming and Euclidean measures provide correspondingly 45% ($P \approx 0.45$) and 65% ($P \approx 0.65$) of correct decisions on average.

WSD experiments were performed with training sets of variable size $S = 10, 15, 55, 75, 100, 200, 500, \ldots$ (up to all contexts except for those included in a trial set) and with proportional expansion of a training set S being 10%, 15%, 20% of E. It seems that the training set S should contain at least 100 unambiguous contexts, while 500 contexts provide the best results. In general, to obtain reliable WSD results, the training set size S should be no less than 20% of the experimental set size E. In other cases the amount of correct decisi-

---

(organizations), *t:constr* (buildings/constructions), *t:space* (space/ places), *t:tool:mus* (musical instruments), *t:perc* (perception), *t:ment* (mental sphere), etc.; 3) mereological classes *pt:partb pc:hum pc:animal* (body parts of humans and animals), *pt:part pc:constr* (parts of buildings/constructions), *pt:set sc:hum* (sets of humans); 4) topological classes *top:contain* (containers), *t:arc* (arcs); 5) derivational markers *der:v* (deverbal nouns), *der:shift dt:partb* (semantic shift from the name of a body part), *der:shift der:metaph* (metaphorical shift).

ons may be reduced because statistical patterns for meanings turn out to be rather 'blurry'.

A series of tests with variable context window size w ([$-i$; $+k$], i, $k \leq N$ (N – context length) was carried out, so that the context window could be symmetric or asymmetric, and could be limited to a clause or a syntactic group. Context analysis with regard to syntactic relations showed an increase in WSD precision by $P = 0.05...0.1$. The best results can be expected if $i \leq 2$, $2 \leq k \leq 4$. In most cases such context window corresponds to noun groups including prepositional (adjectival) and postpositional (nominal, infinitival, etc.) determiners which contain information relevant for meaning disambiguation.

5 WSD based on taxonomy markers, on lexical markers and on morphological tagsets: discussion

Experiments on WSD based on taxonomy markers and on lexical markers gave rather encouraging results. E.g., WSD procedure for the noun *luk* allows to discriminate meanings *luk 'onion'* and *luk 'bow'* given $P \approx 0.825...0.85$ on average, cf. Table 2.

Table 2. Results of WSD based on taxonomy markers and on lexical markers for the noun *luk*

	Amount of correct decisions for separate meanings (P)		Average
	luk 'onion'	*luk 'bow'*	
WSD based on taxonomy markers	0.75	0.95	0.85
WSD based on lexical markers	0.75	0.90	0.825

For the most part, WSD based on taxonomy markers and on lexical markers was equally effective: cf. Table 3, e.g. context (*c*). At the same time, processing of contexts which takes into account taxonomy markers often provides more trustworthy decisions: e.g., the increase of Cosine measure value is noticeable in context (*a*) where the meaning *luk 'onion'* was recognized correctly with the help of both criteria. WSD based on taxonomy markers also helps to evade erroneous interpretations: cf. contexts (*b*) and (*d*) where the meaning of *luk* was chosen correctly in case of WSD based on taxonomy markers.

Table 3. Examples of WSD based on taxonomy markers and on lexical markers for the noun *luk*

luk	WSD based on taxonomy markers		WSD based on lexical markers	
	Meaning	*Cos*	Meaning	*Cos*
(a) *luk 'onion'* Pomn'u hleb s iz'umom, s *lukom*, s kakimi-to korenjami. ([I] remember bread with raisins, with *onion*, and with some spices.)	*luk 'onion'*	0.786	*luk 'onion'*	0.572
(b) *luk 'onion'* Nachinajut prinimat' *luk*, kapustu... ([they] begin to eat *onion*, cabbage...)	*luk 'onion'*	0.514	*luk 'weapon'*	0.502
(c) *luk 'weapon'* Odni tugije *luki*, nad kotorymi neskol'ko chelovek spravit'sa ne mogli, 'igrajuchi' nat'agival'i... (Some [people] 'effortlessly' bent tight *bows* with which several people couldn't cope with...)	*luk 'weapon'*	0.550	*luk 'weapon'*	0.533
(d) *luk 'weapon'* Za spinoj u nego viseli *luk* i kolchan. (He had a *bow* on his back.)	*luk 'weapon'*	0.517	*luk 'onion'*	0.500
...	...	...	...	...

Comparison of WSD results obtained in three modes shows that in general morphological criteria prove to be more reliable than taxonomic and lexical criteria: average P and R for WSD based on morphological annotation are higher than for WSD based on taxonomy markers and on lexical markers. At the same time, differences in WSD results lead to the conclusion that various types of context-dependent meanings determine preferential conditions for application of WSD approaches (cf. example in Table 4).

The correlation between taxonomic, lexical and morphological criteria for WSD was estimated. The Pearson's correlation coefficient is quite low: $|Corr| < 0.4$. Thus, criteria in question should be considered as independent. It is expected that WSD based on combinations of criteria (combinations of taxonomy markers and lexical markers, taxonomy markers and morphological tagsets, etc.) may be more effective.

Table 4. Examples of WSD results obtained in three modes for the noun *vid*: window size w [-5, +5], [-5, +1], [-1, +5]; training set size $S = 20\%\ E$

P	WSD based on taxonomy markers			WSD based on lexical markers			WSD based on morphological tagsets		
	vid 'view'	*vid* 'shape'	*vid* 'kind'	*vid* 'view'	*vid* 'shape'	*vid* 'kind'	*vid* 'view'	*vid* 'shape'	*vid* 'kind'
[-5,+5]	0.4	0.5	0.7	0.75	0.8	0.5	0.65	0.9	0.8
[-5,+1]	0.95	0.35	0.75	0.7	0.85	0.65	0.6	0.95	0.85
[-1,+5]	0.25	0.8	0.75	0.65	0.7	0.85	0.65	0.9	0.85

6 Additional data for meaning identification

WSD procedure also furnished us with additional information relevant for meaning identification, namely, sets of lexical markers of different meanings deduced from contexts (cf. Table 5). In most cases combinations of a word with its lexical markers should be considered as collocations.

Table 5. Lexical markers of meanings induced from contexts for the noun *organ*

Word meanings	Lexical markers
organ 'institution'	uchrezhdenije 'institution', samoupravlenije 'self-government', nachal'nik 'boss', mestnyj 'local', pravoohranitel'nyj 'law-enforcement', etc.
organ 'part of body'	porok 'defect', vrožd'onnyj 'innate', etc.

7 Analysis of errors

Most errors registered in WSD experiments can be explained by insufficiency of contextual information for meaning identification. WSD results for such contexts often show Cosine measure values about 0.500 (cf. contexts (*b*) and (*d*), Table 3). Failures in WSD may also be explained by the use of disambiguated words in constructions and set-expressions, cf. context (*e*) below:

(e) Poroj Elene kazalos', chto vse javlenija i vse predmety mozhno opisat' v treh pozicijah: anfas, profil', *vid* sverhu.

(At times it seemed to Elena that all phenomena and all objects can be described from three positions: front [view], profile, *view* from above.)

Manual WSD: *vid* 'view'

WSD in three modes: *vid* 'kind'

8 Analysis of merged meanings

It is hardly possible to provide unambiguous analysis of certain contexts for some polysemous nouns revealing merged meanings. For example, a noun *dom* forms pairs of meanings which are almost indistinguishable in certain contexts: *dom* 'building & personal space (home)', *dom* 'personal space & family', etc. Of 3 000 contexts for a noun *dom* there are 842 contexts where ambiguity can't be completely resolved. In such cases WSD results compared with manual analysis make it possible to determine a dominating semantic feature in a pair of merged meanings, cf. contexts (*f*) and (*g*), Table 6.

Table 6. Analysis of merged meanings for the noun *dom*: WSD based on lexical markers

dom	Manual analysis	WSD results	*Cos*
(f) ... v *dome* u Jozhika topilas' pech... (... in Jozhik's *house* the stove was burning...)	*dom* 'building & personal space'	*dom* 'building'	0.429
(g) Rodstvenniki u Livii... ludi praktichnyje... jedinstvennyj chelovek, kotoryj uvazhajet jejo v etom *dome*, – eto jejo dvoreckij... (Livia's relatives ... are practically-minded people ... the only person who respects her in this *house* is her butler...)	*dom* 'personal space & family'	*dom* 'family'	0.452

In further experiments additional statistical patterns corresponding to merged meanings were introduced to improve the performance of the WSD system.

9 Conclusion

A set of experiments on statistical WSD were successfully carried out for contexts of polysemous and/or homonymic Russian nouns which had been extracted from the RNC.

WSD was performed in three modes – taking into account (1) lexical markers occurring in contexts; (2) taxonomy markers of context elements; and (3) grammatical markers – morphological tagsets assigned to context elements. All these approaches proved to be reliable, although in controversial cases preference should be given to WSD based on taxonomy markers.

Optimal conditions for WSD in Russian texts were discovered: over 85% (in some cases up to 95%) correct decisions may be achieved through the use of Cosine measure, a training set varying from 100 up to 500 contexts that constitutes at least 20% of the experimental set E, context window size w [$-i$; $+k$] where $i \leq 2$, $2 \leq k \leq 4$.

Further work implies (1) enrichment of WSD software; (2) experiments on WSD based on complex criteria (combinations of taxonomy markers and lexical markers, taxonomy markers and morphological tagsets, etc.); (3) verification of particular linguistic and statistical hypotheses on WSD in Russian texts.The experiments involving machine learning and pattern recognition put into action the key ideas of cognitive semantics which turn out to be of competitive advantage. It is assumed that words of the same lexical-semantic class (which also share the same place in the taxonomy) reveal similar frequency distributions of context features. Thus, WSD for polysemous words of a certain lexical-semantic class (presumably, its core members) may be performed on the basis of the training set of contexts which was previously formed for monosemous (presumably, peripheral) words of the class. It is expected that this approach to WSD may simplify the procedure of selection and analysis of training data (which is time-consuming).

The work discussed in the paper demonstrates practical application of theoretical cognitive linguistics in NLP. Two hypotheses, on entrenchment of word senses in particular context frames [Brooks et al. 1999] and on center (prototype) – periphery structure of lexical semantic categories [Lakoff 1987], proved to be valid in the course of the verification procedure. It appears that these ideas contribute much to the development of effective WSD techniques.

References

Agirre, E. & Ph. Edmonds (eds.). (2007). Word Sense Disambiguation: Algorithms and Applications. Text, Speech and Language Technology, Vol. 33. Springer-Verlag, Berlin, Heidelberg, New York.

Azarova, I.V. & A.S. Marina. (2006). Avtomatizirovannaja klassifikacija kontekstov pri podgotovke dannyh dl'a kompjuternogo tezaurusa RussNet. In: Kompjuternaja lingvistika i intellektual'nyje tehnologii: Trudy mezhdunarodnoj konferencii Dialog–2006. Moscow. P. 13–17.

Azarova, I.V., S.V. Bichineva, & D.T. Vakhitova. (2008). Avtomaticheskije razreshenije leksicheskoj neodnoznachnosti chastotnyh suschestvitelnych (v terminah strukturnych jedinic RussNet). In: Proceedings of the International Conference Corpora 2008, St. Petersburg, Russia, October 6–10, 2008. P. 5–8.

Brooks, P., M. Tomasello et al. (1999). Children's overgeneralization of fixed transitivity verbs: The entrenchment hypothesis. In: Child Development, 70. P. 1325–1337.

Kobricov, B.P., O.N. Lashevskaja, & O.Ju. Shemanajeva. (2005). Sn'atije leksiko-semanticheskoj omonimii v novostnyh i gazteno-zhurnal'nyh tekstah: poverhnostnyje fil'try i statisticheskaja ocenka. In: Internet–matematika 2005: Avtomatičeskaja obrabotka web-dannyh. Moscow . P. 38–57.

Lakoff, G. (1987). Women, Fire, and Dangerous Things. Chicago, IL: University of Chicago Press.

Leacock, C., G.A. Miller, & M. Chodorow. (2002). Using Corpus Statistics and WordNet Relations for Sense Identification. In: Computational Linguistics, 24(1). P. 147–165.

Lukashevich, N.V. & D.S. Chujko. (2007). Avtomaticheskoje razreshenije leksicheskoj mnogoznachnosti na baze tezaurusnyh znanij. In: Internet-matematika 2007. Ekaterinburg. P. 108–117.

Mihalcea, R. (2002). Word Sense Disambiguation Using Pattern Learning and Automatic Feature Selection. In: Journal of Natural Language and Engineering (JNLE), December 2002.

Mihalcea, R. & T. Pedersen. (2005). Word Sense Disambiguation Tutorial. URL: http://www.d.umn.edu/~tpederse/WSDTutorial.html

Mitrofanova, O., P. Panicheva & O. Lashevskaya. (2008a). Statistical Word Sense Disambiguation in Contexts for Russian Nouns Denoting Physical Objects. In: Text, Speech and Dialogue. Proceedings of the 11th International Conference TSD 2008, Brno, Czech Republic, September 8–12, 2008. Springer-Verlag. P. 153–159.

Mitrofanova, O., A. Mukhin, P. Panicheva, V. Savitsky. (2007). Automatic Word Clustering in Russian Texts. In: Matoušek, V., Mautner, P. et al. (eds.): Text, Speech and Dialogue. Proceedings of the Tenth International Conference TSD 2007, Pilsen, Czech Republic, September 3–7, 2007. Lecture Notes in Artificial Intelligence, Vol. 4629. Springer-Verlag. P. 85–91.

Mitrofanova, O., O. Lashevskaya & P. Panicheva. (2008b). Eksperimenty po statisticheskomu razresheniju leksiko-semanticheskoj neodnoznachnosti russkix imen suschestvitel'nyx v korpuse. In: Proceedings of the International Conference Corpora 2008, St. Petersburg, Russia, October 6–10, 2008. P. 284–293.

Navigli, R. (2009). Word Sense Disambiguation: A Survey. In: ACM Computing Surveys, 41(2), 2009. P. 1–69.

Pedersen, T. (2002). A Baseline Methodology for Word Sense Disambiguation. (Pedersen) In: Proceedings of the Third International Conference on Intelligent Text Processing and Computational Linguistics,. pp. 126-135, February 17-23, 2002, Mexico City. P. 126–135.

Rahilina, E.V., B.P. Kobricov, G.I. Kustova, O.N. Lashevskaja, & O.Ju. Shemanajeva. (2006). Mnogoznachnost' kak prikladnaja problema: leksiko-semanticheskaja razmetka v Nacional'nom korpuse russkogo jazyka. In: Kompjuternaja lingvistika i intellektual'nyje tehnologii: Trudy mezhdunarodnoj konferencii Dialog 2006. Moscow. P. 445–450.

Schütze, H. (1998). Automatic Word Sense Discrimination. In: Computational Linguistics, 24(1). P. 97–123.

Toldova, S.Ju., G.I. Kustova, & O.N. Lashevskaja. (2008). Semanticheskije fil'try dl'a razreshenija mnogoznachnosti v nacional'nom korpuse russkogo jazyka: glagoly. In: Kompjuternaja lingvistika i intellektual'nyje tehnologii: Trudy mezhdunarodnoj konferencii Dialog–2008. Moscow. P. 522–529.

ISSN 1736-6305 Vol. 4
http://hdl.handle.net/10062/9206

Towards automatic acquisition of linguistic features

Yves LEPAGE and **Chooi Ling GOH**[1]
GREYC, University of Caen
F-14032 Caen cedex, France
{yves.lepage,chooiling.goh}@info.unicaen.fr

Abstract

This paper proposes a method to acquire linguistic features from a corpus of short sentences by extracting analogous sentences like *what 's the next station ? : where 's the bus station ? :: what is the next stop ? : where is the bus stop ?* The procedures used to construct clusters of analogous sentences are presented. Experiments performed on roughly 40,000 short sentences from the tourism domain in English and Japanese are reported, and the clusters produced are analyzed and interpreted in terms of linguistic features.

1 Introduction

1.1 Linguistic features as dimensions in a vectorial space

To explain the ultimate goal of the research presented in this paper, let us consider an elementary sentence, like: *Can I have a blanket?* and let us analyze it using standard linguistic terminology. We can say that this sentence is interrogative, that its main verb is *to have*, that the noun *blanket* is singular, etc. Many other linguistic characterizations or features of the sentence or of elements in the sentence can be suggested in this way, and the sum of all these characterizations constitutes an analysis of the sentence.

Any such linguistic characterization, i.e., linguistic feature in the sentence can be seen in opposition to other linguistic features that may be realized to produce a different sentence. For instance, the previous sentence is interrogative by opposition to its affirmative form: *I can have a blanket.* Its main verb could be different, like in: *Can I get a blanket?* The noun *blanket* is singular, in opposition to its plural form: *Can I have blankets?* Etc.

Thus, the example sentence forms a pair of *analogous sentences* with any sentence that can be produced by changing any of the linguistic features of the sentence. In this way, we have a pair of analogous sentences with the interrogative and affirmative forms: *Can I have a blanket? : I can have a blanket.* We also have a pair of analogous sentences when *to have* is exchanged for *to get*: *Can I have a blanket? : Can I get a blanket?* And so on.

The final goal of this research is to leverage on large corpora of sentences to automatically perform linguistic analysis, *i.e.*, to characterize any new sentence by its linguistic features. A linguistic feature may be characterized by an example of a pair of sentences, but not any pair of sentences illustrates a linguistic feature. Only if one can find a number of different pairs of analogous sentences can the opposition be thought as reflecting a linguistic feature. For instance, *Can I have a blanket. : I can board on the next flight.* does not reflect any linguistic feature, but the following series does.

Can I have a blan-ket?	*I can have a blan-ket.*
Can I get some small change?	*I can get some small change.*
Can I board on the next flight?	*I can board on the next flight.*

Such a series of analogous sentences constitutes a dimension in the space of sentences and separates this space into three sub-spaces. The first one contains all sentences similar to the sentences on the left in the series, and the second one contains all sentences similar to the ones on the right. The third sub-space contains all those sentences that are similar to none of the sentences in the series because the opposition expressed by the series is not relevant to them. Figure 1 illustrates this view of a space of sentences in a simple configuration. Three pairs of sentences on each axis

---

[1]This author is now with ATR-NiCT, Kyoto 619-0288, Japan. New e-mail: chooiling.goh@nict.go.jp.

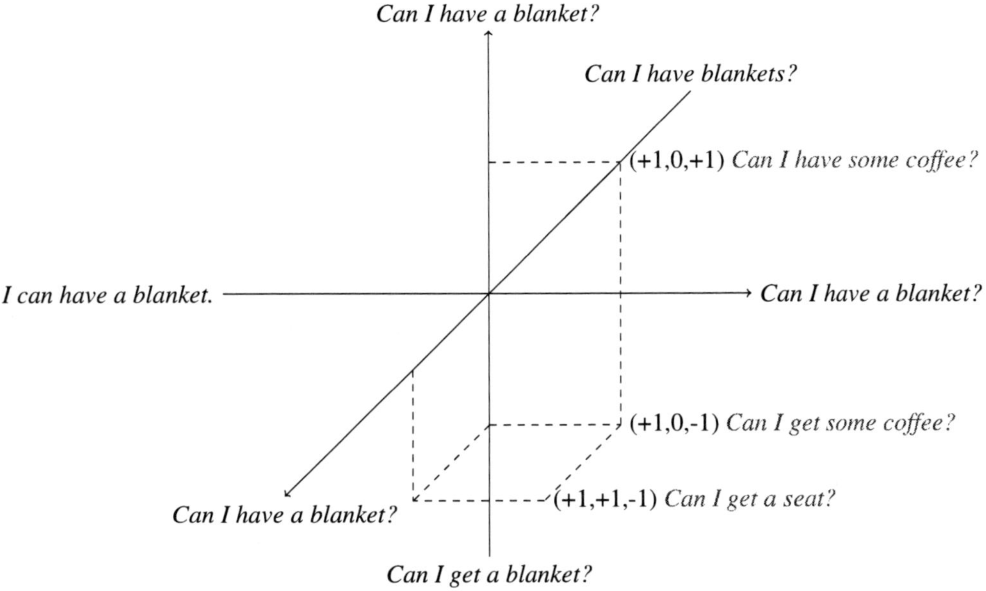

Figure 1: A three-dimensional vectorial space of linguistic features. Each axis stands for the opposition between the two sentences written at both ends.

define three dimensions. Other sentences may be projected in this space according to the possibility for them to enter or not in a series of analogous sentences along any of the dimensions thus taking one of three values: -1 (left), $+1$ (right) or 0 (not relevant) along this dimension.

Such a vectorial space captures those oppositions that are relevant to the sentences of a corpus, thus revealing the linguistic features concealed in that corpus. Such a representation enables the use of any standard vectorial technique for any further desirable computation. The goal of this paper, and the object of the next sections, is not to present such further computations, but to show how it is possible to extract the dimensions defining the space from a corpus of short sentences.

2 Basic Notions

2.1 Analogous Sentences

We follow (Turney, 2006) for the basic notions used in this work:

> Verbal analogies are often written $A : B :: C : D$, meaning *A is to B as C is to D*, for example traffic : street :: water : riverbed.

Following this author, when the relational similarity between two pairs of words is high, we say that

the two pairs of words are *analogous*.[2] In this paper, we concentrate on sentences and extend the notion of analogous pairs of words to analogous pairs of sentences. For instance, the two following pairs of sentences are said to be analogous:

$$\textit{Do you have this in darker green?} : \textit{Do you have this in dark green?} :: \textit{Smaller, please.} : \textit{Small, please.}$$

because the relational similarity between the first sentence and the second one is the same as between the third sentence and the fourth one. Logically, following the term *verbal analogies*, we shall call any such two pairs of sentences *sentential analogies*. Here, the relational similarity consists in opposing the positive and comparative forms of two different adjectives: dark : darker :: small : smaller constitute a verbal analogy that sustain the sentential analogy. However, the sole verbal analogy does not imply the sentential analogy because the context in which the words appear constitutes a part of the sentential analogy.

---

[2] Relational similarity is different from attributional similarity. In this latter case, the correspondence between *attributes* of different words is measured. When this correspondence is high, the two words considered are said to be *synonymous*. In the previous example, water and traffic are not synonymous, clearly showing that relational similarity does not need attributional similarity to exist.

2.2 Series of analogous sentences

When several sentential analogies involve the same pairs of sentences, they form a series of analogous sentences and they can be written on a line like in:

$$A_1 : B_1 :: A_2 : B_2 :: A_3 : B_3 :: \ldots$$

or, in a more convenient way, on a kind of ladder extending over several lines like:

$$A_1 : B_1$$
$$A_2 : B_2$$
$$A_3 : B_3$$
$$\ldots : \ldots$$

A requirement would be that, in such a series of analogous sentences, any two pairs of sentences form a sentential analogy. This is the case in the following example where all the three possible sentential analogies hold (see also Table 2):

Do you have this in : *Do you have this in*
darker green? *dark green?*

Smaller, please. : *Small, please.*

I'll take the longer : *I'll take the long*
one. *one.*

3 Formalization of Verbal and Sentential analogies

3.1 Previous works on verbal analogies

Measuring the degree of relational similarity between words has received much attention in psychology. Gentner (1983) proposed a model called Structure Mapping Theory (SMT) that has been further elaborated until the present days. Hofstadter and his group have also put forward different proposals, among which the CopyCat model (Hofstadter and the Fluid Analogies Research Group, 1994).

The impact of semantics or pragmatics on verbal analogies may lead to situations where a range of different sources of knowledge may be called upon for the interpretation of specific analogies, leading to quite complex situations like the 'monster analogies' listed by Hoffman (1995). For more standard situations like those found in SAT tests,[3] modern·NLP techniques have proved to reach the level of the performance of human beings to identify verbal analogies (Turney and

Littman, 2005). Turney (2008) extends and simplifies the previous techniques to propose a uniform approach to synonyms, antonyms, and word associations, through analogies, an approach that could extend to hypernyms/hyponyms, holonyms, *etc.*

Referring to early but fundamental works in linguistics, linguists like de Saussure (1995) or Paul (1920) considered the role of relational similarity, *i.e.*, analogies, in derivational or flexional morphology and even in syntax, from a purely formal point of view. In this way, they justify both the creation of improper, but regular, morphological forms and the production of correct phrasal units.[4] In this trend, we use a definition of analogy between strings of characters that is based on form only, with the risk of capturing meaningless analogies. This formalization is taken from (Lepage, 2004) where the reported measures show that meaningless analogies represent less than 4% of the analogies captured, on the same kind of data that we use in our experiments.

3.2 Measuring relational similarity for sentential analogies

Lepage (2004) measures relational similarity between two pairs of strings (A, B) and (C, D) by verifying the following constraints:

$$\begin{cases} |A|_x - |B|_x & = & |C|_x - |D|_x \\ d(A, B) & = & d(C, D) \end{cases}$$

$|A|_x$ is the number of occurrences of character x in string A. d is the canonical edit distance that involves only insertion and deletion with equal weights.[5] As B and C may be exchanged in an analogy, the two constraints above have also to be verified for (A, C) and (B, D). With the previous example, where:

$$A = \textit{Do you have this in darker green?}$$
$$B = \textit{Do you have this in dark green?}$$
$$C = \textit{Smaller, please.}$$
$$D = \textit{Small, please.}$$

one verifies $d(A, B) = d(C, D) = 2$ and $d(A, C) = d(B, D) = 36$. The relation on the number of occurrences of characters, which is

---

[3]Scholastic Aptitude Test or Scholastic Assessment Test used in US colleges.

[4]For lack of space, we leave aside the debate about the argument of the poverty of the stimulus (see *The Linguistic Review*, vol. 19, 2003, for arguments and counter-arguments).

[5]This is slightly different from the Levenshtein distance that has substitution as an additional edit operation.

valid for each character, may be illustrated as follows for the character **e**:[6]

$$|A|_\mathbf{e} - |B|_\mathbf{e} \;=\; |C|_\mathbf{e} - |D|_\mathbf{e}$$
$$4 \;-\; 3 \;=\; 3 \;-\; 2$$

The previous characterization of analogies between strings of characters can be expanded in the following way

$$\begin{cases} d(A, B) &=& d(C, D) & (i) \\ |A| - |B| &=& |C| - |D| & (ii) \\ |A|_a - |B|_a &=& |C|_a - |D|_a & (iii.a) \\ |A|_b - |B|_b &=& |C|_b - |D|_b & (iii.b) \\ |A|_c - |B|_c &=& |C|_c - |D|_c & (iii.c) \\ |A|_x - |B|_x &=& |C|_x - |D|_x, \forall x & (iv) \end{cases}$$

where (ii)–$(iii.c)$ are all logically implied by (iv). $|A|$ denotes the length of A. (ii) expresses the fact that the difference in lengths must be the same for the two pairs of sentences.[7] Conditions $(iii.a)$–$(iii.c)$ are just condition (iv) for three specific characters a, b and c. These three characters are computed over a sample of the sentences of the corpus. They are those characters that exhibit the worst correlations among themselves for all possible values of $|A|_x - |B|_x$. The reason for this is to group pairs of sentences into groups as small as possible.

3.3 Non-transitivity and quality of series of analogous sentences

Notwithstanding, the previous formalization has a deceiving aspect. In this setting, analogy is not a transitive relation, *i.e.*, in the general case, $A : B :: C : D$ and $C : D :: E : F$ do not imply $A : B :: E : F$. An example of such a case is given by the following group of three pairs of sentences:

I prefer the longer . *I prefer the long*
one. *one.*

Do you have this in . *Do you have this in*
darker green? *dark green?*

Smaller, please. : *Small, please.*

where the constraint on distances does not hold between the first and the third pairs of sentences (respective distances 25 and 27).

---

[6]Trivially, $|A|_a - |B|_a = |C|_a - |D|_a \Leftrightarrow |A|_a - |C|_a = |B|_a - |D|_a$.

[7]This property obviously holds because the equality in difference of number of occurrences holds for all the characters in the alphabet.

To compromise with the absence of transitivity when building series of analogous sentences, we shall set a minimal threshold, *i.e.*, the *quality* of a series of pairs of analogous sentences will be defined as the number of actual analogies over the total number of possible analogies. In our experiments, we arbitrarily set this quality level to 90%. We shall refer to series of analogous sentences that exceed this quality level as *analogy clusters*.

4 Automatic Construction of Clusters of Analogous Sentences

4.1 The overall process

In order to automatically build analogy clusters from a corpus of sentences, our method proceeds in several steps:

1. for each sentence of the corpus compute its length and the number of occurrences of the three specific characters. This step is linear in the size of the corpus;

2. for each pair of sentences in the corpus, compute their distance. This step is quadratic in the size of the corpus. Previously sorting the sentences by lengths and imposing $|A| \leq |B|$ reduces the computation by half;

3. for each pair of sentences in a group with the same distance, first compute their difference in lengths and in number of occurrences for the three specific characters and then group pairs of sentences with the same difference in lengths and in number of occurrences of the three specific characters, by applying successive sorts. Distribution sort (or bucket sort) ensures a very fast computation;[8]

4. for each group of pairs of sentences, cluster into analogy clusters by using a greedy method.

4.2 Computing distances between sentences

A very efficient way to compute the distance between two sentences seen as strings of characters is to compute their similarity using the fast bit string algorithm described in (Allison and Dix, 1986) and then derive the value of the canonical

---

[8]This is similar in spirit to the technique that consists in building an entire tree-count data-structure as described in (Langlais and Yvon, 2008), but our technique is much more economical as our goal is different and less elaborate.

distance.[9] The above-mentioned algorithm proceeds in two steps, where the first step consists in compiling the first string and the second step computes the similarity. The first step can thus be factored for the computation of the distance between a sentence and all sentences that follow it in increasing lengths, leading to a large speed improvement and to tractable processing time. On a machine with a 2.16 GHz processor, the computation of the distances for 40,000 sentences is achieved in 30 minutes.

4.3 Building analogy clusters

The result of the third step of the process is many groups of pairs of sentences, in which all pairs of sentences share the same distance, the same difference in length and the same difference in number of occurrences for the three specific characters.

Condition (iv) can ultimately be verified between any two pairs of sentences, so as to know whether the analogy holds. For each pair of sentences, the set of other pairs of sentences that form analogies, its analogy set, can be computed and known, so as to know its cardinality.

The clustering process considers the pair of sentences with the largest number of analogies and its analogy set. It successively deletes the pairs of sentences with the least number of analogies from the analogy set until the analogy rate becomes larger than a threshold, 90% in our experiments. The analogy rate is computed as the number of analogies that really exist between all possible pairs of sentences remaining in the analogy set, divided by the square of its cardinality. When the threshold is reached, the cluster is saved and the clustering process proceeds with the next pair of sentences with the largest number of analogies.

5 Experiments

5.1 Corpus used

For experiments, we use an excerpt of the BTEC corpus (Basic Traveling Expressions Corpus). The BTEC corpus is jointly developed by the partners of the C-STAR project.[10] It is a collection of sentences that bilingual travel experts consider useful for people going to or coming from another country. This corpus is widely used in the community of machine translation as it provides translation

equivalents in English, Japanese, Chinese, Arabic *etc.*

The excerpt we use is the part that has been released during the international campaign of evaluation of machine translation systems IWSLT 2007 (International Workshop on Spoken Language Translation) (Fordyce, 2007). The following table summarises some statistics about these data.[11]

	English	Japanese
total number of sentences	39,754	36,774
lengths in characters		
shortest sentence:	4	2
longest sentence:	481	234

5.2 Statistics on the clusters produced

The clustering process could build 123,926 English clusters (42,169 for Japanese; in the sequel, the figures in parentheses are for Japanese), of which 118,386 (39,410). contain only two pairs of sentences (called small clusters in Figure 3). The remaining 5,540 (2,759) clusters contain more than 3 pairs of sentences (called large clusters in Figure 3). After distance 40 for the English data and 20 for the Japanese data, large clusters are almost absent. The maximum size of a cluster is 329 (123), obtained with distance 9 (8). Figure 2 plots the sizes of the largest clusters for each distance value.

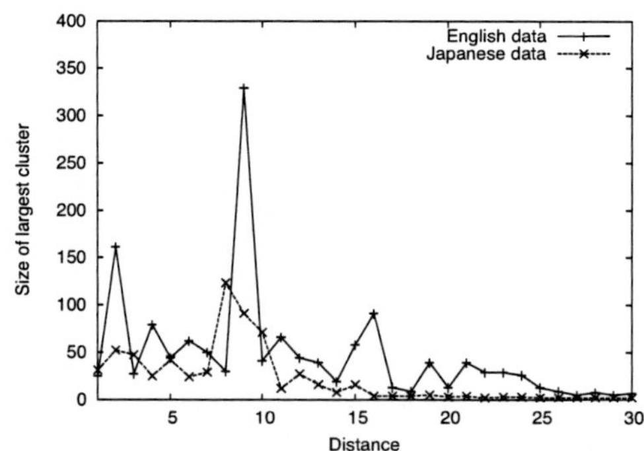

Figure 2: Size of the largest clusters for each distance.

In terms of oppositions, and thus linguistic features, the previous results mean that, for almost

---

[9] $d(A, B) = |A| + |B| - 2 \times s(A, B)$.
[10] www.c-star.org

[11] As the results presented in the following tables and figures will show, the data at our disposal has been preprocessed to separate punctuations from the preceding words (e.g. *what's* becomes *what 's*) and all words have been lowercased. In reality, this is not necessary for the present experiment, as the method processes the sentences in characters and not in words.

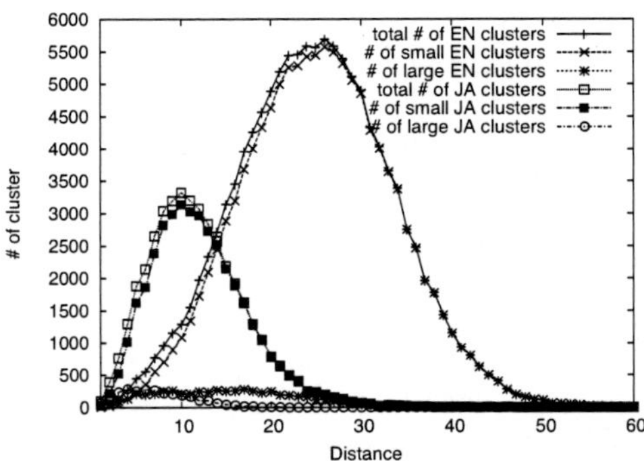

Figure 3: Number of clusters built for each distance.

40,000 English sentences, three times more oppositions could be found that are present in at least two pairs of sentences. However, only 5,500 oppositions are present in more than two pairs of sentences. This leads to a vectorial space of around 5,500 useful dimensions for this corpus.

6 Analysis of the Clusters Produced

In this section, we report on the English data only. Similar trends and explanations can be formulated for the Japanese data.

The largest cluster in our experiment contains 329 pairs of sentences. The interpretation of each cluster has to be made by looking at the opposition between the sentences on the left and the sentences on the right. In this cluster, the pairs of sentences are opposed by the deletion of the ending phrase , *please* . In terms of linguistic feature, one can say that the opposition lies between a neutral and a more polite form of expression. The size of the cluster reflects the optional character of this ending phrase, as one could expect in a corpus that heavily contains expressions of requests.

The next largest cluster contains 161 pairs of sentences. It shows the colloquial use of the contracted form *'s* in place of *is*. One can thus speak about a language level linguistic feature (colloquial vs formal). Again, this is natural in a corpus that necessarily contains traits of oral language.

The third largest cluster contains 91 pairs of sentences. It illustrates the possibility of anteposing *please* at the beginning of a sentence as in: *help me , please* . : *please help me* .

Table 1 shows an example of a cluster where the sentences on the left have the same meaning as the sentences on the right, *i.e.*, they are para-

phrases. The linguistic interpretation of this cluster is that the undefinite article *a* can be dropped in certain contexts, especially when expressing a request (sentences ending with: , *please* .)

Table 2 shows another example of a cluster containing sentences with very similar meaning that show that the phrase *where is the* can be substituted for *is there a*.

Other clusters exhibit similar phenonena. Affirmative sentences introduced by *i 'd like to*, are opposed with interrogative sentences introduced by *can i* ended with a circumstancial *here ?* . This may be seen as a structural transformation for near paraphrasing.

Tables 4 and 5 are clusters in which places (*subway station* and *youth hostel*) or predicates (*keep this baggage* and *draw me a map*) are exchanged in similar situational or illocutionary contexts. Such examples, where left and right sentences are not paraphrases, very frequent with smaller clusters, contradicts the impression of paraphrases that one could get by looking too fastly at larger clusters only (see also the remark at the end of Subsection 2.1 and the footnote there). These kinds of clusters do not reflect an opposition in linguistic features but rather show instantiations of semantic features that would be noted like LOC or PRED.

Other clusters make clear some orthographical variations, like the optional use of an hyphen in compound words *check-out, take-out etc.* or English vs American writing (*colour* vs *color*), thus reflecting a dialect feature.

Many pairs of sentences appearing in smaller clusters of higher distances appear also in larger clusters with a lower distance. For example, the two pairs of sentences below form one of the small clusters (containing only one sentential analogy).

can i borrow an iron ? : *can i have a blanket ?*
may i borrow an iron ? : *may i have a blanket ?*

But they also appear in a different configuration in a cluster that contains 79 pairs of sentences.

can i borrow an iron ? : *may i borrow an iron ?*
can i have a blanket ? : *may i have a blanket ?*

$$\vdots \qquad \vdots \qquad \vdots$$

The first cluster with only one sentential analogy shows the commutation of the phrase *an iron* with the phrase *a blanket* in a limited context, whereas the second cluster shows the commutation of the two modal verbs *can* and *may*.

# of sent. nlgs	Pairs of sentences		
12	i think there 's a mistake in the bill .	:	i think there 's mistake in the bill .
12	a collect call to japan , please .	:	collect call to japan , please .
12	i 'd like a room with a shower .	:	i 'd like a room with shower .
12	i 'll have a whiskey , please .	:	i 'll have whiskey , please .
11	i 'd like a room with a bath .	:	i 'd like a room with bath .
11	is this a train for chicago ?	:	is this train for chicago ?
13	a one -way ticket , please .	:	one -way ticket , please .
13	a table for two , please .	:	table for two , please .
13	is it a direct flight ?	:	is it direct flight ?
13	i 've got a backache .	:	i 've got backache .
11	porter , please .	:	a porter , please .
11	receipt , please .	:	a receipt , please .
11	i 'm a diabetic .	:	i 'm diabetic .

Table 1: A cluster that illustrates the possible deletion of the undefinite article *a* in some context. One can form only 159 analogies among the 13×13 possibilities. The analogy rate of the cluster is thus: $155/(13 \times 13) = 91.72\%$.

# of sent. nlgs	Pairs of sentences		
11	where is the main area for restaurants ?	:	is there a main area for restaurants ?
11	where is the department store ?	:	is there a department store ?
11	where is the duty -free shop ?	:	is there a duty -free shop ?
11	where is the changing room ?	:	is there a changing room ?
11	where is the sleeping car ?	:	is there a sleeping car ?
11	where is the barber shop ?	:	is there a barber shop ?
11	where is the dining car ?	:	is there a dining car ?
11	where is the restaurant ?	:	is there a restaurant ?
11	where is the gift shop ?	:	is there a gift shop ?
11	where is the telephone ?	:	is there a telephone ?
11	where is the pharmacy ?	:	is there a pharmacy ?

Table 2: A cluster that illustrates a substitution pattern of *where is the* with *is there a*. Its analogy rate is 100%.

# of sent. nlgs	Pairs of sentences		
10	i 'd like to cash this traveler 's check .	:	can i cash this traveler 's check here ?
10	i 'd like to make a hotel reservation .	:	can i make a hotel reservation here ?
10	i 'd like to make a reservation .	:	can i make a reservation here ?
10	i 'd like to check my baggage .	:	can i check my baggage here ?
10	i 'd like to leave my baggage .	:	can i leave my baggage here ?
10	i 'd like to leave my luggage .	:	can i leave my luggage here ?
10	i 'd like to reserve a room .	:	can i reserve a room here ?
10	i 'd like to have dinner .	:	can i have dinner here ?
10	i 'd like to check in .	:	can i check in here ?
10	i 'd like to swim .	:	can i swim here ?

Table 3: A cluster that illustrates the structural transformation of *i 'd like to* ... into *can i* ... *here ?*

# of sent. nlgs	Pairs of sentences		
4	is there a subway station around here ?	:	is there a youth hostel around here ?
4	how can i get to the subway station ?	:	how can i get to the youth hostel ?
4	is there a subway station near here ?	:	is there a youth hostel near here ?
4	is there a subway station nearby ?	:	is there a youth hostel nearby ?

Table 4: A cluster that examplifies the exchange of place names: *subway station* vs *youth hostel*.

# of sent. nlgs	Pairs of sentences		
4	could you keep this baggage ?	:	could you draw me a map ?
4	keep this baggage , please .	:	draw me a map , please .
4	will you keep this baggage ?	:	will you draw me a map ?
4	please keep this baggage .	:	please draw me a map .

Table 5: A cluster that examplifies the exchange of predicates: *keep this baggage* vs *draw me a map*.

In terms of vectorial space, this confirms the fact that the same sentence may be characterized along several dimensions.

7 Conclusion

We have presented a method that clusters analogous sentences from a corpus of short sentences and helps highlight the linguistic features concealed in a corpus. Such clusters of analogous sentences allow us to build a vectorial space associated with the sentences of a corpus. In an experiment on a corpus of 40,000 English sentences in the tourism domain, we could automatically collect more than 5,000 significant dimensions that represent linguistic oppositions or features. The ones observed on our data extend over a range of linguistic phenomena:

- orthographical variations;
- fronting of interjections;
- exchange of place names, document names, item names etc.;
- normal vs comparative forms of adjectives;
- structural transformations like interrogative vs affirmative;
- exchange of predicates in the same grammatical subject and object context;
- questions in different levels of politeness;
- etc.

References

Lloyd Allison and Trevor I. Dix. 1986. A bit string longest common subsequence algorithm. *Information Processing Letter*, 23:305–310.

Ferdinand de Saussure. 1995. *Cours de linguistique générale*. Payot, Lausanne et Paris, (1st ed. 1916).

Cameron Shaw Fordyce. 2007. Overview of the iwslt 2007 evaluation campaign. In *Proceedings of IWSLT 2007 (International Workshop on Spoken Machine Translation)*, pages 1–12, Trento.

Dedre Gentner. 1983. Structure mapping: A theoretical model for analogy. *Cognitive Science*, 7(2):155–170.

Robert R. Hoffman. 1995. Monster analogies. *AI Magazine*, 11:11–35.

Douglas Hofstadter and the Fluid Analogies Research Group. 1994. *Fluid Concepts and Creative Analogies*. Basic Books, New York.

Philippe Langlais and François Yvon. 2008. Scaling up analogical learning. In *Proceedings of the22nd International Conference on Computational Linguistics (COLING 2008)*, pages 51–54, Manchester, August.

Yves Lepage. 2004. Analogy and formal languages. *Electronic Notes in Theoretical Computer Science*, 53:180–191.

Hermann Paul. 1920. *Prinzipien der Sprachgeschichte*. Niemayer, Tübingen, (1st ed. 1880).

Peter D. Turney and M.L. Littman. 2005. Corpus-based learning of analogies and semantic relations. *Machine Learning*, 60(1–3):251–278.

Peter D. Turney. 2006. Similarity of semantic relations. *Computational Linguistics*, 32(2):379–416.

Peter Turney. 2008. A uniform approach to analogies, synonyms, antonyms, and associations. In *Proceedings of the 22nd International Conference on Computational Linguistics (Coling 2008)*, pages 905–912, Manchester, UK, August. Coling 2008 Organizing Committee.

ISSN 1736-6305 Vol. 4
http://hdl.handle.net/10062/9206

Building a morphological and syntactic lexicon by merging various linguistic resources

Miguel A. Molinero
Grupo LYS
University of A Coruña
A Coruña, Spain
mmolinero@udc.es

Benoît Sagot
Project ALPAGE
INRIA
Paris, France
benoit.sagot@inria.fr

Lionel Nicolas
Laboratoire I3S (Équipe RL)
Université de Nice-Sophia Antipolis
Sophia Antipolis, France
lnicolas@i3s.unice.fr

Abstract

This paper shows how large-coverage morphological and syntactic NLP lexicons can be developed by interpreting, converting to a common format and merging existing lexical resources. Applied on Spanish, this allowed us to build a morphological and syntactic lexicon, the Le*ffe*. It relies on the Alexina framework, originally developed together with the French lexicon Le*fff*. We describe how the input resources — two morphological and two syntactic lexicons — were converted into Alexina lexicons and merged. A preliminary evaluation shows that merging different sources of lexical information is indeed a good approach to improve the development speed, the coverage and the precision of linguistic resources.

1 Introduction

In the environment of Natural Language Processing (NLP), linguistic resources, such as lexicons and grammars, are required for many high-level applications. However, the current situation for most languages is that several scattered resources exist, with different coverage levels, different linguistic backgrounds and different lexical formalisms. Nevertheless, none of these resources combines in a satisfying way the following properties:

- coverage: all words, including rare ones, in all categories should be included;

- quality: manually and automatically developed resources contain various errors;

- richness: applications such as (deep) parsing require at least morphological and syntactic information, including subcategorization frames.

However, each existing resource for a given language is a provider of valuable lexical information. Merging these resources and expanding them thanks to semi-automatic techniques is therefore a promising idea. Anyhow, this requires to be able to interpret all input resources despite partly incompatible lexical models, to convert them into a common model and format, and then to merge these converted lexicons. None of these three steps is trivial. This approach has been successfully applied on French for developing the syntactic lexicon Le*fff* (*Lexique des formes fléchies du français*), within a lexicon development framework named Alexina (Sagot et al., 2006; Sagot and Danlos, 2008; Danlos and Sagot, 2008).

In this paper, we confirm the validity of this approach by applying it to Spanish, in order to build a wide-coverage morphological and syntactic lexicon for this language, the Le*ffe* (*Léxico de formas flexionadas del español*). Such a lexicon can be directly used in advanced NLP applications, particularly in those involving deep parsing. The Le*ffe* is developed within the same framework as the Le*fff*, the Alexina framework, and distributed under the same free license, the LGPL-LR.[1] The flexibility and completeness of the Alexina format allows for a straightforward integration with deep grammatical formalisms (LFG, LTAG) which require detailed syntactic data for all forms.

The work described in this paper is one of the starting points of the recently created Victoria project, which aims at developing

---

[1]Lesser General Public License for Linguistic Resources

techniques and tools for efficient acquisition and correction of large-coverage linguistic resources with inter-language links. The first phase of the project focuses on Spanish, Galician[2] and French.

This paper is organized as follows: first, in Section 2, we introduce the Alexina model. Section 3 describes the existing Spanish resources we used. Along Section 4 we show how these resources were merged, and in Section 5 we briefly evaluate the resulting lexicon. We present our conclusions and future work in Section 6.

2 Representing lexical information: the Alexina model

A detailed description of all words belonging to a language is needed in order to perform high-level NLP tasks such as deep parsing. This information is usually compiled into a lexicon, which could be defined as a list of words associated with their corresponding morphological and syntactic information. Alexina is a framework compatible with the LMF[3] standard, whose goal is to represent lexical information in a complete, efficient and readeable way (Sagot, 2005; Danlos and Sagot, 2008). The Alexina model allows to describe rich morphological and syntactic lexical information, which can be used in NLP tools relying on various grammatical formalisms.

Alexina is based on two representation levels:

- The intensional lexicon factorizes the lexical information by associating each lemma with a morphological class and deep syntactic information (a deep sub-categorization frame, a list of possible re-structurations, and other syntactic features such as information on control, attributes, mood of sentencial complements, etc.);

- The extensional lexicon, which is generated automatically by *compiling* the intensional lexicon, associates each inflected

form with a detailed structure that represents all its morphological and syntactic information: morphological tag, surface subcategorization frame corresponding to one particular redistribution, and other syntactic features.

The intensional representation is used for an efficent description, while the extensional is directly used by NLP tools such as parsers.

The remainder of this section briefly describes the format of the intensional and extensional lexicons and the formalism used for describing the morphological and syntactic information within the Alexina model.

The first task achieved by the compilation process, which turns an intensional lexicon (an `.ilex` file) into an extensional lexicon (a `.lex` file), is to inflect lemmas according to their morphological class. Morphological classes are defined in a formalized morphological description (Sagot, 2005; Sagot, 2007). In case a lemma inflects in a very specific way, and/or if a lemma has additional inflected forms apart from those generated by its morphological class, these forms are "manually" listed in an additional file (the corresponding `.mf` file).

As sketched above, the compilation process also maps deep syntactic information into surface syntactic information. Deep syntactic information (deep subcategorization frames and other syntactic information) is common to all redistributions, whereas each redistribution corresponds to different surface syntactic information, and therefore to different extensional entries.

For example, here is the intensional entry in the Le*fff* for the French lemma *clarifier*₁ (i.e., *clarifier* in the sense of English *clarify*), slightly simplified:[4]

```
clarifier₁ v-er
        Lemma;v;
        <arg₀:Suj:cln|scompl|sinf|sn,
        arg₁:Obj:(cla|scompl|sn)>;
        %actif,%passif,%passif_impersonnel
```

It describes a transitive entry whose morphological class is **v-er**, the class of so-called first-group verbs. Its semantic predicate can be represented by the **Lemma** as is, i.e., *clarifier*. Its category is *verb*

---

[2]A co-official language in north-west Spain.
[3]Lexical Markup Framework, the ISO/TC37 standard for NLP lexicons.

[4]In particular, additional syntactic features such as control information are not shown, for clarity reasons.

(v). It has two arguments canonically realized by the syntactic functions `Suj` (subject) and `Obj` (direct object).[5] Each syntactic function is associated with a list of possible realizations,[6] which are between brackets if it is faculative. This entry allows for three different redistributions: active (`%actif`), passive (`%passif`), impersonnal passive (`%passif_impersonnel`, *il a été clarifié (par Pierre) que Marie ne viendrait pas*, in English *it has been clarified (by Pierre) that Mary wouldn't come*).

The compilation process builds one extensional entry for each inflected form and each compatible redistribution, by applying formalized definitions of these redistributions (which can be found in file **constructions**). For example, the only inflected forms of *clarifier* that is compatible with the passive redistribution are the past participle forms. The (simplified) extensional passive entry for *clarifiés* is the following (Kmp is the morphological tag for past participle masculine plural forms):

```
clarifiés    v
[pred='clarifier₁<arg₁:Suj:cln|scompl|sn,
arg₀:Obl2:(par-sn)>',@passive,@pers,@Kmp];
%passif
```

As said before, merging linguistic resources requires a careful interpretation of their underlying models, followed by their conversion into a common model that is able to preserve as much (valuable) information as possible. The Alexina model has been evolved over the last 5 years, alongside with the development of the Le*fff* and resources for other languages (Polish, Slovak, and others). The Le*fff* has been mostly developed by semi-automatic acquisition techniques and by merging lexical information extracted from other freely available resources.

It has been used in different NLP tools including deep parsers for French based on various formalisms (LTAG, LFG, etc.). This all has allowed to develop Alexina in order to represent a great range of lexical phenomena. This fact, besides the linguistic proximity between French and Spanish as Romance languages, explains why Alexina already covers all lexical phenomena we encountered while working on Spanish, and no changes in the format were needed.

3   Existing lexical resources for Spanish

Several resources are available for Spanish. However, none of them fulfills all our requirements:

- Large coverage, good precision and satisfying richness (as explained in the introduction);

- Complete separation between lexical and grammatical information;

- Clear and compact format easily readable by humans;

- Freely available in terms of access, modification and distribution;

- Easily linkable with resources describing other languages;

Nevertheless, many valuable information can be found in these existing resources. The following ones were used at some point in the development of the Le*ffe*:

Multext is an international project (Ide and Véronis, 1994) whose goals are to develop standards and specifications for the encoding and processing of linguistic corpora, and to develop tools, corpora and linguistic resources embodying these standards. It includes morphological (but not syntactic) lexicons for several languages, including Spanish, that rely on a widely-used tagset;

The USC lexicon is a large morphological lexicon (Álvarez et al., 1998), created for PoS tagging tasks in the research group *Gramática del Español* of the University of Santiago de Compostela (Spain).

---

[5]The complete set of syntactic functions used in the Le*fff* and in the Le*ffe* is the following: `Suj` (subject), `Obj` (direct object that can be cliticized into an accusative clitic), `Objde` (indirect object canonically introduced by preposition *de* that can be cliticized into a genitive clitic), `Objà` or `Obja` (indirect object canonically introduced by *à* in French or *a* in Spanish), `Loc` (locative), `Dloc` (delocative), `Att` (attribute), `Obl` and `Obl2` (oblique non-cliticizable arguments).

[6]Clitic realizations in French are `cln`, `cla`, `cld`, `en` and `y` for the nominative, accusative, dative, *en* (genitive) and *y* clitic pronouns. Direct realizations are sn, sinf, scompl, qcompl and sa for nominal, infinitive, phrasal, indirect interrogative and adjectival phrases. Prepositional realization are of the form *prep-real*, where *prep* is a preposition and *real* a direct realization.

ADESSE is a database for Spanish verbs developed at the University of Vigo (Spain) (García-Miguel and Albertuz, 2005) with syntactic and some semantic information. It is a high quality work which includes subcategorizarion frames for more than 4,000 verbs. However, it is restricted to verbs and includes no morphological information;

The Spanish Resource Grammar (SRG) is an open-source multi-purpose large-coverage and precise grammar for Spanish (Marimon et al., 2007). It is grounded in the theoretical framework of Head-driven Phrase Structure Grammar (HPSG) and includes a lexicon describing syntactic information for Spanish in a well organized hierarchy of syntactic classes. However, its is not easily readable, and specific to the HPSG formalism.

4 Converting and merging existing resources for building the Le*ffe*

The construction of the Le*ffe* has been sucessfuly achieved by interpreting all input resources mentioned above (despite their partially incompatible lexical models), converting them into the Alexina format, and finally merging the converted lexicons. As said in the previous section, the Multext and the USC lexicons only include morphological information, whereas the SRG and the ADESSE lexicons include syntactic information. Therefore, we decided to proceed in the following way:

1. Build a morphological baseline lexicon by converting the Multext lexicon into the Alexina format and adding some Alexina-specific entries (prefixes, suffixes, named entities, punctuation signs);

2. Converting the USC Lexicon into the Alexina format and merging it with the baseline lexicon extracted from Multext, so as to get the morphological basis of the Le*ffe*;

3. Converting the ADESSE and the SRG lexicon, which are syntactic-only, into the Alexina format;

4. Merging the morphological Le*ffe* from step 2 and both verbal syntactic lexicons

built during step 3; the result is the current Le*ffe*, i.e., the Le*ffe* beta.

We shall now describe sucessively the four following tasks: converting a morphogical lexicon into the Alexina format (steps 1 and 2), converting the ADESSE and SRG syntactic lexicons into the Alexina format (step 3), merging morphologial lexicons (step 4) and merging syntactic lexicons (step 4).

4.1 Converting a morphological lexicon into the Alexina format

A morphological lexicon can be seen as a set of triples of the form *(form,lemma,tag)*. However, in an architecture such as Alexina, which aims at representing also syntactic information, each (intensional) entry corresponds to one lemma. As explained in Section 2, each lemma is associated with a morphological class, which is formally defined in a morphological description of the language. Therefore, in order to convert a morphological lexicon into the Alexina format, such a morphological description has to be extracted automatically from a set of *(form,lemma,tag)* triples.

We developed a fully-automatic technique for extracting morphological classes from such a set of triples. For each lemma, it extracts the longest prefix that is common to all its inflected forms, which is considered as the stem, and builds an ordered list of *(suffix,tag)* pairs.[7] If at least 3 lemmas lead to the same list of *(suffix,tag)* pairs, this list is turned into the definition of a morphological class, and all corresponding lemmas are associated with this class. Moreover, the stems of all these lemmas are analyzed, so as to build the most specific (reasonable) regular pattern that matches them all. This allows to prevent further lemmas to be added with an incompatible morphological class, but also to use the morphological description as an ambiguous lemmatizer with limited overgeneration. For example, while converting the Spanish Multext lexicon, a morphological class is built from a list of *(suffix,tag)* pairs that include the ending *-ar* for the infinitive, *-a* for the third person singular of the indicative present, and *-ué* for the first person singular

---

[7]At this point, the process discards all entries that do not have their lemma as one of their inflected forms.

of the indicative past. An example of such a verb is *halagar* (*to flatter*), which has the inflected forms *halaga* (*he flatters*) and *halagué* (*I flattered*). Because the stems of all lemmas in this class end in -*g*, the regular pattern `.*g` is associated to this morphological class.

Morphological classes that include only one or two lemmas are not built. Instead, the inflected forms of the corresponding lemmas are listed in the corresponding `.mf` file (see Section 2).

We applied this technique to build our baseline lexicon by converting the Spanish Multext lexicon into an Alexina lexicon, including a morphological description of Spanish. The same technique has also been applied to convert the USC lexicon into the Alexina format, which created a different morphological description, since the set of lemmas, the tagsets and sometimes the set of inflected forms for a given lemma are different from one lexicon to another. Section 4.3 explains how we merged these two morphological lexicons.

4.2 Converting the ADESSE and SRG lexicons into the Alexina format

Our most important source of syntactic information is the ADESSE lexicon, a database containing syntantic information for Spanish verbs. ADESSE is a carefully developed resource that includes much valuable information. We parsed and transformed it into the Alexina format as follows. Each verb in the ADESSE lexicon was transformed into one or more Leffe entries with dummy morphological information, by converting ADESSE argument structures into Alexina subcategorization frames. The result is a lexicon with complete and reliable syntactic information for a significant number of Spanish verbs (3,427 unique verb lemmas).

Since some verb lemmas included in Multext or in the USC lexicon are not covered by the ADESSE lexicon and because cross validation is generally useful, we also extracted information from the SRG lexicon. However, we shall see that the technique we used is not fully reliable, and the SRG lexicon itself has a lower precision than the ADESSE lexicon. Thus, we gave a lower level of confidence to syntactic information extracted from SRG, as

explained in Section 4.4.

The SRG classifies lemmas according to a hierarchy of syntactic classes. Mapping one class into the Leffe format allows to extract as many entries as there are lemmas belonging to this class. We used the Lefff as bridge in order to establish a mapping between SRG syntactic classes and Alexina syntactic descriptions. The syntactic proximity between Spanish and French allows to retain Lefff syntactic descriptions in the Spanish lexicon with very few modifications (almost only translating prepositions). The technique can be described as follows: [8]

1. First, a list of the most common verb classes in SRG were extracted;

2. A representative lemma of each of these classes was taken from SRG; this lemma must belong only to a single class in SRG and its translation into French should have the same syntactic behaviour than the Spanish one (something easy to fulfill thanks to the linguistic proximity between French and Spanish).

3. We look into the Lefff for the translation of these lemmas and extracted their associated syntactic information;

4. A link was created between the SRG class and the extracted Lefff syntactic description, manually adapted for becoming a Leffe syntactic description[9];

5. Finally, we assigned to each SRG entry the corresponding Leffe syntactic description.

Such a way to process could lead to some incomplete or erroneous entries. To restrict their impact, we decided to ignore extracted information in case of doubt.

Despite our efforts, it is possible that no syntactic information is found at all for some lemmas of our baseline lexicon. The opposite situation is very rare, that is, not to find morphological information, since it is

---

[8]Steps 1 and 5 were automatically accomplished, while steps 2, 3 and 4 were manually done for the 40 most frequent SRG classes, which covered more than 3,000 verbal lemmas.

[9]In practice, we needed only to translate prepositions.

much more commonly available and easier to acquire. So the very basic condition to acquire a word is to find its morphological information.

4.3 Merging morphological resources

Once in the Alexina format, a morphological lexicon can be seen as a set of *(lemma,class)* pairs, where *class* denotes the inflection class of the entry. Therefore, merging a main morphological lexicon L with an additional morphological lexicon L' consists in converting morphological classes of L' into morphological classes of L. This merging process is applied PoS by PoS, to avoid problems related to cross-PoS homonymy.

In order to achieve this mapping, we rely on lemmas that are common to both lexicons. Given a class from L', we extract from L' all corresponding lemmas that are also in L. Then we look for the classes of these lemmas in L. Usually, the large majority of the lemmas involved have the same class in L, but exceptions do occur. These exceptions correspond to mismatches between L and L', and therefore to errors in L and/or L'. They can be solved automatically by giving the priority to L (or L'), or checking them manually.

We applied this technique with L being the baseline lexicon extracted from Multext (so as to preserve the Multext tagset) and L' being the result of the conversion of the USC lexicon into the Alexina format. The result of this merging process is the morphological part of the Le*ff*e. Section 5 gives quantitative figures about it and compares it to other morphological lexicons.

4.4 Merging syntactic resources

Once the morphological part of the Le*ff*e is obtained, we must complete it with syntactic information. For verbs, this information is obtained by merging the Alexina version of the ADESSE and SRG lexicons, i.e., two intensional lexicons. For other categories, not covered by the ADESSE lexicon, we used the syntactic information extracted from the Alexina version of the SRG lexicon. Finally, some entries (prepositions, auxiliaries, a few very specific verbs) have been written or completed manually.

Contrarily to (Danlos and Sagot, 2008), our two input lexicons did not use the same criteria to distinguish between different entries of a same lemma. Therefore, we were not able to merge intensional entries. Rather, the merging process we used relies on the notion of *expanded intensional lexicon*. As seen above, an intensional entry includes a subcategorization frame in which each syntactic function may be facultatively realized and may have a list of realization alternatives. Such an intensional entry can be converted into a set of *expanded intensional entries*: each of these entries has a subcategorization frame that is *fully-specified* (no alternatives, no facultative argument), in such a way that all these entries, taken together, cover all cases covered by the original intensional entry. For example, an intensional entry with the subcategorization frame `<Suj:cln|sn,Obj:(sn)>` corresponds to 4 expanded intensional entries with the following subcategorization frames: `<Suj:sn>`, `<Suj:cln>`, `<Suj:sn,Obj:sn>` and `<Suj:cln,Obj:sn>`.

The idea is the following: we first expand both our input intensional lexicons (the Alexina versions of the ADESSE and SRG lexicons); then we merge these expanded intensional lexicons; finally, we re-factorize the merging result into an intensional lexicon. The expansion and merging steps are straightforward (here, merging is simply computing the union of all expanded entries). The re-factorization step computes the optimal factorization of a list of (possibly expanded) intensional entries, and involve no particular linguistic knowledge.

The result is a syntactic-only lexicon, which is trivially merged with the morphological lexicon. For those morphological entries that were not covered by the syntactic-only lexicon, we decided to give them the syntactic features that were the most common among entries of the same PoS. This is obviously a baseline. For example, all verbal lemmas that are not covered by ADESSE and by SRG received the following subcategorization frame: `<Suj:sn|cln,Obj:(sn|cla)>` (transitive verb with facultative direct object). However, we rely on existing semi-automatic techniques for extending and correcting our lexicon in the near future (Nicolas et al., 2008).

5   Preliminary Evaluation

In order to evaluate the quality of Le*ff*e, currently in beta version, we performed the following tests: on the one hand, we have compared Le*ff*e with other known Spanish lexicons in terms of coverage; on the other hand, we measured the improvement achieved on the baseline lexicon after adding the information extracted from all other sources.

Regarding coverage, the Le*ff*e beta contains more than 165,000 unique *(lemma,PoS)* pairs, which correspond to approx. 1,590,000 extensional entries that associate a form with both morphological and syntactic information (approx. 680,000 unique *(form,PoS)* pairs). Other lexicons have the following properties:

- SRG: 76,000 unique *(lemma,PoS)* pairs[10] (53.9% less than Le*ff*e), but syntactic information is provided only for some of them;

- Multext: 510,710 unique *(form,PoS)* pairs[11] (24.9% less than Le*ff*e), and no syntactic information is provided;

- Spanish gilcUB-M Dictionary: 70,000 lemmas[11] (57.6% less than Le*ff*e), and no syntactic information is provided;

- USC Lexicon: 490,000 unique *(form,PoS)* pairs (27.95% less than Le*ff*e), and no syntactic information is provided.

We have also tested the morphological coverage of our lexicon in the context of a real application: a morphological preprocessor (Graña et al., 2002; Barcala et al., 2007) developed by group COLE.[12] We performed a first test with our baseline lexicon, and a second one with the Le*ff*e beta.

We have used a corpus of raw text obtained from Wikipedia Sources[13] as an input for this test. It includes more than 4,322,000 words after clearing Wikipedia references and foreign expressions. The evaluation took into account how many words were not tagged by the preprocessor and thus remained unknown. It is worth noting that unknown words are an important cause of PoS-tagging errors. Such problems can be tackled by relying on (very) large coverage lexicons.

As can be observed in Table 1, the process allows noticeable benefits. The Le*ff*e beta has beaten other large lexicons in the morphological preprocessing task[14]. Even if the difference is slight, this demonstrates the interest of merging existing resources to create an enhanced one.

In order to measure the syntactic coverage of the lexicons at all stages of the merging process, we have used the notion of *expanded intensional entry* which describes one fully-specified syntactic behaviour (see Section 4.4). The expanded intensional lexicon acquired from SRG contains 42,689 unique entries, i.e., fully-specified subcategorization frames, while the one from ADESSE contains 39,040. After merging these lexicons, the number of such unique entries jumps to 66,028. Finally, the Le*ff*e beta, which associates default syntactic information with all verbs not covered by the result of this merge, contains 91,507 unique expanded entries. After factorization, the Le*ff*e contains 16,311 verbal entries.

6   Conclusion and future work

For many languages, several lexical resources exist, but usually none of them is satisfying in terms of coverage, richness (morphological and syntactic information is required) or precision.

In this work we have described a process to merge existing Spanish lexical resources into an enhanced one. From our point of view, this approach is nowadays the best way to produce quickly high-quality lexical resources. The theoretical and practical context described here can be used for a similar task in other languages. The resulting lexicon is a large-coverage morphological and syntactic lexicon, the Le*ff*e. This lexicon, currently in beta version, will be distributed under a LGPL-LR license[15] in the near future. Although it is still

---

[10]As provided by Freeling (http://garraf.epsevg.upc.es/freeling/) in a version from April 2008.

[11]According ELRA webpage http://catalog.elra.info, December 2008.

[12]http://www.grupocole.org

[13]http://download.wikimedia.org, January 2009

[14]It is worth noting that the distribution of entries in Multext seems not so natural, since despite being the largest in terms of number of entries, is the worse on this task. Indeed we checked that many common lemmas are missing in Multext.

[15]As explained in this paper, the construction of the Le*ff*e beta involved the Spanish morphological lexicon developed within the Multext project, which is freely

	Total unknown words	Unique unknown words
Multext	228,815	49,673
USC Lexicon	70,026	25,888
Baseline	86,521	27,234
Le*ffe* beta	69,756	24,703

Table 1: Results of applying the morphological preprocessor using different lexicons.

far from perfect, we have shown that the Le*ffe* beta has already overtaken other well known Spanish lexicons in terms of morphological and syntactic coverage.

In the near future, we plan to further evaluate the Le*ffe* as follows: we shall compare the coverage and precision of different deep parsers that rely on the same grammar but on different morphological and syntactic lexicons such as the Le*ffe*. Besides, we will continue improving Le*ffe* using techniques described here with other linguistic resources, and by applying automatic acquisition techniques as additional sources of lexical knowledge.

Acknowledgement Partially supported by Ministerio de Educación y Ciencia of Spain and FEDER (HUM2007-66607-C04-02), the Xunta de Galicia (INCITE08PXIB302179PR, INCITE08E1R104022ES, PGIDIT07SIN005206PR) and the "Galician Network for Language Processing and Information Retrieval" 2006-2009). We would like also to thank group *Gramática del Español* from USC, and especially to Guillermo Rojo, M.ª Paula Santalla and Susana Sotelo, for granting us access to their lexicon.

References

Fco. Mario Barcala, Miguel A. Molinero, and Eva Domínguez. 2007. Xml rules for enclitic segmentation. *Lecture Notes in Computer Science: Computer Aided Systems Theory - EUROCAST 2007, Revised selected papers, pp. 273-281*.

Laurence Danlos and Benoît Sagot. 2008. Constructions pronominales dans dicovalence et le lexique-grammaire – intégration dans le Le*fff*. In *Proceedings of the 27th Lexicon-Grammar Conference*, L'Aquila, Italy.

José M. García-Miguel and Francisco J. Albertuz. 2005. Verbs, semantic classes and semantic roles in the adesse project. In *Proceedings of the Interdisciplinary Workshop on the Identification and Representation of Verb Features and Verb Classes*.

Jorge Graña, Fco. Mario Barcala, and Jesús Vilares. 2002. Formal methods of tokenization for part-of-speech tagging. *Computational Linguistics and Intelligent Text Processing, Lecture Notes in Computer Science*.

Nancy Ide and Jean Véronis. 1994. Multext: Multilingual text tools and corpora. In *Proceedings of COLING'94*.

Montserrat Marimon, Natalia Seghezzi, and Núria Bel. 2007. An open-source lexicon for spanish. In *Sociedad Española para el Procesamiento del Lenguaje Natural, n. 39*.

Lionel Nicolas, Benoît Sagot, Miguel A. Molinero, Jacques Farré, and Éric Villemonte de La Clergerie. 2008. Computer aided correction and extension of a syntactic wide-coverage lexicon. In *Proceedings of COLING'08*.

Benoît Sagot and Laurence Danlos. 2008. Méthodologie lexicographique de constitution d'un lexique syntaxique de référence pour le français. In *Proceedings of the workshop "Lexicographie et informatique : bilan et perspectives"*, Nancy, France.

Benoît Sagot, Lionel Clément, Éric Villemonte de La Clergerie, and Pierre Boullier. 2006. The Le*fff* 2 syntactic lexicon for French: architecture, acquisition, use. In *Proceedings of LREC'06*.

Benoît Sagot. 2005. Automatic acquisition of a Slovak lexicon from a raw corpus. In *Lecture Notes in Artificial Intelligence 3658 (© Springer-Verlag), Proceedings of TSD'05*, pages 156–163, Karlovy Vary, Czech Republic.

Benoît Sagot. 2007. Building a morphosyntactic lexicon and a pre-syntactic processing chain for Polish. In *Proceedings of the 3rd Language & Technology Conference (LTC'05)*, pages 423–427, Poznań, Poland, October.

Concepción Álvarez, Pilar Alvariño, Adelaida Gil, Teresa Romero, María Paula Santalla, and Susana Sotelo. 1998. Avalon, una gramática formal basada en corpus. In *Procesamiento del Lenguaje Natural (Actas del XIV CONGRESO de la SEPLN)*, pages 132–139, Alicante, Spain.

available for research. The Le*ffe* beta is the result of the research work described here. It merges lexical information coming from various resources, most of them with a coverage that is larger than the Spanish Multext lexicon. For this reason, we consider as appropriate to publish the Le*ffe* beta under the LGPL.

ISSN 1736-6305 Vol. 4
http://hdl.handle.net/10062/9206

Using Semantic Features Derived from Word-Space Models for Swedish Coreference Resolution

Kristina Nilsson and Hans Hjelm
Swedish Graduate Schoool of Language Technology (GSLT) and
Computational Linguistics, Department of Linguistics
Stockholm University, SE-106 91 Stockholm
`{kristina.nilsson,hans.hjelm}@ling.su.se`

Abstract

We investigate the effect of using word-space models as an approximation of the kind of lexico-semantic and common-sense knowledge needed for coreference resolution of definite descriptions, that is, definite NPs with a common noun as head, for Swedish news text. We contrast a system using semantic knowledge from the word-space models with a semantically ignorant system and another system drawing its semantic information from a semantic dictionary called SynLex. We demonstrate an improvement in the results for two different evaluation tasks for the system using word space-derived semantic information over both other systems.

1   Introduction

Coreference resolution, that is, the identification of all expressions referring to the same entity within a discourse, is an important preprocessing step in many Natural Language Processing tasks, for example question answering, information extraction, automatic summarization, and machine translation (Mitkov, 2003). For example, extrinsic evaluations of the effect of adding coreference resolution to systems for question answering show that adding referential relationships between noun phrases improves system performance as well as the quality of retrieved answers for passage retrieval (Morton, 2005), and that the coverage of off-line answer extraction is improved (Hendrickx et al., 2008a).

The coreference resolution task, when applied to noun phrases, can be further divided into the following sub-tasks where the classification is based on the type of referring expression:

a) pronoun resolution, e.g., the pronoun 'he' can be used to refer to the NP 'presi-

dent Kennedy' with the Named Entity (NE) 'Kennedy' as head,

b) identification of coreferent NEs, e.g., 'John F. Kennedy', 'Kennedy', 'President Kennedy', and 'JFK' might all refer to the same discourse entity,

c) resolution of definite descriptions, that is, anaphoric definite NPs with a common noun as head, e.g., 'the president of the United States' might refer to the same entity as 'the president' or 'the commander-in-chief' within a discourse.

This paper is concerned with the task 'c', the resolution of coreferent definite descriptions. This is a challenging problem in comparison to Named Entity coreference resolution ('b') and pronoun resolution ('a'). For example, (Strube et al., 2002) report an f-score of 33.94% for definite description resolution using a knowledge-poor, language- and domain-independent approach. The results for definite descriptions are markedly lower than the results for NEs and pronouns (with f-scores of 76.22% and 81.60% respectively) as well as the overall result for the system (an f-score of 67.89%).

But however difficult, it is an important task: in the coreference annotated data used in this experiment, 24% of all subsequent-mention coreferent NPs are pronouns, 32% are NEs, and 44% are definite descriptions. Further, resolution of definite descriptions might be of interest in information access tasks such as information extraction and question answering because definite descriptions carry additional information about the discourse entity in question, for example that the entity denoted by the NE 'John F. Kennedy' in some discourse also is referred to by the definite description 'the president of the United States'.

"

Resolution of definite descriptions in turn includes a number of sub-tasks of varying difficulty; we distinguish between these tasks:

1) *resolution of identical head definite descriptions*: cases where the anaphoric definite description and the antecedent share the same head noun, as in the following example: 'She has a **revenue** of three million a year [...]. The **revenue** of Elly Lagerin's store ...'[1] About 50% of all anaphoric definite descriptions in our data share the same head noun as the antecedent, and thus can be resolved with various string and substring matching techniques combined with morphological analysis;

2) *resolution of non-identical head definite descriptions*: the remaining 50% of all anaphoric definite descriptions are cases where the anaphor has a different head noun than the antecedent. We distinguish between two types of cases based on whether the head of the antecedent NP is a NE or a common noun:

   a) In cases where the antecedent is a NE of a certain type and the head noun of the anaphor is a common noun, as in the antecedent-anaphor pair '<NE type='PERSON'>Hans Stråberg</NE>' - 'the CEO of Electrolux', an estimate of the semantic compatibility of the candidate antecedent and the anaphor might help resolution,

   b) In cases where both the anaphor and the antecedent are definite descriptions but their head nouns are non-identical, resolution might depend on information on lexical relations such as synonymy, hypernymy or hyponymy, or on additional information required for further reasoning and/or keeping track of the current focus.

The main topic of this paper is resolution of non-identical head definite descriptions. We describe an experiment on modeling lexical knowledge on domain-specific data using word-space models. This knowledge is used for deriving

---

[1]This example is an approximate translation from our Swedish data.

features for coreference resolution of candidate antecedent-anaphor pairs. In order to evaluate these semantic features, they are added to a baseline feature set consisting of morphological, lexical, positional, and syntactic features. We also compare the effect of the word-space features to the effect of features based on a semantic dictionary, SynLex.

While coreference resolution is an important preprocessing task for many NLP tasks, the availability of resources needed for the task varies depending on the language and the domain. For the sub-task of resolution of definite NPs with a common noun as head, information on semantic relatedness is essential. The word-space model meet these needs well: it can provide lexico-semantic similarity judgements in any language and domain, as long as the appropriate text material is available. This is our main reason for choosing to work with word-space, or *distributional*, semantics in our experiments.

2   Related Work

Systems for coreference resolution (either for the coreference problem as a whole, or focusing on sub-tasks such as pronoun resolution, or processing of anaphoric definite NPs with common noun heads) commonly use resources such as the lexical database WordNet (Fellbaum, 1998) or its (smaller) European counterparts in EuroWordNet (Vossen, 1998) for adding information on semantic relatedness between NPs.

For example, WordNet was used to test the semantic compatibility of individual NP pairs by assigning the first WordNet sense of the head noun as the semantic class of common noun NPs by (Soon et al., 2001), who found that both a better algorithm for assigning semantic classes and a more refined semantic class hierarchy were needed.

(Ng, 2007) shows that a system for English using automatically induced semantic class knowledge performs better than a system using the WordNet first sense heuristic, while (Hendrickx et al., 2008b) reports that combining features based on automatically generated semantic clusters with features based on synonym and hypernym relations in Dutch EuroWordNet, gives a small but significant improvement.

Other studies have also shown that the knowledge encoded in WordNet is insufficient for coreference resolution, e.g., there are limitations as to coverage of both vocabulary and relations, ambiguity (there might be more than one sense to a concept, and synsets in WordNet are sorted by frequency), and semantically related words might be located far from each other in the WordNet structure (see e.g., (Vieira and Poesio, 2000; Poesio et al., 1998)).

Furthermore, WordNet is a general ontology, while resolution might require domain-specific or context-dependent lexical information. Efforts towards automatically acquiring such information from corpora are described by e.g., (Poesio et al., 1998; Goecke et al., 2007). Again, as mentioned in Sect. 1, we choose to work with word-space semantics, precisely for its ability to provide language and domain-specific lexico-semantic knowledge to our system.

3   Semantic Features for Coreference Resolution

In this experiment, coreference is defined as a relation of identity of reference between two noun phrases. The resolution task is limited to classification of pairs of possibly anaphoric NPs and their candidate antecedents; the subsequent linking of classified pairs into coreference chains will not be discussed here as the aim of the paper is to discuss the influence of semantic features on the classification task.[2]

The task is further limited to resolution of non-identical head anaphora (listed as type '2' in Sect. 1), i.e., cases where we cannot rely on string matching for resolving the anaphoric reference. We also divide the pair-wise classification into two sub-tasks, based on the respective NP types of the candidate antecedent and anaphor:

1. the candidate anaphor is a definite NP with a common noun head, and the candidate antecedent is a NE – listed as '2a' in Sect. 1;

2. the candidate anaphor and the candidate antecedent are both definite NPs with non-identical common nouns as head – listed as '2b' in Sect. 1.

3.1   Semantic relatedness as expressed in SynLex

SynLex[3] is a free dictionary of general vocabulary Swedish synonyms consisting of 25.000 word

pairs (Kann and Rosell, 2006). Synlex was automatically constructed and later manually refined by volunteer users of an on-line dictionary. The users graded each candidate synonym pair according to their intuitive estimate as to how closely the candidate pair was related (semantically), and pairs with a user grade above a certain threshold were included in the dictionary. For each pair of words in SynLex, there is a score between 3.0 and 5.0 representing how the users graded the pair. According to (Kann and Rosell, 2006), pairs with a score of 3.0 are synonymic to a lesser degree, whereas pairs with a score of 4.0 are very good synonyms. SynLex, unlike WordNet, does not distinguish between different word senses.

We use SynLex for deriving two relational features, one binary feature indicating whether the base form of the head word of the candidate antecedent and the base form of the head word of the anaphor are a synonymy pair in SynLex, and one feature consisting of the SynLex score for that word pair (if there is one). For example, the word *företag* ('business') has three synonyms in SynLex, with scores ranging from 3.2 to 4.0:

4.0 firma ('firm')

3.3 bolag ('corporation', 'company')

3.2 affärsverksamhet ('business (activity)')

and the 4.0 synonym *firma*('firm') is in turn listed with four synonyms:

4.4 rörelse ('enterprise')

4.0 företag ('business')

3.1 bolag ('corporation', 'company')

3.1 affärsverksamhet ('business (activity)')

Thus, the word pair *företag* and *bolag* would get a SynLex score of 3.3 in addition to a positive binary feature, whereas the word pair *företag* and *rörelse* would get a SynLex score of 0.0 and a negative binary feature.

3.2   Semantic relatedness in word-space models

Since the early 90's, a large body of research has developed which aims at capturing (lexical) semantic meaning through analyzing word co-occurrence and distribution (Grefenstette, 1994; Schütze, 1998). In analogy with the strongly

---

[2]Any influence on classification is likely to transfer to the complete coreference chains.

[3]URL: http://lexikon.nada.kth.se/synlex.html

related vector-space model, the representational models in these theories are commonly referred to as *word-space* models. Sahlgren (2006) argues that we can classify word-space models into two main groups: one which defines co-occurrence as two words occurring in the same document and one which defines it as two words occurring within a fixed-size sliding window. The first type is claimed to capture *syntagmatic* relations between words, the second type instead captures *paradigmatic* relations. Sahlgren (2006) gives credence to these claims through a series of experiments, but also shows that there is quite a bit of overlap between the two types. We investigate the effectiveness of these two types of models, separately as well as in conjunction, on the current task, using the standard cosine similarity measure.

Many researchers have experimented with applying *singular value decomposition* (SVD) (Golub and van Loan, 1996) to the matrices used by the word-space models to store the co-occurrence data. This process can be used for a dimensionality reduction for the similarity vectors. When the objects represented by the matrix are words and documents, this procedure is often called *latent semantic analysis* (LSA) and it is described in (Deerwester et al., 1990) and given a psychological motivation in (Landauer and Dumais, 1997). The advocates of LSA claim that it allows for capturing "latent" relations among words, that are not accessible through the raw co-occurrence data. In addition to the similarities calculated from the unprocessed matrices, we therefore also examine the effects of using singular value decomposition on the two types of word-spaces described above (again using the cosine similarity measure).

3.2.1 Term selection techniques

Another closely related approach to capturing similarities between words are so-called term selection or term weighting techniques. Just like the word-space models, their modeling capabilities are based on co-occurrence analysis. Where word-space models are based in geometry, term selection techniques are based in statistics or information theory. We use the mutual information (MI) measure (also referred to in (Manning and Schütze, 1999) as expected mutual information) on the two types of co-occurrence mentioned previously (within document or within a sliding window) and compare the results on the current task.

3.2.2 Building the word-space models

The corpus used for training the word-space models comes from the same newspaper and domain as the coreference annotated data (described in Sect. 4.1). It consists of about 1.5 million running words. When training the word-space model, we also include the coreference annotated data in the training data. However, this is not a case of "testing on the training data", since the annotations in the coreference data are not taken into consideration by the word-space model. The word-space model needs to see the words it is modeling as they occur in running text, and the more such examples provided, the better the model will function, typically. The coreference annotated data is just treated as another source for collecting co-occurrence data by the word-space model; the coreference data does not constitute a gold standard for this part of our system.

3.2.3 Word-space features

We thus have three models of similarity: using cosine or mutual information on vectors from the co-occurrence matrices (we merely apply a standard log-2 frequency damping) or using cosine on the dimensionality reduced vectors.

Table 1 gives an overview of all the word-space features, and the three models are represented by the three rows in the table. Each of these three models has two variants: the context window-based (column 'a') and the document-based (column 'b'). The score for the head words of each candidate anaphor-antecedent pair from each model is used as a feature, describing to what degree the two NPs are related within the respective models. We also extract a binary feature for each model, which is positive only for the highest-ranking coreference candidate for each NP within a document (columns 'c' and 'd'). Finally, we create sets consisting of the top 10 most similar coreference candidates for every definite description and proper noun within a document. This is done for each model and similarity measure, with one set containing context window-based (column 'e') and one set containing document-based relations (column 'f'; see also Fig. 1). At least when using the cosine measure on the non-reduced vectors,[4] we are hoping that these sets will help us distinguish between words that are syntagmatically

---

[4]We do not rule out the same effect for the MI measure or for the SVD-reduced matrix, but it has only been demonstrated for the non-reduced vectors and the cosine measure.

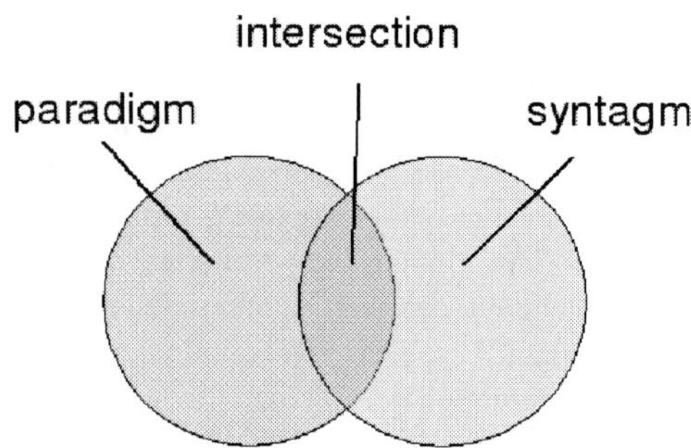

Figure 1: Forming three sets of words: paradigmatically related (window-based co-occurrence), syntagmatically related (document-based co-occurrence) and the intersection of these.

and paradigmatically related. We create a binary feature for each of the three sets formed this way (column 'g' represents the intersection of the previous two), hopefully indicating the type of relation (or lack thereof) in which a particular pair of words stand.

4 Classification of Pairs of Definite Descriptions

4.1 Data

The annotation of the data used in these experiments was done by one of the authors, based on the BREDT annotation guidelines for referential relations developed for Norwegian (Borthen, 2004) with minor modifications for the language (Swedish) and the domain (economic news text). The main goal of the annotation is to mark a select set of anaphoric and cataphoric relations. The most frequent, and thus the most important one, is coreference, which is defined as a relation of *identity of reference*. The annotated data we use here consists of 66 documents; there is a total of 6606 noun phrases of which 1887 (28%) are annotated as coreferent.

The preprocessing includes part-of-speech tagging and lemmatization with Granska (Carlberger and Kann, 1999), dependency parsing with Malt-Parser (Nivre et al., 2007), Named Entity tagging, and NP chunking. For NEs, basic semantic information is added by extending each occurrence of the NE type 'organization' with the synset for *företag, organisation* ('company', 'organization'), and the NE type 'person' with the synset for *människa, person* ('human being', 'person') from the

online version of the Swedish WordNet[5] (Viberg et al., 2002).

Since we define coreference as a relation of identity of reference, each NP within a coreference chain is coreferent with all other NPs within that chain. Thus, in order to construct pairs of anaphors and candidate antecedents, each NP is combined with all other NPs within the document. As stated in Sect. 3, we are concerned with two sub-tasks in these experiments; for the first task there are 269 positive instances, and for the second 328. The data is partitioned so that the instances used in the two experiments are disjoint.

4.2 Features

Our baseline feature set is comprised of language- and domain-independent features used in high-performing coreference resolution systems such as (Soon et al., 2001) and (Strube et al., 2002), some domain-dependent features handling e.g., quoted speech, and some features based on corpus studies on definite descriptions by e.g., (Fraurud, 1992) and (Vieira and Poesio, 2000) describing e.g., NP complexity. This feature set includes 90 features; 58 of these features describe each NP in a candidate anaphor-antecedent pair (including gender, number and definiteness, as well as syntactic function and approximations to salience), and 32 features describe the candidate pair in terms of morphological similarity and syntactic parallelism, location (e.g., whether the two NPs are located within the same sentence, or in adjacent ones), and string similarity (e.g., complete and partial overlap, and the Levenshtein distance). Classification with this feature set is used as a baseline.

In addition to this standard feature set, semantic information is added via two SynLex features (described in section 3.1), and 21 word-space features (described in section 3.2). We group the 21 word-space features into six different configurations as such (please also refer to Table 1):

- **WS**: includes all 21 word-space features (WS stands for word-space)

- **WS cosine**: all features in row 1 in Table 1

- **WS MI**: all features in row 2

- **WS SVD**: all features in row 3 (we use a standard dimensionality of 200 in our experiments)

---

[5]URL: http://www.lingfil.uu.se/ling/swn.html; We do not at present have access to SWN in a machine readable format.

	window	document	window*	document*	paradigm*	syntagm*	intersection*
cosine	1a	1b	1c	1d	1e	1f	1g
MI	2a	2b	2c	2d	2e	2f	2g
SVD	3a	3b	3c	3d	3e	3f	3g

Table 1: Features from word-space models. The *-character indicates that features in the marked column are binary. 'MI' stands for mutual information and 'SVD' for singular value decomposition.

- **WS window**: all features in columns a, c, and e–g; aims to capture paradigmatic relations (we use a standard window size of 3 words to each side of the focus word in our experiments)

- **WS document**: all features in columns b and d–g; aims to capture syntagmatic relations

4.3 Classification

For classification of pairs of definite descriptions, we use 5-fold cross validation with the memory-based learner TiMBL (Daelemans and van den Bosch, 2005). We use the IB1 (k-nn) algorithm with k=5, the distance metric MVDM/overlap, and gain ratio feature weighting, and feature sets adapted for each task.

The classification is evaluated on instance level using the following measures: *precision*, *recall*, and *F-score*. Precision is defined as the number of correct coreference relations given by TiMBL divided by the total number of coreference relations given by the system. Recall is the number of correct coreference relations given by TiMBL divided by the total number of coreference relations in the data. F-score is the harmonic mean of precision and recall.

5 Results

The results in Tables 2 and 3, below, show a positive effect from the semantic features, though not in all configurations. The SynLex features do not provide any useful information to the system – their only effect is to lower the recall slightly. One might argue that the comparison between SynLex and our word-space models is unfair, as SynLex is a general resource whereas the word-space models are domain-specific. But this is in fact the point we wish to make: in order to handle coreference between noun phrases, we need domain-specific models of semantic relatedness. All but one configuration of word-space features produce higher precision than the baseline feature set, and the majority also give a simultaneous increase in recall.

	Precision	Recall	F-score
Baseline	28.3	22.1	24.8
SL and WS	–	–	–
SL	–	–	–
WS	30.7	18.6	23.1
WS cosine	27.7	19.0	22.5
WS MI	33.7	**23.7**	27.8
WS SVD	32.9	22.1	26.5
WS window	31.9	20.9	25.3
WS document	**34.7**	**23.7**	**28.2**

Table 2: Micro-averaged results: antecedent is an NE, anaphor is a common noun. SL stands for 'SynLex'. The feature sets are named and described in Sect. 4.2, above. SynLex does not contain names, therefore we cannot calculate results for settings involving this resource.

	Precision	Recall	F-score
Baseline	42.7	9.8	15.9
SL and WS	48.3	8.8	14.9
SL	42.1	9.8	15.8
WS	49.1	8.8	15.0
WS cosine	**52.9**	11.0	18.2
WS MI	50.7	10.7	17.6
WS SVD	51.2	**12.5**	**20.1**
WS window	43.3	8.8	14.7
WS document	48.6	10.4	17.1

Table 3: Micro-averaged results, both antecedent and anaphor are common nouns.

For the data set where both antecedent and anaphor are common nouns (set '2a' in Sect. 1), we see that the word-space model where we have applied SVD gives the best results, though the "raw" model actually gives higher precision (Table 3). This is not too surprising; given that the SVD is applied in order to uncover latent relations, we can expect a high recall – at the cost of a certain level of noise creeping in, resulting in a lower precision than for the "raw" model.

More surprising was to see that the models with co-occurrence being defined on a document level give better results on both tasks than the ones where it is based on the sliding context windows. We expected the latter to capture paradigmatic relations better than the former, but other factors, perhaps related to data sparseness, seem to influence the results contrary to our intuition. It can be argued, however, that the SVD can manage to capture paradigmatic information even when considering co-occurrence on a document level (features 3b and 3d – 3g in Table 1); that this in fact constitutes part of the "latency" in LSA. Further, in the task where the antecedent is an NE, it may well be that the relation between the two NPs is better thought of as syntagmatic than paradigmatic.

We also see that the 'WS MI' feature setting performs well on the task where the antecedent is an NE. It has been argued (Manning and Schütze, 1999) that the MI measure favors rare cases; something which applies to the NEs, and therefore could explain why this feature setting does well on this task.

The subtask where both antecedent and anaphor are common nouns can conceptually be split further into two cases. First, we have cases that can be resolved using information on lexical relations between the head nouns of the anaphor and the candidate antecedent; relations such as (near) synonymy, as in 'the business' - 'the company', or hypernymy, as in 'mediator' - 'the profession'. Second, we have cases that require additional information for resolution, e.g., common-sense reasoning or real-world knowledge as in 'the period April-June' - 'the second quarter', and/or keeping track of the current focus 'two metal workers' - 'the dismissed (employees)'. We expect the word-space approach to deal better with the former cases than the latter, but we cannot exclude that the latter, too, will display some degree of similarity in a word-space model.

We performed an experiment where we used the word-space features exclusively (no baseline features were used) for classifying the instances. This results in rather low figures in terms of precision and recall, but the successful cases may still give us an idea of the type of information we can hope to extract. E.g., the word-space models correctly predicted a coreference relation between *siffror* and *statistik* ('numbers' and 'statistics'), *anställda* and *personal* ('employees' and 'personel'), and

euroområdet and *euroländerna* ('the Euro area' and 'the Euro countries'). These are all cases of near synonymy, and the results thus support our assumption that the word-space model will handle such cases better than cases where focus or reasoning play a part in the resolution.

We have performed these experiments on Swedish news text, but we have reasons to believe that the results are at least partly generalizable. First of all, the problem of having to resolve non-identical head definite descriptions exists and is relevant for other languages than Swedish, as we discussed in Sect. 1. Secondly, word-space models can be constructed for any language and domain where the tokenization of text into words is not a major issue. Finally, though they do not employ word-space features directly, Hendrickx et al. (2008b) and Ng (2007) show, for Dutch and English, that including semantics from statistically based corpus-methods has positive effects on the accuracy on their systems.

6 Conclusion

Coreference resolution of definite NPs is a complex problem, resulting in higher error rates compared to Named Entity coreference resolution, or pronoun resolution. One reason for this is the problem of acquiring various types of domain-specific lexico-semantic and common-sense knowledge needed for resolution. We present encouraging results from a study on using word-space similarity measures to approximate this knowledge in a system for resolution of definite descriptions.

References

Kaja Borthen. 2004. Annotation scheme for BREDT. Version 1.0. Technical report, University of Bergen.

Johan Carlberger and Viggo Kann. 1999. Implementing an efficient part-of-speech tagger. *Software Practice and Experience*, 29:815–832.

Walter Daelemans and Antal van den Bosch. 2005. *Memory-Based Language Processing*. Studies in Natural Language Processing. Cambridge University Press.

Scott Deerwester, Susan Dumais, Thomas Landauer, George Furnas, and Richard Harshman. 1990. Indexing by Latent Semantic Analysis. *Journal of the American Society of Information Science*, 41(6):391–407.

Christiane D. Fellbaum, editor. 1998. *WordNet: An Electronic Lexical Database*. MIT Press.

Kari Fraurud. 1992. *Processing Noun Phrases in Natural Language Discourse*. Ph.D. thesis, Stockholm University.

Daniela Goecke, Maik Stührenberg, and Tonio Wandmacher. 2007. Extraction and representation of semantic relations for resolving definite descriptions. In *OTT'06. Ontologies in Text Technology: Approaches to Extract Semantic Knowledge from Structured Information. Publications of the Institute of Cognitive Science (PICS) 1-2007*, Osnabrück, Germany.

Gene H. Golub and Charles F. van Loan. 1996. *Matrix Computations*. Johns Hopkins University Press, Baltimore, MD, USA, 3 edition.

Gregory Grefenstette. 1994. *Explorations in Automatic Thesaurus Discovery*. Kluwer Academic Publishers, Boston, MA, USA.

Iris Hendrickx, Gosse Bouma, Frederik Coppens, Walter Daelemans, Veronique Hoste, Geert Kloosterman, Anne-Marie Mineur, Joeri Van Der Vloet, and Jean-Luc Verschelde. 2008a. A coreference corpus and resolution system for Dutch. In European Language Resources Association (ELRA), editor, *Proceedings of the Sixth International Language Resources and Evaluation (LREC'08)*, Marrakech, Morocco, May.

Iris Hendrickx, Véronique Hoste, and Walter Daelemans. 2008b. Semantic and Syntactic Features for Dutch Anaphora Resolution. In *Proceedings of the 9th International Conference on Intelligent Text Processing and Computational Linguistics, CICLing 2008, Haifa, Israel, February 17-23, 2008*, Lecture Notes in Computer Science. Springer.

Viggo Kann and Magnus Rosell. 2006. Free construction of a Swedish dictionary of synonyms. In S. Werner, editor, *Proceedings of the 15th NODALIDA conference, Joensuu 2005*, Ling@JoY : University of Joensuu electronic publications in linguistics and language technology 1, Joensuu. SBN 952-458-771-8, ISSN 1796-1114.

Thomas Landauer and Susan Dumais. 1997. A Solution to Plato's Problem: The Latent Semantic Analysis Theory of Acquisition, Induction, and Representation of Knowledge. *Psychological Review*, 104(2):211–240.

Christopher Manning and Hinrich Schütze. 1999. *Foundations of Statistical Natural Language Processing*. The MIT Press, Cambridge, MA.

Ruslan Mitkov. 2003. Anaphora Resolution. In Ruslan Mitkov, editor, *The Oxford Handbook of Computational Linguistics*, pages 266–283. Oxford University Press.

Thomas Morton. 2005. *Using Semantic Relations to Improve Information Retrieval*. Ph.D. thesis, University of Pennsylvania.

Vincent Ng. 2007. Semantic class induction and coreference resolution. In *Proceedings of the 45th Annual Meeting of the Association of Computational Linguistics*, pages 536–543, Prague, Czech Republic, June. ACL.

Joakim Nivre, Johan Hall, Jens Nilsson, Atanas Chanev, Gülşen Eryiğit, Sandra Kübler, Svetoslav Marinov, and Erwin Marsi. 2007. Maltparser: A language-independent system for data-driven dependency parsing. *Natural Language Engineering*, 13(2):95–135.

Massimo Poesio, Sabine Schulte im Walde, and Chris Brew. 1998. Lexical Clustering and Definite Description Interpretation. In *Proceedings of the AAAI Spring Symposium on Learning for Discourse*, Stanford, CA, March.

Magnus Sahlgren. 2006. *The Word-Space Model: Using Distributional Analysis to Represent Syntagmatic and Paradigmatic Relations between Words in High-Dimensional Vector Spaces*. Ph.D. thesis, Stockholm University, Stockholm, Sweden.

Hinrich Schütze. 1998. Automatic Word Sense Discrimination. *Computational Linguistics*, 24(1):97–123.

Wee Meng Soon, Hwee Tou Ng, and Daniel Chung Yong Lim. 2001. A Machine Learning Approach to Coreference Resolution of Noun Phrases. *Computational Linguistics*, 27(4):521–544.

Michael Strube, Stefan Rapp, and Christoph Müller. 2002. The influence of minimum edit distance on reference resolution. In *Proceedings of the Conference on Empirical Methods in Natural Language Processing (EMNLP)*, pages 312–319, Philadelphia, PA, USA, July. ACL.

Åke Viberg, Karin Lindmark, Ann Lindvall, and Ingmarie Mellenius. 2002. The Swedish WordNet Project. In *Proceedings of Euralex 2002, Copenhagen University*, pages 407–412.

Renata Vieira and Massimo Poesio. 2000. An empirically based system for processing definite descriptions. *Computational Linguistics*, 26(4):539–593.

Piek Vossen. 1998. Introduction to EuroWordNet. *Computers and the Humanities*, 32(2–3), March.

ISSN 1736-6305 Vol. 4
http://hdl.handle.net/10062/9206

Text Categorization Using Predicate–Argument Structures

Jacob Persson
Department of Computer Science
Lund University
S-221 00 Lund, Sweden
jacob.persson@gmail.com

Richard Johansson*
DISI
University of Trento
I-38100 Povo, Italy
johansson@disi.unitn.it

Pierre Nugues
Department of Computer Science
Lund University
S-221 00 Lund, Sweden
pierre@cs.lth.se

Abstract

* Most text categorization methods use the vector space model in combination with a representation of documents based on bags of words. As its name indicates, bags of words ignore possible structures in the text and only take into account isolated, unrelated words. Although this limitation is widely acknowledged, most previous attempts to extend the bag-of-words model with more advanced approaches failed to produce conclusive improvements.

We propose a novel method that extends the word-level representation to automatically extracted semantic and syntactic features. We investigated three extensions: word-sense information, subject–verb–object triples, and role-semantic predicate–argument tuples, all fitting within the vector space model. We computed their contribution to the categorization results on the Reuters corpus of newswires (RCV1). We show that these three extensions, either taken individually or in combination, result in statistically significant improvements of the microaverage F_1 over a baseline using bags of words. We found that our best extended model that uses a combination of syntactic and semantic features reduces the error of the word-level baseline by up to 10 percent for the categories having more than 1,000 documents in the training corpus.

*Research done while at Lund University.

1 Introduction

Text categorization or classification corresponds to the automatic assignment of a document to one or more predefined categories. To carry out this task, techniques using the vector space model (Salton et al., 1974) in combination with a representation based on words – the *bag-of-words* model – are considered to be standard both in practice and for evaluation purposes (Lewis et al., 2004). The bag-of-words model is both simple to implement and enables classifiers to achieve state-of-the-art results.

However as its name indicates, the bag-of-words model ignores possible structures in the text as it only takes into account isolated, unrelated words present in a document. These limits are widely acknowledged and there has been many attempts to break them with more advanced approaches. Approaches include the detection and indexing of proper nouns, complex nominals, phrases, or the identification of word-senses. To date, they have not resulted in any conclusive improvements (Moschitti and Basili, 2004).

In this paper, we describe novel features based on the output of syntactic and semantic parsers – subject–verb–object (SVO) triples and predicate–argument structures – to enrich the document representation. As for the words, these features are automatically extracted from raw text. We use them in the vector space model to extend the word-level representation with syntactic and semantic dimensions.

We evaluated the contribution of the syntactic and semantic representation on the Reuters corpus volume I of newswire articles (RCV1) with a standardized benchmark (Lewis et al., 2004). We used a classifier based on support vector machines

(SVM), where we compared the new representation against the bag-of-words baseline. We could obtain an error reduction ranging from 1 to 10 percent for categories having more than 1,000 documents in the training corpus.

2 Representing Text for Automatic Classification

2.1 The Vector Space Model

In statistical classification, the *vector space model* is the standard way to represent data (Salton et al., 1974). This model uses all features that are extracted from a document collection to build a space, where each feature corresponds to a dimension of this space. A single document is then represented by a vector, where each coordinate indicates the presence of a specific feature and weights it. The document vectors can then be placed in the space and their location can be used to compute their similarity.

2.2 Using a Word-level Representation

The standard features in the vector space model are simply the words in the text. Let us assume that we have a document collection that only contains two documents, whose content is:

D1: Chrysler plans new investment in Latin America.

D2: Chrysler plans major investments in Mexico.

The application of the bag-of-words model on the collection uses all the words in the documents as features and results in the document vectors shown in Table 1. The words are stemmed and the most common ones – the stop words – are not used as features, because they usually appear in all the documents. For each feature, the vector indicates how many times it appeared in the document. This value is known as the *term frequency*, tf.

In Table 1, the document vectors used the raw term frequency for each word and therefore assigning all words equal importance. However, rare features are often more important than features present in many documents of the collection. The spread of a feature is measured using the *document frequency*, which is defined as the number of documents in which a feature can be found. To give rare features more importance, the term frequency is weighted with the *inverted document frequency*, *idf* (1). This weighting scheme

is called $tf \times idf$ and there exist many variants of it. For a list of possible weighting schemes and a comparative study of their influence, see Salton and Buckley (1987) and Joachims (2002).

$$idf = log\left(\frac{collection\ size}{document\ frequency}\right) \quad (1)$$

2.3 Extending the Word-based Representation with Complex Semantic Features

Word-based representations are simple and robust, but this comes at a cost. Using bags of words to represent a document misses the phrase and sentence organization as well as their logical structure. Intuitively, the semantics of sentences in a document should help categorize it more accurately. To account for it, we extracted semantic features from each corpus sentence – predicate–argument tuples, subject–verb–object triples, and word-sense information – and we extended the document vectors with them.

Predicate–argument structures are core constructs in most formalisms dealing with knowledge representation. They are equally prominent in linguistic theories of compositional semantic representation. In the simplest case, predicate–argument tuples can be approximated by subject–verb–object triples or subject–verb pairs and extracted from surface-syntactic dependency trees.

SVO representations have been used in vector-space approaches to a number of tasks (Lin, 1998; Padó and Lapata, 2007). In the widely publicized semantic web initiative, Berners-Lee et al. (2001) advocated their use as *a natural way to describe the vast majority of the data processed by machines*. They also correspond to binary relations in relation algebra on which we can apply a large number of mathematical properties. Nonetheless, as far as we know, strict SVO representations have never been used in automatic text categorization. Fürnkranz et al. (1998) proposed an approximated SVO representation that could increase the precision of some categorization experiments when combined with a low recall ranging from 10 to 40. However, they could not show any decisive, consistent improvement across a variety of experimental settings.

Although they are sometimes equivalent, syntactic parse trees and semantic structures are generally not isomorphic. Tuples directly extracted from dependency trees are susceptible to para-

D#\ Words	chrysler	plan	new	major	investment	latin	america	mexico
1	1	1	1	0	1	1	1	0
2	1	1	0	1	1	0	0	1

Table 1: Document vectors based on the bag-of-words model.

phrasing caused by linguistic processes such as voice alternation, *Chrysler planned investments / investments were planned by Chrysler*, and diathesis alternations such as dative shifts, *We sold him the car / We sold the car to him*.

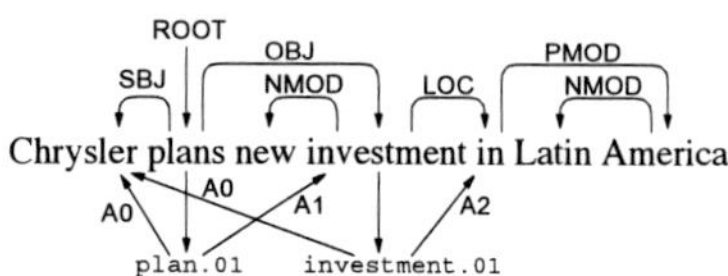

Figure 1: Example sentence with dependency syntax and role semantics annotation. Upper arrows correspond to the dependency relations and the lower ones to the semantic roles.

Role semantics (Fillmore, 1968) is a formalism that abstracts over the bare syntactic representation by means of semantic roles like AGENT and PATIENT rather than grammatical functions such as subject and object.

Figure 1 shows the first example sentence in Sect. 2.2 annotated with syntactic dependencies and role-semantic information according to the PropBank (Palmer et al., 2005) and NomBank (Meyers et al., 2004) standard. The verb *plan* is a predicate defined in the PropBank lexicon, which lists its four possible core arguments: A0, planner, A1, the thing planned, A2, grounds for planning, and A3, beneficiary. Similarly, the noun *investment* is a NomBank predicate whose three possible core arguments are: A0, investor, A1, theme, and A2 purpose. In addition to the core arguments, predicates also accept optional adjuncts such as locations or times.

For each predicate, PropBank and NomBank define a number of *word senses*, such as *plan.01* and *investment.01* in the example sentence. Features based on word sense information, typically employing WordNet senses, have been used in text classification, but have not resulted in any conclusive improvements. For a review of previous studies and results, see Mansuy and Hilderman (2006).

3 Automatic Semantic Role Labeling

Role-semantic structures can be automatically extracted from free text – this task is referred to as *semantic role labeling* (SRL). Although early SRL systems (Hirst, 1983) used symbolic rules, modern systems to a large extent rely on statistical techniques (Gildea and Jurafsky, 2002). This has been made possible by the availability of training data, first from FrameNet (Ruppenhofer et al., 2006) and then PropBank and NomBank. Semantic role labelers can now be applied to unrestricted text, at least business text, with a satisfying level of quality.

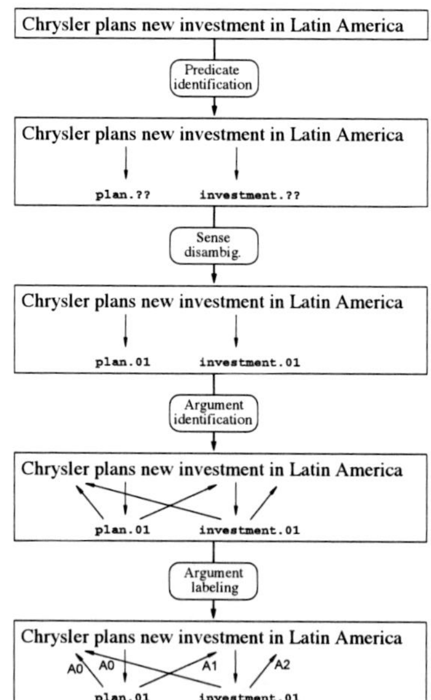

Figure 3: Example processed by the semantic pipeline.

We used a freely available SRL system (Johansson and Nugues, 2008) to extract the predicate–argument structures[1]. The system relies on a syntactic and a semantic subcomponent. The syntactic model is a bottom-up dependency parser and the semantic model uses global inference mechanisms on top of a pipeline of classifiers. The com-

---

[1]Download site: nlp.cs.lth.se.

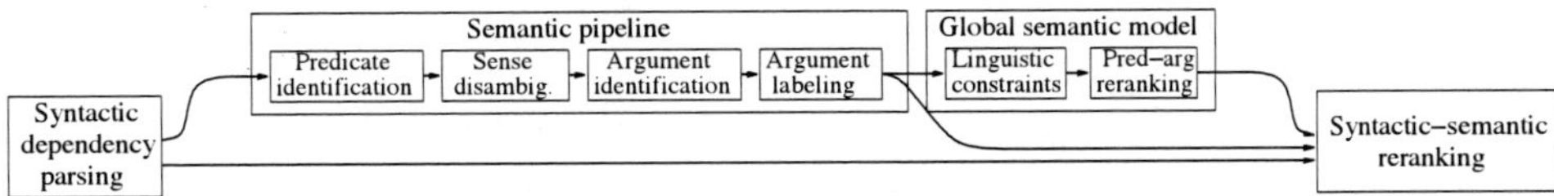

Figure 2: The architecture of the semantic role labeling system.

plete syntactic–semantic output is selected from a candidate pool generated by the subsystems. Figure 2 shows the overall architecture and Figure 3 shows how the example sentence is processed by the semantic subcomponent. The system achieved the top score in the closed challenge of the CoNLL 2008 Shared Task (Surdeanu et al., 2008): a labeled syntactic accuracy of 89.32%, a labeled semantic F_1 of 81.65, and a labeled macro F_1 of 85.49.

4   Experimental Setup

We carried out a series of experiments to determine the contribution of the three sets of syntactic–semantic features: word-sense information, subject–verb–object triples, and role-semantic predicate–argument tuples. They all come as an extension to the baseline word-level representation in the vector space model. We first describe the data sets, then the experimental parameters, and finally the figures we obtained for different combinations of features.

4.1   Corpora

We conducted our experiments on the RCV1-v2 (Lewis et al., 2004) corpus, which is a corrected version of RCV1 (Reuters Corpus Volume 1). We used the LYRL2004 split, which puts articles published between August 20, 1996 to August 31, 1996 in the training set and articles between September 1, 1996 to August 19, 1997 into the test set. We performed the split on the original RCV1-v1 collection which results in 23,307 training documents and 783,484 test documents. RCV1 has three sets of categories called: region code, topic code, and industry code. The region code contains the geographical locations that an article covers. The topic codes try to capture the subjects of an article, and industry codes describe the industry fields mentioned in an article.

4.2   Classification Method

We reproduced the conditions of the SVM.1 classification method described in Lewis et al. (2004).

We used the SVM^{light}(Joachims, 1999) classifier with the standard parameters and the SCutFBR.1 algorithm (Yang, 2001) to choose the optimal threshold.

SCutFBR.1 replaces SVM^{light}'s own method for selecting a partitioning threshold. For each category, SVM^{light} computes a ranking of the documents in the form of a scoring number assigned to each document. This number determines the document rank in the category. The goal is to find a threshold from the ranked training documents that maximizes the number of correct classifications.

The purpose of SCutFBR.1 is to handle cases when there are few training documents for a category. There is then a risk of overfitting, which may lead to too high or too low thresholds. A high threshold results in many misses, which have a negative impact on the macroaverage F_1 while a low threshold results in a potentially large number of documents assigned to a wrong category, which has a negative impact on both the micro and the macroaverage F_1. To avoid this, the F_1 score is calculated for each category in the training set. If the score is too low, the highest ranking is chosen as the threshold for that category.

4.3   Corpus Tagging and Parsing

We annotated the RCV1 corpus with POS tags, dependency relations, and predicate argument structures using the SRL system mentioned in Sect. 3. The POS tagger uses techniques that are similar to those described by Collins (2002).

4.4   Feature Sets

We conducted our experiments with three main sets of features. The first feature set is the baseline bag of words. The second one uses the triples consisting of the verb, subject, and object (VSO) for given predicates. The third set corresponds to predicates, their sense, and their most frequent core arguments: A0 and A1. We exemplify the features with the sentence *Chrysler plans new investment in Latin America*, whose syntactic and semantic graphs are shown in Figure 1.

As first feature set, we used the bags of words corresponding to the pretokenized version of the RCV1-v2 released together with Lewis et al. (2004) without any further processing. Examples of bag-of-words features are shown in Table 1.

For the second feature set, the VSO triples, we considered the verbs corresponding to the Penn Treebank tags: VB, VBD, VBG, VBN, VBP, and VBZ. In each sentence of the corpus and for each verb, we extracted their subject and object heads from the dependency parser output. These dependencies can have other types of grammatical function. We selected the *subject* and *object* because they typically match core semantic roles. We created the feature symbols by concatenating each verb to its subject and object dependents whenever they exist. Verbs without any subject and object relations were ignored. The feature created from the example sentence is: *plan#Chrysler#investment*.

The third feature set considers the predicates of the corpus and their most frequent arguments. We used the semantic output of the SRL system to identify all the verbs and nouns described in the PropBank and NomBank databases as well as their arguments 0 and 1. We combined them to form four different subsets of semantic features. The first subset simply contains the predicate senses. We created them by suffixing the predicate words with their sense number as for instance *plan.01*. The three other subsets corresponds to combinations of the predicate and one or two of their core arguments, *argument 0* and *argument 1*. As with the VSO triples, we created the feature symbols using a concatenation of the predicate and the arguments. The three different combinations we used are:

1. The predicate and its first argument, argument 0. In the example, *plan.01#Chrysler*

2. The predicate and its second argument, argument 1. In the example, *plan.01#investment*

3. The predicate and its first and second argument, arguments 0 and 1. In the example, *plan.01#Chrysler#investment*

We applied the $log(tf) \times idf$ weighting scheme to all the feature sets in all the representations. We used the raw frequencies for the tf component.

5 Results

5.1 Evaluation Framework

Since the articles in RCV1 can be labeled with multiple categories, we carried out a multilabel classification. This is done by applying a classifier for each category and then merging the results from them. For a classification of a single category i, the results can be represented in a contingency table (Table 2) and from this table, we can calculate the standard measures $Precision$ and $Recall$. We summarized the results with the harmonic mean F_1 of $Precision$ and $Recall$.

	+ example	- example
+ classified	a_i	b_i
- classified	c_i	d_i

Table 2: The results of a classification represented in a contingency table.

To measure the performance over all the categories, we use microaveraged F_1 and macroaveraged F_1. Macroaverage is obtained by calculating the F_1 score for each category and then taking the average over all the categories (4), whereas microaverage is calculated by summing all the binary decisions together (2) and calculating F_1 from that (3).

$$\mu Precision = \frac{\sum_{i=1}^{n} a_i}{\sum_{i=1}^{n} a_i + b_i}$$
$$\mu Recall = \frac{\sum_{i=1}^{n} a_i}{\sum_{i=1}^{n} a_i + c_i} \quad (2)$$

$$\mu F_1 = \frac{2 \times \mu Precision \times \mu Recall}{\mu Precision + \mu Recall} \quad (3)$$

$$maF_1 = \frac{1}{n} \sum_{i=1}^{n} F_1^i \quad (4)$$

5.2 Results

The six feature sets create 64 possible representations of our data. We assigned a code to the representations using a six-character string where a 1 at the first location indicates that the bag-of-words set is included and so forth as shown in Table 3.

To get an approximation of the performance of the representations, we conducted tests on the training set. We then ran full tests on the topics categories on the representations that showed the highest effectiveness. We measured and optimized for micro and macroaverage F_1. Table 4 shows the

Feature set	Code
Bag of words	100000
Predicates	010000
VSO triples	001000
Argument 0	000100
Argument 1	000010
Arguments 0 and 1	000001

Table 3: Codes for the features sets. A code for a representation is the result of a bitwise-and between the codes of the included feature sets.

representations we selected from the initial tests and their results with the full test. The representations that include bag-of-words, predicates, and one or more of the argument sets or the VSO set achieved the best performance.

Feature set	Microaverage	Macroaverage
Baseline	81.76	62.31
c110000	81.99	62.09
c111000	**82.27**	62.57
c110100	82.12	62.16
c110010	82.16	**62.77**
c110001	81.81	62.24
c111100	82.17	62.44

Table 4: Effectiveness of microaverage and macroaverage F_1 on the most promising representations. Parameters were set to optimize respectively microaverage and macroaverage F_1. The baseline figure corresponds to the bag of words.

The effectiveness of the individual categories can be seen in Figures 4 and 5. The categories are sorted by training set frequency. The graphs have been smoothed with a local linear regression within a [-200, +200] range.

As scores are close in Figures 4 and 5, we show the relative error reduction in Figures 6 and 7.

We applied the McNemar test to measure the significance of the error reduction. In Table 5, we list how many categories showed a significance under 0.95 out of 103 categories in total.

We also measured the significance by applying a paired t-test on the categories with more than 1000 training documents, where the population consisted of the F_1 scores. The tests showed p-values lower than 0.02 on all representations for both micro and macroaverage optimized F_1 scores.

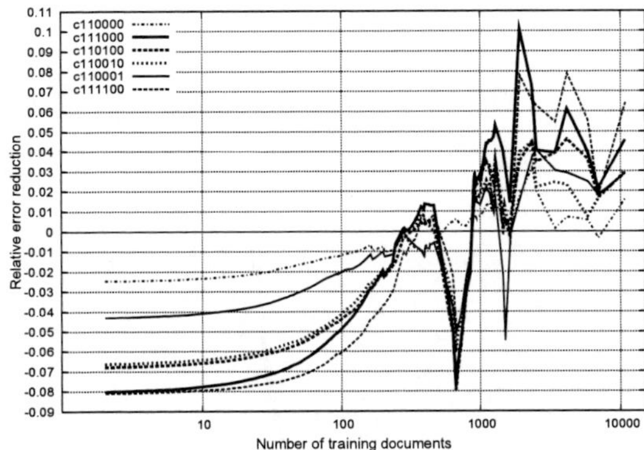

Figure 6: The relative error reduction per category for microaverage optimized classifications.

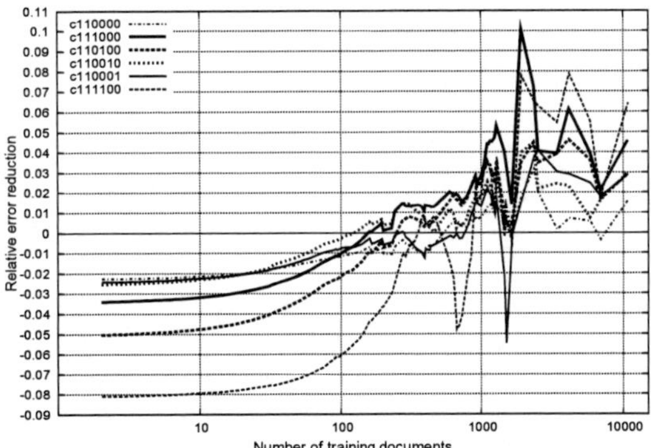

Figure 7: The relative error reduction per category for macroaverage optimized classifications.

Feature set	Microaverage	Macroaverage
c110000	27	23
c111000	**23**	**20**
c110100	**23**	21
c110010	26	25
c110001	25	25
c111100	25	22

Table 5: Number of categories that had an significance under 0.95 when parameters were set to optimize microaverage and macroaverage F_1.

5.3 Conclusion

We have demonstrated that complex semantic features can be used to achieve significant improvements in text classification over a baseline bag-of-words representation. The three extensions we proposed: word-sense disambiguation, SVO

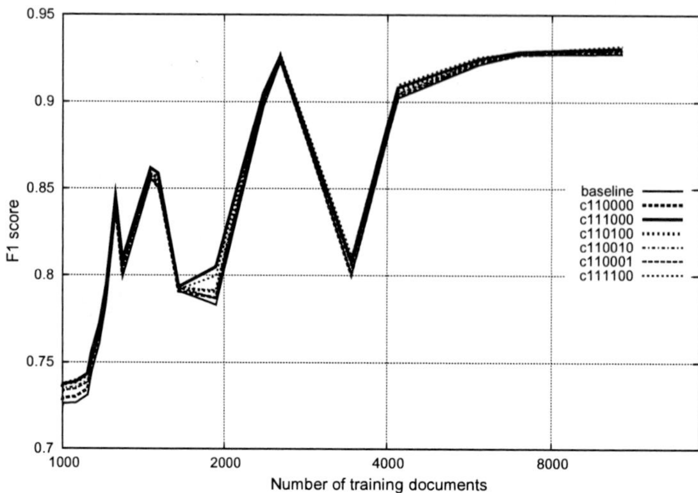

Figure 4: F_1 effectiveness per category on microaverage optimized classifications where there exists more than 1000 training documents.

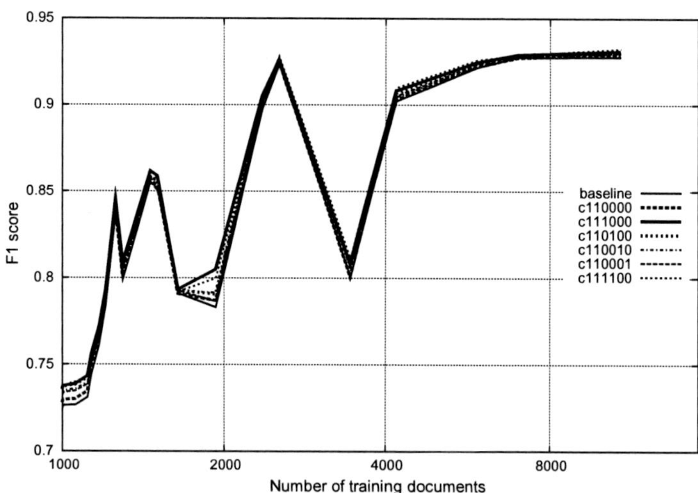

Figure 5: F_1 effectiveness per category on macroaverage optimized classifications where there exists more than 1000 training documents.

triples, and predicate–argument structures, either taken individually or in combination, result in statistically significant improvements of the microaverage F_1. The best results on average are produced by extending the vector space model with dimensions representing disambiguated verb predicates and SVO triples. For classes having more than 2500 training documents, the addition of argument 0 yields the best results.

All results show an improvement over the top microaveraged F_1 result of 81.6 in Lewis et al. (2004) which corresponds to the baseline in our experiment.

Contrary to previous studies (Mansuy and Hilderman, 2006), the sense disambiguation step shows improved figures over the baseline. The possible explanation may be that:

- The PropBank/NomBank databases have simpler sense inventories than WordNet, for example *plan* has four senses in WordNet and only one in PropBank; *investment* has six senses in WordNet, one in NomBank.

- The Penn Treebank corpus on which the semantic parser is trained is larger than SemCor, the corpus that is commonly used to train word-sense disambiguation systems. This means that the classifier we used is possibly more accurate.

We designed our experiments with English text for which high-performance semantic parsers are available. The results we obtained show that using SVO triples is also an efficient way to approximate predicate–argument structures. This may be good news for other languages where semantic parsers have not yet been developed and that only have dependency parsers. We plan to carry out similar experiments with SVO triples in other languages of the Reuters corpus and see whether they improve the categorization accuracy.

Moreover, we believe that our approach can be improved by introducing yet more abstraction. For instance, frame semantics from FrameNet (Ruppenhofer et al., 2006) could possibly be used to generalize across predicates as with *buy/acquisition*. Similarly, structured dictionaries such as WordNet or ontologies such as Cyc could allow generalization across arguments.

References

Tim Berners-Lee, James Hendler, and Ora Lassila. 2001. The semantic web. *Scientific American*, pages 29–37, May.

Michael Collins. 2002. Discriminative training methods for hidden Markov models: Theory and experiments with perceptron algorithms. In *Proceedings of the 2002 EMNLP Conference*, pages 1–8.

Charles J. Fillmore. 1968. The case for case. In *Universals in Linguistic Theory*, pages 1–88. Holt, Rinehart, and Winston.

Johannes Fürnkranz, Tom Mitchell, and Ellen Riloff. 1998. A case study in using linguistic phrases for text categorization on the WWW. In *Learning for Text Categorization: Papers from the 1998 AAAI/ICML Workshop*, pages 5–13.

Daniel Gildea and Daniel Jurafsky. 2002. Automatic labeling of semantic roles. *Computational Linguistics*, 28(3).

Graeme Hirst. 1983. A foundation for semantic interpretation. In *Proceedings of the 21st Annual Meeting of the ACL*, pages 64–73.

Thorsten Joachims. 1999. Making large-scale SVM learning practical. In *Advances in Kernel Methods. Support Vector Learning*. MIT Press.

Thorsten Joachims. 2002. *Learning to Classify Text Using Support Vector Machines*. Kluwer Academic Publishers.

Richard Johansson and Pierre Nugues. 2008. Dependency-based syntactic–semantic analysis with PropBank and NomBank. In *Proceedings of The Twelfth Conference on Natural Language Learning (CoNLL-2008)*.

David D. Lewis, Yiming Yang, Tony G. Rose, and Fan Li. 2004. RCV1: A new benchmark collection for text categorization research. *Journal of Machine Learning Research*, 5.

Dekang Lin. 1998. Automatic retrieval and clustering of similar words. In *Proceedings of the 36th Annual Meeting of the ACL and 17th International Conference on Computational Linguistics*, pages 768–774.

Trevor Mansuy and Robert J. Hilderman. 2006. A characterization of WordNet features in Boolean models for text classification. In *Proceedings of the Fifth Australasian Data Mining Conference (AusDM2006)*, pages 103–109.

Adam Meyers, Ruth Reeves, Catherine Macleod, Rachel Szekely, Veronika Zielinska, Brian Young, and Ralph Grishman. 2004. The NomBank project: An interim report. In *HLT-NAACL 2004 Workshop: Frontiers in Corpus Annotation*, pages 24–31.

Alessandro Moschitti and Roberto Basili. 2004. Complex linguistic features for text classification: a comprehensive study. In *Proceedings of ECIR-04, 26th European Conference on Information Retrieval*.

Sebastian Padó and Mirella Lapata. 2007. Dependency-based construction of semantic space models. *Computational Linguistics*, 33(2).

Martha Palmer, Daniel Gildea, and Paul Kingsbury. 2005. The Proposition Bank: an annotated corpus of semantic roles. *Computational Linguistics*, 31(1).

Josef Ruppenhofer, Michael Ellsworth, Miriam R. L. Petruck, Christopher R. Johnson, and Jan Scheffczyk. 2006. Framenet II: Theory and practice. http://framenet.icsi.berkeley.edu/book/book.html.

Gerard Salton and Chris Buckley. 1987. Term weighting approaches in automatic text retrieval. Technical Report TR87-881, Department of Computer Science, Cornell University.

Gerard Salton, A. Wong, and C. S. Yang. 1974. A vector space model for automatic indexing. Technical Report TR74-218, Department of Computer Science, Cornell University.

Mihai Surdeanu, Richard Johansson, Adam Meyers, Lluís Màrquez, and Joakim Nivre. 2008. The CoNLL–2008 shared task on joint parsing of syntactic and semantic dependencies. In *Proceedings of The Twelfth Conference on Natural Language Learning (CoNLL-2008)*.

Yiming Yang. 2001. A study on thresholding strategies for text categorization. In *Proceedings of the 24th annual international ACM SIGIR conference*, pages 137–145.

ISSN 1736-6305 Vol. 4
http://hdl.handle.net/10062/9206

Part of Speech Tagging for Text Clustering in Swedish

Magnus Rosell
KTH CSC
Stockholm, Sweden
`rosell@csc.kth.se`

Abstract

Text clustering could be very useful both as an intermediate step in a large natural language processing system and as a tool in its own right. The result of a clustering algorithm is dependent on the text representation that is used. Swedish has a fairly rich morphology and a large number of homographs. This possibly leads to problems in Information Retrieval in general. We investigate the impact on text clustering of adding the part-of-speech-tag to all words in the the common term-by-document matrix.

The experiments are carried out on a few different text sets. None of them give any evidence that part-of-speech tags improve results. However, to represent texts using only nouns and proper names gives a smaller representation without worsen results. In a few experiments this smaller representation gives better results.

We also investigate the effect of lemmatization and the use of a stoplist, both of which improves results significantly in some cases.

1 Introduction

Text clustering (see for instance Manning et al. (2008)) aims at dividing a set of texts into groups with coherent content without knowledge of any predefined categories. The result of a clustering could be useful in many different circumstances: it can be used as an intermediate step in a bigger system, or as a tool in its own right, to facilitate exploration of search engine results (Zamir et al., 1997) or for any text set (Cutting et al., 1992).

The result of clustering algorithms is dependent on a definition of a (dis)similarity between the objects. For text clustering the similarity is usually defined via a representation of the texts using some or all the words/tokens that appear in them. Two texts are typically defined as similar if they use the same words. Which words/tokens that are used and how they are preprocessed can have a great effect on the result.

Lemmatization or stemming allows us to treat several related tokens as the same, leading to an increased similarity between texts, using the different forms of a word. Part-of-speech (PoS) tagging can be used to achieve the opposite; separate homographs so that texts are not defined similar when they are using the different meanings of a token.

The rest of this paper is organized as follows. Sections 2 through 4 gives a background to the experiments that we have conducted and present in Section 5. Finally, in Section 6 we summarize and draw some conclusions.

2 Information Retrieval

In Information Retrieval (IR) texts are represented in the common vector space model, see any introductory text, for instance (Manning et al., 2008). Each element of a term-document-matrix is assigned a weight, modeling the importance of the corresponding term to the document. There are several weighting schemes; we use a tf*idf weighting scheme. The similarity between texts (in a search engine: a query and a text) is modeled by a measure that compare their corresponding columns in the matrix. We use the common cosine measure, the cosine of the angle between the vectors.

When building the representation a few preprocessing steps are usually applied after tokenization, depending on the application. Common terms are included in a stoplist and removed, as these usually not contribute to the similarity calculations, being present in many texts. Modern search engines do not use them at all since the original motivation was to save storage space.

Token (or term) normalization, further, reduces classes of related terms to common representatives to increase similarity between texts that contain these. This includes a predetermined way to handle such things as capital letters, hyphenations, abbreviations, etc. From a linguistic point of view, the most interesting part of term normalization is the use of stemming or lemmatization to collapse morphological variants of a word. Stemming is a more ad hoc method that removes affixes and may reduce word derivations having different parts of speech into the same so called stem, while lemmatization refers to replacing each token with its proper lemma. The effect of using stemming on English texts for search engines is somewhat debated. Some studies have shown improvements, while others even a decrease in performance. There have been improvements reported when using stemming and/or lemmatization for several other languages.

In 2001 Hedlund et al. observed that Swedish was poorly known from an IR perspective. They identify a few properties of the Swedish language that are potential problems (as compared to for instance English):

1. The rather rich morphology (inflectional and derivative).

2. The frequent formation of compounds, which appear as one token. (Of words remaining after the use of a stoplist 10 % are compounds, meaning that more than 20 % of the interesting morphemes are found in compounds.)

3. The high frequency of homographic words. (65% of words in running text)

To address these problems they suggest using natural language processing (NLP) tools: word normalization (stemming or lemmatization) for the morphological variation, compound splitting to extract the information in the parts, and part-of-speech tagging with gender for nouns to disambiguate homographic words. However, search queries are usually short and can be hard to part-of-speech tag correctly.

An IR system for Swedish has to take these issues into consideration. There has been a lot of work done on search engines for both mono and cross language retrieval in recent years. A big comparative study of several European languages

is (Hollink et al., 2004). We feel a bit sceptic about the results for Swedish (and Finnish) since they report a substantial increase in performance when removing diacritic characters, indicating that the system does not handle the language very well. They also report substantial improvements using stemming and compound splitting for Swedish.

There are also a lot of studies in CLEF[1] (The Cross-Language Evaluation Forum) that include Swedish, several of which report improvements using morphological analysis.

Carlberger et el. (2001) saw an increase in search engine precision and recall on a newspaper text set when using stemming as compared to not using it. Ahlgren and Kekäläinen (2007) study several user scenarios on newspaper texts and report improvements for morphological analysis, word truncation, and compound splitting.

The results for search engines do not necessarily hold true for other IR methods, such as text clustering.

3 Text Clustering

The vector space model described in Section 2 can be used for text clustering. The reason for doing this is to define similarity between texts and/or groups of texts. Therefore it is not necessary to keep all tokens as in a search engine, where the goal is to be able to retrieve texts containing certain tokens. Hence, the results for search engines are not necessarily valid for text clustering.

Text clustering of Swedish texts has been investigated with respect to stemming and compound splitting (Rosell, 2003) and the use of nominal phrases in the representation (Rosell and Velupillai, 2005). Stemming seems to improve results, but the improvement is small. Compound splitting improves results, but the use of nominal phrases in the representation does not.

We use the K-Means clustering algorithm, see (Jain et al., 1999) for instance. It is fast and efficient and iteratively improves on k centroids (mean vectors) that represent k clusters. In each iteration each text is assigned to the group with the most similar centroid[2]. The algorithm stops when no text changes cluster between iterations. In the experiments presented here we stop after 20 itera-

---

[1] http://clef-campaign.org/

[2] We do not normalize the centroids when calculating similarity, leading to the average similarity between the text and all texts in the cluster.

tions, as the early iterations contribute more to the result.

In K-Means clustering each centroid contains all terms appearing in all texts of its cluster: terms with high weight in a centroid co-occur a lot in the cluster. If there is coherent content groups in the text set K-Means can find them or something related to them via centroids of cooccurring terms.

Homographs with several meanings may appear in several centroids and be disambiguated by the other terms. Synonyms will likely co-occur with the same words, and hence be present in the same centroid(s). In this work we investigate if these effects can be improved by separating homographs of different parts-of-speech.

4   Clustering Evaluation

Evaluation of text clustering can be either internal or external. Internal measures defines the quality of a clustering using the same information available to the clustering algorithm; the representation and/or similarity measure. As we evaluate different representations these are not appropriate here.

External evaluation can be performed by studying the effect of a clustering on a system that uses clustering as an intermediate step, by asking users for their opinions on the clustering result, or by comparing the result to a known categorization. The later is the easiest, fastest, and least expensive.

Among external measures based on comparisons of a clustering C with a known categorization K the mutual information (MI) is good since it compares the entire distribution of texts over the clusters to the entire distribution of texts over the categories (Strehl, 2002):

$$MI(C, K) = \sum_{i=1}^{\gamma} \sum_{j=1}^{\kappa} \frac{m_i^{(j)}}{n} \log(\frac{m_i^{(j)} n}{n_i n^{(j)}}),$$

where γ and κ are the numbers of clusters and categories, n the total number of texts, n_i the number of texts in cluster $c_i \in C$, $n^{(j)}$ the number of texts in category $k^{(j)} \in K$, and $m_i^{(j)}$ the number of texts in both cluster c_i and category $k^{(j)}$.

The normalized mutual information (NMI) takes the distributions of the texts over the clustering and the categorization into account (Strehl and Ghosh, 2003):

$$NMI(C, K) = \frac{2MI(C, K)}{\sqrt{H(C)H(K)}},$$

where $H(C) = -\sum_{i=1}^{\gamma} \frac{n_i}{n} \log \frac{n_i}{n}$ is the entropy for the distribution of texts over the clusters, and $H(K)$ similarly. This makes comparison of evaluations of different clusterings compared to different categorizations theoretically possible. However, the mutual information can never take the the inherent linguistic structure of different text sets into account; although comparable in both size of the entire set and distribution over categories, two text sets need not be similarly hard to cluster!

5   Experiments

We have clustered several text sets, see Section 5.1, with several different text representations described in Section 5.2 to a few different numbers of clusters (5, 10, 50) using the K-Means algorithm. All results presented here are average results over 20 runs with standard deviations in parenthesis.

5.1   Text Sets

We have used the following text sets:

KTH News Corpus (Hassel, 2001) is a set of downloaded news texts. The news are from different sources, some of which have a categorization. For the newspapers *Aftonbladet* and *Dagens Nyheter* the texts are categorized into five sections: Domestic/Sweden, Foreign/World, Economy, Culture/Entertainment, and Sports. We have extracted some small text sets from these:

A is some of the texts with 20 or more words from Aftonbladet.

DN is all of the texts with 20 or more words from Dagens Nyheter.

Occ comes from a questionnaire in The Swedish Twin Registry[3]. This text set is the free text answers from 1998 and 2002 to a question about occupation given to the twins born in and before 1958. All answers were categorized by Statistics Sweden[4] (SCB) according to two hierarchical occupation classification systems:

---

[3] The largest twin registry in the world, containing information about more than 140 000 twins. See (Lichtenstein et al., 2002; Lichtenstein et al., 2006) for a description of the contents and some findings that have come from it and http://www.meb.ki.se/twinreg/index_en.html for more information.

[4] http://www.scb.se

AMSYK is used by AMS (The Swedish National Labour Market Administration) and is based on ISCO88 (The International Standard Classification of Occupations).

YK80 was used in The Swedish Population and Housing Census 1980.

Table 1 gives the number of categories on each of the levels in the classification systems. For the evaluation of these experiments we have used the second level of both.

	L1	L2	L3	L4	L5
AMSYK	11	28	114	361	969
YK80	12	59	288		

Table 1: The Occupation Classification Systems (number of categories per level)

	Text Sets		
	A	DN	Occ
Texts	2424	6395	41949
Categories	5	5	28, 59
$H(K)/\log(\kappa)$	1.00	0.97	0.90, 0.83
Word Forms	12071	37725	17594
Forms/Text	52.29	97.41	15.60
Texts/Form	10.50	16.51	37.20
Lemmas	9050	26451	13873
Lemmas/Text	48.84	88.13	13.70
Texts/Lemma	13.08	21.31	41.29

Table 2: Text Set Statistics

We have used the grammar checking program Granska[5] (Domeij et al., 1999) for tokenization, lemmatization, and to tag each word with its part-of-speech. Table 2 gives some statistics for the text sets after preprocessing to word forms (including delimiters) and lemmas. The number of texts, tokens, and the average number of unique token per text and texts per unique token. We also give the number of categories and the "evenness" of the categorization: $H(K)/\log(\kappa)$, which is 1 for a categorization where all categories have equal size, and lower for other cases.

As can be seen there is a significant decrease in tokens when using lemmas instead of word forms. Even if this does not improve the results it improves the storage requirements for the representations.

5.2 Representation

We have evaluated several different representations, which we describe briefly here. In the next section (Section 5.3) we present the results.

Granska outputs among other things a tokenization that contains word forms, lemmas, the part-of-speech for each token, and some delimiters. The part-of-speech classes are given in Table 3 and is an adaption (Carlberger and Kann, 1999) of the the tag set in the Stockholm-Umeå Corpus (SUC) (Källgren and Eriksson, 1993).

We have used all the tokens in the representation we call *Full* with either word forms or lemmas (*Word Form* and *Lemma* in the tables). To reduce the Full representation one can use either a stoplist or only consider tokens that get a proper wordclass as their part of speech. The *All wordclasses* representation uses all tokens with these, except the delimiters.

For the *Stoplist* representation we removed tokens according to the Swedish stoplist of the snowball stemmer[6], plus all numbers, and words shorter than three characters and longer than 20.

To separate homographs by their part-of-speech we create new features by concatenating the lemma with its part-of-speech tag (*Lemma + PoS*), for instance: "och_kn", "spela_vb", "mittback_nn". We compare the results for this representation to the one using only the lemma. To separate even more homographs we use the gender for nouns as well (*Lemma + PoS + Gender*).

Most parts of speech in Table 3 contain only words that are usually in a stoplist. We have concentrated on the largest wordclasses, as these are also the ones that convey content in an obvious way. In the result tables we indicate which we have used by the abbreviations in Table 3.

When the representation is constructed we remove terms that appear in only one text as these do not contribute to the similarity calculations. We also remove texts that only contain one term.

5.3 Results

We present some results for text set DN in Table 4, and some of the results for text set Occ evaluated against the second level of the AMSYK categorization system in Table 5. The results for text set

---

[5] http://www.nada.kth.se/theory/projects/granska/

[6] http://snowball.tartarus.org/

Abbreviation	Part-of-Speech	Example
nn	noun	bil
pm	proper name	Lars
jj	adjective	grön
rg	number	12
ro	cardinal number	första
vb	verb	springa
ab	adverb	mycket
in	interjection	ja
ha	interrogative/relative adverb	när
dt	determiner	den
hd	interrogative/relative determiner	vilken
ps	possesive pronoun	hennes
hs	interrogative/relative possessive	vems
pn	pronoun	hon
hp	interrogative/relative pronoun	vem
sn	subordinating conjunction	om
kn	coordinating conjunction	och
pp	preposition	till
pc	participle	springande
pl	particle	om
uo	foreign word	the
an	abbreviation	d.v.s.
ie	verb base form marker	att
dl	delimiter	.

Table 3: Part-of-Speech Tags used in `Granska`

A are very similar to the ones for DN, and also the results on text set Occ evaluated against the YK80 categorization system (level 2) are very similar to the results evaluated to the AMSYK categorization.

The tables are divided into sections vertically for different numbers of clusters and horizontally for which features are used in the text representation: Word Form, Lemma, Lemma + PoS, or Lemma + PoS + Gender. Other aspects of the representation are presented as rows; which of the features are used in the representation.

The result of each experiment (20 K-Means clusterings of a particular representation) is presented with two values: the average NMI with standard deviations in parenthesis, and the number of features the representation gives rise to. As we remove texts that have one or fewer features some of the clustering are performed on fewer texts than are presented in Table 2. The number of texts that are removed are under on per cent in all cases.

Most differences are well within the standard deviations and should therefore not be considered significant. The representations are kept constant in the experiments; the varying results are due to the indeterministic K-Means algorithm.

5.4 Discussion

Our attempt to enhance the representation by introducing the part-of-speech tags (and gender) fails miserably. There are no interesting tendencies pointing to any improvements compared to using only lemmas, see Tables 4:b, 4:c, and 5:b. The effect of keeping only some parts-of-speech in the representation is not surprising: adjectives, verbs, and adverbs are not very good, while the nouns and proper names are as good on their own as all parts-of-speeches together. For five clusters on the Occ text set it is even better to only keep the large word classes than using them all (Table 5:b).

We have not tried a combination of the word form and the part-of-speech tag. This would have resulted in a representation with even more features, but might have given better results than the word forms on their own.

The lemmatization might address the homograph problem to some extent in addition to the morphological variants. An other explanation is that the cooccurence statistics gathered in the centroids is quite effective in separating homographs, and is not very dependent on which representation is used. Regardless of whether any of these two explanations are true, a representation extended with PoS tags does not improve results.

The comparison between word form and lemma representation in Tables 4:a and 5:a contains some interesting results. It is almost always beneficial to use lemmatization, and most times it improves results a lot. For text set DN it does not improve results significantly when clustering to five clus-

Clusters	Representation	Word Form		Lemma	
		NMI	Features	NMI	Features
5	Full	0.44 (0.05)	37725	0.52 (0.05)	26466
	Stoplist	0.52 (0.04)	35888	0.51 (0.04)	25604
	All wordclasses	0.47 (0.06)	37705	0.49 (0.04)	26451
50	Full	0.28 (0.01)	37725	0.35 (0.01)	26466
	Stoplist	0.28 (0.01)	35888	0.35 (0.01)	25604
	All wordclasses	0.28 (0.01)	37705	0.35 (0.01)	26451

a) Word Form vs. Lemma

Clusters	Representation	Lemma		Lemma + PoS	
		NMI	Features	NMI	Features
5	All wordclasses	0.49 (0.04)	26451	0.51 (0.04)	27532
	nn, pm, jj, vb, ab	0.50 (0.04)	25923	0.52 (0.05)	26767
	nn, pm	0.54 (0.04)	19507	0.55 (0.05)	19940
	jj, vb, ab	0.28 (0.02)	6729	0.29 (0.02)	6827
	jj, ab	0.20 (0.01)	4231	0.19 (0.01)	4285
	vb	0.27 (0.02)	2542	0.27 (0.02)	2542
50	All wordclasses	0.35 (0.01)	26451	0.34 (0.01)	27532
	nn, pm, jj, vb, ab	0.35 (0.01)	25923	0.34 (0.01)	26767
	nn, pm	0.37 (0.01)	19507	0.37 (0.01)	19940
	jj, vb, ab	0.24 (0.01)	6729	0.24 (0.01)	6827
	jj, ab	0.17 (0.01)	4231	0.17 (0.00)	4285
	vb	0.19 (0.00)	2542	0.19 (0.01)	2542

b) Lemma vs. Lemma + PoS

Clusters	Representation	Lemma + PoS + Gender	
		NMI	Features
5	All wordclasses	0.52 (0.04)	27612
	nn, pm, jj, vb, ab	0.50 (0.05)	26847
	nn, pm	0.51 (0.06)	20020
50	All wordclasses	0.34 (0.01)	27612
	nn, pm, jj, vb, ab	0.35 (0.01)	26847
	nn, pm	0.37 (0.01)	20020

c) Lemma + PoS + Gender

Table 4: Some Results for Text Set DN (about 6400 news articles)

ters, but it does not worsen results. The biggest improvement is for text set Occ clustered to five clusters, more than 50 % on average (standard deviation of about 20 %).

The stoplist improves results for text set Occ, but not for DN. It is particularly in combination with lemmatization, when clustering to few clusters that this can be seen. Perhaps the stop words obscure the representation more in the short texts of Occ. To use only the tokens that have proper wordclasses (All wordclasses) does not improve results. The Full representation does, however, not contain many other tokens in the first place.

Lemmatization effects all words/tokens in the representation. We expected that this global influence should be more obvious in results than the use of a stoplist, which is more local. However, the stop words adds noise; making all texts a bit similar, something which seems to be more important for short texts.

The clustering achieves better results when the number of clusters are roughly the same as the number of categories in the categorization used for the evaluation[7], regardless of the representation. It seems hard to improve results for this "optimal" number of clusters using the different representations we try here.

In these experiments we have used almost all words/tokens as features. It is possible to remove a lot of the features without getting worse results. We have tried a few versions were we remove words that appear in few documents. The general tendencies are still the same. Most notably there is nothing to be gained from using the part of speech tags.

Although results do not always improve with the use of lemmatization and a stoplist they never

---

[7]This is not surprising, considering the definition of NMI. For measures considering only the quality of any single cluster (not the entire clustering) the quality usually improves with more and smaller clusters.

Clusters	Representation	Word Form		Lemma	
		NMI	Features	NMI	Features
5	Full	0.10 (0.02)	17594	0.15 (0.02)	13916
	Stoplist	0.13 (0.02)	16378	0.25 (0.02)	13200
	All wordclasses	0.09 (0.01)	17546	0.15 (0.02)	13873
50	Full	0.25 (0.01)	17594	0.29 (0.01)	13916
	Stoplist	0.29 (0.01)	16378	0.33 (0.01)	13200
	All wordclasses	0.26 (0.01)	17546	0.30 (0.01)	13873

a) Word Form vs. Lemma

Clusters	Representation	Lemma		Lemma + PoS	
		NMI	Features	NMI	Features
5	All wordclasses	0.15 (0.02)	13873	0.15 (0.02)	14151
	nn, pm, jj, vb, ab	0.20 (0.02)	13565	0.20 (0.03)	13704
	nn, pm	0.23 (0.02)	10834	0.23 (0.01)	10841
50	All wordclasses	0.30 (0.01)	13873	0.30 (0.01)	14151
	nn, pm, jj, vb, ab	0.31 (0.01)	13565	0.31 (0.01)	13704
	nn, pm	0.31 (0.01)	10834	0.31 (0.01)	10841

b) Lemma vs. Lemma + PoS

Table 5: Some Results for Text Set Occ (about 42000 short texts)

deteriorate. On the other hand sometimes results improve a great deal. If a minimal representation is required one should consider using only nouns and proper names.

6 Conclusions and Further Work

We conclude that part of speech tagging does not improve results for text clustering of Swedish texts. However, to use only nouns and proper names in the representation often leads to results comparable to using all words, and may decrease the number of features significantly.

Lemmatization improves results a lot in several experiments. To use a stoplist improves results sometimes; in our experiments for short texts.

The cooccurence information in the K-Means centroids is obviously very good at handling homographs as no improvement in clustering results was achieved when introducing lemma-PoS-tag features.

As nouns seems to be very important for clustering, pronoun resolution could perhaps be interesting. However, it would just alter the weighting for the nouns and thus not affect the similarity between texts quite as radically as lemmatization and part of speech tagging.

References

P. Ahlgren and J. Kekäläinen. 2007. Indexing strategies for swedish full text retrieval under different user scenarios. *Inf. Process. Manage.*, 43(1):81–102.

J. Carlberger and V. Kann. 1999. Implementing an efficient part-of-speech tagger. *Softw. Pract. Exper.*, 29(9):815–832.

J. Carlberger, H. Dalianis, M. Hassel, and O. Knutsson. 2001. Improving precision in information retrieval for Swedish using stemming. In *Proc. 13th Nordic Conf. on Comp. Ling. – NODALIDA '01.*

D. R. Cutting, J. O. Pedersen, D. Karger, and J. W. Tukey. 1992. Scatter/Gather: A cluster-based approach to browsing large document collections. In *Proc. 15th Annual Int. ACM SIGIR Conf. on Research and Development in Information Retrieval.*

R. Domeij, O. Knutsson, J. Carlberger, and V. Kann. 1999. Granska – an efficient hybrid system for Swedish grammar checking. In *Proc. 12th Nordic Conf. on Comp. Ling. – NODALIDA '99.*

M. Hassel. 2001. Automatic construction of a Swedish news corpus. In *Proc. 13th Nordic Conf. on Comp. Ling. – NODALIDA '01.*

T. Hedlund, A. Pirkola, and K. Järvelin. 2001. Aspects of Swedish morphology and semantics from the perspective of mono- and cross-language information retrieval. *Information Processing & Management*, 37(1):147–161.

V. Hollink, J. Kamps, C. Monz, and M. De Rijke. 2004. Monolingual document retrieval for european languages. *Inf. Retr.*, 7(1-2):33–52.

A. K. Jain, M. N. Murty, and P. J. Flynn. 1999. Data clustering: a review. *ACM Computing Surveys*, 31(3):264–323.

G. Källgren and G. Eriksson. 1993. The linguistic annotation system of the stockholm: Umeå corpus project. In *Proceedings of the sixth conference on*

European chapter of the Association for Computational Linguistics, pages 470–470, Morristown, NJ, USA. Association for Computational Linguistics.

P. Lichtenstein, U. De faire, B. Floderus, M. Svartengren, P. Svedberg, and N. L. Pedersen. 2002. The Swedish twin registry: a unique resource for clinical, epidemiological and genetic studies. *Journal of Internal Medicine*, 252:184–205.

P. Lichtenstein, P. F. Sullivan, S. Cnattingius, M. Gatz, S. Johansson, E. Carlstrom, C. Bjork, M. Svartengren, A. Wolk, L. Klareskog, U. de Faire M. Schalling, J. Palmgren, and N. L. Pedersen. 2006. The Swedish twin registry in the third millennium: An update. *Twin Research and Human Genetics*, 9(6):875–882.

C. D. Manning, P. Raghavan, and H. Schütze. 2008. *Introduction to Information Retrieval*. Cambridge University Press.

M. Rosell and S. Velupillai. 2005. The impact of phrases in document clustering for Swedish. In *Proc. 15th Nordic Conf. on Comp. Ling. – NODALIDA '05*.

M. Rosell. 2003. Improving clustering of Swedish newspaper articles using stemming and compound splitting. In *Proc. 14th Nordic Conf. on Comp. Ling. – NODALIDA '03*.

A. Strehl and J. Ghosh. 2003. Cluster ensembles — a knowledge reuse framework for combining multiple partitions. *J. Mach. Learn. Res.*, 3:583–617.

A. Strehl. 2002. *Relationship-based Clustering and Cluster Ensembles for High-dimensional Data Mining*. Ph.D. thesis, The University of Texas at Austin.

O. Zamir, O. Etzioni, O. Madani, and R. M. Karp. 1997. Fast and intuitive clustering of web documents. In *Knowledge Discovery and Data Mining*, pages 287–290.

ISSN 1736-6305 Vol. 4
http://hdl.handle.net/10062/9206

What do we need to know about humans?
A view into the DanNet database

Bolette Sandford Pedersen
University of Copenhagen
Denmark
bspedersen@hum.ku.dk

Anna Braasch
University of Copenhagen
Denmark
braasch@hum.ku.dk

Abstract

The first version of the Danish WordNet, DanNet, was released in March 2009 under an open source license similar to the Princeton Licence (cf. www.wordnet.dk). In order to present and discuss the set of encoded semantic information in a focused form and with some empirical data, we dive into a specific ontological type in the WordNet, namely humans. We present and discuss the information types in the lexical semantic resource for this ontological type, and we focus on the information types where DanNet constitutes an extension of the general WordNet framework, namely regarding taxonomical status of a hyponym, qualia structure and connotative information.

1 Introduction

Which kinds of semantic information should be in focus when compiling lexical semantic resources for computational means? And more specifically, if we look into each ontological type, which are the particular ontological characteristics, relations and features that would provide us with the most basic and prototypical dimensions of lexical meaning? In order to answer these questions regarding appropriateness of description from an empirical viewpoint, we dive into a particular ontological type of entities, namely *humans*. The choice has fallen on this ontological type for two reasons: (i) Words referring to humans are *very* frequent in language: Thus, in the modern Danish dictionary, Den Danske Ordbog (DDO), the word *person*

('person') is by far the word with most hyponyms pointing to it: 4246 words refer to it as its closest hyperonym. For comparison, the closest competing word is *del* ('part') with only 764 hyponyms referring directly to it. And (ii) humans are *concrete entities* and thereby belong to a group whose manner of description is relatively well-documented in lexicographical, terminological and NLP literature (in contrast to e.g. abstract entities). At the same time, they are rather complex types in the sense that they encompass a series of semantic properties and connotations. Thus, they constitute a prototypical, but still sufficiently interesting ontological type as to shed light on the appropriate complexity of a lexical semantic resource.

In the following sections we account for and discuss these dimensions on the basis of the empirical data found in the Danish WordNet, DanNet. The first version of DanNet was released as an open source resource in March 2009. This lexical semantic resource has been developed in a collaborative project between a research institute, Centre for Language Technology, University of Copenhagen, and a literary and linguistic society, Det Danske Sprog- og Litteraturselskab under The Danish Ministry of Culture. The WordNet has been semi-automatically compiled on the basis of a traditional dictionary, the aforementioned DDO, and a pilot version of a computational semantic resource built on ontological grounds (SIMPLE-DK developed under the EU project on semantic computational lexica, SIMPLE (Semantic Information for Multifunctional, Plurilingual Lexica)). Currently, DanNet contains 41,000 synsets and will be supplemented during the next two years in order to cover 70,000 of DDO's approx. 100,000 word senses.

The paper is composed as follows: In Section 2 we relate to previous work in the field of lexical semantic resources and briefly discuss the particular, monolingual approach adopted in DanNet, whereas we look in Section 3 into the basic structure and description of humans: Which are the taxonomical principles used and which properties are central to encoding of the specific synsets. How can qualia structure (Pustejovsky 1995) help us organize relations and features in the wordnet, and how can we minimize the so-called ISA-overload problem. In Section 4 we move on to another aspect of the semantic encoding which goes beyond the primary, literary meaning of a synonym set (synset), namely that of connotation. By investigating the DanNet material, we examine the differences in connotational values for men and women, respectively. In Section 5, we exemplify how encodings of semantic relations and features as well as the inheritance mechanism is performed in DanNet, and finally, in Section 6 we conclude by summing up the points where DanNet differs from the standard WordNet framework.

2   Related work

Being a part of the 'WordNet family' (cf. www.wordnet.org), DanNet generally conforms to the framework given in the WordNet Specifications as accounted for in Fellbaum (1998) and Vossen (ed.) (1999). Thus, in DanNet we basically operate with synsets as well as with a fixed set of semantic relations between synsets, the has_hyperonym relation being the central one. However, as already mentioned, two former Danish resources have been reused in the compilation of DanNet, encompassing thereby several aspects of the more lexically driven and far more complex SIMPLE resources as accounted for in Lenci et al. (2000), as well as the linguistic specifications of DDO (Lorentzen 2004). This has resulted in the fact that DanNet includes some information types that are not generally given in WordNets, such as some more specific ontological types, information on taxonomical status of a hyponym minimizing thereby the ISA-overload, qualia structure on nouns, connotative values etc.

The approach of reusing monolingual resources for the building of a WordNet is contrasted by the approaches used in several other recently compiled WordNets of other languages such as the Spanish Wordnet (Fernández-Montraveta et al. 2008), the Arabic WordNet (Rodríguez et al. 2008), and the Hungarian WordNet (Márton et al. 2008). To our knowledge, only one other WordNet, namely the Polish WordNet (Derwojedowa et al. 2008), applies a monolingual approach similar to ours.

Our arguments for applying a monolingual approach to the Danish WordNet (and not an expand approach where translations are performed from Princeton WordNet) are partly linguistic, partly pragmatic, namely that we believe that a WordNet should ideally reflect the *inherent* characteristics of the general vocabulary of the language described, and that SIMPLE and in particular DDO constitute excellent sources for our approach since they are corpus-based, i.e. they reflect contemporary Danish language use. For further accounts of the reuse perspectives in the compilation of DanNet as well as on the general framework of the lexical resource, cf. Asmussen et al. (2007), Pedersen et al. (2008) and Pedersen & Sørensen (2006).

3   Taxonomical Structure and Semantic Properties

A basic assumption in DanNet is that a core part of the vocabulary can and should be organised in terms of strict taxonomical structures. Thus, conforming to the taxonomical principles referred to by Cruse (2002), humans are *a kind of* concrete entities parallel their co-taxonyms such as animals and things. It is further assumed that co-taxonyms are incompatible; thus an entity cannot be a human and an animal at the same time. This is the case in a majority of the synsets established in DanNet, which conforms to what Cruse (2002) refers to as *natural* or *functional kinds*. Natural kinds are found in natural taxonomies: A dahlia is a kind of flower and is incompatible with for instance a rose. Likewise, a needle represents a functional kind which is a type of instrument and which is incompatible with for instance a scalpel[1].

---

[1] Note, however, that *multiple inheritance* is generally accepted in DanNet, i.e. under the ontological type Artifact *a pot* is seen as both a piece of *kitchen equipment* and a *container*.

In this respect, humans constitute a rather special ontological type. If we look into the internal taxonomical structure of humans, it becomes clear that they hardly conform to such principles. For illustration, the following set of hyponyms of *person* may very well have the same referent: *fodgænger* ('pedestrian'), *alkoholiker* ('alcoholic'), *lærer* ('teacher'), *idiot* (idiot) and *skønhed* ('beauty') all at the same time. In other words, these hyponyms of persons are not incompatible since they do not refer to different individuals but rather to specific dimensions of these. Such terms are labelled *nominal kinds* by Cruse (2002). In contrast to natural and functional kinds, nominal kinds cannot be described as *a kind of* or *a type of*. They therefore typically constitute a taxonomical problem which is often referred to as the ISA-overload problem (Guarino 1998, Huang et al. 2008). As a further characteristic, the relation between nominal kinds and their hyperonyms can typically be captured in terms of a single differentiating feature; thus a pedestrian is a person who walks, a teacher a person who teaches, and an alcoholic a person who drinks, etc. This is in clear contrast to the aforementioned natural and functional kinds which require listing of prototypical features and use in order to be defined, i.e. "a needle is a very fine and slender piece of polished metal with a point at one end and a hole or eye for thread in the other, used in sewing" (NODE). To be more precise, nominal kinds call for a classification rather into semantic properties than into taxonomical types. One proposal for such a classification is given in the SIMPLE framework (Lenci et al. 2000a:197-211), where the following dimensions are suggested (Figure 1):

Human (example: *person*)
    People (example: *American*)
    Role (example: *member*)
        Ideo (example: *communist*)
        Kinship (example: *mother*)
        Social Status (example: *lord*)
    Agent of temporary activity
    (example: *student)*
    Agent of persistent activity
    (example: *violinist*)
    Profession (example: *teacher*)

Figure 1: Semantic dimensions of humans encoded in SIMPLE

Note that two of these dimensions, namely People and Professions, however, do expose incompatibility between their own co-hyponyms to a certain degree: Prototypically, an American is not at the same time a French, and a nurse is normally not a doctor at the same time, although specific contexts may permit compatibility.

Agents of temporary activities, on the other hand, are unique in the sense that they do not refer to individuals but rather to events performed by these. If you count monthly customers in a restaurant or passengers on a certain transport route, you are typically not counting individuals but rather the *number of times* that individuals visit the restaurant or take a given train. Several linguistic tests support this ontological distinction, for instance you can add a time specification and say *a frequent customer*, but not **a frequent American* or **a frequent mother*.

In DanNet we have adopted a somewhat simplified way of viewing different semantic properties of persons than the one given in SIMPLE. We apply Pustejovskys four-dimensional qualia structure (Pustejovsky 1995) as a frame also for describing the different properties of persons. The four qualia roles include:

- *the formal role* encompassing the dimension of seeing something as a kind,
- *the constitutive role* encompassing the dimension of seeing something as a whole consisting of parts (in SIMPLE a large number of semantic features and relations typically concerning the internal structure of the concept is expressed via this role[2]),
- *the telic role* encompassing the dimension of seeing something as having a certain function, and finally
- *the agentive role* encompassing the dimension of seeing something from the point of view of its origin.

Excluding here the formal role since it is already described via the hyperonym, the three other qualia roles are interpreted as follows:

- The constitutive role encompasses properties on gender, intellect, appearance or connotation, as expressed implicitly in per-

---

[2] Examples of features are *gender, age* and *connotation*; whereas examples of relations are: *has_colour, lives_in* etc.

son nouns such as *mandsperson* ('man'), *idiot* ('idiot'), *geni* ('genius'), *skønhed* (beauty), and *dværg* ('dwarf').

- The telic role encompasses typical functions as expressed implicitly in nouns such as *lærer* ('teacher', role of agent: to teach) and *chef* ('leader', role of agent: to lead).
- The agentive role focuses on properties that define the following nouns: *fodgænger* ('pedestrian', defining act: to walk), *cyklist* ('cyclist', defining act: to cycle), *alkoholiker* ('alcoholic', defining act: to drink), *kunde* ('customer', defining act: to buy).

On this approach, some of the fine-grained distinctions made in the SIMPLE specifications are excluded, for instance the distinction between properties regarding temporary and persistent activities (which could, however, be added by means of a feature). On the other hand, the qualia structure represents a more basic and generally applicable structure which is resembled all through the DanNet database in the sense that all concrete entities are described within this structure (cf. Pedersen & Sørensen 2006, Pedersen et al. 2008).

4   Connotations

Nominal kinds (to which, as we have seen, most of our human synsets belong) are characterized by the fact that they often include some kind of judgment or connotation. Within the framework of DanNet, connotation is understood as the set of associations implied by a word or lexical item in addition to its primary, literal meaning. The primary meaning of a word is its denotation or its referential meaning[3], e.g. *pige* ('girl') denoting a young female person. Lyons (1977:176) refers to the non-philosophical use of the term "connotation of a word "in semantics [...] as an emotive or affective component additional to its central meaning."

In some cases, a group of lexical items share central (primary) meaning, e.g. young female person. These items can only be distinguished by a difference in their connotations such as the positive

'*sild*' ('bird', 'chick'), and the negative *tøjte* ('tart'), whereas the noun *pige* is emotionally neutral. In DanNet, these words are not considered synonyms, even if they refer to the same entity; they appear in different synsets. In contrast, Cruse (1986:287) discusses a similar case as a sub-type of synonymy from the lexical semantics viewpoint and states that "subordinate [semantic] traits (...) have a role within the meaning of a word analogous to that of a modifier in a syntactic construction".

The connotation associated with a word may express e.g. a value judgment, personal feelings or emotional responses to the entity concerned. Obviously, person nouns frequently imply a connotation because humans judge each other by various remarkable features and traits e.g. in a social context.

Connotation may be of personal or general character. The first depends on the listener/reader's attitude, whereas the last mentioned is common to the language user community and therefore relevant information to be encoded. Further, whether the connotation of a word is activated at all depends on the context in which the word is used. For instance, in somewhat older texts with neutral or objective point of view, the word *tøs* denotes a (very) young, female person ('girl'). In contemporary texts, on the other hand, *tøs* is mainly used derogatively in the sense of 'tart' or 'wench': immorality and a contemptible behavior are associated with the person denoted. In this case the negative connotation is activated. This type of difference gives rise to encoding of separate meanings belonging to two distinct synsets.

The connotative information is based on DDO; it formalizes explicit usage information (e.g. the *nedsættende* 'derogatory' label) and/or implicit information present in the gloss of the word and in the corpus example(s) provided. It is encoded as a distinguishing semantic feature – an attribute – of the constitutive role, like the gender feature. Connotation is always evoked by one or more characteristic features of the person denoted. This feature, e.g. appearance, temper, behavior, morals, manners, mind or intellect, is encoded as a value for the so-called **concerns** relation, which is a DanNet-specific relation that marks an associative relation to the synset. The connotation attribute has two

---

[3] In philosophy and logic the term *extension* is used to refer to the relationship between a lexical item and the class of entities it is applied to. *Intension*, opposed to extension, includes only the defining properties of lexical items (Lyons 1977:159).

explicit polarity values: positive and negative, expressing a subjective attitude to the denoted person, topic, etc. Word senses with neutral attitude have a default, unmarked value.

Currently, 415 person nouns (approximately 10% of the total) are provided with a connotation value, hereof 58 specified by their nearest hyperonym as female and 47 male persons, resp.). The majority of person nouns, such as names of occupations, nationalities, family members, etc. are unmarked. This can be illustrated by the following two synsets: {*børsmægler, børshandler*} ('stock broker', 'stock dealer') denotes an occupation without connotation, whereas {*børsbaron, børshaj, børsspekulant*} ('stock-exchange magnate', 'stock jobber', 'stock speculator') denotes a person risking losses for the possibility of quick, considerable gains in a reprehensible way, which usually evokes a negative connotation.

Since connotations are very often emotional or evaluative in nature, it is interesting to look into the question of which personal characteristics evoke positive and negative associations, respectively. In the following, we present selected examples that are hyponyms of the ontological type *person* ('person'), with the focus on hyponyms of *kvinde, pige* ('woman', 'girl') *mand, dreng* ('man' and 'boy'). We investigate whether there is any difference between the prevalent features and connotation values associated with noun synsets that denote male and female persons, respectively, and we also look briefly into the group of nouns that have both male and female referents.

The features listed in the Tables 1 and 2 may apply also in combination, like appearance and shape, though this fact is ignored in the schematic presentation below. Other traits like manners, temper and mind appear frequently together in dictionary definitions; therefore they are not separated in this presentation either. The order and selection of prevalent features are slightly different in the tables 1 and 2 because of the observation that priority and weight of characterising or striking features seem to differ in case of nouns denoting male and/or female persons.

Feature evoking the connotation	Percentages in the encoded material
sexual behavior	(neg:10; pos:6 =16) 27.5%
temper/mind/manners	(neg:15; pos:0 =15) 26%
appearance	(neg:4; pos:8 =12) 20%
general	(neg:5; pos:2 = 7) 12%
shape/stature	(neg:3; pos: 2 = 5) 8.5%
intellect/ability	(neg:1; pos:2 = 3) 5%
TOTAL	(neg:38 ; pos:20 = 58) 100%

Table 1: Features of female persons (Hyperonyms: *kvinde* 'woman', *pige* 'girl')

Feature evoking the connotation	Percentages in the encoded material
manners/ mind	(neg:14; pos:3 =17) 36%
sexual behavior	(neg: 10; pos:1 = 11) 23.5 %
appearance	(neg: 5; pos:2 =7) 15 %
general	(neg: 4; pos:1 =5) 10.5 %
intellect/ability	(neg: 3; pos:1 =4) 8.5%
physical power	(neg: 1; pos: 2 =3) 6.5 %
TOTAL	(neg:37; pos:10 =47) 100%

Table 2: Features of male persons (Hyperonyms: *mand* 'man', *dreng* 'boy')

The figures and percentages indicate the following distribution tendencies: female persons have more connotations associated to them than male persons, and in general, the connotations are predominantly negative, namely 65% for females and 81% for males.

The most striking traits for both genders seem to concern sexual and social behaviour, but at a more detailed level the figures differ. Female persons are almost equally judged by their sexual behaviour and temper/mind/manners, the latter including a particular way of communication e.g. *rappenskralde* 'battleaxe' (being bad-tempered and cheeky). In case of male persons, their manners/mind is by far the most frequently judged property, e.g. *rod* 'tough, yob' (being ill-mannered and impudent). A large number (319) of person nouns with connotation can denote both male and female persons, e.g. *brokkehoved* ('moaner/ a grouchy person'), though a part of them has a priority of implied gender, e.g. *bulderbasse* ('busterer'). The distribution of connotation polarity in the gender-neutral group shows the same tendency as in the tables, namely 253 nouns with *person* as nearest hyperonym are associated with a negative connotation (79%), whereas only 66

(21%) have a positive connotation. On the other hand, as regards the feature evoking the connotation, the distribution seems to be broader and more scattered, e.g. attitude, position, rank, experience, age, birth, etc.

If we compare the strategy for assigning connotation values in DanNet with other projects, e.g. SentiWordNet (Esuli & Sebastiani, 2006), there are a number of differences. Firstly, DanNet is hand-coded, and connotation is currently provided for a subset of nouns only and without grades of polarity as is the case of SentiWordNet. Secondly, SentiWordNet does not include information parallel to the **concerns** relation in DanNet, information which we believe provide highly relevant lexical semantic information to the word sense.

5   Encodings in DanNet

DanNet currently contains 7057 synsets referring to humans and out of these, 3748 belong to the ontological type Human+Object, 1192 to the type Human+Object+Group, 1944 to the type Human+Occupation+Object, and 183 to the ontological type Human+Object+Part (typically members of something). Each ontological type evokes a specific template with a particular set of relations. For instance, for the ontological type Human+Part, the **has_holo_member** relation is obligatory, i.e. *partimedlem* (party member) **has_holo_member** *parti* (party).[4]

Figure 2 gives an example of the actual encoding of these in the DanNet database. The screen dump regards the encoding of the previously mentioned synset *{brokkehoved, kværulant}* (moaner, grouchy person). The top part of the screen shows the synset identifier, the lemmas of the synset, the gloss taken over from DDO, and the ontological type, in this case Human+Object. The second part regards the semantic features and relations. The connotative value is negative since *{brokkehoved, kværulant}* is conceived as derogative. For the actual synset the constitutive, formal, and telic roles are filled; the constitutive role is filled with the relation **concerns** *{opførsel}* (behavior). The formal role is filled with the **has_hyperonym** *{per-*

son, individ, menneske..}* (person, individual, human being..); this relation is typically automatically inherited from DDO. The **has_hyperonym** relation is further specified by the feature 'ortho' which indicates that *{brokkehoved, kværulant}* is conceived as orthogonal to the taxonomy, i.e. the synset does not form the basic taxonomy because of its being a nominal kind in Cruse's terms (cf. Section 3 on taxonomical structure). The telic role is filled with the relation **role_agent** *{brokke_sig, kværulere}* (moan, make a fuss).

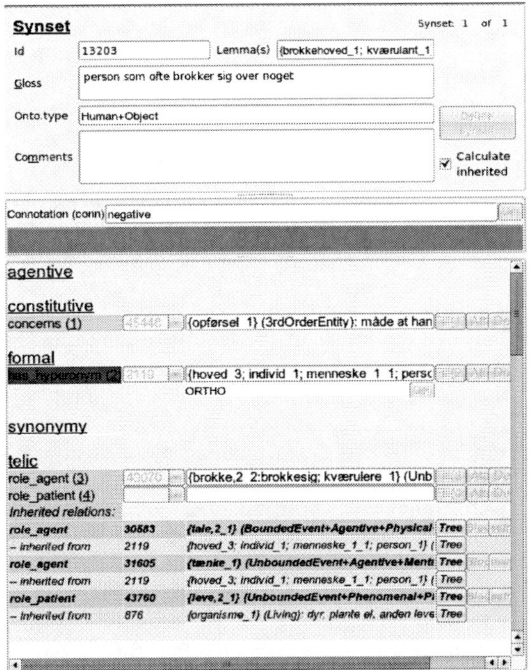

Figure 2: Screen dump of the synset *{brokkehoved, kværulant}* (moaner, grouchy person)

In addition, two relations are inherited from the top synset *{person, individ, menneske..}*, namely **role_agent** *{tænke}* and **role_agent** *{tale}* ('think, talk'). In some (few) cases semantic relations are blocked for inheritance. This facility is applied in cases of non-prototypical behavior, such as for instance a mute who cannot talk.

6   Conclusions

In this paper we have presented and discussed information types on humans as they currently ap-

---

[4] These templates are comparable to Moerdijk's *semagrams*, as presented in Moerdijk 2008.

pear in the DanNet resource, and we have extracted some data from the database in order to examine the actual distribution of various connotative features on humans.

By describing the encodings of humans in DanNet, we have also accounted for four aspects which distinguish this resource from the general WordNet framework:

- The resource is made from a monolingual basis, not by expanding from Princeton WordNet.
- Nominal terms are treated as non-taxonomical (orthogonal to the taxonomy) whereby the ISA-overload is reduced.
- Relations and features are systematically organized along the dimensions of an extended qualia structure.
- Connotative information is provided when relevant in terms of a constitutive feature regarding positive or negative connotation.

The question is to which extent these additions improve the utility of the lexical resource, in this particular case, of the ontological type humans. At the most basic level, the possibility of simply distinguishing humans uniquely from other entities in running text is a much required piece of information asked for repeatedly by DanNet's advisory panel (cf. www.wordnet.dk), an information type provided, however, generally in WordNets. Another question regards whether the subdivision in DanNet of hyponymic relations into taxonomical and non-taxonomical ones will actually ease integration of the lexical resource into formal ontologies or other formal systems where advanced inference mechanisms require a strictly logical structure. Anyhow, the apparently messy structure (from an ontological point of view) of the prototypical WordNet has been eagerly discussed at several Ontolex workshops and in other fora where lexicographers and formal ontologists meet. The organisation of DanNet into taxonomical and non-taxonomical structures is a first attempt to address this problem (see also Huang 2008 for a similar attempt in the Chinese WordNet).

Regarding the description of qualia structure, Pustejovsky (1995) argues that it defines the core elements of meaning of a lexical item, and that these core elements are a prerequisite for resolving several grammatical and semantic hurdles in language analysis such as type shifting, type coercion, and ambiguity. If we, for instance, refer to *en hurtig bilist* (a fast car driver), qualia structure helps disambiguate the often subtle meaning of the adjective (via selective binding), namely that the fastness regards the driving and not anything else.

Finally, the encoding of connotative information can be seen as a way of supplementing the lexical resource with information that goes beyond the pure denotation of words; a feature which in fact has also being investigated in relation to several other WordNets but mostly at an experimental level (Fellbaum & Miller 2006, Veale 2008)). Generally, such information supports the identification of the associations implied beyond the denotative textual level and helps clarify the attitude or bias of a text. In our particular case, we have focused on person nouns with positive or negative connotation and thereby only just shed light on a small corner of this immense semantic field.

The final proof of the pudding is in the eating: In other words, time will show in which kinds of applications the resource can be really useful, and which particular information types are most applicable. Hopefully, experiments will take place in time as to actually give feedback to the second development phase of DanNet running until the end of 2010.

Acknowledgments

Thanks to Nicolai H. Sørensen for providing the statistics on the encoding of synsets referring to humans in DanNet.

References

Asmussen, J. Pedersen, B.S. & Trap-Jensen, L. 2007. DanNet: From Dictionary to WordNet. Kunze, C., Lemnitzer, L. & Osswald, R. (eds.) *GLDV-2007 Workshop on Lexical-Semantic and Ontological Resources*: 1-11. Universität Tübingen, Germany.

Cruse, D.A. 1986. Lexical Semantics. Cambridge University Press.

Cruse, D.A. 2002. Hyponymy and Its Varieties. R. Green, C.A. Bean, & S. H. Myaeng (eds) *The*

Semantics of Relationships: An Interdisciplinary Perspective, Information Science and Knowledge Management: 2–21. Springer Verlag.

Derwojedowa, M. M. Piasecki, S. Szpakowicz, M. Zawislawska & B. Broda. 2008. Words, Concepts and Relations in the Construction of the Polish WordNet. *Global WordNet Conference 2008*: 162–177. Szeged, Hungary.

Esuli, A. & F. Sebastiani. 2006. SentiWordNet: A Publicly Available Lexical Resource for Opinion Mining. *Proceedings of LREC 2006: 417-422*. Genua, Italy

Fellbaum, C. (ed). 1998. *WordNet – An Electronic Lexical Database*. The MIT Press, Cambridge, Massachusetts, London, England.

Fellbaum, C. & G. Miller (2006) *Wither WordNet?* Zampolli Prize Talk at LREC 2006. Available at http://www.lrec-conf.org/lrec2006/IMG/pdf/AZPrize.Christiane%20Fellbaum%20Presentation.LREC06.pdf

Fernández-Montraveta, A, G. Vázquez & C. Fellbaum. 2008. The Spanish Version of WordNet 3.0. In: *Text resources and Lexical Knowledge*: 175–182. Text, Translation, Computational Processing. Mouton de Gruyter, Berlin & New York.

Guarino, N. (1998) Some Ontological Principles for Designing Upper Level Lexical Resources. Proceedings from the First International Conference on Language Resources and Evaluation pp: 527–534, Granada.

Huang, C., Hsiao, P., Su, I., Ke, X. (2008). Paranymy: Enriching Ontological Knowledge in WordNets. *Proceedings of the Fourth Global WordNet Conference*: 221–228, Szeged, Hungary.

Lenci, A., Bel, N., Busa, F., Calzolari, N., Gola, E., Monachini, M., Ogonowski, A., Peters, I. Peters, W., Ruimy, N., Villegas, M. & Zampolli, A. 2000. SIMPLE – A General Framework for the Development of Multilingual Lexicons. T. Fontenelle (ed) *International Journal of Lexicography*, Vol 13: 249–263. Oxford University Press.

Lenci, A. F. Busa, N. Ruimy, E. Gola, M. Monachini, N. Calzolari, A. Zampolli. 2000. *SIMPLE. Linguistics Specifications*. Technical Report. Pisa.

Lorentzen, H. 2004. The Danish Dictionary at large: Presentation, Problems and Perspectives. G. Williams and S. Vessier (eds): *Proceedings of the Eleventh EURALEX International Congress*: 285–294. Lorient, France.

Lyons, J. 1997. *Semantics*. Cambridge University Press.

Márton, M., C. Hatvani, J. Kuti, G. Szarvas, J. Csirik, G. Prószéky, T. Váradi. 2008. Methods and Results of the Hungarian WordNet Project. *Global WordNet Conference 2008*: 311–320. Szeged, Hungary.

Moerdijk, F. 2008. Frames and Semagrams. Meaning Description in the General Dutch Dictionary. *EURALEX 2008*. Barcelona, Spain.

NODE. 1998. *The New Oxford Dictionary of English*. Oxford.

Pedersen, B.S., S. Nimb, L. Trap-Jensen (2008) DanNet: udvikling og anvendelse af det danske wordnet. *Nordiske Studier i Leksikografi, Rapport fra konference om leksikografi i Norden*, Akureyri, Iceland.

Pedersen, B.S. & N. Sørensen. 2006. Towards sounder taxonomies in WordNets. In: Alessandro Oltramari, Chu-Ren Huang, Alessandro Lenci, Paul Buitelaar, Christiane Fellbaum (eds.): *Ontolex 2006*: 9-16. Genova, Italy.

Pustejovsky, J. 1995. *The Generative Lexicon*. The MIT Press, Cambridge, Massachusetts.

Rodríguez, H. D. Farwell, J. Farreres, M. Bertran, M. Alkhalifa, M. A. Martí, W. Black, S. El-kateb, J. Kirk, A. Pease, P. Vossen, & C. Fellbaum (2008). Arabic WordNet: Current State and Future Extension. *Global WordNet Conference 2008*: 387–405. Szeged, Hungary.

Veale, T. 2008. Enriching WordNet with Folk Knowledge and Stereotypes. *Global WordNet Conference 2008*: 453–461. Szeged, Hungary.

Vossen, P. (ed). 1999. *EuroWordNet, A Multilingual Database with Lexical Semantic Networks*. Kluwer Academic Publishers, The Netherlands.

ISSN 1736-6305 Vol. 4
http://hdl.handle.net/10062/9206

Dependency Parsing Resources for French: Converting Acquired Lexical Functional Grammar F-Structure Annotations and Parsing F-Structures Directly

Natalie Schluter
Dublin City University
Dublin 9, Ireland
`nschluter@computing.dcu.ie`

Josef van Genabith
Dublin City University
Dublin 9, Ireland
`josef@computing.dcu.ie`

Abstract

Recent years have seen considerable success in the generation of automatically obtained wide-coverage deep grammars for natural language processing, given reliable and large CFG-like treebanks. For research within Lexical Functional Grammar framework, these deep grammars are typically based on an extended PCFG parsing scheme from which dependencies are extracted. However, increasing success in statistical dependency parsing suggests that such deep grammar approaches to statistical parsing could be streamlined. We explore this novel approach to deep grammar parsing within the framework of LFG in this paper, for French, showing that best results (an f-score of 69.46) for the established integrated architecture may be obtained for French.

1 Introduction

Recent years have seen considerable success in the generation of automatically obtained wide-coverage deep grammars for natural language processing, given reliable and large CFG-like treebanks (for example, (Cahill et al., 2002; Guo et al., 2007; Chrupała and van Genabith, 2006)). For research within Lexical Functional Grammar (LFG) framework, these deep grammars are typically based on an extended PCFG parsing scheme from which dependencies are extracted. However, increasing success in statistical dependency parsing suggests that such deep grammar approaches to statistical parsing could be streamlined. In this paper, we explore this novel approach to deep grammar parsing within the framework of LFG in this paper, for French, showing that best results (an f-score of 69.46) for the established integrated architecture may be obtained for French.

This paper presents a *mise-en-scène* between theoretical dependency syntax and dependency parser practical requirements, an *entrée en scène* for f-structures in the literature for dependency parsing, an approach to representing f-structures in LFG as pseudo-projective dependencies, a first attempt to reconcile parsing LFG and dependency parsing, and, finally, the first treebank-based statistical dependency parsing results for French.

We begin with an brief introduction to LFG, followed by a presentation of the Modified French Treebank (the data source for this research), and an overview of previous parsing architecture of LFG f-structures (Section 2). Following this, we discuss LFG f-structure dependencies, comparing previously mentioned theoretical frameworks for statistical dependency parsing in the literature and showing their pseudo-projectivity (Section 3). In Section 4 we describe the data conversion involved in this research, and we end with the presentation of results of our experiments and a brief discussion (Section 5).

2 Preliminaries

2.1 Lexical Functional Grammar Basics

LFG is a constraint-based theory of language, whose basic architecture distinguishes two levels of syntactic representation : *c-structure* (constituent structure) and *f-structure* (functional structure)—c-structures corresponding to tradiional constituent tree representation, and f-structures to a traditional dependency representation in the form of an attribute value matrix.[1]

Like any attribute-value matrix, f-structures are the minimal solution to a set of functional equations such as $(f\ a) = v$, where f is an f-structure, a is some attribute, and v is the value taken by that attribute, possibly another f-structure.

---

[1] A detailed introduction to LFG may be found in (Dalrymple, 2001).

These two levels of representation (f-structure and c-structure), for a given phrase, are explicitly related by a structural mapping, called the *f-description*, often denoted by ϕ, which maps c-structure nodes to f-structure nodes.

In the LFG framework, this mapping may be given by functional annotations inserted into the c-structure tree, as in Figure 1.

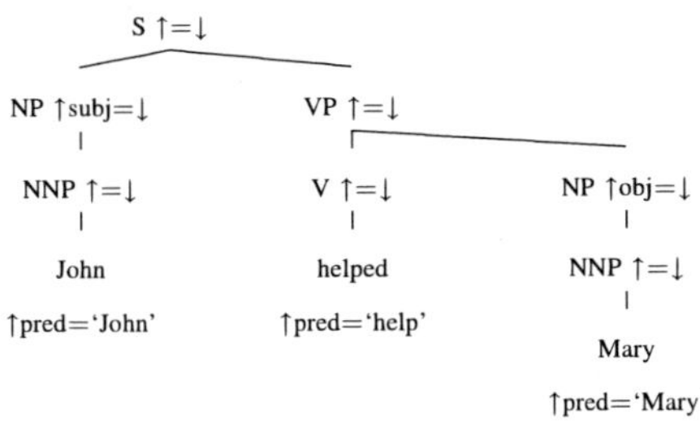

Figure 1: Annotated C-structure for *John helped Mary*.

The metavariables $\uparrow$ and $\downarrow$ refer to the f-structure of the mother node and that of the node itself, respectively. So that if node n, is annotated $\uparrow=\downarrow$, then n's f-structure is mapped to the same f-structure as n's mother's f-structure. Also, if n has the annotation $\uparrow\text{obj}=\downarrow$, this means that the f-structure associated with n is mapped to the value of the mother's f-structure `obj` attribute. LFG also has equations for members of sets, such as $\downarrow\in\uparrow\text{adjunct}$, which states that the node's f-structure is mapped to an element of the mother's ADJ attribute.

2.2 Modified French Treebank

For this research, the treebank adopted is the Modified French Treebank (MFT) (Schluter and van Genabith, 2007). One important feature of the MFT is the extended function tag set, which includes function path tags. Consider the sentence in Example (1), taken directly from the MFT, whose tree structure is given in Figure 2.

(1)   C'est [...] l'URSS [...] qui se
        It is [...] the USSR [...] who herself
        trouve prise
        finds taken
        'It is the USSR that finds itself trapped'[2]

In this example, the Srel constituent takes the functional path tag SUJ.MOD, representing the

[2]Sentence 8151, file flmf3_08000_08499ep.xd.cat.xml.

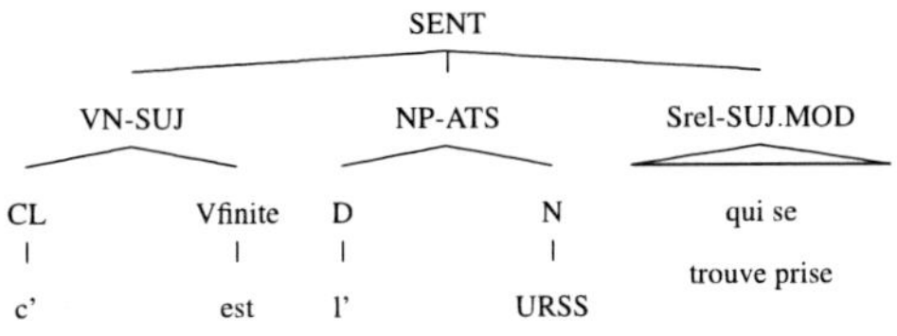

Figure 2: MFT representation of Example (1).

fact that Srel has the function MOD and is dependent on the constituent whose function is SUJ.

For this research, we followed the same random partition as (Schluter and van Genabith, 2008) for the training set (3800 sentences), test set (430 sentences), and development set (509 sentences).

2.3 Previous Parsing Architectures of LFG F-Structures

Previously, the technology for treebank-based acquisition of multilingual LFG probabilistic parsing resources consisted of three main stages, the basic input for which is a CFG-type treebank. These stages include the construction and application of an f-structure annotation algorithm combined with satisfiability verification, subcategorisation frame extraction, and long-distance dependency extraction. Given the resources produced in these initial stages, four CFG-based probabilistic parsing architectures were developed. Figure 3 shows these parsing architectures, with, in bold grey, the additional probabilistic dependency-based integrated architecture that is being presented here. (For more information on these former CFG-based probabilistic parsing architectures for French, see (Schluter and van Genabith, 2008)).

2.3.1 F-Structure Annotation Algorithm

For the creation of the dependency bank for French, to be used as training material, we will use f-structures. In the LFG framework, f-structures may be fully specified by f-structure annotated c-structures. The f-structure annotation algorithm outlined in (Schluter and van Genabith, 2008) will be adopted here, to obtain f-structure annotated c-structures. For French, it uses head-finding principles for a given constituent, to annotate MFT trees according to one of four modules:

1. **LFG Conversion Module:** MFT functional tags are directly translated into LFG function equations with respect to the constituent under consideration. For example, the

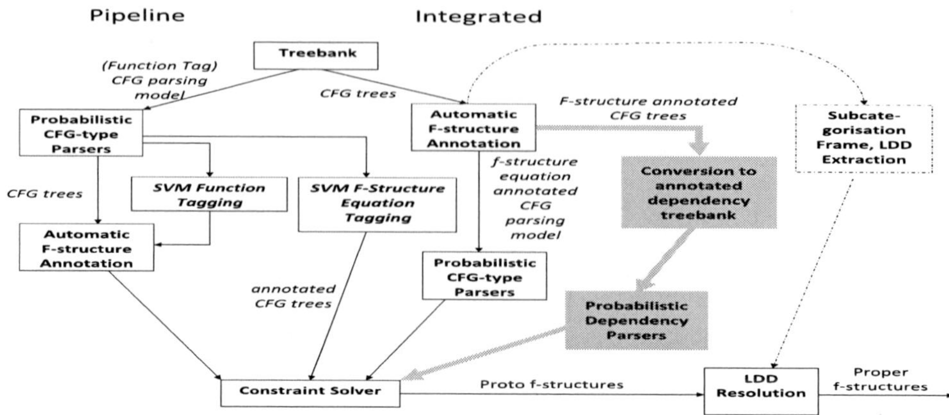

Figure 3: Overview of treebank-based LFG parsing architectures. The proposed dependency-based architecture being outlined in this paper is in bold grey.

functional tag ATO may be mapped to ↑-xcomp=↓, ↑-obj=↓-subj.

2. **Right-Left Annotation Module**: Constituent daughters are annotated with respect to the location of the constituent head. The constituent head is simply annotated as the predicate (↑-pred=*lemma*), or the governor of the predicate (↑=↓).

3. **Verb Combinatorics Module**: Combinations of different verb complexes in the MFT's constituent VN are resolved to predicates with corresponding compound tenses, for a monoclausal f-structural representation of verb phrases.

4. **Catch-all and Clean-up Module**: Any correction of detected overgeneralisations or miscellaneous annotations (such as sentence type) are carried out.

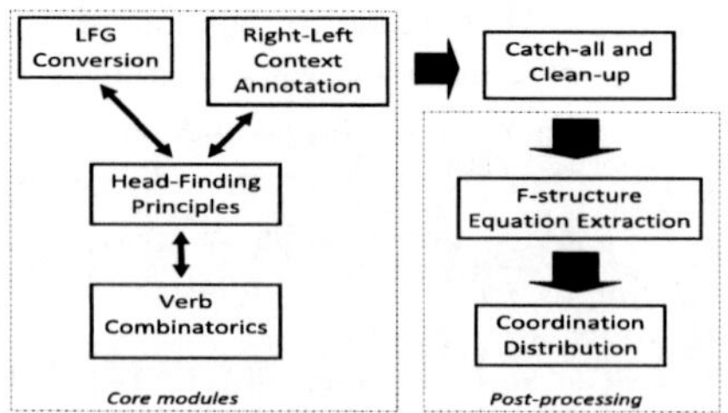

Figure 4: French Annotation Algorithm.

The f-structure annotation algorithm French was evaluated against a hand-corrected gold standard dependency bank. It achieves 98.4% coverage, with a best preds-only f-score of 99.63 (Table 1).

coord dist	precision	recall	f-score
no	98.57	96.38	97.46
yes	99.49	99.77	99.63

Table 1: Preds-only f-structure annotation algorithm performance.

2.3.2 Previous LFG Parsing Results for French

In this paper, because dependency parsers parse relations between actual word-forms and not any other features, we consider only preds-only results for LFG f-structures. That is, we evaluate only along those branches of the f-structures that end in a predicate.

(Schluter and van Genabith, 2008) report parsing results for both the integrated and pipeline architectures, with a best preds-only f-score for the integrated architecture of 67.88.[3]

3 LFG F-structure Dependencies

In this section, we overview the different target frameworks for the conversion of CFG-like data into dependency tree data (Section 3.1). We then

---

[3]The pipeline architecture outperforms the integrated architecture in (Schluter and van Genabith, 2008).

consider projectivity in light of these conversions, and explain why projectivity need not be a problem in LFG dependency parsing as a result of its the property of pseudo-projectivity (Section 3.2).

3.1 A Comparison of Theoretical Frameworks

In the statistical dependency parsing literature, there are generally two sources of modern linguistic theoretical justification behind parsing models: the theoretical framework of the Meaning-Text Theory (Mel'čuk, 1998), and the annotation guidelines of the Prague Treebank (Hajič et al., 1999). Moreover, software converting phrase-structure style treebanks into dependencies for statistical dependency parsing usually quote these two annotation styles in the treatment of hard cases. Therefore, when statistically parsing LFG f-structures, it is vital to consider what sorts of dependencies existing dependency parsers were intended to parse.

Meaning-Text Theory (MTT) represents the syntactic organisation of sentences strictly by dependencies. Under this framework, syntax is separated into surface and deep syntactic dependency-based tree representations. The deep-syntactic structure of a sentence has nodes that are semantically full lemmata (full lexemes); abstraction is made of any auxiliary or structural lemmata at this level. Also, lemmata are subscripted by the grammatical information (grammemes) expressed by their associated word-form(s), not imposed by government and agreement. Arcs are labeled by a selection of around ten language-independent relations. On the other hand, the surface-syntactic structure of a sentence contains all lemmata of the sentence and its arcs are labeled with the names of language-specific surface-syntactic relations, each of which represents a particular construction of the language (Mel'čuk, 2003; Mel'čuk, 1998). Furthermore, communicative functions such as `topic` or `focus` are not associated with a pure syntactic structure in the Meaning-Text Theory (Mel'čuk, 2001).

The Prague Treebank (PT) annotation guidelines (Hajič et al., 1999) also distinguishes between two levels of dependency-based syntactic representation: analytical and tectogrammatical. These guidelines are written in the spirit of Functional Generative Description.[4] These two levels

of syntactic representation roughly correspond to those of the Meaning-Text Theory—the analytical level corresponding to the surface-syntax of the MTT and the tectogrammatical level corresponding to the deep-syntactic level of the MTT (Žabokrtský, 2005). In the PT, word-forms have attributes for their lemmata as well as for grammatical and lexical information expressed morphologically. The syntactic structure of the treebank is given for the analytic level of representation, though work is under way on complementing this with a tectogrammatical level of representation (Sgall et al., 2004). Also similarly to the MTT, communicative structure is not associated with pure syntax in Functional Generative Description, and therefore does not figure among annotations defined for the PT.

LFG does not have a uniform dependency syntax, distinguishing between c-structure and f-structure. These two systems contain different sorts of information, represented by means of phrase-structure trees, for the c-structure, and dependency dags, for f-structures. The f-structure is an abstract functional syntactic representation of a sentence, thought to contain deeper or more language-independent information than the c-structure (Dalrymple, 2001).

There are several important ways in which f-structures differ from the tree-dependencies outlined by the literature on dependency syntax within the MTT framework or the annotation guidelines of the Prague Treebank. For instance, included in the f-structure is communicative information, such as `topic` and `focus`, that LFG theorists consider to be grammaticised or syntacticised components of *information structure*). This introduces the notion of long-distance dependencies. Moreover, subject and object-raising are represented with re-entrancies at the syntactic level in LFG. This creates dags rather than just dependency trees, since some grammatical functions share the same f-structure value; these shared f-structures are called *re-entrancies*. Also, f-structure syntax corresponds, in fact, to a sort of mix of surface and deep dependency MTT syntax (respectively, a mix of analytic and tectogrammatical syntax). Like a surface dependency syntax, some lemmata, like copular verbs, that are not semantically full, appear in f-structures. On the

---

[4]See, for example, (Hajičová and Sgall, 2003) for a discussion of dependency syntax according to Functional Generative Description.

other hand, like deep dependency syntax, some lemmata that are not semantically full are excluded (for example, for the monoclausal treatment of compound tenses of verbs).

Other differences between dependency structures may be found in the notions of grouping and sets. In particular, coordination receives different treatments that must be considered. According to the PT annotation guidelines, coordination is treated as sets (conjuncts are sister nodes, elements of a set of conjuncts). Also, every node of a dependency tree must be associated with a word-form, which makes the coordinating conjunction or punctuation the governor of the set. On the other hand, in the MTT, coordination has a cascaded representation, with the first conjunct as governor. To distinguish between modifiers or arguments of the first conjunct and those of the co-ordinated structure, MTT theorists resort to *grouping*: the first conjunct essentially forms a distinguished group with its modifiers and arguments, much like the notion of constituent (Mel'čuk, 2003). In this sense, the first conjunct grouping is really the governor of the coordination.[5] Also according to the MTT, every node of a dependency tree must be associated with a word-form. But in LFG this is not necessary, in particular, in the representation of both coordination; coordinated elements, like in the PT, are treated as sets. In dag form, it can be seen that these coordinated structures have a *null* governor; that is, they do not have a governor that corresponds to any word-form as the node has no label. Because today's statistical dependency parsers cannot handle null elements, some pre-processing will be needed to convert our LFG representation of coordination (Section 4.1).

Finally, f-structures may be specified in terms of annotated c-structures with the local meta-variables ↑ and ↓, and grammatical function regular paths. This restricts the structure of dependencies actually occurring in LFG f-structure syntax, as we will show in Section 3.2.

3.2 The Breadth of Functional Equations in LFG

LFG's f-structures often have re-entrancies (or shared sub-f-structures)—two functional equations resolve to take the same (f-structure) value—making them dags, rather than simple de-

pendency trees. In LFG, the term *functional uncertainty* describes the uncertainty in the resolution given a simple grammatical function, in the definition of the grammar. The set of options for resolution may be finite and given by a disjunction, in which case resolution is down a chain of f-structure nodes of bounded length, or (theoretically) infinite in which case they are given by a regular expression (including the Kleene star operator) and resolution is down a chain of f-structure nodes of unbounded length. We note, however, that in statistical parsing of f-structures, the functional uncertainty in the resolution of a grammatical function will never be infinite, since the data is finite.

3.2.1 Projectivity

Consider a labeled dependency tree (directed tree) $T = (V, E, L)$, where V is its set of vertices (or nodes), $E = \{(a, l, b) \mid a, b \in V, l \in L\}$ its set of directed edges, and L the set of labels for edges. If $e = (a, l, b) \in E$, we say that a *immediately dominates* b; in this case, we say that a is the governor of b, or that b is a dependent on a. We say that v_1 *dominates* v_n if there is a chain of arcs $e_1, e_2, \ldots, e_{n-1}$, such that $e_1 = (v_1, l_1, v_2), e_2 = (v_2, l_2, v_3), \ldots, e_{n-1} = (v_{n-1}, l_{n-1}v_n)$. In this case, we also say that v_n is a descendent of v_1 or that v_1 is an ancestor of v_n.

An *ordered tree* is a tree having a total order, $(V, \leq)$, over its nodes, which for dependency trees is just the linear order of the symbols (or natural language words) in the generated string. An edge $e = (a, b)$ covers nodes $v_1, v_2, \ldots, v_n$ if $a \leq v_1, \ldots, v_n \leq b$, or $b \leq v_1, \ldots, v_n \leq a$.

An edge, $e = (v_1, l, v_2)$, of a tree is said to be projective if and only for every vertex v covered by e, v is dominated by v_1. A tree T is projective if and only if all its edges are projective (Robinson, 1970). (Gaifman, 1965) explains that a projective dependency tree can be associated with a dependency tree whose constituents are the projections of the nodes of the dependency tree, showing that projectivity in dependency trees corresponds to constituent continuity in phrase-structure trees.

These definitions are easily extended to dags. However in the case of dags, there are sometimes two governors for a single node that must be considered. For f-structure dags, we must additionally consider the mixed surface/deep dependency structure: some lemmata do not appear in f-structures as predicates. For those f-structure dags

---

[5] Grouping may be indicated on labels (Nilsson et al., 2006).

for which there is a one-to-one correspondence between predicates and original word-forms, these extended definitions may easily be applied.

However, LFG's treatment of long-distance dependency resolution and of subject/object raising is non-projective, illustrate non-projective dags. For French, for example, an interesting non-projective structure is found in *en* pronouns and NP extraction.

Projectivity in dependency trees or dags is obviously a result of the definition of the generating dependency grammar. This is true also of cases that are not LFG re-entrancies. For example, (Johansson and Nugues, 2007) propose a conversion of the Penn Treebank into dependency trees that introduces more projective edges than the conversion proposed by (Yamada and Matsumoto, 2003; Nivre, 2006). In addition to long-distance dependencies, for example, their representation of gapping always introduces non-projective branches (Johansson and Nugues, 2007).

LFG is capable of locally representing non-projective dependencies in phrase structures, which should, by definition, be impossible. This is because the only types of non-projective dependencies theoretically represented in LFG are actually pseudo-projectivities.

3.2.2 Non-Projectivity and Pseudo-Projectivity

Dependency trees also model non-projective structures that have no correspondence with any constituent trees—that is, they may be non-projective. This added "increase" in power for dependency grammars is shown to be useful for syntactic representations of certain languages (for example, the cross-serial dependencies of Dutch). However, as (Kahane et al., 1998) explain, pseudo-projective dependency trees may be parsed as projective trees with the aid of a simple transformation.

Consider two non-projective labeled dependency trees, $T_1 = (V, E_1, L_1)$ and $T_2 = (V, E_2, L_2)$. T_2 is called a *lift* if one of the following conditions hold, for some $e = (a, l, b), e' = (b, l', c) \in E_1$.[6]

1. $E_2 = (E_1 - \{e, e'\}) \cup \{(a, l : l', c)\}, L_2 \subseteq L_1 \cup \{l : l'\}$, or

2. T_3 is a lift of T_1 and T_2 is a lift of T_3.

Corresponding to item 1 of the above conditions, the action of creating the tree T_2 from T_1 by removing the edges e, e' and adding the edge e'', will be referred to as *lifting*. A labeled ordered dependency tree T is said to be *pseudo-projective* if there is some lift T' of T that is projective.

(Kahane et al., 1998) explain that (for unlabeled dependency trees) one may make these definitions meaningful through the specification of lifting rules of the form $LD \uparrow SG \ w \ LG$, meaning that a node of category LD can be lifted to its syntactic governor of category LG through a path consisting of nodes of category $C_1, \ldots, C_n$, where C_i is among a specific set of categories (labels) (L_w) for all $i \in \{1, \ldots, n\}$. Equivalently, for a labeled ordered dependency tree, the path w may be specified by a path of labels. In this sense, building a projective tree by means of lifting results in arcs with path labels. Projecting the nodes would result in a sort of annotated c-structure. In this sense, and making abstraction of any contractions resulting from the annotations $\uparrow = \downarrow$, lifting is the opposite of the correspondence ϕ from c-structure to f-structure.[7] Re-entrancies may simply be considered as complex labels. Let us call the transformation opposite to lifting a *de-contraction* (used to undo the lifting transformation). Since generating an f-structure from an annotated c-structure involves simple contractions of the form $\uparrow = \downarrow$ and de-contractions, all f-structures are at most pseudo-projective. That means, we do not have to worry about non-projective structures in the parsing of LFG dependencies in f-structures.

4 Transforming Annotated C-Structures into Dependency Trees

To generate dependency trees, rather than using f-structures, we start with annotated c-structures. The motivation for this choice is straightforward: we need only carry out a certain number of contractions for the equations $\uparrow = \downarrow$ in order to get a projective dependency tree (rather than just a pseudo-projective dependency tree on which we must perform lifts). Moreover, the association of labels for handling re-entrancies is sitting in the annotated tree and does not need to be recalculated. There are some problems that remain in the result.

---

[6]This definition is equivalent to the one given in (Kahane et al., 1998), where a lift was defined as in terms of governance for *unlabeled* dependency trees.

[7](Kahane et al., 1998) remark that the idea of building a projective tree by means of lifting can be compared to the functional uncertainty of LFG.

Firstly, not every terminal will get have a predicate annotation. For example, in causative constructions like for the phrase *faire danser* ('to make dance'), the word-form *faire* would only be annotated with the feature $\uparrow$ `factive` $= +$, not as a predicate. These will simply be turned into f-structures rather than features, by changing annotations such as these to $\uparrow$ `factive:pred =` '*faire'*.

Another problem is that coordination structures have no governor. These structures must be transformed. We choose to follow the annotation guidelines for the PT for this transformation, due to its similarity with LFG analyses. Some coordination structures of the treebank need alternative treatment. In particular, non-constituent coordination and unlike constituent coordination require analyses that are not covered in the those guidelines. We resort to extended dependency tag sets to treat these cases and retain projectivity.

4.1 Coordination Transformations

In general, coordination will be transformed in the spirit of the PT annotation guidelines. If there is a coordinating conjunction, then the last of these will be taken as the governor of the coordination, as in the Figure 5. In the case where there is no coordinating conjunction but there is coordination punctuation (like a comma or semicolon), we will take the last of these as the governor. Otherwise we will take the first conjunct of the coordination as the governor and revert to grouping through extended labels.

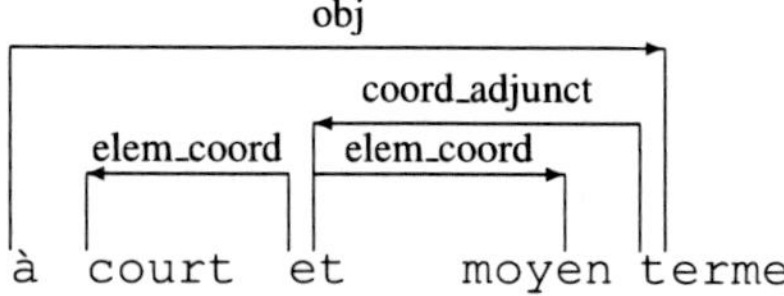

Figure 5: Dependency graph for *a court et moyen terme* ('short and mid-term').

For non-constituent coordination, the goal is twofold: (1) show that the different elements of each of the conjuncts belong together[8] and

(2) show that they are missing something that is present in the first conjunct (done by the function tags). For this reason, the LFG analysis is ideal. However, a surface dependency analysis cannot do this; constituent structure is not simply dependency structure that projects lexical units to terminals. It shows groupings of elements based dependence on a item that is there or not. To do this, we use extended labels, forcing a "fake" lexical head.

5 Dependency Parsing Results

The parsing architecture works as follows. The annotation algorithm is applied to MFT trees, creating f-structure annotated trees that are then transformed into the projective depenendency representation described in Section 4, using the c-structure with the (only) f-structure equations. A dependency parser is then trained on this data, and the test set parsed. The parser output is then transformed back to f-structure equations, which are evaluated against the f-structure gold standard.

Two different dependency parsers were used for this research: MST parser (McDonald et al., 2005) and MALT parser (Nivre et al., 2006). Experiments were done with the simplified architecture (in which long-distance dependencies are given as complex path equations in training), and in the established architecture (with a separated long-distance dependency resolution task).[9] The results are given in Tables 2 and 3.

Parser	coord dist	precision	recall	f-score
MST	*no*	87.46	54.67	67.28
	yes	87.45	54.66	67.27
MALT	*no*	86.23	52.17	65.01
	yes	86.17	51.95	64.82

Table 2: Simplified Architecture Parsing Results

Parser	LDDs resolved	coord dist	precision	recall	f-score
MST	*no*	*no*	86.90	57.07	68.89
		yes	86.89	57.06	68.88
	yes	*yes*	86.48	58.03	69.46
MALT	*no*	*no*	85.98	51.13	64.13
		yes	86.02	50.9	63.96
	yes	*yes*	86.08	51.62	64.54

Table 3: Parsing Results with Long Distance Dependency Resolution

---

[8]The dependency treatment of coordination outlined by (Johansson and Nugues, 2007) for the treatment of gapping also introduced ambiguity for the case where there are more than two conjuncts; in this solution, they have removed the relation that the components of gapping are part of a same element/constituent.

[9]More information on the difference between these two architectures can be found in (Schluter and van Genabith, 2008).

We observe that best results are obtained by the MST parser when LDD recovery separated and coordination distribution is carried out.

6 Concluding Remarks

In this paper, we have shown that best statistical parsing results for French in the integrated LFG parsing architecture are achievable by extending this architecture for statistical dependency parsing. However, best results, in general are still obtained via the original PCFG based LFG parsing approach. Future work would look at extending the use of machine learning to approximate the integrated parsing architecture, which has been shown to improve results in the PCFG based LFG parsing approach.

Acknowledgments

This research was supported by Science Foundation Ireland GramLab grant 04/IN/I527.

References

A. Cahill, M. McCarthy, J. van Genabith, and A. Way. 2002. Automatic annotation of the penn treebank with lfg f-structure information. In A. Lenci, S. Montemagni, and V. Pirelli, editors, *Proceedings of the LREC 2002 workshop on Linguistic Knowledge Acquisition and Representation*, Paris. ELRA.

G. Chrupała and J. van Genabith. 2006. Improving treebank-based automatic lfg induction for spanish. In *Proc. of LFG06*, Konstanz, Germany.

Mary Dalrymple. 2001. *Lexical Functional Grammar*, volume 34 of *Syntax and Semantics*. Academic Press, San Diego.

Haim Gaifman. 1965. Dependency systems and phrase-structured systems. *Information and Control*, 8:304–337.

Y. Guo, J. van Genabith, and H. Wang. 2007. Treebank-based acquisition of lfg resources for chinese. In *Proc. of LFG07*, Stanford, CA.

J. Hajič, J. Panevová, E. Buráňová, Z. Urešová, and A. Bémová. 1999. Annotations at analytical level. instructions for annotators. Technical report, Prague.

E. Hajičová and P. Sgall, 2003. *Dependency Syntax in Functional Generative Description*, pages 570–592. Walter de Gruyter, Berlin and New York.

R. Johansson and P. Nugues. 2007. Extended constituent-to-dependency conversion. In *NODAL-IDA 2007 Conference Proceedings*, pages 105–112, Tartu, Estonia.

S. Kahane, A. Nasr, and O. Rambow. 1998. Pseudo-projectivity: a polynomially parsable non-projective dependency grammar. In *Proceedings of the 17th international conference on Computational linguistics*, pages 646–652.

R. McDonald, K. Crammer, and F. Pereira. 2005. Online large-margin training of dependency parsers. In *Proc. of ACL 2005*.

I. Mel'čuk. 1998. *Vers une linguistique Sens-Texte. Leçon inaugurale*. Collège de France, Paris.

I. Mel'čuk. 2001. *Communicative Organisation in Natural Language. The Semantic-Communicative Structure of Sentences*. Benjamins, Amsterdam and Philadelphia.

I. Mel'čuk, 2003. *Levels of Dependency in Linguistic Description: Concepts and Problems*, volume 1, pages 188–229. Walter de Gruyter, Berlin and New York.

J. Nilsson, J. Nivre, and J. Hall. 2006. Graph transformations in data-driven dependency parsing. In *ACL '06: Proceedings of the 21st International Conference on Computational Linguistics and the 44th annual meeting of the ACL*, pages 257–264.

J. Nivre, J. Hall, and J. Nilsson. 2006. Malt-parser: A data-driven parser generator for dependency parsing. In *Proceedings of LREC'06*.

J. Nivre. 2006. *Inductive Dependency Parsing*. Springer Verlag.

J. J. Robinson. 1970. Dependency structure and transformational rules. 46:259–285.

N. Schluter and J. van Genabith. 2007. Preparing, restructuring, and augmenting a french treebank: Lexicalised parsers or coherent treebanks? In *Proc. of the PACLING 2007*, Melbourne, Australia.

N. Schluter and J. van Genabith. 2008. Treebank-based acquisition of lfg parsing resources for french. In *Proc. of LREC 2008*, Marrakech, Morocco.

P. Sgall, J. Panevová, and E. Hajičová. 2004. Deep syntactic annotation: Tectogrammatical representation and beyond. In A. Meyers, editor, *HLT-NAACL 2004 Workshop: Frontiers in Corpus Annotation*, pages 32–38, Boston, MASS. Association for Computational Linguistics.

Z. Žabokrtský. 2005. Resemblances between meaning-text theory and functional generative description. In J.D. Apresjian and L.L. Iomdin, editors, *Proceedings of the 2nd International Conference of Meaning-Text Theory*, pages 549–557, Moscow, Russia. Slavic Culture Languages Publishers House.

H. Yamada and Y. Matsumoto. 2003. Statistical dependency analysis with support vector machines. In *Proceedings of the 8th International Workshop on Parsing Technologies*, pages 195–206, Nancy, France.

ISSN 1736-6305 Vol. 4
http://hdl.handle.net/10062/9206

Conflict Resolution Using Weighted Rules in HFST-TwoLC

Miikka Silfverberg
Department of General Linguistics
University of Helsinki
Helsinki, Finland
miikka.silfverberg@helsinki.fi

Krister Lindén
Department of General Linguistics
University of Helsinki
Helsinki, Finland
krister.linden@helsinki.fi

Abstract

In this article we demonstrate a novel way to resolve conflicts in two-level grammars by weighting the rules. The rules are transformed into probabilistic constraints, which are allowed to compete with each other. We demonstrate a method to automatically assign weights to the rules. It acts in a similar way as traditional conflict resolution, except that traditionally unresolvable left-arrow rule conflicts do not cause lexical forms to be filtered out. The two-level lexicon and probabilistic two-level grammar are combined using the new transducer operation weighted intersecting composition. The result is a weighted lexical transducer. To the best of our knowledge, this is the first time probabilistic rules have been used to solve two-level rule conflicts. The possible applications of probabilistic lexical transducers range from debugging flawed two-level grammars to computer-assisted language learning. We test our method using a two-level lexicon and grammar compiled with the open source tools HFST-LEXC and HFST-TwoLC.

1 Introduction

In a two-level phonological grammar the rules are parallel constraints whose joint effect determines the surface realizations for lexical analyses. A valid correspondence between a lexical string and its surface realization has to be accepted by all of the rules, otherwise it is filtered out (Koskenniemi, 1983).

Situations where correspondences are filtered out because two rules require a lexical form to be realized in two different ways are called rule conflicts. In the worst case, all surface forms corresponding to a lexical analysis are lost and the analysis is filtered out by the grammar.

Conflict resolution is an automated mechanism in two-level rule compilers, which attempts to find conflicting rules and modify them so that no lexical analyses are lost. Traditional conflict resolution can resolve arbitrary conflicts between right-arrow rules, but it is limited to special cases in the case of left-arrow rule conflicts as we explain in section 2.1.

Instead of traditional conflict resolution we propose a method, which builds on making the whole two-level grammar probabilistic in section 2.2. The rules become weighted violable constraints, which are allowed to compete against each other.

Weighting rules is not a new idea. All statistical parser use the idea. However, casting conflict resolution in probabilistic terms is new. We are not aware, of other systems, which use probabilistic rules for conflict resolution. In finite-state syntax, weighted parallel constraints have been considered by Voutilainen (Voutilainen, 1994). Voutilainen considered the use of weighting to order sentence parses by typicality. The weights could be assigned by a linguist or corpus data could be used. The method he proposes is based on penalty weights like our method.

In section 3 we propose a general method for assigning weights to rules. In section 4 we use this method to weight rules in a way, that parallels traditional conflict resolution, when all rule conflicts are solvable. The difference between traditional conflict resolution and our method is, that our method preserves lexical analyses for surface forms even in conflict situations, although these might not have a preferred order, since their weight may be the same. The rule writer may choose to refine the weighting we propose either according to her intuition or by using corpus-data.

The applications of the new kind of conflict resolution might include identifying typical grammatical errors made by children and language learners or in information retrieval, since the grammar becomes violable and some erroneous forms are retained, although these are less probable, than their correct counterparts. A very significant use is for debugging two-level grammars. Since forms are not filtered out in a conflict situation, the linguist, who is writing the two-level grammar gets a clearer picture of the way the grammar is broken.

In section 5 we use a new transducer operation, weighted intersecting composition to combine a two-level lexicon and a two-level grammar. Weighted intersecting composition allows the weights in the rules to be passed to the resulting lexical transducer. The operation has been modelled on unweighted intersecting composition, which was introduced by Karttunen (Karttunen, 1994).

We test our method using an example lexicon and grammar in sections 6 and 7. The example concerns gradation of stops in Finnish. The example lexicon was compiled using the open source two-level lexicon compiler HFST-LEXC[1] and the example grammar was compiled using the open source two-level grammar compiler HFST-TWOLC[2]. Both compilers belong to the finite-state morphology toolkit HFST Morphology Tools[3].

2   Rule Conflicts

Rule conflicts occur when two-level rules require, that a lexical symbol is realized in two different ways in the same context. Conflict resolution is a process, which aims to modify the two-level grammar in such a way, that rule conflicts vanish. Traditionally it has been restricted to conflicts between several right-arrow rules or two left-arrow rules. We shall make the same restriction, although conflicts occur in other types of rulesets as well (Yli-Jyrä and Koskenniemi, 2006).

2.1   Traditional Conflict Resolution

A number of right-arrow rules, with equal centers are conflicting if their contexts represent different

languages. E.g. the right-arrow rules

$$a{:}b \Rightarrow c \ \_ \ ; \ \text{and} \ a{:}b \Rightarrow d \ \_ \ ;$$

are in conflict. Since the first one limits the realization of lexical a as surface b into contexts where c precedes and the second one into contexts, where d precedes, the result is that a can't be realized as b anywhere. The reasonable way to interpret the two rules, is that $a{:}b$ should occur either in context $c \ \_$ or context $d \ \_$ because we may assume, that the grammar writer intends all rules to be true. Similar considerations apply to other right-arrow rule conflicts as well. Such conflicts may therefore be resolved by joining the conflicting rules into one rule whose context is the union of the contexts of the conflicting rules. Our example becomes

$$a{:}b \Rightarrow c \mid d \ \_ \ ;$$

Obviously right-arrow conflicts may always be resolved.

In contrast to right-arrow rule conflicts, left-arrow conflicts may not always be resolved. Two left-arrow rules concerning the same lexical symbol are in conflict if they require the symbol to be realized in two different ways in the same context. Consider the rules

$$a{:}b \Leftarrow X \ \_ \ ; \ \text{and} \ a{:}c \Leftarrow x \ \_ \ x \ ;$$

where $X = \{x, y, z\}$. In the context $x \ \_ \ x$ the rules have conflicting requirements.

Here the context of the second rule is subsumed by the context of the first rule, so the second rule may be considered a special case of the first rule (Karttunen et al., 1987). The first rule applies everywhere in the context $X \ \_$ except in the context $x \ \_ \ x$. This means that the rule conflict is resolved by modifying the first rule by subtracting the more specific context $x \ \_ \ x$ from the more general $X \ _ \ $. This kind of left-arrow conflicts reflect the fact, that linguists tend to split rules into general tendencies and absolute laws, which are exceptions to those tendencies.

We use the *general restriction* (later GR) operation introduced by Yli-Jyrä (Yli-Jyrä and Koskenniemi, 2004) to compile two-level rules. Rule contexts are compiled into regular expressions, which allows us to operate on them with regular expression operations. Hence, it is possible to resolve a left-arrow conflict by subtracting the context of a sub case rule from the context of a more general rule. It is also possible to resolve right-arrow

---

[1]For documentation:
https://kitwiki.csc.fi/twiki/bin/view/KitWiki/HfstLexC
[2]For documentation:
https://kitwiki.csc.fi/twiki/bin/view/KitWiki/HfstTwolC
[3]For downloading HFST programs:
http://www.ling.helsinki.fi/kieliteknologia/tutkimus/hfst/sources.shtml

conflicts simply by uniting them into one rule. Its context is the union of the contexts of the conflicting rules.

Left-arrow conflicts between rules neither of which is a sub case of the other were not resolved in the first two-level rule compiler (Karttunen et al., 1987). Nor are they resolved by the current Xerox two-level compiler (Karttunen, 1992). The result is that lexical forms are filtered out by the grammar.

2.2 A Probabilistic Interpretation of Rule Conflicts

Consider a grammar, which has two left-arrow rules R_1 and R_2 concerning the lexical symbol x. The rules are defined

$$x{:}y \Leftarrow C_1 \text{ and } x{:}z \Leftarrow C_2$$

respectively. If the set $C_1 \cap C_2$ is nonempty, the rules are conflicting.[4]

Clearly rule R_1 should hold vacuously in the set $C_1 \setminus C_2$ and so should R_2 in the set $C_2 \setminus C_1$. We may interpret the situation probabilistically. The rule R_1 should apply with probability 1 in the context $C_1 \setminus C_2$. Similarly rule R_2 should apply with probability 1 in context $C_2 \setminus C_1$. Since we have no information concerning the relative importance of R_1 and R_2, it is reasonable to assume, that the rules have equally high probability p of applying in the context $C_1 \cap C_2$. Traditional conflict resolution corresponds to assigning p the value 0, but one could equally well argue, that p should have the value 0.5.

In a situation where the rule R_1 is stronger than the rule R_2 it may be given higher probability than R_2, which means that surface realizations derived using rule R_2 are more likely than realizations, which are derived using rule R_1.

Generalizing the idea of rules as tendencies and absolute laws, we get a range of rules with different probabilities of applying, from laws which always hold to less certain tendencies. Compiling a lexical transducer becomes the equivalent of letting the different rules compete with each other, which results in an ordering of possible analyses for lexical forms.

---

[4]We operate with rule contexts like they were regular languages. We do this, because the GR-operation allows us to transform them into regular expressions

3 Conflict Resolution Using Weights

We propose a new method of resolving conflicts, which is based on the idea of making the two-level rules probabilistic. Instead of giving a probability for each rule, we assign a penalty weight for breaking a rule. The principle is, that breaking a more likely rule should always result in a higher penalty, than breaking a less likely one.

The rule R

$$x{:}y \Leftarrow C$$

is combined with a penalty weight transducer using weighted union of transducers (Allauzen et al., 2007), so after conflict resolution it becomes the weighted rule R'

$$R \cup (\Sigma^*_{\langle \text{WEIGHT} \rangle})$$

The expression $\Sigma^*_{\langle \text{WEIGHT} \rangle}$ denotes the language of all strings of feasible pairs, where every string receives weight WEIGHT.

In the transducer R', correspondences which break the rule R receive weight WEIGHT and correspondences which do not break the rule R receive weight 0. This happens, because we use the *tropical semi-ring* to represent weights, as we will see in section 5. In the tropical semi-ring addition of weights, performed by the weighted union, corresponds to taking the least of the weights.

The two-level grammar is equivalent to the intersection of the weighted rule transducers. The best paths corresponding to a surface realization for a lexical string are those for which the sum of the weight given by each rule transducer is the lowest.

When two rules compete, the correspondences which break the rule whose penalty weight is lower get a lower penalty than the ones that break a rule with a higher penalty. Conflict resolution thus becomes the task of finding suitable weights for the rules in a grammar.

4 Compiling Two-Level Rules and Weighting them

We now demonstrate a way to weight the rules in a two-level grammar, which will give the same results as ordinary conflict resolution, when all rule conflicts are solvable. The process may be completely automated.

The right-arrow rules will be compiled in the same way as usual, but we need to find penalty weights associated with the left-arrow rules in the grammar.

We precompile the contexts of all $x{:}y \Leftarrow L$ _ R ; into context expressions $L \diamond \Sigma^* \diamond R$, where Σ is the alphabet of the two-level grammar.

We define a relation *context-inclusion* in the grammar. We say that context-inclusion holds between two rules R_1 and R_2,whose centers have the same lexical symbol,

$$x{:}y \Leftarrow Cl_1 \_ Cr_1 \; ; \text{ and } x{:}z \Leftarrow Cl_2 \_ Cr_2 \; ;$$

iff

$$(Cl_1 \diamond \Sigma^* \diamond Cr_1) \subset (Cl_2 \diamond \Sigma^* \diamond Cr_2).$$

Context-inclusion is a partial ordering, so we use the symbol $<$ for it and write $R_1 < R_2$.

Let $\{X_1, ..., X_n\}$ be a set of rules in the two-level grammar. The set is a *chain* beginning at X_1, iff

$$X_1 < \; ... \; < X_n.$$

Specifically any set of size 1 is a chain.

We now give each rule R a penalty weight according to the length of the longest chain beginning at R.

Suppose there is a conflict between the rules R and S. If the conflict is resolvable and R is a sub case of S, then $R < S$. Since every chain beginning at S may be extended to a chain beginning at R, breaking the rule R will result in a greater penalty weight than breaking the rule S.

Conflicts, which couldn't be solved using traditional conflict resolution will not result in filtered out lexical forms using our conflict resolution, even though there might not be a preferred order for realizations of a lexical form. This happens because all left-arrow rules are violable.

Other ways of assigning weights for rules might be conceivable, e.g. using corpus data to extract probabilistic two-level rules or to extract lexical contexts in the form of n-grams. This could also be used to fine-tune a grammar obtained using our method. In addition the linguist writing the two-level grammar could assign penalty weights for breaking the rule. The penalty weight v pre-assigned by the linguist and the weight w given by our conflict resolution may be combined. The actual penalty weight received for breaking the compiled rule becomes $v \otimes w$, where $\otimes$ is the multiplication of the weight semi-ring.

A limitation of our system is, that a correspondence violating a rule receives the same

weight	surface form
1	ay
1	az
1	bz
2	by

Table 1: surface forms corresponding to ax.

penalty weight regardless of how many positions in the correspondence violate the rule, since equal penalty weights are assigned for all correspondences violating a rule. This might not be a problem in practice, since correspondences exhibiting the same rule conflict multiple times may be rather rare.

Other possible limitations stem from complex rule-interferences. E.g. let the alphabet Σ be

$$\Sigma = \{a, \; a{:}b, \; x{:}y, \; x{:}z\}$$

and consider the somewhat strange rules

$$x{:}y \Leftarrow a{:} \_ \; ; \text{ and } x{:}z \Leftarrow a{:}b \_ \; ;$$

of a two-level grammar with alphabet Σ.

The second rule is a sub case of the first one, so our method of weighting the rules will give it a higher penalty weight. If these are the only rules for the lexical symbol x, then the first rule gets penalty weight 1 and the second gets penalty weight 2. Now, consider the rule

$$a{:}b \Leftarrow \_ x{:}y \; ;$$

If it is the only rule concerning the lexical symbol a, it will get the penalty weight 1.

The conceivable realizations for the lexical string ax ordered by weight are given in Table 1.

Among the three best correspondences, there is one, which breaks the third rule, which was not in a left-arrow or a right-arrow conflict with either of the other rules. This example is rather contrived and we are not sure, whether actual phonologies contain these kinds of phenomena.

A further limitation of our system is that, it is possible that surface forms which would not have received any analyses, if they would have been compiled in the normal way, receive analyses. Since our system deals with relative weights, it is not possible to see, if a form is likely to be a good surface form for a lexical form, without generating the best surface forms corresponding to the lexical analysis. We will see an example of this in section 7

5 Combining a Two-Level lexicon and a Probabilistic Two-Level Grammar

As usual, we combine the two-level lexicon and rules to form a lexical transducer. Traditionally this can be done using the operation *intersecting composition* introduced by Karttunen (Karttunen, 1994). Since our rules are weighted, we need to modify the operation slightly. We call the modified operation *weighted intersecting composition*.

The result of unweighted intersecting composition is equivalent to composing the two-level lexicon with the intersection of the two-level rules. The operation was developed, since sequential intersection followed by composition could be rather slow, as computing the intersection of the rule transducers is a resource demanding operation. In intersecting composition the composition and intersections are carried out simultaneously. This allows both the lexicon and the rules to limit the size of the result of the operation without large intermediate results.

Weighted intersecting composition is a modification of intersecting composition for weighted lexicons and rules. The result of the operation is equivalent to weighted composition of the lexicon and the weighted intersection of the rules as defined in (Allauzen et al., 2007).

A probability p can be interpreted as a penalty weight w, using the standard conversion $w = -\log(p)$. This means that high probabilities corresponds to low penalty weights.

We use the tropical semi-ring $\mathcal{T} = (\mathbb{R}_+, \bar{0}, \bar{1}, \oplus, \otimes)$ to represent penalty weights. Here $\mathbb{R}_+$ are the reals, $\bar{0} = \infty$, $\bar{1} = 0$ and the binary operations

$$\oplus : \mathbb{R}_+ \times \mathbb{R}_+ \to \mathbb{R}_+ \text{ and } \otimes : \mathbb{R}_+ \times \mathbb{R}_+ \to \mathbb{R}_+$$

are defined

$$x \oplus y = \min(\{x, y\})$$

and

$$x \otimes y = x + y$$

respectively. The operation $+$ is the regular addition of the reals.

A weighted transducer has one initial state s_0 and may have several final states. A state s is final, if its final weight $s[w] \neq \bar{0} = \infty$

Let e be a transition from state s to state t with the pair $x{:}y$ and weight w. We represent it as a four tuple $e = (s, t, w, p)$ where $s = e[s]$ is the source state, $t = e[t]$ is the target state, $w = e[w]$ is the weight and $p = e[p]$ is the pair $x{:}y$ of the transition.

A *final path* P in the transducer is a sequence of transitions

$$P = e_0, ..., e_n$$

where the source state of e_0 is s_0, i.e. $e_0[s] = s_0$, $e_{i+1}[s] = e_i[t]$ for all $0 \leq i < n$ and the target of the last transition is a final state, i.e.

$$(e_n[t])[w] \neq \bar{0} = \infty.$$

We define the weight of P

$$w(P) = (e_n[t])[w] \otimes \bigotimes_i e_i[w]$$

For a transducer T and pair-string

$$x{:}y = x_1{:}y_1 \ ... \ x_n{:}y_n$$

we define the set of final paths

$$P_{x:y,T} = \{P = (e_0, ..., e_n) \mid e_i[p] = x_i{:}y_i, \\ w(P) \neq \bar{0}\}$$

and the weight of $P_{x:y,T}$

$$w(P_{x:y,T}) = \bigoplus_{P \in P_{x:y,T}} w(P).$$

The weight of the string $x{:}y$ is $w(P_{x:y,T})$.

Let $\mathcal{L}$ be a weighted two-level lexicon and $R_1, ..., R_m$ weighted two-level rules. We mark their intersecting composition by

$$\mathcal{L} \circ \cap (R_1, ..., R_m).$$

It contains paths corresponding to a pair-string

$$x{:}z = x_1{:}z_1, ..., x_n{:}z_n,$$

if there are pair-strings

$$x{:}y = x_1{:}y_1, ..., x_n{:}y_n,$$

and

$$y{:}z = y_1{:}z_1, ..., y_n{:}z_n,$$

s.t. $P_{x:y,L} \neq \emptyset$ and $P_{y:z,R_i} \neq \emptyset$ for each i. Following from the definitions of weighted composition and intersection, the weight for $x{:}z$ is

$$w(P_{x:y,L}) \otimes \bigotimes_i w(P_{y:z,R_i}).$$

The weighted rule transducers are more complex, than unweighted ones, so the role of intersecting composition is even bigger in the weighted situation. It might not even be feasible to compute the intersection of weighted rule transducers.

6 A Test Grammar: Gradation of k in Finnish

We tested weighted conflict resolution using a small two-level lexicon and grammar. The grammar consists of three rules governing the gradation of k in Finnish. The grammar we used is a part of a two-level grammar for Finnish gradation of k, p and t, which appeared in (Karttunen et al., 1987).

Gradation is an alternation in the stems of a number of Finnish words. The quality of the final stop k, p or t depends on, whether it is in an open (CV) or closed syllable (CVC). The lenited form of the stop may be a fricative, or the stop may vanish. This is determined by the phonological context.

We use K to mark the morphophoneme participating in k-gradation. In surface forms, it may be realized as 0, j, k, or v. The correspondence K:k is the default correspondence. Our rules govern the realization of K as 0, j and v.

The compiler we use is HFST-TwoLC, an open source two-level rule.compiler, whose syntax is very similar to Xerox TwolC. The sets we use in the rules are We also use the named regular

```
Cons = h j k l n r s t v ;
Vowel = a e i o u ;
Liquid = l r ;
HighLabial = u y ;
```

expressions

```
ClosedOffset =
    Cons: [ Cons: | #:0 ] ;

ClosedCoda =
    Vowel: ClosedOffset ;
```

where `ClosedCoda` is the coda of a closed syllable.

The grammar has three rules

```
"Gradation of K to 0"
 K:0 <=>
 [h | Liquid | Vowel:] _ ClosedCoda;

"Gradation of k to j"
 K:j <=>
 [Liquid | h] _ [:i | e:] ClosedOffset;

"Gradation of k to v"
 K:v <=>
 Cons :HighLabial _ :HighLabial
 ClosedOffset;
```

All the rules are double-arrow rules and will be split down into a left-arrow rule and a right-arrow rule (this is usually done when two-level rules are compiled).

E.g. the rule `Gradation of K to 0` will be broken down into two sub-rules

```
K:0 <=
[h | Liquid | Vowel:] _ ClosedCoda;

K:0 =>
[h | Liquid | Vowel:] _ ClosedCoda;
```

We call the left-arrow rules, which are formed, L_0, L_j and L_v and the right-arrow rules R_0, R_j and R_v according to the surface symbol in their center. Our grammar now has six rules.

The two-level lexicon we use is defined by the HFST-LexC file.

```
Multichar_Symbols K +NOUN +NOM +GEN +SG

LEXICON Root

arki+NOUN:arK CASE1 ;
arka+NOUN:arKa CASE2 ;
luku+NOUN:luKu CASE2 ;

LEXICON CASE1

+SG+NOM:0i# # ;
+SG+GEN:en# # ;

LEXICON CASE2

+SG+NOM:0# # ;
+SG+GEN:n# # ;
```

It covers the singular nominative and singular genitive cases of three words *arki* (workday), *arka* (timid) and *luku* (number) exhibiting different kinds of gradation of k. The surface forms, which correspond to the cases, are given by Table 2.

	K:0	K:j	K:v
sg. nom.	arka	arki	luku
sg. gen.	ar0an	arjen	luvun

Table 2: Surface Forms

7 Weighting the rules and Compiling the Test Grammar

We proceed to identifying conflicts. There are no right-arrow conflicts, since all of the rules have different centers. There are two left-arrow conflicts, however. One occurs between the rules L_0 and L_j and the other between L_0 and L_v. There is no conflict between the rules L_j and L_v, since their contexts are disjoint.

To begin resolving the conflicts in the grammar, we first order the left-arrow rules according to context-inclusion

$$L_j < L_0 \text{ and } L_v < L_0$$

We can see that the longest chain starting at L_0 has length 1, since the context of rule L_0 is not included in any other rules. The longest chains beginning at L_j and L_v have length two, since both of the rules are sub cases of the rule L_0.

We now compile the rules using the GR operation and and weight the rule transducer. Weighting the three left-rule transducers, we obtain the weighted transducers

$$
\begin{aligned}
L'_0 &= L_0 \cup \Sigma^*_{\langle 1 \rangle}, \\
L'_j &= L_j \cup \Sigma^*_{\langle 2 \rangle} \\
L'_v &= L_v \cup \Sigma^*_{\langle 2 \rangle}
\end{aligned}
$$

Let the transducer obtained by compiling the HFST-LexC file in the example be $\mathcal{L}$. The lexicon $\mathcal{L}$ and the unweighted rules R_0, R_j and R_v may be converted into weighted transducers, following the principle that all transitions get weight $\bar{1}$, all final states get final weight $\bar{1}$ and all other states get final weight $\bar{0}$. Since all states in a weighted transducer get a final weight and only those states, whose final weight is infinite are non-final, we must give the non-final states weight $\bar{0}$.

We now compile the lexical transducer using weighted intersecting composition. It is given by the expression

$$\mathcal{L} \circ \cap(R_0, R_j, R_v, L'_0, L'_j, L'_v)$$

The result is a weighted acyclic transducer. The pair-strings it accepts, together with their weights are shown below as pair-strings[5].

As might be expected, the correspondences with weight 0.0 are those, that adhere to of all the rules.

The pair-strings with weight 1.0 are those, that violate the general rule L_0, but don't violate either of the more specific rules L_j and L_v. One of these is `arka+NOUN:0+SG:n+GEN:0` which is erroneous, but there is a better correspondence `ark:0a+NOUN:0+SG:n+GEN:0` with weight 0.0.

---

[5]A pair-string `a:bcd` corresponds to the string-pair `acd:bcd`

```
WEIGHT  PATH

0.0  ark:0a+NOUN:0+SG:n+GEN:0
0.0  arka+NOUN:0+SG:0+NOM:0
0.0  luku+NOUN:0+SG:0+NOM:0
0.0  arki:0+NOUN:0+SG:i+NOM:0

1.0  arka+NOUN:0+SG:n+GEN:0
1.0  luk:vu+NOUN:0+SG:n+GEN:0
1.0  ark:ji:0+NOUN:0+SG:e+GEN:n

2.0  luk:0u+NOUN:0+SG:n+GEN:0
2.0  ark:0i:0+NOUN:0+SG:e+GEN:n

3.0  luku+NOUN:0+SG:n+GEN:0
3.0  arki:0+NOUN:0+SG:e+GEN:n
```

The forms `ark:ji:0+NOUN:0+SG:e+GEN:n` and `luk:vu+NOUN:0+SG:n+GEN:0` are the correct sg. gen. forms. They are the best correspondences given the lexical strings `arki+NOUN+SG+GEN` and `luku+NOUN+SG+GEN`.

Lexical forms, which occur in a rule conflict, have no unweighted surface realizations. This is because rule conflicts are situations, where it isn't possible to avoid breaking some rule.

The form `arka+NOUN:0+SG:n+GEN:0` demonstrates, that we can get slightly erroneous forms with larger weight, than the best forms. This might be useful e.g. for finding and identifying common errors in the writing of a child or a language learner.

All paths with weight 2.0 or 3.0 are erroneous. The paths with weight 2.0 violate the specific rules, but keep the more general rule. The paths with weight 3.0 violate both a specific rule and the general one. The weight 3.0 is a maximum. There are no paths with weight 5.0, although such paths might be conceivable. This is a consequence of the fact that the rules L_j and L_v never apply at the same time, so a correspondence can't violate both of them.

Note, that the surface form `lujun` of `luku+NOUN+SG+GEN` is not possible, since the right-arrow rule R_j limits the distribution of the pair `K:j`. The right-arrow rules R_0, R_j and R_v hold vacuously.

8 Discussion and Further Work

The test, which we conducted in sections 6 and 7 shows that our method of conflict resolution works. However, a more extensive test should be conducted to ascertain, that the method is practical even when used on complete two-level lexicons and grammars. There is some worry, that the lexical transducer may become rather large, because it contains both grammatical and ungrammatical forms with different weights. Complex grammars with more intricate interplay between the rules should also be tested.

Since the rules are weighted, standard look up will have to be replaced by an n-best algorithm, which will slow down the parsing process.

Previously improvements to conflict-resolution have been considered by Yli-Jyrä, who proposes an unweighted method for resolving general rule conflicts (Yli-Jyrä and Koskenniemi, 2006). In addition to left-arrow conflicts and right-arrow conflicts, the method also resolves other kinds of rule conflicts, but it diverges from traditional conflict resolution, since it does not prefer rules, which are sub cases of more general rules. Still, it would be interesting to compare our method to the one Yli-Jyrä proposes especially in regard to conflicts, which represent other types of conflicts than right-arrow or left-arrow conflicts.

The uses of our method, without modifications, are probably limited by the fact, that ungrammatical surface forms may receive analyses (as was seen in section 7). It is possible to check the best surface forms matching an analysis, but this means that every surface string for which the best analysis receives a penalty greater than 0.0 requires an extra look up in the lexical transducer. This is feasible for diagnostics purposes e.g. in applications related to computer assisted language learning.

Applications, which require error tolerance could still benefit from our method. Our method might be used both in applications, which test two-level grammars and in computer assisted language learning applications. Increasing recall in information retrieval systems, through error tolerant analysis of queries, is also a possible area of applications. Related to information retrieval is the task of finding corrections for forms, which have been tagged as ungrammatical by a speller.

9 Acknowledgements

We would like to thank Kimmo Koskenniemi, Anssi Yli-Jyrä and the anonymous referees for their comments on the paper. We would also like to thank our colleagues Erik Axelson and Tommi Pirinen in the HFST team for making development of open source finite-state tools an interesting and rewarding experience.

References

Cyril Allauzen, Michael Riley, Johan Schalkwyk, Wojciech Skut, and Mehryar Mohri. 2007. OpenFst: a general and efficient weighted finite-state transducer library. In Proceedings of the 12th International Conference on Implementation and Application of Automata (CIAA 2007). volume 4783 of Lecture Notes in Computer Science, pages 11–23, Prague, Czech Republic, July 2007. Springer-Verlag, Heidelberg, Germany.

Kimmo Koskenniemi. 1983. *Two-Level Morphology: A General Computational Model for Word-Form Recognition and Production.* University of Helsinki, Department of General Linguistics, Helsinki.

Lauri Karttunen. 1994. *Constructing Lexical Transducers.* The Proceedings of the 15th International Conference on Computational Linguistics COLING 94, I, pages 406–411. Association of Computational Linguistics, Morristown, NJ.

Lauri Karttunen, Kimmo Koskenniemi and Ronald M. Kaplan. 1987. A Compiler for Two-level Phonological Rules. In Dalrymple, M. et al. Tools for Morphological Analysis. Report CSLI-87-108. Center for the Study of Language and Information. Stanford University.

Lauri Karttunen. 1992. *CA:Two-Level Rule Compiler - Xerox XRCE.* http://www.xrce.xerox.com/competencies/content-analysis/fssoft/docs/twolc-92/twol92.html

Atro Voutilainen. 1994 *Designing a Parsing Grammar.* University of Helsinki, Department of General Linguistics, Helsinki.

Anssi Yli-Jyrä and Kimmo Koskenniemi. 2004. *Compiling Contextual Restriction on Strings into Finite-State Automata.* In L. Cleophas and B. W. Watson, eds., Proceedings of the Eindhoven FASTAR Days 2004. Computer Science Reports 04/40. The Netherlands: Technische Universiteit, Eindhoven.

Anssi Yli-Jyrä and Kimmo Koskenniemi. 2006. *Compiling Generalized Two-Level Rules and Grammars* . In Advances in Natural Language Processing, Springer Berlin/Heidelberg

ISSN 1736-6305 Vol. 4
http://hdl.handle.net/10062/9206

A linear time extension of deterministic pushdown automata[*]

Anders Søgaard
Center for Language Technology
University of Copenhagen
Njalsgade 140–142
DK-2300 Copenhagen S
soegaard@hum.ku.dk

Abstract

A linear time extension of deterministic pushdown automata is introduced that recognizes all deterministic context-free languages, but also languages such as $\{a^n b^n c^n \mid n \geq 0\}$ and the MIX language. It is argued that this new class of automata, called λ-acyclic read-first deterministic stack+bag pushdown automata, has applications in natural language processing.

1 Introduction

This article presents a linear time extension of deterministic pushdown automata (DPAs). DPAs have numerous applications in computer science, as many programming languages can be recognized by such automata, but they are not expressive enough for natural language parsing. There are at least two reasons for this; namely, that natural languages are heavily ambiguous, and that natural languages exhibit non-context-free constructions. Deterministic stack+bag pushdown automata introduce a limited form of nondeterminism, since information can be stored in bags. The bag construction also gives us limited context-sensitivity. It is argued that at least for some of the complex constructions in natural languages the degrees of nondeterminism and context-sensitivity are adequate. Our example in Sect. 6 concerns German scrambling.

Thanks to Thomas Hanneforth for pointing out previous work on ϕ-transitions to me. This work was done while the author was a Senior Researcher at the Dpt. of Linguistics, University of Potsdam, supported by the German Research Foundation.

2 Formal preliminaries

A **stack+bag pushdown automaton** (SBPA) is a 6-tuple $P = \langle Q, \Sigma, \Gamma, \delta, q_0, F \rangle$ where Q is a finite set of states, Σ the finite alphabet, Γ the finite stack symbols, $q_0 \in Q$ the initial state, $F \subseteq Q$ the final states, and $\delta \subseteq Q \times (\Sigma \cup \{\lambda\}) \times (\Gamma \cup \{\lambda\}) \times Q \times (\Gamma \cup \{\lambda\}) \times \{\{\gamma_1, \ldots, \gamma_n\}_M \mid \gamma_1 \ldots \gamma_n \in \Gamma, n \geq 0\}$ a finite set of transitions, where $\{\ldots\}_M$ is a bag or a multiset, i.e. $\{\{\gamma_1, \ldots, \gamma_n\}_M \mid \gamma_1, \ldots, \gamma_n \in \Gamma, n \geq 0\}$ is the set of multisets over elements of Γ.

The elements of δ, e.g. $\delta(q_i, a, A) = (q_j, \lambda, \{A\}_M)$, are transitions between states augmented with instructions to read or process string elements from the alphabet and pop and push stack symbols from the stack and the bag. The transition $\delta(q_i, a, A) = (q_j, \lambda, \{A'\}_M)$ is, for example, an instruction to read a, move from q_i to q_j and pop a stack symbol A from either the stack or the bag and push a symbol A' into the bag. If the transition had been $\delta(q_i, a, A) = (q_j, A', \emptyset_M)$ A' had been pushed onto the stack instead of into the bag.

The notion of an instantaneous description $(q, w, \gamma, \gamma') \in Q \times \Sigma^* \times \Gamma^* \times \{\{\gamma_1, \ldots, \gamma_n\}_M \mid \gamma_1 \ldots \gamma_n \in \Gamma, n \geq 0\}$ is introduced to define the language of a SBPA, where q is the state the SBPA is currently in, w the input string still to be processed, γ the contents of the stack, and γ' the contents of the bag. The derivability relation is the transitive, reflexive closure ($\vdash^*$) of the following binary relation over the class of instantaneous descriptions (ID), $\vdash \subseteq \text{ID} \times \text{ID}$, where

- $(q, xw, z\gamma, \gamma') \quad \vdash \quad (q', w, \alpha\gamma, \gamma')$ if $(q', \alpha, \emptyset_M) \in \delta(q, x, z)$, [pop z from stack, push α to stack]

- $(q, xw, z\gamma, \gamma') \quad \vdash \quad (q', w, \gamma, \alpha' \cup \gamma')$ if

$(q', \lambda, \alpha') \in \delta(q, x, z)$, [pop z from stack, push α' to bag]

- $(q, xw, \gamma, \{z\}_M \cup \gamma') \vdash (q', w, \alpha\gamma, \gamma')$ if $(q', \alpha, \emptyset_M) \in \delta(q, x, z)$, and [pop z from bag, push α to stack]

- $(q, xw, z\gamma, \{z\}_M \cup \gamma') \vdash (q', w, \gamma, \alpha' \cup \gamma')$ if $(q', \lambda, \alpha') \in \delta(q, x, z)$, [pop z from bag, push α' to bag],

with $x \in \Sigma \cup \{\lambda\}$, $z \in \Gamma \cup \{\lambda\}$, $\alpha \in \Gamma^*$, and $\alpha' \in \{\{\gamma_1, \ldots, \gamma_n\}_M \mid \gamma_1 \ldots \gamma_n \in \Gamma, n \geq 0\}$. The definition of the language of a SBPA S is now as follows:

$$
\begin{aligned}
L(S) \;=\; & \{w \mid (q_0, w, \lambda, \emptyset_M) \vdash^* \\
& (q, \lambda, \lambda, \emptyset_M) \land q \in F\}
\end{aligned}
$$

The languages that can be recognized by SBPAs are called stack+bag pushdown languages.

A SBPA S is called **deterministic** if for all possible instantaneous descriptions over S at most one transition in S is applicable. The languages that can be recognized by deterministic SBPAs are called deterministic stack+bag pushdown languages. Note that it can be assumed without loss of generalization that a deterministic SPBA for any state $q \in Q$ contains no λ-transitions or cycles of λ-transitions from q to q.

If a transition that reads an element of the alphabet is always chosen over a transition that reads λ, a read-first strategy is said to have been adopted. A SBPA S is said to be **read-first deterministic** if it is always clear what transition to apply under a read-first strategy, i.e. if for all instantaneous descriptions over S at most one transition of the form $(q, a, A) = \ldots$ where $a \in \Sigma$, and at most one transition of the form $(q, \lambda, A') = \ldots$, is applicable. If an automaton is *not* read-first deterministic it thus means that there are two transitions in δ of the form:

$$
\begin{aligned}
\delta(q_i, a, A) &\in (q_i', \ldots, \ldots) \\
\delta(q_i, a, A'') &\in (q_i'', \ldots, \ldots)
\end{aligned}
$$

or two transitions of the form:

$$
\begin{aligned}
\delta(q_j, \lambda, A) &\in (q_j', \ldots, \ldots) \\
\delta(q_j, \lambda, A') &\in (q_j'', \ldots, \ldots)
\end{aligned}
$$

and it is either *not* the case that A, A' never occur in the same bag, or it is not the case that A can never be the top element with A' in the bag, or vice versa, or both. The languages that can be recognized by read-first deterministic SBPAs running in read-first mode are called read-first deterministic

stack+bag pushdown languages.[1] Obviously, the read-first deterministic stack+bag pushdown languages include the deterministic stack+bag pushdown languages.

Finally, we say that a read-first deterministic stack+bag pushdown automaton is λ-**acyclic** if it is impossible to apply a transition

$$
\delta(q, \lambda, \ldots) \in \ldots
$$

more than once without reading an element from the input string first. The languages that can be recognized by λ-acyclic read-first deterministic SBPAs are called λ-acyclic read-first deterministic stack+bag pushdown languages.

3   Related work

This section compares our work to three rather disparate strands of research, namely (i) work on ϕ-transitions in the automata literature, (ii) deterministic parsing strategies for shift-reduce parsers and (iii) recent work on linguistically motivated extensions of tree-adjoining grammar. The first two comparisons serve to provide a bit of background on the read-first strategy. The third provides a bit of background on our use of bags.

Aho and Corasick (1975) design a class of automata for bibliographic search in which transitions are replaced by a function $g : Q \times \Sigma \to Q$ that maps pairs of states and input symbols into states or the failure message *fail*. There are no empty transitions, i.e. $\lambda \notin \Sigma$; instead a failure function $f : Q \to Q$ is consulted whenever g returns *fail*. It is not difficult to see that this is equivalent to a read-first strategy.

The read-first strategy is also related to work on deterministic shift-reduce parsers, e.g. Nivre (2003) for projective dependency grammars. A projective dependency grammar annotates a finite string $w_1 \ldots w_n$ with directed edges E, i.e. governor-dependent relations, such that the string positions, decorated by words, and the edges form an acyclic connected graph $G = \langle \{w_1 \ldots w_n\}, E \rangle$ in which each node has at most one governor and the edges are wellnested. Call such a graph a projective dependency graph. The deterministic shift-reduce parser introduced in Nivre (2003) begins with a 3-tuple $\langle \mathbf{nil}, \lambda, \emptyset \rangle$, in which the first element is the empty stack and the third element is the empty graph, and

---

[1]Below it is assumed that read-first deterministic SPBAs always run in read-first mode.

terminates when the string has been read, i.e. in $\langle T, w_1 \ldots w_n, G \rangle$ where T is a possibly non-empty stack. The string is accepted if G is a projective dependency graph. The algorithm applies four transitions to these states in a prioritized way, i.e. **Left-Arc** first if applicable, otherwise **Right-Arc**, then **Reduce**, and finally, if nothing else works, **Shift**.[2]

- The first transition **Left-Arc** adds an edge to the graph that encodes that the first element on the stack n is a dependent of the initial position n' in the substring still to be processed. The edge is licensed by a grammar rule that relates the two words that decorate the nodes in question in this way, i.e. R is a set of such word-to-word rules. The requirement that n is not governed by anything else is also necessary. The node n is removed from the stack to avoid cycles.

- The second transition **Right-Arc** adds an edge to the graph that encodes that the initial position in the substring to be processed is a dependent of the first element on the stack. The edge is again licensed by the grammar, and it is required that the dependent is not already governed. The dependent node is immediately shifted; again, to prevent cycles.

- The third transition **Reduce** simply pops the first element of the stack. Note that an element can only be popped this way if it is already assigned a governor.

- The fourth transition **Shift** pushes the next position onto the stack.

While this is technically a bit different from the read-first strategy adopted in our proposal, the intuition is the same: The constructive transitions **Left-Arc** and **Right-Arc** are tried out first, and only if no constructive transitions are applicable can the λ-transitions be applied. The underlying if-then-else structure means that the procedure remains deterministic. The three algorithms introduced in Nivre (2003) all terminate in linear time.

Other related classes of automata include extended pushdown automata (Vijay-Shanker,

1987), weakly equivalent to tree-adjoining grammars, which use nested stacks to provide an additional control layer, and thread automata (Ville-monte de La Clergerie, 2002), weakly equivalent to simple range concatenation grammar. These classes are not discussed here, but it should be noted that they were constructed to capture the expressivity of linguistic theories, while the class of automata introduced here "cross-cuts the Chomsky hierarchy" in a non-standard way. It restricts expressivity in some ways (by read-first determinism and λ-acylicity), but adds expressivity in other ways (by introducing a bag).

In the conclusion, once we have established the necessary results, our proposal is also compared to Bertsch and Nederhof (1999). Bertsch and Nederhof (1999) define another linear time extension of deterministic pushdown automata, but their extension remains context-free.

Finally, our use of bags is related to the use of sets of elementary trees in certain linguistically motivated extensions of tree-adjoining grammar, incl. Becker et al. (1991) and Lichte (2007). A very brief summary of tree-adjoining grammar: Tree substitution grammar is a variation over context-free grammar. Instead of production rules of the form

$$S \quad \rightarrow \quad NP \; VP$$

tree fragments of the following form are introduced:

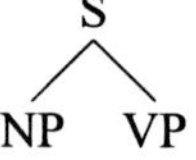

In derivation, trees with root labels A are plugged into trees with leaf nodes labeled by A. If a tree is obtained with root label S (the start symbol) and all leaf nodes are labeled by terminal symbols, the tree is a parse of its yield. Tree-adjoining grammar extends this context-free formalism by an operation on trees called adjunction, e.g.:

---

[2]In fact this simple set-up is only used to obtain a baseline in Nivre (2003). Two superior parsing algorithms are introduced that complicates this simple scenario by introducing limited lookahead. The details are unimportant for our purposes.

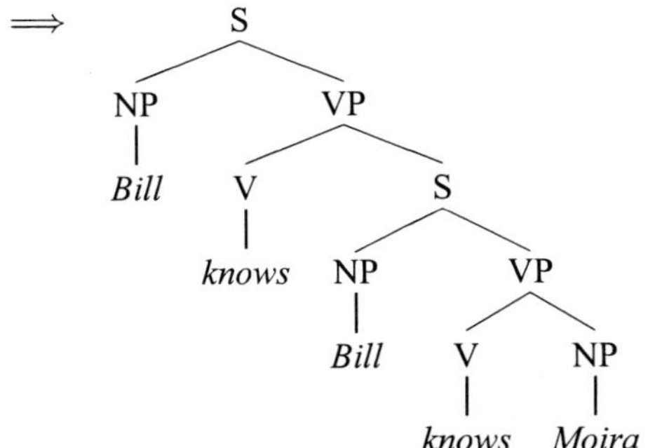

If an auxiliary tree t, with a root node and a leaf node both labeled A, is adjoined at some node n also labeled A in a derived tree t', the subtree s' (of t') rooted at n is replaced by t, and s' is then inserted at the leaf node of t.

The adjunction operator buys us limited context-sensitivity. In particular, tree-adjoining grammar is weakly equivalent to linear indexed grammar (Vijay-Shanker and Weir, 1994a) or level 2 control grammars (Weir, 1992). The universal recognition problem and the parsing problem can both be solved in time $\mathcal{O}(|G|n^6)$ (Vijay-Shanker and Weir, 1994b).

The formalism presented in Becker et al. (1991) is called (nonlocal) multicomponent tree-adjoining grammar (MCTAG). In fact, MCTAG comes in a number of varieties, but the intuition behind all of them is to introduce sets of auxiliary trees rather than just singular trees. Scrambling is now obtained when a set of multiple auxiliary trees is used in a relatively unconstrained context. The set must be emptied, i.e. each element must be adjoined, but the adjunctions can in unconstrained contexts result in any possible permutation of the yields of the auxiliary trees. See also Kallmeyer and Yoon (2004) for an analysis of scrambling in Korean in MCTAG.

Lichte (2007) replaces sets of auxiliary trees with 2-tuples $\langle t, \{a_1, \ldots, a_n\} \rangle$ where t can be any kind of tree, and $a_1, \ldots, a_m$ are auxiliary trees. This separation is similar to what is adopted in our analysis of German scrambling below.

4 Weak generative capacity

Lemma 4.1. *The stack+bag pushdown languages strictly include the context-free languages.*

Proof. The languages that can be recognized by pushdown automata, i.e. stack+bag pushdown automata without bags, are exactly the context-free languages (Chomsky, 1962). The languages that can be recognized by pushdown automata can be recognized by stack+bag pushdown automata, by definition, and thus stack+bag pushdown automata recognize context-free languages. It is not difficult to show that the inclusion is strict either. Simply note that the SBPA $S_1 = \langle \{q_0, q_1, q_2, q_3\}, \{a, b, c\}, \{A, B, C\}, \delta, q_0, \{q_3\} \rangle$ with the following transitions δ generates the language $L(S_1) = \{a^n b^n c^n \mid n \geq 0\}$ which is non-context-free by the Bar-Hillel pumping lemma (Aho and Ullman, 1972):

$$
\begin{aligned}
\delta(q_0, \lambda, \lambda) &\in \delta(q_0, \lambda, \{A, B, C\}_M) \\
\delta(q_0, \lambda, \lambda) &\in \delta(q_3, \lambda, \emptyset_M) \\
\delta(q_0, a, \lambda) &\in \delta(q_1, \lambda, \emptyset_M) \\
\delta(q_1, b, \lambda) &\in \delta(q_2, \lambda, \emptyset_M) \\
\delta(q_2, c, \lambda) &\in \delta(q_3, \lambda, \emptyset_M) \\
\delta(q_1, a, A) &\in \delta(q_1, \lambda, \emptyset_M) \\
\delta(q_2, b, B) &\in \delta(q_2, \lambda, \emptyset_M) \\
\delta(q_3, c, C) &\in \delta(q_3, \lambda, \emptyset_M)
\end{aligned}
$$

The automaton pushes an arbitrary number of A, B, C's into the bag in transitions from state q_0 to state q_0. Since the stack symbols are pushed into the bag simultaneously, it is guaranteed that the bag always contains the same number of A's, B's and C's in state q_0. Unless the automaton recognizes the empty string, in which case it does not push any stack symbols into the bag, but proceeds immediately to the final state q_3, it will first have to remove an A from the bag by moving into state q_1. In fact it has to remove *all* A's, since if it moves to q_2 by removing a B, it is no longer possible to remove the A's that remain, and the input string will not be recognized. Once the A's have been removed, it proceeds to q_2 to remove B's, and so on. Note that the automaton reads an a, resp. b or c, whenever it removes an A, resp. B or C. Since it is guaranteed that the bag always contains the same number of A's, B's and C's in state q_0, the strings that are recognized by this automaton will be of the form $a^n b^n c^n$ for $n \geq 0$. Since the stack+bag pushdown languages include the context-free languages and at least one language that is not context-free, namely $\{a^n b^n c^n \mid n \geq 0\}$, it follows that they strictly include the context-free languages. $\qquad\square$

It is not difficult to see how the automaton in the proof of Lemma 4.1 can be modified to recognize the MIX language, i.e. the language that consists of any permutation of a string in $\{a^n b^n c^n \mid n \geq 0\}$. This is of some interest, since the MIX language is conjectured not to be recognized by any linear indexed grammar (Gazdar, 1988).[3] The context-free languages constitute the first level of the hierarchy of controlled languages (Weir, 1992), the linear indexed languages the second level. Lemma 4.3 below relates the stack+bag pushdown languages to the entire hierarchy and shows that they are not included in the kth level of the hierarchy for any fixed k either.

Lemma 4.2. *The stack+bag pushdown languages include the MIX language.*

Proof. The SBPA $S_2 = \langle\{q_0\}, \{a,b,c\}, \{A,B,C\}, \delta, q_0, \{q_0\}\rangle$ with the following transitions δ generates the MIX language:

$$
\begin{aligned}
\delta(q_0, \lambda, \lambda) &\in \delta(q_0, \lambda, \{A, B, C\}_M) \\
\delta(q_0, a, A) &\in \delta(q_0, \lambda, \emptyset_M) \\
\delta(q_0, b, B) &\in \delta(q_0, \lambda, \emptyset_M) \\
\delta(q_0, c, C) &\in \delta(q_0, \lambda, \emptyset_M)
\end{aligned}
$$

In the light of our description of the automaton in Lemma 4.1 it should be easy to see how the automaton works. It recognizes the empty string, since the initial state is also a final state, and it recognizes all permutations of strings in $\{a^n b^n c^n \mid n \geq 0\}$, since the transitions that forced us to first remove A's, then B's, and so on, in the above, have been removed. □

Note that none of the two automata S_1, S_2 in the lemmas above are deterministic. Consider, for instance, the instantaneous descriptions $(q_0, aabbcc, \lambda, \emptyset_M)$ when S_1 reads the string $aabbcc$. In this case there are three applicable transitions (the first three on the list).

Note also that the two automata are both read-first deterministic. Another language that is non-deterministic and read-first deterministic is the language of palindromes $\{ww^R \mid w \in \Sigma^*\}$.

Finally, the automaton for the MIX language is λ-acyclic, but the one for $\{a^n b^n c^n \mid n \geq 0\}$ isn't. It is easy to see that there are equivalent stack+bag pushdown automata for $\{a^n b^n c^n \mid n \geq 0\}$ that are λ-acyclic. Consider, for instance, the SBPA $S_3 = \langle\{q_0, q_1, q_2\}, \{a,b,c\}, \{B,C\}, \delta, q_0, \{q_2\}\rangle$ with the following transitions δ:

$$
\begin{aligned}
\delta(q_0, \lambda, \lambda) &\in \delta(q_2, \lambda, \emptyset_M) \\
\delta(q_0, a, \lambda) &\in \delta(q_0, \lambda, \{B, C\}_M) \\
\delta(q_0, b, B) &\in \delta(q_1, \lambda, \emptyset_M) \\
\delta(q_1, b, B) &\in \delta(q_1, \lambda, \emptyset_M) \\
\delta(q_1, c, C) &\in \delta(q_2, \lambda, \emptyset_M) \\
\delta(q_2, c, C) &\in \delta(q_2, \lambda, \emptyset_M)
\end{aligned}
$$

When the automaton reads an a it pushes a B and a C into the bag. The first input b takes the automaton to its second state q_1 in which subsequent bs (if any) are read; the first input c takes the automaton to its final state q_2 in which subsequent cs (if any) are read. Each reading of a b, resp. c, removes a B, resp. C, from the bag. Consequently, for each a there is exactly one b and one c. The transitions between the three states ensure that the as precede the bs, and that the bs precede the cs.

Lemma 4.3. *The stack+bag pushdown languages are not included in the kth level of the hierarchy of control languages (Weir, 1992) for any fixed k.*

Proof. It is known that there exists a k-level control grammar for the language $\{a_1^n \ldots a_{2k}^n \mid n \geq 0\}$, but not for $\{a_1^n \ldots a_{2k+1}^n \mid n \geq 0\}$ (Palis and Shende, 1995). It is easy to see by inspection of the automaton S_1 that we can always build a SBPA that accepts $\{a_1^n \ldots a_{2k+1}^n \mid n \geq 0\}$ for any fixed k. □

It can be seen in the same way by inspection of the automaton S_3 that the same holds for λ-acyclic read-first deterministic stack+bag pushdown languages.

Corollary 4.4. *The λ-acyclic read-first deterministic stack+bag pushdown languages are not included in the kth level of the hierarchy of control languages (Weir, 1992) for any fixed k.*

Note also that the λ-acyclic read-first deterministic stack+bag pushdown languages include the deterministic context-free ones, since a deterministic pushdown automaton will never visit a λ-transition more than once without processing a string, since, equivalently, for any state $q \in Q$ it contains no λ-transitions or cycles of λ-transitions from q to q. This observation is stated as a lemma for further reference:

Lemma 4.5. *The λ-acyclic read-first deterministic stack+bag pushdown languages include the deterministic context-free languages.*

5 Complexity

In this section it is shown that the universal recognition problem of λ-acyclic read-first determinis-

---

[3]Bill Marsh's stronger original conjecture, from an unpublished 1985 ASL paper, is that the MIX language is not even an indexed language.

tic stack+bag pushdown automata can be solved in linear time.

Theorem 5.1. *The universal recognition problem of read-first deterministic stack+bag pushdown automata can be solved in time quadratic in the length of the input string, and in linear time for λ-acyclic ones.*

Proof. Consider the universal recognition problem if for some string $w_1 \ldots w_n$ and some read-first stack+bag pushdown automata $P = \langle Q, \Sigma, \Gamma, \delta, q_0, F \rangle$ with start ID $(q_0, w_1 \ldots w_n, \lambda, \emptyset_M)$. The string $w_1 \ldots w_n$ is recognized by P iff the procedure in Figure 1 returns *true* on the start ID when called recursively.

Under the assumption that the procedure halts and outputs *false* when it reads the same state and string for the nth time,[4] this procedure will loop at most n^2 many times if P is read-first deterministic. If P is also λ-acyclic, the number of loops required is at most $2n$.

Step 2 can be done in time $\mathcal{O}(|F|)$, and **read** and **print** are obviously linear time. The complicated steps are 4 and 7. The reason is of course that $\vdash$ has not been computed, so it must be checked if there is a transition in δ that licenses the relevant derivation, say

$$(q, w_i \ldots w_n, \gamma_1, \gamma_2) \vdash (q', w_{i+1} \ldots w_n, \gamma_1', \gamma_2')$$

This is linear in $|\delta|$, but on a naïve implementation it may also depend on the size of the bag, which again depends on the length of the input string and the maximum number of stack symbols a transition can push to the bag. Consequently, on such an implementation, the overall runtime would be cubic in the length of the input string for unrestricted read-first SBPAs, and quadratic for λ-acyclic ones. A more efficient option is to keep a table of stack symbols with numerical counters of size $|\Gamma|$. If a stack symbol A is pushed to the bag the value of the counter in column A is increased by one; if A is popped the value decreases. The overall runtime, with such a counter, is in $\mathcal{O}(n^2 \times |\Gamma| \times |\delta| \times |F|)$ for otherwise unrestricted read-first deterministic pushdown automata, and in $\mathcal{O}(n \times |\Gamma| \times |\delta| \times |F|)$ for λ-acyclic ones.[5] $\square$

---

[4]This move is safe. It is left for the reader to verify this.

[5]One of our reviewers observe that the bit complexity of this algorithm is actually $\mathcal{O}(n \log n \times |\Gamma| \times |\delta| \times |F|)$ for λ-acyclic read-first deterministic pushdown automata. The distinction here is comparable to bit complexity vs. word complexity in graph theory.

6 Scrambling in German

This section presents an indication that it is possible to analyze German scrambling phenomena in λ-acyclic read-first deterministic SBPAs in ways similar in spirit to what has been presented in Becker et al. (1991) and Lichte (2007). Unlike these formalisms, both extensions of tree-adjoining grammars, λ-acyclic read-first deterministic SBPAs are computationally efficient. The formalism used in Becker et al. (1991), called non-local MCTAG, recognizes NP-complete languages (Rambow and Satta, 1992).[6]

The phenomenon of scrambling is illustrated by the example in Figure 2:

The point in this case is that all possible permutations of the four NPs are grammatical in German. They can be scrambled in any way. One of the relevant syntactic construction involved in scrambling is of the following form, ignoring the internal syntax of the verb cluster:

dass $permute(\mathrm{NP}_1 \ldots \mathrm{NP}_{n-1}\, \mathrm{NP'})\ \mathrm{V}_1 \ldots \mathrm{V}_n$

where NP_i is the object complement of V_i for $1 \leq i < n$. The NP' is the subject of the finite verb V_n. This construction is recognized by the SBPA $S_4 = \langle \{q_0, q_1, q_2, q_3\}, \{NP_1, \ldots, NP_{n-1}, NP', V_1, \ldots V_n\}, \{NP_1, \ldots, NP_{n-1}, NP', V_1, \ldots V_n\}, \delta, q_0, \{q_3\} \rangle$ with the following transitions δ:[7]

---

[6]Its set-local variant (Weir, 1988), which may not suffice for analyses of scrambling (Rambow et al., 1992), though see Xia and Bleam (2000) for discussion, is weakly equivalent to simple range concatenation grammar whose universal recognition problem can be solved in deterministic time $\mathcal{O}(|G|n^{6k})$, where k, intuitively, is the number of (possibly scrambled) complements a verb may take. The complexity is to be precise $\mathcal{O}(|G|n^{2k(l+1)})$ where l is the maximum number of RHS nonterminals/predicates. See Boullier (1998) for an example of a parsing algorithm, applicable via the conversion described in Weir (1988). Set-local MCTAG is more succinct than simple range concatenation grammar, however, and its universal recognition problem can be shown to be NP-complete (Søgaard et al., 2007). The formalism used in Lichte (2007) has also been shown to be NP-complete (Søgaard et al., 2007).

[7]The indeces here should not lead the reader to think that we are not accounting for an unbounded number of dependencies. If the NPs in the above example are all the same, say *John*, and $n-1$ of the verbs are *let*, except the transitive, most embedded one, our automaton only needs two transitions for reading NPs (no matter how long the sentence is).

```
1.     read (q, w_i … w_n, γ_1, γ_2)
2.     if q ∈ F, w_i … w_n = λ, γ_1 = λ, γ_2 = ∅_M
3.     print true
4.         elsif (q, w_i … w_n, γ_1, γ_2), (q', w_{i+1} … w_n, γ'_1, γ'_2) ∈ ⊢
5.         print (q', w_{i+1} … w_n, γ'_1, γ'_2)
6.         return
7.         elsif (q, w_i … w_n, γ_1, γ_2), (q', w_i … w_n, γ'_1, γ'_2) ∈ ⊢
8.         print (q', w_i … w_n, γ'_1, γ'_2)
9.         return
10.        else
11.            print false
```

Figure 1: Recognition procedure for read-first deterministic stack+bag pushdown automata.

dass	der	Dedektiv	dem	Klienten	den	Verdächtigen	des	Verbrechens
that	the	detective.NOM	the	client.DAT	the	suspect.ACC	the	crime.GEN
zu	überführen	versprochen	hat					
to	indict	promised	has					

'that the detective has promised the client to indict the suspect of the crime.'

Figure 2: Example from Becker et al. (1991).

$$\delta(q_0, \lambda, \lambda) \in \delta(q_1, \lambda, \{NP', V_n\}_M)$$
$$\delta(q_1, NP_1, \lambda) \in \delta(q_1, \lambda, \{V_1\}_M)$$
$$\vdots$$
$$\delta(q_1, NP_{n-1}, \lambda) \in \delta(q_1, \lambda, \{V_{n-1}\}_M)$$
$$\delta(q_1, NP', \lambda) \in \delta(q_2, \lambda, \emptyset_M)$$
$$\delta(q_2, V_1, V_1) \in \delta(q_2, \lambda, \emptyset_M)$$
$$\vdots$$
$$\delta(q_2, V_{n-1}, V_{n-1}) \in \delta(q_2, \lambda, \emptyset_M)$$
$$\delta(q_2, V_n, V_n) \in \delta(q_3, \lambda, \emptyset_M)$$

In the transition from q_0 to q_1 a requirement that there is a main verb that has a subject, intuitively, is pushed into the bag. In the cyclic transitions in q_1, the NPs, incl. the subject of the finite verb V_n, are read, and when NP_i for $1 \leq i < n$ is read the stack symbol for the corresponding embedded verb V_i is pushed into the bag. The verbs are read in the cyclic transitions in q_2. Finally, the finite verb V_n is read.

7 Conclusion

This article presents a class of extended pushdown automata, i.e. λ-acyclic read-first deterministic stack+bag pushdown automata, that recognize a class of languages that strictly includes the deterministic context-free languages (Lemma 4.5), but also languages conjectured not to be indexed languages (by the observation that the automaton in Lemma 4.2 is λ-acyclic and read-first

deterministic). In fact, the λ-acyclic read-first deterministic stack+bag pushdown languages are not included in the kth level of the hierarchy of control languages for any fixed k (Corollary 4.4). It was shown that the universal recognition problem for this class of pushdown automata can be solved in linear time (Theorem 5.1).

Similar classes of linear time recognizable languages have been identified in the literature. Bertsch and Nederhof (1999) also identify a class of linear time recognizable pushdown languages, namely the class of all languages that are in the regular closure of the class of deterministic pushdown languages. This class includes a number of ambiguous context-free languages, incl. $\{a^m b^m c^n\} \cup \{a^m b^n c^n\}$ which is probably not a read-first deterministic stack+bag pushdown language, but no non-context-free languages. It follows, if so, that this class and the class of λ-acyclic read-first deterministic stack+bag pushdown languages are strict extensions of their intersection.

Since the paper was first submitted, a parser has been implemented in Python. The parser hardwires a read-first strategy and warns the user about nondeterminism and λ-cycles. It is of course difficult to test if the degree of nondeterminism given to us by bags is adequate for natural language processing, but a toy automaton has been constructed that parses attachment ambiguities, verbs with different subcategorization frames, and recursive modifiers.

References

Alfred Aho and Margaret Corasick. 1975. Efficient string matching: an aid to bibliographic search. *Communications of the Association for Computing Machinery*, 18(6):333–340.

Alfred Aho and Jeffrey Ullman. 1972. *The theory of parsing, translation and compiling*. Prentice-Hall, London, England.

Tilman Becker, Aravind Joshi, and Owen Rambow. 1991. Long-distance scrambling and tree adjoining grammars. In *Proceedings of the 5th Conference of the European Chapter of the Association for Computational Linguistics*, pages 21–26, Berlin, Germany.

Eberhard Bertsch and Mark-Jan Nederhof. 1999. Regular closure of deterministic languages. *SIAM Journal on Computing*, 29(1):81–102.

Pierre Boullier. 1998. Proposal for a natural language processing syntactic backbone. Technical report, INRIA, Le Chesnay, France.

Noam Chomsky. 1962. Context-free grammars and pushdown storage. Quarterly Progress Report 65, Research Laboratory of Electronics, Massachusetts Institute of Technology, Boston, Massachusetts.

Gerald Gazdar. 1988. Applicability of indexed grammars to natural languages. In Uwe Reyle and Christian Rohrer, editors, *Natural language parsing and linguistic theories*, pages 69–94. Reidel, Dordrecht, the Netherlands.

Laura Kallmeyer and Sin-Won Yoon. 2004. Treelocal MCTAG with shared nodes. In *Proceedings of the Traitement Automatique des Langues Naturelles*, Fes, Marocco.

Timm Lichte. 2007. An MCTAG with tuples for coherent constructions in German. In *Proceedings of the 12th Conference on Formal Grammar*, Dublin, Ireland.

Joakim Nivre. 2003. An efficient algorithm for projective dependency parsing. In *Proceedings of the 8th International Workshop on Parsing Technologies*, pages 149–160, Nancy, France.

Michael Palis and Sunil Shende. 1995. Pumping lemmas for the control language hierarchy. *Mathematical Systems Theory*, 28:199–213.

Owen Rambow and Giorgio Satta. 1992. Formal properties of nonlocality. In *Proceedings of the 2nd International Workshop on Tree Adjoining Grammars*, Philadelphia, Pennsylvania.

Owen Rambow, Tilman Becker, and Michael Niv. 1992. Scrambling is beyond LCFRS. Manuscript, University of Pennsylvania.

Anders Søgaard, Timm Lichte, and Wolfgang Maier. 2007. On the complexity of linguistically motivated extensions of tree-adjoining grammar. In *Proceedings of Recent Advances in Natural Language Processing 2007*, Borovets, Bulgaria.

K. Vijay-Shanker and David Weir. 1994a. The equivalence of four extensions of context-free grammars. *Mathematical Systems Theory*, 27:511–546.

K. Vijay-Shanker and David Weir. 1994b. Parsing some constrained grammar formalisms. *Computational Linguistics*, 19(4):591–636.

K. Vijay-Shanker. 1987. *A study of tree-adjoining grammar*. Ph.D. thesis, University of Pennsylvania, Philadelphia, Pennsylvania.

Éric Villemonte de La Clergerie. 2002. Parsing mildly context-sensitive languages with thread automata. In *Proceedings of the 19th International Conference on Computational Linguistics*, pages 1–7, Taipei, Taiwan.

David Weir. 1988. *Characterizing mildly context-sensitive grammar formalisms*. Ph.D. thesis, University of Pennsylvania, Philadelphia, Pennsylvania.

David Weir. 1992. A geometric hierarchy beyond context-free languages. *Theoretical Computer Science*, 104:235–261.

Fei Xia and Tonia Bleam. 2000. A corpus-based evaluation of syntactic locality in TAGs. In *Proceedings of the 5th International Workshop on Tree Adjoining Grammars and Related Formalisms*, Paris, France.

ISSN 1736-6305 Vol. 4
http://hdl.handle.net/10062/9206

Verifying context-sensitive treebanks and heuristic parses in polynomial time[*]

Anders Søgaard
Center for Language Technology
University of Copenhagen
Njalsgade 140–142
DK-2300 Copenhagen S
soegaard@hum.ku.dk

Abstract

A polyadic dynamic logic is introduced in which a model-theoretic version of nonlocal multicomponent tree-adjoining grammar can be formulated. It is shown to have a low polynomial time model checking procedure. This means that treebanks for nonlocal MCTAG, incl. all weaker extensions of TAG, can be efficiently corrected and queried. Our result is extended to HPSG treebanks (with some qualifications). The model checking procedures can also be used in heuristics-based parsing.

1   Introduction

First order logics and monadic second order logics have been used to query standard treebanks of context-free derivation structures (Kepser, 2004). The model checking problems for both logics are known to be PSPACE-complete (Blackburn et al., 2001), however. Moreover, treebanks are now being constructed that replace context-free derivation structures with context-sensitive ones, incl. The Prague Dependency Treebank (Hajičová et al., 2001), The Danish Dependency Treebank (Buch-Kromann, 2007), The LinGO Redwoods Treebank (English) (Oepen et al., 2002), and BulTreeBank (Simov et al., 2004).

Maier and Søgaard (2008) show that even German standard treebanks such as TIGER and NeGra contain mildly context-sensitive derivation structures. The dependency treebanks also use mildly

context-sensitive derivation structures (Kuhlmann and Möhle, 2007); the frequency of non-context-free structures in these treebanks is estimated in Nivre (2006) and is similar to the frequency of such strucures in TIGER and NeGra (Maier and Søgaard, 2008). The HPSG treebanks (Redwoods and BulTreeBank) also contain context-sensitive derivation structures (and beyond). The obvious question to ask now is: Are there less complex logics that can be used to correct and query context-sensitive treebanks?

This paper introduces a polyadic modal logic called *decharge logic*. Its model checking problem can be solved in low polynomial time; a model checking algorithm is spelled out. It is shown that decharge logic captures context-sensitive nonlocal multicomponent tree-adjoining grammars (MC-TAGs) (Becker et al., 1991) in the following sense: For each non-local MCTAG G, there exists a decharge logic D such that $\omega \in L(G)$ iff $\exists M.M \models_D \omega$, i.e. if a string is recognized by the grammar G it is satisfiable in the corresponding logic. D is thus a model-theoretic characterization of G.

Nonlocal MCTAG is context-sensitive, but not mildly context-sensitive (Rambow and Satta, 1992), and its fixed and universal recognition problems are NP-complete. Head-driven phrase structure grammar (HPSG) (Pollard and Sag, 1994) is strictly more expressive, i.e. it is possible to reconstruct nonlocal MCTAGs in the HPSG formalism (Søgaard, 2007). In other words, every nonlocal MCTAG is, formally, a HPSG. This doesn't tell us much, since, formally, most things are HPSGs: most formalizations of HPSG are Turing complete (Hegner, 1996). Even the model checking problem of the standard logical formalization of HPSG – known as relational speciate

---

The model checking procedure described in this paper uses constructs from a model checking procedure introduced in joint work with Martin Lange. Thanks also to Laura Kallmeyer, Timm Lichte and Wolfgang Maier for introducing me to various extensions of tree-adjoining grammar, incl. nonlocal MCTAG.

reentrant logic (RSRL) (Richter, 2004) – is undecidable (Søgaard, 2007). HPSG is captured in the above sense (with some qualifications) by an extended version of decharge logic whose model checking problem remains low polynomial time solvable (Søgaard and Lange, 2009).

Note on style: Knowledge of tree-adjoining grammar and HPSG is assumed for brevity. Instead a more detailed introduction is given to the concepts from modal logic used in decharge logic. See Joshi and Schabes (1997) for a recent introduction to tree-adjoining grammar. Since the paper covers some ground, proofs are only presented as informal proof sketches.

In general, the point of the paper is to present decharge logic and its extension and to argue that these logics may be relevant for natural language processing. The technical results are sketched, but only informally. No motivation is provided for the move to context-sensitive formalisms itself. The point is simply: *if* you want to use context-sensitive treebanks and query them, decharge logic has better computational properties than the other logics proposed in the literature for linguistic theories such as nonlocal MCTAG and HPSG. The model checking algorithms can also be used in heuristics-based parsing. Since neither nonlocal MCTAG nor HPSG has efficient parsing procedures, real-life parsing will typically be heuristics-based. A derivation structure is guessed (though not in a completely arbitrary fashion), rather than derived, and model checking can be used to check if the derivation structure satisfies whatever linguistic principles not guaranteed by the heuristics.

2 Decharge logic

2.1 Modal and dynamic logic

The logics covered in this brief introduction are all modal extensions of propositional logic. Propositional logic is the classic logic over propositional variables and Boolean connectives. Basic modal logic extends propositional logic with monadic operators $\Diamond_i, \Diamond_j, \ldots$, or in a notational variant $\langle i \rangle, \langle j \rangle, \ldots$, known as "diamonds" and their duals known as "boxes" (written $\Box_i, \Box_j, \ldots$ or $[i], [j], \ldots$). See Blackburn et al. (2001) for an introduction. The monadic operators introduce binary relations. The diamonds intuitively mean "there is a relation from the current state to a state for which it holds that". For example, the formula $\langle i \rangle p$ means that there is a relation (indexed by i) from the current state to a state in the denotation of p. The relation indeces are called labels (Labels), and the propositional variables are called atoms (Atoms). The syntax of basic modal logic over a signature $\langle \mathsf{Labels}, \mathsf{Atoms} \rangle$ is:

$$\phi, \psi \; \dot{=} \; p \mid \phi \wedge \psi \mid \neg\phi \mid \langle a \rangle \phi$$

where $a \in \mathsf{Labels}$ and $p \in \mathsf{Atoms}$. $[a]\phi \; \dot{=} \; \neg\langle a \rangle \neg\phi$ for all $a \in \mathsf{Labels}$.

Semantics is defined in terms of satisfaction definitions over Kripke models (henceforth, models) $M = \langle \mathbb{W}, \{R_a \in a \in \mathsf{Labels}\}, \mathcal{V} \rangle$ where $\mathbb{W}$ is a finite set of states (or worlds), $R_a \subseteq \mathbb{W} \times \mathbb{W}$, and $\mathcal{V} : \mathsf{Atoms} \to 2^{\mathbb{W}}$ a valuation function. The satisfaction definitions are as follows:

$$
\begin{aligned}
M, w &\models p && \text{iff} && w \in \mathcal{V}(p) \\
M, w &\models \phi \wedge \psi && \text{iff} && M, w \models \phi \;\&\; M, w \models \psi \\
M, w &\models \neg\phi && \text{iff} && M, w \not\models \phi \\
M, w &\models \langle a \rangle \phi && \text{iff} && \exists w'. R_a(w, w') \;\&\; M, w' \models \phi'
\end{aligned}
$$

Example 2.1. The model

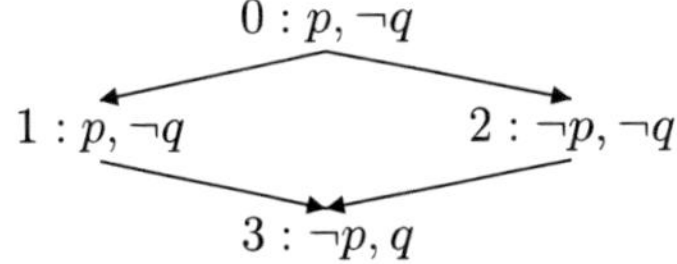

with all edges in R_a, except $(2, 3) \in R_b$, satisfies the formulas (i) $\langle b \rangle \top \to \langle b \rangle q$, since all edges in R_b lead to states in the denotation of q, and (ii) $\neg[a]\neg q$, since not all edges in R_a lead to states in the complement of the denotation of q.

Clearly, basic modal logic is not powerful enough to capture HPSG, since modal logic has the tree model property (Blackburn et al., 2001), i.e. if there exists a model that satisfies ϕ it is possible to unravel this model into a tree. Since reentrancies are used discriminatively in HPSG, it is clear that any logic that has the tree model property is too weak to capture HPSG. The reason that basic modal logic is too weak to capture nonlocal MCTAG is more subtle. Basic modal logic is invariant under generated substructures (Blackburn et al., 2001), i.e. if ϕ is true in all states of a model it is also true in all states of a submodel (by the tree model property also a subtree) generated in one of those states. Since set saturation, used in both nonlocal MCTAG and HPSG, relies on an "upwards query", i.e. if a set (labeled by some FEATURE in the case of HPSG) is introduced in a state w, then w must be dominated by a state with an empty set (labeled by some FEATURE in the case of HPSG), it is clear that any logic that is invariant under generated substructures is too weak to capture nonlocal MCTAG (and HPSG).

Propositional dynamic logic (PDL) is an extension of modal logic in which it is possible to do up- and downwards indeterministic queries such as "somewhere down/up the model it holds that". The syntax of PDL over a signature $\langle$Labels, Atoms$\rangle$ not only defines a set of formulas, but also a set of programs Programs. Diamonds and boxes can now be indexed by programs rather than just labels, and relations are induced over models:

$$\phi, \psi \;\dot=\; p \mid \phi \wedge \psi \mid \neg\phi \mid \langle\alpha\rangle\phi$$
$$\alpha, \beta \;\dot=\; \epsilon \mid a \mid \alpha;\beta \mid \alpha^* \mid \alpha\cup\beta \mid \alpha^{-1} \mid \phi?$$

where $a \in$ Labels and $p \in$ Atoms. The satisfaction definitions are the same as for basic modal logic, except the last clause is generalized to programs:

$$M, w \models \langle a\rangle\phi \quad \text{iff} \quad \exists w'.R_a(w,w') \,\&\, M, w' \models \phi'$$

Each program α, as already mentioned, induces a relation R_α over a model with states $\mathbb{W}$ that is inductively defined:

$$
\begin{aligned}
R_\epsilon &\;\dot=\; \{(w,w) \mid s \in \mathbb{W}\} \\
R_{\alpha;\beta} &\;\dot=\; \{(w,w') \mid \exists(w,v) \in R_\alpha \,\&\, (v,w') \in R_\beta\} \\
R_{\alpha^*} &\;\dot=\; \textstyle\bigcup_k R_{\alpha^k} \text{ w. } R_{\alpha^0} = R_\epsilon \,\&\, R_{\alpha^{k+1}} = R_{\alpha;\alpha^k} \\
R_{\alpha\cup\beta} &\;\dot=\; R_\alpha \cup R_\beta \\
R_{\alpha^{-1}} &\;\dot=\; \{(w,v) \mid (v,w) \in R_\alpha\} \\
R_{\phi?} &\;\dot=\; \{(w,w) \mid M, w \models \phi\}
\end{aligned}
$$

Intuitively, ϵ is the empty transition, $\alpha;\beta$ is composition, α^* is Kleene closure, $\alpha\cup\beta$ is union, α^{-1} is converse and $\phi?$ is a test.

Example 2.2. The model

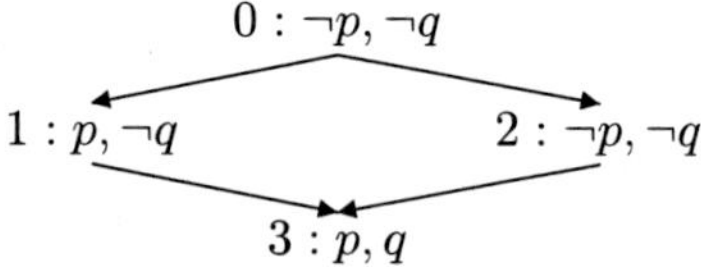

with all edges in R_a satisfies the formulas (i) $\neg[a^*]p$, since $0 \notin \mathcal{V}(p)$, and (ii) $\langle a\rangle q$, since any state dominates a state in the denotation of q.

Note that PDL is not invariant under generated substructures. The formula $\langle(a^*)^{-1}\rangle p$, for example, is true in the model:

$$
\begin{array}{c}
0 : p \\
1 : \neg p \qquad 2 : \neg p \\
3 : \neg p
\end{array}
$$

with all edges in R_a, but not in any of its proper generated submodels. PDL still has the tree model property and is thus not adequate for HPSG (nor as a stand-alone logic for non-local MCTAG). A

slight extension of PDL, namely PDL with intersection, has been proposed for simpler unification-based formalisms and basic tree-adjoining grammar (Keller, 1993; Blackburn and Spaan, 1993). The extension simply adds a clause $\alpha \cap \beta$ to the syntax of programs with semantics:

$$R_{\alpha\cap\beta} \;\dot=\; R_\alpha \cap R_\beta$$

PDL with intersection does not have the tree model property, since, for example, $\langle a \cap b\rangle\top$ is not satisfied by any tree-like model. The model checking problem for PDL with intersection can be solved in linear time (Lange, 2006). Consequently, querying simpler unification-based treebanks and treebanks based on tree-adjoining grammar can be done in time linear in the size of structures and in the length of queries.

PDL with intersection is not powerful enough to capture the kind of set saturation found in non-local MCTAG and HPSG in an intuitive way.[1] Decharge logic is an extension of PDL with intersection specially designed for this purpose. The standard logic for HPSG, which is adequate for nonlocal MCTAG too by the general inclusion result (Søgaard, 2007), as already mentioned has an undecidable model checking problem. So the main result of this paper is that decharge logic is adequate for nonlocal MCTAG and (with some qualifications) HPSG and has a low polynomial time model checking procedure.

2.2 Decharge logic

Decharge logic is a polyadic extension of deterministic PDL with intersection in the following sense. Our signatures are as usual. Our models, however, differ a bit from ordinary Kripke models.

Definition 2.3 (Semi-deterministic polyadic Kripke models). A semi-deterministic polyadic Kripke model (SPKM) is a tuple $M = \langle\mathbb{W}, \{R_a \mid a \in$ Labels$\}, \mathcal{V}\rangle$ such that $\mathbb{W}$ is a set of worlds or states. Let $R_\dagger = \{(s_1, ..., s_n) \mid \forall i = 1, \ldots, n.\forall j = i + 1, \ldots, n.s_i \neq s_j\}$ be the relation consisting of all tuples of worlds without multiple occurrences. Furthermore, for each $a \in$ Labels, $R_a \subseteq R_\dagger$ is a polyadic relation over $\mathbb{W}$. All atomic programs are

---

[1] Given a specific treebank, the maximum set size can be fixed. In this case, PDL with intersection may suffice as a logical query language, albeit less intuitive, but generally it is not expressive enough. Finally, such a trick is not possible in heuristics-based parsing.

required to be deterministic, i.e. whenever $\{(s, t_1, \ldots, t_n), (s, u_1, \ldots, u_m)\} \subseteq R_a$ for some $a \in$ Labels then $n = m$ and $t_i = u_i$ for all $i = 1, \ldots, n$. Finally $\mathcal{V} : \mathbb{W} \to 2^{\mathsf{Atoms}}$ interprets propositional variables in worlds.

Note that labels are not associated with a particular arity. Relations may contain tuples of different lengths, since they will be used to encode set values in nonlocal MCTAG and HPSG.

Definition 2.4 (Syntax of decharge logic). Formulas (ϕ, ψ) and programs (α_i) of decharge logic over the signature $\langle$Labels, Atoms$\rangle$ are defined as:

$$
\begin{aligned}
\phi, \psi &\doteq p \mid \phi \wedge \psi \mid \neg\phi \mid \langle\alpha\rangle(\phi_1, \ldots, \phi_n) \\
\alpha_1, \alpha_2 &\doteq \epsilon \mid a \mid \alpha_1; a \mid \beta_1^* \mid \alpha_1 \cup \alpha_2 \mid \alpha_1 \cap \alpha_2 \\
&\quad\mid \ominus(\gamma, a, \alpha_3) \\
\beta_1, \beta_2 &\doteq \epsilon \mid a \mid \beta_1 \cup \beta_2 \\
\gamma_i &\doteq \epsilon \mid a \mid \gamma_i; a
\end{aligned}
$$

where $a \in$ Labels and $p \in$ Atoms.

$\ominus$ is called the decharge operator. The semantics of the PDL operators are as usual, but over SPKMs, and the relation induced by the decharge operator is defined as follows:

$$
\begin{aligned}
R_{\ominus(\alpha_1, \alpha_2, \alpha_3)} &\doteq \{(w, v_1, \ldots, v_{j-1}, v_{j+1}, \ldots, v_n) \mid \\
&\quad \exists (w, w') \in R_{\alpha_1}, \exists (w', v_1, \ldots, v_n) \\
&\quad \in R_{\alpha_2}, \exists (w, v_j) \in R_{\alpha_3}\}
\end{aligned}
$$

$\ominus$ is a complement operator that nondeterministically removes an element from a list. Intuitively, α_1 is a pointer to somewhere in the structure, α_2 is the set value at the node that is pointed out, and α_3 the place where we put the element that has been removed. $\cap$ can then be used to place the new set.

2.2.1 Model checking

There exists a model checking procedure for decharge logic whose worst-case complexity is in $\mathcal{O}(|\phi|^2 \times |\mathbb{W}|^4)$ where ϕ is the input formula and $\mathbb{W}$ the world set of the SPKM. The proof goes as follows:

Let M be a SPKM with world set $\mathbb{W}$ and ϕ a decharge logic formula. First find all subformulas of the form $\alpha\langle\psi\rangle$ in ϕ. This can be done in time $\mathcal{O}(|\phi|)$. Then for each subformula compute the relation R_α over M. This can be done in time $\mathcal{O}(|\alpha| \times |\mathbb{W}|^4)$ by Lemma 5.4 in Søgaard and Lange (2009). Add R_α to M under a new atomic program name a_α in time $\mathcal{O}(|\mathbb{W}|^2)$ (the bound on the size of the new relations). Let M' be the resulting SPKM, and let ϕ' result from ϕ by replacing every $\langle\alpha\rangle\phi$ with $\langle a_\alpha\rangle\phi$ in a bottom-up fashion. Now $M, w \models \phi$ iff $M', w \models \phi'$, and $M', w \models \phi'$ is an instance of the model checking problem of

ordinary polyadic modal logic (Blackburn et al., 2001) known to be solvable in time $\mathcal{O} = (|M'| \times |\phi'|)$ (Lange, 2006). Overall this gives an upper bound of $\mathcal{O}(|\phi|^2 \times |\mathbb{W}|^4)$ on the time needed to perform model checking for decharge logic.

2.3 Extended decharge logic

Decharge logic is not rich enough to cover all the basic constructs in HPSG (Pollard and Sag, 1994). Extended decharge logic bridges this gap (in part) without changing the worst-case complexity of the model checking problem. Formulas (ϕ, ψ) and programs (α_i) of extended decharge logic over a signature $\langle$Labels, Atoms$\rangle$ are defined as follows:

$$
\begin{aligned}
\phi, \psi &\doteq p \mid \phi \wedge \psi \mid \neg\phi \mid \langle\alpha\rangle(\phi_1, \ldots, \phi_n) \\
\alpha_1, \alpha_2 &\doteq \epsilon \mid a \mid \alpha_1; a \mid \beta_1^* \mid \alpha_1 \cup \alpha_2 \mid \alpha_1 \cap \alpha_2 \mid \\
&\quad \alpha_1 \sqcap \alpha_2 \mid \mathbf{app}(\gamma_1, \gamma_2, \gamma_3, \gamma_4) \mid \\
&\quad \ominus(\gamma_1, a, \alpha_1) \\
\beta_1, \beta_2 &\doteq \epsilon \mid a \mid \beta_1 \cup \beta_2 \\
\gamma_i &\doteq \epsilon \mid a \mid \gamma_i; a
\end{aligned}
$$

where $a \in$ Labels and $p \in$ Atoms. Note that two new operators are introduced, namely $\sqcap$ and **app**. $R_{\alpha \sqcap \beta}$ is defined as $\{(w, w') \mid \exists(w, v_1, \ldots, v_n) \in R_\alpha \text{ and } \exists(w, u_1, \ldots, u_m) \in R_\beta, \exists i, j.w' = v_i = u_j\}$, while $R_{\mathbf{app}(\alpha_1, \alpha_2, \alpha_3, \alpha_4)}$ is defined as $\{(x, \bar{y}_1, \ldots, \bar{y}_m, \bar{z}_1, \ldots, \bar{z}_n) \in R_\dagger \mid \forall i, j.\exists x', x''.(x', \bar{y}_i) \in R_{\alpha_2}, (x'', \bar{z}_j) \in R_{\alpha_4}, (x, \ldots x' \ldots) \in R_{\alpha_1}, (x, \ldots x'' \ldots) \in R_{\alpha_3}, (x, \bar{y}_1, \ldots, \bar{y}_m, \bar{z}_1, \ldots, \bar{z}_n) \in R_\dagger\}$.

Intuitively, the append operator (**app**) works this way: α_1 and α_3 are pointers to nodes in a feature structure. The operator then takes the arguments of α_2 and α_4 at the nodes to which the pointers lead, and conjoins them. In a sense, this gives us a virtual list value, a list value that is nowhere in the derivation structure; the notion of virtual lists and sets is similar to the notion of a chain in Richter (2004), albeit a very restricted one. The intersection operator is used to place this virtual list value somewhere in the structure. In extended decharge logic, lists are used as canonical representations of sets. The even richer logic in Søgaard and Lange (2009) represents all linearizations of sets in models, but has a PSPACE-complete model checking procedure.

The low polynomial time model checking procedure can be extended to this extension of decharge logic, as shown in Theorem 5.5 in Søgaard and Lange (2009). Consequently, the new operators do not add to asymptotic complexity.

3 Nonlocal multicomponent tree-adjoining grammar

Multicomponent tree-adjoining grammar (MC-TAG) (Becker et al., 1991) is an extension of tree-adjoining grammar in which adjunction is simultaneous adjunction of all trees in a finite set (of fixed size) of auxiliary trees rather than just adjunction of a single tree. Tree-local and set-local MCTAG impose further restrictions on adjunction, while nonlocal MCTAG imposes no further restrictions.

MCTAG was primarily invented to implement analyses of scrambling in languages such as German (Becker et al., 1991) and Korean (Kallmeyer and Yoon, 2004). A recent alternative to MCTAG uses tree tuples rather than sets (TT-MCTAG) (Lichte, 2007), also motivated by scrambling phenomena.

The key idea in all these analyses is to factorize the verb and its complements into different auxiliary trees that can then be permuted in derivation. For each verb with its complements a new tree set is adjoined.

3.1 Computational complexity and generative capacity

Rambow and Satta (1992) present a proof that the fixed recognition problem of nonlocal MCTAG is NP-hard, generalized to a few restricted variants in Champollion (2007), while Søgaard et al. (2007) present a (weaker) proof of the NP-hardness of the universal recognition problem that is generalized to all variants of MCTAG. It follows from the linear upper bound on the size of derivation structures that the universal recognition problem can also be solved in nondeterministic linear space, which also implies that nonlocal multicomponent tree-adjoining languages can be recognized by linear bounded automata. Since any language that can be represented by a linear bounded automaton is context-sensitive (Landweber, 1963), it holds that nonlocal MCTAG is context-sensitive. It also follows from the result obtained in this paper, namely that model checking can be done in low polynomial time, that the universal recognition problem is in NP and thereby NP-complete. It is possible to nondeterministically guess a derivation structure linear in the length of the input string and verify it in low polynomial time.

On the other hand it is easy to prove that nonlocal MCTAG is *not* mildly context-sensitive; see also Rambow and Satta (1992). Consider the

grammar with the auxiliary tree set:

and the initial tree:

This grammar generates the MIX language which according to Marsh's conjecture is not even an indexed language. Tree-local MCTAG, on the other hand, is weakly (but not strongly) equivalent to tree-adjoining grammar and thus mildly context-sensitive.

3.2 Model-theoretic characterization

A model-theoretic version of nonlocal MCTAG in which a grammar is a set of axioms in decharge logic, and the language is the set of strings whose logical descriptions are satisfiable in conjunction with the grammar, is briefly sketched.

The first step of the reconstruction of nonlocal MCTAG in logical terms is similar to the model-theoretic characterization of tree-adjoining grammar in Keller (1993). Consider the translation of a case of adjunction in below, presented in Figure 1 in the more readable AVM notation known from HPSG and also used in Keller (1993), Blackburn and Spaan (1993) and Richter (2004), i.e. AVMs can, if we ignore the issue of underspecification for now, be seen as deterministic Kripke models (Blackburn and Spaan, 1993).

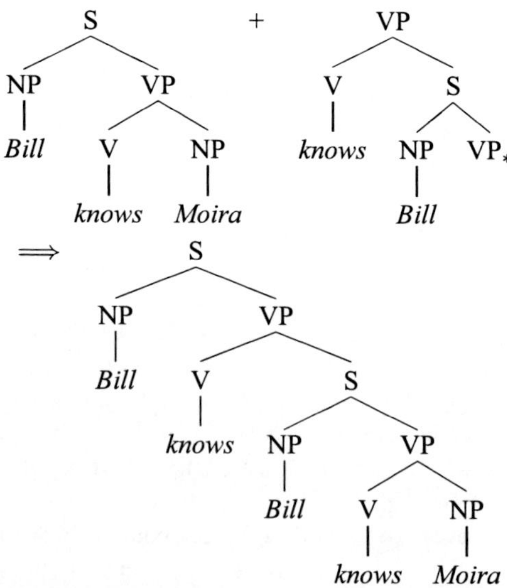

$$
\begin{bmatrix}
\text{CAT S} \\
\text{IDTRS}\left\langle
\begin{bmatrix}\text{CAT NP}\\ \text{IDTRS}\langle Bill\rangle\end{bmatrix},\;
\boxed{2}\begin{bmatrix}\text{CAT VP}\\ \text{IDTRS}\left\langle\begin{bmatrix}\text{CAT V}\\ \text{IDTRS}\langle knows\rangle\end{bmatrix},\begin{bmatrix}\text{CAT NP}\\ \text{IDTRS}\langle Moira\rangle\end{bmatrix}\right\rangle\end{bmatrix}
\right\rangle
\end{bmatrix}
\;+\;
\boxed{2}\begin{bmatrix}
\text{CAT VP}\\
\text{DTRS}\left\langle\begin{bmatrix}\text{CAT V}\\ \text{IDTRS}\langle knows\rangle\end{bmatrix},\begin{bmatrix}\text{CAT S}\\ \text{IDTRS}\left\langle\begin{bmatrix}\text{CAT NP}\\ \text{IDTRS}\langle Bill\rangle\end{bmatrix},\begin{bmatrix}\text{CAT VP}\\ \text{IDTRS}\;\boxed{1}\end{bmatrix}\right\rangle\end{bmatrix}\right\rangle\\
\text{IDTRS}\;\boxed{1}
\end{bmatrix}
\;\Longrightarrow
$$

$$
\begin{bmatrix}
\text{CAT S}\\
\text{IDTRS}\left\langle\begin{bmatrix}\text{CAT NP}\\ \text{IDTRS}\langle Bill\rangle\end{bmatrix},\begin{bmatrix}\text{CAT VP}\\ \text{DTRS}\left\langle\begin{bmatrix}\text{CAT V}\\ \text{IDTRS}\langle knows\rangle\end{bmatrix},\begin{bmatrix}\text{CAT S}\\ \text{IDTRS}\left\langle\begin{bmatrix}\text{CAT NP}\\ \text{IDTRS}\langle Bill\rangle\end{bmatrix},\begin{bmatrix}\text{CAT VP}\\ \text{IDTRS}\left\langle\begin{bmatrix}\text{CAT V}\\ \text{IDTRS}\langle knows\rangle\end{bmatrix},\begin{bmatrix}\text{CAT NP}\\ \text{IDTRS}\langle Moira\rangle\end{bmatrix}\right\rangle\end{bmatrix}\right\rangle\end{bmatrix}\right\rangle\end{bmatrix}\right\rangle
\end{bmatrix}
$$

Figure 1: Adjunction in AVM notation

The idea behind the translation is that we duplicate trees. So we have an initial constituent structure embedded under IDTRS that adjunction can modify; if no adjunction takes place, the IDTRS and DTRS tree structures are unified. The axiomatization of TAG is such that every node in a model must be either a terminal node, an adjunction site or IDTRS and DTRS must be unified. See Keller (1993) for details.

The trick is now to introduce an additional feature TSET to encode sets of auxiliary trees. The discharge operator $\ominus$ is used to nondeterministically remove auxiliary trees from these sets one at a time in derivation. Saturation is ensured by the converse operator, as already described above.

4 Head-driven phrase structure grammar

HPSG (Pollard and Sag, 1994) is a popular, but very complex deep grammar theory or, perhaps more adequately, a complex deep grammar architecture. Its earliest version was unification-based, but this is no longer the case. It is, unlike nonlocal MCTAG, supposed to be model-theoretic. Consequently, logical formalizations already exist. Conventionally, an HPSG grammar is defined as a tuple $\langle\langle \text{Types}, \sqsubseteq\rangle, \text{Principles}\rangle$, where $\langle\text{Types}, \sqsubseteq\rangle$ is the inheritance hierarchy, a finite bounded complete partial order, and Principles is a set of linguistic principles. The linguistic principles correspond intuitively to generative rules, but are con-

straints over a set of legitimate derivation structures. The inheritance hierarchy is formally simple and can be reconstructed in propositional logic (Moens et al., 1989). Consequently, the tricky part is the linguistic principles. The main challenges are set saturation, covered in extended discharge logic by the discharge operator, and union of sets. Note that set union cannot be expressed by the discharge operator.

Example 4.1. An example of a linguistic principle in HPSG that uses set union is the Nonlocal Feature Principle (Pollard and Sag, 1994):

> For each nonlocal feature, the INHERITED value on the mother is the union of the INHERITED values on the daughters minus the TO-BIND value on the head daughter.

In Pollard and Sag (1994), there are three nonlocal features on INHERITED, SLASH, QUE, REL.

4.1 Related formalizations

Reape (1994) formalizes an earlier version of HPSG in terms of a quantified hybrid logic $\mathcal{L}^{++}$. $\mathcal{L}^{++}$ is an extension of propositional logic with n-ary modalities, nominals and quantification over nominals. Nominals are a subset of the set of propositional variables that only denote singleton subsets in a model. Quantification is similar to first order logic. $\mathcal{L}^{++}$ is a polyadic version of $H(\exists)$. Set union is implemented in a first order theory of sets. The model checking problem is obviously PSPACE-hard.

(Hegner, 1996) defined a decidable extension of the Schönfinkel-Bernays class as a formalization of HPSG. In this logic, quantifiers or variables are typed relative to the inheritance hierarchy, and prefixes of the form $\forall_t \exists_t$ are allowed iff t, t' are incompatible types.The logic is clearly more expressive than the Schönfinkel-Bernays class, but it does not capture strong welltypedness (Carpenter, 1992). Consider, for instance, the HPSG-style strong welltypedness condition on phrases:

$$\forall x.\textit{hd-phr}(x) \rightarrow \exists y.\textit{head-dtr}(x, y)$$

saying that a headed phrase has a head daughter. The trouble is that a head daughter can itself be a headed phrase, so this condition cannot be expressed in the logic of (Hegner, 1996). In general, no decidable standard prefix-vocabulary class of first order logic characterizes the deterministic, connected and strongly welltyped structures used in HPSG (Søgaard, 2007).

The logic proposed in Richter (2004), RSRL, is an extension of description logic with global quantification similar to what can be obtained in PDL with intersection by $(a_1 \cup \ldots \cup a_n)^*$ with Labels $= \{a_1, \ldots, a_n\}$, i.e. the master modality. RSRL is much more complex than PDL with intersection, though. In fact its model checking problem is known to be undecidable. Sets are still decomposed as in the first order theory of sets.

The relevant complexity results (and proofs thereof) for $\mathcal{L}^{++}$ and RSRL are presented in Søgaard (2007). PSPACE-hardness of model checking $\mathcal{L}^{++}$ and RSRL can be proven by reduction of Geography (Garey and Johnson, 1979), the undecidability of satisfiability by the tiling problem, and the undecidability of model checking RSRL can be proven by the Post correspondence problem.

The main difference between decharge logic and $\mathcal{L}^{++}$ and RSRL is that sets are first class citizens in decharge logic, i.e. sets of tuples denoted by relations of variable arity. This complicates the logical machinery in some respects, but means that first order machinery that leads to PSPACE-complete model checking, can be avoided.

4.2 Model-theoretic characterization

Here is possible formalization of the Nonlocal Feature Principle in Example 4.1 in extended decharge logic in the feature geometry in Pollard and Sag (1994) (w. *hd-dtr* = headed daughter):

$$\textit{hd-phr} \quad \rightarrow \quad \langle\texttt{elem}(\ominus(\epsilon, \pi, \texttt{dtrs;hd-dtr;synsem;} \\ \texttt{nonlocal;to-bind;f)}\cap \\ \texttt{synsem;nonlocal;} \\ \texttt{inherited;f)}\rangle\top$$

with $\langle\textbf{elem}(\pi \cap \textbf{app}(\texttt{all-dtrs,} \texttt{synsem;nonlocal;inherited;f}, \epsilon, \epsilon))\rangle\top$ and $\pi \in$ Labels. F is a placeholder for the nonlocal features SLASH,QUE,REL.

See Søgaard and Lange (2009) for more examples. Our qualifications, mentioned multiple times in the above, are also made precise in Søgaard and Lange (2009). There are a few somewhat controversial HPSG principles, i.e. the Trace Principle and the Binding Theory, that do not seem to be definable in extended decharge logic.

5 Conclusion

This paper introduced a polyadic dynamic logic called decharge logic and an extension thereof to provide query languages for context-sensitive treebanks, e.g. treebanks with non-projective dependency structures, incl. the Prague Dependency Treebank and the Danish Dependency Treebank, the LinGO Redwoods Treebank and the BulTree-Bank.

Common query tools for treebanks include CorpusSearch, ICECUP III (Wallis and Nelson, 2000) and TGrep2, but as pointed out by Kepser (2004) the query languages used in these tools are not even expressive enough to perform arbitrary queries on context-free derivations. They are, according to Kepser (2004), all subsumed by the existential fragment of first order logic. Other more expressive logics that have been introduced to characterize context-sensitive grammar formalisms (Reape, 1994; Richter, 2004) have model checking procedures with exponential runtime. It was shown that decharge logic and its extension have low polynomial time model checking procedures. The two logics thus make querying context-sensitive treebanks feasible.

Using decharge logics for querying treebanks is similar to using more common query tools. Say the following is a sentence in a treebank in TGrep2 input format:

```
(TOP (NP (NP (NN Budget)) (VP (VBD
        increased))))
```

In TGrep2, the following three lines of text are examples of queries:

```
(i)     NP ≺≺ NN
(ii)    NP ≺ NN
(iii)   NP !≺ NN
```

(i) matches all nodes labeled by NP that dominate a node labeled by NN (2 nodes); (ii) matches all nodes labeled by NP that immediately dominate a node labeled by NN (1 node); and (iii) matches all nodes labeled by NP that do not immediately dominate a node labeled by NN (1 node). The queries correspond to the following formulas in decharge logic:

$$
\begin{array}{ll}
\text{(i')} & np \wedge \langle (\texttt{down}; \texttt{right}^*)^* \rangle nn \\
\text{(ii')} & np \wedge \langle \texttt{down}; \texttt{right}^* \rangle nn \\
\text{(iii')} & np \wedge \neg \langle \texttt{down}; \texttt{right}^* \rangle nn
\end{array}
$$

The query tools thus essentially model check the derivation structure wrt. some formula ϕ and output the set of nodes (states) that satisfy ϕ.

Decharge logic and its extension can also be used to verify heuristic parses.

References

Tilman Becker, Aravind Joshi, and Owen Rambow. 1991. Long-distance scrambling and tree adjoining grammars. In *EACL'91*, pages 21–26, Berlin, Germany.

Patrick Blackburn and Edith Spaan. 1993. A modal perspective on the computational complexity of attribute value grammar. *Journal of Logic, Language and Information*, 2(2):129–169.

Patrick Blackburn, Maarten de Rijke, and Yde Venema. 2001. *Modal logic*. Cambridge University Press, Cambridge, England.

Matthias Buch-Kromann. 2007. Computing translation units and quantifying parallelism in parallel dependency treebanks. In *ACL'07, Linguistic Annotation Workshop*, pages 69–76.

Bob Carpenter. 1992. *The logic of typed feature structures*. Cambridge University Press, Cambridge, England.

Lucas Champollion. 2007. Lexicalized non-local MCTAG with dominance links is NP-complete. In *MOL'07*, Los Angeles, California.

Michael Garey and David Johnson. 1979. *Computers and intractability*. W. H. Freeman & Co., New York, New York.

Eva Hajičová, Jan Hajič, Barbora Hladká, Martin Holub, Petr Pajas, Veronika Řezníčková, and Petr Sgall. 2001. The current status of the Prague Dependency Treebank. In *LNCS 2166*, pages 11–20. Springer, Berlin, Germany.

Stephen Hegner. 1996. A family of decidable feature logics which support HPSG-style set and list constructions. In *LACL'96*, Berlin, Germany.

Aravind Joshi and Yves Schabes. 1997. Tree-adjoining grammars. In *Handbook of Formal Languages*, volume 3, pages 69–124. Springer, Berlin, Germany.

Laura Kallmeyer and Sin-Won Yoon. 2004. Tree-local MC-TAG with shared nodes. In *TALN'04*, Fes, Marocco.

Bill Keller. 1993. *Feature logics, infinitary descriptions and grammar*. CSLI Publications, Stanford, California.

Stephan Kepser. 2004. Querying linguistic treebanks with monadic second-order logic in linear time. *Journal of Logic, Language and Information*, 13:457–470.

Marco Kuhlmann and Mathias Möhle. 2007. Mildly context-sensitive dependency languages. In *ACL'07*, pages 160–167, Prague, Czech Republic.

Peter Landweber. 1963. Three theorems on phrase structure grammars of type 1. *Information and Control*, 6(2):131–136.

Martin Lange. 2006. Model checking propositional dynamic logic with all extras. *Journal of Applied Logic*, 4:39–49.

Timm Lichte. 2007. An MCTAG with tuples for coherent constructions in German. In *FG'07*, Dublin, Ireland.

Wolfgang Maier and Anders Søgaard. 2008. Treebanks and mild context-sensitivity. In *FG'08*, Hamburg, Germany.

Marc Moens, Jo Calder, Ewan Klein, Mike Reape, and Henk Zeevat. 1989. Expressing generalizations in unification-based grammar formalisms. In *EACL'89*, Manchester, England.

Joakim Nivre. 2006. Constraints on non-projective dependency parsing. In *EACL'06*, pages 73–80, Trento, Italy.

Stephan Oepen, Kristina Toutanova, Stuart Shieber, Cristopher Manning, Dan Flickinger, and Thorsten Brants. 2002. The LinGO Redwoods Treebank. In *COLING'02*, pages 1253–1257, Taipei, Taiwan.

Carl Pollard and Ivan Sag. 1994. *Head-driven phrase structure grammar*. The University of Chicago Press, Chicago, Illinois.

Owen Rambow and Giorgio Satta. 1992. Formal properties of nonlocality. In *TAG+'92*, Philadelphia, Pennsylvania.

Mike Reape. 1994. A feature value logic with intensionality, nonwellfoundedness and functional and relational dependencies. In *Constraints, language and computation*, pages 77–110. Academic Press, San Fransisco, CA.

Frank Richter. 2004. *A mathematical formalism for linguistic theories with an application in head-driven phrase structure grammar*. Phd thesis (2000), Universität Tübingen, Tübingen, Germany.

Kiril Simov, Petya Osenova, Alexander Simov, and Milen Kouylekov. 2004. Design and implementation of the Bulgarian HPSG-based treebank. *Research on Language and Computation*, 2(4):495–522.

Anders Søgaard and Martin Lange. 2009. Polyadic dynamic logics for HPSG parsing. *Journal of Logic, Language and Information*, 18(2):159–198.

Anders Søgaard, Timm Lichte, and Wolfgang Maier. 2007. On the complexity of linguistically motivated extensions of tree-adjoining grammar. In *RANLP'07*, Borovets, Bulgaria.

Anders Søgaard. 2007. *Complexity, expressivity and logic of linguistic theories*. Ph.D. thesis, University of Copenhagen, Copenhagen, Denmark.

Sean Wallis and Gerald Nelson. 2000. Exploiting fuzzy tree fragment queries in the investigation of parsed corpora. *Literary and Linguistic Computing*, 15(3):339–361.

ISSN 1736-6305 Vol. 4
http://hdl.handle.net/10062/9206

Predictive Features in Semi-Supervised Learning
for Polarity Classification and the Role of Adjectives

Michael Wiegand and **Dietrich Klakow**
Spoken Language Systems
Saarland University
D-66123 Saarbrücken, Germany
{Michael.Wiegand|Dietrich.Klakow}@lsv.uni-saarland.de

Abstract

In opinion mining, there has been only very little work investigating semi-supervised machine learning on document-level polarity classification. We show that semi-supervised learning performs significantly better than supervised learning when only few labeled data are available. Semi-supervised polarity classifiers rely on a predictive feature set. (Semi-)Manually built polarity lexicons are one option but they are expensive to obtain and do not necessarily work in an unknown domain. We show that extracting frequently occurring adjectives & adverbs of an unlabeled set of in-domain documents is an inexpensive alternative which works equally well throughout different domains.

1 Introduction

There has been an increasing interest in *opinion mining* in *natural language processing* in recent years. The highly interactive *Web 2.0* contains a huge amount of opinionated content. Advanced search engines and question answering systems should, therefore, be able to distinguish between factoid and opinionated content. Moreover, the classification of polarity in opinionated utterances or entire documents into positive and negative content, known as *polarity classification*, is another important functionality. This classification task, in particular, relies very much on *polar expressions*, i.e. key words indicating a specific polarity.

In this paper we investigate *whether semi-supervised learning for document-level polarity classification works, what the best possible classifier is, what kind of feature set is most appropriate*, and, in particular, *how adjectives & adverbs perform as features*.

Semi-supervised learning is a class of machine learning methods that makes use of both labeled and unlabeled data for training, usually a small amount of labeled data and a large amount of unlabeled data. A classifier using unlabeled and labeled data can produce better performance than a classifier trained on the labeled data alone. Since labeled data are expensive to produce, semi-supervised learning is an inexpensive alternative to supervised learning.

The primary objective of our work is not to exceed the performance of supervised classifiers given a sufficient amount of labeled data as reported in previous research. Instead, we want to find out whether and how semi-supervised learning can produce better performance than supervised classifiers when only minimal amounts of labeled training data are available. Discriminative feature sets are far more important in this classification task than in supervised learning since there is less reliable information contained in small labeled datasets. We provide evidence that standard feature selection methods from semi-supervised topic classification (i.e. just using frequently occurring words) are not optimal for polarity classification. Polarity lexicons are an alternative option, however, they are expensive to create and their individual effectiveness may vary across different domains. We show that a small list of frequently occurring adjectives & adverbs cheaply extracted from an unlabeled in-domain dataset usually has competitive performance.

We consider polarity classification as a binary classification problem. That is, we assume that each document to be classified is subjective. We neglect the distinction between objective and subjective content since this classification is usually solved independently (Pang and Lee, 2004; Ng et al., 2006). Besides Ng et al. (2006) report that document-level subjectivity detection is a rather easy task compared to (binary) document-level polarity classification.

In our experiments, we primarily use the standard dataset from Pang et al. (2002) comprising movie reviews. To substantiate that our insights carry over to other domains, we also use a multi-domain dataset we created from *Rate-It-All*[1].

To the best of our knowledge, this is the first time that several semi-supervised classifiers are evaluated on this learning task in depth, in particular, in combination with various feature sets.

2 Related Work

Fully supervised polarity classification has been extensively explored. Both discriminative methods, such as *support vector machines (SVMs)*, and generative methods have been applied (Pang et al., 2002; Salvetti et al., 2006). Discriminative methods usually perform significantly better. If sufficient labeled data are available, supervised classifiers offer a reasonable performance even without dedicated feature selection. Various linguistic features, such as part-of-speech information, syntactic dependency information and semantic relations have been shown to increase performance of standard bag-of-words feature sets, (Ng et al., 2006; Gamon, 2004). However, Ng et al. (2006) report that the same improvement can be obtained by using higher order n-grams. We omit advanced linguistic features in this work, since, usually, the gain in performance hardly justifies the computational overhead of these methods (Gamon, 2004).

There are several *domain-independent* polarity lexicons containing important *polar expressions*. The most prominent manual lexicons are *General Inquirer*[2], the subjectivity lexicon from the *MPQA-project* (Wilson et al., 2005), and *Appraisal Groups* (Whitelaw et al., 2005). They have been successfully applied to polarity classification (Kennedy and Inkpen, 2005; Wilson et al., 2005; Whitelaw et al., 2005).

Moreover, several methods have been proposed to automatically induce polarity lexicons. Turney (2002) applies *Pointwise Mutual Information* in order to find similar words to a given list of polar seed words on web data. The polarity scores which are thus computed for each word can be used for a completely unsupervised classification algorithm of documents. A document is assigned the polarity derived from the average of the po-

larity scores of the words occurring within the document. The most recent semi-automatic lexicon is *SentiWordNet* (Esuli and Sebastiani, 2006) which assigns polarity to word senses in WordNet[3] known as *synsets*. The polarity of manually annotated seed synsets is expanded onto the remaining synsets of the WordNet ontology by measuring the overlap between their respective glosses.

The only works dealing with semi-supervised learning on this classification task we know of are Beineke et al. (2004) who combine Turney's web mining approach with evidence from labeled training data, and Aue and Gamon (2005) who focus on domain adaptation. Neither different algorithms nor feature sets are compared in these works.

In this paper, we look into adjectives & adverbs as features in detail. Pang et al. (2002) use feature sets exclusively comprising adjectives for supervised polarity classification but report performance to be worse than a standard bag-of-words representation. However, Ng et al. (2006) increase performance significantly by adding to a standard feature set higher order n-grams in which adjectives are replaced by their in-domain polarity which has been established via manual annotation.

3 Semi-Supervised Methods

Throughout the next sections, we adhere to the following notation: A document is denoted by $\vec{x}_i$. In total, there are N documents encompassing L labeled and U unlabeled documents. The label of an individual document $\vec{x}_i$ is $y_i \in \{-1, 1\}$. We tested three popular state-of-the-art semi-supervised classifiers in our experiments: *expectation maximization algorithm (EM)*, *transductive support vector machines (TSVMs)*, and *spectral graph transduction (SGT)*.

We use EM for a multinomial Naive Bayes classifier, similar to EM-λ proposed in Nigam et al. (2000). Since in all datasets we use the distribution of the classes is uniform, we omit the estimation of the class prior.

TSVMs use an extended objective function of SVMs: $OF_{tsvm} = \frac{1}{2}\|\vec{w}\|^2 + C\sum_{i=0}^{L}\xi_i + C^*\sum_{j=0}^{U}\xi_j^*$ which includes in addition to a weight vector $\vec{w}$, a regularizer C and a set of slack variables ξ_i for all labeled instances, an extra regularizer C^* and an extra set of *slack variables* ξ_j^*

---

[1] http://www.rateitall.com

[2] http://www.wjh.harvard.edu/~inquirer

[3] http://wordnet.princeton.edu

for unlabeled instances. A full account of the optimization is given in Joachims (1999).

In SGT (Joachims, 2003), all documents $\vec{x}_i$ of a collection (i.e. labeled and unlabeled) are represented as a symmetrized and similarity-weighted k nearest-neighbor (knn) graph G. Its adjacency matrix is defined as $A = A' + A'^T$ where

$$A'_{ij} = \begin{cases} \frac{sim(\vec{x}_i, \vec{x}_j)}{\sum_{\vec{x}_k \in knn(\vec{x}_i)} sim(\vec{x}_i, \vec{x}_k)} & \text{if } \vec{x}_j \in knn(\vec{x}_i) \\ 0 & \text{else} \end{cases} \quad (1)$$

and $sim(\cdot, \cdot)$ is any common similarity function. The graph G is decomposed into its spectrum. For this, the smallest 2 to $d + 1$ eigenvalues and eigenvectors of the normalized Laplacian $L = B^{-1}(B - A)$ where B is the diagonal degree matrix with $B_{ii} = \sum_j A_{ij}$ are computed. The spectrum is used for minimizing the normalized graph cut: $\min_{\forall y_i} \frac{cut(G^+, G^-)}{|\{i:y_i=1\}||\{i:y_i=-1\}|}$ where G^+ and G^- denote the set of positive and negative classified vertices in the graph. The cut-value $cut(G^+, G^-) = \sum_{i \in G^+} \sum_{j \in G^-} A_{ij}$ is the sum of the edge-weights of a cut partitioning the graph into two clusters.

4 The Different Feature Sets

The task of feature selection is to remove features that are irrelevant or noisy for a particular classification task. The reduction of these features does not only result in an increase in efficiency but may also improve the accuracy of a classifier.

4.1 Term Frequency Cut-off

The simplest feature selection method is using a term-frequency cut-off. The rationale behind this is that rarely observed terms do not contribute to a good classifier. Usually, this selection method is combined with stop-word removal[4]. Very frequently occurring terms, in particular function words, are not considered to be predictive for a particular class label, since they are uniformly distributed throughout all classes.

4.2 Polarity Lexicons

In our experiments we use Appraisal Groups (AG), General Inquirer (GI), the subjectivity lexicon from the *MPQA project* (MPQA), and SentiWordNet (SWN). From GI we use all polar expressions and from AG we only consider *orientation words* that are not neutral (Whitelaw et al., 2005). From MPQA, we use both *weak* and *strong* subjective words (Wilson et al., 2005) with either positive or negative prior polarity[5].

SentiWordNet (SWN) does not specify the polarity of individual words but synsets (i.e. senses of words). The database provides a non-negative polarity score $senseScore(s, p)$ for each synset s and polarity $p \in \{+, -\}$. Neutral polarity strength is denoted by 0. Usually, words have different senses associated with them. There are even words which have both senses with positive and negative polarity. Therefore, most words have various polarity scores associated with them. Our goal is to derive a unique polarity for each word with a corresponding score denoting its strength. We use the unique scores in order to find a subset of SWN with highly polar expressions. We estimate the strength of a word w and a polarity p, i.e. $wordScore(w, p)$, by: $wordScore(w, p) = \max_s [senseScore(s, p)]$ where $s \in synsets(w)$. The final polarity of the word, i.e. $pol(w)$, is the polarity with the maximum polarity score: $pol(w) = \arg\max_p [wordScore(w, p)]$. The unique score denoting the polarity strength is defined as: $strength(w) = \max_p [wordScore(w, p)]$. By using only the subset of SWN instead of the total (we chose all words with $strength(w) \geq 0.5$), we increased the accuracy of the semi-supervised classifiers by approximately 1.5% on average. We reduced the size of the initial version by 70% which substantially increased the efficiency of model learning. A subset of SWN based on taking the average rather than taking the maximum produced slightly worse results.

4.3 Adjectives & Adverbs

Adjectives, such as *superb* or *poor*, are usually regarded as very predictive words for polarity classification. The impact on semi-supervised learning has not yet been examined. Even if this feature set is too small for supervised learning (Pang et al., 2002; Salvetti et al., 2006), it might still be effective in semi-supervised learning. In contrast to supervised learning, large feature sets which are noisy cannot be compensated by the information contained in many labeled documents. Smaller

---

[4]We use a publicly available list of stopwords:
`http://www.dcs.gla.ac.uk/idom/`
`ir_resources/linguistic_utils/stop_words`

[5]Note that just focusing on the strong entries resulted in a decrease in performance.

Feature Set	Type	#Words
Top n words	statistical selection	3000
Top n non-stopwords	statistical selection	2000
Top n adjectives & adverbs	stat. & linguistic select.	**600**
Appraisal Groups (AG)	manual polarity lexicon	2014
General Inquirer (GI)	manual polarity lexicon	2882
Subjectivity Lexicon (MPQA)	manual polarity lexicon	4615
SentiWordNet (SWN)	semi-automatic pol. lex.	11366

Table 1: Optimal size of the different feature sets.

but more predictive feature sets are preferable. We use feature sets of frequently occurring adjectives & adverbs in our document collection. The feature sets are extracted using C&C part-of-speech tagger[6]. After manually annotating the 600 most frequent stemmed adjectives & adverbs from the movie domain dataset (Pang et al., 2002), we estimate that more than 20% of the expressions are ambiguous with regard to part of speech[7]. Thus, our selection method if combined with stemming also captures some polar verbs and nouns. By looking at the list of extracted adjectives & adverbs from other domains, we observed that unlike current polarity lexicons this method allows both some colloquial expressions, such as *crappy*, and highly domain-dependent polar expressions, such as *creamy* or *crunchy* from the food domain, to be detected.

4.4 Optimal Feature Size

Table 1 lists the optimal size[8] of the different feature sets we used in our experiments[9]. Note that the subset selection for the polarity lexicons has been explained in Section 4.2. By far, the smallest feature set are adjectives & adverbs; the largest feature set is SWN.

5 Experiments

The results of *all* our experiments below are reported on the basis of 20 randomized partitionings. Each partitioning comprises a labeled dataset of varying length for training, and another dataset

comprising 1000 documents used as unlabeled training data and test data[10]. We also experimented with larger amounts of unlabeled data but did not measure any improvement in performance. The labeled training data and the test data are always mutually exclusive. We report the results of experiments carried out on the movie review database (Pang et al., 2002) (benchmark dataset) and the results of cross-domain experiments using reviews from *Rate-It-All*. The movie dataset comprises 2000 reviews whereas for the other domains we could only acquire 1800 documents per domain. All datasets are balanced. We report statistical significance on the basis of a paired t-test using 0.05 as the significance level. We only state the results of the optimally sized feature sets (see Section 4.4). Since there is no difference in performance between the optimally sized feature set with the most frequent words and the most frequent non-stopwords, we only evaluated the latter feature set. We used *SVMLight*[11] for SVMs and TSVMs and *SGTLight*[12] for SGT. Feature vectors consist of tf-idf weighted words appearing in the pre-defined feature set normalized by document length. This produced best results throughout our experiments. Further modifications of the standard configuration of *SVMLight* (e.g. changing regularization parameters) did not improve performance. We also confirm the results from Aue and Gamon (2005) where further modifications on EM, i.e. by weighting the unlabeled data[13], did not improve performance. For *SGTLight* we mainly adhered to the standard configuration (as discussed in Joachims (2003)). Since we had no development data for optimizing the only task-sensitive parameter k we simply took the optimized value for the only text classification corpus tested in Joachims (2003) (i.e. *Reuters collection*). The current choice (i.e. $k = 800$) should thus guarantee a fairly unbiased setting. EM is smoothed by absolute discounting (Zhai and Lafferty, 2001). All classifiers are run with a reasonable parameter setting but we did not attempt to tune the parameters to the current task. We also stem the entire text since some polarity lexicons we use also include lemmas of inflectional words,

---

[6]http://svn.ask.it.usyd.edu.au/trac/candc

[7]e.g. *interesting* (adj) and *interests* (noun) are both reduced to *interest*

[8]The optimal size was determined by testing all semi-supervised algorithms trained on various amounts of labeled documents and 1000 unlabeled documents.

[9]Due to the stemming we applied some of the entries in the original polarity lexicons were conflated.

---

[10]It is not uncommon to use test data as unlabeled training data in semi-supervised learning (Aue and Gamon, 2005; Joachims, 1999; Joachims, 2003).

[11]http://svmlight.joachims.org

[12]http://sgt.joachims.org

[13]Note that this is similar to regularization in TSVMs.

SWN	AG	GI	MPQA	GI+Turney
54.20	54.45	59.90	61.95	63.30

Table 2: Accuracy of unsupervised algorithm using different polarity lexicons (movie domain): *best classifier is GI+Turney.*

such as nouns and verbs. Moreover, stemming has considerable advantages for the feature set comprising adjectives & adverbs (see discussion in Section 4.3). In-domain feature sets (i.e. frequent non-stopwords and frequent adjectives & adverbs) are obtained by considering the entire dataset of a particular domain.

5.1 Experiments on the Movie Domain

5.1.1 Unsupervised Algorithms using Different Polarity Lexicons

Before comparing the different polarity lexicons in the context of semi-supervised learning, we shortly display their performance using a completely unsupervised algorithm. A test document is assigned the polarity with the majority of polar expressions in that document. This experiment should give an idea of the intrinsic predictiveness of the polarity lexicons. Table 2 lists the results. Though all lexicons perform significantly better than the random baseline (i.e. 50%), the best performance of MPQA with 61.95 is still very low.

We also evaluated an extension GI+Turney which weights the polar expressions in GI according to the association scores to a very small number of manually selected highly polar seed words, such as *excellent* or *poor* (Turney and Littman, 2003)[14]. The scores for entries in GI are calculated in the same way as the scores for words in the web-based lexicon induction method using *Pointwise Mutual Information* (Turney, 2002). The improvement is significant, even though the scores have been gained by domain-independent web-data.

In the following, we show that very small amounts of labeled in-domain documents can produce significantly better results using semi-supervised learning.

5.1.2 Comparison of the Different Polarity Lexicons with Other Feature Sets

Table 3 displays the performance of different classifiers on different feature sets. On average, polar-

---

[14]Unfortunately, currently only the weights for entries of GI were available to us.

ity lexicons perform significantly better than the top 2000 non-stopwords. The same holds for an inexpensive small feature set of in-domain adjectives & adverbs. On EM, we achieved even the best performance with the latter feature set. The best performing feature set for the movie dataset is AG. With the exception of EM, it is significantly better than any other feature set using semi-supervised learning.

5.1.3 Complex Feature Sets that Do Not Improve Performance

Contrary to our expectations, adding explicit polarity information to the feature set by including the number of positive and negative polar expressions according to the pertaining polarity lexicon did not improve performance. We assume that the meaning of these polar expressions, occasionally even their polarity, varies across different contexts, therefore a unique polarity in the polarity lexicons may not always be correct.

We also experimented with more expressive features by adding bigrams with one token being either a polar expression, an adjective or an adverb. On semi-supervised learning we did not measure any increase in performance. We assume that this is due to data-sparseness. Similar to Ng et al. (2006), we observed an increase in performance by approximately 2% on supervised classifiers (when more than 400 labeled documents are used).

5.1.4 Semi-Supervised Classifiers

We compared all different learning algorithms using their respective best feature sets. Figure 1 displays the results. All semi-supervised algorithms are better than the strict supervised baseline (i.e. SVMs trained on AG) on small amounts of labeled data. EM gets worse than SVMs trained on AG when more than 400 labeled documents are used, but still outperforms SVMs trained on top 2000 non-stopwords when less than 700 labeled documents are used. TSVMs and SGT, on the other hand, constantly perform better than SVMs. Clearly, the best classifier is SGT which, with the exception of 1000 labeled data, is always significantly better than any other classifier tested. At approximately 200 labeled documents, SGT already performs as well as SVMs trained on a standard feature set (i.e. top 2000 non-stopwords) using 1000 labeled documents. The best supervised performance at 80.6% is similar to the one pre-

	20 Labeled Documents						200 Labeled Documents					
	Top 2000	**SWN**	**MPQA**	**GI**	**AG**	**Adj**	**Top 2000**	**SWN**	**MPQA**	**GI**	**AG**	**Adj**
SVM	59.81	61.24	*63.07*	61.48	62.22	61.44	72.05	74.93	74.35	72.72	*75.88*	73.14
EM	67.50	67.31	68.73	66.63	69.44	*69.54*	73.44	76.46	75.02	73.80	75.46	*77.32*
TSVM	64.57	67.04	66.58	65.53	*68.87*	68.37	73.48	76.80	75.73	74.72	*77.89*	75.12
SGT	62.60	67.39	67.10	66.14	***70.28***	66.58	70.91	77.55	77.78	75.12	***80.21***	76.90

Table 3: Accuracy of different classifiers on different feature sets using 20 and 200 labeled documents (movie domain): *best configuration is SGT+AG.*

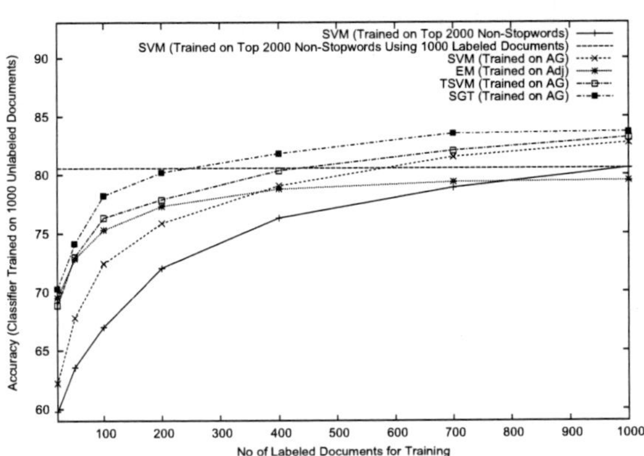

Figure 1: Performance of different learning algorithms on the best respective feature set (movie domain): *SGT+AG save 800 labeled documents in comparison to SVM+Top 2000 trained on 1000 labeled documents.*

sented in Pang et al. (2002). They report 81.4% with their most similar configuration using 1400 labeled documents and training on 2633 words. Just using 20 labeled documents offers an increase by 7% in performance in comparison to the best unsupervised classifier (i.e. GI+Turney displayed in Table 2).

5.2 Cross-Domain Experiments

In order to validate our findings from Section 5.1, we extracted reviews from *Rate-It-All*. In particular, we want to know whether semi-supervised learning works there as well, whether SGT outperforms other classifiers, whether polarity lexicons improve performance, and whether adjectives and adverbs produce classifiers competitive to average polarity lexicons. We do not attempt to carry out detailed domain studies which would be beyond the scope of this section. We chose four domains from the list of *Topic Categories* of the website which we thought are very different from

the movie domain and for which we could extract sufficient training data. We took *Computer & Internet (computer)*, *Products (products)*, *Sports & Recreation (sports)* and *Travel, Food, & Culture (travel)*. We follow the method from Blitzer et al. (2007) to infer the polarity of the reviews. Ratings with less than 3 stars are considered negative reviews whereas ratings with more than 3 stars are positive reviews. We decided not to consider *mixed* reviews, i.e. reviews rated with 3 stars. In general, we found far fewer mixed reviews[15]. On those domains which provided a reasonable amount of data, our initial supervised learning experiments showed that mixed polarity can only be poorly distinguished from definite polarity[16]. Manual inspection of a random sample of reviews also showed that a great part of these documents are actually negative reviews. We only extracted reviews having at least 3 sentences in order to rule out too fragmentary instances. We did not filter out mislabeled entries though we are aware of their presence in our set.

Table 4 lists the average performance of all classifiers on different feature sets using 20 labeled documents. For the sake of completeness we also include the results from the movie domain. There is no significant difference among the feature sets using SVMs, but there is a difference between top 2000 non-stopwords and the remaining feature sets on semi-supervised classification (with the exception of EM). All polarity lexicons and adjectives & adverbs perform significantly better than top 2000 non-stopwords using TSVMs and SGT. On average, the performance of EM is significantly worse than any of the other semi-supervised classifiers. The results of TSVMs

---

[15]In the *computer* domain, for example, there were only approximately 200 reviews.

[16]A binary classifier trained on 900 mixed and 900 definite polar reviews from the *travel* domain only produced an accuracy of 63.1% on a three fold crossvalidation and the best feature set.

are similar with our previous observations on the benchmark dataset. SGT is the best performing classifier (in particular in combination with adjectives).

Table 5 shows the performance on the individual domains and feature sets using 20 labeled documents on SGT. On average, semi-supervised learning improves performance significantly over supervised learning. On some domains (e.g. *computer*) using a standard feature set (i.e. using top 2000 non-stopwords in the collection) produces good results. However, in some other domains, such as *travel*, there is no improvement whatsoever. Polarity lexicons can perform significantly better than top 2000 non-stopwords (e.g. GI on *travel* or, most notably, AG on *movie*) but there can also be a domain where they are actually worse than the standard feature set (e.g. the *sports* domain). There is no polarity lexicon which consistently outperforms all other polarity lexicons on all domains. A feature set comprising in-domain adjectives & adverbs, however, is more robust: Firstly, it never performs worse than the standard feature set. Secondly, it is never significantly worse than the average performance of polarity lexicons and, thirdly, there might be some domain, such as *sports*, where it significantly outperforms any other feature set. Considering the low effort to generate such a feature set should make it particularly attractive.

Figure 2 displays the performance of SGT on various feature sets averaged over all domains using various amounts of labeled training data. SGT only significantly outperforms SVMs when less than 200 labeled documents are used. Therefore, we restricted the figure to the range ending at that size. The lower performance of the averaged results must be due to some properties of the *Rate-It-All* data (either noise or the dataset is more difficult) since the individual performance of the semi-supervised classifiers on the movie domain was significantly better. Despite the lower performance, we can still use the averaged results to characterize the relation between the different feature sets in semi-supervised learning. Both polarity lexicons and adjectives & adverbs are significantly better than top 2000 non-stopwords and there is no significant difference between polarity lexicons and adjectives & adverbs.

All these results support both the competitiveness of adjective & adverbs and the robustness

of SGT. Given the best feature set in a particular domain, the average gain in improvement compared to SVMs only trained on 20 labeled documents using top 2000 non-stopwords is approx. 8.5% when SGT is used. This is a clear indication that semi-supervised learning for polarity classification works across all domains when only tiny amounts of labeled data are used.

	Top 2000	SWN	MPQA	GI	AG	Adj
SVM	**61.17**	61.13	60.81	**61.17**	60.77	60.68
EM	64.41	65.09	64.08	63.88	65.10	**65.22**
TSVM	63.87	66.79	66.51	66.26	65.98	**67.20**
SGT	64.60	66.92	67.69	67.83	67.22	**68.30**

Table 4: Average accuracy of different semi-supervised classifiers across all domains using different feature sets (trained on 20 labeled documents & 1000 unlabeled documents): *best configuration is SGT+Adj*.

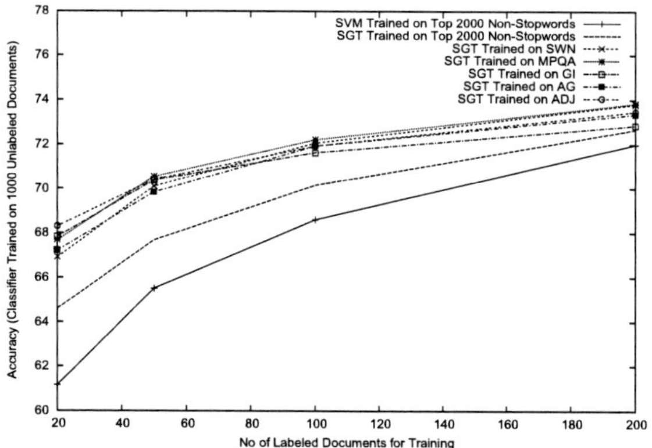

Figure 2: SGT trained on different amounts of labeled data and different feature sets averaged over all domains (1000 unlabeled documents): *polarity lexicons and Adj are very similar among each other and significantly better than top 2000 non-stopwords.*

6 Conclusion

In this paper we have shown that semi-supervised learning can be successfully applied to document-level polarity classification. Significant improvement over supervised classification can be achieved across all domains when less than 200 labeled documents are available. On the movie domain we even achieved improved performance

	SVM	SGT					
Domain	**Top 2000**	**Top 2000**	**SWN**	**MPQA**	**GI**	**AG**	**Adj**
computer	67.75	73.88	*75.77*	74.77	73.95	73.74	74.51
products	62.38	67.20	68.45	68.40	*69.84*	68.44	68.79
sports	57.96	61.83	57.57	59.80	60.62	58.53	*63.55*
travel	57.95	57.48	65.44	68.37	*68.62*	65.09	68.05
movies	59.81	62.60	67.39	67.10	66.14	*70.28*	66.58
average	61.17	64.60	66.92	67.69	67.83	67.22	**68.30**

Table 5: Accuracy of SGT on different domains using different feature sets (trained on 20 labeled documents & 1000 unlabeled documents): *on an individual domain either some polarity lexicon or Adj is the best feature set; on average Adj is the best feature set.*

across all amounts of labeled training data. SGT is the classifier which produces significantly better results than all other semi-supervised classifiers used in our experiments. On average, polarity lexicons and adjectives & adverbs perform better than just using frequent in-domain non-stopwords. Adjectives & adverbs are less expensive to obtain and more robust throughout different domains.

Acknowledgements

The authors would like to thank Grzegorz Chrupała, Sabrina Wilske and Theresa Wilson for interesting discussions. We, in particular, thank Stefan Kazalski for pre-processing the web documents from *Rate-It-All*. Michael Wiegand was funded by the German research council DFG through the International Research Training Group between Saarland University and University of Edinburgh.

References

A. Aue and M. Gamon. 2005. Customizing Sentiment Classifiers to New Domains: a Case Study. In *Proc. of RANLP*.

P. Beineke, T. Hastie, and S. Vaithyanathan. 2004. The Sentimental Factor: Improving Review Classification via Human-Provided Information. In *Proc. of ACL*.

J. Blitzer, M. Dredze, and F. Pereira. 2007. Biographies, Bollywood, Boom-boxes and Blenders: Domain Adaptation for Sentiment Classification. In *Proc. of ACL*.

A. Esuli and F. Sebastiani. 2006. SentiWordNet: A Publicly Available Lexical Resource for Opinion Mining. In *Proc. of LREC*.

M. Gamon. 2004. Sentiment Classification on Customer Feedback Data: Noisy Data, Large Feature Vectors, and the Role of Linguistic Analysis. In *Proc. of COLING*.

T. Joachims. 1999. Transductive Inference for Text Classification Using Support Vector Machines. In *Proc. of ICML*.

T. Joachims. 2003. Transductive Learning via Spectral Graph Partitioning. In *Proc. of ICML*.

A. Kennedy and D. Inkpen. 2005. Sentiment Classification of Movie Reviews Using Contextual Valence Shifters. In *Workshop on the Analysis of Formal and Informal Information Exchang during Negotiations*.

V. Ng, S. Dasgupta, and S. M. Niaz Arifin. 2006. Examining the Role of Linguistic Knowledge Sources in the Automatic Identification and Classification of Reviews. In *Proc. of ACL*.

K. Nigam, A. McCallum, S. Thrun, and T. Mitchell. 2000. Text Classification from Labeled and Unlabeled Documents Using EM. *Machine Learning*.

B. Pang and L. Lee. 2004. A Sentimental Education: Sentiment Analysis Using Subjectivity Summarization Based on Miminum Cuts. In *Proc. of ACL*.

B. Pang, L. Lee, and S. Vaithyanathan. 2002. Thumbs up? Sentiment Classification Using Machine Learning Techniques. In *Proc. of EMNLP*.

F. Salvetti, C. Reichenbach, and S. Lewis. 2006. Opinion Polarity Identification of Movie Reviews. In J. Shanahan, Y. Qu, and J. Wiebe, editors, *Computing Attitude and Affect in Text: Theory and Applications*. Springer-Verlag.

P. Turney and M. Littman. 2003. Measuring Praise and Criticism: Inference of Semantic Orientation from Association. In *Proc. of TOIS*.

P. Turney. 2002. Thumbs up or Thumbs down?: Semantic Orientation Applied to Unsupervised Classification of Reviews. In *Proc. of ACL*.

C. Whitelaw, N. Garg, and S. Argamon. 2005. Using Appraisal Groups for Sentiment Analysis. In *Proc. of CIKM*.

T. Wilson, J. Wiebe, and P. Hoffmann. 2005. Recognizing Contextual Polarity in Phrase-level Sentiment Analysis. In *Proc. of HLT/EMNLP*.

C. Zhai and J. Lafferty. 2001. A Study of Smoothing Methods for Language Models Applied to Information Retrieval. In *Proc. of SIGIR*.

ISSN 1736-6305 Vol. 4
http://hdl.handle.net/10062/9206

An Efficient Double Complementation Algorithm for Superposition-Based Finite-State Morphology

Anssi Yli-Jyrä
Department of General Linguistics
HFST Research Group
University of Helsinki
Finland
`anssi.yli-jyra helsinki.fi`

Abstract

This paper presents an *efficient compilation algorithm* that is several orders of magnitude faster than a standard method for context restriction rules. The new algorithm combines even hundreds of thousands of rules in parallel when the alphabet is large but the resulting automaton is sparse. The method opens new possibilities for representation of context-dependent lexical entries and the related processes. This is demonstrated by encoding complete HunSpell dictionaries as a single context restriction rule whose center placeholder in contexts is replaced with a new operation, called *underline operation*. The approach gives rise to new *superposition-based* context-dependent lexicon formalisms and new methods for on-demand compilation and composition of two-level morphology.

1 Introduction

The use of the context restriction rule of two-level morphology (Koskenniemi, 1983) has traditionally been limited to relatively simple phonological rules. The purpose of this paper is to make this operation more widely applicable in finite-state morphology, by improving its compilation methods and by developing new ways to encode morphological processes with this operation.

1.1 Prior Art

Compilation of compound context restrictions is a problem that has inspired a series related solutions:

- Kaplan and Kay's method (Karttunen et al., 1987; Kaplan and Kay, 1994) requires that the occurrences of the center in each string are bracketed. Then it applies double complementation (if-then idioms) to restrict the context of each bracket. The method needs separate brackets for each context.

- A related approach (Grimley-Evans et al., 1996; Kiraz, 1997; Kiraz, 2000) handles similar single-tuple rules directly with double complementation, being a special case a star-free compilation method of Yli-Jyrä (2003).

- Yli-Jyrä (2003) uses star-free regular operations to show that the context restriction rule with overlapping multi-tuple centers is definable in first-order predicate logic.

- Yli-Jyrä and Koskenniemi (2004; 2006) and Hulden (2009) use first-order quantification over substrings in order to express the same semantics more abstractly and efficiently.

- Additional bracketing can express disjoint but not necessarily contiguous centers (Yli-Jyrä, 2008a; Yli-Jyrä, 2008b). Kiraz (2000) uses it with contiguous centers.

The prior art suggests that complementation is an essential part of context restriction whereas bracketing has a supplementary role.

1.2 The Problem

Complementation can be really difficult to implement efficiently due to its transition complexity. This is illustrated in Fig. 1.

Automaton of Fig. 1(a) is a deterministic acceptor for the language $(a|b)^* \diamond^* a(a|c)^*$, and automaton of Fig. 1(b) accepts its complement

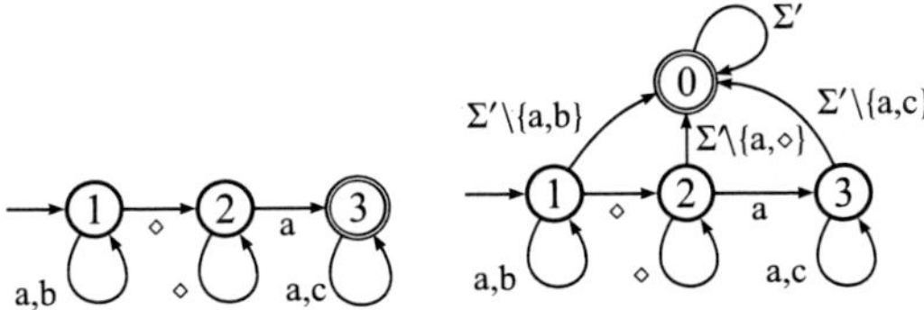

Figure 1: (a) A DFA and (b) its complement.

with respect to the universal language Σ'^* where $a, b, c, \diamond \in \Sigma'$. By complementation, only one state is added, but the number of transitions grows significantly. With an alphabet of *e.g.* 500 symbols and a deterministic automaton with 2 million states, we can easily end up with an automaton with 1 billion (10^9) transitions. Such a blow-up is not only a problem for complementation itself but also for further processing.

Finding an efficient compilation method for context restrictions is particularly important because it would pave the way for a similar efficient solution for an even more general-purpose operation, *generalized restriction (GR)* (Yli-Jyrä and Koskenniemi, 2004; Yli-Jyrä, 2008a). GR admits context restriction as one of its special cases. Other interesting uses of the GR operation include:

- conventional, partition-based and generalized two-level grammars (Silfverberg and Lindén, 2009; Barthélemy, 2007b; Yli-Jyrä and Koskenniemi, 2006; Yli-Jyrä, 2008a)

- replace rules (Yli-Jyrä, 2008b) and tree linearization (Barthélemy, 2007a).

The combinatorial properties of the GR operation are parallel to a first-order predicate logic (Hulden, 2009). Thanks to these combinatorial properties, the double-arrow rules of two-level morphology (Karttunen, 1991) and some other rules can be reduced into context-restriction rules. This underlines the importance of the efficient compilation method for context restriction rules.

1.3 The Contributions of This Paper

The first significant contribution of this paper is an algorithm that compiles context restriction rules much more efficiently than the prior approaches to the underlying double complementation. The new algorithm has been inserted to a branch of SFST code base (Schmid, 2005) and it is in the process of migrating from there to the HFST API and the HFST family of tools (Koskenniemi and

Yli-Jyrä, 2009; Lindén et al., 2009). The algorithm can be used to compile also other two-level operations such as prohibition and coercion rules. Furthermore, the algorithm can be embedded into a new operation, *superposing composition*. This operation compiles and composes the lexicon and the two-level grammar in parallel.

The second significant contribution of the current paper is to initially demonstrate that large context restrictions can be used to address a wide range of context-dependent morphological processes. In particular, we will show that it can be used for

- synthesis of cyclic lexicons

- context-dependent concatenation and truncation for prefixing and suffixing

- context-dependent circumfixing (with aid of a postprocessing step).

Moreover, we have reasons to believe that this list could be extended with a number of other morphological and phonological processes. In particular, we propose *underlined expressions and languages* as a convenient means for representing context-dependent processes through co-incidences and superposition. The current algorithm and other efficient implementations for such underlined languages give rise to *superposition-based* lexicon formalisms that are more general than concatenation-based LEXC (Karttunen, 1993) and truncation/concatenation-based Hun-Spell (Németh et al., 2004).

1.4 The Structure of the Paper

The paper is structured as follows: The definitions and notations are given in Section 2. Section 3 motivates the aimed semantics, simplifies its representation and generalizes it to capture a variety of rules. Section 4 presents the new algorithm that implements this semantics procedurally. Section 5 presents applications of the new algorithm to morphological processes. Section 6 evaluates the efficiency using tiny examples and huge HunSpell dictionaries, and then discusses further optimizations and generalizations. The paper is concluded by Section 7.

2 Preliminaries

Denote the empty language with $\emptyset$ and the empty string with ϵ. If x is string, the set $\{x\}$ is denoted alternatively with x. Let A and B be regular languages and let k be a positive integer. Concatenation AB, intersection $A \cap B$, union $A \cup B$, complement $\overline{A}$, asymmetric difference $A \backslash B$, Kleene's closure A^* and bounded iteration $A^{\leq k}$ are defined as usual.

A deterministic finite automaton (DFA) is a tuple (A, Q, i, F, δ) where A is the *finite input alphabet*, Q is the *finite set of states*, $i \in Q$ is the *initial state*, $F \subseteq Q$ is the *set of final states*, $\delta : Q \times A \rightarrow Q$ is the *transition relation*. Extended transition relation $\hat{\delta} : Q \times A^* \rightarrow Q$ is defined in such a way that $\hat{\delta}(q, \epsilon) = q$ and $\hat{\delta}(q, aw) = \hat{\delta}(\hat{\delta}(q, a), w)$ for all $q \in Q$, $a \in \Sigma$ and $w \in \Sigma^*$. The automaton *accepts* a string $w \in \Sigma^*$ if and only if $\hat{\delta}(i, w) \in F$. The language recognized by the automaton is the set $\{w | \hat{\delta}(i, w) \in F\}$.

Two-level systems (Koskenniemi, 1983; Kiraz, 2000) and their rules describe binary or n-ary regular same-length relations between strings. However, these systems and their rules can be viewed also as descriptions of languages over a tuple alphabet. In this paper, two-level rules describe languages over a set of tuples, Σ. For related conventions and the definitions of Id, Range, Domain, and composition $\circ$, see (Kaplan and Kay, 1994).

2.1 Context Restriction

A *(compound) context restriction (CR)* rule (Koskenniemi, 1983; Kaplan and Kay, 1994) is conventionally written in the form

$$X \Rightarrow \#L_1 \_ R_1 \#, \ldots, \#L_n \_ R_n \#. \tag{1}$$

where the *center* X and the left and right parts $L_i, ..., L_n, R_1, ..., R_n$ of *contexts* are regular languages over a known alphabet Σ. It is reasonable to assume that $\epsilon \notin X$. For strings $v, y \in \Sigma^*$, denote condition $v \in L_i \wedge y \in R_i$ by expression $v\_y \in L_i\_R_i$. The semantics of the CR rule is a set of strings given by

$$\{w | w \in \Sigma^* \wedge (\forall v \in \Sigma^*)(\forall x \in X)(\forall y \in \Sigma^*)$$
$$w \neq vxy \vee (\exists L_i\_R_i)v\_y \in L_i\_R_i\}.$$

2.2 Generalized Restriction

Generalized restriction (GR) (Yli-Jyrä, 2008a) is an operation whose operands consist of the universal language Σ^*, a set of markers M, a language $W \subseteq \Sigma^*(M\Sigma^*)^{\leq k}$ and a language $W' \subseteq (\Sigma \cup M)^*$. Set M is such that $M \cap \Sigma = \emptyset$ and it contains, conventionally, symbols $\diamond, \diamond_1, \diamond_2, \ldots$ that are called

diamonds. Languages W and W' are called *generalized precondition* and *generalized postcondition*, respectively. The relationship between the syntax and the semantics of GR is defined by equation

$$[W \overset{\Sigma, k, M}{\Longrightarrow} W'] = [W \overset{M}{\Longrightarrow} W'] = \Sigma^* \backslash h_M(W \backslash W')$$

where $h_M : (\Sigma \cup M)^* \rightarrow \Sigma$ is a morphism that deletes the markers from strings.

3 The Aimed Semantics

The GR operation (Yli-Jyrä and Koskenniemi, 2006) yields the semantics of a CR rule by

$$[X \Rightarrow \#L_1 \_ R_1 \#, \ldots, \#L_n \_ R_n \#]$$
$$= [\Sigma^* \diamond X \diamond \Sigma^* \overset{M}{\Longrightarrow} \cup_{i=1}^n L_i \diamond X \diamond R_i] \tag{2}$$
$$= \Sigma^* \backslash h_M((\Sigma^* \diamond X \diamond \Sigma^*) \backslash (\cup_{i=1}^n L_i \diamond X \diamond R_i)). \tag{3}$$

While formula (2) looks elegant, it actually employs, in (3), complementation of rather complex languages. In the following, we will simplify the representation of the centers and contexts and arrive at formula (13) that captures the meaning of a CR rule set. After this, we will add to this rule set two special CR rules that account for a restricted universe and prohibition rules.

3.1 Simplifications

3.1.1 Decomposition of Generalized Centers

CR rule centers are, in general, subsets of Σ^+ rather than subsets of Σ. In the GR semantics, CR rules can be reduced to a GR of more limited kind with a decomposition technique.[1] The technique expresses that every symbol in the restricted strings must have separately a valid context. By decomposition, (2) gives

$$[\Sigma^* f(X) \Sigma^* \overset{M}{\Longrightarrow} \cup_{i=1}^n L_i \, g(X) \, R_i]. \tag{4}$$

employs two functions $f, g : \Sigma^+ \rightarrow \Sigma^* \diamond^* \Sigma^+$, that are given by

$$f(x) = h_M^{-1}(x) \cap \Sigma^* \diamond \Sigma^+ \tag{5}$$
$$g(x) = h_M^{-1}(x) \cap \Sigma^* \diamond^* \Sigma^+. \tag{6}$$

3.1.2 Combining Sets of Rules

In a set of context restriction rules, separate rules may induce right arrow conflicts. The right-arrow conflicts of two (or more) context restrictions can

---

[1] For related techniques, see (Yli-Jyrä and Koskenniemi, 2006; Yli-Jyrä, 2008a).

be resolved using the *coherent intersection operation* ⋒ (Yli-Jyrä, 2008a) of generalized restrictions:

$$[W \overset{M}{\Longrightarrow} W'] \barwedge [U \overset{M}{\Rightarrow} U'] \qquad (7)$$

$$= [(W \cup U) \overset{M}{\Rightarrow} ((W \cap W') \cup (U \cap U'))]. \qquad (8)$$

The same operation can be used to combine context restrictions that are not in conflict. Thus, coherent intersection operation combines arbitrary many context restrictions and resolves also any right-arrow conflicts. This gives equation

$$\overset{m}{\underset{r=1}{\barwedge}} [X_r \;=>\; \#L_{r,1}\_R_{r,1}\#, \ldots, \#L_{r,n_r}\_R_{r,n_r}\#]$$

$$= [\cup_{r=1}^{m} \Sigma^* f(X_r) \Sigma^* \overset{M}{\Rightarrow} \cup_{r=1}^{m} \cup_{i=1}^{n_r} L_{r,i}\, g(X_r)\, R_{r,i}]. \qquad (9)$$

3.1.3 Constrained Center Alphabet

Let $S \subseteq \Sigma$ be the alphabet of centers of rules in such a way that $\cup_{r=1}^{m} X_r \subseteq S^*$. In fact, traditional two-level grammars admit $S = \cup_{r=1}^{m} X_r$. Even when $\cup_{r=1}^{m} X_r \not\subset \Sigma$, it is reasonable to assume that $S \subseteq \cup_{r=1}^{m} X_r$. From this, it follows that $\Sigma^* \diamond S \Sigma^* = \cup_{r=1}^{m} \Sigma^* f(X_r) \Sigma^*$. This equation (9) to

$$[\Sigma^* \diamond S \Sigma^* \overset{M}{\Rightarrow} \cup_{r=1}^{m} \cup_{i=1}^{n_r} L_{r,i}\, g(X_r)\, R_{r,i}]$$

$$= [\Sigma^* g(S) \Sigma^* \overset{M}{\Rightarrow} \cup_{r=1}^{m} \cup_{i=1}^{n_r} L_{r,i}\, g(X_r)\, R_{r,i}]. \qquad (10)$$

3.1.4 Rearranging the Contexts

The right hand side of (10) can be viewed in such a way that the contexts are arranged according to the symbol that follows the marker:

$$[\Sigma^* g(S) \Sigma^* \overset{M}{\Rightarrow} \cup_{a \in S} \cup_{i=1}^{n_a} L_{a,i}\, g(a)\, R_{a,i}] \qquad (11)$$

3.1.5 The Underline Operator

For notational convenience, introduce an *underline* operator $\underline{X} = g(X)$. With this operator, (11) can be rewritten as

$$[\Sigma^* \underline{S} \Sigma^* \overset{M}{\Rightarrow} \underset{a \in S}{\cup} \overset{n_a}{\underset{i=1}{\cup}} L_{a,i}\, \underline{a}\, R_{a,i}]. \qquad (12)$$

3.1.6 Underlined Expressions and Languages

Regular expressions with the underline operator admit Boolean combinations between the right-hand sides. *E.g.* $\underline{KiTaB} \cup Ki\underline{TaB} = \underline{KiTaB} \cap Ki\underline{TaB}$. The underline operator gives a compact representation for gapped centers. *E.g.*

$$[\Sigma^* \{i, a\} \Sigma^* \overset{M}{\Rightarrow} (\underline{KiTaB} \cup Ki\underline{TaB})]$$

$$= [\Sigma^* \{i, a\} \Sigma^* \overset{M}{\Rightarrow} K\underline{i}T\underline{a}B].$$

Due to the closure properties of languages with underline, we view (12) more generally as:

$$[\Sigma^* \underline{S} \Sigma^* \overset{M}{\Rightarrow} C] \qquad (13)$$

where $C \subseteq (\Sigma \cup \{\diamond\})^*$ and $h(C) \subseteq C$.

3.2 Additional Context Restrictions

3.2.1 Constraining the Universe

The prior two-level systems present two approaches to the treatment of non-center symbols $\Sigma \backslash S$:

- the alphabet Σ gathered from the centers (Kiraz, 2000); thus $\Sigma \backslash S = \emptyset$.

- the strings $(\Sigma \backslash S)^*$ are not restricted by the rules (Koskenniemi, 1983).

There is an approach that can emulate both the prior approaches: in our approach, all strings are restricted by non-underlined contexts $h(C) \subseteq C$ with an additional CR rule:

$$[\Sigma^* \overset{M}{\Rightarrow} h(C)]$$

$$= [\Sigma^* \overset{M}{\Rightarrow} C]. \qquad (14)$$

By combining formulas (13) and (14),[2] we obtain:

$$[\Sigma^* \underline{S} \Sigma^* \cup \Sigma^* \overset{M}{\Rightarrow} C]. \qquad (15)$$

3.3 Center Prohibition Rules

The rule operator of a center prohibition rule is $/<=$ (Karttunen, 1991). The semantics a set of intersected prohibition rules is given by

$$\cap_{r=1}^{p} [X_r \;/<=\; \#L_{r,1}\_R_{r,1}\#, \ldots, \#L_{r,n_r}\_R_{r,n_r}\#]$$

$$= [\cup_{r=1}^{p} i \cup_{i=1}^{n_r} (L_{r,i}\, X_r\, R_{r,i}) \overset{M}{\Rightarrow} \emptyset] \qquad (16)$$

Let $P = \cup_{r=1}^{p} i \cup_{i=1}^{n_r} (L_{r,i}\, X_r\, R_{r,i})$. Because the universe is already restricted to $h(C)$, we can assume that $P \subseteq h(C) \subseteq C$. Combining (16) with (15) gives

$$[\Sigma^* \underline{S} \Sigma^* \overset{M}{\Rightarrow} C] \cap [\Sigma^* \overset{M}{\Rightarrow} C] \cap [P \overset{M}{\Rightarrow} \emptyset]$$

$$= [\Sigma^* \underline{S} \Sigma^* \overset{M}{\Rightarrow} C] \barwedge [\Sigma^* \overset{M}{\Rightarrow} C] \barwedge [P \diamond_2 \overset{M}{\Rightarrow} \emptyset]$$

$$= [(\Sigma^* \underline{S} \Sigma^* \cup \Sigma^* \cup P \diamond_2) \overset{M}{\Rightarrow} C]$$

$$= \Sigma^* \backslash h((\Sigma^* \diamond S \Sigma^* \cup \Sigma^* \cup P \diamond_2) \backslash C). \qquad (17)$$

Observe that coherent intersection admits intersection when both the preconditions and the postconditions are disjoint, or the postconditions are equivalent.

---

[2] Formula (14) reminds us from a prior formula where no markers are in use (Kiraz, 2000, 87).

4 The Algorithm

The algorithm to compute (17) is given in Fig. (2).

```
Superpose((Σ ⊎ {◇, ◇₂}, Q, i, F, δ) ∈ DFA, S ⊆ Σ)
 1: assert{ δ : Q × (Σ ⊎ {◇, ◇₂}) → Q}                              %1
 2: I' ← {(i, 1)}∪{(q, 2)|(i, ◇, q)∈δ}; Q' ← {I'}                   %1%3
 3: M ← ∅; B ← ∅                                                    %1
 4: for q ∈ {q|(q, ◇₂, q') ∈ δ} do                                 %2
 5: |  if {a|(q, a, q) ∈ δ} = Σ then                                %2
 6: |  |  B ← B ∪ {q}                                               %2
 7: while ∃P'(P' ∈ Q'\M) do                                        %1
 8: |  M ← M ∪ {P'}                                                 %1
 9: |  P ← {p | (p, r)∈P'}                                          %1
10: |  c ← |{q | {(q, 3)∈P'}|                                       %4
11: |  if P'∩(F × {1}) ≠ ∅ then                                    %1
12: |  |  if δ∩(P×{◇₂}×Q) = ∅ then                                 %2
13: |  |  |  if {q|(q, 3)∈P'}\F = ∅ then                           %4
14: |  |  |  |  F' ← F' ∪ {P'}                                      %1
15: |  for all a ∈ Σ do                                            %1
16: |  |  C[a] ← 0; N[a] ← ∅; L[a] ← (a ∉ S)                        %1%3
17: |  for all (q, a, q') ∈ δ ∩ (P×Σ×Q) do                         %1
18: |  |  for all (q, 1) ∈ P' do                                   %1
19: |  |  |  N[a] ← N[a] ∪ {(q', 1)}                                %1
20: |  |  if a ∈ S then                                            %3
21: |  |  |  for all (q, 2) ∈ P' do                                %3
22: |  |  |  |  N[a] ← N[a] ∪ {(q', 3)}                             %3
23: |  |  |  |  L[a] ← true                                         %3
24: |  |  for all (q, 3) ∈ P' do                                   %4
25: |  |  |  N[a] ← N[a] ∪ {(q', 3)}                                %4
26: |  |  |  C[a] ← C[a] + 1                                        %4
27: |  for all b∈Σ s.t. N[b]≠∅ do                                  %1
28: |  |  for all (q, 1) ∈ N[b] ∧ (q, ◇, q') ∈ δ do                %3
29: |  |  |  N[b] ← N[b] ∪ {(q', 2)}                                %3
30: |  |  if N[b] ∩ (B × {1, 2, 3}) = ∅ then                       %2
31: |  |  |  if L[b] then                                          %3
32: |  |  |  |  if C[b] = c then                                   %4
33: |  |  |  |  |  Q' ← Q' ∪ {N[b]}                                 %1
34: |  |  |  |  |  δ' ← δ' ∪ {(P', a, N[b])}                        %1
35: return (Σ, Q', I', F', δ')                                     %1
```

Figure 2: An algorithm that computes $\Sigma^*\backslash h(\ (\Sigma^*\diamond S\Sigma^* \cup \Sigma^* \cup P\diamond_2)\backslash C)$ from $C \cup P\diamond_2$.

Theorem 1 *When G is a DFA that recognizes the language $C \cup P\diamond_2$, algorithm* Superpose(G, S) *in Fig. 2 returns a DFA that recognizes the language $\Sigma^*\backslash h((\Sigma^*\diamond S\Sigma^* \cup \Sigma^* \cup P\diamond_2)\backslash C)$.*

Proof. Basically, the algorithm performs a subset construction over the state space $Q \times \{1, 2, 3\}$, using a transition function $\delta_2 : (Q \times \{1, 2, 3\}) \times (\Sigma \cup \{\diamond, \diamond_2\}) \times (Q \times \{1, 2, 3\})$ defined in such a way that $\delta_2([q, 1], \diamond) = [\delta(q, a), 2]$, $\delta_2([q, 2], a) = [\delta(q, a), 3]$ and $\delta_2([q, r], a) = [\delta(q, a), r]$ for all $a \in \Sigma$ and $r \in \{1, 3\}$. The lines marked with comment %1 copy a subautomaton $Q\times\{1\}$ whose transitions are labeled with ordinary symbols Σ. This aspect of the algorithm computes $\Sigma^*\backslash h(\Sigma^*\backslash C) = \Sigma^* \cap C$. The lines marked with %2 subtract from this

subautomaton another deterministic subautomaton whose final states are those that have a leaving transition on $\diamond_2$. Line 13 alone performs the subtraction, but the other lines with comment %2 implement an optimization that prevents insertion of states that correspond to language $\Sigma^* \cup \Sigma^*\diamond_2$. This aspect of the algorithm computes $\Sigma^*\backslash h(P\diamond_2)$. Lines marked with %3 compute correct prefixes $\Sigma^*\backslash h((\Sigma^*\diamond S)\backslash(L_{a,i}\diamond a))$ by testing that every symbol $a\in S$ is preceded by a diamond. Finally, the lines marked with %4 ensure that whenever the prefix $v\diamond$ of a context string $v\diamond ay\in C$ has provided a necessary and unique (since G is deterministic) diamond for prefix va, the path accepting $v\diamond ay \in C$ will continue (lines 10, 26, and 32) and finally reach a final state (line 13) when the $\diamond$-free string $vay \in h(C)$ ends. Together with %3-lines, this aspect ensures that if the resulting automaton accepts a string $x \in \Sigma^*$, then $x \in \Sigma^*\backslash h((\Sigma^*\diamond S\Sigma^*)\backslash C)$. The four aspects constrain one another. In sum, the algorithm computes the language $\Sigma^*\backslash h((\Sigma^*\diamond S\Sigma^* \cup \Sigma^* \cup P\diamond_2)\backslash C)$. □

5 Applications to Morphology

The presented algorithm has several applications.

Two-Level Grammars The algorithm can be used to compile traditional two-level grammars (Koskenniemi, 1983) where left-arrow conflicts have already been resolved. For this purpose, (1) the center alphabet S is collected from the CR rules, (2) the centers of CR rules are moved to the contexts with the underline operator, (3a) the union of resulting languages and the universal language Σ^* is assigned to C, (4) all surface (and lexical) coercion rules are converted into prohibition rules, (5) the union of the prohibition rules becomes P, (6) the union $C \cup P\diamond_2$ is converted to a minimal deterministic automaton G. The compiled grammar automaton T_G is returned by Superpose(G, S).

It is well known that the size of the compiled two-level grammar may be prohibitively large in practice. The size blow-up can be avoided by restricting the compiled grammar T_G with the lexicon transducer T_L (Karttunen, 1994) in composition $T_L \circ T_G$. Following this general approach, we could define *superposing composition* where the current algorithm is embedded into a composition algorithm and compiles both the lexicon and the grammar at the same time.

Continuation Classes The superpose algorithm can be used to compile continuation classes that are an essential part of the widely used LEXC formalism (Karttunen, 1993). Consider the following entry in a LEXC sublexicon:

$$\text{LEXICON Verbs}$$
$$\text{talk V ;} \qquad (18)$$

In order to compile the lexicon, (1) put the sublexicon names into the center alphabet: $S = \{$<Root>, <Verbs>, <V>, ..., <#>$\}$, (2) compute the alphabet Σ as a union of S and the normal symbols occurring in the lexical entries, (3) convert each entry into a regular expressions with underline, *e.g.* <#>Σ^*<u><Verbs></u> t a l k <V>Σ^*, (4) compute the union of these expressions, (5) add to the union the expression $(\Sigma^*$<u><#></u>$) \cup ($<u><#></u><Root>$\Sigma^*)$, (6) this union, C, is converted to a minimal deterministic automaton G. The compiled lexicon automaton T_L is returned by SUPERPOSE(G, S).

This approach extends to HunSpell dictionary (.dic) format. For example, the entry

$$\text{glossy/TSP} \qquad (19)$$

corresponds to underlined regular expression <#>Σ^*<u><Root></u> g l o s s y {<T>, <S>, <P>, <#>}Σ^*. In the terminology of LEXC, we could say that the .dic-file contains only the Root sublexicon, and its each entry has an implicit continuation to the word boundary class #.

Context-Dependent Affixation and Truncation
The prefix and suffix rules of HunSpell work largely in a symmetrical way. A HunSpell (Németh et al., 2004) suffix rule,

$$\text{SFX T y iest [\^aeiou]y,} \qquad (20)$$

specifies continuation class T, affix iest, truncation y, condition [^aeiou]y and the implicit continuation class #. The combination of (19) and (20) is encoded as string <#><Root>gloss<D>y<T><-D>iest<#> where <D> and <-D> are additional center symbols that bracket the truncated part. The affix rule corresponds to an underlined expression: <#>Σ^*[^aeiou]<u><D></u>y<u><T></u><u><-D></u>iest<#>Σ^*.[3] To make the pieces to work together, the entry for glossy is extended with optional <D>-brackets.

---

[3]This reminds of alternation rules that are triggered by lexical features (Kiraz, 1997)

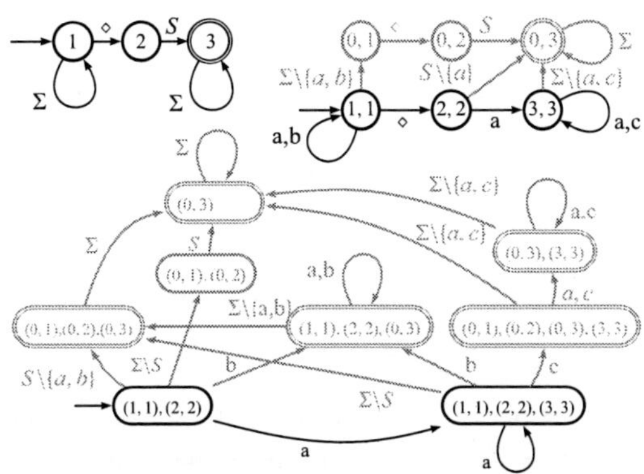

Figure 3: Minimal DFAs for languages $W' = \{a, b\}^*\underline{a}\{a, c\}^*$ and $\overline{W'} = \Sigma\backslash(\{a, b\}^*\underline{a}\{a, c\}^*)$ are displayed in Fig. 1. Let $S = \{a, b, c\}$. The three DFAs in this figure (in clockwise order) recognize languages (a) $W = \Sigma^*\diamond S\Sigma^*$, (b) $W \backslash W' = W \cap \overline{W'}$, (c) $h(W \backslash W')$. The shadowed states and transitions do not contribute to the final result that is $a^* = \Sigma^*\backslash h(W \backslash W')$.

Circumfixing The prefix-suffix pair un+iable can be viewed, however, as a circumfix because the prefix cannot be attached alone to some stems. Our encoding for word unidentifiable is <#>un<U-><Root>identif<D>y<U><D>iable<#>. In principle, each circumfix could be described as a gapped underlined expression, but because the superposition algorithm works from left to right, it does not see in the beginning of the word if suffix iable is encountered in the end of the word. This uncertainty generates alternative paths and slows down the algorithm. Often this effect is seen already during the determinization of the input DFA G. A practical solution is to compile prefixes and suffixes as separate entries and then check afterwards that for each bracket <U-> in a prefix there is a matching bracket <U> in a suffix.

6 Discussion

6.1 Efficiency

When the input DFA G is known, the size complexity of the result (17) can be analyzed: The complement of C is in $O(|\Sigma| \cdot |Q|)$. When $|H|$ is the number of states of a recognizer for language $\Sigma^*\diamond S\Sigma^*$, automaton for $H\backslash C$ is in $O(|\Sigma| \cdot |Q| \cdot |H|)$. A $\diamond$-removal of $H\backslash C$ results in size $O(|\Sigma| \cdot (|Q| \cdot |H|)^2)$. Finally, determinizing and complementing automaton $h(H\backslash C)$ results in size $O(|\Sigma| \cdot 2^{(|Q| \cdot |H|)^2})$. In addition, computing $\Sigma^*\backslash h((\Sigma^* \cup P\diamond_2)\backslash C)$ results in $O(|Q| + |E|)$. In sum, computing of (17) results in a DFA of size $O(c^{|Q|})$.

In comparison to a standard step-wise approach (=the baseline method) in Fig. 3, the superpose algorithm avoids creating many useless transitions and states because it does not construct state subsets that contain states $(0, 1), (0, 2), (0, 3) \in (Q \cup \{0\}) \times \{1, 2, 3\}$ of Fig. 3b. These are reached only with strings $w \in h(W \backslash W')$ none of which belongs to the aimed result.

The algorithm was tested with some HunSpell lexicons.[4] The execution time of the superpose algorithm was roughly proportional to the sizes of the input and the output (Table 1) and several orders of magnitude faster than the baseline. With the superpose algorithm, the number of arcs did not typically grow, but the number of states would grow by a small factor before minimization.

6.2 Optimization

We can optimize the superpose algorithm in several ways.

When the automaton G recognizing $C \cup P\diamond_2$ is minimized, information about the prohibitive role of strings $w \in P\diamond_2$ could be used. In particular, final states that have a transition on $\diamond_2$ could be turned non-final, which may cause more pruning to take place during minimization. Optionally, one could substitute $C \cup (h^{-1}(P)\diamond_2)$ for $C \cup P\diamond_2$, which would extend pruning even to strings in $C \backslash h(C)$, but this can actually make G bigger.

The data structures could be improved as well. For example, using failure transitions (Mohri, 1997) reduces the memory footprint of G and optimizes the computation of accessible subsets during the subset construction.

During the two-level grammar compilation procedure (Sect. 5), we could restrict the shared tape of T_L and T_G in the result T_G as follows: (3b) Add markers to the tape that is extracted from T_L i.e. $U = \mathrm{Id}(h^{-1}(\mathrm{Range}(T_L)))$. (3c) Restrict the lexical side of C with U: $C \leftarrow U \circ C$. Continue the compilation procedure from (4).

6.3 Possible Extensions

Some generalizations to the semantics of the algorithm would be desirable.

---

[4]The Hungarian lexicon (hu) used 26 GB in the original format and it had the total alphabet of 301 characters (letters and continuation class symbols). The induced underlined expression took 83 GB and the minimized result automaton 3.2 MB in the SFST file format.

dic	aff	arcs i/o/m			nodes i/o/m			time b/s	
sw	48	0	98	69	69	28	28	28	756	2
sv	55	.4	291	299	119	58	182	51	19005	17
en	46	1	483	549	116	50	333	48	n/a	95
hu	841	21	7876	2366	359	418	1265	113	n/a	503

Table 1: The total number of root dictionary and affix entries (in *thousands*), DFA transition and state set sizes (input/superpose output/minimized) (in *thousands*), and execution time of baseline/superpose algorithm (in seconds).

We would like to deal with infixes and inserted characters like <D> more abstractly without a need to add them to the root dictionary as optional characters. Such characters should emerge "out of the blue" when needed. The idea could be based on a simplified notion of multi-tape automata where multiple tapes are projected to a single tape.

The current algorithm and its deterministic input are not the most efficient ways to handle nested (Barthélemy, 2007a) or crossing bracketing. A more efficient approach would be based on layered, iterative construction of the result. A layerization method for bracketing constraints is given (Yli-Jyrä and Koskenniemi, 2004), but it assumes that all rules are compiled separately.

The current algorithm cannot compile two-level grammars that have left-arrow conflicts. There are ways to resolve the conflicts when the prohibition rules are combined into one automaton.

There exist already three other algorithms that generalize the idea of superposition to weighted automata (Yli-Jyrä, 2009).

7 Conclusions

The paper presents a new direct algorithm to compilation and combination of context restriction rules. It does not need to know the total alphabet and it is several orders of maginitude faster than a standard, stepwise approach. The presented solution has applications in computational morphology and phonology, predicate logic and in general-purpose finite-state calculus.

In addition, regular expressions with the underline operator are introduced. Underlined expressions and languages are a natural way to describe context restriction rules, context-dependent lexical entries and non-concatenative phenomena.

Acknowledgements

The HunSpell compilation problem was introduced to the author by András Kornai, Péter Halácsy, György Gyepesi, Dániel Varga and Viktor Trón during his visit to BUTE in Hungary.

References

François Barthélemy. 2007a. Multi-grain relations. In *CIAA*, volume 4783 of *LNCS*, pages 243–252. Springer.

François Barthélemy. 2007b. Using Mazurkiewicz trace languages for partition-based morphology. In *Proceedings of ACL 2007*.

Edmund Grimley-Evans, George Anton Kiraz, and Stephen G. Pulman. 1996. Compiling a partition-based two-level formalism. In *16th COLING 1996, Proc. Conference*, volume 1, pages 454–459.

Måns Hulden. 2009. Regular expressions and predicate logic in finite-state language processing. In *Proceedings of FSMNLP 2008*, pages 82–97. IOS Press.

Ronald M. Kaplan and Martin Kay. 1994. Regular models of phonological rule systems. *Computational Linguistics*, 20(3):331–378.

Lauri Karttunen, Kimmo Koskenniemi, and Ronald M. Kaplan. 1987. A compiler for two-level phonological rules. Report CSLI-87-108, Center for Study of Language and Information, Stanford University, CA.

Lauri Karttunen. 1991. Finite-state constraints. In *Proceedings of the International Conference on Current Issues in Computational Linguistics*, Universiti Sains Malaysia, Penang, Malaysia.

Lauri Karttunen. 1993. Finite-state lexicon compiler. Technical Report ISTL-NLTT-1993-04-02, Xerox Palo Alto Research Center.

Lauri Karttunen. 1994. Constructing lexical transducers. In *15th COLING 1994, Proceedings of the Conference*, volume 1, pages 406–411, Kyoto, Japan.

George Anton Kiraz. 1997. Compiling regular formalisms with rule features into finite-state automata. In *35th ACL 1997, 8th EACL 1997, Proceedings of the Conference*, pages 329–336.

George Anton Kiraz. 2000. Multitiered nonlinear morphology using multitape finite automata: A case study on Syriac and Arabic. *Computational Linguistics*, 26(1):77–105.

Kimmo Koskenniemi and Anssi Yli-Jyrä. 2009. Clarin and free open source finite-state tools. In Jakub Piskorski *et al.*, editor, *Finite-State Methods and Natural Language Processing - Postproceedings of the 7th International Workshop FSMNLP 2008*, volume 191 of *Frontiers in Artificial Intelligence and Applications*. IOS Press.

Kimmo Koskenniemi. 1983. *Two-level morphology: a general computational model for word-form recognition and production*. Number 11 in Publications. Department of General Linguistics, University of Helsinki, Helsinki.

Krister Lindén, Miikka Silfverberg, and Tommi Pirinen. 2009. HFST tools for morphology – an efficient open-source package for construction of morphological analyzers. In *Proceedings of SFCM 2009 (to appear)*, Zurich, Switzerland.

Mehryar Mohri. 1997. String-matching with automata. *Nordic Journal of Computing*, 2(2):217–231.

László Németh, Viktor Trón, Péter Halácsy, András Kornai, András Rung, and István Szakadát. 2004. Leveraging the open source ispell codebase for minority language analysis. In *Proceedings of the SALTMIL Workshop at LREC 2004*, pages 56–59.

Helmut Schmid. 2005. A programming language for finite state transducers. In *Pre-proceedings of FSMNLP 2005*, pages 280–281.

Miikka Silfverberg and Krister Lindén. 2009. Conflict resolution using weighted rules in HFST-TWOLC. In *Proceedings of NODALIDA 2009 (to appear)*, Odense, Denmark.

Anssi Yli-Jyrä and Kimmo Koskenniemi. 2004. Compiling contextual restrictions on strings into finite-state automata. In *The Eindhoven FASTAR Days, Proceedings*, Eindhoven, The Netherlands.

Anssi Yli-Jyrä and Kimmo Koskenniemi. 2006. Compiling generalized two-level rules and grammars. In *Proceedings of FinTAL 2006*, LNAI.

Anssi Yli-Jyrä. 2003. Describing syntax with star-free regular expressions. In *11th EACL 2003, Proc. Conference*, pages 379–386, Budapest, Hungary.

Anssi Yli-Jyrä. 2008a. Applications of diamonded double negation. In *Finite-State Methods and Natural Language Processing, 6th International Workshop, FSMNL-2007, Potsdam, Germany, September 14–16, Revised Papers*, pages 6–30. Universitätsverlag, Potsdam.

Anssi Yli-Jyrä. 2008b. Transducers from parallel replacement rules and modes with generalized lenient composition. In *Proceedings of FSMNLP 2007*, Potsdam, Germany, forthcoming.

Anssi Yli-Jyrä. 2009. Context-dependent alignments in ambiguous weighted automata. Manuscript.

ISSN 1736-6305 Vol. 4
http://hdl.handle.net/10062/9206

IV Regular Short Papers

Automatic Semantic Role Annotation for Spanish

Eckhard Bick
Institute of Language and Communication
University of Southern Denmark
eckhard.bick@mail.dk

M. Pilar Valverde Ibáñez
Departamento de Lengua Española
Universidade de Santiago de Compostela
pilar.valverde@usc.es

Abstract

This paper describes and evaluates the automatic annotation of clause-level complements with semantic roles in a Spanish Web corpus, using a rule- and dependency-based approach. In all, 52 different role tags, like agent (§AG), experiencer (§EXP), location (§LOC) etc. are distinguished. The annotator uses a role grammar of 568 hand-written Constraint Grammar rules that take as input the syntactic analysis of the HISPAL parser. A rough evaluation of 5000 running words was performed, where the role annotation achieved an F_1 of 81,6% on raw text and 90,0% on syntactically revised input. A Spanish Internet corpus of 11.2 million words has been compiled and automatically annotated with our semantic role grammar, allowing us to provide some linguistic and statistical interpretations about the relationship between semantic roles on the one hand and syntactic functions, part of speech and semantic prototypes on the other.

1 Semantic roles

A semantic role is the underlying relationship that a syntactic constituent has with a predicate. Therefore, assigning semantic roles to the arguments of a verb is a way of adding deep semantic information to the analysis of a sentence. With this type of information, we can answer questions like who, when, where or what happened, which is useful in systems that require the comprehension of sentences, like dialogue systems, information retrieval, information extraction or automatic translation.

The idea of semantic roles has a long linguistic tradition, originated in the concept of case roles (Fillmore 1968), later termed thematic or theta roles in Government & Binding theory (Jackendoff 1982).

A higher level of abstraction often implies less consensus on category definitions in the linguistic community, and in semantic role annotation the level of agreement among different projects, as well as inter-annotator agreement and annotation consistency is affected by this tendency. For Spanish, the ADESSE database (García-Miguel and Albertuz 2005) uses a set of 143 roles, the AnCora corpus (Taulé et al. 2008) 20 roles and the Sensem corpus (Alonso et al. 2007) 24 roles. Only the AnCora corpus assigns a semantic role to all the complements of the clause, while the rest only treat valency-bound complements.

In our corpus, we use a set of 52 semantic roles, adopting the set of roles used by Bick (2007) for the annotation of Portuguese texts. These cover the major categories of the tectogrammatical annotation layer of the Prague Dependency Treebank (Hajicova et al. 2000), as well as those of the Spanish AnCora project.

The rules of the grammar use syntactic-semantic information available in the input (lemma, semantic prototype of the head, type of preposition, etc.) as well as information extracted from corpus-based resources, such as the ADESSE database (García-Miguel and Albertuz 2005) and the Spanish CorpusEye corpora (http://corp.hum.sdu.dk).

2 The grammar

We have developed a role grammar of 568 hand-written Constraint Grammar rules that exploit syntactic and semantic information to assign role tags to the clause-level complements. Input to the semantic role grammar is provided by the HISPAL parser (Bick, 2006a). Linguistically, the three main difficulties to overcome in the assignment of syntactic roles were (a) the relative lack of lexical-semantic information, (b) the fact that there is no clear correspondence between syntactic functions and semantic roles, and (c) the behaviour of the multi-ambiguous particle *se*.

2.1. Semantic information
We used the ADESSE database, that contains syntactic-semantic information about the clauses

and verbs of a Spanish corpus of 1.5 million words, to study the relationship between the syntactic functions and the role of valency-governed clause-level complements. All in all, 96 sets of verb lexemes that typically allow a given role with a given syntactic function have been defined[1], moving part of the lexical information into the grammar. For example, the following LIST of verbs (V-SP-SUBJ) contains verbs whose subject is usually a speaker.

(a) LIST V-SP-SUBJ = "contar" "decir" "hablar" ...;
(to tell, to say, to speak)

With the list in (a) and the following rule, the grammar assigns the role "speaker" (§ SP) to any subject (or agent complement in the passive voice) (§ARG1&) whose dependency-parent (p) is one of the verbs of the list.

(b) MAP (§SP) TARGET §ARG1& (p V-SP-SUBJ);

In addition, the semantic features of the head were also used, exploiting the semantic prototype information from the HISPAL lexicon. For example, the following rule (c) assigns the role "destination" (§DES) to a dependent of preposition (@P<) if its semantic prototype is in the set N-LOC (that contains the semantic prototypes related with a locative meaning) and its parent is in the set of prepositions PRP-DES (that contains prepositions that typically introduce this role, like *hasta (till)*, *en dirección a (towards)*, etc.).

(c) MAP (§DES) TARGET @P< (0 N-LOC LINK p PRP-DES);

2.2. Diathesis alternation
The tags §ARG0& and §ARG1& are used to systematize diathesis alternation, and assigned to two types of arguments, respectively: the argument semantically closest to the predicate (0) (that corresponds to the subject in active voice) and the second closest one (1) (that corresponds to the accusative object of transitive verbs in active voice). Specifically, §ARG1& is assigned to the subject of passive clauses or unaccusative verbs and to the accusative object of the rest of verbs. §ARG0& is assigned to the rest of subjects and to the passive agent of the passive voice. The grammar takes the active voice as a reference, and the roles that would be assigned to the subject in the active voice are instead assigned to §ARG0&, and the roles that would be

assigned to the accusative object in the active voice, are assigned to §ARG1&.
Three annotation principles were followed:

a) All clause-level complements (valency governed or not), are systematically assigned a semantic role, including relative pronouns and adverbial subclauses.

b) The role tags are assigned to semantic dependency heads at the token level, CG-style, i.e. alongside syntactic and other tags. However, the semantic head is not necessarily equivalent to the syntactic head. Thus, pp's were role-tagged not on the preposition, but on its dependent. In (sub)clauses, the syntactic head is the first verb of a verb chain, while the semantic head is the last one.

c) Only one role is allowed for each token, with the exception of clause-heading verbs which besides §PRED (predicator) also carries the "external" function for its clause as a whole.

2.3. The particle *se*
So-called "se-constructions", covering not only true reflexive use, but also others (pronominal, unaccusative, passive and impersonal), constitute one of the main sources of ambiguity in the automatic syntactic analysis of Spanish, and thus in further levels of analysis like the semantic one. These sentences are syntactically similar, but their argument structure is different.

3   Constraint Grammar (CG)

Our Constraint Grammar uses the new CG3 compiler, that was developed by the Danish company GrammarSoft in an open source framework, in cooperation with the VISL project at the University of Southern Denmark (for documentation, see http://beta.visl.sdu.dk/constraint_grammar.html). In fact, the semantic role annotation project served as a kind of test bed for a number of CG3 features, allowing the authors to influence compiler development according to their needs.

Like previous incarnations of the Constraint Grammar paradigm (Karlsson 1995), CG3 is basically a disambiguation and information mapping methodology operating on token-based grammatical tags that can be added, removed or changed in an incremental and context-sensitive fashion. Unlike previous editions of the formalism, however, CG3 explicitly moves beyond shallow syntax, by allowing the direct creation and use of dependency and other binary rela-

---

[1]   The problem of semantic verb ambiguity was limited, since listing the same verb in 2 different lists was only necessary where a semantic difference corresponded to a difference in syntactic subcategorization frames.

tions. CG3 also provides for hybridization with other major parsing paradigms, integrating corpus-derived statistical information and feature-attribute unification. Finally, CG3 allows the use of regular expressions, increasing rule and tag set economy and permitting the on-the-fly reference to lexical information by reference to e.g. grammatical morphemes and affixes.

In CG3's direct use of dependency links, as we have seen in rule (c), topological methods (here searching leftward from a noun, for the nearest preposition with nothing in between but determiners) are replaced with p (parent), c (child) or s (sibling) relations. Thus, the context "p PRP LINK p V LINK c @SUBJ LINK 0 §AG" could be used to establish a preposition-link independent of the actual distance between the preposition and its argument, and to check for the agent-hood of the clause's subject (through its verb).

4 Evaluation

A soft evaluation has been carried out by manually revising the role labels in a fragment of 5000 running words[2]. Overall, the automatic role annotation achieved 89.0% recall, 75.4% precision and 81.6% F_1 (tp=1062, fp=347, fn=131)[3].

As expected, the results of an automatic role labelling system depend to a large extent on the precision of the previous syntactic analysis (Gildea and Palmer, 2002). If we only take into account the errors that can be attributed to the role grammar itself, ignoring the errors due to wrong input[4], a promising 91.4% recall, 88.6% precision and 90.0% F_1 are achieved (tp=1249, fp=160, fn=117).

One purpose of the evaluation was to identify error sources that could be fixed in a second development phase. For example, 20 of the false negatives (fn) are due to the fact that, by mistake, one of the rules of the role grammar included the passive clitic *se* as a target only when it was placed to the right of the verb. False positives role tags (fp) were often due to the lack of a clear-cut division between related tags. Thus, 32 errors concerned the role §BEN (benificiary) and

12 §DES (destination), both of which conflict with §REC (recipient). Those three functions constitute an important source of error not only in the automatic annotation but also in the manual annotation of Spanish corpus with semantic roles (cf. Vaamonde 2008)[5].

A relatively high pay-off can thus be expected from tackling the most problematic categories. Using the grammar for corpus creation, we intend to create a bootstrapping cycle facilitating such work, followed by more precise evaluation allowing a comparison with other role labelling systems for Spanish that are based on machine learning (e.g. Márquez et al. 2007 and Morante et al. 2007), achieving an F_1 of around 86%.

5 Corpus results

We used our semantic role grammar to create a new, annotated internet corpus of Spanish (11.2 million words), which allowed us – with a certain margin of error - to infer some tendencies about the relationship between syntactic information and semantic roles. In the table below, the most frequent correspondences are listed for some major roles (by order of role frequency), covering (a) syntactic function, (b) part of speech and (c) semantic prototype (nouns).

Role	Syntactic function[6]	Part of speech[7]	Semantic prototype[8]
§TH	ACC (61%)	N (57%)	sem-c (10%)
§AG	SUBJ> (91%)	N (45%)	Hprof (7%)
§ATR	SC (75%)	N, ADJ, PCP	act (7%)
§BEN	ACC (55%)	INDP (35%)	HH (13%)
§LOC-TMP	ADVL (64%)	ADV (34%)	per (31%)
§EV	ACC (54%)	N (85%)	act (33%)
§LOC	ADVL (57%)	PRP-N (55%)	L (10%)
§REC	DAT (73%)	PERS (41%)	H (9%)
§TP	FS-ACC (34%)	VFIN (33%)	sem-c (14%)
§PAT	SUBJ> (73%)	N (55%)	sem-c (7%)

Table 3: roles, syntax and lexical categories

---

[2] Due to our diferent and much larger role set, it was not possible to use pre-existing evaluation material from SemEval 2007 (the AnCora corpus)

[3] tp = number of correctly detected cases; fp = number of incorrectly detected cases; fn = number of non-detected cases. Recall = tp / (tp+fn) ; Precision = tp / (tp+fp) ; F1 = (2 * precision * recall) / (precision+recall)

[4] In the manual evaluation, errors were classified into 2 types: those attributed to a previous incorrect syntactic analysis and those attributed to the role grammar alone.

[5] Obviously, role-specific differences in performance will be of interest also beyond the evaluation phase, but figures from the current development-level grammar were not deemed to be of interest as such.

[6] SUBJ=subject, ACC=direct object, DAT=dative object, SC=subject complement, ADVL=adverbial, FS-ACC=que-subclause

[7] N=noun, PERS=personal pronoun, INDP=non-inflecting nominal pronoun, VFIN=finite verb, PRP-N=prepositional phrase (pp) with noun,

[8] H=human, Hprof=professional, HH=human group/organisation, sem-c=cognitive semantic product, f=feature, act=action, L=location,, per=period

As percentages in the first column indicate, every role can be fulfilled by multiple syntactic functions, §AG (agent) and its subcategories §SP (speaker) and §COG (cognizer) having the smallest spread (subject and passive agent). "Easiest" are roles like §SP and §COG, since they can be determinde from the head verb alone, while roles like §AG and §TH (theme) cover a wide range of verbs and semantic features. Inversely, the dominant functions, subject and object, both can correspond to around 20 different roles, depending on the target's semantic features, the governing verb, etc. However, certain tendencies can be observed, which might be of interest to descriptive linguistics, and could also be exploited in parser design. Thus, §AG has the highest and §BEN and §TP (topic) the lowest subject/object ratio.

Role	Frequency	Subject/object ratio	Left/Right ratio
§TH	14.6 %	25.4 %	31.0 %
§AG	6.6 %	97.2 %	78.4 %
§ATR	6.0 %	-	21.7 %
§BEN	5.0 %	3.2 %	59.2 %
§LOC-TMP	4.0 %	23.7 %	42.6 %
§EV	3.7 %	43.4 %	30.0 %
§LOC	3.0 %	0.0 %	23.0 %
§REC	1.6 %	87.8 %	44.7 %
§TP	1.5 %	4.0 %	7.5 %
§PAT	0.4 %	80.0 %	68.5 %

Table 4: frequency, function and position ratios

Our data also permit to judge the markedness of pre- or postverbal position. Thus, as expected, typically human roles (§AG, §PAT, §BEN, §REC) often occur left of the verb, while non-human roles (§TH, §LOC, §TP) are more frequent to the right. Interestingly, the rightward tendency is less marked in temporal (§LOC-TMP) than in spatial (§LOC) constituents.

For annotation examples, we refer to the grammatical search interface we established for our internet corpus, with both concordances and statistics (http://corp.hum.sdu.dk).

6   Conclusion and future work

We have shown that it is possible to use a rule-based approach for the semantic-role annotation of Spanish. However, given problems like (a) the interdependence between syntactic and semantic annotation, (b) the scarcity of necessary linguistic and corpus information and (c) a certain gradual nature of role definitions, more work has to be done. Here, we expect a positive bootstrap-ping effect from the construction of corpora automatically annotated with semantic roles, such as our Spanish web corpus.

References

Alonso, L.; Capilla, J.; Castellón, I.; Fernández, A. and Vázquez, G. (2007): "The Sensem Project: Syntactico-Semantic Annotation of Sentences in Spanish", *Recent Advances in Natural Language Processing IV. Selected papers from RANLP 2005. Current Issues in Linguistic Theory,* John Benjamins Publishing Co, , pp. 89--98.

Bick, E. (2006): "A Constraint Grammar-Based Parser for Spanish", *Proceedings of TIL 2006 - 4th Workshop on Information and HLT.*

Bick, E. (2007): "Automatic Semantic Role Annotation for Portuguese", *Proceedings of TIL 2007 - 5th Workshop on Information and Human Language Technology / Anais do XXVII Congresso da SBC*, pp. 1713--1716.

Fillmore, C. (1968): "The case for case", *in* E. Bach and R. Harms (ed.), *Universals in linguistic theory*, Holt, Reinehart and Winston, New York.

García-Miguel, J. and Albertuz, F. (2005): "Verbs, semantic classes and semantic roles in the ADESSE project", in K.Erk; A. Melinger and S. Schulte im Walde (ed.), *Proceedings of the Interdisciplinary Workshop on the Identification and Representation of Verb Features and Verb Classes.*

Gildea, D. and Palmer, M. (2002): "The necessity of parsing for Predicate Argument Recognition", *ACL 2002.*

Hajicova, E.; Panenova, J. and Sgall, P. (2000): *A Manual for Tectogrammatic Tagging of the Prague Dependency Treebank*, Technical report, UFAL/CKL Technical Report TR-2000-09, Charles University, Chzech Republic.

Jackendoff, R. (1972): *Semantic interpretation in Generative Grammar*, The MIT Press, Cambridge.

Karlsson et al. (1995): *Constraint Grammar - A Language-Independent System for Parsing Unrestricted Text.* Natural Language Processing, No 4. Berlin & New York: Mouton de Gruyter.

Morante, R. and den Bosch, A. V. (2007): "Memory-based semantic role labelling", *Proceedings of RANLP-2007*, pp. 388-394.

Màrquez, L.; Villarejo, L. and Martí, M. (2007): "Semeval-2007 Task 09: Multilevel semantic annotation of Catalan and Spanish", *Proceedings of SemEval 2007*, pp. 42-47.

Taulé, M.; Martí, M. and Recasens, M. (2008): "AnCora: Multilevel Annotated Corpora for Catalan and Spanish", *Proceedings of LREC 2008.*

Vaamonde, G. (2008): "Algunos problemas concretos en la anotación de papeles semánticos. Breve estudio comparativo a partir de los datos de AnCora, SenSem y ADESSE", *Procesamiento del lenguaje natural*, n° 41, pp. 233--240.

ISSN 1736-6305 Vol. 4
http://hdl.handle.net/10062/9206

Voting and Stacking in Data-Driven Dependency Parsing

Mark Fishel
University of Tartu
Tartu, Estonia
`fishel@ut.ee`

Joakim Nivre
Uppsala University
Uppsala, Sweden
`joakim.nivre@lingfil.uu.se`

Abstract

We compare the techniques of voting and stacking for system combination in data-driven dependency parsing, using a set of eight different transition-based parsers as component systems. Experimental results show that both methods lead to significant improvements over the best component system, and that voting gives the highest overall accuracy. We also investigate different weighting schemes for voting.

1 Introduction

System combination is a general technique that can be used to boost accuracy in natural language processing tasks. By combining several models for performing the same task, we can exploit the unique advantage of each model and reduce some of the random errors. In this paper, we study two techniques for combining data-driven dependency parsers: *voting* and *stacking*.

In parser combination by *voting*, the outputs of (at least three) independent parsers are combined to produce an analysis supported by a majority of component systems. This technique was first proposed by Zeman and Žabokrtský (2005) and further refined by Sagae and Lavie (2006), who showed that it could be construed as a special form of spanning tree parsing. In parser combination by *stacking*, the outputs of one or more parsers are used as features for a data-driven parser that can learn from the predictions of other models. Parser stacking was recently used by Nivre and McDonald (2008) to advance the state of the art on the multilingual test sets from the CoNLL-X shared task (Buchholz and Marsi, 2006).

We describe a series of experiments, where we first try to optimize the voting strategy, by investigating different schemes for assigning weights to the votes of different systems. We then compare voting to the alternative method of stacking. The paper is organized as follows. Section 2 describes the tools, resources and methods, common to all experiments, as well as the component parsers, used for voting and stacking. Optimizations of voting are introduced and evaluated in Section 3, and stacking is treated in Section 4. The paper is concluded with Section 5.

2 Common Resources and Methodology

We used the corpora from the closed part of the CoNLL 2008 shared task (Surdeanu et al., 2008), including a training corpus (39,279 sentences), a development corpus (1,334 sentences), an in-domain test corpus (labeled WSJ, 2,399 sentences) and an out-of-domain test corpus (labeled Brown, 425 sentences). The available features included word forms, lemmas, and part-of-speech. A more detailed description of the corpora can be found in Surdeanu et al. (2008).

In all voting experiments the training corpus was used to train the component systems and the development corpus was used to learn weights. In the case of stacking, the development corpus was too small to train the joint parsing system. Thus 4-fold cross-validation on the training set was used with the common systems, and the joint system was trained on the resulting training set.

All results are evaluated using the *labeled attachment score*, which is the percentage of tokens with correctly determined heads and dependency relations in the test corpus. Intermediate models are evaluated on the WSJ testing corpus, whereas the final scores are presented for both WSJ and Brown.

All component parsers (as well as the stacking parser) were trained using MaltParser (Nivre et al., 2006), a data-driven dependency parser generator that implements two parsing algorithms: the shift-reduce algorithm proposed by Nivre (2003), in an arc-eager and an arc-standard variant (*Nivre-Eager* and *Nivre-Std*), and the incremental parsing algorithm first described in Covington (2001), in a projective and a non-projective variant (*Cov-Proj* and *Cov-NonProj*).

We used eight component parsers, defined by the four algorithm variants times two directions (forward and reverse), which is the same setup as in Samuelsson et al. (2008). Feature models and parameter settings were taken from Hall et al. (2007). The scores of the eight parsers on the two test corpora are presented in Table 1. The highest score is obtained with Nivre-Eager forward, which may be partly due to the fact that this is the setup used for feature selection and parameter tuning by Hall et al. (2007).

	WSJ	Brown
Nivre-Eager forward	86.47%	78.76%
Nivre-Eager reverse	82.94%	76.29%
Nivre-Std forward	84.87%	76.34%
Nivre-Std reverse	84.52%	76.88%
Cov-Proj forward	85.14%	77.61%
Cov-Proj reverse	83.41%	76.59%
Cov-NonProj forward	85.75%	78.09%
Cov-NonProj reverse	83.61%	77.23%

Table 1: Labeled attachment score of the component parsers on WSJ and Brown.

3 Voting

System combination by voting was first proposed for dependency parsing by Zeman and Žabokrtský (2005). Since the task of a dependency parser is to select one head and one dependency relation for each input word, letting component systems vote is a straightforward strategy for combining their predictions. One problem is that using the majority vote for each word may not result in a valid dependency tree – it may result in a graph with cycles, for example – but Sagae and Lavie (2006) showed that this problem can be solved using the maximum spanning tree algorithm previously proposed for dependency parsing by McDonald et al. (2005). If all dependency arcs proposed by some parser are stored in a graph and weighted by their number of votes, then extracting the maximum spanning tree (MST) from this graph yields the optimal dependency tree.

Sagae and Lavie (2006) also showed that accuracy can be further improved if votes are weighted by the accuracy of the component parser on all arcs where the dependent token has the same part of speech. This weighting scheme, which we will refer to as the default model, was later used by Hall et al. (2007) to achieve the best overall score in the CoNLL 2007 shared task by combining six different parsers. Samuelsson et al. (2008) used a variation on the default model, where weights are first set according to accuracy but are then iteratively updated using the following simple principle: at each iteration the MST is compared to the reference parse, after which all weights of correct arcs are given a small increase and all incorrect ones a small decrease. This technique resulted in minor score improvements over the default model.

In order to obtain a baseline, the default model was applied to the eight component systems, resulting in a score of 88.14%, which is a considerable improvement over the best component system (1.67% absolute score improvement, 12.35% error reduction). In addition to the baseline an upper-bound was computed by using the reference parse as an ideal oracle parse, giving correct arcs a weight of 1 and incorrect ones a weight of 0. The resulting upper-bound score is 93.84%.

The first optimization attempt consisted of using other categories or category combinations than the part of speech of the dependent token (POS) to group the individual weights. As a result, three features that improved scores were found: the dependency relation of the dependent token (DE-PREL) (88.28%), the part of speech of its head (H-POS) (88.27%), and the dependency relation of its head (H-DEPREL) (88.30%). However, all improvements are rather marginal.

In the next step we tested composite categories, consisting of subsets of the three successful features and the original part of speech, getting improvements for the following combinations: POS, DEPREL (88.48%), POS, H-POS (88.40%), and POS, H-DEPREL (88.45%). We also tried replacing the original part-of-speech tags with more general categories, obtained by taking the first two characters of the original tags (which are two or three characters long). This resulted in 32 tags (instead of 47) and generally improved scores, but again only marginally.

All results from our weight grouping experiments can be found in Table 2. In general, it can

	POS WSJ	PO WSJ	PO Brown
POS (default)	88.14%	88.15%	80.64%
DEPREL	88.28%	-	80.88%
H-POS	88.27%	88.29%	80.84%
H-DEPREL	88.30%	-	80.77%
POS, DEPREL	88.48%	88.49%	80.96%
POS, H-POS	88.40%	88.50%	81.14%
POS, H-DEPREL	88.45%	88.50%	81.05%
DEPREL, H-POS	88.24%	88.28%	80.92%
DEPREL, H-DEPREL	88.26%	-	80.82%
H-DEPREL, H-POS	88.26%	88.27%	80.81%
All but H-DEPREL	88.18%	88.42%	81.05%
All but H-POS	88.21%	88.30%	80.91%
All but DEPREL	88.14%	88.38%	81.12%
All but POS	87.99%	88.11%	80.67%
All four	87.74%	88.15%	80.67%
Upper bound	93.84%	-	88.66%

Table 2: Labeled attachment score for voting systems with weights grouped by different combinations of the token part of speech (POS), the first two letters of the part-of-speech tag (PO), the token dependency relation (DEPREL), the head part of speech (H-POS), and the head dependency relation (H-DEPREL).

be concluded that the part-of-speech of the dependent token, used in the default model, is an important feature for grouping weights, but the system can benefit from combining it with other features of dependency arcs.

The second optimization attempt was to apply gradient descent learning to the problem of finding optimal weights. We defined the error function as follows:

$$\mathcal{E} = \sum_i (w_i^{ref} - w_i^{hyp})^2$$

where w_i^{hyp} are the current weights and w_i^{ref} are the golden reference weights, which equal 1 if the arc is present in the reference parse and 0 otherwise. Thus, minimizing the error function causes the weights to get closer to the golden reference, and the weight of the corresponding category and system is "rewarded" for each correct guess.

Gradient descent learning gave results on a par with the default model but never exceeded them by more than 0.05% despite tweaking the learning rate, replacing categories or switching between initializing the weights to the default model or to random values. In our opinion, this strongly indicates that the default model is either optimal or very close to optimal.

4 Stacking

A completely different way of using the results of several different systems is to include their outputs as input features to a joint system. This is known as *stacking* and has the potential advantage that it allows the joint system to learn from the predictions of the component parsers, as opposed to merely combining the predictions. Stacking for dependency parsing was used by Nivre and McDonald (2008) to combine MaltParser (Nivre et al., 2006) and MSTParser (McDonald et al., 2005). The results showed significant improvements in accuracy when using either of the parsers to generate features for the other, with the largest improvement when MSTParser could learn from features generated by MaltParser.

In our experiments, this approach was tested with the eight component parsers described in Section 2 as input systems. The joint system was essentially the same as the best performing component parser (*Nivre-Eager*) but trained on features that include both the original feature set from Hall et al. (2007) and the new features from the input system outputs. The latter included the hypothesized incoming arcs and dependency relations of the token on top of the stack and the next input token. The joint system achieved a labeled attachment score of 87.67% (1.20% absolute score improvement, 8.87% error reduction).

We then tried removing some of the new feature groups, for example, only using the arc features, or only the dependency relation features. The best combination was achieved by excluding the dependency relation features of the token on the top of the stack (87.76%). The final results for the best models are presented in Table 3. Although some models achieved improvements over the best component system, all of them remained below the best voting system, described above in Section 3.

	WSJ	**Brown**
Baseline	86.47%	78.76%
Stacking, all features	87.67%	80.05%
Stacking, all but input DEPREL	87.15%	79.77%
Stacking, all but stack DEPREL	87.76%	79.83%
Stacking, all but arcs	87.73%	80.07%
Stacking, only input DEPREL	87.71%	79.92%

Table 3: Labeled attachment score of the stacking parsers.

5 Conclusions

This paper focused on the voting technique, which uses the output of many dependency parsers to combine their individual advantages and compute a joint parse. We conducted several experiments, empirically evaluating some adjustments to the technique, and also compared it to the alternative technique of stacking.

The experimental results first of all confirmed that voting may result in considerable quality improvements over their component parser systems. Our attempts to find better ways of grouping arcs when assigning weights showed marginal improvements, in particular when introducing more general part-of-speech categories, while the experiments on replacing the default weighting scheme with gradient descent learning mainly showed that the default model is close to optimal in itself.

The experiments on stacking also showed improvements over its baseline but generally resulted in lower scores than all voting systems. We believe that better results can be achieved by thoroughly

selecting the features of the joint parser, but it is also possible that stacking works better when the differences between the input parsers and the joint parser are greater. For example, whereas all our parsers were instantiations of the transition-based approach implemented in MaltParser, Nivre and McDonald (2008) combined one transition-based parser and one graph-based parser, models that have different characteristic error distributions.

References

Sabine Buchholz and Erwin Marsi. 2006. CoNLL-X shared task on multilingual dependency parsing. In *Proc. of CoNLL*, pages 149–164.

Michael A. Covington. 2001. A fundamental algorithm for dependency parsing. In *Proc. of the Annual ACM Southeast Conference*, pages 95–102.

Johan Hall, Jens Nilsson, Joakim Nivre, Gülsen Eryigit, Beáta Megyesi, Mattias Nilsson, and Markus Saers. 2007. Single malt or blended? a study in multilingual parser optimization. In *Proc. of CoNLL Shared Task*, pages 933–939.

Ryan McDonald, Fernando Pereira, Kiril Ribarov, and Jan Hajič. 2005. Non-projective dependency parsing using spanning tree algorithms. In *Proc. of HLT/EMNLP*, pages 523–530.

Joakim Nivre and Ryan McDonald. 2008. Integrating graph-based and transition-based dependency parsers. In *Proc. of ACL*, pages 950–958.

Joakim Nivre, Johan Hall, and Jens Nilsson. 2006. Maltparser: A data-driven parser-generator for dependency parsing. In *Proc. of LREC*, pages 2216–2219.

Joakim Nivre. 2003. An efficient algorithm for projective dependency parsing. In *Proc. of IWPT*, pages 149–160.

Kenji Sagae and Alon Lavie. 2006. Parser combination by reparsing. In *Proc. of NAACL*, pages 129–132.

Yvonne Samuelsson, Oscar Täckström, Sumithra Velupillai, Johan Eklund, Mark Fishel, and Markus Saers. 2008. Mixing and blending syntactic and semantic dependencies. In *Proc. of CoNLL*, pages 248–252.

Mihai Surdeanu, Richard Johansson, Adam Meyers, Lluís Màrquez, and Joakim Nivre. 2008. The conll 2008 shared task on joint parsing of syntactic and semantic dependencies. In *Proc. of CoNLL*, pages 159–177.

Daniel Zeman and Zdeněk Žabokrtský. 2005. Improving parsing accuracy by combining diverse dependency parsers. In *Proc. of IWPT*, pages 171–178.

ISSN 1736-6305 Vol. 4
http://hdl.handle.net/10062/9206

MedEval
Six test collections in one

Karin Friberg Heppin
University of Gothenburg
Gothenburg, Sweden
`karin.friberg@svenska.gu.se`

Abstract

Information retrieval is a field of research reaching from computer and information science to lingusitics. As a linguist in the information retrieval field, I leave the quest for effective search engines and evaluation models to others, and focus on language aspects. Words, and parts of words such as compound constituents, which are successful in queries, what features do they have in common? Does the domain of search terms have impact in a domain specific environment? Can search terms with certain features help users of different categories find documents suited for them?

This paper describes the making of an information retrieval test collection which made it possible to study these questions. The test collection will be used to **Eval**uate search strategies to retrieve **Med**ical documents, hence the name.

To study language aspects of information retrieval a new test collection was called for, a collection which was domain specific, which regarded user groups, and which had double indexes for split and unsplit compounds. Since there was no such collection we built **MedEval**, a Swedish medical test collection, with documents marked for target groups, professionals and laypersons, with a system allowing choice of user group, and with two indexes, treating compounds in different ways.

In accordance with the Cranfield Paradigm the MedEval test collection is based on three parts: A set of **documents**, a set of **topics**, and a set of known **relevant documents** with respect to each of the topics (Cleverdon, 1967).

1   The Document Collection

The MedEval test collection is built on documents from the MedLex corpus (Kokkinakis, 2004). MedLex consists of scientific articles from medical journals, teaching material, guidelines, patient FAQs, health care information, etc. The set of documents used in MedEval is a snapshot of MedLex in October 2007, approximately 42 200 documents or 15.2 million tokens. See Table 1.

For the MedEval test collection the documents are stored in the trectext format. The documents have IDs that reveal the source, and they are tokenized and tagged.

Table 1: The genres of the MedEval document sources. (D. Kokkinakis, p.c.)

Type of source	Number of documents	Percent of documents	Number of tokens	Percent of tokens
Journals and periodicals	8 453	20.0	5.3 million	34.6
Specialized sites	14 631	34.6	2.9 million	19.1
Pharmaceutical companies	9 200	21.8	2.3 million	14.8
Faculties, institutes, hospitals and government	2 955	7.0	2.0 million	13.3
Health-care communication companies	4 036	9.6	1.7 million	11.3
Media (TV, daily newspapers)	2 980	7.1	1.0 million	6.9
Total	42 255	100.1	15.2 million	100

2   The Indexes

The terms of the documents and their positions in each document are listed in inverted files. For each term, the ID of each document containing this term is listed along with the positions of the term in the document. This makes it possible to search for phrases or put conditions on queries, for example that terms must appear in a certain order or within a certain distance of each other.

The MedEval test collection has two indexes. One that contains the documents converted to lower case, tokenized and lemmatized, and one that also has compounds split before lemmatization. The compounds are indexed as one orthographic word, as in the first index, but also by each part separately. For example *spiralformad* 'spiral formed', indexed as *spiralformad, spiral,* and *formad*. Example 1 shows part of a document prepared for the first index. Example 2 is the same text prepared for the second index, with split compounds.

Example 1. A document prepared for the first index. It is tagged and the words are converted to lower case, tokenized and lemmatized.

```
<DOC>
<DOCNO> FLKB-0004 </DOCNO>
<TITLE> cell vävnad kropp organisation
</TITLE>
<DATE> 2006-04-xx </DATE>
<TEXT> http://www.folkbildning.net ...
senare uppstå dna deoxiribonukleinsyra en
spiralformad molekyl uppbyggd av kolhydrat
fosfat och kvävebas det vara också möjlig att de
första dna-molekyl sprida som ett smittämne från
någon annan plats i rymd där levande organism
redan finna för att cell skola överleva och dess-
utom trivas vara det viktig att miljö ...

</TEXT>
</DOC>
```

Example 2. A document prepared for the second index. The text contains the compounds as a whole, as well as the parts.

```
<DOC>
<DOCNO> FLKB-0004 </DOCNO>
<TITLE> cell vävnad kropp organisation
</TITLE>
<DATE> 2006-04-xx 2006-04- xx </DATE>
<TEXT> http://www.folkbildning.net ...
senare uppstå dna deoxiribonukleinsyra
deoxiribo nuklein syra en spiralformad spiral
formad molekyl uppbyggd upp byggd av
kolhydrat kol hydrat fosfat och kvävebas det
vara också möjlig att de första dna-molekyl
dna- molekyl sprida som ett smittämne smitt
ämne från någon annan plats i rymd där levande
organism redan finna för att cell skola överleva
```

över leva och dessutom trivas vara det viktig att miljö ...

```
</TEXT>
</DOC>
```

3   Topics

When the documents were assessed, it was the relevance of a document in accordance to a topic that was judged. The topics are static and are used as a base for posing queries. Queries, on the other hand, are created by the user and put to the system in order to find documents that satisfy the topic. They are specific for each run and can be modified if the user is not satisfied with the results.

The process of developing topics, which is described below, is inspired by INEX 2006 Guidelines for Topic Development (Larsen and et al., 2006).

Two medical students were consulted to create topics. They were instructed to make the topics models of realism, sufficiently abstract to be assessed by others. The topics should have varying but suitable numbers of relevant documents, not lower than 5 and possibly up to 50 or more.

The topic creators made queries to the system to get an indication of the amount of relevant documents. Too many hits is an indication that the query is too general. With too many hits there is no room to test strategies for possible improvements. Of course it is equally important to check that relevant documents do exist.

The next step was to explore the collection again, more thoroughly, to see if the topics were suitable to enable assessors to consistently judge and grade documents for relevance. These trial runs helped the creators to decide the complexity of the topics.

When the main idea and title of a topic were ready, the narrative was constructed. The narrative explains in detail what makes a document relevant. It was the narratives that the assessors later used as guides when deciding the grade of relevance of the documents.

After the narrative, the description, in essence the topic itself, was written. A description is a natural language interpretation of the topic, written in one or two sentences. It is usually in the form of a question or a request.

The topics were converted to XML format, just as the documents. Each topic is surrounded by tags and also contains tags for topic number, title, description, and narrative.

Example 3. Example of a topic with ID number, title, description and a more informative narrative.

```
<TOP>
<TOPNO> 23 </TOPNO>
<TITLE> Risker vid användning av neuroleptika <TITLE>
<DESC> Vilka risker är förknippade med användandet av neuroleptika? </DESC>
<NARR> Relevanta dokument skall innehålla generell information gällande neuroleptika, deras indikationer, biverkningar och behandlingsalternativ.  Information om de olika sjukdomstillstånd där neuroleptika används för behandling är relevant.
</NARR>
</TOP>
```

4 Relevance Assessments

With the topics created, documents were assessed for relevance with respect to each topic. Four new medical students were consulted, as the topic creators could not stay on. For each of 62 topics, an assessor read through the documents to be assessed and decided, for each document, the intended group of readers and the degree of relevance to the topic. The documents for each individual need were assessed by one and the same assessor for reasons of consistency.

The assessor began by studying a topic so that (s)he became familiar with it. (S)he was also instructed to keep a written copy of the need at hand when reading the documents. The assessor read every document carefully, marking, in the margins, paragraphs contributing to the topic. After reading a document through, the assessor looked through the marked paragraphs and decided which degree of relevance the document should be assigned.

Each document was judged on its own merits. That is, seeing a piece of information for the umpteenth time should not tempt the assessor to judge it less relevant to the topic than it was the first time.

In the MedEval test collection the **relevance assessments** were made on a four graded scale, 0-3, according to the recommendation by Sormunen (2002). See Table 2. Four levels, instead of the usual two, allow for a subtler differentiation in the evaluation of search strategies, when it comes to

retrieval of highly relevant documents compared to moderately relevant documents. The scale is easily turned into a binary scale if one regards documents graded 0 or 1, as well as unassessed documents, as non-relevant and documents graded 2 or 3 as relevant. The relevance judged here is the **topical relevance**, how well the document corresponds to the topic. The assessors were instructed not to involve **user relevance** in this grade, that is how relevant a document is to a certain user at a certain point of time.

When assessing the documents for **target group** the assessors decided for each document which group of readers was the intended. The assessors marked the documents with a **P**, for patients, if a document was written for laymen, or with an **L**, for *läkare* 'doctor', if it was written for medical professionals. The assessors were forced to mark either a **P** or an **L**. The assumption is that doctors and patients could both have a certain, although not equal, interest in most documents. A third category including both doctors and patients would open up for the risk of having the majority of the documents ending up there.

The marking of target group was done to make it possible to evaluate search strategies, not only considering relevance to the topic, but also considering if the retrieved documents were aimed at the correct user profile.

5 Selecting Documents to Assess

In the ideal test collection every document would be assessed for relevance with respect to every topic. With a collection of over 42 000 documents and 62 topics, taking 8 minutes to assess each document, it would take four persons more than 40 years working 40 hours per week to finish the assessments.

Instead, only the documents that were considered most likely to be relevant to each topic were assessed. The documents were filtered out by use of a series of queries using different strategies. The documents for each topic were sorted by document ID and duplicates were removed so that the assessors would not know how high a document had been ranked, or in how many searches it was retrieved. For each topic and each of the four search methods the 100 highest ranked documents were selected, if, in fact, there were that many. This means that for every topic between 100 and 400 documents were assessed. The mean number of assessed documents for a topic was 224, and the

Table 2: The four graded scale of topical relevance, according to Sormunen (2002).

Value	Relevance	Description
0	Non-Relevant	The document does not contain information relevant to the topic.
1	Marginally relevant	The document does not contain other information relevant to the topic than what is in the description of the topic.
2	Fairly relevant	The document contains more information about the topic than the description, but it is not exhaustive. If it is a topic with several aspects, only some aspects are covered.
3	Highly relevant	The document discusses all themes of the topic. If it is a topic with several aspects, all or most of them are covered.

mean number of documents judged relevant for a topic was 20. Selecting documents in this manner made the work load reasonable, but one must remember that all relevant documents may not have been assessed. Given more funding, we will in a later stage assess additional sets of document selected with other search engines and other queries.

6   Six Collections in One

The MedEval test collection allows the user to state **user group**: *None* (No specified group), *Doctor* or *Patient*. This choice directs the user to one of three scenarios. The *None* scenario contains the original relevance grades. The *Doctor* scenario contains the same grades with the exception that the grades of the documents marked for patient target group are downgraded by one. In the same way the *Patient* scenario has the documents marked for doctor target group downgraded by one. This means that for a doctor user patient documents originally given relevance 3, are graded with 2, documents given relevance 2 are graded 1 and documents given relevance 1 are graded 0. The same is done in the patient scenario with the doctor documents. The idea is that a document that is written for a reader from one user group but retrieved for a user from the other group will not be non-relevant, but less useful than a document from the correct target group. More precisely, a document intended for a patient target group would (hopefully) contain background facts that most doctors already know. On the other hand, documents intended for the doctor target group, even though they might be topically relevant for a patient's need, the risk is that they are written in such a way that the patient has difficulty grasping the content.

In addition to indicating user group, the user must choose which index to search in, with or without split compounds. This choice is present for all three user scenarios. This means that the same query in connection with the same topic will give six different results depending on which user scenario and which index are chosen.

7   Using MedEval

A Swedish medical test collection such as MedEval with double indexes containing split and unsplit compounds, as well as the marking of document target group combined with the possibility to choose user group, will open up new linguistic aspects of Swedish information retrieval. How does one best deal with compounds? How does one get search results suited for different groups of users? And are there certain aspects to consider when searching in a domain specific environment.

Once the copyright issues are settled, we plan to let the MedEval collection be available to whomever wishes to use it.

References

C.W. Cleverdon. 1967. The cranfield tests on index language devices. In *Aslib Proceedings*, volume 19, pages 173–192.

Dimitrios Kokkinakis. 2004. Medlex: Technical report. Technical report, Department of Swedish Language, University of Gothenburg.

Birger Larsen and Andrew Trotman et al., 2006. *INEX 2006 Guidelines for Topic development.* [www] <http://inex.is.informatic.uni-duisburg.de/2006/inex06/pdf/TD06.pdf>.

Eero Sormunen. 2002. Liberal relevance criteria of trec - counting on negligible ocuments? In *Proceedings of the 25th Annual International ACM SIGIR Conference on Research and Development in Information Retrieval.*

ISSN 1736-6305 Vol. 4
http://hdl.handle.net/10062/9206

Active Learning in Example-Based Machine Translation

Rashmi Gangadharaiah
Carnegie Mellon University
Pittsburgh, PA
rgangadh@cs.cmu.edu

Ralf D. Brown
Carnegie Mellon University
Pittsburgh, PA
ralf@cs.cmu.edu

Jaime Carbonell
Carnegie Mellon University
Pittsburgh, PA
jgc@cs.cmu.edu

Abstract

In data-driven Machine Translation approaches, like Example-Based Machine Translation (EBMT) (Brown, 2000) and Statistical Machine Translation (Vogel et al., 2003), the quality of the translations produced depends on the amount of training data available. While more data is always useful, a large training corpus can slow down a machine translation system. We would like to selectively sample the huge corpus to obtain a sub-corpus of most informative sentence pairs that would lead to good quality translations. Reducing the amount of training data also enables one to easily port an MT system onto small devices that have less memory and storage capacity. In this paper, we propose using Active Learning strategies to sample the most informative sentence pairs. There has not been much progress in the application of active learning theory in machine translation due to the complexity of the translation models. We use a pool-based strategy to selectively sample instances from a parallel corpora which not only outperformed a random selector but also a previously used sampling strategy (Eck et al., 2005) in an EBMT framework (Brown, 2000) by about one BLEU point (Papineni et al., 2002).

1 Introduction

An EBMT system uses source-target sentence pairs present in a parallel corpus to translate new input source sentences. The input sentence to be translated is matched against the source sentences present in the corpus. When a match is found, the corresponding translation in the target language is obtained through sub-sentential align-ment. The translation is generated from the partial target phrasal matches using a decoder. The motivation for using these systems is that they can quickly be adapted to new language pairs. EBMT systems in general have been found to require large amounts of data to function well and the quality of the target translations produced continues to improve as more and more data is added. However, many of the sentence pairs present in a parallel corpus do not contribute much to the translation quality. This could be due to the presence of poorly word-aligned sentence pairs, poorly translated sentences, spelling mistakes, repetition or redundancy in data. Using large amounts of data slows down the generation of the target sentence. In this paper, we use active learning to select useful sentence pairs from a large bilingual corpus.

Active Learning is a paradigm in Machine Learning, where a learner selects as few instances as possible (to be labelled by a labeller) and iteratively trains itself with the new examples selected. Supervised learning strategies require a large set of labeled instances to perform well. In many applications, unlabeled instances may be abundant but obtaining labels for these instances could be expensive and time-consuming. Active Learning was introduced to reduce the total cost of labeling.

The process of collecting the most useful examples for training an MT system is an active learning task, as a learner can be used to select these examples. This active learning strategy is not to be confused with translation model adaptation. In active learning, the assumption is that the test data is not available or known at selection time.

Different techniques exist for active learning (for a review see (Settles, 2009)), (i) membership query synthesis, (ii) stream-based selective sampling and (iii) pool-based active learning. Pool-based active learning is the most widely used technique. It assumes that there is a small set of labeled data and a large pool of unlabeled data. The learner evaluates and ranks the unlabeled instances before selecting the best query.

There are a number of strategies a learner can follow to generate queries. In uncertainty sampling the learner queries instances that it is least certain how to label. In query-by-committee, multiple models are trained and the instance on which most models disagree is chosen as the query. Another strategy is to query the instance that would cause greatest change to the current model. Unfortunately these strategies are prone to outliers, which are common in MT systems. Instances can also be queried based on expected future error. This strategy is better resistant to outliers as it uses the unlabeled pool when estimating the future error. Density-weighted sampling strategy is also very common and is based on the idea that informative instances are those that are uncertain and representative of the input distribution. In this paper we will investigate these last two strategies.

Although active learning has been well studied in many natural language processing tasks, such as, Named-Entity Recognition (Shen et al., 2004), Parsing (Thompson et al., 1999), Word-sense disambiguation (Chen et al., 2006), not much work has been done in using these techniques to improve machine translation. (Eck et al., 2005) used a weighting scheme to select more informative sentences, wherein the importance is estimated using the unseen n-grams in the sentences that were previously selected. The length of the source sentence and actual frequency of the n-grams is used in their weighting scheme. Their experiments were based on the assumption that target sentences are not available at selection time, hence, no information from the target half of the data was used. Sentences were also weighted based on TF-IDF which is a widely used similarity measure in information retrieval. TF-IDF was used to find the most different sentence compared to the already selected sentences by giving it the highest importance i.e., the sentence with the lowest TF-IDF score is selected next. The TF-IDF approach did not show improvements over the other approach.

In (Eck et al., 2005) the system was evaluated against a weak baseline that selected sentences based on the original order of sentences in the training corpus. As adjacent sentences tend to be related in topic the number of new words added every iteration is low. A random selector would have been a stronger baseline. We show in this paper that random strategy would outperform (Eck et al., 2005) for EBMT systems. In this paper, we use a pool-based strategy that maximizes a measure of expected future improvement, to sample instances from a large parallel corpora. We also sample instances based on density of the input distribution and show that this modified sampling further improves the performance. Although the method is evaluated on a single language-pair in an EBMT paradigm, we expect to obtain improvements for other language pairs and other MT paradigms.

2 Description of the Method

Based on the properties of different active learning strategies (as described in the previous section), we conclude that a pool-based approach that selects sentence pairs based on expected future improvements is best suited for our EBMT task. The large corpus from which we select sentence pairs will be called the learner selector set, LSS. The sampled set with sentence pairs added so far into the active learning training set will be called the learner trained set, LTS. In a machine translation task there could be many possible ways to estimate the future improvement, such as translation BLEU scores. This would require retraining the MT system after adding each possible new sentence pair from the LSS into LTS, computing the BLEU score of the trained MT model on the remaining sentence pairs in LSS, and then adding the sentence pair which results in the best improvement in BLEU over the previous iteration to the LTS. Such a strategy is computationally infeasible, and so we suggest some modifications to the basic strategy that result in a substantial increase in speed without much loss in performance.

In this paper, we use a set of features that are much easier to compute than the BLEU score, noting that preliminary experiments indicated that they were good indicators of the sentence pair that would lead to best improvement in BLEU score over a test set. Also, to avoid having to estimate the improvement for every sentence pair in the LSS, we follow a cluster-then-sample approach that leads to a much smaller set (reduced set) that is still a representative of the LSS. We use a batch processing modification that speeds up the algorithm even further. We now describe the features used and the final score calculated from them.

$feature1$(Translation Score): Sentence pairs with high word alignment probabilities and new word

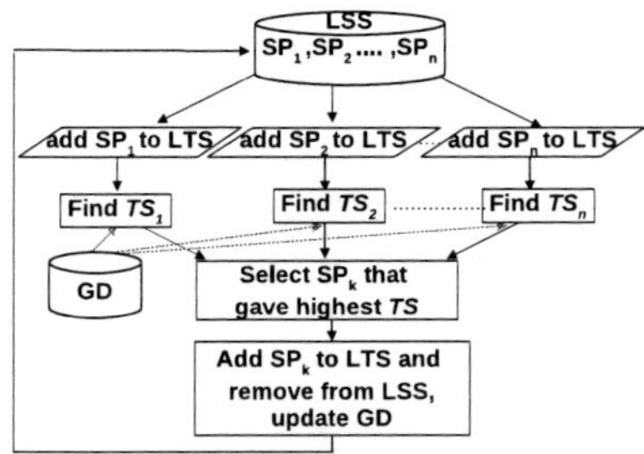

Figure 1: Active Learning strategy.

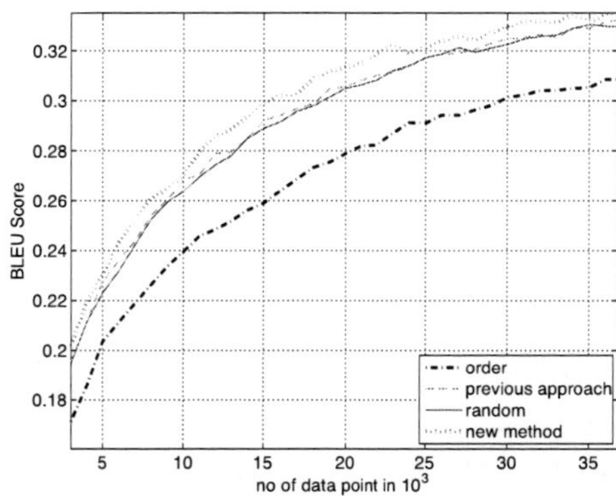

Figure 2: Comparison of (Eck et al., 2005), our method, random selection, selection based on the sentences in original order.

pair counts are arguably the most informative and are good candidates to improve translation quality. We start with a word-aligned bilingual corpus. In every iteration, a global dictionary (GD) which contains all word pairs added so far into LTS is consulted (Fig. 1). A scoring function is used to score each sentence pair (SP) in LSS and is defined as the sum of alignment scores in the reduced set of all those word pairs that are not present in GD but are present in the sentence pair. This score is then divided by the number of alignment scores that contributed to the summation. Normalizing the summation ensures that the word pairs added to GD are of high quality.

$feature2$(Alignment Score): the average of all word-alignment probabilities in the sentence pair. The two features are linearly combined to obtain the totalscore(TS),

$$TS_{sentence\ pair} = \lambda_1 feature1 + \lambda_2 feature2$$

The sentence pair with the highest TS is added into the LTS and GD is updated with the new word pair entries found in the newly selected sentence pair. The feature values were normalized to have a mean of 0 and a variance of 1. For our preliminary experiments we gave equal weights to both the features ($\lambda_1 = \lambda_2 = 1$). To speed up the process further, a batch procedure is adopted. In every iteration, S sets with P points are randomly selected, where, S and P are parameters selected based on the amount of computation available. In this paper, $S = 100$ and $P = 10$. Each of these sets are scored using TS. The highest scoring set is added to the LTS in every iteration.

3 Experimental Setup and Preliminary results

A set of word-aligned 100k sentence pairs from FBIS English-Chinese data (NIST, 2003) was used for the experiments. The reduced set was collected from 100k sentence pairs by first clustering the sentence pairs using the Lemur Clustering Application (Ogilvie and Callan, 2002) and picking sentence pairs randomly from each cluster such that it resembled the distribution of the entire word-aligned parallel corpus i.e., more sentence pairs were picked from denser regions and fewer from the less dense regions. The resulting set had 2056 sentence pairs. For the test set, 2500 sentence pairs were randomly chosen which had no overlap with the reduced set. To create the initial LTS, the remaining data was clustered using the Lemur Cluster Application and the centroid sentence-pairs were picked and ranked in the order of density with centroids from higher density regions appearing at the top. An initial LTS was formed by picking the first 2000 centroids. The remaining sentence pairs were used as the LSS.

3.1 Previous approach versus our method

We compared the method suggested in (Eck et al., 2005) with two baselines tested on the test set, one in which the sentence pairs were selected based on the original order of the sentences in the corpus, the other with sentence pairs randomly selected. The same LTS was used for (Eck et al., 2005). From Fig. 2, it can be seen that (Eck et al., 2005) outperforms the first baseline but there is no clear improvement over the second random baseline.

Our method was also compared with the same two baselines. From Fig 2, it can be seen that our method outperforms both baselines and (Eck et al., 2005) by 1 BLEU point. All the approaches were run until the LTS contained 65,000 sentence pairs, the plot in Fig 2 shows BLEU scores only up to 37,000 sentence pairs as after this point the scores for the approach (Eck et al., 2005), our method and random had no significant difference.

3.2 Incorporating Density Information

Density weighted sampling performs uncertainty or query-by-committee sampling from dense regions. Since density weighted sampling strategies sample points from maximal-density regions, they help in forming the initial decision boundary where it affects the most remaining unsampled points. Density-based sampling methods are known to perform well in the initial iterations when the amount of data in LTS is small. We performed an initial experiment to see if this was true even in MT. For our preliminary experiments, we only sampled sentence pairs from the dense regions and did not use uncertainty or query-by-committee strategies. What we aim to sample here are the centroids which we believe are a good representation of dense regions. For this, the LSS was first clustered using the Lemur Cluster Application. In an iteration, P centroids from the most dense regions were sampled and their performance was tested on the test set (Fig 3). In the next iteration, P centroids from the next most P dense regions were picked. This process was iteratively performed until there were no clusters (with more than 3 sentence pairs) left. This took roughly 800 iterations to exhaust the centroids. For the remaining iterations, the method explained in Fig 1 was applied. As predicted, from Fig 3, it can be seen that this method performs better than the approach in Fig 1 up to 11,000 sentence pairs but its performance drops when more data is added to the LTS using the approach in Fig 1.

4 Conclusion and Future work

In this paper, we used a pool-based strategy to selectively sample instances from a word aligned parallel corpora which not only outperformed a random selector but also a previously suggested sampling strategy in an EBMT framework. As future work, we would like to perform experiments with different sizes of initial LTS and larger sizes of LSS where we expect to see more improvements. In our batch processing framework, we sampled S sets each of size P randomly, it would be interesting to see the performance when we use

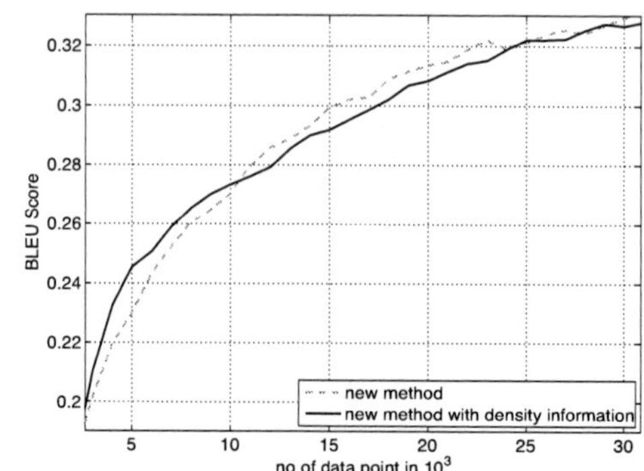

Figure 3: Comparison of the density-based method and the non-density method in Fig 1.

density or uncertainty strategies to pick samples. We also used a density-based sampling strategy which was found to help only in the initial iterations, and as future work, we would like to combine it with other sampling strategies.

References

B. Settles. 2009. Active Learning Literature Survey. *Computer Sciences Technical Report 1648,* University of Wisconsin-Madison.

C. A. Thompson, M. E. Califf, R. J. Mooney 1999. Active Learning for Natural Language Parsing and Information Extraction. *Proc. of ICML.*

D. Shen, J. Zhang, J. Su, G. Zhou, C. L. Tan. 2004. Multi-criteria-based active learning for named entity recognition. *Proc. of the 42nd Annual Meeting of the ACL.*

J. Chen, A. Schein, L. Ungar, M. Palmer. 2006. An empirical study of the behavior of active learning for word sense disambiguation. *Proc. of HLT/NAACL.*

K. Papineni, S. Roukos, T. Ward, and W. Zhu. 2002. BLEU: A Method for Automatic Evaluation of Machine Translation. *Proc. of the 20th Annual Meeting of the ACL.*

M. Eck, S. Vogel, and A. Waibel. 2005. Low Cost Portability for Statistical Machine Translation based on N-gram Frequency and TF-IDF. *Proc. of IWSLT.*

P. Ogilvie and J. Callan 2002. Experiments using the Lemur toolkit. *Proc. of TREC 2001,* NIST, special publication 500-250.

R. D. Brown 2000. Example-Based Machine Translation at Carnegie Mellon University. *The ELRA Newsletter, vol 5:1.*

S. Vogel, Y. Zhang, A. Tribble, F. Huang, A.Venugopal, B. Zhao, and A. Waibel. 2003. The CMU Statistical Translation System. *Proc. of MT Summit IX.*

ISSN 1736-6305 Vol. 4
http://hdl.handle.net/10062/9206

Context-Sensitive Spelling Correction and Rich Morphology

Anton K. Ingason **Skúli B. Jóhannsson** **Hrafn Loftsson** **Sigrún Helgadóttir**
Eiríkur Rögnvaldsson
Árni Magnússon Institute
University of Iceland Reykjavik University for Icelandic Studies
Reykjavík, Iceland Reykjavík, Iceland Reykjavík, Iceland
`{antoni,skulib,eirikur}@hi.is` `hrafn@ru.is` `sigruhel@hi.is`

Abstract

Context-sensitive spelling correction is the task of correcting spelling errors which result in valid words. We present work in progress where we adapt established methods from English to a morphologically rich language and conclude that the rich morphology negatively affects performance. However, our system is still good enough to be useful in regular word processing.

1 Introduction

Context-sensitive spelling correction is the task of correcting spelling errors which result in valid words. For example, in the sentence *I want a peace of cake*, *peace* is a valid word in isolation but an error in this context (should be *piece*). Most spelling correction systems check one word at a time and do not correct such errors. Context-sensitive errors account for 25% to 50% of observed errors (in English data) (Kukich, 1992) and thus it is important to address this problem. A variety of methods have given good results for English but little attention has been paid to how well such methods perform on languages with very rich morphology. No earlier attempts at this task exist for the language of our study, Icelandic.

In this paper, we aim to shed light on the issue of morphological richness and ambiguity in context-sensitive spelling correction by presenting a system (a work in progress) for Icelandic, whose morphology is both rich and highly ambiguous. We adapt methods used in previous work on English to be used on Icelandic and evaluate the performance of the system.

The paper is organized as follows. In Sect. 2 we review some of the previous work carried out on the subject. Sect. 3 describes our method and its evaluation which estimates the accuracy of the system to be 87.2%. We conclude in Sect. 4.

2 Context-Sensitive Spelling Correction

In the literature, the problem of context-sensitive spelling correction is commonly formulated as a disambiguation task (Roth, 1998) where the ambiguity among words is modeled by confusion sets. A confusion set $C = \{W_1, ..., W_n\}$ means that each word W_i in the set is ambiguous with each other word in the set. Thus, if $C = \{piece, peace\}$ and either *piece* or *peace* is encountered in a text, the task is to decide which one was intended.

Such errors can be categorized in various ways (Kukich, 1992). One distinction is whether the contrast between the contexts of the members of the confusion set is semantic, grammatical or both. (1) Semantic contrast (piece/peace): Different words with different meaning but they belong to the same distributional class (in this case they are both nouns) and behave identically with respect to the syntactic context. (2) Grammatical contrast (he/him): Different forms of one word which behave differently with respect to the syntactic context. (3) Semantic and grammatical contrast (cite/site): Different words with different meanings and different syntactic properties (verb vs. noun). We evaluate the performance of a data-driven approach against all the above types of errors.

2.1 Related Work

Our focus is on data-driven systems which are able to handle disambiguation between members of confusion sets without relying entirely on syntactic structure. We can divide these into two categories based on whether they can be trained using only a corpus or whether they require external semantic databases like WordNet (Fellbaum, 1998).

Solutions which do not rely on external semantic databases extract semantic and grammatical features from the contexts of members of confusion sets using corpora and take advantage of general purpose classifiers. Successful methods used for this purpose include Bayesian classifiers (Golding, 1995) and Winnow-based classifiers (Golding and Roth, 1999).

Solutions which do rely on external semantic databases take advantage of the fact that semantic relations within the lexicon of a given language provide useful evidence for semantic disambiguation. If we have a confusion set $C = \{a, b\}$ and many words in the context are semantically related to a but few are semantically related to b, then this is evidence that the intended form is a. A few such methods are compared in Budanitsky and Hirst (2006). It is a feasible option to take advantage of knowledge-rich resources in context-sensitive spelling correction but the problem is the cost of developing such resources. For example, there exists no WordNet-like resource for Icelandic suitable for this purpose.

2.2 Morphological Richness

We take Icelandic as our test-case for a morphologically rich language. Icelandic has rich inflection and morphosyntactic categories are encoded using affixes which are often quite ambiguous. This is reflected in the tagset normally used when PoS-tagging the language which has about 700 different PoS-tags (originally developed by Pind et al. (1991)). This leads to data sparseness when collecting evidence from a corpus. The sparseness of the features used for disambiguation can furthermore make it more difficult to effectively prune the number of features without losing important evidence, thus making scalability a more serious problem. To counter the data sparseness problem it is possible to normalize the data in the corpus. For normalization we used the Lemmald lemmatizer (Ingason et al., 2008). Lemmald is a data-driven system but it still employs some linguistic knowledge about Icelandic grammar. Note that the problems caused by the morphological richness also apply to the lemmatization itself. The lemmatizer achieves an accuracy of 98.54%.

The rich morphology and the corresponding large tagset also affect the accuracy of the PoS-tagging. Various taggers and combinations of taggers have been tried out for Icelandic PoS-tagging (Helgadóttir, 2005; Loftsson, 2006; Loftsson, 2008; Dredze and Wallenberg, 2008). The highest reported tagging accuracy for a data-driven solution is 92.06% (Dredze and Wallenberg, 2008) but

the rule-based IceTagger achieves 91.54% accuracy (Loftsson, 2008) and runs considerably faster (2.700 tokens/sec vs. 179 tokens/sec). We used IceTagger in our experiments. Note that, while performance is low compared to the over 97% reported performance for state-of-the-art English taggers (Shen et al., 2007; Giménez and Màrquez, 2004), the tagging of only the word class actually has a similar accuracy as the state-of-the-art taggers for English – most mistakes are made in tagging other features such as case.

3 Machine Learning Approach

3.1 Feature Extraction

The choice of features is the result of experiments with different combinations of features intended to bring out important evidence of context. More work is needed to evaluate the actual contribution of specific types of features. We extracted three types of features from the corpus in our experiments. (1) Context Words: Word forms occuring at a distance of ≤ 5 from the confusion word; (2) Context Lemmas: Lemmas (base forms of words) occuring at a distance of ≤ 5 from the confusion word; (3) Collocations with words and tags combined (all such possible tri-grams including the confusion word). The Context Word and Context Lemma feature extractors simply collect all words and base forms of words which occur within a window of 5 tokens on either side of the confusion word. The Collocation feature extraction combines word forms and PoS-tags and every such possible tri-gram is a potential feature.

(1) *Listamaður frá   Reykjavík hefur ákveðið að*
     Artist   from Reykjavík has   decided to
     sýna verk sín á listahátíð.
     show work his at art festival

     'An artist from Reykjavík has decided to show his work at an art festival.'

Sentence (1) contains the word *sýna* 'show' which is sometimes confused with *sína* 'his/her/its' because in Modern Icelandic there is no phonetic difference between 'í' and 'ý' (and spelling mistakes are common in many words in which those letters occur). The window we use for our Collocation feature extractor is shown in (2) where the second line displays the PoS-tags for the corresponding tokens. The confusion word is represented as '_'.

(2) *ákveðið að* _ *verk sín*
     ssg   cn _ nhfo fehfo
     decided to _ work his

Confusion set	F_{Total}	F_1	F_2
sína 'his', sýna 'show'	951	521	430
list 'art', lyst 'appetite'	177	150	27
kvatt 'said bye', hvatt 'encouraged'	170	100	70
mig 'I-acc', mér 'I-dat'	895	558	337
vil 'want-1.p.', vill 'want-3.p.'	803	480	322
fínn 'fine-masc', fín 'fine-fem'	203	110	93
leiti 'search,hill', leyti 'respect'	606	439	167
himinn 'sky-nom', himin 'sky-acc'	192	101	91
deyi 'die', degi 'day'	462	420	42
líkur 'similar', lýkur 'finishes'	807	414	393
honum 'he-dat', hann 'he-nom'	2829	2068	761

Table 1: Frequencies of confusion words in training corpus: F_{Total}=Total frequency of members of confusion set, F_1=Frequency of more common member, F_2=Frequency of less common member

Confusion set	F_T	F_S	F_1	F_2
sína, sýna	871	419	229	223
list, lyst	176	88	86	2
kvatt, hvatt	168	113	33	22
mig, mér	821	547	217	57
vil, vill	720	349	252	119
fínn, fín	169	116	25	28
leiti, leyti	567	319	58	190
himinn, himin	188	138	20	30
deyi, degi	447	101	331	15
líkur, lýkur	801	315	292	194
honum, hann	2674	1518	944	212

Table 2: Number of features extracted for each confusion set: F_T=Total number of features, F_S=Shared features (which belong to both members of the set), F_1=Features which belong to the former member exclusively, F_2=Features which belong to the latter member exclusively

We then generate all possible tri-gram combinations of word forms and tags from the window. Those are shown in (3).

(3) ákveðið að _ ; ssg að _ ; ákveðið cn _ ; ssg cn _ ;
     cn _ verk ; að _ nhfo ; _ verk sín ; _ nhfo sín ;
     _ verk fehfo ; _ nhfo fehfo ; að _ verk ; cn _ nhfo

For evaluation purposes we extracted features for 11 confusion sets from a selected part of the SÁ corpus[1] according to the methods described above. Table 1 shows the 11 confusion sets and their frequency in the corpus.

To reduce the number of features we remove all features which occur less than 4 times in the training data. Table 2 shows the number of features extracted for each confusion set, first the total number of features, then the features that occur in the context of both members of the confusion set, then the features which belong only to the former member and finally the features which belong only to the latter member.

As Table 2 shows, the amount of evidence varies quite a lot between confusion sets. For some of the confusion sets there are many features which belong exclusively to one of the two members but for others, such as *lyst* 'appetite', there is a serious data sparseness problem.

3.2 Evaluation

The features extracted according to the description in the previous section were fed to data-driven classification algorithms implemented in the Weka algorithm collection (Witten and Frank, 2005).

Confusion set	Baseline	NaiveBayes	Winnow
sína, sýna	55.0%	96.0%	92.6%
list, lyst	85.0%	87.6%	71.8%
kvatt, hvatt	58.0%	77.6%	64.1%
mig, mér	62.0%	81.2%	77.8%
vil, vill	60.0%	95.3%	94.9%
fínn, fín	54.0%	80.8%	72.9%
leiti, leyti	72.0%	84.5%	83.0%
himinn, himin	53.0%	83.3%	73.4%
deyi, degi	91.0%	93.5%	92.2%
líkur, lýkur	51.0%	92.2%	87.0%
honum, hann	73.0%	87.5%	80.2%
Average	**64.9%**	**87.2%**	**80.9%**

Table 3: Evaluation of the performance of two classification algorithms from the Weka algorithm collection when given the task of disambiguating the members of each confusion set.

We tried two methods that have performed well for English: Naive Bayes and Winnow. We also compared the result with a baseline classifier which always chooses the more common member of the confusion set. All tests were performed using a 10-fold cross validation on all sentences which contained the confusion set in question. The results of these tests are displayed in Table 3.

The results show lower accuracy than what has been reported for English (Golding, 1995; Golding and Roth, 1999) but the performance is still close to 90% which is probably enough for a real world application to be useful. It is unexpected that the Naive Bayes method outperforms Winnow which has been more successful for English (cf. the references above) and we do not have an ex-

---

[1]Textasafn Orðabókar Háskólans.   [SÁ Corpus.] www.lexis.hi.is/corpus/leit.pl

planation for this.

It is not unexpected that the results are worse for a morphologically rich language like Icelandic than for morphologically simple English. Data sparseness and errors in PoS-tagging and normalization are the most likely reasons for this. Even if we include all the features described in the previous section, context-sensitive spell checking for Icelandic lags behind comparable systems for English.

4   Conclusion and Future Work

As expected, morphological complexity negatively affects performance. However, our system is still a viable option for everyday word processing. We have begun integrating our system into the LanguageTool platform (Naber, 2003) which provides easy integration into OpenOffice.org. Our system must still be viewed as work in progress and some issues require further study. We hope to gain a better understanding of why a Winnow-based classification method does not perform well for Icelandic. We also hope to construct semantic resources for Icelandic to complement the method we use for semantic disambiguation.

Acknowledgments

The work in this paper was supported by the Icelandic Research Fund, grant 070620022.

References

Alexander Budanitsky and Graeme Hirst. 2006. Evaluating WordNet-based Measures of Lexical Semantic Relatedness. *Computational Linguistics*, 32:13–47.

Mark Dredze and Joel Wallenberg. 2008. Further Results and Analysis of Icelandic Part of Speech Tagging. Technical report, University of Pennsylvania, Department of Computer and Information Science.

Christiane Fellbaum. 1998. *WordNet: An Electronic Lexical Database (Language, Speech, and Communication)*. The MIT Press.

Jesús Giménez and Lluís Màrquez. 2004. SVMTool: A general POS tagger generator based on Support Vector Machines. In *Proceedings of the 4th International Conference on Language Resources and Evaluation*, pages 43–46.

Andrew R. Golding and Dan Roth. 1999. A Winnow-Based Approach to Context-Sensitive Spelling Correction. In J. Mooney and Claire Cardie, editors, *Machine Learning*, pages 107–130.

Andrew R. Golding. 1995. A Bayesian hybrid method for context-sensitive spelling correction. In *Proceedings of the Third Workshop on Very Large Corpora*, pages 39–53.

Sigrún Helgadóttir. 2005. Testing Data-Driven Learning Algorithms for PoS Tagging of Icelandic. In H. Holmboe, editor, *Nordisk Sprogteknologi 2004*. Museum Tusculanums Forlag, Copenhagen.

Anton Karl Ingason, Sigrún Helgadóttir, Hrafn Loftsson, and Eiríkur Rögnvaldsson. 2008. A Mixed Method Lemmatization Algorithm Using a Hierarchy of Linguistic Identities (HOLI). In *GoTAL '08: Proceedings of the 6th international conference on Advances in Natural Language Processing*, pages 205–216, Berlin, Heidelberg. Springer-Verlag.

Karen Kukich. 1992. Techniques for automatically correcting words in text. *ACM Computing Surveys*, 24(4):377–439.

Hrafn Loftsson. 2006. Tagging Icelandic text: An experiment with integrations and combinations of taggers. *Language Resources and Evaluation*, 40(2):175–181.

Hrafn Loftsson. 2008. Tagging Icelandic text: A linguistic rule-based approach. *Nordic Journal of Linguistics*, 31(1):47–72.

Daniel Naber. 2003. A Rule-Based Style and Grammar Checker. Diploma thesis, University of Bielefeld.

Jörgen Pind, Friðrik Magnússon, and Stefán Briem. 1991. *Íslensk orðtíðnibók [The Icelandic Frequency Dictionary]*. The Institute of Lexicography, University of Iceland, Reykjavik, Iceland.

Dan Roth. 1998. Learning to Resolve Natural Language Ambiguities: A Unified Approach. In *AAAI '98/IAAI '98: Proceedings of the 15th national/10th conference on Artificial Intelligence/Innovative applications of Artificial Intelligence*, pages 806–813, Menlo Park, CA, USA. American Association for Artificial Intelligence.

Libin Shen, Giorgio Satta, and Aravind Joshi. 2007. Guided Learning for Bidirectional Sequence Classification. In *Proceedings of the 45th Annual Meeting of the Association for Computational Linguistics*. The Association for Computer Linguistics.

Ian H. Witten and Eibe Frank. 2005. *Data Mining: Practical Machine Learning Tools and Techniques, Second Edition (Morgan Kaufmann Series in Data Management Systems)*. Morgan Kaufmann Publishers Inc., San Francisco, CA, USA.

ISSN 1736-6305 Vol. 4
http://hdl.handle.net/10062/9206

PolArt: A Robust Tool for Sentiment Analysis

Manfred Klenner & Angela Fahrni & Stefanos Petrakis
Computational Linguistics
Zurich University, Switzerland
{klenner, petrakis}@cl.uzh.ch
angela.fahrni@swissonline.ch

Abstract

We introduce PolArt, a robust tool for sentiment analysis. PolArt is a pattern-based approach designed to cope with polarity composition. In order to determine the polarity of larger text units, a cascade of rewrite operations is carried out: word polarities are combined to NP, VP and sentence polarities. Moreover, PolArt is able to cope with the target-specific polarity of phrases, where two neutral words combine to a non-neutral phrase. Target detection is done with the Wikipedia category system, but also user defined target hierarchies are allowed. PolArt is based on the TreeTagger chunker output, and is customised for English and German. In this paper we evaluate PolArt's compositional capacity.

1 Introduction

Sentiment detection aims at identifying the positive or negative polarities of portions of a text – words, phrases[1] and sentences. Normally, the evaluation of dedicated objects is focussed on, e.g. persons or products and their features and attributes (e.g. the *appearance* of a person, the *price* of a product). Our system, PolArt, uses the Wikipedia category system to derive these domain specific target concepts (targets are sometimes called 'features' in the literature).

The polarity of larger text units comprising two or more polarity tagged words is compositional (Moilanen and Pulman, 2007). For example, a 'bad joke' is negative, since a negative adjective and a positive noun yield a negative noun phrase. Besides bearing a negative or positive polarity, words can be polarity shifters. Negation is the most common form, the 'not' in 'this is not a bad joke' shifts the negative polarity of 'bad joke' to a positive polarity. In the simplest case, word polarities are given by a polarity lexicon, e.g.(Esuli and Sebastiani, 2006). Of course, ambiguity turns out to be a problem: 'a cheap meal' is positive if 'cheap' means 'low price' but negative if it means 'low quality'. Moreover, there are target-specific

---

[1]We do not cope with collocations, currently.

polarities that emerge from the combination of two neutral words (e.g. the negative 'warm beer'). No prior polarity lexicon can cope with this problem. Even worse, the same neutral word might take, depending on the target object, both polarities, positive and negative. For example, 'cold burger' is negative, while 'cold beer' is positive. However, 'cold burger' could also be used ironically. We have no means to detect pragmatic usages.

We introduce PolArt, a robust tool for sentiment analysis. PolArt is based on the output of the TreeTagger chunker (Schmid, 1994) and it uses Wikipedia categories for target detection. It has a pattern-based compositional sentiment semantics that is based on lexicons that code the prior polarity of words, but also on a target-specific lexicon induced from a seed lexicon and the analysis of additional texts, cf. (Fahrni and Klenner, 2008). Currently, PolArt is customised for English and German. In this paper, we focus on the evaluation of PolArt's sentiment composition, readers interested in the Wikipedia-based target detection and the induction of the target-specific polarity lexicon are referred to (Fahrni and Klenner, 2008).

2 PolArt as a Tool

PolArt is a tool to detect and visualise how targets are evaluated in texts. Figure 1 depicts PolArts's output for texts taken from the fast food domain. On the left-hand side, the recognised targets such as 'coffee' or 'cheeseburger' are shown together with their polarities in the text. With a click on a polarity value of a target (e.g. 'positive') all phrases evaluating the target in the selected way and their frequency appear on the right upper window. A click on a phrase displays the context in the right bottom window highlighting all phrases interpreted by the tool in different colours. The advantages of this output are twofold. First, it enables an engineer to analyse the effect of an annotation rule in a fast way. Secondly, it allows

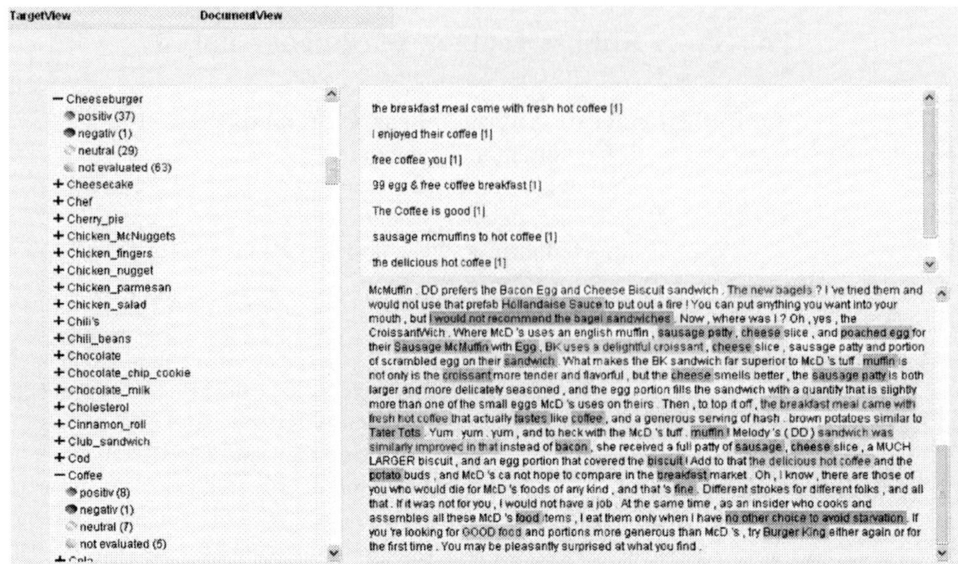

Figure 1: Output of PolArt

users of the tool to quickly get an overview how targets of interest are evaluated in texts and which text passages are important.

3 Target-specific Polarity

As (Turney, 2002) has pointed out, the polarity of some adjectives is domain-dependent. For example, an 'unpredictable plot' clearly increases suspense and as such is positive. An 'unpredictable (behaviour of a) friend' on the other hand is undesirable and thus negative. Please note that the problem with 'unpredictable' has nothing to do with word sense ambiguity (both examples adhere to WordNet word sense 1: not capable of being foretold). Even if the word sense is identified, the polarity still might be open. We call this the *target-specific polarity* of adjectives. An adjective is target-specific, if it takes a polarity dependent on the accompanying noun, e.g. 'old wine' (positive) as compared to 'old bread' (negative). See (Fahrni and Klenner, 2008) for a description and evaluation of that part of our model.

4 Sentiment Composition

The polarity of larger text units comprising two or more words that have a sentiment orientation is compositional. The sentiment orientation of a word comes either from a pre-compiled polarity lexicon or - if it is target specific – has to be learned from domain-specific texts. Available

polarity lexicons are e.g. SentiWordNet (Esuli and Sebastiani, 2006) (semi-automatically derived from WordNet) and the subjectivity lexicon introduced in (Wilson et al., 2005). In our experiments, we have used the subjectivity lexicon comprising 8000 words (adjectives, verbs, nouns, adverbs) and their polarities. Our tests with SentiWordNet have been less successful, but see (Fahrni and Klenner, 2008) for an attempt to use a lexicon derived from SentiWordNet.

We have implemented our sentiment composition as a cascade of transducers operating on the prior polarities of the subjectivity lexicon, the output of the TreeTagger chunker (Schmid, 1994) and our pattern-matching rules. The rules for NP level composition comprise the following regularities:

ADJ	NOUN	→	NP	Example
NEG	POS	→	NEG	disappointed hope
NEG	NEG	→	NEG	a horrible lier
POS	POS	→	POS	a good friend
POS	NEG	→	NEG	a perfect misery
POS	NEU	→	POS	a perfect meal
NEG	NEU	→	NEG	a horrible meal

At each cascade the matching parts (from the TreeTagger output) are rewritten (simplified). NP rules are applied first, followed by PP rules, verb rules and negation. Given 'He doesn't fail to verify his excellent idea', the cascade is (indices indicate succession, 'excellent' is positive, idea is 'neutral' according to the prior lexicon):

'excellent idea'	$\rightarrow$	POS_1
verify POS_1	$\rightarrow$	POS_2
fail POS_2	$\rightarrow$	NEG_3
not NEG_3	$\rightarrow$	POS_4

We have designed a rule language to facilitate the customisation of rules for sentiment composition. Consider these three slightly simplified examples:

```
1. advc_pol=SHIFT;vc_pol=NEG-->POS  % not regret
2. ?nc_no=dt,pol=NEG-->POS          % no problem
3. ?nc_no=dt,pol=POS-->NEG          % no help
```

Rule 1 captures the case where an adverbial chunk (advc) with a polarity shifter (e.g. not) is immediately followed by a verb chunk (vc) with a negative polarity (which has been derived by the application of another rule, or which is simply given by the prior polarity of the verb). The result is a larger chunk with a positive polarity. Rule 2 and 3 are complementary, they capture noun chunks (nc) where a negation (here ' no') precedes a negative or positive word. Again, the polarity is inverted in these cases. Similar rules are designed to determine the polarity of such examples like 'I don't have any complaints' or 'I can't say I like it'. Of course, the flat output structure of a chunker poses limitations on the expressive capacity of such rules. We also have to find ways to evaluate the usefulness of a single rule, i.e an error analysis in terms of false positives and false negatives. We currently work with 70 rules. Since the rules of sentiment composition are domain independent, only the lexicon need to be exchanged (in parts) in order to switch to another domain.

Another, yet experimental part of PolArt, is polarity strength. Each word has a polarity strength that ranges from 0 to 1 (strong positive or negative). Polarity strength adds up while rules are applied. For example, 'good friend' yields a positive NP polarity, the polarity strength is the sum of the polarities of 'good' and 'friend' (currently 1 respectively). Intensifiers duplicate the polarity. So 'a very good friend' has a polarity strength of 4. Shifter such as 'not' invert the polarity without altering the strength. In order to determine sentence level polarity all phrase-level polarities are added up and the polarity class with the highest strength is chosen (e.g. a sentence has positive polarity, if the sum of positive strength is higher than the sum of negative strength).

5 Empirical Evaluation

We have evaluated PolArt in two steps. The evaluation of the target specific component was done on our own data set (3000 manually annotated noun phrases). The details can be found in (Fahrni and Klenner, 2008). In this paper, we present the evaluation of our composition rules. We have used customer reviews as described in (Ding and Liu, 2007). The authors have manually annotated a number of texts from Amazon[2]. They have identified the targets of the domain (e.g. 'installation software', 'camera') and have numerically qualified their polarity strength (-3 to +3). Here are two examples taken from the dataset:

```
color screen[+2]##it has a nice color screen.
phone[+2],warranty[-2]##this is a very nice
        phone , but there is no warranty on it.
```

In order to generate a gold standard from that data, we have selected those sentences (1511) that contain at least one evaluated target. Gold standard sentence polarity is derived by adding up the polarity strength of all targets of the sentence. If the sum is > 0 then sentence polarity is positive, a zero yields a neutral polarity and a sum of < 0 is negative. For example: 'phone book[+2] speaker-phone[+2]' indicates a positive polarity (since the sum of +2 and +2 is > 0). Cases where two or more targets with inverse polarities are present are, however, problematic. So 'phone[+2],warranty[-2]' indicates a neutral polarity, but 'phone[+2],prize[-1]' would be still positive. In both cases, PolArt would assign a neutral polarity (producing a non-avoidable misclassification), since currently it does not have a full-fledged metric of polarity strength.

The accuracy of the polarity classification at the sentence level in our experiments is 72.46%. Without any rule application, i.e. by just taking the majority class from the sum of the word-level polarities (as a baseline), accuracy is 68.03%. The effect of our compositional component thus amounts to 4.5 %. Unfortunately we can not compare our result with the result of (Ding and Liu, 2007), since these authors have only evaluated their feature extraction component.

Sentence polarity might be regarded as an artificial notion[3], since normally the *targets* appearing in a sentence are getting evaluated. Only in simple cases (sentence with one target) are both viewpoints identical. It is the target-level polarity that is relevant for applications (i.e. which product feature is evaluated 'good', 'poor' etc.). The accu-

---

[2]cf. www.cs.uic.edu/~liub/FBS/sentiment-analysis.html.
[3]It is, however, an important theoretical problem to determine sentence level polarity.

racy of the polarity classification of the targets is 87.72%. That is: given an evaluated target, PolArt assigns it the right polarity (orientation) in about 9 out of 10 cases. However, 60% of the targets do not receive an evaluation from PolArt, so the accuracy values reported here refer to the found targets (i.e. 40%). The problem here is – among others – that the gold standard data is not very reliable, as some randomly chosen examples suggest. Consider the sentence 'many of our disney movies do not play on this dvd player'. The authors have identified 'disney movie' as a target with a negative evaluation. Neither is true: it is not a target, but if so, it was not negatively evaluated.

As a prior lexicon we have used the subjectivity lexicon from (Wilson et al., 2005). We have added 'not' as a valency shifter and have removed some words that PolArt has identified as target-specific (e.g. low - 'low price' versus 'low quality'). We have also added polarity strengths, but we did it uniformly (strength of 1). Only selected words are given a fine-grained polarity strength - in order to carry out some experiments.

We have turned off our Wikipedia-based target detection, since the targets are already part of the gold standard information. Note that target detection actually is crucial. For example in the movie domain (another often used domain for sentiment detection), one must well distinguish between content (of a movie) and evaluation. A horror film might get enthusiastic ratings, although the review talks of frightened people, bloodshed and eternal perdition.

6 Related Work

Only a limited number of approaches in the field of sentiment analysis copes with the problem of sentiment composition. A fully compositional account to sentence level sentiment interpretation on the basis of a manually written grammar is presented in (Moilanen and Pulman, 2007). Since based on a normative grammar, their approach is brittle, while our pattern-matching approach operates well in the presence of noise. More recently, (Choi and Cardie, 2008) have introduced a machine learning approach to sentiment composition, but they also have experimented with a pattern-matching approach. Their empirical results are based on the MPQA corpus (Wilson et al., 2005). In the near future, we shall also experiment with the MPQA corpus to enable a more direct com-

parison (including the pattern-matching part).

7 Conclusion

We have demonstrated that robust sentiment composition with a cascade of polarity rewrite operations and based on a moderate sized polarity lexicon is successful. Our 70 pattern-matching rules are domain-independent, although domain-specific tuning is possible. Domain dependence was one of the main reasons, why pattern-matching approaches have been discarded in the past and have been replaced by machine-learning approaches. This problem is not present in the area of sentiment detection, since polarity composition rules are not specific to the domain of application - only the (target-specific) polarity lexicon is. It has always been acknowledged that carefully designed pattern-based approaches are at least as good as machine learning approaches. A pattern-based approach to sentiment analysis thus seems to be a sensible choice. But domain-specific lexicon induction is a good candidate for machine learning.

Acknowledgement This work is partly funded by the Swiss National Science Foundation (grant 105211-118108).

References

Y. Choi and C. Cardie. 2008. Learning with compositional semantics as structural inference for subsentential sentiment analysis. In *Proc. of EMNLP*.

Xiaowen Ding and Bing Liu. 2007. The utility of linguistic rules in opinion mining. In *SIGIR*.

Andrea Esuli and Fabrizio Sebastiani. 2006. SentiWordNet: A publicly available lexical resource for opinion mining. In *Proc. of LREC-06*, Genova, IT.

A. Fahrni and M. Klenner. 2008. Old wine or warm beer: Target-specific sentiment analysis of adjectives. In *Symposion on Affective Language in Human and Machine, AISB Convention*, pages 60 – 63.

Karo Moilanen and Stephen Pulman. 2007. Sentiment composition. In *Proc. of RANLP-2007*, pages 378–382, Borovets, Bulgaria, September 27-29.

Helmut Schmid. 1994. Probabilistic part-of-speech tagging using decision trees. In *Proc. of Intern. Conf. on New Methods in Language Processing*.

Peter Turney. 2002. Thumbs up or thumbs down? Semantic orientation applied to unsupervised classification of reviews. In *Proc. of ACL*, pages 417–424.

Theresa Wilson, Janyce Wiebe, and Paul Hoffmann. 2005. Recognizing contextual polarity in phrase-level sentiment analysis. In *Proc. of HLT/EMNLP 2005*, Vancouver, CA.

ISSN 1736-6305 Vol. 4
http://hdl.handle.net/10062/9206

The Open Source Tagger HunPoS for Swedish

Beáta B. Megyesi

Department of Linguistics and Philology
Uppsala University
`beata.megyesi@lingfil.uu.se`

Abstract

HunPoS, a freely available open source part-of-speech tagger—a reimplementation of one of the best performing taggers, TnT—is applied to Swedish and evaluated when the tagger is trained on various sizes of training data. The tagger's accuracy is compared to other data-driven taggers for Swedish. The results show that the tagging performance of HunPoS is as accurate as TnT and can be used efficiently to tag running text.

1 Introduction

In the last decade, several data-driven part-of-speech taggers have been successfully developed, such as MXPOST (Ratnaparkhi, 1996) based on the maximum entropy framework, the memory-based tagger (MBT) (Daelemans et al., 1996), Brill's tagger (TBL) based on transformation-based learning (Brill, 1995), and Trigram 'n' Tags (TnT) based on Hidden Markov models (Brants, 2000). These taggers are freely available for research purposes but not for industrial use, and in many cases they are not open in the sense that the user does not have access to the source files, hence she/he cannot make any changes to fit the tagger to his/her needs.

One of the best performing taggers among the data-driven tools is the Trigrams 'n' Tags, shortly TnT (Brants, 2000). Recently, HunPoS (Halácsy et al., 2007), a reimplementation of TnT was released, allowing the user to tune the tagger by using different feature settings.

The goal of our work is to find out how the open source tagger HunPos performs when applied to Swedish compared to other data-driven taggers. We apply HunPos to Swedish by training the tagger on the Stockholm Umeå Corpus. We vary the size of the training data and the features used for tagging unknown and known tokens. We then compare the results to other data-driven taggers when applied to Swedish.

The paper is structured as follows. First, we briefly describe HunPoS and the data sets used for training and testing the tagger. Then, we present the experiments with different feature settings while we vary the size of the training data followed by the comparison to other taggers. Lastly, we conclude the paper.

2 HunPoS Applied to Swedish

HunPoS is based on Hidden Markov Models with trigram language models similar to TnT with the difference that the tagger also estimates lexical/emission probabilities based on the current tag and previous tags. For the treatment of unseen words, TnT's suffix guessing algorithm is also implemented where the length of the last characters can be varied as well as the frequency required for a particular word to appear in in order to be taken into account in the learning for guessing the tag for unknown words.

In our study, the tagger is trained with various feature settings in order to find out which setting is the most appropriate for Swedish. In addition, these feature settings were tested on training data of various sizes from one thousand tokens to one million.

For the tagging experiments we use the Stockholm Umeå Corpus (Ejerhed and Källgren, 1997), henceforth SUC, which is a balanced corpus, consisting of over one million tokens. The tokens in the corpus are lemmatized, and tagged with their syntactically correct part-of-speech and morphological features. The corpus is publicly available and free for research purposes.[1] For annotation scheme, we use the PAROLE tagset (Ejerhed and Ridings, 1997) consisting of 156 tags.

---

[1]For more information about SUC, see
`http://www.ling.su.se/DaLi/projects/SUC/`.

data size	t2,e2	t2,e1	t1,e2	t1,e1
1000	68.07	68.25	**68.71**	68.70
2000	75.11	75.23	**75.75**	75.65
5000	81.29	81.41	82.15	**82.19**
10000	84.55	84.67	85.12	**85.23**
20000	88.03	88.10	88.24	**88.26**
50000	91.19	**91.22**	91.11	91.10
100000	93.13	**93.15**	92.95	92.95
200000	**94.35**	94.34	93.98	93.93
500000	**95.34**	95.27	94.87	94.80
1000000	**95.90**	95.79	95.38	95.25

Table 1: Tagger performance with various tag- and emission order given various size of training data.

To train the tagger on various sizes of data, we reuse the same split as has been used previously for the comparison of different data-driven taggers when applied to Swedish, as described in (Megyesi, 2002). From a randomly ordered set extracted from SUC, the training sets and the test data were taken. The size of the training data varies from 1 000, 2 000, 5 000, 10 000, 20 000, 50 000, 100 000, 200 000, 500 000 to 1 000 000 tokens, and the separate test set contains 117 685 tokens containing 7 464 sentences.

2.1 Experiments with Feature Settings

We run several experiments to train the tagger with different feature settings. First, we experiment with the order of tag transitions $(-t)$ using either bigram tagging $(-t1)$ or default trigram tagging $(-t2)$. As for the lexical probabilities, we test emission order e by either setting the tag order NUM to 1, where $NUM = 1 \rightarrow P(w_i|t_i)$ or using the default tag order NUM set to 2 where $NUM = 2 \rightarrow P(w_i|t_{i-1}t_i)$. The results of the combination of these features are shown in Table 1. Not surprisingly, bigram models better fit to smaller training data containing less than 50 000 tokens while trigram models are to prefer when we use larger data sets, over 50 000 tokens, for training.

For unknown words, there is a possibility to vary the length of the suffixes that the tagger uses to build a suffix tree. In this study, we tested suffixes of length 10 (default), 9, and 5 to see if a decrease in suffix length can increase performance. Looking at the results given in the second and third columns in Table 2, we can conclude that there is an increase in error rate by reducing the length of the suffixes independently of the size of the training data. For Swedish, suffix length set to 10 yields best results.

As the next step, we also vary the frequency with which a word can occur to be added to the suffix tree. Column four and five in Table 2 show that for small amounts of training data consisting of less than 100 000 tokens, tagger performance can be improved by reducing the frequency requirement for words to be added to the suffix tree. For larger training corpora, the default setting of the tagger can be used, i.e., setting the frequency to 10.

2.2 HunPoS Compared to other Data-Driven Taggers

Lastly, given the default feature setting of the tagger, we compare the result achieved by HunPoS to other taggers' performance when trained on the same data set and evaluated on the separate but same test set. Table 3 lists the data size, the baseline—calculated by assuming unknown words to be common nouns (NCUSNIS), and when capitalized, proper nouns (NP00N0S) and known words receiving their most frequently occurring tag—followed by the accuracy of the MBT tagger (MBT), the MXPOST tagger (ME), Brill's tagger (TBL), TnT, and lastly HunPoS with default settings (HP-default) and HunPoS optimized (HP-best). HunPoS has highest accuracy when trained on small training data consisting of less than 20 000 tokens, while TnT achieves highest performance for the other data sets with the exception of training on one million tokens where both taggers achieve comparable results. The difference in performance between TnT and Hun-PoS when trained on the largest data set is not significant using McNemar's test ($p <= 0.827$ with 95% confidence level) and the freely available open source system is therefore a good alternative to use.

3 Concluding Remarks

We applied a freely available open source tagger HunPoS to Swedish and trained with different feature settings for the tagging model and lexical probabilities, as well as for the treatment of unknown words. We can conclude that for larger training data consisting of above 200 000 tokens, the default settings of the tagger can be used while for smaller data sets, features for lexical proba-

data size	s10-s9+f10	s5+f10	s10+f9	s10+f5
1000	68.07	**68.08**	68.17	**68.45**
2000	**75.11**	75.10	75.11	**75.32**
5000	**81.29**	81.27	81.29	**81.47**
10000	**84.55**	84.52	84.56	**84.57**
20000	**88.03**	88.02	**88.04**	**88.04**
50000	**91.19**	91.14	91.18	91.18
100000	**93.13**	93.08	93.13	**93.14**
200000	**94.35**	94.30	**94.35**	94.34
500000	**95.34**	95.29	**95.34**	**95.34**
1000000	**95.90**	95.86	**95.90**	95.89

Table 2: Tagger performance for unknown words with different feature settings and using the default model ($t2, e2$) given various size of training data.

data size	baseline	MB	ME	TBL	TnT	HP-default	HP-best
1000	48.68	62.91	53.41	61.10	67.98	68.07	**68.71**
2000	50.90	69.36	61.86	63.44	74.87	75.11	**75.75**
5000	58.19	75.90	72.73	70.49	81.72	81.29	**82.19**
10000	63.60	79.30	78.08	74.62	85.05	84.55	**85.23**
20000	67.19	82.84	82.96	80.32	88.25	88.03	**88.26**
50000	72.77	86.47	88.06	85.33	**91.34**	91.19	91.22
100000	76.89	88.87	90.69	89.84	**93.23**	93.13	93.15
200000	80.18	90.51	92.53	92.40	**94.41**	94.35	94.35
500000	83.55	92.30	94.18	93.45	**95.39**	95.34	95.34
1000000	85.49	93.94	—	92.74	95.89	95.90	**95.90**

Table 3: Performance of taggers given various size of training data.

bilities and treatment of unknown words shall be adapted. Lastly, we also compared the tagging accuracy of HunPoS to the performance of other data-driven taggers applied to Swedish. We conclude that HunPoS is a good alternative to TnT which is one of the best performing taggers today.

References

Thorsten Brants. 2000. Tnt - a statistical part-of-speech tagger. In *Proceedings of the 6th Applied Natural Language Processing Conference (ANLP-00)*, Seattle, Washington, USA.

Eric Brill. 1995. Transformation-based error-driven learning and natural language processing: A case study in part-of-speech tagging. *Computational Linguistics*, 21:543–566.

W. Daelemans, J. Zavrel, P. Berck, and S. Gillis. 1996. A memory-based part of speech tagger generator. In E. Ejerhed and I. Dagan, editors, *Proceedings of the Fourth Workshop on Very Large Corpora*, pages 14–27.

Eva Ejerhed and Gunnel Källgren. 1997. Stockholm Umeå Corpus. Version 1.0. Produced by Department of Linguistics, Umeå University and Department of Linguistics, Stockholm University. ISBN 91-7191-348-3.

Eva Ejerhed and Daniel Ridings. 1997. PAROLE→SUC and SUC→PAROLE. http://spraakbanken.gu.se/parole.

Péter Halácsy, András Kornai, and Csaba Oravecz. 2007. Hunpos - an open source trigram tagger. In *Proceedings of the 45th Annual Meeting of the Association for Computational Linguistics*, volume Companion Volume, Proceedings of the Demo and Poster Sessions, pages 209–212, Prague, Czech Republic. Association for Computational Linguistics.

Beata Megyesi. 2002. *Data-Driven Syntactic Analysis: Methods and Applications for Swedish*. Ph.D. thesis, KTH: Department of Speech, Music and Hearing.

Adwait Ratnaparkhi. 1996. A maximum entropy model for part-of-sppech tagging. In *Proceedings of the Conference on Empirical Methods in Natural Language Processing (EMNLP)*.

ISSN 1736-6305 Vol. 4
http://hdl.handle.net/10062/9206

English-Latvian SMT: knowledge or data?

Inguna Skadiņa
Institute of Mathematics and Comput-
er Science, University of Latvia
Riga, Latvia
Inguna.Skadina@lumii.lv

Edgars Brālītis
Institute of Mathematics and Comput-
er Science, University of Latvia
Riga, Latvia
Edgars.Bralitis@lumii.lv

Abstract

In cases when phrase-based statistical machine translation (SMT) is applied to languages with rather free word order and rich morphology, translated texts often are not fluent due to misused inflectional forms and wrong word order between phrases or even inside the phrase. One of possible solutions how to improve translation quality is to apply factored models. The paper presents work on English-Latvian phrase-based and factored SMT systems and, using evaluation results, demonstrates that although factored models seem more appropriate for highly inflected languages, they have rather small influence on translation results, while using phrase-model with more data better translation quality could be achieved.

1 Introduction

In the last decade statistical machine translation (SMT) has become one of the most popular approaches in the field of automated translation. SMT started with word-based models, but significant advances were made with the introduction of phrase-based models.

Statistical Machine Translation tries to generate translations on the basis of statistical models, with parameters derived from the analysis of bilingual text corpora. SMT approach is language independent, but it requires large bilingual corpora for training. If such corpora are available, good results can be achieved in translating texts of a similar kind. The main advantage of SMT approach is a possibility to build up the system in a relatively small period of time.

One of the prerequisites for classical SMT systems is availability of large parallel corpus which computer then uses in the training process. The lack of large parallel corpus is the main reason why experiments with SMT in Baltic countries have been started only recently, i.e., implementation of Estonian-English (Fishel et al., 2007) and English-Latvian (Skadiņa and Brālītis, 2007) SMT systems have been reported only in 2007.

Phrase-based models (Koehn et al., 2003) typically deals with words or phrases thus often generating wrong form if the text is translated into morphologically rich language. In factored translation models (Koehn and Hoang, 2007), the surface forms are augmented with factors, such as grammatical information and base form. Thus factored models usually improve machine translation performance for problems such as morphology, free word order, and sentence-level grammatical coherence. For instance, English-Czech factored SMT reached 27.04% BLEU for all morphological features and 27.45% BLEU for selected morphological features, in comparison to the baseline of 25.82% BLEU (Koehn and Hoang, 2007).

The paper presents application of factored approach to English-Latvian SMT and discusses evaluation results, demonstrating that simple factored models have no enough influence on translation quality, i.e., with phrase-based models and more data better results could be achieved as with factored models and less data.

2 English-Latvian factored translation model

Latvian language is typical representative of morphologically rich languages. Almost all open word classes, i.e., nouns, adjectives, numerals, pronouns, and verbs, are inflective.

Latvian nouns and pronouns have 6 cases in both singular and plural. Adjectives, numerals and participles have 6 cases in singular and plural, 2 genders and definite and indefinite form. In Latvian conjugation system there are two numbers, three persons and three tenses (present, future and past tenses), both simple and compound and 5 moods. Moreover, inflected forms are highly ambiguous. Nouns in Latvian have 29 graphically different endings and only 13 of them are unambiguous, adjectives have 24 graphically different endings and half of them are ambiguous, verbs have 28 graphically different endings and only 17 of them are unambiguous. The most common ambiguity classes are feminine singular genitive vs. feminine plural nominative and masculine singular accusative vs. masculine plural genitive.

Initially the phrase-based model was built for JRC Acquis 2.2. corpus (Steinberger et al., 2006). Human analysis of translation results allowed us to conclude that one of the central problems, which make translation abstruse, is wrong inflectional form (Skadiņa and Brālītis, 2007). Selection of wrong inflectional form not only influences fluency of translation, but in complex sentences (as most of legal texts) makes translation abstruse. Therefore, to improve translation quality, factored SMT system which uses Latvian morphological analyzer was built (Figure 1).

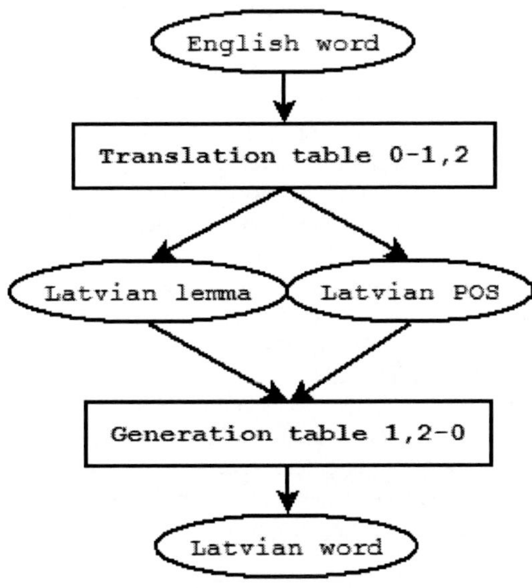

Figure 1. English-Latvian factored SMT

For Latvian language three factor model was chosen: inflected form (0), base form (or lemma) (1) and morphological tag (2). The translation process has been decompiled into the following steps:

1. English sentence has been translated into sequence of Latvian factors 1 and 2, using translation table 0-1,2

2. Sequence of Latvian factors 1 and 2 were translated into factor 0, using generation table 1,2-0

In addition three Latvian language models were implemented for each factor. All language models have the same weight during translation process.

The system was built using well known tools and techniques: after text normalization (texts were converted to lower-case, empty lines deleted, punctuation marks were separated from words) the GIZA++ tool (Och and Ney, 2003) was used for translation models. For Latvian language models SRI LM Toolkit (Stolcke, 2002) with recommended parameters (modified Kneser-Ney discounting and interpolation) were used. We used Latvian morphological analyzer by Paikens (2007) and Latvian tagger developed by Virza (unpublished work). For decoding Moses decoder (Koehn, 2004) was used.

3   Evaluation

For test purposes two test collections were created. For automatic evaluation sentences were selected randomly (1 from 1000) from JRC 3.0 corpus after omitting sentences from JRC2.2 corpus, and excluding sentences with possibly wrong alignment. As result text collection for automatic evaluation contains 843 sentences. For human evaluation 200 sentences were chosen from the test collection. Sentences which were included into test collections were deleted from JRC3.0 and JRC2.2 corpora before the training.

The evaluation was performed for four systems: phrase-based model built from JRC2.2 corpus, factored model built from JRC2.2 corpus, phrase-based model built from JRC3.0 corpus and factored model built from JRC3.0 corpus.

At first influence of different parameters, i.e., n-grams in language model, target language corpus, choice of decoder, on phrase-based models was evaluated (Table 1). As it is shown below the size of corpora has considerable influence on BLEU score (Papineni et al., 2002), while choice of decoder and number of n-grams in language model has relatively small influence on translation quality.

Phrase table data	Total number of words	Decoder	Language model			
			Order	Training data		
					JRC Acquis 2.2	JRC Acquis 3.0
JRC Acquis 2.2	EN – 9 932 536, LV – 8 129 497	Pharaoh	3		**26.20**	**29.91**
			5		23.91	26.43
JRC Acquis 2.2	EN – 9 932 536, LV – 8 129 497	Moses	3		26.37	31.82
			5		26.45	**32.41**
			7		**26.63**	32.37
JRC Acquis 3.0	EN -55 537 910, LV – 44 703 607	Moses	3		31.68	43.28
			5		**31.99**	44.93
			7		31.74	**44.97**

Table 1. Evaluation results (Bleu scores) for phrase-based models

While influence of size of training corpora on translation quality is obvious result, our main goal was to evaluate the influence of factored models on translation quality (Table 2). The first results show that it is possible to increase translation performance using factored models as it is in case of phrase-based model built form JRC Acquis 2.2 corpus and corresponding (same training data, language model order and other parameters) factored model. Factored model built from JRC3.0 Acquis corpus is slightly outperformed by corresponding phrase-based model.

SMT	BLEU score
JRC Acquis 2.2. phrase-based	26.37
JRC Acquis 2.2. factored	28.96
JRC Acquis 3.0 phrase-based	43.28
JRC Acquis 3.0 factored	42.98

Table 2. Influence of factored model on translation quality

Although JRC Acquis 2.2. corpus is almost five times smaller than JRC Acquis 3.0 corpus, it is sufficient for translation dictionary of EU legislation domain: in test corpus of 200 sentences and 5313 running words in Latvian reference translation, only 33 words have been left without translation, in 9 cases word was not translated by all SMT systems, thus only in 24 cases English word was not in JRC Acquis 2.2. translation model.

To compare automatic evaluation results with human intuition, the simple human evaluation was performed. The evaluator compared translations of four systems: phrase-based model built from JRC2.2 corpus, factored model built from JRC2.2 corpus, phrase-based model built from JRC3.0 corpus and factored model built from JRC3.0 corpus, by answering two questions for each sentence in test collection:

1. Which translation is better?
2. Is translation understandable easily?

Evaluator may select several translations in case the output of systems is similar. Evaluation results are summarized in Table 3.

	Chosen as the best (or one of best)	Easily understandable translations
JRC Acquis 2.2 phrase-based	20	12
JRC Acquis 2.2 factored	42	18
JRC Acquis 3.0 phrase-based	57	30
JRC Acquis 3.0 factored	74	28
All	71	15

Table 3. Results of human evaluation

The human evaluation showed the similar tendency – the size of training corpus has great influence on translation performance. 58 translations (29%) generated by systems trained on JRC Acquis 3.0 corpus are evaluated as understandable, while for systems trained on JRC Acquis 2.2 only 30 translations (15%) are evaluated as understandable. In 71 cases (35.5%) human evaluator has classified all translations as equal in translation quality; however, most of them are not easily understandable.

4 Conclusions

The paper presents first results of English-Latvian factored SMT systems showing that at current stage, better results could be achieved with more data as by intelligence, i.e., factored models.

We plan to make deeper and more precise human evaluation of current systems for further elaborations. We plan to research reasons why factored models have not demonstrated sufficient improvements in translation quality, especially for system trained on large (JRC Acquis 3.0) corpus and research possibilities to elaborate factored models.

Recent versions of SMT systems presented here are available at eksperimenti.ailab.lv/smt.

Acknowledgments

The work presented was supported by Latvian Council of Science through projects Evaluation of Statistical Machine Translation Methods for English-Latvian Translation system (2005-2008) and Application of Factored Methods in English-Latvian Statistical Machine Translation System (2009-2012). We would also like to thank reviewers for useful comments.

References

Fishel Mark, Kaalep Heiki-Jaan, Muischnek Kadri. 2007. Estonian-English Statistical Machine Translation: the First Results. Nivre J., Kaalep H., Muischnek K., Koit M. (eds.) *Proceedings of the 16th Nordic Conference of Computational Linguistics NODALIDA-2007.* Tartu, 278–283.

Koehn Philipp. 2004. Pharaoh: a beam search decoder for statistical machine translation. In: *6th Conference of the Association for Machine Translation in the Americas, AMTA*, Lecture Notes in Computer Science. Springer.

Koehn Philipp, Och Franz Josef, and Marcu Daniel. 2003. Statistical phrase based translation. *Proceedings of the Joint Conference on Human Language Technologies and the Annual Meeting of the North American Chapter of the Association of Computational Linguistics (HLT-NAACL).* Edmonton, Canada, pp. 48-54.

Koehn Philipp and Hieu Hoang. 2007. Factored Translation Models. *Proceedings of the 2007 Joint Conference on Empirical Methods in Natural Language Processing and Computational Natural Language Learning,* Prague, pp. 868–876.

Och Franz Josef, Ney Hermann. 2003. A Systematic Comparison of Various Statistical Alignment Models, *Computational Linguistics*, volume 29, number 1, pp. 19-51.

Papineni Kishore, Roukos Salim, Ward Tood, Zhu Wei-Jing. 2002. BLEU: a method for automatic evaluation of machine translation. *Proceedings of the 40th Annual Meeting of the Association of Computational Linguistics (ACL)*, Pennsylvania, pp. 311-318.

Paikens Pēteris. Lexicon-Based Morphological Analysis of Latvian Language.2007. *Proceedings of the 3rd Baltic Conference on Human Language Technologies*, Kaunas, pp. 235–240.

Skadiņa Inguna, Brālītis Edgars. 2007. Experimental Statistical Machine Translation System for Latvian. *Proceedings of the 3rd Baltic Conference on Human Language Technologies*, Kaunas, 2007, pp. 281-286.

Steinberger Ralf, Pouliquen Bruno, Widiger Anna, Ignat Camelia, Erjavec Tomaž Erjavec, Dan Tufiş, Dániel Varga. 2006. The JRC-Acquis: A multilingual aligned parallel corpus with 20+ languages. *Proceedings of the 5th International Conference on Language Resources and Evaluation (LREC'2006).* Genoa, pp. 2142-2147.

Stolcke Andreas. 2002. SRILM - an extensible language modeling toolkit, *ICSLP-2002*, 901-904.

ISSN 1736-6305 Vol. 4
http://hdl.handle.net/10062/9206

Cross-lingual porting of distributional semantic classification

Lilja Øvrelid
Department of Linguistics
University of Potsdam
Germany
`lilja@ling.uni-potsdam.de`

Abstract

This article presents experiments in the porting of semantic classification between two closely related languages, Swedish and Danish. We show that a classifier for the semantic property of animacy, trained on morphosyntactic distributional data for one language may be applied directly to data from another language with little loss in terms of accuracy.

1 Introduction

Semantic classification of natural language has in recent years received extensive attention.[1] Most approaches to these tasks make use of language-specific, annotated data or lexical resources, such as FrameNet and WordNet, a fact which complicates a multilingual perspective on semantic annotation and classification. One way of approaching this is found in work on projection of semantic classifications, such as semantic roles, making use of parallel corpora and hence the relation of translation to acquire semantic relations for new languages (Pado and Lapata, 2005; Johansson and Nugues, 2006).

Much recent work in semantic classification assumes that the syntactic distribution of lexical items constitutes a reliable predictor of semantics or meaning, at the *type* level (Lin, 1998). In the task of verb classification, for instance, it has been shown that features motivated in typological generalizations and found to be highly predictive for classification in one language (English) may be 're-used' for the classification of verbs in other languages, such as Italian (Merlo et al.,

2002). The semantic property of animacy influences linguistic phenomena in a range of different languages, and has been shown to correlate quite reliably with other semantic, syntactic and information-structural properties, such as agentivity, argumenthood and topicality (de Swart et al., 2008). In computational linguistic work, animacy has been shown to provide important information in anaphora resolution (Orăsan and Evans, 2007), argument disambiguation (Dell'Orletta et al., 2005) and syntactic parsing in general (Øvrelid and Nivre, 2007).

In this article we will explore the porting of a semantic classifier from one language to another, investigating the application of a semantic classifier trained on distributional data for one language directly to data from another language. We present first experiments examining the porting of automatic classification for the semantic property of animacy between the closely related languages of Swedish and Danish. Unlike previous work, we do not assume a parallel corpus or a gold standard annotation for the second language (Danish).

2 Swedish animacy classification

Talbanken05 is a Swedish treebank converted to dependency format, containing both written and spoken language (Nivre et al., 2006b).[2] In addition to information on part-of-speech, dependency head and relation, Talbanken05 distinguishes animacy for all nominal constituents.[3]

The dimension of animacy roughly distinguishes between entities which are alive and entities which are not. Table 1 presents an overview

---

[1] Parts of the research reported in this paper has been supported by the *Deutsche Forschungsgemeinschaft* (DFG, *Sonderforschungsbereich 632*, project D4).

[2] The written sections of the treebank consist of professional prose and student essays and amount to 197,123 running tokens, spread over 11,431 sentences.

[3] To be precise, the annotation in Talbanken05 distinguishes between 'person' and 'non-person'.

Class	Types	Tokens covered
Animate	644	6010
Inanimate	6910	34822
Total	7554	40832

Table 1: The animacy data set from Talbanken05; number of noun lemmas (Types) and tokens in each class.

of the animacy data for common nouns in Talbanken05. It is clear that the data is highly skewed towards the 'inanimate' class, which accounts for 91.5% of the data instances. Due to the small size of the treebank we classify common noun *lemmas*. Following a strategy in line with work on verb classification (Merlo and Stevenson, 2001; Stevenson and Joanis, 2003), we set out to classify the lemmas based on their morphosyntactic distribution in a considerably larger corpus. For the animacy classification of common nouns, we construct a general *feature space* for animacy classification, which makes use of distributional data regarding syntactic properties of the noun, as well as various morphological properties. The syntactic and morphological features are presented below:

Syntactic features subject (SUBJ), object (OBJ), prepositional complement (PA), root (ROOT), apposition (APP), conjunct (CC), determiner (DET), predicative (PRD), complement of comparative subjunction (UK).

Morphological features gender (NEU/UTR), number (SIN/PLU), definiteness (DEF/IND), case (NOM/GEN).

For each noun lemma w, relative frequencies of the morphosyntactic features f_i are calculated from the corpus: $\frac{freq(f_i,w)}{freq(w)}$. For extraction of distributional data for the Talbanken05 nouns we make use of the Swedish Parole corpus of 21.5M tokens,[4] and to facilitate feature extraction, we part-of-speech tag the corpus and parse it with MaltParser[5] (Nivre et al., 2006a), which assigns a dependency analysis.[6]

Classification is performed with Support Vector Machines (SVMs) and we make use of the LIB-SVM package (Chang and Lin, 2001) with a RBF kernel ($C = 8.0, \gamma = 0.5$).[7] For training and testing of the classifiers, we make use of leave-one-out cross-validation.

We obtain results for animacy classification, ranging from 97.1 accuracy to 93.7 depending on the sparsity of the data.[8] With an absolute frequency threshold of 10, we obtain an accuracy of 95.1%, which constitutes a 46.7% reduction of error rate compared to a majority baseline which assigns the class of inanimate to all instances (90.8).

3 Danish distributional data

The Swedish classifier has been trained on distributional data which generalizes over the distribution of individual nouns. In order to apply the animacy classifier trained on Swedish and described in section 2 above, we will need morphosyntactic distributional data for Danish noun lemmas along the same set of features as those employed for the classification of Swedish nouns.

3.1 Data

We employ the freely available Danish corpus Korpus2000 which contains approximately 22 million words.[9] In order to obtain both morphological and syntactic information regarding the nouns in the corpus, we part-of-speech tag and parse the corpus, employing MaltTagger and Malt-Parser, both trained on the analysis found in the Danish Dependency Treebank (DDT) (Kromann, 2003).[10]

3.2 Features

For application of the animacy classifier to Danish data, we must also represent our data set within the same feature space as the one defined for the Swedish classification task. As mentioned earlier, Korpus2000 has been parsed with a parser which assigns a dependency analysis, and followingly has much in common with the dependency analysis in Talbanken05. Even so, the syntactic anal-

---

[4]Parole is available at http://spraakbanken.gu.se

[5]http://www.maltparser.org

[6]For part-of-speech tagging, we employ the MaltTagger – a HMM part-of-speech tagger for Swedish (Hall, 2003). For parsing, we employ MaltParser with a pretrained model for Swedish, which has been trained on the tags output by the tagger.

[7]Parameter optimization, i.e., choice of kernel function, C and γ values, is performed on 20% of the total data set with the easy.py tool, supplied with LIBSVM.

[8]With a threshold of 1000 instances in Parole, the accuracy is 97.1, whereas it is 93.7 with no threshold. It is not surprising that a method based on distributional features suffers when the absolute frequencies approach 1.

[9]http://korpus.dsl.dk/korpus2000/.

[10]http://www.id.cbs.dk/ mtk/treebank/

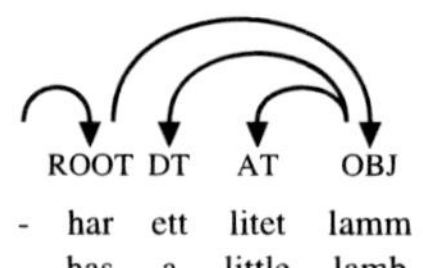

Figure 1: Talbanken05 annotation

Figure 2: DDT annotation

	Animate			Inanimate		
	Prec	Rec	Fscore	Prec	Rec	Fscore
Swedish >10	81.9	64.0	71.8	96.4	98.6	97.5
Danish >10	74.5	45.5	56.5	95.5	98.7	97.1

Table 2: Precision, recall and F-scores for the two classes in the Swedish experiments, as well as the Danish experiments, evaluated through translational equivalents on the Talbanken05 data set.

yses of the two treebanks, hence parsers, are not completely isomorphic.

One point of difference between the two treebanks is in the head status of so-called functional categories, such as determiners and prepositions. Talbanken05 treats the nouns as heads with functional dependents, as illustrated in figure 1 where the determiner *ett* 'a' is a dependent of the noun *lamm* 'lamb'. The syntactic annotation in DDT, on the other hand, treats functional categories as heads with nominal dependents (nobj), as illustrated by figure 2, where the noun is a dependent of the determiner *et* 'a'. In extracting the distributional data for Danish, we wish to distinguish between various types of nominal argument relations such as subject, object and prepositional object. We therefore assign to the nouns the dependency relation of their head, e.g. the noun *lam* 'lamb' in figure 2 is assigned the `dobj`-relation of its determiner head.

With a few adjustments, we may thus employ the feature sets described in section 2 above to represent the Danish distributional data. With a frequency treshold of 10, to ensure sufficient distributional data, we end up with 18240 noun lemmas for classification. We apply the Swedish classifier to the Danish distributional data, resulting in a total of 16692 inanimate instances (91.5%) and 1548 animate instances (8.5%).

4 Evaluation

Evaluation of the resulting classification is not entirely straightforward, due to the fact that we do not have a Danish gold standard. Whereas this fact formed part of the motivation for this work, it also poses a challenge when we wish to evaluate the resulting classifier.

4.1 Evaluation through translation

If we assume that central semantic properties, such as animacy, do not differ between translational equivalents, we may use the Swedish gold standard annotation in order to evaluate the Danish classification.

We compile a Danish-Swedish lexicon from freely available, on-line resources.[11] The resulting dictionary contains a total of 5885 Danish-Swedish word pairs.[12] With this resource, we find a Swedish translation for 2555 of our classified Danish noun lemmas (18240 in total). Out of the set of classified Danish lemmas with a Swedish translation, 978 noun lemmas furthermore have a gold standard animacy annotation in the Talbanken05 data set. In the resulting gold-standard, the proportion of inanimate instances is 92.1, giving us a baseline for evaluation.[13]

The method for evaluation clearly only gives us an evaluation for a small subset of our classified lemmas. Even so, it might still give us a reasonable idea about the general quality of the ported classifier.

4.1.1 Results

The accuracy of the classifier when evaluated against the translated Talbanken05 data is 94.5, which constitutes a 30.3% reduction in error rate compared to the baseline. We find that the acquired classification furthermore is significantly better than the baseline (p<.001).[14]

The result for Danish is similar to the result obtained for the Swedish nouns of same frequency (95.1). Recall however that the Swedish and Dan-

---

[11]The free dictionaries project at http://www.dicts.info/ and dictionaries found at http://www.danska-svenska.se and http://dictionary.japplis.com/danish-swedish.html

[12]The lexicon consists of all types of word classes, not only nouns. Furthermore, the on-line resources from which the lexicon was compiled have largely been constructed automatically, hence are by no means perfect.

[13]Note however, that the baseline does not necessarily reflect the true distribution of animate vs. inanimate instances in Danish. The fact that it is higher than in the Swedish data is an indication that it might be artificially high due to arbitrary properties of the dictionaries used for evaluation.

[14]For calculation of the statistical significance of differences in the performance of classifiers tested on the same data set, McNemar's test is employed.

ish classifiers are evaluated on different data sets. The Swedish classifier is evaluated on the total Talbanken05 data set presented in table 1,[15] whereas the Danish classifier is evaluated on the nouns in this data set for which there is a Danish-Swedish translation *and* more than 10 instances in the Korpus2000 corpus.

With respect to the classes of 'animate' and 'inanimate', table 2 reports the class-based measures of precision, recall and F-score for the Swedish and Danish classifiers. The baseline F-score for the animate class is 0, and a main goal in classification is therefore to improve on the rate of true positives for animate instances, while limiting the trade-off in terms of performance for the majority class of inanimates, which start out with F-scores approaching 100. We find that the performance for the minority class of 'animate' is generally lower than in the Swedish results. Like the Swedish results, however, we find that the classifier is consevative in terms of assignment of the minority class of 'animate' and shows a fairly high precision (74.5), combined with a lower recall (45.5) for this class. For the majority class of 'inanimate', the performance for the two languages are highly similar, with F-scores between 97.1-97.5.

5 Conclusions and future work

The porting of a classifier for the semantic property of animacy, trained on distributional frequencies for noun lemmas, turns out to work quite well for the highly related language-pair Swedish-Danish. Distributional data describing the general morphosyntactic distribution of nouns was extracted for the new language, Danish, and a classifier trained on corresponding data for the source language, Swedish, was then applied. We evaluated the resulting classification by means of translation to the gold standard annotation in Swedish and found that the resulting classifier gave significant improvements over a majority baseline. We obtain an accuracy of 94.5 on the Danish evaluation data set, constituting a 30.3% reduction of error rate. Using only a large, automatically annotated corpus for the second language, Danish, we were able to obtain animacy annotation for a total of 18240 noun lemmas. This clearly gives us a better coverage than one what one might expect

---

[15]With the restriction that it occurs more than 10 times in the Parole corpus.

from an approach relying on translation by means of lexical resources.

In terms of future work, we are interested in the application of a similar methodology (i) to other language pairs, both highly related, e.g., German-Dutch, Spanish-Italian, and less related ones, and (ii) to other semantic classification tasks, such as verb or adjective classification.

References

Chih-Chung Chang and Chih-Jen Lin. 2001. LIBSVM: A library for support vector machines. Software available at http://www.csie.ntu.edu.tw/~cjlin/libsvm.

Peter de Swart, Monique Lamers, and Sander Lestrade. 2008. Animacy, argument structure and argument encoding: Introduction to the special issue on animacy. *Lingua*, 118(2):131–140.

Felice Dell'Orletta, Alessandro Lenci, Simonetta Montemagni, and Vito Pirrelli. 2005. A maximum entropy model of subject/object learning. In *Proceedings of the 2nd Workshop on Psychocomputational Models of Human Language Acquisition*.

Johan Hall. 2003. A probabilistic part-of-speech tagger with suffix probabilities. Master's thesis, Växjö University, Sweden.

Richard Johansson and Pierre Nugues. 2006. A FrameNet-based semantic role labeler for Swedish. In *Proceedings of COLING/ACL*.

Matthias Trautner Kromann. 2003. The Danish Dependency Treebank and the DTAG treebank tool. In *Proceedings of the Second Workshop on Treebanks and Linguistic Theories (TLT)*.

Dekang Lin. 1998. Automatic retrieval and clustering of similar words. In *Proceedings of the 17th International Conference on Computational Linguistics (COLING)*, volume 2, pages 768–774.

Paola Merlo and Suzanne Stevenson. 2001. Automatic verb classification based on statistical distributions of argument structure. *Computational Linguistics*, 27(3):373–408.

Paola Merlo, Suzanne Stevenson, Vivian Tsang, and Gianluca Allaria. 2002. A multilingual paradigm for automatic verb classification. In *Procs. of the 40th Meeting of the Association for Computational Linguistics (ACL '02)*.

Joakim Nivre, Johan Hall, and Jens Nilsson. 2006a. Maltparser: A data-driven parser-generator for dependency parsing. In *Proceedings of the Conference on Language Resources and Evaluation (LREC)*.

Joakim Nivre, Jens Nilsson, and Johan Hall. 2006b. Talbanken05: A Swedish treebank with phrase structure and dependency annotation. In *Proceedings of the Conference on Language Resources and Evaluation (LREC)*.

Constantin Orăsan and Richard Evans. 2007. NP animacy resolution for anaphora resolution. *Journal of Artificial Intelligence Research*, 29:79–103.

Lilja Øvrelid and Joakim Nivre. 2007. When word order and part-of-speech tags are not enough – Swedish dependency parsing with rich linguistic features. In *Proceedings of Recent Advances in Natural Language Processing (RANLP)*.

Sebastian Pado and Mirella Lapata. 2005. Cross-lingual projection of role-semantic information. In *Proceedings of HLT/EMNLP 2005*.

Suzanne Stevenson and Eric Joanis. 2003. Semi-supervised verb class discovery using noisy features. In *Proceedings of the Conference on Computational Natural Language Learning (CoNLL)*, pages 71–78.

ISSN 1736-6305 Vol. 4
http://hdl.handle.net/10062/9206

V Student Papers

Prominence detected by listeners

for future speech synthesis application

Maria Eskevich
Saint Petersburg State University
Saint Petersburg, Russia
`maria.eskevich@gmail.com`

Abstract

The point of interest in the present investigation is to find out and to make a pilot statistical presentation of the prominence distinguished by native speakers in read aloud texts taken from the Russian corpus for text-to-speech unit-selection synthesis.

The TTS system uses the linguistic information encoded in the input text. Therefore the parameters which are easily extracted from the text (part of speech classes, number of syllables) are admitted as the basis for the classification of the words detected as prominent by listeners.

On further steps the TTS system has to assign prosodic structure and its suprasegmental acoustic parameters. The professionally made phonetic segmentation and analysis of syntagmatic structures of the material are compared with the judgments of native speakers in order to find some of these acoustic correlates.

1 Introduction

Prediction of word prominence might help us to build more natural synthesized speech and pay more attention to some parts of speech in process of speech recognizing because it brings more valuable information. The person who is making it prominent (speaker or writer) is doing it consciously, however it is probably that this person is not aware of the physical mechanism (changing of pitch, intensity or syllable duration).

According to Taylor (2008) there are different levels of prominence:

(1) conceived by the author of some written text which normally is not intended to be read and therefore in this text special constructions are used to emphasize important things (e.g. he said it *angrily*, he said *aloud*)

(2) conceived by people who are reading the text aloud

(3) conceived by people who are talking and emphasizing something in their utterances

In all these cases, native speakers understand where the authors put the emphasis and the speech seems natural and normal for them.

While doing speech synthesis we have to predict prominence by using information available in the text. In the sentence we have word-accent and sentence-level stress. The former is put according to the rules of the language (for example on the last syllable as in French) or according to the dictionary (as in English or in Russian). The latter is put according to the meaning of the sentence and communicative intention.

We have also to distinguish three levels of word accents: accented, unaccented, and clitisized. Clitisized words are unaccented, but additionally lack word stress (Cole, 1997).

On the other hand, we may distinguish the words according to main lexical classes – function words and content words (Holmes at al., 2001). Function words (or grammatical words) are words that have little lexical meaning or have ambiguous meaning, but instead serve to express grammatical relationships with the other words within sentence, or specify the attitude or mood of the speaker (Skrelin at al., 1997). Content words always have meaning (Noun names the object; Verb, Adjective and Adverb name its features). Function words and Pronouns belong to the closed-class words and content words to the open-class words.

It seems that content words should have accent and can have prominence. The clitisized function words (as particles in Russian) may add some extra meaning, and in this way they may increase prominence of the content word.

The structural data of the input text are processed by the algorithm which predicts the prosodic structure and the prominence of some words. Later on the TTS system changes the acoustic characteristics of concatenated units in a way the researchers suppose it has to be realized in the signal.

Streefkerk at al. (2001) tried to predict prominence using rules based mainly on the word-class classification and achieved the score of 92.6 % right prediction. The prominence was considered as gradual parameter and the value was counted as the sum of marks assigned while applying the rules. Content words received one mark, then additional mark for special parts of speech within content words) and also on the polysyllabic structure of content words (polysyllabic words from the classes Pronoun, Verb, Adverb). The information about the word-class of the previous word was partially used, only for the case of the Noun preceded by an Adjective. This limitation seems reasonable since the other research confirmed that the word class and the clause position are more relevant for prominence prediction than word class of context. For Russian the experiments of the perception of the combination Noun + Adjective and Adjective + Noun also did not reveal strong difference in prominence perception (Altuhova, 2007).

In the prosodic organization of Russian text-to-speech synthesis there were several stages of accentuation assignment: content words were unified with cliticized words; on the level of phrase the content words received stress; then the last content word in phrase received additional syntagmatic stress; and in the end special logic stress derived from the special syntactic factors (Skrelin at al., 1997). These words marked with phrasal stress and special logic stress are supposed to be perceived by listeners as prominent.

2 Experiment

2.1 Material/Method

Corpus for Russian text-to-speech unit-selection synthesis is created at the Saint Petersburg State University. For this pilot experiment 100 sentences read by 2 speakers (male (MS) and female (FS)) were taken. Both speakers are professional announcers that is why it is possible to assume that the quality of their voice is not going to change and become more monotonous due to tiredness caused by reading.

The speech material was presented via headphones and judgments were made on printout of the text. There was no response time limitation. The subjects could decide for themselves how many times to replay the utterance.

8 Russian native speakers (3 male and 5 female), aged from 25 to 31, passed the listening tests and gave their responses regarding the prominence in each sentence and its position in each phrase. It was not explained in details what kind of prominence they should find. The request was to indicate the prominence where they hear it and to evaluate it from 1 to 10 points. The amount of points assigned to the word is the level of prominence intensity felt by the native speaker.

As a result the statistics was built on the basis of the judgments made by listeners. The word was considered prominent if at least four listeners marked it as prominent. Since the data might be affected by the restricted number of speakers (just two voices) the results are given separately.

3 Results

The average length of the sentence is 8.79 words. The total amount of words is 863.

All words in text are divided into two general classes – content words (Verbs, Nouns, Pronouns, Adverbs, Adjectives, Numerals) and function words (Conjunctions, Propositions, Particles and Interjections).

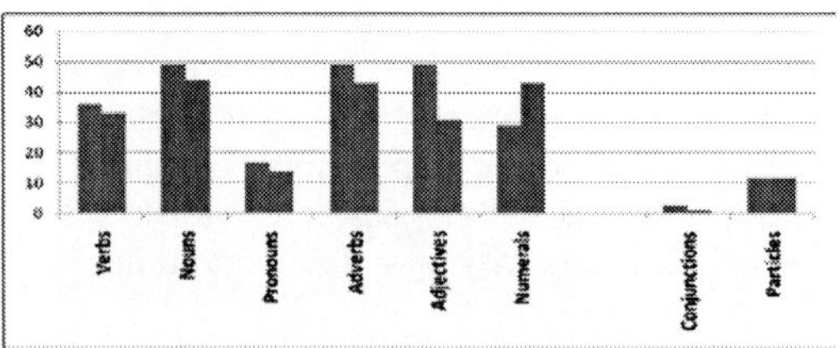

Figure 1. Distribution of the words according to the parts of speech classification (percentage). First column – Male speaker, second column – Female speaker

Figure 1 shows the distribution of words used in experiment among the parts of speech and the number of words (percentage) within corresponding part of speech detected as prominent by listeners. The data for the male and the female speakers are given separately. 29 % of the words in the male speaker's sentences and 25 % of the words in the female speaker's sentences were marked as prominent. It means that each sentence had one or more prominent words. The number of prominent content words (239 for MS and 206 for FS) is much greater than the number of prominent function words (13 for MS and 11 for FS) as it was expected and found by Widera at al. (1997) for German.

Even though different speakers have their own style of pronunciation, they are giving a comparable level of prominence to the words since they read the same text. The slight difference in percentage may consequently show individual characteristics and tendency to emphasize more or less, but the order of numbers stays the same. This implies that the text contains some linguistic information.

The average length of prominent words is presented in Figures 2. It shows the percentage of the words with 1-6 syllables in each part of the speech (only prominent words). It turns out that the content words, such as Verbs, Nouns, Adverbs and Adjectives, which contain 2-3 syllables are more prominent (2 syllables - 40-50% and 3 syllables – 30-40 % of all prominent words). Among the content parts of speech only pronouns are mainly presented by 1-syllable words. It can be explained by the average length of this class of words in Russian (1-2 syllables) and the fact that this is a closed-class.

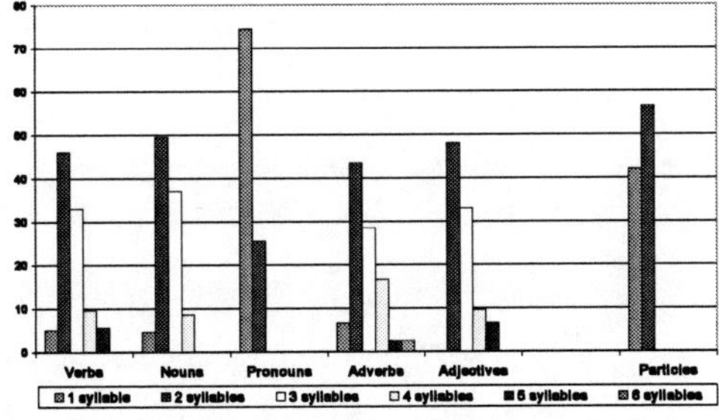

Figure 2. Average number of prominent words of each part of speech (%) with corresponding number of syllables (for 2 speakers).

3.1 Discussion

The distribution of the prominence assignment among content words shows that the part of speech tagging of the input text might help to predict prominence. For Dutch the additional marks were given to Noun, Adjective, Numeral and Negation (Streefkerk at al., 2001), but the results of experiment shows that for Russian these extra marks can be added to Verb as well. The polysyllabic structure in Russian also differs and the results show that for Russian the polysyllabic Verb, Noun, Adverbs, Adjectives and monosyllabic Pronouns can receive such additional marks.

All the data were listened by a phonetician to assign logical stress which is supposed to be consistently perceived by native speakers as prominence.

When the logical stress coincides with phrasal stress, it is perceived by listeners in 92 % for MS and 82 % for FS. There are some cases when less than three listeners perceive prominence, but there are no cases when it is not perceived at all. It means that this type of pattern can be used for sentences with predicted prominence. The other question is how to derive the information about logical stress from written text when it is emphasized by font and has to be done by means of syntactic analysis.

On the other hand, there are 33 occurrences (22 for MS and 10 for FS) when logical stress does not coincide with phrasal stress. And these cases are perceived by speakers as prominent in 64 % for MS and 60 % for FS. It is interesting that in 25 % cases for both speakers only two listeners marked prominence. These listeners differ from other ones as they received musical education and seem to have ear for music that might be the reason for detecting pitch changing as good as phoneticians. However there are some cases that are not perceived as prominence at all.

3.2 Conclusion and Future Work

As the experiment has shown, listeners quite easily distinguish prominent words and are mainly uniform in assigning it. Further interrelated directions of research are prediction of prominence on the basis of the text (part of speech classification and assigning of prominence) and further acoustical analysis of words marked as prominent and the pitch contours they make part in, thus investigating how to set prominent parameters for which words have to be emphasized according to the previous written text analysis. It was found that the distribution of the prominence within part of speech classification can be added for Russian speech synthesis as well as it is added for other languages. The coincidence of marks of professional phonetician segmentation and of native speakers means that the correlates of prominence are presented in the signal and can be found in further acoustic analysis.

References

Cole R., Mariani J., Uszkoreit H., Zaenen A. and Zue V., 1997 *Survey of the state of the art in human language technology*, Cambridge University Press.

Holmes, J. and Holmes, W. 2001. *Speech synthesis and recognition. London and New York.*

Taylor P., 2008. *Text-to-Speech Synthesis* Cambridge University Press.

Widera C. and Portele T., 1997. *Prediction of word prominence.* In Proc. European Conf. on Speech Communication and Technology.

Streefkerk, B. M., Pols, L. C. W., and Bosch, L. F. M., 2001. *Up to what level can acoustical and textual features predict prominence*", Proc. Eurospeech'01, Vol. 2, Aalborg, Denmark: 811-814,

Raux A. and A. Black, 2003. *A unit selection approach to F0 modeling and its application to emphasis.* ASRU 2003, St Thomas, US Virgin Islands.

Altuhova E., 2007. *Changing of the pitch on an adjective followed by a noun and its' interpretation for intonation division.* Materials of the XXXVI International Philological conference [in Russian]

Skrelin P.A., Svetozarova N.D. and Volskaja N.B., 1997. *Modelling of prosodic organization of Russian speech.* In Bulletin of Phonetic Fund of Russian language. N. 7. Saint Petersburg-Bohum. [in Russian]

ISSN 1736-6305 Vol. 4
http://hdl.handle.net/10062/9206

A comparison and combination of segmental and fixed-frame signal representations in NMF-based word recognition

Okko Räsänen
Department of Signal Processing and
Acoustics, Helsinki University of
Technology, Espoo, Finland
Okko.Rasanen@tkk.fi

Joris Driesen
Department of Electrical Engineering,
Katholieke Universiteit Leuven, Leuven,
Belgium
Joris.Driesen@esat.kuleuven.be

Abstract

Segmental and fixed-frame signal representations were compared in different noise conditions in a weakly supervised word recognition task using a non-negative matrix factorization (NMF) framework. The experiments show that fixed-frame windowing results in better recognition rates with clean signals. When noise is introduced to the system, robustness of segmental signal representations becomes useful, decreasing the overall word error rate. It is shown that a combination of fixed-frame and segmental representations yields the best recognition rates in different noise conditions. An entropy based method for dynamically adjusting the weight between representations is also introduced, leading to near-optimal weighting and therefore enhanced recognition rates in varying SNR conditions.

1 Introduction

Structural characteristics of signal representations are an important aspect in all pattern discovery and speech recognition tasks. There are numerous different methods for describing speech signals that use different types of signal transformations, including, e.g., FFT, cepstra and LP-coefficients. These approaches describe local spectral properties of the signal as feature frames at a specific point in time. However, it is well known that also the way that temporal aspects of the signal are included in the analysis is important. Most approaches in speech recognition, including state-of-the-art HMMs, use *fixed-frame* windowing where the chosen features are extracted from approximately 20-25 ms long windows at fixed temporal intervals, e.g., every 10 milliseconds (see Gales and Young, 2008).

Speech signals, however, have a very special temporal structure, which can be described in terms of hierarchically organized linguistically motivated units like utterances, words, syllables and phones. This structure has to exist in the speech signal in order for the receiver to be able to decode it. For example, human listeners are able to locate and segment phone-like segments in speech signal, although the reliability and accuracy of the location of phone-phone boundaries is often quite inaccurate (+/- 20 ms at best). Phone structure, or at least phone-like units, can then also be detected automatically using automatic segmentation algorithms that often use information about spectral changes in the signal in order to provide hypotheses about possible phone-boundary locations. These phone-like segments can then be described with chosen features to next levels of processing instead of fixed windowing, or the phone boundary information can be utilized in processing of fixed frame representations as was done in this study to form *segmental representations*. The way that temporal information is embedded in the feature stream has important implications for the next steps in the processing of the signals.

The aim of this paper is to present findings from comparison of fixed-frame and segmental based vector quantized representations of the speech signal in a NMF-based word learning and recognition task (Van hamme, 2008a; Van Hamme, 2008b; Ten Bosch et al., 2008), where a weakly supervised speech recognition system is trained with these two types of signal representations and then tested in word recognition accuracy.

1.1 Properties of signal representations

In theory, the use of temporal segmental information should have several advantages. It synchronizes the feature stream to phonetically meaningful units in speech and the features can be extracted from desired temporal locations aligned with each segment. Phonetic synchrony facilitates the co-occurrence of subsequent phonetic units in temporally coherent manner (or at fixed lags in NMF) as the temporal deviations resulting from, e.g., different speaking rates or badly aligned windows are removed. This may aid pattern discovery methods, including NMF, in detection of recurring patterns (see Stouten et al., 2008). Segmental knowledge can be also used for compression of the feature data describing the signal, since each segment can be represented with a fixed number of features that incorporate all essential aspects of a segment. Segmental descriptions have the potential of being more robust in noisy situations when compared to fixed-frame representations, as they can integrate spectral information over large temporal units.

The use of fixed frame representations, on the other hand, has several advantages, too. It provides a stable stream of information about the speech signal without being affected by the underlying signal content. For example, in situations where a segmentation algorithm misses transitions from phone to another and therefore leads to deletions in the label sequence, the fixed frame representation provides systematical information of the spectral content in the transient signal. Temporal resolution of fixed frames is also good if the window step size is sufficiently small, which means that the quantized label sequences can describe short-term details in the signal whereas segmental information is often an 'average' description of the content of a detected phone-like unit.

2 Algorithms used in experiments

2.1 Signal representations

For the experiments, fixed-frame signal representations were first created using vector quantization (VQ) and then segmental information was utilized to derive segmental version of the representations. The signals were first pre-emphasized and then MFCC-features were extracted every 10 ms. Quantization of the signal frames was performed using codebooks created by *k-means* algorithm: one codebook for static MFCCs, one for Δ-, and one for $\Delta\Delta$- coefficients. Corresponding VQ codebook sizes were 150, 150 and 100 labels, respectively. Each codebook was used as a separate input stream to the system.

Segmental information was provided using a blind segmentation algorithm that tracks sudden changes in the spectral content of the signal using cross-correlation of spectral frames. The algorithm detects approximately 75 % of the segmental boundaries defined in a manually annotated reference of a test-set in the TIMIT corpus (with maximum deviation of ± 20 ms; Räsänen, 2007). Segmental representations were created using the information about segmental boundaries to group fixed-frame representation into segments, and then compressing these groups of VQ labels in each stream into overall descriptions of the segments. In order to do this, a number of labels had to be chosen to represent each segment according to some decision criteria. Preliminary experiments indicated that the best method for picking up N labels for each segment was to take the mode of labels (the most frequent label) inside each of the N pre-defined sub-segment. This smoothens out small variability inside segments and picks only the most dominant label for the chosen sub-segment. When one label was chosen to represent a segment, the mode was taken from labels between 5 % and 95 % of the entire segment duration. In case of two labels per segment, the segment was divided to two sub-segments from 5 % to 45 % and from 55 % to 95 % of segment duration and modes were taken from these sub-segments. In case of three labels, corresponding sub-segment ranges were from 5 % to 40 %, from 30 % to 70 %, and from 60 % to 95 % in terms of segment duration.

2.2 Word-learning algorithm

The utilized non-negative matrix factorization (NMF) algorithm for word recognition is described in detail in the work of (Van hamme 2008a). The NMF in general is a mathematical technique to decompose a complex high-dimensional data-matrix as a product of two lower-dimensional matrices (see Lee and Seung, 2001). It has shown to be a powerful language-learning algorithm, capable of acquiring and robustly detecting at least a dozen keywords (see Van hamme, 2008a; Ten Bosch et al., 2008; Van hamme, 2008b).

The idea of the method is as follows. Firstly, speech utterances are converted to a vectorized form by accumulating the co-occurrences of labels from a single stream (statics, velocity and acceleration) in the signal at different time offsets (lags) and putting them in a histogram. The histograms determined on the different label streams can be concatenated into a single high-dimensional vector. This representation, which is called the Histogram of Acoustic Co-occurrences (Van hamme 2008a), is very convenient for performing NMF, due to the non-negativeness of its elements and the fact that it is by approximation entirely composed of non-negative subparts, namely the HAC-representations of the words constituting the original utterances. Concretely, the NMF algorithm can be written as:

$$\mathbf{V} \approx \mathbf{W}\,\mathbf{H} \qquad (1)$$

in which $\mathbf{V}$ is a matrix, each column of which is the HAC-representation of an utterance from the input data. The columns of $\mathbf{W}$ contain non-negative parts that make up the data, and the columns of $\mathbf{H}$ contain the extent to which each of these parts is present in each utterance. If the inner dimension (i.e. the number of columns in W) of the factorization is cleverly chosen, typically a bit higher than the total number of different words to be learned in the data, the non-negative parts contained in the columns of W will approximately model the HAC-representations of those words after convergence (Van hamme, 2008a; Van hamme, 2008b).

Given an utterance from the test set, $\mathbf{W}$ can be used to calculate an activation level for each trained word. If our objective is to detect one single keyword in the utterances of the test set, the answer for each utterance will consist of the word that is maximally activated by this utterance.

3 Experiments

3.1 Material

A corpus recorded as a part of the ACORNS project[1] was used. The chosen subset of the corpus (UK Y1) consists of 4000 English utterances spoken by four different native English speakers (two males). The sentences in the material simulate linguistic input to infants less than one year of age. Each utterance contains a keyword surrounded by

a carrier sentence (total 11 different keywords: *bath, book, bottle, car, daddy, mommy, nappy, shoe, telephone, Angus, Ewan*). Each utterance is also paired with a meta-tag that indicates the presence of a keyword in the utterance. This simulates a multimodal information source in a situation where there is an object of interest in the environment and the learning agent is paying attention to it, making it possible to model acoustic content in association to some other information source. The training material consisted of 2999 randomly selected utterances and the test material of the remaining 1000 utterances (one signal was removed due to an apparent recording problem). In the evaluation, the algorithm had to provide most likely keyword for each utterance that was then compared to the manual annotation.

3.2 Baseline experiments

After training the system with the 2999 utterances in the training material using 10 ms fixed-frame VQ-labels, a baseline result of 0.1 % WER was obtained for word recognition. When information about segmental boundary locations was utilized, keyword recognition accuracy depended on the amount of labels used for describing each segment. WER of 3.2 % was obtained using 1 label per segment. Interestingly, with two labels, only WER of 3.3 % was obtained after profuse experimenting with parameters, whereas for three labels the WER decreased to 2.8 %, being slightly below one label condition.

While it is not exactly clear why the error rate does not decrease when two labels are used instead of one, a possible explanation may be that the co-occurrence of labels becomes disturbed when the mode of labels is chosen from relatively large temporal areas that mainly represent left and right phone transitions (from the previous phone to the current phone and from the current phone to the next phone), whereas selecting one label per segment smoothens out these left and right transitions into one overall segmental description. However, transitional information should be still somewhat systematic at least for those phones that are not in the beginning or at the end of the word that is being modeled. Despite this, it may be that one overall description is better than two more context dependent descriptions, since counting co-occurrences of context-dependencies of adjacent phones may be more sensitive to variations in, e.g.,

---

[1] http://www.acorns-project.org

speaking rate and long-range phonetic context.

In case of three labels per segment, the segmental description contains both left and right context and a sort of "locus" description from the middle of each segment that seems to carry important information regarding the underlying phonetic content. This is still significantly worse than the 0.1 % WER baseline with fixed frame representation.

This concludes that the compression to segmental level descriptions loses some fine details in the speech signal that are meaningful in order to differentiate between words. Three labels per segment yields the best recognition results for segmental based signal representations but falls still far behind fixed frame accuracies.

However, using only one label per segment has a noteworthy impact on computational complexity of further processing, since the signal representation is compressed into approximately 1/11 (9.1 %) of the original 10 ms fixed-frame size. The accuracy with this approach is almost as good as with three labels per segment, but due to data reduction, it speeds up execution of the NMF algorithm greatly.

3.3 Introducing noise

In order to see how well the representations and NMF perform in noise, two different types of noise were introduced to the system: 1) white noise added to the acoustic input, and 2) artificial noise added to the already quantized label sequences. In these experiments, the fixed frame signal representations were compared with segmental labels with one label per segment (mode of fixed frame symbols inside the segment).

In the first noise condition, five levels of (white Gaussian) noise were added to the acoustic input before signal quantization. Corresponding signal-to-noise ratios were baseline level (set to 60 dB for visualization purposes), 40 dB, 30 dB, 20 dB, and 10 dB, mean noise level being computed over each utterance, including small silent portions in the beginning and in the end of the signals. For the remaining of this paper, this type of noise shall be called *acoustic white noise* (*AWN*).

The second type of noise, which shall be called *channel noise* (*CN*), was introduced to the recognition process by directly scrambling the label sequences at random indices. A manually defined percentage of labels were changed to a

random label from the VQ codebook (using a uniform distribution). Five levels of SNR^2 were used: ∞, 22dB, 8.5dB, 0dB, and -8.5dB (SNR = $10\log([1\text{-}p_{scrambled}]/p_{scrambled})$, where $p \in [0,1]$). This type of scrambling simulates noise originating from somewhere inside the system, e.g., by errors in the transmission channel, and can be used to examine the nature of representations needed for reliable pattern discovery.

It was also of interest whether fixed frame and segmental representations would contain complementary information. Therefore activations of keyword representations in NMF were combined together with a formula:

$$act_{combined} = \alpha \times act_{fixed} + (\alpha - 1) \times act_{segmental} \quad (2)$$

where $\alpha \in [0,1]$ and act_{fixed} and $act_{segmental}$ are word activations caused by fixed-frame input and segmental input, respectively.

In addition, reliability of segmentation in noisy conditions is also a central issue in this type of comparison. Boundary detection accuracy of the used segmentation algorithm has been found reasonably robust at least down to 0 dB SNR, however leading to increase in over-segmentation rate as the noise becomes more dominating (still approximately 75 % of boundaries are correctly detected at SNR = 20 dB with less than 10 % of over-segmentation; Räsänen, in preparation). In order to confirm these findings in word recognition experiments instead of previous comparison to reference annotation, the segmentation was also performed in parallel with both noisy input and clean input to see differences between these two situations.

3.4 Experiments with acoustic white noise

The system, including VQ codebook and NMF representations, was first trained using clean speech and then tested in word recognition with VQ-labels produced at different levels of AWN. Figure 1 displays the results at different SNR levels. As can be seen, the results are very similar for both representations at SNR = 40 dB, but as the SNR goes further down, the segmental representation of the signal performs significantly better than the fixed 10 ms frames approach. Increasing and varying the lag parameter of NMF

---

[2] Note that SNR is here defined as a ratio of corrupted versus uncorrupted VQ-labels instead of using momentary noise and signal amplitude or power.

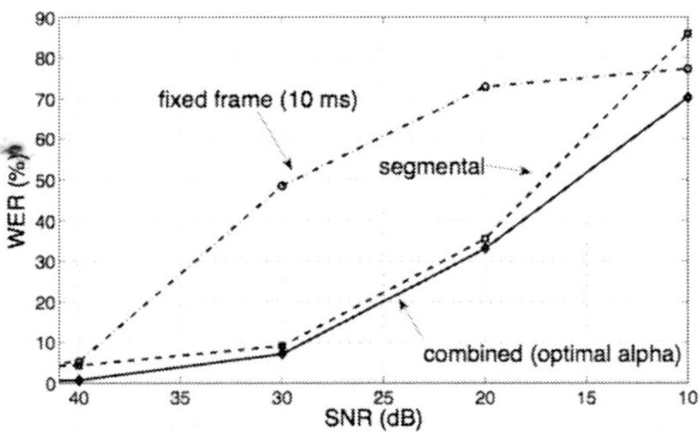

Figure 1: Word-error rates as a function of SNR for fixed frames labels every 10 ms, segmental labels (one label per phone-like segment) and these two combined in case of acoustic white noise. Combination of these representations has complementary value and increases the recognition accuracy.

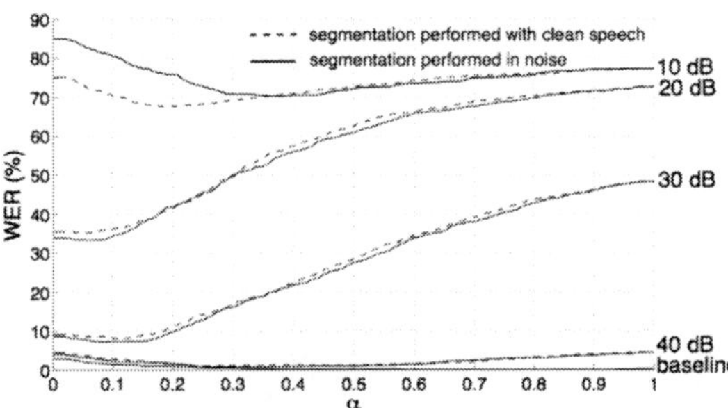

Figure 2: Word-error rates shown for different SNR levels (acoustic white noise) as a function of representation weighting factor alpha. The left edge (alpha = 0) shows results for pure segmental representation whereas the right edge (alpha = 1) shows results using only fixed frame information.

did not affect the WER significantly from the original 50 ms and 90 ms lags in fixed-frame condition.

When word model activations from both representations are combined using eq. 2, WER further decreases, suggesting that they contain complementary information at all noise levels (alpha optimized separately for each SNR level). Figure 2 displays the word-error rates for combined representations at different SNR levels as a function of alpha, both with segmentation performed in noise (solid lines) and with clean speech (dashed lines).

As the fixed frame representation performs better at low noise levels, the optimal alpha for these levels is rather high. However, as soon as the SNR starts to drop, the optimal alpha starts to decrease fast. At very high noise levels the

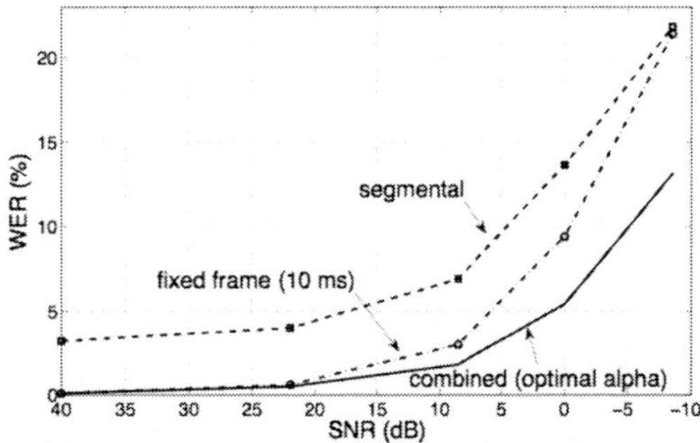

Figure 3: Word-error rates in channel noise as a function of SNR for fixed frames labels every 10 ms, segmental labels (one label per phone-like segment) and these two combined. Combination of these representations has complementary value and increases the recognition accuracy.

segmental descriptions seem to degrade badly and alpha shifts back towards fixed frames. This was found to be due to fact that at very high noise levels the vector quantization process tends to attract most of the feature vectors into a handful of *'noise-like'* clusters. As these labels start to become the majority in the utterance related sequences, taking the mode of labels for all segments results in same (noise) symbols representing most of the segments. However, the overall recognition rates at 10 dB are extremely poor with all values of alpha.

Figure 2 also shows that the difference between blind segmentation performed in clean and noisy speech is not being significantly affected by the increase of noise all the way down to $SNR = 20$ dB. Only at SNR of 10 dB the degradation of segmentation quality becomes clearly visible in terms of recognition rate. This suggests that the information about segmental boundaries can be considered reliable at moderate white noise levels.

3.5 Experiments with channel noise

When noise is introduced directly to label sequences after quantization, the situation changes significantly as the noise affects only some of the quantized frames. The results show that the qualities of both representations start to degrade in a fairly similar manner as the SNR increases (figure 3), fixed frame representation being more effective all the way down to SNR = -8.5 dB. Increasing the number of lags or varying the lag lengths did not decrease the WER significantly

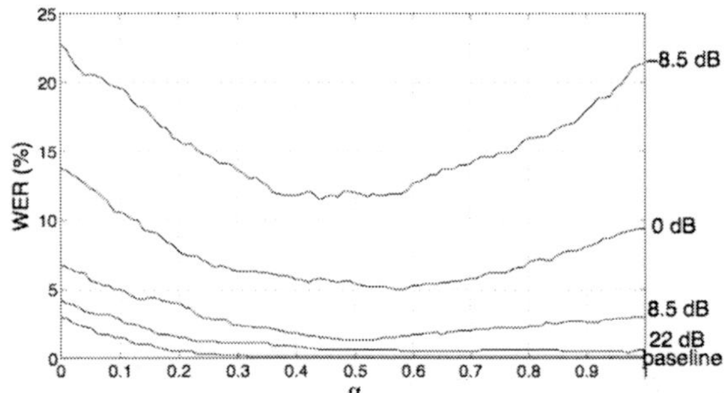

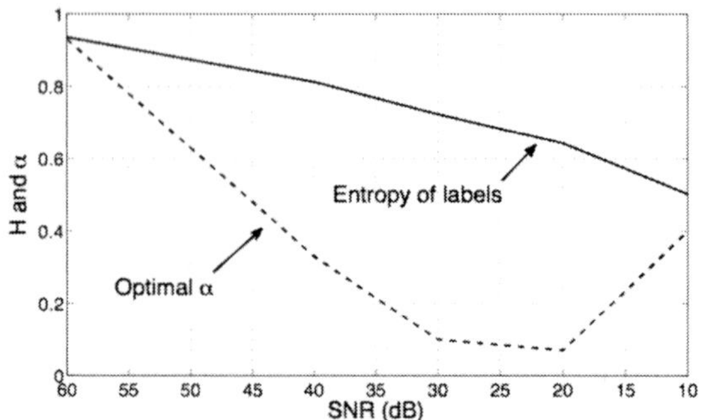

Figure 4: Word-error rates shown for different SNR levels (channel noise) as a function of alpha. The left edge (alpha $\alpha = 0$) shows results for pure segmental representation whereas the right edge (alpha = 1) shows results using only fixed frame information.

Figure 5: Entropy and optimal alpha values for acoustic white noise are shown as a function of signal-to-noise ratio.

from the original 50 ms and 90 ms lags in fixed frame conditions or 1, 2, 3, 4, and 5 segments in segmental conditions. A value for alpha was again optimized for each SNR level separately by finding the value resulting in the minimum WER. Figure 4 shows the recognition rates at different noise levels and with different values of alpha.

A combination of the two different representations yields again the best recognition results, suggesting that the information about larger scale units (speech segments) can aid in the recognition process when the input is distorted. Next we will consider how this combination can be performed automatically when the signal conditions change.

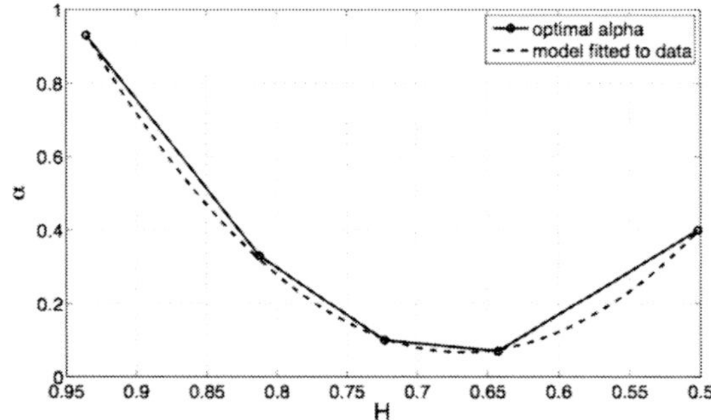

Figure 6: Optimal alpha values as a function of entropy and the 2nd order polynomial fitted to data. A nearly optimal value for alpha in different noise conditions can be chosen dynamically by estimating entropy of the input sequences.

4 Automatic weighting of representations

4.1 Alpha in acoustic white noise

It was shown that combining fixed frame and segmental information is useful when noise is introduced to the system. But how does the system know how to weight small details (fixed frames) or larger units (segments), i.e., how can it automatically find a proper value for alpha in varying conditions when word-error rates are not available for optimization?

One method is to build a SNR dependent model for alpha so that value of alpha can be adjusted based on signal conditions. For on the fly estimation of SNR of the input, entropy is computed from the sequential label input X:

$$H(X) = -\sum_{i=1}^{n} p(x_i) \log_n p(x_i) \qquad (3)$$

where n is the number of labels in the codebook and p is the probability distribution function of X that describes the frequency proportion of each symbol in the input. By measuring the entropy in different noise conditions, it is possible to find a mapping between SNR and the optimal alpha values. For white noise, entropy measured in the baseline SNR condition sets a maximum value for the entropy range, where $H(X) = 1$ would be obtained if signal content was entirely random (note that base of the logarithm is the size of the codebook). Figure 5 shows both entropy and the optimal alpha value as a function of SNR in the AWN condition. As the amount of noise increases, the entropy decreases as the noise-like clusters in the codebook start to become more probable.

By taking entropy estimates and optimal alpha values for the test signals at several noise levels, a good estimate for alpha can be described as a 2nd order polynomial function of entropy of the input sequences.

$$\alpha = a_2 H^2 + a_1 H + a_0 \qquad (4)$$

The coefficients a_2, a_1, and a_0 of the equation will depend on the used codebook, and therefore it is necessary to estimate entropy and WER values as a function of noise level and define these parameters in the development/training phase of the system. For VQ codebooks of size 150/150/100 (static, Δ, and $\Delta\Delta$ labels) used in the experiments, $a_2 = 12.07$, $a_1 = -16.1$, and $a_0 = 5.4$ were obtained. The parabolic fit to the data used in the experiments is extremely good (correlation > 0.999; figure 6) and therefore recognition rates are basically identical between entropy-based and manually optimized alpha, and are not therefore plotted separately (see fig. 3 for the results). In practice some deviation between these two may occur if the alpha is adjusted on the fly, depending on the temporal length of input used for estimating the entropy.

4.2 Alpha in channel noise

Entropy based alpha estimation can also be used in channel noise situation. In contrast to AWN, the entropy now increases as SNR decreases since labels at random locations become replaced with random labels. A reasonably good fit between entropy and alpha values can be obtained with a 1st order polynomial using eq. 4. However, even a more straightforward approach to select a proper alpha exists. It can be grossly approximated from figure 4 that the valleys of the curves are located in the middle section of the alpha range. Fixing α to 0.5 is then a trivial and computationally efficient method to combine information from both temporal resolutions in both clean sequences and noisy sequences.

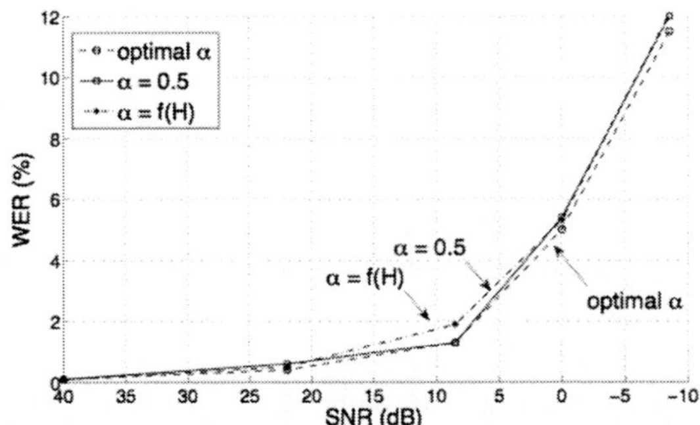

Figure 7: WER as a function of SNR for alpha optimized for each noise level separately, calculated from signal entropy, and $\alpha = 0.5$ for all noise levels. Weighting segmental and fixed frame information equally in all conditions leads to nearly same recognition accuracy as in optimized situation.

Figure 7 displays results from the recognition task in channel noise as was performed previously, now also including results with entropy based alpha estimation and the manually defined α. The difference between recognition rates using optimal alpha values and alphas estimated from the input entropy are small. However, having fixed alpha of 0.5, that is, weighting the segmental and fixed frame information equally, leads to even better accuracy than the entropy based estimation. This suggests that this type of noise that does not take into account the spectral content of the speech, but uniformly affects entire quantized sequences, can be compensated by equally weighting fixed frame and segmental sized representations with NMF.

4.3 Discussion about noise experiments

An important finding here is that the information from larger temporal scales seems to become more and more important as the signal-to-noise ratio becomes worse (figures 2,4,5). Changes in the SNR of the input can be approximated with entropy after it is known how the entropy behaves at different levels of noise. This information can be then used to adjust the weight between scales dynamically.

When noise is introduced to the acoustic signal before vector quantization (e.g., external noise source), the quality of quantized labels suffers greatly as the spectral structure of the input becomes dominated by the noise, biasing the NMF word activations towards specific word models. It seems that integrating temporal information over phone-like speech segments helps to form more systematic representations than treating each small time-scale unit as a meaningful event in the presence of external (white) noise. Combining these two representation leads to better recognition accuracy than using either of them alone.

If noise is introduced directly to label sequences after quantization, weighting of small- and large-scale temporal information equally at all noise levels is much more straightforward and leads to similar or even better results than dynamic entropy estimation. It may be so that the balance between activations emerging in NMF representations on different temporal scales is automatically adjusted by the ambiguity of the incoming patterns at each scale, since this type of noise does not bias the representations in any specific direction (except towards general randomness). When small-scale (more detailed) patterns match well with the small-scale representations, they dominate large-scale information in activation levels due to richness of information. When the small-scale patterns are distorted, previously learned large-scale patterns in the memory start to become more dominant. This linear weighting of cues has an interesting relation to perceptual processing in humans, where such summation of different cues embedded in the input takes place in, e.g., vision (Bruce et al., 2003; Oruc et al., 2003).

5 Conclusions

The use of segmental representations instead of fixed 10 ms frames degrades the recognition accuracy noticeably with clean speech. The magnitude of difference between these two is slightly surprising, as there are supposed to be several advantages of using segmental information, as was discussed in the introduction. However, it was found out that the segmental information is helpful in noisy conditions, adding robustness to the recognition decisions and therefore reducing the word-error rates. The weighting between segmental and fixed frame information can be estimated by utilizing entropy measure to the vector quantized labels. Parameters for this adaptive process have to be estimated in advance with well-defined input so that approximate entropy values for clean speech and several noise levels can be obtained.

In case of uniformly distributed random channel noise, simply using constant equal weight for both small and large temporal scales results in nearly optimal results. This may be because the strength of activation of internal representations in NMF at different temporal scales seems to follow the amount of previously learned structure available at these scales. This has striking similarity to theories of linear summation of cues from different scales of processing. Why this type of self-adjustment does not occur in case of AWN is not certain, but it may be due to the fact that the noise in quantization input changes the process systematically (reducing entropy). As such, it biases activations of internal representations towards a specific set of words instead of uniformly impeding all internal representations.

Acknowledgements

This research is funded as part of the EU FP6 FET project Acquisition of Communication and Recognition Skills (ACORNS), contract no. FP6-034362.

References

Vicki Bruce, Patrick R. Green and Mark A. Georgeson. 2003. *Visual perception: Physiology, psychology and ecology*. Lawrence Erlbaum Associates, UK.

Louis ten Bosch, Hugo Van hamme and Lou Boves. 2008. *A Computational Model of Language Acquistition: Focus on Word Discovery*. In Proc. Interspeech, Brisbane, Australia.

Mark Gales and Steve Young. 2008. *The Application of Hidden Markov Models in Speech Recognition*. Foundations and Trends in Signal Processing. 1(3):195-304.

Daniel D. Lee and Sebastian H. Seung. 2001. *Algorithms for Non-Negative Matrix Factorization*. In Advances in Neural Information Processing Systems ,13(1):556-562.

Ipek Oruç, Laurence T. Maloney and Michael S. Landy. 2003. *Weighted linear cue combination with possibly correlated error*. Vision Research, 43(23):2451-2468.

Okko J. Räsänen. 2007. *Speech Segmentation and Clustering Methods for a New Speech Recognition Architecture*. Master's Thesis, TKK, Finland, http://lib.tkk.fi/Dipl/2007/urn010123.pdf.

Okko J. Räsänen, Unto Laine and Toomas Altosaar, in preparation. *A Blind Speech Segmentation Algorithm Utilizing Non-linear Filtering and Temporal Masking of Spectral Frame Distances*.

Veronique Stouten, Kris Demuynck and Hugo Van hamme. 2008. *Discovering Phone Patterns in Spoken Utterances by Non-negative Matrix Factorization*. IEEE Signal Processing Letters, 15(1):131-134.

Hugo Van hamme. 2008. *HAC-models: a Novel Approach to Continuous Speech Recognition*. In Proc. Interspeech, Brisbane, Australia.

Hugo Van hamme. 2008. *Integration of Asynchronous Knowledge Sources in a Novel Speech Recognition Framework*. ISCA Tutorial and Research Workshop (ITRW), Aalborg.

ISSN 1736-6305 Vol. 4
http://hdl.handle.net/10062/9206

Verb Argument Browser for Danish

Bálint Sass
Pázmány Péter Catholic University
Budapest, Hungary
sass.balint@itk.ppke.hu

Abstract

The Verb Argument Browser is a linguistically relevant corpus query tool, which can be used for investigating argument structure of verbs. The original tool was developed for Hungarian corpora but the methodology is claimed to be language independent because of the dependecy grammar based representation. This paper examines this language independency applying the methodology to a language with different structure, namely: Danish. We will see that the methodology can be applied straightforwardly, and the resulting tool shows the same properties as the original version. The Verb Argument Browser for Danish is available at http://corpus.nytud.hu/vabd (username: nodalida, password: vabd).

1 Introduction

The Verb Argument Browser (VAB) is a corpus query tool which is suitable for investigating the argument structure of verbs (Sass, 2008). The paper cited defines the term *argument* as a phrase that appears in a syntactic relationship with the verb in a clause; and so we will use this term – as a synonym for *dependent* – for complements and adjuncts both.

In the VAB approach basic units are clauses: a verb together with its dependents. Dependents are represented by the lemma of their head and their surface relationship to the verb. These surface relationships are called *positions*, and can be defined by order (e.g. subject or direct object), by a preposition or a case marker etc. According to this terminology, in the sentence *"26 personer kom på hospitalet."*, we have the word *person* in subject position and *hospital* in *på* position.

The tool performs collocation extraction using the association measure *salience* (Kilgarriff and Tugwell, 2001). It can answer the following typical research question: what are the most important collocates of a given verb (or verb frame) in a particular position. The VAB has the important property that it can treat not just a single word but a whole verb frame (a verb together with some arguments) as one unit in collocation extraction. In other words, instead of collecting salient objects of a verb, it can collect for example salient objects of a given subject–verb pair or even salient locatives of a given subject–verb–object triplet and so on. In such a way we can outline the salient patterns of a verb "recursively".

This dependency grammar based model outlined above should be suitable for the description of a broad class of languages. In (Sass, 2008) it is stated but not tested that "the methodology can be extended to other languages and corpora". The aim of the present paper is to test this statement.

We chose the Danish language as testbed because its structure is considerably different from Hungarian. They use different linguistic markers to express arguments. In brief, while Danish has fixed word order and a system of prepositions, Hungarian has a rich case system and its word order is relatively free.

2 Representation

As we mentioned, the basic unit of the VAB is the clause (a verb together with its dependents), and dependents are represented by their position (surface relationship to the verb) and the lemma of their head.

We can say that this is a kind of *mixed* clause model: a one-level-deep dependency structure, where the dependents are phrases. The verb has dependents in some particular relationship but dependents do not have internal dependency structure; they are treated as phrases instead, represented by their heads.

We can define positions as we like. Dealing with Danish we will have: subject position (*subj*), direct object position (*dobj*) and a position for every preposition (*i*, *til*, *på* etc.).

Thus, the above example in VAB input format looks like the following:

```
26 personer kom på hospitalet.
stem=komme subj=person på=hospital
```

We treat clausal dependents in two ways. As they are clauses per se, they are separate units in our representation: they have a verb and some dependents of it internally. From the main clause point of view they are dependents, so they are represented by position and the lemma of their head.

As we see the VAB is not just a classic concordancing tool – like e.g. (Dura, 2006) –, because it has a special corpus representation for the verb–argument structure which can also handle free word order.

3   Converting a Treebank for the VAB

To integrate a corpus into the VAB, the representation described above should be worked out. First, we need to extract the clauses then we need to identify the depedents, their heads and their relations to the verb.

There are two possibilities. On the one hand, we can set out from a POS-tagged corpus and develop a full-fledged chunking system with clause boundary detection. On the other hand, we can set out from a treebank and extract only the information needed. We chose the (obviously cheaper) second possibility. Although treebanks are usually about two orders of magnitude smaller than POS-tagged corpora, for our testing purposes they suffice. The chosen treebank is the 90000 word Danish Dependency Treebank (Trautner Kromann, 2003) because it is freely available with extensive documentation.

Converting the treebank we made the following steps:

- We detected clause boundaries with a simple rule: when we found a comma preceding a conjunction (with CC or CS msd code) then we split the sentence into two parts. Such a way we obtained approximate clauses.

- To detect the main verb we started from the root node of the tree of the given clause. If the root node was not a verb we descended

the tree along `vobj` dependencies to search for the verb. If the verb found had a `vobj` dependent too, we selected that child node to discard auxiliary verbs and obtain the main verb which owns the formal dependents of the auxiliary verb semantically. This example shows the representation of a sentence with an auxiliary verb:

```
Med én ræv kan man ikke sidde på to
heste.
stem=sidde subj=man med=ræv på=hest
```

- Collecting all first level dependencies, to identify subject and direct object was straightforward (by the `subj` and `dobj` relations). We detected prepositional phrases using other relations (e.g. `pobj`, `lobj`), and recorded the prepositions as they are the units which correspond to positions in the representation.

- We identified the heads of phrases descending the `nobj` and `possd` relations.

4   VAB for Danish

The answer screen of the resulting tool can be seen in Fig. 1. The user interface (at the top of Fig. 1) is built up determined by the representation: after entering the verb stem, three arguments (dependents) can be given by position, by lemma or both.

In the example in Fig. 1 we are searching for salient collocates of the Danish verb *have* in the direct object position. We can enter 'subj' or 'dobj' or any preposition into the position field. (The 'Distribution' radio button on the right determines the position in question. Setting it becomes relevant only if we specify two or three dependents.) The most salient collocates are shown in variable font size below the input form: *brug*, *plan*, *masse*, *kontakt* etc.

Salient collocates collected by the VAB tool can be divided into two parts (Sass, 2008):

1. frequent words with literal meaning, often forming a semantically coherent class – like kinds of food as the direct objects of *to eat*;

2. words that form a *multiword verb* together with the verb – like *part* in *take part in* or *rid* in *get rid of*.

We see that this holds for the Danish version, even at such a small corpus size. While *plan* is a frequent concept which people usually have, *have*

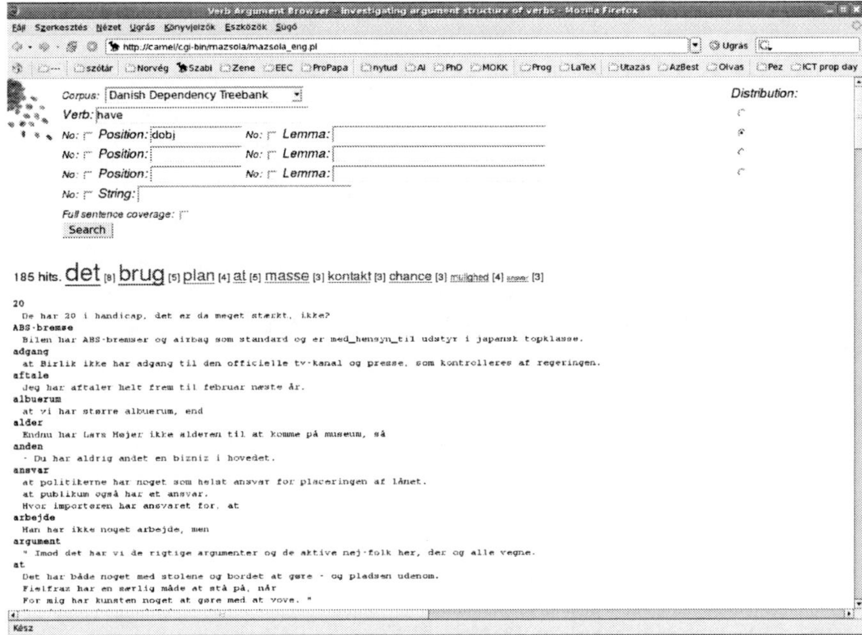

Figure 1: *have* + *dobj* (direct object) in the Danish VAB.

brug for (to need sg) is an authentic multiword verb.

Testing the tool with other (frequent) verbs and positions, we can get different multiword verbs, e.g. *være i tvivl om* (to be in doubt about), *være i forbindelse med* (to be in connection with), *være på vej* (to be on the road), *være på besøg* (to visit) or *få lov til* (to allow).

Apart from verbs, prepositions and nouns can also be investigated, if we leave the verb and/or the position field blank in the input form. This way we can discover important noun phrases, e.g. *ved bord* (at the table), *til gengæld* (in exchange) or *på en måde* (in a way).

5 Comparison with a Treebank Viewer

VAB for Danish can be seen as an alternative to the interactive treebank viewer for the Danish Dependency Treebank (available at: `http://treebank.dk/cdt-map/MapDep.html`) Important differences are:

- The treebank viewer is made to query exactly one graph edge; the VAB has a different approach, it can bring together several entities of a clause, e.g. the verb, the subject and the object.

- The VAB treats verbs and dependents as potential units in collocations, and applies a specific collocation extraction method, instead of just showing some parts of the corpus.

- For the VAB, a verb frame is "worth" exactly the same, not only as a top level structure of the sentence, but also as an embedded one. The VAB sums up all instances of a verb (frame), and does statistics on the whole list.

- The treebank viewer focuses on dependencies (relations); while in the VAB we can also specify and study the lemmas.

- In the treebank viewer we can see every edges of the tree; while in the flat representation of the VAB most of the edges are removed, only the verb and its one-level-deep dependents remain, together with their heads. Such a way VAB does some generalisation on verb frames.

In actual fact, the VAB can also be considered as a treebank viewer, however, not only (computational) linguists but e.g. language learners can benefit from its use.

6 Conclusion

The main message of this paper is that the language independency of the Verb Argument Browser approach (Sass, 2008) holds. The Danish version shows the same properties as the original Hungarian: it can be used to collect mulitword verbs and other important verb frames of the language.

Thus, the Danish version can also be used to support corpus-driven lexicographic work or can be used in corpus-driven language teaching, as it provides the most important verb phrase constructions. Using the VAB a special learners' dictionary can be compiled, which "helps students to write and speak idiomatically" (Hanks, 2008).

A VAB can be created for (hopefully) any language if we have the representation needed. We showed that a treebank can be converted to this representation with ease. The other approach of starting with a POS-tagged corpus and building a suitable chunker is more expensive but POS-tagged corpora are much larger so the resulting tool will have a more impressive coverage.

Most corpora are either large, and have no syntactic annotation (e.g. the so called "national corpora" with POS-tagging); or small with rich syntactic annotation (treebanks). A VAB would work well with a middle-sized chunked corpus, thus such tools set up a claim for a third type, which is in the middle in both respects and often missing: few ten million word shallow parsed corpora.

The Verb Argument Browser for Danish is available at `http://corpus.nytud.hu/vabd` (temporary username: `nodalida`, password: `vabd`). For free individual access or if you want to build a VAB for another language, please contact the author.

References

Elzbieta Dura. 2006. CULLER – a user-friendly corpus query system. In *Proceedings of the Fourth International Workshop on Dictionary Writing Systems*, pages 47–52, Torino, Italy.

Patrick Hanks. 2008. The lexicographical legacy of John Sinclair. *International Journal of Lexicography*, 21(3):219–229.

Adam Kilgarriff and David Tugwell. 2001. Word Sketch: Extraction and display of significant collocations for lexicography. In *Proceedings of the 39th Meeting of the Association for Computational Linguistics, workshop on COLLOCATION: Computational Extraction, Analysis and Exploitation*, pages 32–38, Toulouse.

Bálint Sass. 2008. The Verb Argument Browser. In *Sojka P. et al. (eds.): 11th International Conference on Text, Speech and Dialogue. LNCS, Vol. 5246.*, pages 187–192, Brno, Czech Republic.

Matthias Trautner Kromann. 2003. The Danish Dependency Treebank and the DTAG treebank tool. In *Proceedings of the Second Workshop on Treebanks and Linguistic Theories (TLT 2003)*, Växjö, Sweden.

ISSN 1736-6305 Vol. 4
http://hdl.handle.net/10062/9206

VI Demos

DeepDict –
A Graphical Corpus-based Dictionary of Word Relations

Eckhard Bick
GrammarSoft & University of Southern Denmark
eckhard.bick@mail.dk

Abstract

In our demonstration, we will present a new type of lexical resource, built from grammatically analysed corpus data. Co-occurrence strength between mother-daughter dependency pairs is used to automatically produce dictionary entries of typical complementation patterns and collocations, in the fashion of an instant monolingual Advanced Learner's dictionary. Entries are supplied to the user in a graphical interface with various thresholds for lexical frequencies as well as absolute and relative co-occurrence frequencies. DeepDict draws its data from Constraint Grammar-analysed corpora, ranging between tens and hundreds of millions of words, covering the major Germanic and Romance languages. Apart from its obvious lexicographical uses, DeepDict also targets teaching environments and translators.

1   Lexicographical motivation

From a lexicographer's point of view, a corpus-based dictionary has a potentially better coverage and legitimacy than a traditional dictionary built on introspection and literature quotes. Many modern dictionaries do therefore make use of corpus data, striving to balance their data with regard to domain, register etc. However, the ultimate product is usually still a traditional dictionary, even in electronic versions, because corpus data are used more for exemplification and simple frequency counts than for dictionary generation proper. Notable exceptions are the *Sketch Engine* (Kilgariff et al. 2004), which uses n-gram collocations and grammatical relations in a systematical way, and the Leipzig University *Wortschatz* project (Biemann et al. 2004), that automatically creates lexical similarity nets from monolingual corpora.

In addition, even where corpora are used selectively or systematically, not all information – especially structural information – is readily accessible, because most corpora of the necessary size will be text corpora without any deeper grammatical annotation. Optimally, the extraction of lexical patterns should not only be based on lemmatized and part-of-speech annotated text, but also exploit true linguistic relations (e.g. subject, object etc.) rather than mere adjacency (n-grams). Finally, even given all of the above, and using a statistics-integrating interface, a lexicographer will only be able to look at one pattern at a time – a tedious process for not least verbs with a complex phrasal and semantic potential. Also, he may not find what he isn't looking for, because the search interface only allows textual searches or because the one resource that might do the job – a syntactic treebank – is usually produced by hand and too small for lexicographical work[1].

The dictionary tool presented here, DeepDict, strives to address both the linguistic quality of available corpus information, and the issue of how to present this information so as to permit a more complete and simultaneous overview of usage patterns for a given word. DeepDict was developed at GrammarSoft and launched commercially at <u>gramtrans.com</u> in September 2007.

2   Ordinary dictionary users

From an ordinary dictionary user's point of view, the following advantages of electronic dictionaries over paper dictionaries should be addressed:

1. There are no size limitations, so the individual entry for an infrequent word can be assigned as much space as for a frequent word, and the exclusion of rare patterns should not be absolute, but governed by user-controlled thresholds.
2. On paper, it is easier to create passive ("definitional") dictionaries than active ("productive-contextual") ones, because the former address native speakers of the target language (TL) , while the latter have to provide a lot of detailed usage information, semantic con-

---

[1] Size restraints on coverage and statistical salience are mentioned by Kaarel Kaljurand for his *depdict* listings derived from an Estonian treebank, also based on CG, of 100,000 words (http://math.ut.ee/~kaarel/NLP/Programs/Treebank/DepDict/)

"

straints and complementation patterns to a user not familiar with the TL, e.g. A gives x to B (where A, B = +HUM and x,y = -HUM).

3. An electronic dictionary can offer unlimited (linked) corpus examples, on demand, without complicating the entry as such.

3 Assembling the data

Motivated by the arguments discussed in chapters 1 and 2, we opted for Constraint Grammar (Karlsson et al. 1995) as the underlying annotation technique, firstly because of its robustness and good lexical coverage, secondly because its token-based dependency syntax is computationally easier to process. The following method was followed to build the necessary lexico-relational database.

First, for each language, available corpora were annotated with CG parsers and – subsequently – a dependency parser using CG function tags as input (Bick 2005), effectively turning almost a billion words of data into treebanks, with functional dependency links for all words in a sentence[2]. For a number of corpora, only the last step was part of the DeepDict project, since CG annotation had already been performed by the corpus providers for their CorpusEye search interface (http:// corp.hum.sdu.dk). Table 1 provides a rough overview over data set sizes and parsers used.

	Corpus size[3]	Parser[4]	Status[5]
Danish	67+92M mixed	DanGram	+
English	210M mixed	EngGram	+
Esperanto	18N mixed	EspGram	+
French	[67M Wi, Eu]	FrAG	-
German	44M Wi, Eu	GerGram	+
Norwegian	30+20M Wi	Obt / NorGram	+
Portuguese	210M news	PALAVRAS	+
Spanish	50+40M Wi,Eu	HISPAL	+
Swedish	60M news, Eu	SweGram	+

Table 1: Corpora and parsers

In the token-numbered annotation example below, the subject 'Peter' (1. word) and the object 'apples' (6. word) both have dependency-links

(#x->y) to the verb 'ate' (2. word).

Peter "**Peter**" <hum> PROP @**SUBJ** #1->2
ate "eat" V IMPF #2->0
a couple of ....
apples "**apple**" <fruit> N P @**ACC** #6->2

From the annotated corpora, dependency pairs ("dep-grams") were harvested – after some filtering between syntactic and semantic head conventions-, using lemma, part of speech and syntactic function. For prepositional phrases both the preposition and its dependent were stored as a unit, de facto treating prepositions like a kind of case marker. For nouns and numerals, in order to prevent an explosion of meaningless lexical complexity, we used category instead of lemma. For nouns, semantic prototypes were stored as a further layer of abstraction (e.g. <hum> and <fruit> in our example). For a verb like 'eat', this would result in dep-grams like the following[6]:

PROP_SUBJ -> eat_V
cat_SUBJ -> eat_V
apple_ACC -> eat_V
mouse_ACC -> eat_V

With little further processing, the result could be represented as a summary "entry" for eat in the following way:

{PROP, cat, <hum>, ...} SUBJ --> eat <-- {apple, mouse, <fruit>, ...} ACC

Obviously, the fields in such an entry would quickly be diluted by the wealth of corpus examples, and one has to distinguish between typical complements and co-occurrences on the one hand, and non-informative "noise" on the other. Therefore, we used a statistical measure for co-occurrence strength[7] to filter out the relevant cases, normalizing the absolute count for a pair a->b against the product of the normal frequencies of a and b in the corpus as a whole:

$$C * \log(p(a\text{->}b) \char94 2/ (p(a) * p(b)))$$

where p() are frequencies and C is a constant introduced to place measures of statistical significance in the single digit range.

---

[2] Our long-range dependencies provide complete-depth trees, as in constituent treebanks, CG3 dependencies (beta.visl.sdu.dk/constraint_grammar.html) or Functional Dependency Grammar (www.connexor.fi).

[3] Wi = Wikipedia (http://www.wikipedia.com), Eu = the Europarl corpus (Koehn 2005)

[4] More information about the parsers is available at http://beta.visl.sdu.dk/constraint_grammar.html.

[5] The Portuguese, Swedish and Esperanto DeepDicts have unlimited free access, the others have regulated access

[6] Of course, beyond the examples given here, all other relations, such as prepositional objects and adverbials, are equally treated in both the analysis and the interface.

[7] The difference from Church's *Mutual Information* measure is the higher (square) weighting of the actual cooccurrence. This was deemed more supportive of lexicographical purposes – preventing strong but rare or wrong collocations from drowning out common ones.

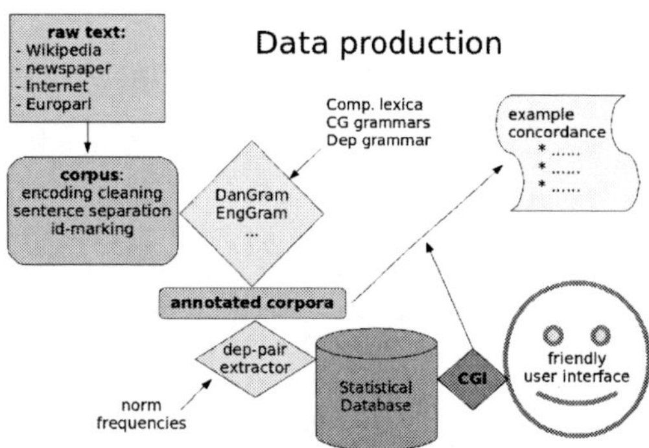

Fig. 1: Data production

The resulting database would then contain, for each dep-gram pair, both its absolute frequency, co-occurrence strength, as well as an index of relevant sentence ID's in the source corpus. Even for a single language, parsing all corpus material and creating the databases, may take days or weeks, and the resulting datasets are so big (currently 90 GB) that querying them in a straightforward fashion would cause unacceptable delays to the user. Hence, special file structures and querying algorithms had to be devised by our interface programmer, Tino Didriksen.

4 The user interface

In order to to meet the requirements outlined in chapter 2, dictionary entries are composed on the fly, respecting user-set significance thresholds[8], and allowing simultaneous overview (a "lexicogram") over a words combinatorial potential. For grammatical reasons, and in order to resolve class ambiguities (e.g. house_N vs. house_V), each word class has its own "lexicogram" template. As can be seen in fig. 2, the lexicogram for the noun 'voice' not only captures typical multi-word expressions like "voice actor" and "voice recorder", but also shows typical qualities (loud, deep, husky) and the polysemy implied in "passive voice". The fields of the DeepDict lexicograms are designed to support "natural" reading - which is why the English DeepDict places attributes left and heads right for nouns and adjectives, or subjects left and objects right for verbs, and why other fields are flanked by frame text to create the illusion of a sentence: "one can {recog-

nize, hear, lower, lend, raise} a voice". A minimum of classifier information is provided together with the head word, i.e. gender, transitivity and countability. However, even this information is partly corpus based. Thus, countability/mass is deduced from certain trigger-dependents such as numerals and quantifiers.

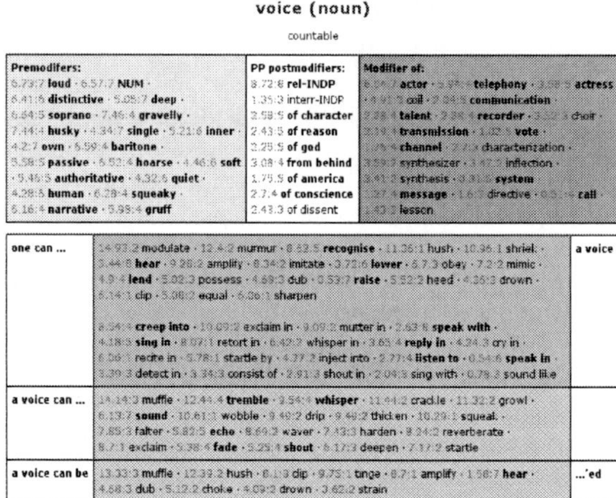

Fig. 2: DeepDict noun template

The co-occurrence strength between the lookup word and a given relation is presented in red numbers in front of the context word, separated by a colon from the absolute frequency class (an integer representing the dual logarithm of the actual frequency[9]. Ordering is a function of these 2 values, and to give further salience to important correlations, frequency classes of 4 and above are in bold face. At the same time, the red numbers serve as clickable links to a corpus concordance for the relation in question – allowing lexicographers to check DeepDict's analysis in rare or problematic cases, especially if low significance thresholds have been set by the user.

Personal and quantifier pronouns are so frequent that exact statistical measures are of little interest. However, they may provide semantic information in a prototypical fashion, and they are therefore listed - by order of frequency - at the top of subject and object fields. Personal pronouns may help classify activities as typically male (he) or female (she), or mark objects as inanimate (it) or mass nouns (much). Even sociolinguistic deductions are possible: Thus the DeepDict entry for the verb "caress" (Fig. 3) shows, that males (he) are more likely to caress females (she) than vice versa.

---

[8] There are 4 types of threshold: (a) minimum occurrence, designed to filter out corpus errors and hapaxes, (b) minimum co-occurrence strength, with a default at 0, (c) maximum number of hits shown per field, and (d) minimum lexical frequency of relation words, for language learners, so rare words will be explained with ordinary word contexts rather than vice versa.

[9] In its default settings, the interface cuts out relations with frequencies < 4, to avoid errors caused by misspellings and other corpus anomalies, or faulty analysis.

caress (verb)

total of 527 relations

Subjects:	Accusative objects:
PERS: we, he, they, she	PERS: her, one another
6.21:2 PROP · 4.79:2 finger ·	6.62:2 cheek · 5.12:2 skin · 5.83:1 fingertip · 4.74:2 hair · 4.24:2 breast ·
4.62:1 breeze · 4.44:1 thumb ·	4.7:1 spine · 3.45:2 face · 4.42:1 jaw · 3.86:1 neck · 2.71:2 body ·
2.89:2 hand · 1.47:1 eye	3.71:1 PROP · 2.59:2 bad · 3:1 length · 0.25:1 head

caress ...	5.54:2 gently · 3.71 sensuously
caress to ...	4.48:1 waist
caress with ...	4.01:1 tongue · 1.5:1 hand
caress in ...	0.23:1 way

Fig. 3: DeepDict: part of verb template

The example also illustrates metaphorical usage – the lexicogram not only lists the bodyparts that do the caressing (subject) and the ones that are caressed (objects), but also mentions 'eyes' and even 'breeze' as caressors. Finally, it shows how prepositions (*with tongue/hand*) are linked into the verb template. For other verbs, it is here we will find prepositional valency, too.

Adverb-verb collocations may appear in several functional shades, ranging from (a) free temporal, locative and modal adverbs (work *where/when/how*) to (b) valency bound adverbial complements (feel *how,* go *where*) and (c) verb-integrated particles (give *up,* fall *apart*). In some cases, it may even be difficult to decide on one or other category (eat *out*). Since DeepDict is basically intended as a dictionary tool, syntactic hair splitting is less important, and only the verb particles (c) are singled out, to cover phrasal verbs, presenting the rest in a single (brown) field ('gently/sensuously' for the verb 'caress').

spise (verb)

total of 28482 relations

Subjects:	Subclauses:	Accusative objects:
PERS: jeg, vi, de, du, hun, han, man, dere,	2.56:2 interr	PERS: hva
som, den, det, ingen, en		9.72:9 middag · 10.2:7 lunsj · 8.19 <food-h> ·
9.59:7 PROP-hum · 1.38:8 <H> ·		9.55:7 frokost · 7.23:5 <food-m-h> ·
3.45:5 <Adom> · 2.74:3 katt · 1.46:4 folk ·		6.52:8 <food-c-h> · 6.15:8 <food-m> · 6.93:7 mat ·
2.21:3 larve · 1.85:3 gjest · 2.72:3 mamma		3.84:8 <food> · 7.92:2 brødskive · 6.67:8 kjøtt ·
· 2.53:2 ku · 0.38:4 barn · 3.14:1 fanden ·		8.46:4 kveldsmat · 4.62:7 <Aich> · 6.59:9 PROP-hum
3.02:1 bikkje · 9.02:1 kathunge ·		3.34:8 <temp> · 5.08:6 fisk · 5.39:5 brød · 6.32:4 kake
2.89:1 passasjerbåt · 2.77:1 lefse ·		· 4.13:6 <food-c> · 7.07:3 matpakke · 6.4 pizza ·
1.54:2 elg · 0.35:3 dyr ·		5.99:4 kjeks · 7.99:7 <occ> · 4.62:5 frukt ·
2.33:1 spekthogger · 1.26:2 dame ·		6.59:3 potetgull · 2.26.6 <Azo> · 1.53:6 <amount> ·
0.22:3 hund · 0.85:3 mor · 1.97:1 jaguar ·		3.39:5 <Aent> · 1.87:5 <B> · 1.73:5 <Aom> ·
1.98:1 pappa · 0.61:2 fange ·		1.35:5 <Adom> · 1.3.5 <A> · 1.29.5 <cm> ·
0.58:2 pasient		1.22:5 <drink-h> · 1.27:4 <drink-c-h> · 0.36:1 PROP
		Verbal particles:
		4.67:7 opp · 4.26:7 sammen · 1.69:2 stille

Fig. 4: Semantic prototypes

In the parsers providing the corpus data behind DeepDict, nouns are classified according to semantic prototype class[10], e.g. as <Hprof> (professional human) or <tool-cut> (cutting tool) or <Vair> (air vehicle), and this semantic generalisation has been made available for some Deep-

---

[10] Depending on the language, about 160-200 prototypes are used (http://beta.visl.sdu.dk/semantic_prototypes_overview.pdf). For our purposes, semantic prototypes were preferred to classical wordnets because the latter have too many (and sometimes usage-dependent) subdistinctions and do not clearly state where in a hyperonomy chain to find the best classifier.

Dict languages. In the conference demo linked to this paper DeepDict will be accessible through an internet portal at (http://www.gramtrans.com).

5 Conclusion and future work

We have shown how syntactically related word pairs can be harvested from Constraint Grammar-annotated dependency corpora and fed into a statistical database that will allow the on-the-fly creation of so-called "DeepDict lexicograms" – semi-graphical overview pages for dictionary words, with information about head and modifier selection restrictions, verb complementation and phrasal collocations. The tool allows lexicographers to mine corpora not only for examples of structures and lexical relations, but for the structures and relations themselves. DeepDict can be chained to other lexical resources - tradional definition dictionaries, ontologies or bilingual dictionaries (cp. the QuickDict dictionaries at gramtrans.com). Since the DeepDict method can be run from scratch on any language data accessible to a CG parser, it should be possible in the future to provide researchers, lexicographers and teachers with individual DeepDict instalments for specific user corpora, reflecting a specific domain, genre or language variety.

References

Bick, Eckhard. (2005) "Turning Constraint Grammar Data into Running Dependency Treebanks". In: Civit, Montserrat & Kübler, Sandra & Martí, Ma. Antònia (red.), *Proceedings of TLT 2005*, Barcelona, December 9th - 10th, 2005), pp.19-27

Bick, Eckhard (2006): "A Constraint Grammar-Based Parser for Spanish", *Proceedings of TIL 2006 - 4th Workshop on Information and HLT.*

Biemann, Chris & Stefan Bordag & Uwe Quasthoff & Christian Wolff (2004). "Language-Independent Methods for Compiling Monolingual Lexical Data". In *Comp. Linguistics and Intelligent Text Processing.* Springer: Berlin, pp. 217-228

Church, Ken and P. Hanks 1991. Word Association Norms, Mutual Information and Lexicography. Computational Linguistics, Vol.16:1, pp. 22-29.

Karlsson, Fred et al. (1995): *Constraint Grammar - A Language-Independent System for Parsing Unrestricted Text.* Natural Language Processing, No 4. Berlin & New York: Mouton de Gruyter.

Kilgarriff, Adam, Rychlý, P., Smrž, P. & Tugwell, D. (2004). "The Sketch Engine". Paper presented at EURALEX, Lorient, France, July 2004.

Koehn, Philipp (2005). Europarl: A Multilingual Corpus for the Evaluation of Machine Translation. MT Summit X, Sept.12-16, 2005.Phuket,Thailand.

ISSN 1736-6305 Vol. 4
http://hdl.handle.net/10062/9206

SubTTS: Light-weight automatic reading of subtitles

Sandra Derbring
Peter Ljunglöf
Maria Olsson
DART: Centre for AAC and AT
Gothenburg, Sweden

Abstract

We present a simple tool that enables the computer to read subtitles of movies and TV shows aloud. The tool extracts information from subtitle files, which can be freely downloaded or extracted from a DVD, and reads the text aloud through a speech synthesizer.

The target audience is people who have trouble reading subtitles while watching a movie, for example people with visual impairments and people with reading difficulties such as dyslexia. The application will be evaluated together with user from these groups to see if this could be an accepted solution to their needs.

1 Background

1.1 Why read subtitles aloud?

Spoken subtitles could be a solution if, due to sight disorder or poor reading skills, a person is unable to read subtitles and the language spoken in the movie is unknown, or not known good enough.

A speech synthesizer able to read the text file of the DVD could make the text audible. This would make the vast sea of foreign language movies and TV shows on DVDs accessible to people with reading disabilities and visual handicaps.

Swedish Association of the Visually Impaired (Synskadades Riksförbund)[1] has around 12,000 members but there are most likely more people with poor eyesight. The number of people with reading disabilities is unknown, but according to the Swedish Dyslexia Association[2] between 5 and 8 percent of the population have significant difficulties to read and write. A survey by OECD (Organisation for Economic Co-operation and Development) in 1996 showed that "8 per cent of the adult population [in Sweden] encounters a severe literacy deficit in everyday life and at work" (OECD, 2000, p. xiii). For other countries, the problems were even bigger: "In 14 out of 20 countries, at least 15 per cent of all adults have literacy skills at only the most rudimentary level" (OECD, 2000, p. xiii).

To hear the subtitles along with the original audio track of the movie may not suit everyone, but making these movies and shows accessible could bring a huge value for people who would use it.

To reduce the risk of a large amount of auditive information disrupting the experience of watching the movie, we plan to investigate what kind of speech synthesis is best suited and what modifications can be made to the sound in the synthesis as well as in the movie.

1.2 Previous work

There have been some previous work done on automatic reading of subtitles.

A project by the Swedish Association of the Visually Impaired, in cooperation with Svenska Enter Rehabilitering AB,[3] developed a prototype that used OCR to interpret subtitles, which then were spoken aloud using TTS. The project estimated that a batch product would cost around 2500€, which they concluded would be too much for ordinary users (Eliasson, 2006, pp. 63–64).

Swedish Public Service Television (SVT) uses speaking subtitles since 2005.[4] The speech is transmitted through a second channel, which means that the user needs two digital boxes. This solution only works on SVT's own programs.

---

[1] `http://www.srfriks.org`

[2] `http://dyslexiforeningen.se/om_dyslexi.html`

[3] "Framtagande av TV-textläsare för syntetisk uppläsning av TV:s textremsa" (Development of a TV text reader for synthetic reading of TV subtitles)

[4] `http://svt.se/svt/jsp/Crosslink.jsp?d=22138&a=274311`

Very similar to our project is Hanzlíček et al. (2008), who describe a system for reading Czech subtitles aloud. Their motivation is similar to ours, but they focus their attention on technical details on how to synchronize speech and subtitles.

1.3 Problems with existing solutions

The main problems with the existing solutions (apart from those in the Czech project described above) are that:

- they are overly complicated, by for example using OCR to scan the subtitles.

- they are closed, which means that they do not work for all kinds of movies and formats.

2 Implementation

Our prototype implementation is very simple. It consists of a script that reads a subtitle file and calls a speech synthesizer at the correct times.

To provide the speech synthesizer with input, the texting from the program needs to be extracted. There are different techniques for producing subtitles onto a TV show or a movie. Soft or closed subtitles are plain text files that are run separately from the video file, which makes them easy to edit and to extract information from. This format is often used in the subtitles available from the Internet. The files consist of the spoken lines together with time stamps that signals when the text should be displayed during playback:

```
00:00:41,549 --> 00:00:42,419
You have to go.
```

The above example means that the subtitle should be displayed 41.549 seconds into the movie and disappear at 42.419 seconds.

Subtitles are available from several sites on the Internet,[5] both in the original language and in translations into different other languages. For our purpose, the Swedish translations are of interest. In addition, subtitles are also available in purchased DVDs, often in multiple languages. Those are called prerendered subtitles and are separate video frames laid over the original streams during playback. They are usually made as an image, which makes them hard to edit. However, there is special software that can be used to extract and convert the information into soft subtitles with the help of OCR.

The present implementation is a script that extracts information from the subtitles file and uses it to provide input when communicating with the speech synthesizer. The script is currently run in parallel with the media player, but a future extension includes having it automatically synchronized.

3 Discussion

3.1 Social and pedagogical advantages

People with visually impairments and/or reading difficulties often use text-to-speech to cope with school work, and to keep up with society. Spoken subtitles further increase the accessibility of foreign movies and TV shows for these people.

Hypothetically, people with reading difficulties may also learn better how to read by using spoken subtitles. The theory is that looking at the text as it is spoken by the speech synthesis, may benefit the reading process but this is yet to be tested.

3.2 Future work

To further ease the user friendliness and the availability, the current implementation is planned to be built into a module for the open-source and cross-platform VLC Media Player.[6]

According to Hanzlíček et al. (2008), 44 percent of the Czech subtitles had overlaps when spoken with TTS. Even though we have no figures for Swedish, some overlap is to be expected also here, which is an issue that should be addressed. One possible simple solution is to modify the speech rate.

An important factor for the experience of the speech synthesizer together with a video playback would be the settings of the audio channels. Hypothetically, a listener would want to keep both the original background cues, like music, and the original voices. However, these sounds must not interfere with the speech synthesizer that is the source of information for the listener. Balancing these two criteria to get the optimized result is of great interest.

We also have plans to evaluate the application together with different users in the target groups. The aim is to discover if this approach is appreciated and if it could be an accepted solution to

---

[5]Two examples are http://www.undertexter.se and http://www.opensubtitles.org

[6]http://www.videolan.org/vlc/

the need of text interpretation during movie playback. Factors that could be evaluated and used to improve the implementation could be, for example, type of voice, type of speech synthesizer, and filter settings on the audio channels.

If the program would be used for language learning, or to help slow readers to comprehend, the feature of highlighting the word that is spoken could be a very useful additional feature.

Acknowledgements

We are greatful to three anonymous referees for their valuable comments.

References

Folke Eliasson. 2006. *IT i praktiken – slutrapport*. Hjälpmedelsinstitutet, Sweden.

Zdeněk Hanzlíček, Jindřich Matoušek, and Daniel Tihelka. 2008. Towards automatic audio track generation for Czech TV broadcasting: Initial experiments with subtitles-to-speech synthesis. In *ICSP '08, 9th International Conference on Signal Processing*, Beijing, China.

OECD. 2000. *Literacy in the Information Age: Final Report of the International Adult Literacy Survey*. OECD Publications, Paris.

ISSN 1736-6305 Vol. 4
http://hdl.handle.net/10062/9206

TRIK: A Talking and Drawing Robot for Children with Communication Disabilities

Peter Ljunglöf
Staffan Larsson
University of Gothenburg
Gothenburg, Sweden

Katarina Mühlenbock
Gunilla Thunberg
DART: Centre for AAC and AT
Gothenburg, Sweden

Abstract

This paper describes an ongoing project where we develop and evaluate setup involving a communication board (for manual sign communication) and a drawing robot, which can communicate with each other via spoken language. The purpose is to help children with severe communication disabilities to learn language, language use and cooperation, in a playful and inspiring way. The communication board speaks and the robot is able to understand and talk back. This encourages the child to use the language and learn to cooperate to reach a common goal, which in this case is to get the robot to draw figures on a paper.

1 Introduction

1.1 Dialogue systems

Most existing dialogue systems are meant to be used by competent language users without physical or cognitive language disabilities – either they are supposed to be spoken to (e.g., phone based systems), or one has to be able to type the utterances (e.g., the interactive agents that can be found on the web). The few dialogue systems which are developed with disabled people in mind are targeted at persons with physical disabilities, who need help in performing common acts.

Dialogue systems have also been used for second language learning; i.e., learning a new language for already language competent people. Two examples are the artificial agent *"Ville – The Virtual Language Tutor"* (Beskow et al., 2004), and *"SCILL – Spoken Conversational Interface for Language Learning"*, a system for practicing Mandarin Chinese (Seneff et al., 2004).

However, we are not aware of any examples where a dialogue system has been used for improving first language learning.

1.2 Target audience

Our intended target group are children with severe communication disabilities, who needs help to learn and practice linguistic communication. One example can be children with autism spectrum disorders, having extensive difficulties with representational thinking and who therefore will have problems in learning linguistic communication. Many children with autism are furthermore hindered in their speech development by the fact that they also have physical disabilities. Our dialogue system will give an opportunity to explore spoken language – content as well as expression.

Another target audience which we believe will benefit from our system are children whose physical disabilities are very extensive, usually as a consequence of Cerebral Palsy (CP). The abilility to control a robot gives a fantastic opportunity to play, draw and express oneself in spoken language, which otherwise would be very difficult or even impossible.

1.3 Language development

To be able to learn a language one must have practice in using it, especially in interplay with other language competent people. For the communication to be as natural as possible, all participants should use the same language. For that reason there is a point in being able to express oneself in spoken language, even if one does not have the physical or cognitive ability. If one usually expresses oneself by pointing at a communication board, it is thus important that the board can express in words what is meant by the pointing act. This is even more important when learning a language, and its expressions and conventions (Sevcik and Romski, 2002; Thunberg, 2007).

When it comes to children with autism, learning

appears to be simpler in cooperation with a technical product (e.g., a computer), since the interaction in that case is not as complex as with another human (Heimann and Tjus, 1997). Autistic persons have difficulties in coordinating impressions from several different senses and different focuses of attention. When one is expected to listen to, look at and interpret a number of small signals, all at the same time, such as facial expressions and gazes, human communication can become very difficult.

All children need repetition to learn things. Children with disabilities often need even more repetition in their language learning, because of their lack of communicative functions. Adapted techniques, and in this case the speech-controlled drawing robot, can offer the required repetition as an exciting complement to human communication.

2 Project description

Our basic idea is to use a dialogue system to support language development for children with severe communicative disabilities. There are already communication boards connected to speech synthesis in the form of communication software on computers. The main values that this project add to existing systems are that

1. the child can explore language on her own and in stimulating cooperation with the robot;

2. it can be relieving and stimulating at the same time, with a common focus on the dialogue together with a robot;

3. the child is offered an exciting, creative and fun activity.

By being able to use a picture- or symbol-based communication board the children are given an exciting opportunity to explore language; to play and in the same time learn to use a method for alternative and augmentative communication.

2.1 A talking communication board and a talking robot

In our goal scenario the child has a communication board which can talk; i.e., when the child points at some symbols they are translated to an utterance which the board expresses via speech synthesis, and in grammatically correct Swedish. This is recognized by a robot which can move around on a

paper and draw at the same time. The robot executes the commands that was expressed by the communication board; e.g., if the child points at the symbol for *"draw a figure"*, and the symbol with a flower, the utterance might be *"draw a flower, please"*, which the robot then performs.

The dialogue system comes into play when the robot is given too little information. E.g., if the child only points at the symbol for *"draw a figure"*, the robot does not get enough information. This is noticed by the dialogue system and the robot asks a follow-up question, such as *"what figure do you want me to draw?"*.

2.1.1 Functionality of the robot

Our robot is a variant of the LOGO-robot which was developed at Massachusetts Institute of Technology for learning children to use computers and program simple applications (Papert, 1993). The robot can move forward and backward, and turn right and left. It also has a pen which it can lift (for not drawing) or lower (for drawing). The robot can also be programmed to execute command sequences; e.g., it is possible to define that a *"square"* is to first move forward, turn left 90 degrees, and then redo the same thing three more times.

2.2 Pedagogical advantages

By having the communication board and the robot talking to each other there is a possibility for users in an early stage of language development to understand and learn basic linguistic principles. For the linguistically more advanced child the robot offers the possibility of understanding basic properties of dialogue such as turn-taking, asking and answering questions, the importance of providing sufficient information, and cooperating to achieve a shared goal. In addition, the child learns to plan its actions in order to achieve a goal; e.g., getting the robot to draw a flower.

At yet more advanced stages, the child may learn simple "programming" to get the robot to repeatedly perform a complex action. For example, the child may provide a step-by-step instruction for drawing a square, and then name this shape *"square"*. Subsequently, the robot can be told to draw new squares using a single command (*"draw a square"*). This provides further practice in using dialogue to achieve more complex goals.

As discussed in section 3.2 later, the setup works without the robot and the communication board actually listening to each others' speech – instead, they communicate wirelessly. However, there is an important pedagogical point in having them (apparently) communicate using spoken language. It provides the child with an experience of participating in a spoken dialogue, even though the child does not speak.

2.3 Generality of the approach

One reason for choosing a drawing robot is that is provides a simple yet infinitely variable arena of behaviour. A further reason is that no advanced sensors or motors are needed to build such a robot. An alternative which is equally understandable and useful to the user could be a robot building towers using wooden blocks, but in this case the robot would need to be more advanced and difficult to construct.

This does not mean that the technique cannot be applied to other domains. There is nothing about the idea itself – a talking communication board communicating with a robot via a dialogue system – which dictates what the robot can be used for. To adapt the setup to a new domain, one needs to specify the relevant domain knowledge to the GoDiS dialogue system, and perhaps provide new signs for the communication board which are appropriate to the new domain.

3 Implementation

This section describes some technical aspects of the implementation of the TRIK system.

3.1 Components

The final TRIK setup consists of the following components:

- a simple LEGO robot which can turn and move in all directions, and has a pen that can be lifted and lowered;

- a touch-screen which functions as a communication board with pictograms/symbols;

- a computer with a dialogue system and speech synthesis, which is physically attached to the communication board and communicates wirelessly with the robot.

The computer will seem like it is a part of the communication board, but it also controls the robot, both movements and speech. Every utterance by the robot will be executed by the speech synthesizer, and then sent to the robot via radio.

3.2 Perfect speech recognition

Typically, the most error-prone component of a spoken dialogue system is speech recognition; i.e., the component responsible for correctly interpreting speech. This of course becomes even more problematic when working with language learning or communication disorders, since in these sitations it is both more difficult and more important that the computer correctly hears and understands the user's utterances. An advantage of the TRIK setup is that we will, in a sense, have "perfect speech recognition", since we are cheating a bit. The (dialogue system connected to the) robot does not actually have to listen for the speech generated by the (computer connected to the) communication board; since the information is already electronically encoded, it can instead be transferred wirelessly. This means that the robot will never hear *"go forward and then stop"* when the communication board actually says *"go forward seven steps"*.

3.3 Existing resources

This section describes the technical resources which are used in TRIK.

3.3.1 The GoDiS dialogue manager

A dialogue system typically consists of several components: speech recognizer, natural language interpreter, dialogue manager, language generator, speech synthesizer and a short-term memory for keeping track of the dialogue state. One can make a distinction between dialogue *systems*, which (ideally) are general and reusable over several domains, and dialogue system *applications*, which are specific to a certain domain. The dialogue manager is the "intelligence" of the system, keeping track of what has been said so far and deciding what should be said next.

The GoDiS dialogue manager (Larsson, 2002) is designed to be easily adaptable to new domains, but nevertheless be able to handle a variety of simpler or more complex dialogues. For example, GoDiS can either take initiative and prompt a user for information, or take a back seat and let the experienced user provide information in any desired order, without having to wait for the right question from the system.

3.3.2 The grammar formalism GF

Grammatical Framework (GF) (Ranta, 2004) makes it easy to quickly design the language in-

Peter Ljunglöf, Staffan Larsson, Katarina Mühlenbock and Gunilla Thunberg

terpretation and generation components of a dialogue system. In addition, GF is a multilingual formalism, which means that it is well suited for use in translation between different languages. Since, e.g., the graphical Blissymbolics system can be regarded as a language in itself, it is possible to write GF grammars for translating between symbols and spoken Swedish (Lidskog, 2007).

3.3.3 LEGO Mindstorms

The robot itself is built using LEGO Mindstorms NXT,[1] a kind of technical lego which can be controlled and programmed via a computer. Apart from being cheap, this technology makes it easy to build a prototype and to modify it during the course of the project.

4 Evaluation

During April–June 2009, the system will be evaluated by a number of users with linguistic communication disorders.

4.1 Design

The evalation process is designed as a case study with data being collected before and after interventions. The children will also be video recorded when playing with the robot, to enable analysis of common interaction patterns.

4.2 Users

The users will consist of children with a diagnose within the autism spectrum, and children with a CP diagnosis. The chronological age of the children may vary but the intention is to both include children in an early stage of language development, and children who have developed further and where there is a need to develop and train grammatical skills.

4.3 Evaluation method

After the children's families and/or personnel have been instructed about the use of the robot, they will be using it during 2 months. The children will have the opportunity to play with the robot about 2 to 3 times per week.

Before the robot is used, the parents answer a survey about how they perceive their interaction with their children. They will also estimate the communicative abilities of their children. The surveys will be complemented with questions based

on the vocabulary which will be included in the children's communication boards. When the trial period is over, the surveys are repeated. During the trial period, the children will be filmed twice while using the robot, in the beginning and towards the end. The videos will then be analysed using suitable methods, such as Activity-Based Communication Analysis, developed at the University of Gothenburg. Furthermore, all interaction between the communication board and the robot will be logged by the system, providing valuable information to include in the overall analysis.

Acknowledgements

We are greatful to three anonymous referees for their comments. The TRIK project is financed by the Promobilia foundation and Magn. Bergvall's foundation.

References

Jonas Beskow, Olov Engwall, Björn Granström, and Preben Wik. 2004. Design strategies for a virtual language tutor. In *INTERSPEECH 2004*.

Mikael Heimann and Tomas Tjus. 1997. *Datorer och barn med autism*. Natur och Kultur.

Staffan Larsson. 2002. *Issue-based Dialogue Management*. Ph.D. thesis, Department of Linguistics, University of Gothenburg.

Johanna Lidskog. 2007. Swedish Bliss: Grammar based translation from Swedish into Bliss. Master's thesis, University of Gothenburg.

Seymour Papert. 1993. *Mindstorms: Children, Computers, and Powerful Ideas*. Basic Books.

Aarne Ranta. 2004. Grammatical Framework, a type-theoretical grammar formalism. *Journal of Functional Programming*, 14(2):145–189.

Stephanie Seneff, Chao Wang, and Julia Zhang. 2004. Spoken conversational interaction for language learning. In *InSTIL/ICALL 2004 Symposium on Computer Assisted Learning*.

Rose Sevcik and Mary Ann Romski. 2002. The role of language comprehension in establishing early augmented conversations. In I. J. Reichle, D. Beukelman, and J. Light, editors, *Exemplary Practices for Beginning Communicators*, pages 453–475. Paul H. Brookes Publishing.

Gunilla Thunberg. 2007. *Using speech-generating devices at home*. Ph.D. thesis, Department of Linguistics, University of Gothenburg.

---

[1] http://mindstorms.lego.com/

ISSN 1736-6305 Vol. 4
http://hdl.handle.net/10062/9206

CAOS – A tool for the Construction of Terminological Ontologies

Bodil Nistrup Madsen
Copenhagen Business School
Copenhagen, Denmark
bnm.isv@cbs.dk

Hanne Erdman Thomsen
Copenhagen Business School
Copenhagen, Denmark
het.isv@cbs.dk

Abstract

This paper presents some principles of terminological ontologies implemented in the prototype that has been developed in the research project CAOS - Computer-Aided Ontology Structuring. Furthermore some issues, that have to be faced to further develop facilities for automatic consistency checking and automatic changes to ontologies, are discussed. The presentation will illustrate central facilities of the current version of the CAOS prototype, which is interactive and presupposes an end-user with a background in terminology rather than in formal ontology.

1   Introduction

A terminological ontology is a domain specific ontology, cf. for example the categorization of ontologies by Guarino (1998). We use the term terminological ontology as synonym to the term concept system, which is normally used in terminology work, cf. for example (ISO 704, 2000).

The principles of terminological ontologies, presented here, build on the principles of terminology work as presented in (ISO 704, 2000), but have been further developed in the research and development project CAOS - Computer-Aided Ontology Structuring - whose aim is to develop a computer system designed to enable semi-automatic construction of concept systems, or ontologies, cf. (Madsen et al., 2005).

Terminological ontologies model concepts and the relations between them, and a concept is described by means of characteristics that denote properties of individual referents belonging to the extension of that concept. Other ontologies most commonly model classes, described by means of properties, and the relations between classes.

It is possible to use all types of concept relations in CAOS. The system offers a set of concept relations organized in a taxonomy, cf. (Madsen et al., 2002). Also it is possible for the user to introduce user defined relations. For other presentations of concept relations, see for example (Nuopponen, 2005).

2   The CAOS Prototype

The backbone of terminological concept modeling in CAOS is constituted by characteristics modeled by formal feature specifications, i.e. attribute-value pairs, cf. (Carpenter, 1992). The use of feature specifications is subject to a number of principles and constraints.

Figure 1 presents part of an ontology for prevention created in CAOS. As can be seen, the graphical presentation is UML-based.

2.1   Consistency checking in CAOS

The technology developed in CAOS enables validation of inheritance of characteristics when a single new concept is introduced into a concept system. In a type hierarchy, subordinate concepts inherit characteristics from their superordinate concepts, and hence it is possible to validate whether the position of a given concept allows for the characteristics associated with it.

The facilities for semi-automatic construction of ontologies and for consistency checking in CAOS are among other things based on the introduction of dimensions and dimension specifications. A dimension of a concept is an attribute occurring in a (non-inherited) feature specification of one of its subordinate concepts, i.e. an attribute whose possible values allow a distinction between some of the subconcepts of the concept in question. A dimension specification consists of a dimension and the values associated with the corresponding attribute in the feature specifications of the subordinate concepts: dimension: [value1| value2| ...]. In this way, the principle of subdivision criteria that has been used for many years in terminology work, has been formalized in CAOS.

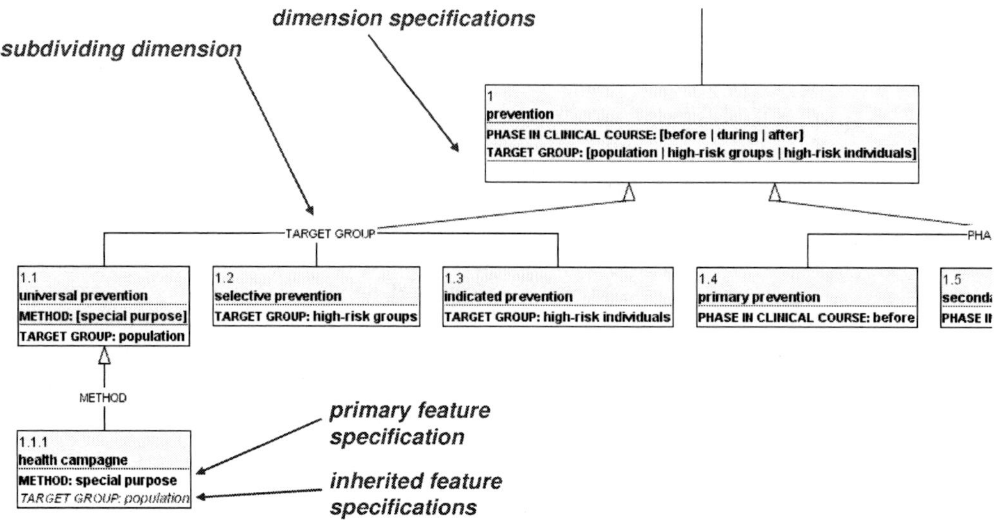

Figure 1. Extract of an ontology for prevention

One or more of the dimensions of a concept must be chosen as subdividing dimensions. Subdividing dimensions must be chosen in such a way that each daughter concept has one and only one feature specification containing as an attribute a subdividing dimension of the mother concept. This ensures that there are no overlapping subdividing dimensions, and hence no overlap in partitions.

In the following a brief description of some important principles of CAOS will be given: grouping by subdividing dimensions, including choice of subdividing dimensions and no overlapping of subdividing dimensions, uniqueness of primary feature specifications and uniqueness of dimensions.

2.2 Grouping by subdividing dimensions

From figure 1 it is seen that *prevention* may differ with respect to both target group and phase in clinical course. However, in the case of the three concepts *universal prevention, selective prevention* and *indicated prevention* it is obvious that TARGET GROUP must be chosen as the subdividing dimension (subdivision criterion). If the user tries to choose a second dimension as subdividing dimension for the three mentioned subordinate concepts, CAOS will not allow it, and will consequently warn the user. The feature specifications comprising the subdividing dimension (referred to as the delimiting feature specifications) will form the basis for the definition of the three concepts.

Constraints in CAOS related to subdivision criteria are:

- A concept (with only one mother concept) may contain at most one delimiting feature specification
- A concept (of level 2 or below) must contain at least one delimiting feature specification

Another constraint is that an attribute may only be associated with one value in a feature structure (a combination of two or more feature specifications on a concept is called a feature structure). If the user attempts at creating a concept *universal selective prevention* with two superordinate concepts within the same group (dimension TARGET GROUP), this would mean that the attribute TARGET GROUP would be associated with two values in the feature structure for *universal selective prevention*: TARGET GROUP: population and TARGET GROUP: high-risk groups. CAOS will not allow this 'illegal polyhierarchy'. This type of error is also known as a partition error (Góméz-Péréz et al. 2003).

In Protégé[1] this can be handled be adding a new superordinate concept to a concept on the basis of the formal definition of the concepts in question. However, this treatment is not feasible for the end users we have in mind, who have no training in formal logic or similar.

---

[1] http://protege. stanford.edu/

2.3 Uniqueness of dimensions

The principle of uniqueness of dimensions says that a given dimension may occur on only one concept in an ontology. Uniqueness of dimensions helps to create coherence and simplicity in the ontological structure because concepts that are characterised by means of primary feature specifications with the same dimension must appear as coordinate concepts on the same level having a common superordinate concept.

2.4 Uniqueness of feature specifications

The principle of uniqueness of feature specifications stipulates that a feature specification may occur only once in a terminological ontology as primary. A primary feature specification is entered on a concept directly by the terminologist, as opposed to inherited feature specifications, which are inherited from superordinate concepts.

Uniqueness of dimensions (the previous principle) means that a given primary feature specification can only appear on concepts that are daughters of the concept containing the relevant dimension. Uniqueness of primary feature specifications means that a given primary feature specification can only appear on one of these daughters. If the terminologist tries to insert the primary feature specification [TARGET GROUP: population] on the concept *selective prevention*, CAOS will report that [TARGET GROUP: population] is already specified on the concept 1.1 *universal prevention*.

The motivation of the principle of uniqueness of primary feature specifications is that

- characteristics will always serve to distinguish concepts, and
- common characteristics should be located on a common superordinate concept (this principle may contribute to the identification of potential gaps in the ontology).

2.5 Characteristics of the CAOS prototype compared to other ontology editors

Several other tools for creating ontologies have been (or are being) developed, e.g. Protégé and WebODE[2].

The main difference between the system for terminological ontologies, described here, and other systems is that in the latter, terminological information cannot be modeled and presented in the same way. This information, i.e. subdivision criteria and dimension specifications, is crucial in the development of terminological ontologies. Furthermore, in order to check conformance to the constraints mentioned in section 2.2 – 2.4, the end user has to be able to formulate formal constraints for each subdivision criterion. In CAOS, the constraints are part of the system.

3 Further Development of the CAOS Prototype

In a new project we aim to develop an additional prototype that will be able to automatically build a first draft ontology on the basis of a domain-specific text corpus. This prototype will be based on a combination of existing and new methods and principles for automatic extraction of concepts and information about concepts, i.e. characteristics and concept relations.

Another aim is to further develop CAOS so that it may be used for automatic validation of draft ontologies that are the result of the automatic concept extraction. The new prototype will not just be able to detect errors, it will also propose corrections of errors. For example it will automatically handle partition errors. To our knowledge no other systems have such capabilities.

To further develop facilities in CAOS for automatic consistency checking and automatic changes to ontologies, various issues have to be dealt with.

3.1 Validation of an ontology vs. validation of one concept

First of all, the technology currently used in CAOS validates one concept at a time, while the new prototype will need to validate an entire ontology provided by the knowledge extraction module.

3.2 Characteristics vs. relations

In CAOS, a concept may have both feature specifications and relations to other concepts. However a given characteristic of a concept can be modeled either as an attribute-value pair or a relation-concept pair, e.g. in Figure 1, the characteristic modeled by the feature specification [TARGET GROUP: population] could have been modeled as a relation (HAS_TARGET_GROUP) to another concept (*population*).

The ontology extraction module will not be able to distinguish between attributes and relations, so in the new prototype relations (other than type relations) and attributes of characteris-

---

tics will have to be treated identically. In validation they will be treated as attributes of characteristics, and the related concepts will be treated as values. This raises a theoretical research issue: is it necessary to differentiate relations and characteristics? If so, what is the difference?

3.3 Multiple values

A problem related to the above is that CAOS technology allows a given concept to have only one value for a given attribute, while it may be related to several other concepts with the same relation. The extraction tool is bound to deliver more than one concept for a given relation (or value for a given attribute) for any concept. The CAOS technology needs to be modified to handle this.

Some relations may only be applied to a given concept once. For example, no concept can have more than one instance of the relation HAS_LENGTH_IN_CM. This corresponds to the CAOS principle mentioned above, i.e. that for a given attribute a concept can have at most one value. Hence a research issue to be investigated is whether these relations can be distinguished from those allowing for multiple instances, since this is important for validation.

3.4 Specialized values

An issue relating to characteristics is that of specialized values. In order to handle this, the CAOS technology needs to be enhanced to include a type hierarchy of values (or related concepts). The use of value hierarchies has been implemented e.g. in the Lexical Knowledge Base system (LKB) first developed by Ann Copestake for lexical semantics and further enhanced for HPSG[3] purposes, c.f. (Copestake, 1993).

3.5 Automatic positioning

A prerequisite for making automatic changes in the ontology based on the validation is to be able to position a concept in an existing type hierarchy by employing the characteristics registered for that concept. Techniques for positioning concepts and making automatic changes to the ontology are to be developed.

4 Perspectives

Terminological ontologies offer very detailed information about concepts, e.g. feature specifications, subdivision criteria and dimension speci-

fications. The question is whether this information is useful in the various applications of ontologies. No doubt, this information is needed for concept clarification, for example with a view the definition of central concepts in the use of IT systems for information storage and retrieval.

In the SIABO project, Semantic Information Access through Biomedical Ontologies, cf. http://siabo.org, it is planned to test whether terminological ontologies will also add value to systems for ontology-based information retrieval.

References

Carpenter, Bob. 1992. *The Logic of Typed Feature Structures*. Cambridge University Press, UK.

Copestake, Ann. 1993 *The Compleat LKB, Technical Report No. 316*, University of Cambridge.

CWA 15045. 2005. *CEN Workshop Agreement: Multilingual Catalogue Strategies for eCommerce and eBusiness.*

Gómez Pérez, Asunción, Mariano Fernández-López, Oscar Corcho: (2003) "Ontological Engineering". Advanced Information and Knowledge Processing series. ISBN 1-85233-551-3. Springer Verlag.

Guarino, Nicola. 1998. Formal Ontology and Information Systems. *Formal Ontology in Information Systems, Proceedings of the First International Conference (FOIS'98)*, June 6-8, Trento, Italy, 3-15. Ed. Nicola Guarino. Amsterdam: IOS Press.

ISO 704. 2000. *Terminology work — Principles and methods*. Genève: ISO.

Madsen, Bodil Nistrup, Hanne Erdman Thomsen & Carl Vikner. 2005. Multidimensionality in terminological concept modelling. Bodil Nistrup Madsen, Hanne Erdman Thomsen (eds.): *Terminology and Content Development, TKE 2005, 7th International Conference on Terminology and Knowledge Engineering*, Copenhagen: 161-173.

Madsen, Bodil Nistrup, Bolette Sandford Pedersen & Hanne Erdman Thomsen. 2002. The Role of Semantic Relations in a Content-based Querying System: a Research Presentation from the OntoQuery Project. Simov, Kiril & Atanas Kiryakov (eds.): *Proceedings from OntoLex '2000, Workshop on Ontologies and Lexical Knowledge Bases*, Sept. 8-10 2000, Sozopol, Bulgaria: 72-81.

Nuopponen, Anita. 2005. Concept Relations. Bodil Nistrup Madsen, Hanne Erdman Thomsen (eds.): *Terminology and Content Development, TKE 2005, 7th International Conference on Terminology and Knowledge Engineering*, Copenhagen, 127-138.

---

[3] Head Driven Phrase Structure Grammar

ISSN 1736-6305 Vol. 4
http://hdl.handle.net/10062/9206

The Nordic Dialect Database: Mapping Microsyntactic Variation in the Scandinavian Languages

Arne Martinus Lindstad
University of Oslo
Oslo, Norway
a.m.lindstad@iln.uio.no

Anders Nøklestad
University of Oslo
Oslo, Norway
a.noklestad@iln.uio.no

Janne Bondi Johannessen
University of Oslo
Oslo, Norway
j.b.johannessen@iln.uio.no

Øystein A. Vangsnes
University of Tromsø
Tromsø, Norway
oystein.vangsnes@hum.uit.no

Abstract

We describe the development of a database containing informant judgments on a range of test sentences. The database is intended as a research resource for linguists interested in morphosyntactic variation across Scandinavian dialects. We present the data types contained in the base, and how they are used to create a user-friendly search interface. The database forms part of the efforts undertaken under the ScanDiaSyn project umbrella, currently run at ten universities in Denmark, The Faroe Islands, Finland, Iceland, Norway and Sweden. The database has been developed by the Text Laboratory at the University of Oslo, Norway.

1 Introduction

The Nordic Dialect Database is part of the achievements of the Scandinavian Dialect Syntax (ScanDiaSyn) project umbrella. ScanDiaSyn is a collaborative effort run by individual research groups at ten universities in the Nordic countries. The main purpose of ScanDiaSyn is to chart and study morphological and syntactic variation in Scandinavian dialects. The outcome of the project will be a pan-Scandinavian dialect research resource, made available to the research community via a user-friendly web interface. The data collected for the project are of three kinds:

- Speaker intuitions, i.e. speakers' evaluation of test sentences presented to them in a questionnaire.

- A corpus of transcribed audio and video recordings of interviews of and conversations between the informants.

- "Translation" of constructions into dialect from the standard language.

In this paper, we focus on the speaker intuition data. First, we sketch some background in section 2, then discuss the data types that form the basis for the database in section 3, before showing how the data is made available and searchable via a web resource in section 4. Section 5 briefly presents technical aspects of the database, and section 6 discusses future improvements to the system not yet implemented.

2 Background

Somewhat unevenly distributed across the countries, ScanDiaSyn has gathered data at 270 measure points in Scandinavia.

The data from the questionnaire part of the project forms the basis for the database we have built. A subset from a common pool of around 1400 sentences is tested at each measure point. In Norway, 140 sentences are tested, while in Denmark up to 240 sentences are tested at each point. It is up to each research group to decide exactly which sentences are tested, based on individual interest and on what is considered relevant in each dialect.

Though the number of sentences tested is not very high, it is demanding for the informants, as evaluating grammaticality is an unusual task for most speakers.

The database developed so far is based primarily on data from the Norwegian and Danish parts of the project. Data from the other languages will be added when they are available.

3 Data types

Compared to the spoken language data in the corpus (see section 1), the amount of data comprising the database is relatively small, and not very much preprocessing is required. In this section, we describe the various data types that enter into the database.

3.1 Test sentences and constructions

The data collection for the database is inspired by a generative syntax approach to grammatical variation (in terms of parameters). Test sentences are constructed to reflect well-known patterns of variation described in the literature, or they are based on expected patterns of syntactic variation across the dialects.[1]

3.2 Speaker evaluations

Following standard practice within generative linguistics (Chomsky 1965), speaker intuitions (or judgments) on the grammaticality of syntactic constructions are considered crucial for a comprehensive theory of language. Informants are asked to judge test sentences on a five-point scale, where 1 is bad and 5 is fully acceptable.

3.3 Linguistic categorisation

Each test sentence has been appended with a number of linguistic features – or categories – describing in as much detail as possible the linguistic property that is tested by that particular sentence. An illustration is given in (1) and (2), *wh*-questions differing in the placement of the finite verb:

(1) Hva   du   heter?
     what you   is.called
     'What is your name?'
(2) Hva   heter du?
     what is.called you
     'What is your name?'

---

[1] Note that the informants never see the test sentences visually. We "translate" each test sentence into the local dialect and record a local speaker reading them aloud. The sentences are then presented to the informants aurally.

The linguistic categories appended to these example sentences are the following:

(3) word order, interrogative, question, constituent question, simple *wh*-word

In addition, a category describing the placement of the finite verb distinguishes the sentences from each other: "V3" for (1) and "V2" for (2).

3.4 Metadata: Demographic information

In the Norwegian subproject, the number of informants per measure point is four, one of each sex below the age of 30, and one of each sex above the age of 50. Following traditional sociolinguistic practice, various types of demographic information about the informants are gathered before the recordings are undertaken. This is described in more detail in section 4.

The charting of demographic information and linguistic background ensures that the individual informant is a genuine speaker of the dialect in question.

4 The user interface

As mentioned in section 3, the amount of data is rather small. The challenge lies in structuring, displaying and making the actual content available to researchers in a user-friendly fashion. Various criteria and variables can be applied for performing searches in the database. Figure 1 is a screen dump of the search interface, illustrating the search possibilities. In this section we describe the search possibilities in detail.

4.1 Main search options: categories and test sentences

For most syntacticians, a search for a given feature in a dialect will typically be based on a special interest in a particular syntactic phenomenon such as variation in the placement of the finite verb in constituent questions (*wh*-questions), as above. This is a phenomenon that splits the Norwegian dialect continuum into regions (cf. Vangsnes (2005) for an overview and further literature on the subject). In Figure 1, a search with categories has been performed. This is done by activating category search in the upper left box of the screen. Categories are listed in the drop-down menu at the top of this box. Selecting a given category pops up a sub-menu with all other categories appearing together with the selected category in the description of any sentence

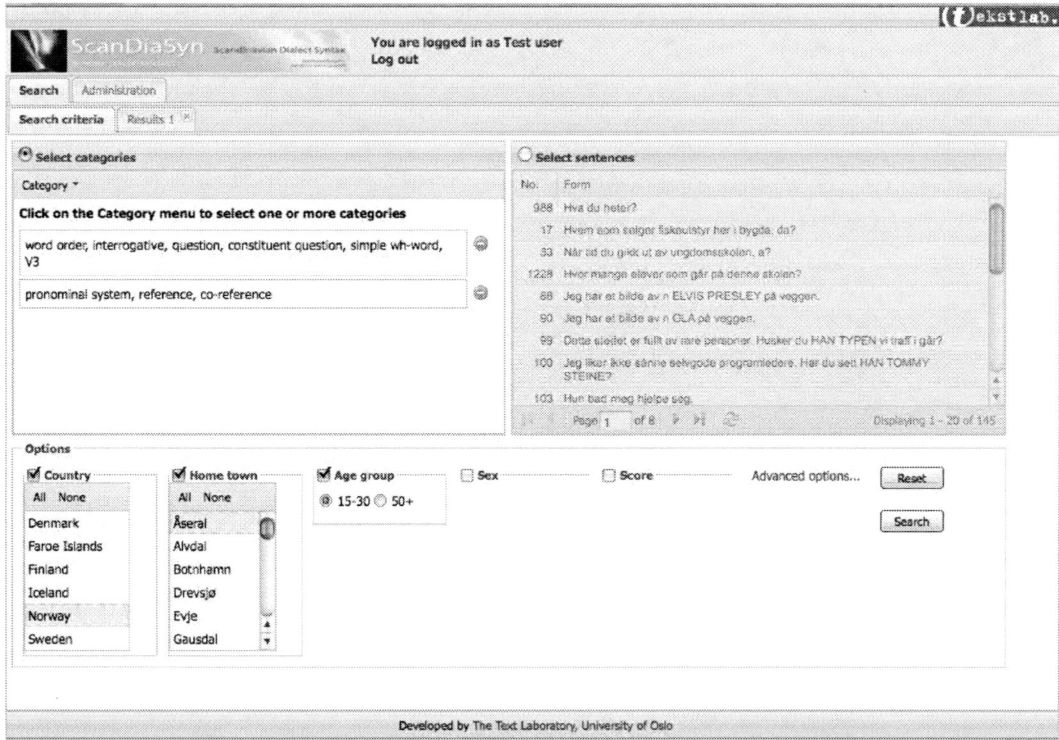

Figure 1: Search interface.

in the database. This way, the search is narrowed, and returns a smaller set of sentences. Several category searches can be specified simultaneously, enabling listing of covariance between phenomena.

This is also illustrated in Figure 1: the user specifies two sets of categories (search criteria), each of which is defined by a comma-separated list. Each set of categories returns a set of one or more test sentences, and the final search result is the union of these sentence sets.

As a second option, the database is searchable by test sentence, i.e., a single sentence or a set of sentences can be selected in the upper right box.

4.2 Restricting the search

While it is possible to search for all judgments for a given test sentence regardless of any variables, it will sometimes be useful to narrow down the search in various ways to obtain a manageable output. This is obviously so if one is looking for covariance between phenomena.

The search can be restricted using the information provided by the various data types described in section 3. In the search interface (Figure 1), this can be accomplished by using the five drop-down menus at the lower end of the screen.

Leftmost, the search can be restricted geographically to a single country or to a combination of countries. This narrows down the set of measure points in the next menu. *Norway* is selected above, and a list of all measure points in Norway is provided in the next menu. Any combination of measure points can be selected for comparison on the features specified in the category search, or on the particular sentences selected in a test sentence search.

If there is agreement between the informants on a particular phenomenon, one can say something meaningful about the dialect in question. Irrespective of dialectal variation, one can also compare the language of e.g. men and women or of young and old speakers over a user-defined geographical area. This is accomplished by specifying the age group and/or the sex in the relevant drop-down menus. For illustrative purposes, the age group 15-30 is selected in Figure 1.

Finally, in the rightmost drop-down menu it is possible to restrict the selection to those sentences that have been given specific scores by the informants, e.g. high acceptance scores, such as 4 and 5 (see section 3.2).

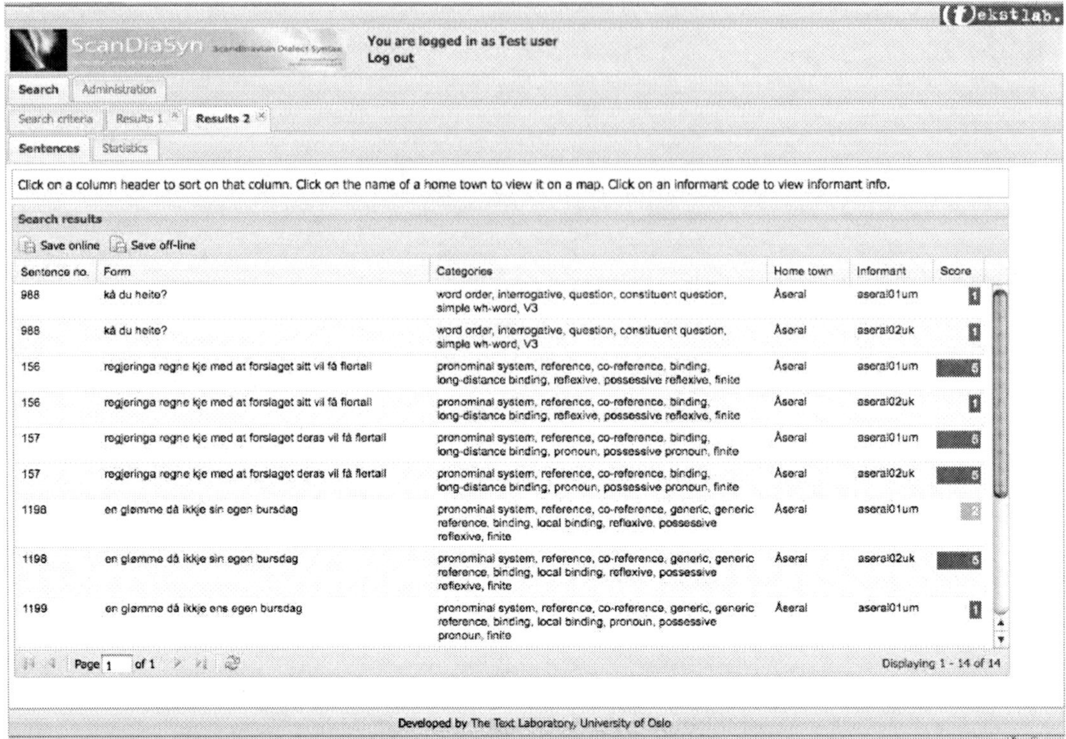

Figure 2: Results page.

4.3 Displaying the results

The results from a given search are displayed in a new tab next to the "Search criteria" tab. Each new search opens a new tab (cf. "Results 1" and "Results 2" in Figure 2). A search can be saved on- or off-line for further processing. Search results are abandoned by closing the tab.

The search results can be sorted in various ways by clicking column headers in the results page, a measure point can be displayed on a map by clicking its name, and demographic information about the informants can be obtained by clicking the informant code.

Throughout, our efforts have been aimed at creating a user-friendly system that can easily adjust to the needs of linguists of any theoretical orientation, and the system is open for easy addition of further variables and search criteria.

5 Technical issues

The server side of the system runs on the Ruby on Rails web application framework[2] with a MySQL database.[3] The web browser interface has been created using the Ext JS JavaScript framework.[4]

6 Refinements: maps and statistics

As a refinement in the future, and for the ease of the eye, a map function will be implemented that can illustrate the presence of a linguistic feature at given places in the dialect continuum. This will enable drawing of isoglosses. Given the dynamic search possibilities the system provides, any covariance between linguistic properties (features, categories) can be easily illustrated in a graphic fashion. We are also planning to provide statistical measures that can be used to detect significant patterns of dialect variation.

References

Chomsky, Noam. 1965. *Aspects of the Theory of Syntax*. MIT Press, Cambridge, Massachusetts.

ScanDiaSyn: http://uit.no/scandiasyn

The Text Laboratory: http://www.hf.uio.no/tekstlab

Vangsnes, Øystein Alexander. 2005. Microparameters for Norwegian *wh*-grammars. *Linguistic Variation Yearbook*, 5: 187-226.

---

[2] http://rubyonrails.org
[3] http://www.mysql.com

[4] http://extjs.com

ISSN 1736-6305 Vol. 4
http://hdl.handle.net/10062/9206

Author Index

Association for Computational Linguistics
209 N. Eighth Street
Stroudsburg, Pennsylvania 18360

ISBN 978-1-5108-3465-1